CORPORATE COMPLIANCE

ANSWER BOOK

2017 Edition

VOLUME 1

PRACTISING LAW INSTITUTE®

PLI'S COMPLETE LIBRARY OF TREATISE TITLES

ART LAW

Art Law: The Guide for Collectors, Investors, Dealers & Artists

BANKING & COMMERCIAL LAW

Asset-Based Lending: A Practical Guide to Secured Financing
Documenting Secured Transactions: Effective Drafting and Litigation
Equipment Leasing–Leveraged Leasing
Hillman on Commercial Loan Documentation
Import Practice Answer Book: Customs and International Trade Law
Maritime Law Answer Book

BANKRUPTCY LAW

Bankruptcy Deskbook
Personal Bankruptcy Answer Book

BUSINESS, CORPORATE & SECURITIES LAW

Accountants' Liability
Anti-Money Laundering: A Practical Guide to Law and Compliance
Antitrust Law Answer Book
Broker-Dealer Regulation
Conducting Due Diligence in a Securities Offering
Consumer Financial Services Answer Book
Corporate Compliance Answer Book
Corporate Legal Departments: Practicing Law in a Corporation
Corporate Political Activities Deskbook
Corporate Whistleblowing in the Sarbanes-Oxley/Dodd-Frank Era
Covered Bonds Handbook
Cybersecurity: A Practical Guide to the Law of Cyber Risk
Derivatives Deskbook: Close-Out Netting, Risk Mitigation, Litigation
Deskbook on Internal Investigations, Corporate Compliance and White Collar Issues
Directors' and Officers' Liability
Doing Business Under the Foreign Corrupt Practices Act
EPA Compliance and Enforcement Answer Book
Exempt and Hybrid Securities Offerings
Fashion Law and Business: Brands & Retailers
Financial Institutions Answer Book: Law, Governance, Compliance
Financial Product Fundamentals: Law, Business, Compliance
Financial Services Regulation Deskbook
Financially Distressed Companies Answer Book
Global Business Fraud and the Law: Preventing and Remedying Fraud and Corruption
Hedge Fund Regulation
Initial Public Offerings: A Practical Guide to Going Public
Insider Trading Law and Compliance Answer Book
Insurance and Investment Management M&A Deskbook
International Corporate Practice: A Practitioner's Guide to Global Success
Investment Adviser Regulation: A Step-by-Step Guide to Compliance and the Law
Life at the Center: Reflections on Fifty Years of Securities Regulation
Mergers, Acquisitions and Tender Offers: Law and Strategies
Mutual Funds and Exchange Traded Funds Regulation
Outsourcing: A Practical Guide to Law and Business
Privacy Law Answer Book
Private Equity Funds: Formation and Operation
Proskauer on Privacy: A Guide to Privacy and Data Security Law in the Information Age
Public Company Deskbook: Complying with Federal Governance & Disclosure
    Requirements

SEC Compliance and Enforcement Answer Book
Securities Investigations: Internal, Civil and Criminal
Securities Law and Practice Handbook
The Securities Law of Public Finance
Securities Litigation: A Practitioner's Guide
Social Media and the Law
Soderquist on Corporate Law and Practice
Sovereign Wealth Funds: A Legal, Tax and Economic Perspective
A Starter Guide to Doing Business in the United States
Technology Transactions: A Practical Guide to Drafting and Negotiating Commercial
    Agreements
Variable Annuities and Variable Life Insurance Regulation

COMMUNICATIONS LAW

Advertising and Commercial Speech: A First Amendment Guide
Sack on Defamation: Libel, Slander, and Related Problems
Telecommunications Law Answer Book

EMPLOYMENT LAW

Employment Law Yearbook
ERISA Benefits Litigation Answer Book
Labor Management Law Answer Book

ESTATE PLANNING AND ELDER LAW

Blattmachr on Income Taxation of Estates and Trusts
Estate Planning & Chapter 14: Understanding the Special Valuation Rules
International Tax & Estate Planning: A Practical Guide for Multinational Investors
Manning on Estate Planning
New York Elder Law
Stocker on Drawing Wills and Trusts

HEALTH LAW

FDA Deskbook: A Compliance and Enforcement Guide
Health Care Litigation and Risk Management Answer Book
Health Care Mergers and Acquisitions Answer Book
Medical Devices Law and Regulation Answer Book
Pharmaceutical Compliance and Enforcement Answer Book

IMMIGRATION LAW

Fragomen on Immigration Fundamentals: A Guide to Law and Practice

INSURANCE LAW

Business Liability Insurance Answer Book
Insurance Regulation Answer Book
Reinsurance Law

INTELLECTUAL PROPERTY LAW

Copyright Law: A Practitioner's Guide
Faber on Mechanics of Patent Claim Drafting
Federal Circuit Yearbook: Patent Law Developments in the Federal Circuit
How to Write a Patent Application
Intellectual Property Law Answer Book
Kane on Trademark Law: A Practitioner's Guide
Likelihood of Confusion in Trademark Law
Patent Claim Construction and *Markman* Hearings
Patent Law: A Practitioner's Guide
Patent Licensing and Selling: Strategy, Negotiation, Forms
Patent Litigation
Pharmaceutical and Biotech Patent Law
Post-Grant Proceedings Before the Patent Trial and Appeal Board

Substantial Similarity in Copyright Law
Trade Secrets: A Practitioner's Guide

LITIGATION

American Arbitration: Principles and Practice
Class Actions and Mass Torts Answer Book
Electronic Discovery Deskbook
Expert Witness Answer Book
Evidence in Negligence Cases
Federal Bail and Detention Handbook
How to Handle an Appeal
Medical Malpractice: Discovery and Trial
Product Liability Litigation: Current Law, Strategies and Best Practices
Sinclair on Federal Civil Practice
Trial Evidence Brought to Life: Illustrations from Famous Trials, Film and Fiction
Trial Handbook

REAL ESTATE LAW

Commercial Ground Leases
Friedman on Contracts and Conveyances of Real Property
Friedman on Leases
Holtzschue on Real Estate Contracts and Closings: A Step-by-Step Guide to Buying and
    Selling Real Estate
Net Leases and Sale-Leasebacks

TAX LAW

The Circular 230 Deskbook: Related Penalties, Reportable Transactions, Working Forms
The Corporate Tax Practice Series: Strategies for Acquisitions, Dispositions, Spin-Offs,
    Joint Ventures, Financings, Reorganizations & Restructurings
Foreign Account Tax Compliance Act Answer Book
Internal Revenue Service Practice and Procedure Deskbook
International Tax & Estate Planning: A Practical Guide for Multinational Investors
International Tax Controversies: A Practical Guide
Langer on Practical International Tax Planning
The Partnership Tax Practice Series: Planning for Domestic and Foreign Partnerships,
    LLCs, Joint Ventures & Other Strategic Alliances
Private Clients Legal & Tax Planning Answer Book
Transfer Pricing Answer Book

GENERAL PRACTICE PAPERBACKS

Anatomy of a Mediation: A Dealmaker's Distinctive Approach to Resolving Dollar
    Disputes and Other Commercial Conflicts
Attorney-Client Privilege Answer Book
Drafting for Corporate Finance: Concepts, Deals, and Documents
Pro Bono Service by In-House Counsel: Strategies and Perspectives
Smart Negotiating: How to Make Good Deals in the Real World
Thinking Like a Writer: A Lawyer's Guide to Effective Writing & Editing
Working with Contracts: What Law School Doesn't Teach You

Order now at www.pli.edu/pubs
Or call (800) 260-4754 Mon.–Fri., 9 a.m.–6 p.m.

Practising Law Institute
1177 Avenue of the Americas
New York, NY 10036

When ordering, please use Priority Code NWS9-X.

CORPORATE COMPLIANCE

ANSWER BOOK

2017 Edition

VOLUME 1

HOLLAND & KNIGHT LLP

Edited by
Christopher A. Myers
&
Kwamina Thomas Williford

Practising Law Institute
New York City

#170717

This work is designed to provide practical and useful information on the subject matter covered. However, it is sold with the understanding that neither the publisher nor the author is engaged in rendering legal, accounting, or other professional services. If legal advice or other expert assistance is required, the services of a competent professional should be sought.

QUESTIONS ABOUT THIS BOOK?

If you have questions about billing or shipments, or would like information on our other products, please contact our **customer service department** at (800) 260-4PLI.

For library-related queries, **law librarians** may call toll-free (877) 900-5291 or email: libraryrelations@pli.edu.

For any other questions or suggestions about this book, contact PLI's **editorial department** at: editorial@pli.edu.

For general information about Practising Law Institute, please visit **www.pli.edu**.

Legal Editor: Paul Matsumoto

ISBN: 978-1-4024-2658-2
LOC: 2010924112

About the Editors

CHRISTOPHER A. MYERS is chair of Holland & Knight's Compliance Services Team and a member of the firm's White Collar Defense Team. He is a former federal prosecutor and has experience in a broad range of complex matters affecting heavily regulated industries, including healthcare, government contracts, financial institutions, real estate, securities, and other companies. He has represented clients with respect to matters involving civil and criminal fraud investigations, corporate governance, anti-money laundering, design and implementation of compliance programs, and administrative litigation. In addition to his practice, Mr. Myers has been a faculty member at a wide variety of continuing legal education and law school programs relating to enforcement and compliance issues, investigations, records retention programs, e-discovery issues, and risk assessments. Mr. Myers is a Certified Anti-Money Laundering Specialist and a Certified Compliance & Ethics Professional. He was selected to both *Washington, D.C. Super Lawyers* and *Virginia Super Lawyers* in the fields of White Collar Criminal Defense and Corporate Governance and Compliance. Mr. Myers also has been selected for inclusion in *The Best Lawyers in America* guide in the field of white collar criminal defense since 2013.

KWAMINA THOMAS WILLIFORD is a partner with Holland & Knight's Litigation Department and a member of the firm's Compliance Services Team. She represents clients in internal investigations responding to and anticipating inquiries by various government agencies related to alleged fraudulent activity, such as the False Claims Act. Ms. Williford draws upon her experience to advise clients on the design and implementation of compliance programs for institutions of higher education, government contractors, healthcare companies, and other highly regulated entities. Prior to joining Holland & Knight, Ms. Williford served as a law clerk for the Honorable Gerald Bruce Lee in the U.S. District Court for the Eastern District of Virginia.

About the Contributors

Nathan A. Adams IV represents educational and religious institutions, including private universities and schools. For public institutions, his practice includes providing advice on diversity in admissions, financial aid, and hiring; compliance with Title VI, Title VII, and Title IX; distance learning; and academic freedom and tenure. Dr. Adams provides general counsel for a number of private institutions, including advice about compliance with church-state law. He has experience working with the Florida Department of Education, Board of Governor's Florida Commission for Independent Education and the U.S. Department of Education. Dr. Adams holds a Ph.D. in international political economy from the University of Florida, a J.D. from the University of Texas School of Law, and a B.A. from Wheaton College in Wheaton, Illinois. He is a Florida Bar-Certified Specialist in Education Law and the immediate past Chair of the Florida Bar Education Law Committee. He is a frequent guest lecturer, has published extensively in law reviews and trade journals, and has argued multiple federal and state cases in trial and appellate courts. He is admitted to the U.S. Supreme Court and multiple federal appellate and district courts, as well as all courts in Florida, Colorado, and the District of Columbia.

Gregory Baldwin has specialized in anti-money laundering since 1982, when he became a federal anti-money laundering prosecutor in Miami, Florida. As a federal prosecutor in Miami, Mr. Baldwin was assigned to "Operation Greenback," the first federal multi-agency anti-money laundering prosecution task force in the United States, and served as its Chief in 1985 and 1986. Mr. Baldwin served as Assistant Counsel to the United States Permanent Subcommittee on Investigations from 1980–82 and as Special Trial Attorney with the U.S. Department of Justice Organized Crime and Racketeering Section from 1974–80. Mr. Baldwin has been a frequent speaker and lecturer at national and international conferences on anti-money laundering criminal and regulatory compliance. He is a Certified Anti-Money Laundering Specialist and a member of the American Bar Association Task Force on the Gatekeeper Initiative. He has been elected by his peers to appear in *The Best Lawyers in America*

(2006–13) for Corporate Governance and Compliance Law and for White Collar Criminal Defense, in *South Florida Legal Guide* as a "Top Lawyer" (2007–13), and in Florida's *Super Lawyers* magazine (2010–13). Mr. Baldwin received his law degree from Cornell Law School in 1974. He joined Holland & Knight in 1986 and was made a partner in 1989. He continues to specialize in anti-money laundering, particularly the USA PATRIOT Act, the Bank Secrecy Act, and the Money Laundering Control Act. He also specializes in anti-money laundering compliance program development and implementation.

Timothy D. Belevetz is a partner in Holland & Knight's Washington, D.C. and Northern Virginia offices. A former assistant U.S. attorney and U.S. Securities and Exchange Commission attorney, he focuses his practice on white collar criminal defense, SEC enforcement matters, internal investigations, government investigations, and compliance matters. He has extensive trial and investigative experience, having served as counsel in numerous federal trials and investigations involving Foreign Corrupt Practices Act violations, securities and corporate fraud, tax offenses, healthcare fraud, fraudulent investment schemes, money laundering, bank fraud, and arson. He assists companies and individuals facing government scrutiny for criminal, civil, and regulatory enforcement matters and advises clients with regard to compliance policies and procedures.

Thomas H. Bentz, Jr. practices insurance law with a focus on cyber liability, D&O liability, and other management liability insurance policies. Mr. Bentz leads Holland & Knight's D&O and Management Liability Insurance Team, which provides insight and guidance on ways to improve policy language and helps insureds maximize their possible insurance recovery. Using an extensive library of insurance forms and endorsements, along with the experience of reviewing numerous insurance policies each year, Mr. Bentz analyzes policy forms and works with brokers to negotiate improvements to policy wordings. He also provides policy comparisons and coverage summaries for management and boards of directors. In the event of a claim, Mr. Bentz offers policyholders strategic and technical advice on coverage matters such as notice, "duty to defend," retention of defense counsel, rescission, and severability. Mr. Bentz also advises clients on policy interpretation and how to respond to reservation of rights and denial letters from insurers, and provides advice on risk mitigation and management, coordination of coverage (including cyber insurance), and crisis management. He has extensive experience with insurance issues related to mergers and acquisitions and other high-risk transactions, including extended reporting periods (or "tail" coverage), reps and warranties insurance, and indemnification agreements. He also assists clients with their bylaw indemnification provisions. Mr. Bentz regularly publishes articles on cyber and D&O insurance and is a frequent commentator on insurance issues.

David S. Black practices in the area of government contracts counseling and dispute resolution. His practice includes representing contractors in protests, claims under the Contract Disputes Act, responding to government investigations and audits, False Claims Act investigations and litigation, terminations for default and convenience, prime-subcontractor disputes, compliance programs, and counseling on a variety of contract administration and procurement issues.

Maximillian J. Bodoin is a member of Holland & Knight's Intellectual Property Group and the Data Privacy and Security Team. Mr. Bodoin focuses his practice on intellectual property licensing, information technology, and outsourcing transactions and electronic commerce. He advises clients on a variety of intellectual property and information technology matters including software development and licensing, IT outsourcing, master services agreements for IT professional services, online social networking, commercialization of technology and IT, and security-related employee policies. Mr. Bodoin also has significant experience advising clients on data security compliance efforts as well as preparing for and responding to data security incidents. Such advice includes assisting with preparing and implementing information security programs, policies, and procedures, overseeing internal investigations, notifying impacted data subjects and regulators, responding to regulator investigations, as well as developing and implementing mitigation efforts following data breaches.

Thomas M. Brownell is a partner in Holland & Knight's Northern Virginia office. He has over thirty-five years of experience in all aspects of government contract law, including bid protests, claims and disputes, subcontractor litigation, False Claims Act litigation, and state and local contracts. He is admitted to practice and tries cases in the courts of Virginia, Maryland, and the District of Columbia, as well as the Court of Federal Claims and the Boards of Contract Appeals.

John A. Canale is an associate in Holland & Knight's Los Angeles office, practicing in the area of general commercial litigation. He represents clients in a variety of commercial disputes, including litigation matters involving product liability, construction defects, contract disputes, and unfair trade practices. Mr. Canale represents clients at the trial and appellate level and in state and federal courts. He has co-authored several articles regarding compliance issues.

Christopher DeLacy is the leader of the Political Law Group at Holland & Knight. He advises clients on compliance issues related to lobbying, ethics, pay-to-play, and campaign finance. He represents clients before the Federal Election Commission, House and Senate Ethics Committees, the Office of Congressional Ethics, and related state and local agencies. Prior to entering private practice, Mr. DeLacy worked in the U.S. Senate, the U.S. House of Representatives, and the Virginia General Assembly. Mr. DeLacy received his J.D. from the William & Mary School of Law and his B.A. from the University of Virginia.

Jonathan M. Epstein's practice focuses on international trade and aviation law. His trade practice includes advising clients in the aerospace, electronics, agrochemical, biochemical, and other high-technology industries on export, import, and related trade issues. His aviation practice focuses on representing clients before the Federal Aviation Administration and the Department of Transportation, and assisting clients in corporate jet transactions and structuring of corporate aircraft operations to comply with FAA regulations.

Vince Farhat is a partner in Holland & Knight's Los Angeles office and is a member of the West Coast Litigation Group, Compliance Services Team, and Healthcare & Life Sciences Team. Mr. Farhat has extensive jury trial experience and focuses his practice on representing companies in criminal and civil investigations and prosecutions by government enforcement agencies, as well as healthcare enforcement matters and complex federal litigation. He also advises companies in connection with complex and sensitive internal investigations. Prior to joining Holland & Knight, Mr. Farhat served as an assistant U.S. attorney in the Major Frauds Section of the U.S. Attorney's Office for the Central District of California. While in Major Frauds, Mr. Farhat served as the criminal healthcare fraud coordinator for the U.S. Attorney's Office and oversaw the investigative activities of the U.S. Department of Justice Medicare Fraud Strike Force for the Central District. Before becoming a criminal prosecutor, Mr. Farhat was an assistant U.S. attorney in the Civil Division of the U.S. Attorney's Office, where he represented the United States in commercial litigation and other civil cases. He served as a law clerk to U.S. District Court Judge Edward Rafeedie.

Mark A. Flessner is a partner in Holland & Knight's Chicago office. He has a broad range of industry experience, having represented clients in many areas, including healthcare, retail, manufacturing, insurance, and finance. He also has substantial experience investigating wrongdoing within the corporate world. Mr. Flessner has extensive trial experience—this includes bringing more than forty cases to verdict and arguing more than thirty-five cases on appeal. He advises clients on litigation risk and assists clients facing government scrutiny for criminal, civil, and regulatory matters. Additionally, Mr. Flessner represents clients facing complex commercial litigation, internal corporate investigations, grand jury inquiries, and issues involving the Foreign Corrupt Practices Act. Prior to entering private practice, Mr. Flessner was a federal prosecutor at the U.S. Attorney's Office in Chicago for twelve years. He led major investigations involving sophisticated and complex financial funds. His prosecutions included public corruption, bank fraud, insurance fraud, securities fraud, white collar crime, gangs, and narcotics cases. Mr. Flessner has also investigated international money laundering, terrorism, and cases involving national security.

Robert J. Friedman leads Holland & Knight's practice in the area of ERISA, employee benefits, and executive compensation. Mr. Friedman advises clients on their benefit and compensation plans in general and in the context of business and investment transactions. Mr. Friedman also counsels employers and executives in the negotiation and drafting of employment agreements and termination agreements. His clients include publicly traded and private corporations. Mr. Friedman has been elected by his peers to appear in *The Best Lawyers in America* each year since 1995 and has been selected

xiii

among the nation's leading practitioners by *Chambers USA: America's Leading Business Lawyers 2009–2016*.

David Gebler, J.D., is a founder and President of Skout Group, LLC, a global consultancy focused on reducing people-based risks while improving productivity and corporate reputation. Mr. Gebler advises global organizations on understanding how culture impacts ethics and compliance risks, and then developing strategies to reduce those risks by aligning the values of the organization's people with business goals. The results are training programs and leadership strategies that are targeted to an organization's specific risk factors. Mr. Gebler is the author of *The 3 Power Values: How Commitment, Integrity and Transparency Clear the Roadblocks to Performance* (Jossey-Bass 2012) and is also a Senior Lecturer on Business Ethics at Suffolk University, where he serves on the International Advisory Board of Suffolk University's Graduate Program in Ethics and Public Policy.

Steven D. Gordon practices in the areas of white collar crime and complex civil litigation, including appeals. He conducts internal investigations and represents companies and individuals who are being audited or investigated or who have been charged with criminal offenses. Many of his cases involve suspected fraud, waste, or abuse with respect to federal contracts or programs. He has substantial experience in defending government contractors and program participants against civil False Claims Act suits brought by the Department of Justice or by whistleblowers. He also has represented numerous clients facing suspension or debarment from participating in federal contracting or other federal programs.

William F. Gould is a partner in Holland & Knight's National White Collar Defense and Investigations team. He represents corporations and individuals in civil and criminal matters, with a focus on responding to government investigations, litigation, and negotiations, particularly in heavily regulated industries such as healthcare and government contracts. Prior to joining Holland & Knight, Mr. Gould was a federal prosecutor with the Department of Justice and on the faculty of the University of Virginia School of Law, where he taught trial practice and criminal law. He also served as a law clerk for federal District Court Judge Morton A. Brody. He graduated from the University of Virginia School of Law.

Lynne M. Halbrooks is a member of Holland & Knight's White Collar Defense & Investigations and Government Contracts teams. She is a former federal prosecutor and acting inspector general, and her practice focuses on representing corporate and individual clients responding to inquiries, audits, and investigations by the federal government. Many of her cases involve defending government contractors against false claims act allegations and conducting internal investigations on their behalf. Prior to joining Holland & Knight, Ms. Halbrooks held a number of senior positions in the federal government. From 2009 through April 2015, she was general counsel and then principal deputy inspector general at the Department of Defense's Office of Inspector General. During this time, she served as the acting inspector general for twenty-one months. She was previously the general counsel for the Office of the Special Inspector General for Iraq Reconstruction and spent four years with the U.S. Senate sergeant at arms, first as general counsel and then as deputy sergeant at arms. She began her federal career as a prosecutor in the Eastern District of Wisconsin and also served as a deputy director in the Executive Office for U.S. Attorneys at the Department of Justice.

Mitchell E. Herr exclusively concentrates his practice in securities litigation, primarily SEC and FINRA enforcement matters, in which he defends corporate clients and their directors and officers, financial institutions including broker-dealers, registered investment advisers and their associated registered persons, mutual funds, and hedge funds. Mr. Herr joined Holland & Knight in 2000, after serving for over five years as the chief trial counsel for the SEC's regional office in Miami, where he was responsible for its litigation in eight states and two territories. At the SEC, he successfully handled many significant and complex SEC cases, including several of first impression. Mr. Herr graduated with honors from the University of Chicago Law School, where he served as Associate Editor of the *Law Review* and was elected to the Order of the Coif.

Richard J. Hindlian has practiced law in Boston for more than twenty-five years and before that was an accountant with Ernst & Ernst in Boston for two years. Mr. Hindlian concentrates his practice in taxation, including employee benefit plans, corporate finance, and commercial law for publicly held and private corporations, banks, individuals, and nonprofit corporations and public entities in connection with a wide variety of transactions including mergers and acquisitions, public and private offerings of debt and equity securities, venture capital financings, debt and equity restructuring, leveraged buyouts, ESOPs and other qualified plans, equipment leasing transactions, low-income housing, and other commercial matters, including arbitrations, tax litigation, commercial litigation, estate planning, and foreign investments made in the United States and overseas.

Jerome W. Hoffman is a partner at Holland & Knight practicing in the area of commercial litigation, with special emphasis on antitrust, consumer fraud, RICO, government investigations, Medicaid and Medicare fraud, and healthcare regulatory matters.

John S. Irving IV is a partner in the Washington, D.C. office of Holland & Knight. He is a former federal prosecutor with significant trial and investigative experience whose practice focuses on corporate internal investigations, effective compliance and ethics programs, and white collar defense in a variety of substantive areas, including the Foreign Corrupt Practices Act, False Claims Act, environmental statutes, and congressional investigations.

Kenneth A. Jenero is a partner in Holland & Knight's Labor, Employment & Benefits Practice Group. He serves as the leader of that group's national Healthcare & Life Sciences Team and co-leader of the group in the firm's Chicago office. Mr. Jenero is an experienced trial lawyer and business advisor, who has devoted his entire professional career to litigation and client counseling in all areas of labor and employment law, including employment discrimination, civil rights, and affirmative action; wage-and-hour law; union-management relations; wrongful discharge, retaliation, and common law employment torts; trade secrets, non-compete agreements, and other post-employment restrictive covenants; and occupational safety and health. Mr. Jenero represents employers nationally in a wide range of industries, including healthcare, manufacturing, distribution, temporary staffing, transportation and inter-modal operations, construction, landscaping, environmental services and recycling, security, insurance, financial services, not-for-profit organizations, commercial printing, retail, travel and tourism, hospitality, restaurants and food service, and professional services. Throughout his career, Mr. Jenero has served as outside labor and employment counsel for a wide range of business clients, including large publicly held companies, middle-market companies, and family-owned businesses. His practice includes auditing companies' labor and employment policies, rules, and practices to identify potential areas of exposure and develop comprehensive compliance plans and strategies.

Charles E. Joern, Jr. (charles.joern@joernlaw.com), based in Oak Brook, Illinois, focuses his practice in the area of consumer product safety laws and product liability. During his more than thirty years in practice he has served as lead trial counsel for a number of *Fortune 500* corporations in high-value product liability and commercial litigation cases, obtaining favorable results at both the trial and appellate levels. He has represented clients in a wide range of matters, including consumer product safety compliance, product liability litigation, punitive damages, RICO litigation, and commercial claims, in jurisdictions across the country. A significant portion of his work involves counseling clients on the application of the U.S. Consumer Product Safety Improvement Act and representing businesses before the U.S. Consumer Product Safety Commission.

Bonni F. Kaufman is a partner in the Public Policy and Regulation Group of Holland & Knight, where she focuses on the practice of environmental law. Ms. Kaufman represents clients in a wide variety of matters relating to regulatory enforcement and compliance, environmental aspects of corporate and real estate transactions, and litigation. She has counseled clients with respect to compliance with requirements under FIFRA, the Clean Air Act, RCRA, CERCLA, TSCA, and state law and has successfully resolved many substantial enforcement actions and litigation related to violations of environmental regulations and migration of contamination.

Paul G. Lannon, Jr. is a partner in the Litigation Section of Holland & Knight, the Co-Chair of the firm's Education Team, a member of the firm's national Labor, Employment, and Benefits practices, Education and Energy practices, and is Chair of the Non-Competition, Trade Secrets, and Employee Defection team. Mr. Lannon represents public and private companies in complex civil litigation, counsels businesses on asset protection and workplace issues, and advocates for management in employment disputes. Mr. Lannon devotes a large part of his practice to advising private educational institutions on a broad range of matters, including tenure disputes, campus security, student safety and discipline, policies and handbooks, Title IV compliance, governance, contracts, regulatory issues, and preventative training. He acts as general outside counsel to several colleges and secondary schools. He also represents educational institutions in state and federal courts and before the U.S. Department of Education and other administrative agencies. Mr. Lannon is a member of the National Association of College and University Attorneys, a Steering Committee member and former Co-Chair of the Boston Bar Association Section on College and University Law, a former editor of the *Journal of College and University Law*, and a former Chair of the Editorial Board for the *Boston Bar Journal*. United Educators named Mr. Lannon a select counsel for the defense of secondary and post-secondary institutions. He has written and presented widely on education issues. Mr. Lannon has been honored in education law as one of the Best Lawyers in America, Boston's Best Lawyers, Massachusetts Super Lawyers, and Who's Who. Mr. Lannon clerked for the Honorable Joseph R. Nolan, Associate Justice of the Supreme Judicial Court of Massachusetts (1992–93).

Ieuan G. Mahony is a partner at Holland & Knight concentrating his practice in intellectual property licensing and litigation and electronic commerce. Mr. Mahony is the firm-wide Technology Partner and Chair of the firm's Technology Advisory Council. Mr. Mahony has counseled clients on, and has litigated, a wide range of intellectual property and technology matters, including matters involving traditional and open-source software, software development and integration, IT outsourcing transactions, distance education, "best practices" in data privacy and protection, value-added medical and financial data, traditional and online media, medical devices, and domain names. Mr. Mahony's cases and licensing matters have involved rights under patent, copyright, trade secret, and trademark law, as well as rights of publicity. Mr. Mahony is active in community service, focusing his efforts on tutoring grade school students at the nearby Boston Renaissance Charter School.

Michael Manthei is a partner in the Boston office of Holland & Knight. He devotes his practice to the representation of clients in the healthcare and life sciences industries. Mr. Manthei represents clients primarily in healthcare fraud, abuse and compliance matters, in privacy matters, and in other healthcare regulatory

This is your new

Corporate Compliance Answer Book
2017 Edition
Holland & Knight LLP

Edited by Christopher A. Myers & Kwamina Thomas Williford

PLI's *Corporate Compliance Answer Book (2017 Edition)* has the information you need to understand what an effective compliance and ethics program is, how it should operate, and what issues and risks it must address in a variety of heavily regulated industries. Most importantly, it helps make the case to management and the board as to why your company needs such a program. The attorneys at Holland & Knight have assembled a team of experts not just to ask the right questions, but to give you all the answers.

Presented in a clear, easy-to-use Q&A format, *Corporate Compliance Answer Book (2017 Edition)* is loaded with dozens of case studies, invaluable compliance facts and tips, checklists, charts, and tables. This two-volume set provides the targeted guidance you need to design, implement, and enforce compliance programs that detect and prevent wrongdoing and minimize the legal and financial damage it can cause. Highlights of this year's edition of the *Answer Book* include the following:

The False Claims Act. The False Claims Act has become an extraordinarily popular and powerful addition to the government's enforcement arsenal, with a rapid increase in qui tam suits and recoveries in recent years. Chapter authors Lynne M. Halbrooks and Timothy J. Taylor have updated the *Answer Book*'s coverage of the FCA, the government's premier tool to recover government money lost to fraud and abuse, including the DOJ's recent emphasis on its commitment to holding individual wrongdoers accountable; conduct that most commonly leads to FCA liability; the importance of a company having an effective compliance program; and a number of recent and illustrative FCA case studies.

(continued on reverse)

Practising Law Institute
1177 Avenue of the Americas
New York, NY 10036
#170717

Government Contractors. The *Answer Book*'s coverage of contractor compliance includes a discussion of recent executive orders signed by President Obama that regulate employment practices in the government contracting industry and that a company should account for in its contractor compliance plan policies and procedures.

Environmental Law. In June 2016, President Obama signed into law the **Frank R. Lautenberg Chemical Safety for the 21st Century Act**, which substantially amends the Toxic Substances Control Act, including revising the standard under the TSCA used to determine whether regulatory control of certain chemicals is warranted. *See* Q 19.9.3 for further discussion of this new legislation's requirements.

Affordable Care Act: Compliance and Enforcement. Coverage of reporting, compliance, and antifraud provisions under the ACA includes details of the long-awaited **CMS final rule for reporting and returning Medicare overpayments**, providing answers to questions about how overpayments are identified; what the standard is for finding constructive knowledge of an overpayment; what obligations a provider or supplier has to investigate potential overpayments; quantifying overpayments; the time frame for reporting and returning overpayments; and how overpayments are reported and returned. *See* QQ 27.12.1–27.12.9.

SEC Investigations of Public Companies. The *Answer Book* provides the latest facts and figures on SEC enforcement (*see, e.g.*, QQ 32.1.2 and 32.3), as well as detailed answers to questions about the SEC's **whistleblower program** (*see* Q 32.1.4), how the SEC uses **data analytics** in its enforcement process (*see* Q 32.1.5), the kinds of charges the SEC can bring (*see* Q 32.27), and the differences between SEC enforcement actions brought in federal court and those pursued in **administrative proceedings** (*see* QQ 32.28–32.28.1).

Anti–Human Trafficking and Forced Labor. California continues to lead the charge in state enforcement of laws aimed at human trafficking and forced labor. In cooperation with the U.S. attorney's office, the L.A. County Sheriff's Department will establish the **Los Angeles Human Trafficking Task Force**, which is intended to be a model for the nation in the development of comprehensive and proactive interdisciplinary strategies (*see* Q 38.3). A number of notable suits were filed in federal district courts in California in connection with **violations of the California Act**, whose anti–human trafficking supply chain regulations apply to all "California businesses" (*see* QQ 38.5, 38.7.1). And California Attorney General Kamala Harris recently sponsored a bill to create the Statewide Interagency Human Trafficking Task Force (*see* Q 38.8).

An **Index** is included to assist in your research.

Practising Law Institute is proud to publish *Corporate Compliance Answer Book (2017 Edition)*. If you have any questions, please contact customer service at 1-800-260-4PLI.

matters. He regularly represents clients before state and federal regulatory and law enforcement authorities such as the Department of Justice, the Center for Medicare and Medicaid Services, and the Office of Inspector General for the Department of Health and Human Services. He speaks and writes frequently on healthcare fraud and abuse matters.

Stacy Watson May practices environmental law in the Jacksonville, Florida office of Holland & Knight, and is a Florida Qualified Arbitrator and a Florida Supreme Court Certified Circuit Mediator in all judicial circuits of the State of Florida. She previously served as in-house counsel with CSX Transportation. Ms. Watson May counsels clients in environmental compliance and enforcement actions across multiple states as well as at the federal level, regularly negotiating reduced penalties. She represents property owners in litigation and transactions involving the purchase, sale, and redevelopment of environmentally impacted properties, including due diligence in mergers and acquisitions, and property acquisition for significant residential, commercial, and condominium developments. She has handled numerous CERCLA matters including litigation and remediation projects. She also handles litigation involving environmental cost recovery claims, indoor air quality issues, Legionnaires' disease, and toxic torts.

Jeffrey W. Mittleman is a partner in the Business Section of Holland & Knight, is the Transactions leader of the firm's national Health and Life Sciences Team, and is a member of the firm's Compliance Services Team. He practices in the area of health, regulatory, and corporate law. With over ten years' experience, he represents clients in a variety of sectors of the healthcare industry including health plans (both fully and self-insured), PPOs, HMOs, insurers, pharmaceutical manufacturers, medical device companies, retail pharmacies, long-term care pharmacies, specialty pharmacies, mail order pharmacies, wholesale drug distributors, e-health, disease management, and healthcare technology companies. Mr. Mittleman represents clients in a variety of corporate and contractual transactions, including mergers and acquisitions, joint ventures, licensing, financing, and services-related transactions. He also advises clients in fraud and abuse defense, the structuring of compliance and ethics programs, Medicare, Medicaid, ERISA, HIPAA, licensing, state insurance, and managed care law. In addition, Mr. Mittleman has significant experience in advising health plans on drafting of plan documents, ASO contracting, and other regulatory issues.

David G. O'Leary's practice is concentrated primarily in the areas of employee benefits, employee stock ownership plans, executive compensation, and ERISA. A member of Holland & Knight's Private Wealth Services Group, he also has considerable experience advising clients in family business matters, estate planning, and related taxation.

Ronald A. Oleynik is chair of Holland & Knight's International Trade Regulatory Group. His experience involves a broad range of industrial security, customs, export, FCPA, and international trade matters. In the area of customs, his experience includes custom classification and valuation, rules of origin, and special duty programs such as GSP, NAFTA, CBI, and CBPTA, as well as trade policy representation before the Executive Branch and Congress regarding the WTO, CBI, CBPTA, and other multilateral and bilateral trade negotiations. In the area of U.S. export control, Mr. Oleynik counsels a broad range of clients on licensing, compliance, and enforcement issues under the export control regimes of the Departments of State, Commerce, and Treasury. In the area of industrial security, Mr. Oleynik has been involved in a significant percentage of all foreign investment review proceedings before the Committee on Foreign Investment in the United States and is one of the leading practitioners in the area of foreign direct investment in the U.S. defense industry under the U.S. regulations regarding foreign ownership, control, and influence.

William M. Pannier practices in the area of government contracts. Mr. Pannier has worked with a wide spectrum of federal, state, and local agencies, and he has handled cases before the Government Accountability Office, U.S. Court of Federal Claims, various boards and offices of hearings and appeals, and California courts. He also has experience in compliance and enforcement defense matters, including internal investigations, voluntary and mandatory disclosures, and civil false claims. Before joining Holland & Knight, Mr. Pannier served in the U.S. Air Force JAG Corps, where he concentrated in government contracts, advising on all aspects of the procurement process from acquisition strategy to source selection, award and contract administration.

Jenna C. Phipps Bigornia is an associate in Holland & Knight's Litigation Practice Group. She is a graduate, cum laude, of Suffolk University Law School, where she was Editor-in-Chief of the *Suffolk Journal of Trial & Appellate Advocacy* and served on the Moot Court Board. She received a master's degree in Public Health from Boston University and graduated cum laude from Simmons College with a degree in Biochemistry. She is admitted to practice in Massachusetts.

Shannon Hartsfield Salimone is a Board Certified Specialist in health law in Florida, advising clients on state and federal healthcare regulatory matters including compliance, data privacy, licensure, prescription drug distribution, and fraud and abuse. She is a past Chair of the eHealth Privacy and Security Interest Group of the American Bar Association's Health Law Section. The clients she serves include assisted living facilities, health plans, medical technology companies, disease management companies, nursing homes, pharmaceutical manufacturers and distributors, tissue banks, hospitals, medical management companies, and other members of the healthcare industry.

William N. Shepherd is a partner in Holland & Knight's West Palm Beach office and is a member of the Litigation Group, Compliance Services Team, and White Collar Team. Mr. Shepherd is a trial lawyer who defends individuals and corporations in state and federal government investigations and grand jury investigations. He also assists the general counsel of public and private companies in conducting sensitive internal inquiries. Mr. Shepherd's extensive trial practice background also serves to support his practice in complex civil litigation involving fraud and the False Claims Act. Prior to joining Holland & Knight, Mr. Shepherd served, at the appointment of the attorney general, as the Statewide Prosecutor of Florida and earlier in his career, as a prosecutor in Miami, Florida. Mr. Shepherd is the chair of the American Bar Association's 20,000-member Criminal Justice Section, a member of its Global Anti-Corruption Task Force, and former division director of its White Collar Crime Division. He served as a law clerk to U.S. District Court Judge Stephen N. Limbaugh.

Daniel I. Small practices in the area of litigation, focusing on witness preparation, government and internal investigations, white collar criminal law, and complex civil litigation. He has extensive investigation, jury trial, and other litigation experience. Prior to entering private practice, Mr. Small was a prosecutor for the U.S. Department of Justice, during which time he tried RICO, corruption, financial, and regulatory cases. Mr. Small received various awards and commendations for his work. He also was General Counsel for a publicly traded healthcare management firm, where he oversaw in-house legal and risk management staff, outside counsel, litigation, compliance, and facility, entity, and physician contracting. Mr. Small has written several books on litigation for the ABA, including *Preparing Witnesses* (4th ed. 2014) and *Going To Trial*, used in CLE programs he gives throughout the country, and was a Lecturer on Law at Harvard Law School. He is a frequent television, radio, and newspaper commentator. Mr. Small has represented witnesses, plaintiffs, and defendants in a wide range of internal and external investigations, administrative proceedings, and civil and criminal litigation. These have included issues of healthcare, education, regulation, insider trading, revenue recognition, and others.

Ilenna J. Stein is an associate in Holland & Knight's Boston office. She is a member of the firm's Healthcare & Life Sciences Team and the Mergers and Acquisitions Practice Group. She advises clients on healthcare regulatory matters, fraud, abuse and compliance matters, and corporate transactional matters in various sectors of the healthcare industry. This includes pharmaceutical and medical device manufacturers, pharmacies (retail, specialty, long-term care, and mail order), pharmacy benefits managers, insurers, e-health, and wholesale drug distributors. Ms. Stein also assists in a variety of corporate and contractual transactions for healthcare and life sciences companies.

Sonya Strnad practices in the litigation department of Holland & Knight and has experience in both federal and state courts, regulatory investigations, congressional investigations, and internal investigations. Her practice encompasses internal and government investigations into FCPA compliance, fraud, and embezzlement, as well as securities class actions, federal securities fraud, and derivatives litigation. Ms. Strnad is a Certified E-Discovery Specialist. She is a member of the Sedona Working Groups on Electronic Document

Retention and Production (WG1) and International Electronic Information Management, Discovery and Disclosure (WG6), as well as the firm's National Electronic Data Discovery Team. She has extensive experience in e-discovery, and forensic and document retention arenas, and frequently lectures on these topics for businesses, for Continuing Legal Education classes, and internally within the firm. Ms. Strnad also counsels clients on document management practices outside of litigation.

Timothy J. Taylor is a litigation attorney in Holland & Knight's Northern Virginia office. His practice focuses on civil and criminal litigation and related enforcement issues, including False Claims Act defense, federal and internal investigations, corporate compliance, and white collar matters. He has particular experience representing and advising clients in the government contracts and life sciences industries, including in matters before courts, the GAO, and the boards of contract appeals. Before joining Holland & Knight, Mr. Taylor served as a judicial clerk to the Honorable Harris L. Hartz of the U.S. Court of Appeals for the Tenth Circuit and the Honorable Charles F. Lettow of the U.S. Court of Federal Claims. While attending Harvard Law School, Mr. Taylor served as a research assistant to professors John Manning, Jim Greiner, and the late Bill Stuntz. He also served as an editor of the *Harvard Law Review*.

Antonia I. Tzinova practices in the areas of international trade, foreign direct investment, and industrial security. She advises on defense and high-technology exports, U.S. trade embargoes and economic sanctions, and customs matters. She regularly represents clients before the Committee on Foreign Investment in the United States (CFIUS) and advises on measures to mitigate Foreign Ownership, Control, or Influence (FOCI) in cross-border mergers and acquisitions of U.S. government and defense contractors. She counsels foreign investors on structuring investments in the defense, high-tech, and critical infrastructure sectors of the U.S. economy. Recent transactions include advising on measures to mitigate FOCI in portfolio investments by private equity firms in government contractors with security clearances for performance on classified contracts, as well as representation before the CFIUS in foreign government investment in a U.S. port and refueling facility. Ms. Tzinova also has extensive experience in assisting technology exporters, government contractors, and research universities in developing and implementing export compliance programs and conducting company-wide compliance training. Enhancing compliance under the International Traffic in Arms Regulations (ITAR), the Export Administration Regulations (EAR), and Office of Foreign Assets Control (OFAC) regulations often includes conducting confidential internal investigations and submission of voluntary disclosures to mitigate potential export compliance violations. Ms. Tzinova also advises on inbound movement of goods in import matters, including classification, valuation, country of origin, and import licensing under the U.S. Customs and Border Protection, the U.S. Bureau of Alcohol, Tobacco, Firearms and Explosives, and other U.S. trade regulations.

Richard T. Williams is a partner in the Commercial Litigation Practice Group in the Los Angeles office of Holland & Knight and a member of the firm's Antitrust, Class Action, and Product Liability Teams. In several dozen federal and state trials, both jury and nonjury, and in arbitrations, both domestic and international, Mr. Williams represented a wide variety of domestic and overseas corporations as well as foreign governments. Mr. Williams is a graduate of Stanford University (A.B. 1967, M.B.A. 1972, J.D. 1972) and has been recognized in *The Best Lawyers in America* and *Who's Who in America*.

James D. Wing is a senior litigator in Miami experienced in representing officers and directors of public companies in a variety of contexts. He also represents accountants and accounting firms in tax, Sarbanes-Oxley 404, and indemnity and document access issues arising from government white collar enforcement activities. Mr. Wing is the Chairman of the D&O Insurance Subcommittee of the ABA Business Section's Director and Officer Liability Committee and a national speaker on these issues. He is also a frequent speaker and active practitioner in the area of commercial arbitration. Mr. Wing is a summa cum laude, Phi Beta Kappa graduate of Beloit College, holds an M.A. degree from the University of Chicago in Germanic Languages as a Ford Foundation scholar, holds a law degree from the University of Chicago Law School, and is listed in *The Best Lawyers in America* (2008) and *Who's Who in the World*.

Don Zarin is a partner in the International & Cross Border Transactions practice group in the Washington, D.C. office of Holland &
Knight. He is co-head of the International Trade Practice Group and
head of the Foreign Corrupt Practices Act Team, a part of the White
Collar Defense and Corporate Compliance Team. Mr. Zarin has
represented and counseled U.S. and foreign companies on a wide
range of international trade and international commercial matters,
including multilateral and bilateral trade agreements, antidumping
duty proceedings and other trade remedy laws, customs matters,
export control issues, U.S. anti-boycott laws, and trade legislative
issues, as well as overseas joint venture projects and international
commercial agreements. He has represented foreign governments
on trade policy matters, in treaty negotiations, and in the drafting of
a constitution. Mr. Zarin is a leading attorney in the area of the
Foreign Corrupt Practices Act and anti-corruption practices. He is
the author of PLI's *Doing Business Under the Foreign Corrupt Practices Act*, a leading textbook on this subject. He has been appointed
by the Department of Justice to serve as an independent Compliance Monitor in a major FCPA enforcement case.

Acknowledgments

Holland & Knight LLP and the authors and contributors of this book wish to acknowledge the extraordinary and invaluable contributions of former Holland & Knight attorney Suzanne Foster, who is now Vice President and General Manager of Medtronic Advanced Energy, located in Portsmouth, New Hampshire. Ms. Foster not only wrote and/or edited several chapters in this publication's first edition, *Corporate Compliance Answer Book 2009*, she also took on many of the organizational responsibilities that helped bring the book to fruition.

Table of Chapters

VOLUME 1

VOLUME 2

Table of Contents

PART II
FCPA's Accounting Provisions

VOLUME 2

Table of Contents

cxxxix

Introduction

"We are a good company. We don't need a compliance program. What is a 'compliance program' anyway?"

"I am sure we have a compliance program, I just can't tell you where it is."

"We would like to have a compliance program; we just don't have the resources right now. Our financial performance last quarter wasn't so good."

These are just a few of the variations on the common theme frequently heard from companies we speak with about compliance and ethics programs. Many companies instinctively react negatively to the suggestion that they spend time and often scarce resources on a compliance and ethics program. They initially don't see a positive and direct impact on their bottom line. But this attitude is short-sighted and potentially disastrous, as corporate debacles too numerous to count can attest.

Frequently, however, when corporate executives see the fallout from an Enron, a WorldCom, or any one of hundreds of multi-million-dollar fraud settlements with healthcare organizations, government contractors, financial institutions, and others, they often disassociate their companies from the "bad" companies that commit fraud and other offenses. The reality, however, is that bad things happen to "good" companies too. Despite the best intentions on the part of boards, management, and employees, many companies involved in heavily regulated industries are easily tripped up by one or more of the complex regulatory regimes that govern their operations. This includes, among numerous others:

- public companies, which must comply with the Sarbanes-Oxley Act and the Dodd-Frank Act;

- government contractors, which must comply with the Federal Acquisition Regulation and other procurement regulations;

- health and life sciences companies, which must comply with Medicare, Medicaid, FDA, the Affordable Care Act ("Obamacare"), and a host of many other federal and state regulations; and

- financial institutions, which must comply with the Bank Secrecy Act and now must deal with the investigations and regulations flowing out of the financial system meltdown.

Sometimes companies make the same mistakes over and over again because they misunderstand a government requirement. The impact of such mistakes often depends on the "intent" or mindset of the individuals involved. Did they misunderstand a complex regulation despite a good-faith effort to comply and thus make an honest error? Did they fail to pay attention to the regulations that they knew governed their operations, and thus commit "reckless disregard" and subject themselves to civil penalties? Did they intentionally violate a known regulation in an effort to cheat the government, the investing public, or others to whom they owed a responsibility to be honest, and thus commit a criminal violation? What is inside the heads of the key actors, management, and sometimes the board, is the crucial determining factor in whether the company simply has to repay any overpayment it has received, or whether it is hit with crippling penalties, damage to reputation, and possible suspension, debarment, or exclusion from future government business.

Often it is government investigators, prosecutors, or plaintiff's lawyers who must make judgments about the company's intent or state of mind. Gleaning a corporation's intent from documents and witness statements is a process that involves judgment and sometimes guesswork. The persons making those judgments and guesses often don't have the best interests of the corporation as their top priority. Investigating agents are trained to be skeptical; prosecutors sometimes seek the thrill of bringing down a big industry player. For example, an Assistant U.S. Attorney in a healthcare fraud investigation of one of our clients once said, "Anyone who is making money in the Medicare system is committing fraud." How does an organization respond and prove something government agents and prosecutors are programmed not to believe?

The one thing that has proven to be most useful in persuading regulators, prosecutors, and judges of the good faith and good intent of companies is an "effective," fully implemented and supported compliance and ethics program. Recent studies have demonstrated empirically that, in addition to the ability to deflect investigations into possible regulatory and other violations, companies with good systems of governance and compliance have numerous financial advantages in terms of access to capital, lower insurance costs, and higher stock prices.

This *Corporate Compliance Answer Book* provides information intended to help busy corporate counsel and compliance officials understand what an effective compliance and ethics program is, how it should operate, and what issues and risks it must address in a variety of heavily regulated industries. Most importantly, it helps make the case to management and the board as to why your company needs to have such a program.

CHRISTOPHER A. MYERS

1

The Business Case for Compliance Programs

Christopher A. Myers & Michael Manthei *

Good governance matters, if for no other reason than bad governance is so costly.

Buy the Board
Morgan Stanley US Investment Strategy

There is much confusion among counsel and other officials of companies in heavily regulated industries about what it means to have a compliance and ethics program. There is also much confusion about the costs and benefits of such programs. This chapter provides an overview of what a compliance and ethics program really is and why companies in heavily regulated industries need them. It also provides empirical evidence demonstrating that compliance programs are not just a cost center but can provide measurable financial returns on the investment.

* The authors wish to acknowledge Suzanne M. Foster, Mary Anne H. McElroy, and Jennifer A. Short for their contributions to this chapter.

Compliance and Ethics Programs Overview

Definitions

Q 1.1   What is a compliance program?

The most commonly used definition of a compliance program comes from chapter eight of the *U.S. Sentencing Guidelines Manual*, dealing with the sentencing of organizations.

---

§ 8B2.1. Effective Compliance and Ethics Program

(a) To have an effective compliance and ethics program,
    . . . an organization shall—
    (1) exercise due diligence to prevent and detect
        criminal conduct; and
    (2) otherwise promote an organizational culture that
        encourages ethical conduct and a commitment to
        compliance with the law.

> Such compliance and ethics program shall be reason-
> ably designed, implemented, and enforced so that the
> program is generally effective in preventing and
> detecting criminal conduct. The failure to prevent or
> detect the instant offense does not necessarily mean
> that the program is not generally effective in
> preventing and detecting criminal conduct.[1]

The Society of Corporate Compliance and Ethics has a very practical definition of "compliance program" that can be useful in communications with company management and the board of directors:

> On a very basic level it is about education, definition, preven-
> tion, detection, collaboration, and enforcement. It is a system
> of individuals, processes, and policies and procedures devel-
> oped to ensure compliance with all applicable federal and state
> laws, industry regulations, and private contracts governing the
> actions of the organization. A compliance program is not
> merely a piece of paper or a binder on a shelf; it is not a quick
> fix to the latest hot problem; it is not a collection of hollow
> words. A compliance program—an *effective* compliance
> program—must be a living, ongoing process that is part of the
> fabric of the organization. A compliance program must be a
> commitment to an ethical way of conducting business and a
> system for helping individuals to do the right thing.[2]

Q 1.1.1   What does the Federal Sentencing Guidelines' definition mean by "due diligence"?

The U.S. Sentencing Commission's definition cited above goes on
to define what it means by "due diligence" and to describe what
promoting "an organizational culture that encourages ethical
conduct and a commitment to compliance with the law" requires.
The Federal Sentencing Guidelines enumerate seven elements that
are considered the minimum requirements of an effective compliance
program.[3] (These seven elements are discussed in detail in chapter
2.) In addition, the Federal Sentencing Guidelines require a periodic
compliance risk assessment and designing and implementing compli-

3

ance procedures to address the risks identified.[4] (The risk assessment process is discussed in detail in chapter 4.)

Q 1.1.2 Should the primary focus of a compliance program be on criminal conduct?

Because of the nature of its mission (criminal sentencing), the U.S. Sentencing Commission guidance speaks to a compliance and ethics program preventing and detecting *criminal* conduct. In commentary and in other communications, however, the Commission made clear that the better practice would be for the program to address all legal, regulatory, and ethical risks facing the organization, not just the risk of criminal conduct.

Thus, most organizations at the forefront of thinking about compliance and ethics programs use them in the context of comprehensive enterprise risk management programs.[5] In this way, organizations can address their commitment to compliance with laws and regulations, their commitment to ethical business practices, and fixing problems internally before they fester and expose the organization to legal, regulatory, or reputational damage.

"Effective" Compliance Programs

Q 1.2 What makes a compliance program "effective"?

The qualifying word almost always seen in the context of compliance programs is "effective": Does the organization have an *effective* compliance and ethics program? This issue is key.

Enron had a "compliance program" in the sense that, when the FBI went into company offices after the investigation had begun, they found a written compliance manual on a bookshelf. Unfortunately for Enron, its compliance program had never been implemented. Its written procedures were not followed. In the view of government investigators it was a "paper program"; it was not an "effective" program.

An effective compliance and ethics program should:

- communicate to employees, customers, and the government that your company is committed to compliance with laws and regulations and ethical business conduct;
- provide an outlet, an internal place, to report possible problems or violations and to ask questions;
- provide compliance training and guidance to help employees understand proper procedures and how to conform their behavior to the regulatory requirements;
- provide an internal mechanism for appropriately investigating potential wrongdoing;
- provide for periodic audits of compliance with key laws, regulations, and company procedures;
- identify problems early and provide a process for correcting them before they fester or cause unhappiness in employees that can result in reports to the government;
- provide oversight and organization of compliance procedures throughout the company, allowing for more effective oversight by both senior management and the board;
- provide a process for and source of documentation of compliance-related activities;
- be integrated into customer service and quality control activities to provide better service to customers;
- properly implement the growing number of state and federal regulations that have made compliance program components mandatory in certain areas such as healthcare, financial services, and government contracts; and
- periodically assess compliance and enforcement risks and effectiveness of company procedures to address them.

COMPLIANCE FACT

Studies have shown that most employees would rather have a problem dealt with internally than report it to the government. If a company's program and management demonstrate a commitment to compliance, employees will feel more comfortable reporting issues through the internal mechanism.

An effective compliance and ethics program brings all of the company's compliance activities under one umbrella. This allows for objective oversight and documentation that the company is meeting its obligations. It provides a process for making sure that individual employees and management are receiving the training they need and that the board receives the information it needs to provide proper oversight. It organizes compliance activities into a comprehensible bundle. And it provides a process for evaluating existing and developing risks and making sure that the organization is prepared to meet them appropriately.

Without the structure of a compliance and ethics program, an organization's compliance activities can be disjointed, inconsistent, and difficult to identify. They are often overseen by the very people who are required to comply and who may have other reasons, both business and personal, to take compliance shortcuts, often with disastrous results for the organization.

The Role of a Compliance and Ethics Program

Ethical Conduct and the Corporate Culture

Q 1.3   How does a compliance program help prevent unethical or illegal conduct from occurring?

The regulatory and ethical guidelines, training, reporting, and disciplinary requirements incorporated into a program set corporate-wide standards. These standards clearly identify hazards and establish policies to guide conduct away from them. In the event that unethical or illegal conduct occurs, a program will include mechanisms to report the misconduct, to enforce appropriate disciplinary action, to conduct an investigation and to implement changes that will prevent similar conduct in the future.

Q 1.3.1   How can a program change a corporate culture?

Initially, by adopting a program, the company declares the ethical and legal values and standards by which it wishes to be judged and by which it will measure its employees, vendors, and customers. In turn, the program becomes a central coordinating mechanism for furnishing and disseminating to employees information and training on their ethical and legal obligations. The program provides a mechanism—typically a confidential one—allowing employees to report potential ethical and legal problems and to seek information and guidance before problems become crises. It also provides a framework for rapid responses to any potential ethical or legal misconduct and gives warning of the consequences of such conduct.

In order for a compliance program to support an ethical culture, however, it must be supported and nurtured by senior management and the board. Employees have an uncanny ability to see through programs that are supported only on paper or through lip service.

Why Businesses Need Compliance and Ethics Programs

Q 1.4   Why does my organization need a compliance and ethics program?

Most companies, whether public or private, doing business in the United States and/or overseas, are subject to a wide range of local, state, federal, and/or international laws and regulations. Violation of these laws and regulations often comes with significant reputational damage, as well as civil and/or criminal penalties. An effective compliance and ethics program can mitigate the problems, costs, and damages of such violations and the investigations they often trigger.

Participation in activities that are the subject of complex regulatory requirements is a high-risk activity, make no mistake about it. The rewards from such participation are frequently high, but the risks of failing to meet one or more of the regulatory requirements are also high, even for the best-intentioned organization. Compliance programs provide a significant level of insurance against such risks. For the boards and management of organizations involved in government programs, receiving government money, or subject to regulatory regimes, it is literally a breach of fiduciary duty not to have a compliance program in place.[6]

Also, in government enforcement actions involving almost all agencies, a condition of most settlement agreements involving companies that do not have a demonstrably effective compliance and ethics program is the implementation of such a program. Organizations that already have a program in place are typically allowed to simply revise and enhance their existing programs to correct any problems discovered during the government investigation. Organizations without a program are required to implement one, often with onerous and expensive bells and whistles, including frequent outside audits and the appointment of an outside compliance program overseer or monitor.

Finally, many governmental agencies and regulatory programs now specifically mandate compliance programs as a condition of participation. These include healthcare, government contractors, and financial institutions, to name just a few.

Q 1.4.1   Can't we just start a compliance program after we get hit with a government investigation?

Not if you want to get credit for the program. The Department of Justice, along with numerous other federal agencies, formally gives credit to companies for having a compliance and ethics program. DOJ policy instructs federal prosecutors to consider a number of unique factors in determining whether or not to charge a corporation with a criminal violation. Among those factors is "the existence and effectiveness of the corporation's *pre-existing* compliance program."[7] In evaluating potential criminal charges against business entities, a prosecutor will evaluate whether the organization's compliance program was already in existence at the time the investigation was begun, or at the time the organization first became aware of it. "Prosecutors should therefore attempt to determine whether a corporation's compliance program is merely a 'paper program' or whether it was designed, implemented, reviewed, and revised, as appropriate in an effective manner."[8]

The *U.S. Attorneys' Manual* provides extensive guidance to prosecutors on the factors that should be evaluated to determine whether or not the program is "truly effective."

Compliance programs that are begun or implemented only after the company learns of a government investigation are viewed with skepticism by prosecutors and agents. To receive the full benefit from an "effective" program, the company must be able to demonstrate that it was implemented voluntarily, because the company wanted to "do the right thing" and had an ethical approach to business relationships, particularly those involving government funding. A company that begins its program after learning of an investigation is viewed as developing a conscience only under duress.

Amendments to the Federal Sentencing Guidelines for organizations in 2004 and 2010 also make it clear that programs developed and implemented at the last minute will not receive credit as "effective." The 2004 amendments added a requirement that, in addition to a program of legal compliance to prevent and detect criminal conduct, an effective program must establish and maintain an organizational culture that "encourages ethical conduct and a commitment to compliance with the law."[9] The 2004 amendments also added an eighth "element," providing that, "In implementing [an effective compliance program], the organization shall periodically assess the risk of criminal conduct and shall take appropriate steps to design, implement, or modify each requirement [for an effective compliance program] to reduce the risk of criminal conduct identified through this process."[10]

In 2010, the Federal Sentencing Guidelines again were amended to include the following:

- **Reporting Requirements:** Compliance officers must have regular and direct access to the board or appropriate committee (typically, the Audit Committee) and report periodically (at least annually) on the effectiveness of the compliance and ethics program.[11] The board must also receive regular compliance training and exercise reasonable oversight over the program.[12]
- **Response to Criminal Conduct:** If criminal conduct is detected, an organization must consider restitution or other reparations to victims, self-disclosure and cooperation with the government,[13] and modifications to its program to ensure that similar conduct will not take place in the future.[14]

In our view, it is virtually impossible to implement these requirements under duress or on short notice.[15]

Q 1.4.2   What happens if we don't have a compliance program, learn of a government investigation, and *still* don't implement a program?

You likely will be viewed by the government as having a cavalier attitude about your legal and ethical obligations. In fact, in at least one case, the government has taken the view that, in heavily regulated industries like healthcare, not having a comprehensive compliance program is itself evidence supporting an intent to commit fraud (*see United States v. Merck-Medco* case study, *infra*). As a result, all companies that derive revenue from federal funding should ensure that they have compliance and ethics programs and that their programs are "effective" under applicable legal standards and industry practices.

Compliance and the Law

Q 1.5   Does the law require businesses to have compliance and ethics programs?

As discussed in chapter 2, the Federal Sentencing Guidelines provide a basic framework for all compliance programs. However, there also are many statutes and regulations that require companies to implement various compliance measures.[16] For instance, the Bank Secrecy Act mandates that banks and other financial institutions adopt programs to prevent the "laundering" and deposit of proceeds from illegal activities such as drug trafficking and the financing of terrorist activities.[17] The Sarbanes-Oxley Act of 2002[18] requires that publicly traded companies establish audit committees and compliance procedures to better promote the integrity of a company's internal accounting controls and financial reporting. Certain government contractors are also required to have compliance and ethics programs.[19]

The Patient Protection and Affordable Care Act of 2010 (ACA), also known as the Healthcare Reform Act,[20] requires providers and suppliers enrolled in federal healthcare programs to create and maintain compliance programs as a condition of their continued participation.[21] The ACA further empowers the Health and Human Services Department Office of Inspector General (HHS-OIG) to disenroll noncompliant providers and suppliers and/or to impose civil monetary penalties or other immediate sanctions.[22] In addition to the general compliance program requirement, the ACA also imposes much more detailed compliance and ethics program requirements for skilled nursing facilities and nursing facilities.[23]

Q 1.5.1   Are there state law requirements related to compliance and ethics programs?

Yes. States also have begun to experiment with direct legislative requirements. California has passed legislation requiring all pharmaceutical manufacturers to certify that they have adopted a compliance program that is in accordance with HHS-OIG guidance and that incorporates the guidelines of the Pharmaceutical Research and Manufacturing Association's Code of Conduct related to interactions with healthcare professionals.[24] Maine requires manufacturers and labelers of prescription drugs to report on marketing costs and expenses, and imposes prohibitions on advertising and disclosures regarding clinical trials.[25] New York requires all Medicaid providers to develop, adopt, and implement effective compliance programs.[26] Numerous other states have passed, or are considering, statutes intended to restrict activities related to marketing and advertising of pharmaceutical and medical device products, all with the intent of limiting or driving down the costs of drugs and/or devices and related products and services.[27]

Q 1.5.2   Do some agencies require (rather than recommend) compliance programs?

Yes. Several agencies that oversee compliance issues require formal compliance programs. The trend throughout the federal government is to remove compliance and ethics programs from the "recommended" list to become a clear requirement for participation. As time passes, more and more federal agencies are expected to mandate compliance procedures, including codes of conduct, ethical business practices, training, auditing, etc.

For example, in December 2007 and again in November 2008, the Department of Defense (DOD), the General Services Administration (GSA), the National Aeronautics and Space Administration (NASA), and the Office of Federal Procurement Policy (OFPP) adopted final rules amending the Federal Acquisition Regulation (FAR) to require most federal contractors and subcontractors to:

11

CASE STUDY:
United States v. Merck-Medco Managed Care LLC [28]

The government contended that Merck's failure to maintain an adequate compliance program demonstrated that it acted with reckless disregard or deliberate ignorance of the falsity of the claims it had submitted. Merck moved to dismiss on the grounds that the lack of a compliance program was insufficient to establish that the company or its upper management acted in reckless disregard in submitting such claims. The court, however, denied the motion, holding as a matter of law that the failure to have an adequate compliance program "satisfied"—for pleading purposes—the allegation that the company acted with reckless disregard of the truth or falsity of the claims.

This case arose out of a civil action brought by the Department of Justice under the False Claims Act, which provides that companies that "knowingly" submit false claims paid with federal funds are liable for *three times* the actual damages suffered by the government, plus additional penalties of up to $11,000 *per claim*. These per-claim penalties alone can snowball into astronomical amounts for a company that submits thousands of claims for payment each year. Because the government is *not* required to prove the company had *actual* knowledge that a claim was false in order to find that it acted in "reckless disregard" or "deliberate ignorance" of the truth or falsity of its claims—a much easier legal standard for the government to meet—a company that is merely sloppy or careless in the preparation of claims can get caught in a quagmire of complex litigation and substantial liability, even though it intended no wrongdoing.

- have a code of business ethics and conduct within thirty days of contract award;
- develop internal controls to support the code within ninety days of contract award;
- implement a formal "awareness" or training program on the code within ninety days of contract award;
- exercise "due diligence" to prevent and detect improper conduct;
- promote an organizational culture that encourages ethical conduct and a commitment to compliance with the law;
- display a hotline poster;
- report "credible evidence" of any violation of federal criminal law involving fraud, conflict of interest, bribery, or gratuity violations found in title 18 of the U.S. Code, or a violation of the civil False Claims Act; and
- "fully cooperate" in government audits, investigations or corrective actions relating to contract fraud and corruption.[29]

Federal banking law requires a variety of mandatory compliance measures, including anti-money laundering programs;[30] the SEC mandates other compliance measures;[31] the Deficit Reduction Act of 2005 requires all organizations that receive more than $5 million per year in funding from the Medicaid program to have healthcare fraud prevention policies and procedures in place as a condition of payment;[32] and all companies with access to confidential health information must have privacy and security programs under the Health Insurance Portability and Accountability Act (HIPAA),[33] to name just a few.

Q 1.5.3   What have the courts said about compliance programs?

Courts increasingly are beginning to recognize that a corporation's failure to have a functioning and operational compliance plan may give rise to considerable legal exposure. In the landmark case *In re Caremark International, Inc. Derivative Litigation*,[34] the Delaware Court of Chancery held that corporate directors violate their fiduciary duty if they fail to assure that corporations implement "information and reporting systems" to appropriately supervise and monitor the corporation and to prevent wrongdoing. In *Caremark*, the shareholders brought a derivative action against the board of directors alleging that the board breached its fiduciary duty of care to the corporation by failing to monitor actively or to give appropriate attention to the corporation's performance. The court explained that directors have an "obligation" to attempt in good faith to assure that a corporate information and reporting system exists and that the failure to do so can render a director liable for losses caused by noncompliance by the corporation with applicable legal standards.

Specifically, the shareholders blamed the board of directors for failing to detect and prevent numerous violations of the anti-kickback statute[35] and of the False Claims Act,[36] which in turn gave rise to civil and criminal investigations by various federal agencies. Caremark ultimately settled the underlying investigations by pleading guilty to one count of mail fraud. It also paid civil and criminal fines totaling $250 million.

In *United States v. Merck-Medco Managed Care, LLC,*[37] the court found that, as a matter of law, a company's alleged failure to maintain an appropriate program suffices to state a claim that the company acted with reckless disregard of its legal obligations by submitting false claims to the government. The court held that Merck-Medco, a large pharmacy benefits manager, could be held liable for violating the False Claims Act as a result of failing to have a program to prevent the submission of false or fraudulent claims for payment to the government. At the very least, the government's charge that the company's compliance program was inadequate was sufficient to support a False Claims Act allegation that the company acted with reckless disregard of the truth or falsity of the claims it submitted to federal healthcare programs.[38]

Your Compliance Program

The Costs

Q 1.6   Can our business afford a program?

The better question may be whether you can afford *not* to have a program. The cost of implementing and maintaining a program always will be much less than the cost of responding to an investigation or the cost of settling civil or criminal claims.

In recent years, ruinous corporate scandals have brought down several large companies in the United States: WorldCom, Adelphia, Tyco, Enron, Arthur Andersen, and BellSouth. Other companies have suffered severe reputational and/or financial damage from compliance failures, sometimes even from allegations of failures.[39] In addition to corporate damage, the government has ratcheted up criminal prosecutions of corporate executives it believes are responsible for wrongdoing.[40]

A fully implemented program with commitment from top leadership might have prevented each of these corporate downfalls. In the Enron case there is the now-famous story of how, when investigators searched the office of Enron CFO Andrew Fastow, they found a copy of the company's compliance program and procedures still sealed in the plastic wrapping in which it had arrived. It was the ultimate in what DOJ considers a "paper program."

Many of these cases started with whistleblowers who, instead of reporting wrongdoing to company, went to the government. In many instances, the employees tried to report wrongdoing to company officials, but there was no effective internal mechanism. In others, the corporate culture discouraged reporting wrongdoing or actively encouraged the wrongdoing in the first place. Perhaps warnings were ignored or the employee was written off as "difficult" or as an "underperformer" because of his or her refusal to engage in questionable conduct. Either way, an effective program could have addressed these issues and given the company a chance to prevent illegal or unethical conduct or at least stop it at its earliest and least expensive stages.

Q 1.7   What are the potential costs of an investigation?

Responding to government investigations, internal or external reports of violations, fraud audits, and the like is extremely expensive. Sometimes just responding to government subpoenas or requests for information can cost millions of dollars;[41] and in many cases, these out-of-pocket costs of defense counsel and related consultants are only the tip of the iceberg. (See the extensive discussion of the Boeing Company case below for a vivid illustration of the costs—monetary and otherwise—of an investigation.) Furthermore, criminal and civil penalties can reach into the hundreds of millions, or even billions, of dollars (in 2012, DOJ recovered a record $9 billion in corporate settlements); these penalties are sometimes accompanied by suspensions, debarments, exclusions, or other prohibitions from doing business with the government or receiving specified government benefits.

 CASE STUDIES

Pfizer paid $2.3 billion to resolve criminal and civil allegations that it had illegally marketed a prescription pain killer. Announced in September 2009, it was the largest healthcare fraud settlement and largest criminal fine of any kind in U.S. history.

Tenet Healthcare paid the government $900 million for alleged billing violations that included manipulation of payments from Medicare as well as kickbacks, up-coding, and bill padding.

Columbia HCA paid the government $840 million to settle a False Claims Act case. The federal government's suit against HCA alleged numerous frauds such as billing for lab tests that were not medically necessary, up-coding medical services to get higher reimbursements, billing the government for advertising under the guise of community education, and billing the government for non-reimbursable costs.

TAP Pharmaceuticals paid $860 million to settle a whistleblower lawsuit based on alleged kickbacks to doctors. Abbott Laboratories paid over $600 million to settle similar allegations.

Abbott Laboratories, Inc. pleaded guilty and agreed to pay $1.5 billion to resolve its criminal and civil liability arising from allegedly unlawful promotion of the prescription drug Depakote for uses not approved by the FDA.

GlaxoSmithKline agreed to a combined criminal and civil False Claims Act settlement of $3 billion, as the DOJ reported in a press release issued on July 2, 2012. The pharmaceutical company's settlement was for promoting certain of its antidepressant drugs for unapproved uses and failing to report safety data.

Additionally, if the target of the investigation is a public company, the stock price frequently takes a significant tumble, thus damaging shareholders. This, in turn, often leads to shareholder suits against management and the board. Dealing with these problems distracts executives and employees from their duties, and time is consumed in responding to subpoenas, customer inquiries, grand jury testimony, and civil and administrative discovery demands. No company can keep its eye totally on business in the midst of an investigation.

COMPLIANCE FACT

On June 7, 2015, the two co-chief executives of Deutsche Bank, the world's sixth largest investment bank, announced their resignations amid "legal problems and accusations of misconduct that have weighed on Deutsche Bank's profit and undercut its reputation."[42] Following the financial crisis, "Deutsche Bank became embroiled in a series of official investigations of wrongdoing. In April, Deutsche Bank agreed to pay $2.5 billion to the United States and British authorities to settle accusations that some employees conspired to rig benchmark interest rates. . . . Partly because of the $2.5 billion settlement, Deutsche Bank's profit in the first three months of the year sank by about half. . . . Legal costs more than offset a 24 percent increase in quarterly revenue."[43]

Q 1.7.1   Why not just pay the fine and move on?

Studies have shown that the impact of fraud on a company can be enormous. "Estimates of the cost of white-collar crime to companies in the United States range from $200 billion (Touby, 1994) to $600 billion per year (Association of Certified Fraud Examiners (ACFE, 2002))."[44] White-collar fraud impacts a typical company between 1% and 6% of annual sales.[45] Such compliance violations are reported to have caused 30% of new business failures.[46] An analysis of 114 companies (matched pairs of companies, half of which had suffered a white-collar fraud event and half of which did not) revealed that "a firm's clarity of policies and procedures, formal communication, contingent pay for employees [compensation tied to performance criteria], . . . audit committees, contingent pay for board members and codes of conduct are also associated with fewer crimes."[47]

Busy executives sometimes view compliance and ethics programs only as overhead items that do not add to the bottom line, and compliance officers as nay-sayers, reasoning that bad things that happen at other companies won't happen to "good" companies and "good" people like ours. However, true commitment to ethical behavior and compliance with laws and regulations is becoming an important *competitive advantage* for companies.

Q 1.7.2   Shouldn't compliance programs be viewed as cost centers?

No. An increasing number of sources are demonstrating that strong compliance and governance programs have a positive impact on the bottom line. They can help to:

- improve production and profitability;
- enhance and build brand loyalty;
- maintain customer retention and growth;
- enhance vendor relationships;
- prevent damage to reputation;
- prevent damage to brand;
- enhance director retention and recruitment;
- lower D&O insurance premiums;
- enhance employee retention and recruitment;
- prevent loss of intellectual property;
- avoid damage to business operations such as:
  - denial of export licenses;
  - loss of security clearances;
  - prohibition of stock trading;
  - suspension/debarment/exclusion;
  - FDA approval denials;
  - elimination of product lines;
  - loss of suppliers and business partners;
  - loss of IPO opportunities;
  - loss of M&A opportunities;
  - damage to post-merger integration.

The Benefits

Q 1.8   What other benefits does an effective compliance program provide?

As noted above, it is the formal policy of the Department of Justice that, before making a decision on whether or not to bring criminal charges against a company, the prosecutor must, among other things, take into account whether or not the company has in place an "effective" compliance program.[48] Experience shows that, for the most part, companies that have an "effective" compliance and ethics program in place when the investigation begins are not charged criminally. Of course, the program, and the company's commitment to it, must be real. The company should, ideally, have a program that is well-documented and includes all of the elements identified in the Sentencing Commission's guidance on compliance programs.[49]

Included in the *U.S. Sentencing Guidelines Manual*'s chapter devoted to the sentencing of organizations[50] is a series of exacerbating or mitigating factors that, when relevant, are combined to create a final "culpability score," which, in turn, is used to develop a recommended sentencing range.[51] Of all of the mitigating factors that combine to benefit an organization being sentenced, the largest reduction in sentence comes from having an effective compliance and ethics program.[52] Of course, the goal is not to have to face a criminal sentencing at all, and a strong compliance and ethics program can help organizations to avoid prosecution altogether.

Several federal agencies have "voluntary disclosure" programs.[53] These programs are intended to provide organizations with incentives to self-audit and self-report regulatory violations and to repay any moneys that may have been improperly paid. One of the best known is that of the Health and Human Services Department's Office of Inspector General (OIG).[54] The OIG Self-Disclosure Protocol (the "OIG Protocol") and similar programs at other agencies are designed to encourage self-reporting of compliance failures by companies that have business relationships with the government, receive government funding, or are covered by regulatory schemes.[55] In 2008, the Federal Acquisition Regulation was amended to require mandatory disclosure of violations of certain integrity focused criminal statutes and the civil False Claims Act. (For details, see chapter 14, Government Contractors.)

An effective compliance and ethics program can protect a company from the government and private litigants.

 CASE STUDY: *Morgan Stanley*

On April 25, 2012, the Department of Justice announced that a former managing director for Morgan Stanley's real estate division in China had pled guilty to criminal charges of conspiracy to evade Morgan Stanley's internal accounting controls required under the Foreign Corrupt Practices Act (FCPA). In addition, however, DOJ announced that it was not prosecuting Morgan Stanley for any part in these violations. This was because "Morgan Stanley maintained a system of internal controls meant to ensure accountability for its assets and to prevent employees from offering, promising or paying anything of value to foreign government officials."[56] (The court documents went on to detail the extensive efforts made by Morgan Stanley to ensure that its employees knew of and followed company policies against violations of the FCPA. It was these compliance efforts that drove DOJ's decision not to prosecute the company, as it so often does in similar circumstances.)

Time will tell, but this may be part of a response by DOJ to requests for clearer recognition of legitimate and comprehensive compliance programs and identification of specific instances in which companies receive the benefits of their efforts to promote compliance and ethical behavior.[57]

The numerous whistleblower provisions of the federal, state, and even local False Claims Acts are the scourge of almost all types of organizations that receive federal, and increasingly, state funding of any kind. An effective compliance and ethics program is a tremendous bulwark against whistleblower complaints. In many respects, it is an insurance policy, protecting the organization against potentially catastrophic damage from highly risky activities. (The various false claims acts are discussed in detail in chapter 11.)

COMPLIANCE FACT

The Department of Justice has pending at any one time literally hundreds of such whistleblower suits that it must investigate.[58] In FY 2014 alone, there were 713 new qui tam False Claims Act suits filed. This is the second year in a row that qui tam suits have exceeded 700.[59]

Finally, in addition to the protective reasons for having a compliance program outlined above, an increasingly extensive body of research demonstrates that companies with good compliance and governance structures receive a number of financial benefits, or return on investment, flowing from such programs.

Q 1.8.1   What is the proof that there is a link between corporate governance and corporate performance?

Evaluations of compliance and governance returns on investment are becoming more and more prevalent. Independent research, university studies, and a variety of corporate surveys demonstrate the positive impact of strong compliance and governance systems.

TIP: One factor companies should consider in designing their compliance and ethics programs is whether to make the program "compliance-based" or "values-based." Under a compliance-based program, the focus is on the rules that govern the corporation's activities and compliance with those rules. The basis for such programs is avoidance of penalties. For example, the Federal Sentencing Guidelines with their traditional "seven elements" for effective compliance programs can reduce the potential for criminal penalties by up to 95%, while companies without programs that meet these criteria can have fines increased by up to 400%.[60] Studies have shown that:

21

> even if fear of punishment or the anticipation of reward,
> which we term risk, is sometimes a viable way to
> encourage compliance, it is a poor way to motivate,
> *voluntary* commitment to rules . . . which is almost totally
> responsive to legitimacy and to whether employees view
> management practices as moral. Voluntary acceptance is
> important because it motivates employees to comply
> when detection for violations is unlikely.[61]
>
> Thus, "[i]f employees have a personal commitment to the
> organization, and if they believe the rules are morally right, they
> are motivated to obey the rules even in the absence of
> monitoring."[62]

Independent Research. In 2006, GMI,[63] which at the time was an agency that conducted independent corporate governance and risk research and rating activities, an independent corporate governance research and rating agency, reported that "[i]n recent years traditional investor safeguards—broker research, credit rating agencies, accounting firms—fell short, leading to enormous losses and a crisis in confidence."[64] This has caused investors to "place a premium on the quality of information and quality of earnings, not just earnings growth."[65] Through a proprietary ratings system, GMI prepared corporate governance ratings on thousands of companies traded on certain public exchanges. The ratings are based on "hundreds of metrics organized into six broad categories of analysis:

- Board Accountability
- Financial Disclosure and Internal Controls
- Shareholder Rights
- Executive & Director Remuneration
- Market for Control/Ownership Base
- Corporate Behavior/Corporate Accountability."[66]

Over a multi-year period of analysis, GMI was able to demonstrate a "consistent link between total shareholder returns and GMI ratings. . . ."[67] Additional findings showed that the benefits of good governance included:

- lower cost of capital;
- lower D&O insurance premiums;
- enhanced reputation as an aid to recruiting;
- lower chance of shareholder suits; and
- increased shareholder returns.

Furthermore, a company's good governance factored into credit risk models by commercial banks and was used as a screen by director and executive search firms.[68]

On the other hand, poor governance ratings demonstrated that governance and compliance issues were an "early warning system" for future problems and that there was a strong correlation between compliance and governance red flags and subsequent problems.[69]

University Studies. The GMI findings are supported by independent analyses undertaken by several universities. Researchers from the University of Iowa and the University of Wisconsin found that "firms with better governance have a lower cost of equity. Better governed firms, on average, have a cost of equity that is 88 basis points lower than firms with weaker governance after controlling for known risk factors."[70]

Similarly, a team of researchers from Harvard, Yale, and Stanford found that firms with "stronger shareholder rights" had:

- higher firm value;
- higher profits;
- higher sales growth; and
- lower capital costs.[71]

In an interview with Harvard Business School's "Working Knowledge for Business Leaders," Harvard Business School Professor Lynn S. Paine discussed the conclusions of her book *Value Shift*:[72]

> In recent years, however, I have seen more attention being paid to the positive side of ethics. More managers are waking up to the ways in which positive values contribute to a company's effective day-to-day functioning, as well as its reputation and long-term sustainability. In the book, I trace these connections

in some detail and show how they play out in practice—sometimes in surprising ways.[73]

Among the ways that having a positive value system can add to the bottom line, Paine identifies:

- better access to talent;
- enhanced employee commitment;
- better information sharing;
- greater creativity; and
- enhanced reputation.[74]

Corporate Surveys. A Global Investor Opinion survey conducted by McKinsey & Co. in 2002 concluded: "An overwhelming majority of investors are prepared to pay a premium for companies exhibiting high governance standards."[75] McKinsey further found that:

- 57% of institutional investors said that good corporate governance determined whether they increased or decreased their holdings in a company.
- Investors are willing to pay a premium of up to 41% for good governance.
- By moving from worst to best practices in governance, companies can expect a 10%–12% gain in market valuation.

Two employees of the SEC said it well:

> Many issuers might prefer to avoid the costs associated with even minimal corporate governance measures, particularly if they can give the appearance of maintaining high corporate governance standards without actually having to do so. Yet, as American president Abraham Lincoln almost said, you can't fool all of the investors all of the time. Pyramid schemes inevitably collapse. Holes in corporate accounts are uncovered, if only because bills eventually go unpaid. Furthermore, recent empirical research—not to mention common sense—suggests a correlation between poor corporate governance and poor corporate performance, as well as a link between strong corporate governance standards and superior corporate performance. If nothing else, investors will notice these performance differences, and punish or reward issuers accordingly.[76]

Ethisphere magazine reported that the World's Most Ethical Companies for the year 2010 had outperformed the S&P 500.[77] Over a five-year period, the magazine found a "53% return for the 2010 class of companies, compared to a 4% return in the S&P."[78] Upon hearing this news, investment writer Doug Cornelius researched the performance of *Ethisphere*'s World's Most Ethical Companies from 2007. The results were that the World's Most Ethical Companies "dramatically outperformed the broader market."[79]

COMPLIANCE FACT

A recent study has confirmed that a good corporate reputation and avoidance of wrongdoing is crucial to company success.

- "Executives estimate that, on average, 60% of their firms' market value is attributable to its reputation."[80]
- In the United States, 61% of consumers stop buying a product when they discover it is made by a company they do not like.[81]
- "[C]onsumers make purchase decisions based on company reputation, not just on the goods or services they buy."[82]
- "[C]orporate brands are more important than ever because they provide an anchor of trust and credibility in a sea of dynamic, continual change."[83]
- "[C]ompany wrong-doing overshadows many of the good deeds and community engagement that a company participates in."[84]
- "Consumers want assurance that their well-earned [money is] spent on products produced by companies that share their values."[85]
- Employee treatment and wrongdoing are now staples of consumer discussions, so executives should be vigilant about building better internal cultures and being transparent.[86]

Q 1.8.2   What if I have a program and wrongdoing still occurs?

Having an effective program is an important factor that prosecutors consider in deciding whether to pursue criminal charges against a corporation. The U.S. Department of Justice recently revised the criteria it uses in deciding on whether to prosecute corporations. Three of the key criteria that guide the prosecutor's decision are:

(1)   the corporation's timely and voluntary disclosure of wrongdoing and willingness to cooperate in an investigation;
(2)   the existence and adequacy of the corporation's *pre-existing* program; and
(3)   the corporation's remedial actions, including any efforts to implement an effective program or to improve an existing one.

Having a program also makes a company a less attractive target to prosecutors. Prosecutors and juries often have some sense of fairness, and prosecutors may forego indicting a company if the company has made a real effort through its program to comply with the law. Programs do not guarantee that all unethical or criminal misconduct will be prevented. Rather, a comprehensive program helps minimize the risk that criminal misconduct will occur. In the event that misconduct occurs, having an adequate and operational program is tangible proof to prosecutors that the company was and is serious about preventing violations of the law, and permits the company to argue better that it is in fact a victim of such misconduct as opposed to the beneficiary or the promoter of the conduct.

Identifying Whether You Already Have One

Q 1.9   How do I tell if my company already has a compliance program?

If you have to ask the question, you do not have a complete or comprehensive program.

Fully effective compliance and ethics programs are visible, known entities within the organization. If employees are surveyed on the question of whether their organization has a compliance program, they will overwhelmingly answer "Yes." They will have at least a basic understanding of its structure and know how to make a report of a potential violation or obtain guidance on compliance issues.

COMPLIANCE FACT

Studies have shown that the most effective programs have a number of common features. They include the following:

- The guiding values and commitments make sense and are clearly communicated.
- Company leaders are personally committed, credible, and willing to take action on the values they espouse.
- The espoused values are integrated into the normal channels of management decision making and are reflected in the organization's critical activities.
- The company's systems and structures support and reinforce its values.
- Managers throughout the company have the decision-making skills, knowledge, and competencies needed to make ethically sound decisions on a day-to-day basis.[87]

Q 1.9.1   If we do not already have a functioning compliance program in place, how do we start from "zero" to build one?

Even if your company does not have a fully operational compliance and ethics program that would be recognized as "effective" under the Federal Sentencing Guidelines criteria, it is quite likely that many pieces of a compliance program are already in place. It is extremely rare that a company will have to start completely from scratch in developing a compliance program.

For example, your human resources department may have procedures in place to comply with regulations affecting employees, such as wage and hour laws, labor laws, employment discrimination, and unemployment insurance laws. Your accounting or finance department may already have procedures in place to comply with Sarbanes-Oxley section 404 requirements. Manufacturing units may have

27

CASE STUDY: *Boeing Company*

Boeing Co. believed that it was a "good" company that made useful products. At a Boeing Leadership Meeting on January 5, 2006, however, Boeing's Executive Vice President and General Counsel Doug Bain laid out the reasons why Boeing should have paid more attention to its compliance and ethics requirements.[88] Bain described the initial shock of federal prosecutors and others that Boeing was under investigation for ethical violations:

> They say, "You guys are the Boeing Company. You build things that are larger than life. You do things that are larger than life. You're not a sleazy company. How did this happen?" And the question that they always ask: Where was the leadership?

By the end of six years of investigations, some still ongoing, Bain reported that the prosecutors had changed their view of Boeing.

> [T]here are some within the prosecutors' offices that believe that Boeing is rotten to the core. . . . They talk to us about pervasive misconduct and they describe it in geographic terms of spanning Cape Canaveral to Huntington Beach, to Orlando, to St. Louis to Chicago. . . . The U.S. Attorney in Los Angeles is looking at indicting Boeing for violations of the Economic Espionage Act, the Procurement Integrity Act, the False Claims Act and the Major Frauds Act. . . . The U.S. Attorney in Alexandria, Virginia, is looking at indicting us for violation of the conflict-of-interest laws. And both are looking to throw in a few conspiracy and aiding-and-abetting charges for good measure.

How did a company with a strong reputation for good work and integrity, and that is highly knowledgeable about government contracts, end up with government officials, the public, and many of Boeing's own employees believing that company officials "just don't get it"? Bain suggested there was an unwritten code of silence that resulted in employees' failing to report suspected wrongdoing when they saw it and management's not following up when reports finally reached them.

For the alleged use of proprietary documents that a former Lockheed employee brought with him to Boeing:

- Boeing lost $1 billion of launches and was suspended from the launch business for twenty months;
- Boeing was sued by Lockheed for more than $1 billion;
- Boeing employees were fired and indicted.

A separate investigation into violations of conflict-of-interest laws related to the hiring of government employees:

- lost Boeing the U.S. government tanker market and made Italy its only customer;
- forced Boeing to re-compete the C-130 AMP [Avionics Modernization Program] and the small-diameter bomb;
- caused the "biggest hit" to Boeing's reputation;
- forced a senior executive to plead guilty to one felony count of aiding and abetting a violation of the conflict-of-interest laws, serve time in a federal prison, pay a fine of $250,000, and "forfeit approximately $5 million in equity-based compensation."

Indirect costs related to these scandals included:

- denial of export licenses;
- potential loss of security clearances;
- re-suspension or debarment;
- potential prohibition of use and possession of explosive devices (used to trigger airplane door "actuators");

- denial of State Department licenses; plus
- additional millions in fines and penalties.

Bain challenged Boeing's leadership to change the culture that allowed these and other violations to occur without being reported internally until it was too late. He pointed out that it was important to continue talking about these problems. "Our job as [leaders] is to establish a culture that ensures that there is no next time. And frankly the choice is ours."

On June 30, 2006, the DOJ announced it had reached a "record" settlement with Boeing: a $565 million civil fraud settlement and a $50 million penalty related to a separate criminal agreement.[89] This settlement and the other costs related above do not include what must have been additional millions in attorney fees and related investigation costs.

procedures in place to comply with environmental regulations. Shipping departments may have procedures in place to comply with import and export laws. All of these are pieces of a comprehensive compliance program.

What is missing from these examples is the structure to tie the pieces together—the process and documentation to be able to demonstrate to employees, management, the board, stakeholders, regulators, and the outside world that your company is committed to act in accordance with industry rules and standards, to meet its commitments and contracts, and to act ethically and with integrity in its dealings.

Q 1.9.2   What happens as my business grows and changes over time?

A program is not static. A company continually must evaluate its legal and ethical risks, character, and behavior; collect reports on and learn from violations or lapses that may occur; and plan for correcting any violations or ethical lapses that may occur in the future. A well-run program will be integrated into the business operations of an organization. It is a part of the long-term strategic plan to achieve business goals by providing proactive guidance and protection as new challenges arise. Continued risk analysis and modification to address growth as well as legal, business, and operational changes is an essential part of any program.

Notes to Chapter 1

1. U.S. SENTENCING GUIDELINES MANUAL § 8B2.1 (Nov. 2011).
2. THE COMPLETE COMPLIANCE AND ETHICS MANUAL (Society of Corporate Compliance and Ethics 2004).
3. *See* U.S. SENTENCING GUIDELINES MANUAL § 8B2.1(b)(1)–(7).
4. *Id.* § 8B2.1(c) and Commentary.
5. See *infra* chapter 31 for a discussion of the work of the Committee of Sponsoring Organizations of the Treadway Commission (COSO), which has published guidance for an integrated framework for enterprise risk management and legal and regulatory compliance. In many respects, the U.S. Sentencing Commission's guidance for effective compliance and ethics programs is similar to the COSO guidance.
6. *See* Stone v. Ritter, 911 A.2d 362 (Del. 2006), in which the Delaware Supreme Court affirmed the standard set forth in *In re* Caremark Int'l, Inc. Derivative Litig., 698 A.2d 959 (Del. Ch. 1996), holding that corporate boards of directors have an affirmative duty, in heavily regulated industries, to see that the company has implemented a compliance program and to exercise reasonable oversight of that program. They have this duty even if they do not have any reason to believe that there has been wrongdoing within the company. *See also* Miller v. McDonald, et al., 385 B.R. 576 (Bankr. D. Del. 2008), which held that corporate officers, and in particular the general counsel, can be held personally liable for corporate wrongdoing even if they do not have personal knowledge of, involvement in, or benefit from the underlying wrongful activities.
7. U.S. ATTORNEYS' MANUAL ch. 9-28.300, www.justice.gov/usam/usam-9-28000-principles-federal-prosecution-business-organizations#9-28.300.
8. *Id.* ch. 9-28.800.
9. U.S. SENTENCING GUIDELINES MANUAL § 8B2.1(a)(2).
10. *Id.* § 8B2.1(c).
11. *Id.* § 8B2.1(b)(2) and Commentary, n.3.
12. *Id.* § 8B2.1(b)(2)(A) and Commentary, n.3.
13. Government contractors are now required to disclose certain criminal and civil False Claims Act violations and to "fully cooperate" with government investigators. See chapter 14, Government Contractors, for more information on this issue.
14. U.S. SENTENCING GUIDELINES MANUAL § 8B2.1(b)(7) and Commentary, n.6.
15. For further information on the design and implementation of an effective compliance and ethics program, see chapter 2, Implementation of Effective Compliance and Ethics Programs and the Federal Sentencing Guidelines.
16. Compliance requirements for specific industries are discussed in greater detail in the industry-specific chapters.

17. 31 U.S.C. §§ 5311–30; 12 U.S.C. §§ 1818(s), 1829(b), and 1951–59; 12 C.F.R. § 21.21. The Bank Secrecy Act is discussed in chapter 29.

18. Pub. L. No. 107-204, 116 Stat. 745, also known as the Public Company Accounting Reform and Investor Protection Act of 2002. *See* chapter 30, *infra.*

19. *See* 48 C.F.R. §§ 3.10, 52.203-13, and 52.203-14. (These are sections of the Federal Acquisition Regulation [hereinafter FAR], which is codified at 48 C.F.R.) *See also* chapter 14 on government contractors.

20. Patient Protection and Affordable Care Act (ACA), Pub. L. No. 111-148, 124 Stat. 119 (Mar. 23, 2010).

21. *Id.* § 6401(a)(7).

22. *Id.*

23. *Id.* § 6102.

24. *See* California Marketing Compliance Law, CAL. HEALTH & SAFETY CODE §§ 119400–119402.

25. *See* ME. REV. STAT. ANN. tit. 22, §§ 2698-A and 2700-A.

26. N.Y. SOC. SERV. LAW § 363-d.

27. In 2007 alone, twenty-seven states were considering some form of compliance legislation requiring reporting of or restrictions on marketing of pharmaceutical and medical device products to healthcare professionals.

28. United States v. Merck-Medco Managed Care, LLC, 336 F. Supp. 2d 430 (E.D. Pa. 2004).

29. FAR 52.203-13, 52-203-14. For further discussion, see chapter 14 on government contractors.

30. *See* chapter 29 on anti-money laundering compliance.

31. *See* chapters 30 and 32 on Sarbanes-Oxley and the SEC.

32. *See* chapter 22 on healthcare organizations.

33. *See* chapter 26 on HIPAA compliance.

34. *In re* Caremark Int'l, Inc. Derivative Litig., 698 A.2d 959 (Del. Ch. 1996).

35. 42 U.S.C. § 1320a-7b.

36. 31 U.S.C. § 3729 *et seq.*

37. United States v. Merck-Medco Managed Care, LLC, 336 F. Supp. 2d 430 (E.D. Pa. 2004).

38. The False Claims Act is discussed in detail in chapter 11.

39. On April 23, 2012, the *New York Times* reported that, "Wal-Mart's stock fell almost 5 percent on Monday, accounting for about one-fifth of the losses in the Dow Jones industrial average, as investors reacted to a bribery scandal at the retailer's Mexican subsidiary and a report that an internal investigation was quashed at corporate headquarters in Arkansas."

40. On November 21, 2011, the *Wall Street Journal* reported that, "A former Synthes Inc. executive was sentenced Monday to nine months in prison for his role in the medical-device maker's promotion of a bone cement for unauthorized uses. The sentence is likely to be viewed as a victor for the Justice Department, which has stepped up efforts to hold individual executives criminally responsible for corporate violations of food and drug laws."

41. In one recent tax fraud case, defense counsel estimated the cost of a "reasonable defense" to be "anywhere from $10 million to $44 million." Beth Bar, *Defense Cost Estimates Offered in KPMG Case*, N.Y.L.J., July 13, 2007.

42. Jack Ewing, *Co-Chiefs Announce Resignation at Deutsche*, N.Y. TIMES, June 8, 2015, at B1.

43. *Id.*

44. K. Schnatterly, *Increasing Firm Value Through Detection and Prevention of White-Collar Crime*, STRATEGIC MGMT. J. vol. 24, 587–614 (2003).

45. *Id.*

46. *Id.*

47. *Id.* at 588.

48. *See* U.S. ATTORNEYS' MANUAL, *supra* note 7, at 4, 12–15.

49. U.S. SENTENCING GUIDELINES MANUAL § 8B2.1.

50. *Id.* ch. 8.

51. *Id.* § 8C.

52. *Id.* Additional mitigation is provided for self-reporting of wrongdoing. *See id.* § 8C2.5(g).

53. For more information, see chapter 8.

54. Provider Self-Disclosure Protocol, 63 Fed. Reg. 58,400 (Oct. 30, 1998).

55. Other agency programs include, but are not limited to: credit in debarment proceedings (FAR 9.406-1(a)(2)); credit for defense contractors (DFARS 203.7001(a)(6)); Department of Defense Voluntary Disclosure Program; Department of Justice Antitrust Division, Corporate Leniency Program; The Environmental Protection Agency Voluntary Environmental Self-Policing and Self-Disclosure Interim Policy Statement.

56. Press Release No. 12-534, U.S. Dep't of Justice, Former Morgan Stanley Managing Director Pleads Guilty for Role in Evading Internal Controls Required by FCPA (Apr. 25, 2012), www.justice.gov/opa/pr/2012/April/12-crm-534.html.

57. On August 7, 2012, the Department of Justice announced a settlement with Pfizer H.C.P. Corporation of $15 million to resolve a foreign bribery investigation. News Release No. 12-980, U.S. Dep't of Justice, Pfizer H.C.P. Corp. Agrees to Pay $15 Million Penalty to Resolve Foreign Bribery Investigation (Aug. 7, 2012), www.justice.gov/opa/pr/pfizer-hcp-corp-agrees-pay-15-million-penalty-resolve-foreign-bribery-investigation. The settlement agreement in that case specifically states that the government credited Pfizer's robust compliance program in its decision not to require a corporate monitor as part of the settlement.

> The agreement recognizes the timely voluntary disclosure by Pfizer H.C.P.'s parent company, Pfizer Inc.; the thorough and wide-reaching self-investigation of the underlying and related conduct; the significant cooperation provided by the company to the department and the SEC; and the early and extensive remedial efforts and the substantial and continuing improvements Pfizer Inc. has made to its global anti-corruption compliance procedures.

> Pfizer H.C.P. received a reduction in its penalty as a result of
> Pfizer Inc.'s cooperation in the ongoing investigation of other
> companies and individuals. In addition to the $15 million
> penalty, the agreement requires Pfizer Inc. to continue to
> implement rigorous internal controls and to cooperate fully
> with the department.
>
> Due to Pfizer Inc.'s extensive remediation and improvement of
> its compliance systems and internal controls, as well as the
> enhanced compliance undertakings included in the agreement,
> Pfizer H.C.P. is not required to retain a corporate monitor, but
> Pfizer Inc. must periodically report to the department on
> implementation of its remediation and enhanced compliance
> efforts for the duration of the agreement.
>
> *Id.*

58. *See* U.S. DEP'T OF JUSTICE, CIVIL DIV., FRAUD STATISTICS—OVERVIEW: OCTOBER 1, 1987–SEPTEMBER 30, 2014 [hereinafter 2014 Fraud Statistics Overview], www.justice.gov/civil/pages/attachments/2014/11/21/fcastats.pdf; *see also* Press Release No. 14-1300, U.S. Dep't of Justice, Justice Department Recovers Nearly $6 Billion from False Claims Act Cases in Fiscal Year 2014 (Nov. 20, 2014), www.justice.gov/opa/pr/justice-department-recovers-nearly-6-billion-false-claims-act-cases-fiscal-year-2014 ("The U.S. Department of Justice obtained a record $5.69 billion in settlements and judgments from civil cases involving fraud and false claims against the government in the fiscal year ending September 30, Acting Associate Attorney General Stuart F. Delery and Acting Assistant Attorney General Joyce R. Branda for the Civil Division announced today. This is the first time the department has exceeded $5 billion in cases under the False Claims Act, and brings total recoveries from January 2009 through the end of the fiscal year to $22.75 billion—more than half the recoveries since Congress amended the False Claims Act 28 years ago to strengthen the statute and increase the incentives for whistleblowers to file suit.").

59. *See* 2014 Fraud Statistics Overview, *supra* note 58.

60. Tom Tyler, John Dienhart & Terry Thomas, *The Ethical Commitment to Compliance: Building Value-Based Cultures*, 50 CAL. MGMT. REV., no. 2, at 31–51 (Winter 2008). *See* www.jstor.org/stable/41166434.

61. *Id.* at 35.

62. *Id.*

63. GMI was acquired in 2014 by MSCI. *See* MSCI, *ESG Integration*, www.msci.com/esg-integration (last visited June 25, 2015).

64. Corporate Governance, Risk and Rewards, Presentation Prepared for the Conference Board Ethics and Compliance Conference, by Chief Operating Officer, Howard Sherman (May 11, 2006).

65. *Id.*

66. *Id.*

67. *Id.*

68. *Id.*

69. *Id.*

70. Hollis Ashbaugh (University of Wisconsin), Daniel Collins (University of Iowa) & Ryan LaFond (University of Wisconsin), Working Paper, Corporate Governance and the Cost of Equity Capital (Dec. 2004), at 3.

71. Paul Gompers, Joy Ishii & Andrew Metrick, *Corporate Governance and Equity Prices*, Q. J. ECON. (Feb. 2003).

72. LYNN S. PAINE, VALUE SHIFT: WHY COMPANIES MUST MERGE SOCIAL AND FINANCIAL IMPERATIVES TO ACHIEVE SUPERIOR PERFORMANCE (McGraw Hill 2003).

73. Where Morals and Profits Meet: The Corporate Value Shift, Harvard Business School Working Knowledge for Business Leaders, Q&A with Lynn S. Paine, by Carla Tishler, *reprinted in* HBS Working Knowledge, Harvard Business School's weekly newsletter, Nov. 18, 2002.

74. *Id.*

75. Michael Emen, Senior Vice President NASDAQ Listing Qualifications, Corporate Governance: The View from NASDAQ (2004), *reprinted in* GLOBAL CORPORATE GOVERNANCE GUIDE 2004: BEST PRACTICE IN THE BOARDROOM (Globe White Page Ltd. 2004).

76. Ethiopis Tafara & Robert J. Peterson, SEC, *The True Value of Corporate Governance, in* GLOBAL CORPORATE GOVERNANCE GUIDE 2004: BEST PRACTICE IN THE BOARDROOM, *supra* note 75, at 60.

77. Doug Cornelius, *Should You Invest in Ethical Companies?*, INVESTMENT CHOICE (Mar. 24, 2010, 8:00 A.M.), www.compliancebuilding.com/2010/03/24/should-you-invest-in-ethical-companies/.

78. *Id.*

79. *Id.* "If you bought one share in each of the 52 companies on June 1, 2007, you would have realized a -6.34% return. In comparison, the S&P 500 had a -19.57% return and the Dow Jones Industrial Average had a -15.80% return." *Id.*

80. WEBER SHANDWICK, THE COMPANY BEHIND THE BRAND: IN REPUTATION WE TRUST, at 18 (2011).

81. *Id.* at 11.

82. *Id.* at 7.

83. *Id.* at 4 (quoting Micho Spring, Weber Shandwick, Global Corporate Chair).

84. *Id.* at 15.

86. *Id.* at 21.

87. *Id.*

88. Lynn Sharp Paine, *Managing for Organizational Integrity*, HARV. BUS. REV., Mar.–Apr. 1994, at 112.

89. Speech by Doug Bain, Boeing Senior Vice President and General Counsel, at Boeing Leadership Meeting, Orlando, Fla. (Jan. 5, 2006), *reprinted in Transcript of Speech by Boeing's Doug Bain*, SEATTLE TIMES, Jan. 31, 2006 (Business & Technology section).

89. Press Release No. 06-412, U.S. Dep't of Justice, Boeing to Pay United States Record $615 Million to Resolve Fraud Allegations (June 30, 2006), www.justice.gov/opa/pr/2006/June/06_civ_412.html.

2

Implementation of Effective Compliance and Ethics Programs and the Federal Sentencing Guidelines

*Steven D. Gordon**

How should a company go about designing and implementing a compliance program? While other chapters address the specifics of compliance programs in particular industries, this chapter considers issues relating to designing and implementing compliance and ethics programs generally. The biggest influence on the design and implementation of a compliance program is guidance from the U.S. Sentencing Commission contained in the Federal Sentencing Guidelines that apply to companies convicted of federal criminal offenses. The Sentencing Guidelines set standards that have become the norm for virtually all companies, even though relatively few

* The author wishes to acknowledge Michael Manthei, Christopher A. Myers, and Jonathan Strouse for their contributions to this chapter.

37

will ever be prosecuted or convicted. In fact, the most useful benefit from using the Guidelines to design and implement a compliance and ethics program is that it can help companies avoid investigations and convictions in the first place.

In addition to complying with the Sentencing Guidelines, if the company is publicly held, it must comply with the Sarbanes-Oxley Act of 2002. And if the company is a federal government contractor or subcontractor, the Federal Acquisition Regulation (FAR) comes into play. Other compliance requirements apply to other industries. Fortunately, these various guidelines and requirements do not conflict and, instead, tend to complement each other.

Sentencing Guidelines Basics

Q 2.1   What are the Federal Sentencing Guidelines?

Since 1991, the sentencing of corporations and other business entities convicted of federal criminal offenses has been governed by the Federal Sentencing Guidelines ("Sentencing Guidelines"), established by the U.S. Sentencing Commission. These Sentencing Guidelines were mandatory, but in 2005, the Supreme Court ruled that it is unconstitutional to apply them in mandatory form. The Court left them intact as voluntary guideposts that federal courts should consult but are not bound to follow.[1]

In addition to providing guidance on how convicted companies should be sentenced, the Sentencing Guidelines also contain detailed guidance from the Sentencing Commission on what it means to have an "effective" compliance and ethics program. This guidance, contained in chapter eight of the *Guidelines Manual*,[2] is used by hundreds of companies to design and implement their compliance programs and is also the standard used by many government agencies to evaluate company compliance and ethics programs.

Q 2.2   How do the Sentencing Guidelines relate to an effective compliance program?

A company convicted of a federal offense is eligible for a reduced sentence under the Sentencing Guidelines if it has an effective compliance and ethics program and the offense occurred despite the program.[3] The Sentencing Guidelines spell out the basic elements of an effective compliance program.[4] Additionally, a prosecutor might exercise his or her discretion not to bring criminal charges if the company has a compliance program that meets the Sentencing Guidelines' requirements.

Q 2.2.1   Why should my company care about the Sentencing Guidelines if it conducts business honestly and is unlikely ever to face criminal prosecution?

If the business is a corporation, its management probably has a duty to ensure that the business has an adequate compliance program. The Delaware Chancery Court, in the leading *Caremark* decision,[5] held that corporate management has such a duty under Delaware law in light of the Sentencing Guidelines. Also, having an effective compliance program can show that the corporation was not at fault if an employee does engage in criminal or unethical conduct.

Even ethical companies get investigated. In the event of an investigation, enforcement authorities will look at a variety of factors to determine whether there has been wrongdoing, who is at fault, and whether to bring criminal, civil, administrative, or no claims against the company. Among the most significant factors influencing these decisions is whether the company has a compliance program that meets the Sentencing Guidelines' requirements.

Components of an Effective Compliance Program

Q 2.3   What policies and procedures should my company implement to meet the Sentencing Guidelines' requirements?

You are required to have written standards and procedures. After performing a thorough assessment of your company's legal, compliance, and reputational risks, you should create policies addressing those risk areas. The number and types of standards and procedures a company requires depend on a number of factors, including the industry in which the company operates.

Q 2.3.1   What are the elements of an effective compliance program that will satisfy the Sentencing Guidelines?

The Sentencing Guidelines state that the two fundamental elements of an effective compliance and ethics program are:

(1)   exercising due diligence to prevent and detect criminal conduct; and

(2)   otherwise promoting an organizational culture that encourages ethical conduct and a commitment to compliance with the law.[6]

Q 2.3.2   What specific steps must our company take to create an effective compliance program?

The Sentencing Guidelines provide that, at a minimum, a company must do the following in order to have an effective compliance and ethics program:

(1)   Establish standards and procedures to prevent and detect criminal conduct.

(2)   Ensure that the company's governing authority (board of directors, etc.) understands the content and operation of the program and exercises reasonable oversight with

respect to its implementation and effectiveness. Specific senior manager(s) shall have overall responsibility to ensure the implementation and effectiveness of the program. Specific individuals shall be delegated day-to-day operational responsibility for the program and shall be given adequate resources and authority. They shall report periodically to senior management and shall have direct access to the board of directors or a subgroup thereof.

(3)   Keep bad actors out of managerial ranks (or other key positions). Reasonable steps should be taken to screen out persons whom the company knows, or should know through the exercise of due diligence, to have a history of engaging in illegal activity or other misconduct.

(4)   Take reasonable steps to communicate periodically and in a practical manner its standards and procedures to its officers, employees, and, as appropriate, its agents, by conducting effective training programs and otherwise disseminating information.

(5)   Take reasonable steps to
    (a)   ensure that the program is followed, including using monitoring and auditing to detect criminal conduct;
    (b)   evaluate periodically the program's effectiveness; and
    (c)   have a system whereby employees and agents may report or seek guidance regarding potential or actual criminal conduct without fear of retaliation (although a mechanism for anonymous reporting is not required).

(6)   Promote and enforce the program through appropriate incentives and disciplinary measures for engaging in criminal conduct and for failing to take reasonable steps to prevent or detect criminal conduct.

(7)   Take reasonable steps to respond appropriately to criminal conduct and to prevent further similar criminal conduct, including making any necessary modifications to the compliance and ethics program.[7]

Q 2.3.3   Is there a standard compliance program that most companies can use?

No. There is no "one-size-fits-all" solution. The Sentencing Guidelines recognize that an effective program must be tailored to the particular company.

The Sentencing Guidelines require a company to engage in periodic risk assessments in designing, implementing, and modifying its compliance and ethics program.[8] Each company must examine the nature of its business and its own prior history to determine what sorts of criminal conduct pose the greatest risk, and then take steps designed to prevent and detect such misconduct.

For example, if your company employs sales personnel who have flexibility in setting prices, you must have established standards and procedures designed to prevent and detect price-fixing. If you employ sales personnel who have flexibility to represent the material characteristics of a product, you must have established standards and procedures designed to prevent fraud. Your company should prioritize the risks that you face in terms of the severity of the criminal conduct and its likelihood of occurring, and tailor your compliance and ethics program accordingly.[9]

Designing and Implementing a Compliance Program

Relevant Factors and Considerations

Q 2.4   Are industry practice and standards considered in assessing the effectiveness of a compliance program?

Yes. The Sentencing Guidelines recognize that the particulars of an effective compliance and ethics program are likely to be affected by applicable industry practice or the standards called for by any applicable governmental regulation. For publicly traded corporations, applicable governmental regulations would include the requirements of the Sarbanes-Oxley Act of 2002. A company's failure to incorporate and follow applicable industry practice or to comply with applicable government regulations will weigh against a finding that its compliance program is an effective one.[10] For healthcare companies the Department of Health and Human Services, through its Office of Inspector General, has issued a number of very specific compliance program guidances targeting specific business sectors such as hospitals and pharmaceutical manufacturers.

Q 2.4.1   Does the company size matter?

Size is a relevant factor in structuring a compliance and ethics program. A large company generally should devote more formal operations and greater resources to its program than a small company.

Q 2.4.2   What are the differences between compliance programs for large companies and small companies?

- The governing authority in a small company may directly manage the compliance and ethics efforts.
- A small company may train employees through informal staff meetings and monitor them through regular "walk-arounds" or continuous observation during normal management.
- A small company may use available personnel, rather than separate staff, to carry out the compliance and ethics program.[11]

Requirements; Risk Areas

Q 2.5   When it comes to putting a compliance program together, where do we start?

A first step is to determine whether the compliance program must satisfy the mandates of the Sarbanes-Oxley Act[12] in addition to the Sentencing Guidelines. Sarbanes-Oxley, if applicable, imposes fairly detailed requirements that focus on the company's internal control over financial reporting and its disclosure controls and procedures. A good compliance program should also address the prevention of other employee misconduct that may impose civil liability on the company or that may victimize the company itself.

The foundation for designing a good compliance program is to identify the principal risks of misconduct that must be safeguarded against. This is a task that requires input from counsel and senior management. The effectiveness of the compliance program likely will be directly proportional to the time and effort invested in designing it.

Q 2.5.1   What are the most common risk areas that we may need to address in our compliance program?

Consider the following fifteen areas:

1.   Accounting practices. Sarbanes-Oxley has made internal control over financial reporting and disclosure controls and procedures the foremost risk area for every public company. It also spells out in detail the procedures that must be used to address this risk area.[13]

Private companies must also protect against the risk that an officer or employee may "cook" or alter the books in order to boost performance or hide problems. Common examples include improper revenue recognition, intentional overstatement of assets, or understatement of liabilities, as well as false entries to cover up employee embezzlement and theft, or expenditures for improper or illegal purposes such as bribes.

2.   USA PATRIOT Act. The PATRIOT Act aims to cut off sources of financing for terrorists by strengthening anti-money laundering laws. The PATRIOT Act greatly expanded the definition of "financial institutions" covered by anti-money laundering laws to include not only banks, savings associations, and credit unions, but also securities broker-dealers; investment companies; hedge funds; commodities brokers; mutual funds; issuers or redeemers of travelers checks; operators of credit card systems; insurance companies; telegraph companies; loan or finance companies; automobile, airplane, and boat dealers; real estate brokers; persons or companies involved in real estate closings and settlements; currency exchanges; money transmitters; pawn brokers; travel agencies; dealers in precious metals, stones, or jewels; and casinos.[14]

The PATRIOT Act requires that "*each* financial institution *shall* establish anti-money laundering programs" unless the Treasury Department issues a specific exemption. These programs must include written policies and procedures; a designated compliance officer; employee training; and periodic auditing and monitoring.[15] Further, financial institutions must implement special account opening procedures and "Know Your Customer" due diligence.[16]

In addition, banks, securities broker-dealers, money services businesses, and casinos are required to file reports of suspicious transactions with the Treasury Department's Financial Crimes Enforcement Network.[17] Finally, all persons (not only financial institutions) who receive in excess of $10,000 in cash in one transaction, or two or more related transactions, in the course of their trade or business are required to file a currency transaction report.[18]

3.   Conducting business with suspected terrorists. Following the September 11 attacks, Executive Order 13224 mandated creation of a list of persons, entities, and groups believed to be connected with terrorism. This order bans *anyone* in the United States from conducting *any* business with *any* person, entity, or group on the list, which is maintained by the Treasury Department's Office of Foreign Assets Control (OFAC).[19] The OFAC list is constantly updated and now is quite lengthy, consisting of thousands of names, aliases, and "doing business as" designations. Businesses, particularly those with some international component, must ensure that they are complying with the provisions of the Executive Order. Specifically, before entering into or continuing any financial relationship, businesses should check the identities of existing and potential clients and customers against the latest OFAC List.

4.   Conflicts of interest; corporate opportunities. Conflicts of interest are an issue for every company. The code of ethics mandated by Sarbanes-Oxley specifically requires a company to promote the ethical handling of actual or apparent conflicts of interest between personal and professional relationships.[20] Common breeding grounds for conflicts of interest include employee relationships with the company's suppliers and outside employment.

The corporate opportunity doctrine forbids employees, officers, and directors of a company from

(i)   taking for themselves personally opportunities that are discovered through the use of corporate property, information, or position;

(ii)   using corporate property, information, or position for personal gain; and

(iii)   competing with the company.

45

The New York Stock Exchange (NYSE) has adopted rules requiring each issuer listed on the Exchange to adopt a code of conduct that addresses, separately, both conflicts of interest and corporate opportunities.[21]

Further, Sarbanes-Oxley, in order to strengthen protections against conflicts of interest, prohibits public companies from making personal loans to any director or executive officer.[22]

5.   Bribes, kickbacks, improper payments, inappropriate gifts. Improper payments to government officials are a potential issue for many companies, especially if the government is a customer or if the business is subject to significant government regulation. Giving bribes or gratuities to U.S. government officials is prohibited by federal law,[23] and bribery of foreign government officials is prohibited by the Foreign Corrupt Practices Act.[24] Kickbacks are explicitly prohibited, both at the prime contractor and subcontractor levels, in connection with any federal government contract.[25] Kickbacks also are prohibited in exchange for the referral of business for which payment is made under federal healthcare programs, such as Medicare and Medicaid.[26] In addition, a number of states have criminal commercial bribery statutes that prohibit payments to influence the conduct of an agent or employee with respect to the affairs of the agent's employer.[27]

6.   Antitrust issues. Antitrust issues such as price-fixing, collusive bidding, and market allocation are a concern in many industries.

7.   Confidential information and trade secrets. For many companies, protection of confidential information and trade secrets is a significant issue. In the healthcare industry, protection of individual health information is critical. Often such information may be a key company asset and, under Sarbanes-Oxley, the safeguarding of company assets is one of the elements of internal control over financial reporting.[28] In order to protect its proprietary data and trade secrets, a company must take the requisite steps to preserve confidentiality. At a minimum, this includes reminding employees, during the course of their employment and upon their departure, of their continuing duty to safeguard such information. In addition, written confidentiality agreements may be desirable.

Further, companies must ensure that they do not become liable for misappropriating trade secrets belonging to their competitors or third parties. Employees should be warned against acquiring a competitor's confidential or trade secret information—and against bringing such information with them from a prior employer when they join the company.

8.   Product safety. If the company manufactures or processes tangible products, especially consumer goods, then product safety may well be a key risk area. Indeed, in highly regulated industries that implicate public health and safety, such as food and drugs, product safety is likely to be the single most important risk issue. Where public health and safety are implicated, defective products may trigger strict criminal liability for the company as well as its senior managers.[29]

9.   Workplace safety. In industries such as manufacturing, construction, or extraction of natural resources, workplace safety may be a significant issue.

10. Environmental issues. For many businesses, compliance with environmental laws is a significant concern. Some environmental statutes are drafted in such sweeping terms as to create something approaching strict criminal liability in the event of a violation.[30]

11. Government contracts issues. As detailed in chapter 14 on government contractors, new mandatory compliance and ethics program requirements went into effect in 2008 for many government contractors and subcontractors. The new requirements amend the Federal Acquisition Regulation (FAR) and are modeled to a large extent on the Federal Sentencing Guidelines criteria for effective compliance and ethics programs.[31] In addition to the specific elements of a compliance and ethics program that must be implemented, the new FAR provisions also require mandatory reporting of violations of federal criminal law, violations of the civil False Claims Act, and "significant" overpayments.

Companies engaged in contracting with the federal government are especially vulnerable to liability for business misconduct. A number of statutes impose civil liability upon government contractors for engaging in fraudulent conduct or failing to comply with applicable procurement and contracting rules.[32] Further, an array of criminal statutes may be applied to contractors who engage in fraud or other misconduct.[33]

The most common types of fraud encountered in government contracting include defective pricing, cost mischarging, product substitution, progress payment fraud, antitrust violations, kickbacks, bribery, gratuities, and conflicts of interest.[34]

12. Insider trading. Another risk for publicly held companies is that directors, officers, or employees may engage in insider trading in the company's shares. The NYSE considers this risk so significant that it identifies insider trading as one of the issues to be addressed by the code of conduct it requires for listed companies.[35]

13. International business practices. U.S. laws that may create significant risks for companies engaged in international business include export control laws and the Foreign Corrupt Practices Act (FCPA). Export control laws and regulations prohibit the export of certain commercial products, strategic goods, defense articles and their related technologies, and the furnishing of defense services, unless licensed by the appropriate federal agency—either the Department of Commerce or the Department of State.

Note that an "export" can occur anywhere when equipment or technical data is released or made available to a foreign person, whether within the United States or abroad.

The FCPA prohibits bribery in the conduct of business abroad. In general, the FCPA prohibits corrupt payments to foreign officials or political parties (whether made directly or through intermediaries) for the purpose of obtaining or keeping business.[36]

14. Employee relations. Discrimination and harassment issues are a concern for virtually all employers. Federal statutes and regulations forbid discrimination in the workplace based on race, color, sex, religion, national origin, marital status, age, or disability.[37] Discrimination or harassment can subject a company to civil liability for compensatory damages and, in cases involving malice or reckless indifference, to punitive damages as well.[38]

15. Other issues. There are a number of additional issues that are less common but very significant to particular businesses or industries. Certain highly regulated industries, such as banking and healthcare, face numerous compliance risks that derive from the specialized laws and regulations that govern their conduct. Other businesses, though not highly regulated, may have particular attributes that create significant compliance risks. For example, marketing organizations are vulnerable to charges of fraudulent sales techniques. Compliance programs must be designed to combat these risks.

Code of Conduct

Q 2.6   Is a code of conduct a required part of a compliance program?

A code of ethical conduct is a centerpiece of a compliance program. The Sentencing Guidelines and Sarbanes-Oxley now make a code of ethics virtually mandatory for all companies. Furthermore, both the NYSE and NASDAQ have rules that mandate that listed companies adopt codes of business conduct and ethics.[39]

Sarbanes-Oxley effectively requires every publicly traded corporation to adopt a code of ethics that applies to its principal executive officer, principal financial officer, principal accounting officer or controller, or persons performing similar functions.[40]

Q 2.6.1   What are the legal requirements for a code of conduct?

Sarbanes-Oxley mandates that the code consist of written standards that are reasonably designed to deter wrongdoing and to promote:

(1)   honest and ethical conduct, including the ethical handling of actual or apparent conflicts of interest between personal and professional relationships;

(2)   full, fair, accurate, timely, and understandable disclosure in reports and documents that a registrant files with, or submits to, the SEC and in other public communications made by the registrant;

(3)   compliance with applicable governmental laws, rules, and regulations;

(4)   the prompt internal reporting of violations of the code to an appropriate person or persons identified in the code; and

(5)   accountability for adherence to the code.[41]

The Sentencing Guidelines impose more general requirements for a code of conduct. They require that the company establish standards and procedures to prevent and detect criminal conduct, and take reasonable steps to communicate periodically and in a practical manner its standards and procedures to all employees and agents by conducting training programs and otherwise disseminating information.

Q 2.6.2   What are the elements of a good code of conduct?

A corporate code of ethical conduct should accomplish several distinct, but related, objectives:

1. *Address, in a direct, practical manner, the compliance risk issues that are relevant to the particular company.* The code should alert employees to the principal risks and spell out their duty to avoid them. Some of the most effective codes follow up their discussion of the relevant standards with sample questions and answers applying the standard(s) to common situations that employees are likely to encounter.

2. *Identify the personnel who administer the company's compliance program, from the senior executive(s) in charge of the program down through any lower-level contact personnel.* In addition, the code should outline the system for reporting suspected misconduct. Employees and agents must be able to report or seek guidance regarding potential or actual criminal conduct without fear of retaliation.

Furthermore, it is desirable (and sometimes required) that the system permit confidential, anonymous reporting.[42] The code should state unequivocally that any employee may contact compliance personnel to discuss potential violations of the code without fear of retribution and, if applicable, that anonymous reporting is an option. The code should encourage employees to contact compliance personnel whenever an ethical issue arises and they are uncertain about whether or how the code applies.

3.   *Announce that employees who violate code provisions will be sanctioned for their misconduct, indicating the range of sanctions that may be applied.* The sanctions may range from a reprimand for minor or unintentional violations up to termination for cause for serious violations. The Sentencing Guidelines note that disciplinary actions sometimes may need to be taken not only against the actual offender but also against individuals who fail to take reasonable steps to prevent or detect the misconduct.[43] Thus, the code should also state that an employee who witnesses a violation and fails to report it may be subject to discipline, as may a supervisor or manager to the extent that the violation reflects inadequate supervision or lack of diligence.

4.   *Be distributed to all company employees and agents in writing and/or by making it available on the company's website.* Many companies require that employees certify that they have received and read the code of conduct. Some companies make this an annual ritual. Such certifications can provide useful evidence of the company's good faith and diligence if an issue ever arises. However, the certifications can end up undercutting the company's position if they are incomplete or out of date. Thus, if a company decides to utilize employee certifications, it must diligently monitor them to ensure that they are complete and up to date.

Q 2.6.3   How many codes of conduct should a company have?

Sarbanes-Oxley mandates a code of ethics only for a select group of senior corporate officials: a company's principal executive officer, principal financial officer, principal accounting officer or controller, or persons performing similar functions. In contrast, the Sentencing Guidelines and the NYSE and NASDAQ rules require a code that is broadly applicable to a company's officers, employees, and (as appropriate) agents.

For most companies, it would seem simplest to have only one code of conduct that applies to all officers, employees, and agents, and that either applies the Sarbanes-Oxley standards to all such persons, or else "adds on" the specific Sarbanes-Oxley requirements for the specified senior officers who are subject to them. Multiple codes of conduct applicable to different groups of officers and/or employees are likely to breed problems for the company.

Compliance Program Administration

Q 2.7   How do we administer and enforce a compliance program?

1.   Establish comprehensive written policies and procedures that implement the Code of Conduct and that address the specific risk areas you have identified.

2.   Conduct effective training programs and otherwise disseminate information about the compliance program to officers and employees.

3.   Establish and publicize a system for reporting violations.

4.   Promptly and carefully investigate any reports of suspected misconduct and take corrective action if appropriate.

5.   Provide feedback to employees who have reported suspected misconduct so that they know that you took their allegations seriously and that an appropriate resolution was reached. Employees who believe that you have ignored their complaints are far more likely to become "whistleblowers" initiating litigation against the company than are employees who believe that their complaints have been considered and addressed.

6.   Document the complaints you receive and the steps that you take to resolve them. Although there is a risk that such documentation may later be discoverable by adverse parties, it is simply not an option for the company to keep no records regarding the workings of its compliance program. Among other things, a failure to keep records would make it difficult or impossible to audit the workings of the program, which is a process required by Sarbanes-Oxley and the Sentencing Guidelines.

7.   Actively check for misconduct and periodically evaluate the effectiveness of its compliance program.

> **TIP:** Be mindful that the results of an internal investigation can
> end up providing a roadmap of corporate misconduct to adverse
> parties such as the government, civil litigants, or disaffected
> shareholders. It may be wise to place an attorney in charge of
> investigating matters that appear to involve serious misconduct
> in order to secure the protections of the attorney-client privilege
> and attorney work-product doctrines insofar as possible. To the
> extent that the compliance program, or any aspect(s) thereof, is
> administered by non-legal personnel, such as the audit
> department or H.R., it is likely that the results of their work will
> be discoverable in subsequent proceedings.

In addition to investigating reports of suspected misconduct, the
Sentencing Guidelines require a company to engage in proactive
enforcement efforts by monitoring and auditing to detect criminal
conduct.[44] Sarbanes-Oxley requires management to evaluate and
disclose the effectiveness of the company's internal control over
financial reporting by utilizing a recognized control framework such
as the COSO Internal Control—Integrated Framework. The assessment of a company's internal control must be based on procedures
sufficient both to evaluate its design and test its operating effectiveness.[45]

Q 2.7.1   Who should administer the compliance program?

The Sentencing Guidelines provide that the company must
appoint senior managers who must have overall responsibility for the
compliance program. Additionally, several different departments
within the company may have significant roles to play in administering the compliance program. These include the inside audit or
accounting department, the security department, human resources,
and the legal department. They probably already perform compliance functions in their respective areas. Their various compliance
efforts must be coordinated as part of a single program and specific
senior manager(s) must be responsible—and accountable—for overseeing compliance efforts.[46]

53

Q 2.7.2   Which senior executive(s) should be placed in charge of the compliance program?

For public companies, Sarbanes-Oxley makes the audit committee (and, by extension, the entire board of directors) directly responsible for ensuring that a company's internal control over financial reporting functions properly and that all requisite disclosures are made. Otherwise, there is no single, required approach for assigning responsibility for management of the compliance program. Many companies, especially smaller ones, will designate one compliance officer. Larger organizations often designate individual compliance officers by substantive areas and may utilize a compliance committee in lieu of a single compliance officer, or a combination of an individual compliance officer who is supported by a committee from different areas. Increasing the number of compliance officers presents problems of communication, possible inconsistency, and lack of accountability.[47]

Q 2.7.3   What role does top management have in administering a compliance program?

The Sentencing Guidelines require that the company's governing authority (board of directors, etc.) understand the content and operation of the compliance program and exercise reasonable oversight with respect to its implementation and effectiveness. At least annually, but more often if practicable, the board should receive an update as to the status and operation of the compliance program, including usage of reporting mechanisms, reports of wrongdoing, reports of disciplinary action, reports of new risk areas, and other pertinent information.

Specific senior manager(s) must be assigned overall responsibility to ensure the implementation and effectiveness of the program. The individuals delegated day-to-day operational responsibility shall be given adequate resources and authority. Moreover, they shall report periodically to senior management and shall have direct access to the board of directors.[48]

Sarbanes-Oxley places responsibility for the creation and operation of a company's compliance program on both senior management and the audit committee of the board of directors, which it requires to be comprised of outside, independent directors.[49] The audit committee must establish procedures for (1) the receipt, retention, and treatment of complaints about accounting, internal accounting controls, or auditing matters, and (2) the confidential, anonymous submission by employee of concerns regarding questionable accounting or auditing matters.[50]

Sarbanes-Oxley imposes compliance responsibilities on senior corporate officials by requiring the principal executive officer and the principal financial officer, or persons performing similar functions, to make a series of certifications in each annual and quarterly report filed with the SEC. Each of these officers must certify that:

(1) he/she has reviewed the report;

(2) based on his/her knowledge, the report does not contain any untrue statement of a material fact or omit to state a material fact;

(3) based on his/her knowledge, the financial information in the report fairly presents in all material respects the financial condition, results of operations, and cash flows of the company;

(4) he/she and the company's other certifying officials are responsible for establishing and maintaining the company's disclosure controls and internal control over financial reporting;

(5) the disclosure controls and procedures have been designed to ensure that material information relating to the company and its consolidated subsidiaries is made known to the certifying officials by others in the company;

(6) the internal control over financial reporting has been designed to provide reasonable assurance regarding the reliability of financial reporting and the preparation of financial statements for external purposes in accordance with generally accepted accounting principles;

(7) he/she and the company's other certifying officials have evaluated the effectiveness of the disclosure controls and procedures and presented in this report their conclusions about their effectiveness as of the end of the period covered by the report;

(8) he/she and the company's other certifying officials have disclosed in the report any change in the company's internal control over financial reporting that occurred during the

most recent fiscal quarter that has materially affected or is reasonably likely to materially affect the company's internal control over financial reporting; and

(9) he/she and the company's other certifying officials have disclosed to the company's outside auditors and the audit committee of the board of directors

    (a) all significant deficiencies and material weaknesses in the design or operation of internal control over financial reporting that are reasonably likely to adversely affect the company's ability to record, process, summarize, and report financial information; and

    (b) any fraud, whether or not material, that involves management or other employees who have a significant role in the company's internal control over financial reporting.[51]

The overriding need to protect the investing public drives the Sarbanes-Oxley requirement for disclosure of any material weaknesses in the company's internal control over financial reporting or in its disclosure controls and procedures.

Q 2.7.4   What is meant by a "culture" of compliance?

Government enforcement authorities look to determine if there is executive "buy-in" regarding compliance programs and expect company officers to set the tone. As one SEC official recently stated,

> We're trying to get the fundamentally honest, decent CEO or CFO or General Counsel—the one who wouldn't break the law—to say to herself when she wakes up in the morning: "I'm going to spend part of my day today worrying about, and doing something about, the culture of my company."[52]

This is what is meant by a "culture" of ethics and compliance, and of the top setting the tone. Chapter 3 also offers an in-depth discussion of assessing and managing an ethical culture.

Q 2.7.5   How can we demonstrate a culture of ethics and compliance?

- Give the compliance officer "dotted line" reporting to the board as a whole, as well as its audit committee or other appropriate subgroup.
- Give periodic compliance program reports to the board.
- Involve senior management in compliance working groups, created by the company to assist the compliance officer in his or her duties.

Q 2.7.6   What are reasonable efforts to exclude bad actors?

There is no sure-fire way to root out each and every employee who possibly could act improperly. Companies are, however, expected to make *reasonable* efforts not to hire or retain as managers or other higher-level employees any individuals who have engaged in illegal or unethical conduct.

TIP: Background Checks and Other Due Diligence

Potential employers should check lists of "excluded persons" within their particular industry.

For example, healthcare companies should check their employees against the Department of Health and Human Services Office of Inspector General List of Excluded Individuals/Entities, http://oig.hhs.gov/fraud/exclusions/listofexcluded.html. Government contractors should utilize the General Services Administration's Excluded Parties List System (EPLS), accessible via www.sam.gov.

Training

Q 2.8   What is required in the way of training and communication?

Training should be provided upon hiring or transfer of an existing employee to a new position. Training should be provided at least annually thereafter, but more often if the circumstances dictate. Training can be provided using any number of means. It can be in-person, computer-/Internet-based, lecture-style, or by any other method that is appropriate to the content and reasonably calculated to provide a meaningful training experience.

It should never be forgotten that Enron seemed on the surface to have a compliance program, including a code of conduct. As it turned out, however, all Enron had was a "paper" program, and nothing of substance. In the words of Enron whistleblower Sharon Watkins, "It's not just a snappy little code of conduct or code of ethics that makes sure things are done right."[53] Instead, a company must ensure that *all* employees receive training on the code and policies that are relevant and applicable to their particular jobs within the company.

Good training is the cornerstone of an effective compliance and ethics program. A company can have the best-drafted code of conduct and the most thorough ethics policies money can buy, but if the company's employees are not trained on them, they are worthless paper.

Q 2.8.1   Who within our organization needs to be trained?

The Sentencing Guidelines state that, for an effective compliance and ethics program, the following individuals must receive training:

- members of the company's governing authority (for example, board of directors);
- high-level personnel;
- substantial authority personnel;
- employees; and
- agents, as appropriate.

Q 2.8.2   Do we need to educate every employee about every policy?

No; that would be a waste of the company's resources. A front-line cashier of a nationwide retailer does not need to be trained on the company's import/export controls policy. Instead, the company should determine which categories of employees (for example, sales, human resources, management) need training on the company's various policies.

Q 2.8.3   We hold a training session for new employees. Is a thorough, one-time training session on our code and policies enough?

No. The Sentencing Guidelines require *periodic* communication of the company's written standards and procedures. A company that trains its employees only during an orientation program does not have an effective compliance program. As time goes by, laws and regulations affecting a company will change, sometimes dramatically, and the company's written standards and policies must change accordingly. If individuals within that company do not receive education on the revised policies, those policies may as well not exist in the eyes of any governmental or other auditor or investigator.

Audits

Q 2.9   How can my company maintain the compliance program's effectiveness?

Conducting regular, periodic audits and monitoring of its program are effective means for a company to determine whether its compliance program is actually being followed. The audit can be done internally under the direction and supervision of the compliance officer, or it can be done externally. If an external audit is performed, it should be performed by outside counsel, due to the protections of the attorney-client privilege. The audit should be performed by evaluators with expertise in the relevant federal and state laws and regulations that affect the company's business.

In addition, a company's monitoring procedures should include a reporting system, discussed in greater detail below. Additionally, the company should conduct an investigation any time potential wrong-doing is revealed through the company policy.

Q 2.9.1   What should an audit of the program be examining?

The audit should be the company's method of determining whether the company does indeed have all of the elements of an effective compliance and ethics program in place. The following is just a sampling of the questions that auditors should be asking in an evaluation of the program:

❐ Does the company have in place all of the standards and procedures that are necessary, given the applicable legal and regulatory framework?

❐ Has the company appropriately distributed those written standards and procedures, including its code of conduct?

❐ Has the company provided ongoing training programs to educate its employees, officers, and (where appropriate) agents and contractors?

❐ Has the company devoted adequate resources to the operations of its compliance program, and does the compliance officer have sufficient authority within the organization?

❐ Are employees actually following the company program?

❐ Have there been any internal investigations of alleged noncompliance with the program? If so, what were the results?

❐ If internal investigations have taken place, were the proper procedures for investigations followed?

❐ Were remedial actions taken upon discovery of wrong-doing?

Q 2.9.2   What is internal auditing?[54]

The Institute of Internal Auditors has developed the globally accepted definition of internal auditing:

Internal Auditing is an independent, objective assurance and consulting activity designed to add value and improve an organization's operations. It helps an organization accomplish its objective by bringing a systematic, disciplined approach to evaluate and improve the effectiveness of risk management, control, and governance process.

Independence is established by the organizational and reporting structure while objectivity is achieved by an appropriate mind-set. The internal audit activity evaluates risk exposures relating to the organization's governance, operations, and information systems for: effectiveness and efficiency of operations; reliability and integrity of financial and operational information; safeguarding of assets; and compliance with laws, regulations, and other legal documents.

Q 2.9.3 Why should an organization have internal auditing?[55]

A cornerstone of strong governance, internal auditing bridges the gap between management and the board, assesses the ethical climate and the effectiveness and efficiency of operations, and serves as an organization's safety net for compliance with rules, regulations, and overall best business practices.

Management is responsible for establishing and maintaining a system of internal controls within an organization. Internal controls are those structures, activities, processes, and systems which help management effectively mitigate the risks to an organization's achievement of objectives. Management is charged with this responsibility on behalf of the organization's stakeholders and is held accountable for this responsibility by an oversight body (for example, board of directors, audit committee, elected representatives).

Q 2.9.4 What is internal auditing's role in preventing, detecting, and investigating fraud?[56]

Internal auditors support management's efforts to establish a culture that embraces ethics, honesty, and integrity. They assist management with the evaluation of internal controls used to detect or mitigate fraud, devalue the organization's assessment of fraud risk, and are involved in any fraud investigations.

Although it is management's responsibility to design internal controls to prevent, detect, and mitigate fraud, the internal auditors are an appropriate resource for assessing the effectiveness of the internal control structure that management has implemented.

Q 2.9.5   What is the appropriate relationship between the internal audit activity and the audit committee of the board of directors?[57]

The audit committee of the board of directors and the internal auditors are interdependent and should be mutually accessible, with the internal auditors providing objective opinions, information, support, and education to the audit committee; and the audit committee providing validation and oversight to the internal auditors.

Reporting Systems/Whistleblowing/Non-Retaliation

Q 2.10   What type of reporting system does my company need to have?

The Sentencing Guidelines require a reporting system that allows employees (1) to report ethical or legal concerns or (2) to seek guidance on particular ethical or legal matters. To achieve these goals, companies typically use a hotline. However, the reporting system a company chooses should be tailored to the size and geographical range of the company. A smaller company may decide to set up an internal telephone extension as its hotline, or—better yet—may use a toll-free number that allows callers to leave a voicemail message. A larger, geographically diverse company should at the very least have a toll-free number. Companies may also choose to set up an email account for the reporting of potential violations or seeking guidance.

Some external vendors can manage the reporting system, setting up internal and external websites that allow for anonymous reporting but also allow employees to check back in with the system to determine whether their reports are being investigated by the company. This type of two-way communication can provide employees with confidence that their concerns are being taken seriously by the company, and thus tends to cultivate company loyalty.

Although reporting systems may vary depending on the company, there are some across-the-board requirements. The system must:

- allow for anonymous and/or confidential reporting;
- be accompanied by a non-retaliation policy.

Q 2.10.1   What is a non-retaliation policy?

A non-retaliation policy should explain that a company will not retaliate against any employee who, in good faith, reports a potential violation. All employees should be made aware that any attempt at retaliation against an employee who uses the reporting system or engages in any kind of whistleblowing in good faith will result in immediate disciplinary action. A company should also instruct employees to contact the compliance officer immediately if they feel they are being retaliated against.

A non-retaliation policy is critical if your reporting system is to be more than "just for show." Without such a policy, employees and others will not feel secure reporting potential problems internally. In addition, they will not feel comfortable seeking guidance on some of the complex laws and regulations that govern many businesses and will, therefore, be less likely to prevent problems.

Rewards/Discipline

Q 2.11 How can my company effectively enforce the compliance program?

With both discipline and positive reinforcement. Companies should make compliance and ethics an integral part of employee evaluations. The promotions process should also take into account an employee's commitment to compliance. For example, has the employee been cooperative when asked to answer questions as part of an internal investigation? Has the employee brought ethical concerns to the attention of his or her supervisor, in an effort to ensure that the company's operations were aboveboard?

Conversely, companies need to dispense punishment as necessary and appropriate where employees have broken the law, have violated the company's written standards and procedures, or have otherwise acted counter to the goals of the compliance and ethics program. Companies will need to administer disciplinary actions that are suitable for given violations (for example, suspensions without pay or termination).

Q 2.11.1 Despite our best efforts to promote a culture of honesty and integrity, some criminal or unethical conduct has occurred. How should the company respond?

Promptly discipline individuals who engage in criminal or unethical conduct. Once those individuals have been dealt with appropriately, take steps to prevent further similar conduct—for example, by reviewing your compliance and ethics program to determine where the weak links are (Was there enough training conducted on certain policies? Were there gaps in your company's compliance auditing process?), and by modifying the program accordingly.

Depending on the industry involved and the nature and severity of the misconduct, self-disclosure to regulatory or law enforcement authorities may be prudent or required. For example, government contractors and subcontractors must make written disclosure to the government whenever they have credible evidence of a violation of federal criminal law or a violation of the civil False Claims Act.[58]

Notes to Chapter 2

1. United States v. Booker, 543 U.S. 220 (2005).
2. U.S. SENTENCING GUIDELINES MANUAL § 8B2.1.
3. *Id.* § 8C2.5(f)(1).
4. *Id.* § 8B2.1.
5. *In re* Caremark Int'l, Inc. Derivative Litig., 698 A.2d 959, 970 (Del. Ch. 1996).
6. U.S. SENTENCING GUIDELINES MANUAL § 8B2.1(a).
7. *Id.* § 8B2.1(b). In 2010, the Federal Sentencing Guidelines were amended in several respects. The most significant amendment permits a company's "culpability score" to be reduced by three levels for having an effective compliance program even when high-level personnel (a director, an executive officer or a person in charge of a major business unit) are involved in an offense if:

> (1) the company's compliance personnel have direct reporting authority to the board or audit committee on any matter involving criminal conduct and, at least annually, on the effectiveness of the compliance program;
>
> (2) the compliance program detected the offense before it was discovered by outsiders;
>
> (3) the company promptly reported the violation to the appropriate authorities; and
>
> (4) no individual with operational responsibility for the compliance program was involved in the offense.

Second, the corrective steps a company should take if criminal conduct is detected have been elaborated to include: (i) taking reasonable steps to remedy the harm resulting from the criminal conduct, which may include, where appropriate, providing restitution to identifiable victims; and (ii) preventing further similar criminal conduct by assessing the compliance program and making any necessary program changes, possibly with the help of an outside professional advisor.

8. *Id.* § 8B2.1 cmt. (n.7).
9. *Id.* § 8B2.1 cmt. (n.2).
10. *Id.* § 8B2.1 cmt. (n.2(B)).
11. *Id.* § 8B2.1 cmt. (n.2(C)(iii)).
12. Pub. L. No. 107-204 (Sarbanes-Oxley), 116 Stat. 745 (codified in scattered sections of titles 11, 15, 18, 28, and 29 U.S.C.).
13. Certification of Disclosure in Companies' Quarterly and Annual Reports, Securities Act Release No. 8124 (Aug. 30, 2002), www.sec.gov/rules/final/33-8124.htm.
14. *See* 31 U.S.C. § 5312(a)(2) and (c)(1).

15. 31 U.S.C. § 5318(h)(1).

16. *Id.* § 5318(*l*).

17. 12 C.F.R. § 21.11; 31 C.F.R. §§ 103.18, 103.19, 103.20, 103.21.

18. 31 C.F.R. §§ 103.22, 103.30.

19. This list can be found at www.treas.gov/offices/enforcement/ofac/sanctions/terrorism.html.

20. Sarbanes-Oxley § 406, 15 U.S.C. § 7264.

21. NYSE MANUAL § 303A.10 (Code of Business Conduct and Ethics), http://nysemanual.nyse.com/lcm/Help/mapContent.asp?sec=lcm-sections&title=sx-ruling-nyse-policymanual_303A.10&id=chp_1_4_3_11.

22. Sarbanes-Oxley § 402, 15 U.S.C. § 78m(k).

23. *See* 18 U.S.C. § 201.

24. 15 U.S.C. §§ 78a, 78m, 78dd-1, 78dd-2, 78ff.

25. 41 U.S.C. § 51 *et seq.*

26. 42 U.S.C. § 1320a-7b(b).

27. *See* United States v. Parise, 159 F.3d 790, 804 & n.1 (3d Cir. 1998) (Garth, J., dissenting) (collecting state commercial bribery statutes).

28. *See* 68 Fed. Reg. 36,636, 36,640 (2003).

29. *See* United States v. Park, 421 U.S. 658 (1975); United States v. Dotterweich, 320 U.S. 277 (1943); United States v. Cattle King Packing Co., 793 F.2d 232, 240 (10th Cir.), *cert. denied*, 479 U.S. 985 (1986).

30. *See, e.g.*, United States v. Weitzenhoff, 1 F.3d 1523, 1529 (9th Cir.), *reh'g denied and amended*, 35 F.3d 1275 (9th Cir. 1993) (construing criminal provision of the Clean Water Act).

31. *See* FAR subpt. 3.10, [48 C.F.R.] §§ 9.406-2, 9.407-2, 52.203-13, 52.203-14; 73 Fed. Reg. 67,064, FAR Case 2007-006, Contractor Business Ethics Compliance Program and Disclosure Requirements (Nov. 12, 2008).

32. *E.g.*, False Claims Act, 31 U.S.C. § 3729; claim forfeiture statute, 28 U.S.C. § 2514; anti-kickback statute, 41 U.S.C. § 51 *et seq.*; Procurement Integrity Act, 41 U.S.C. § 423; Contract Disputes Act, 41 U.S.C. § 601 *et seq.*; Truth in Negotiations Act, 10 U.S.C. § 2306a.

33. *E.g.*, 18 U.S.C. § 1001 (false statements); 18 U.S.C. § 287 (false claims); 18 U.S.C. § 371 (conspiracy to defraud the United States); 18 U.S.C. § 1031 (major fraud against the United States).

34. *See* DEP'T OF DEFENSE, HANDBOOK ON FRAUD INDICATORS FOR CONTRACT AUDITORS, IGDH 7600.3 (Mar. 31, 1993), www.dodig.mil/resources/policyreferences/Audit/igdh7600.pdf; Inspector General, Dep't of Defense Pub. No. IG/DOD 4075.1-H (1987).

35. NYSE MANUAL § 303A.10 (Code of Business Conduct and Ethics), *supra* note 21.

36. 15 U.S.C. § 78dd-1.

37. *See* Title VII of the Civil Rights Act of 1964, 42 U.S.C. § 2000e; Americans with Disabilities Act of 1990, 42 U.S.C. §§ 12101–213.

38. Civil Rights Act of 1991, 42 U.S.C. § 1981.

39. NYSE MANUAL § 303A.10 (Code of Business Conduct and Ethics), *supra* note 21.

40. Sarbanes-Oxley § 406, 15 U.S.C. § 7264; 17 C.F.R. §§ 228.406, 229.406. If the company does not adopt a code of ethics, it must explain why not. *Id.*
41. 17 C.F.R. §§ 228.406, 229.406.
42. *See* Sarbanes-Oxley § 301, 15 U.S.C. § 78f(m)(4).
43. U.S. SENTENCING GUIDELINES MANUAL § 8B2.1(b)(6).
44. *Id.* § 8B2.1(b)(5).
45. 68 Fed. Reg. 36,636, 36,642–43 (2003).
46. U.S. SENTENCING GUIDELINES MANUAL § 8B2.1(b)(2).
47. *See* JEFFREY M. KAPLAN, JOSEPH E. MURPHY & WINTHROP M. SWENSON, COMPLIANCE PROGRAMS AND THE CORPORATE SENTENCING GUIDELINES § 8.11 (1995).
48. U.S. SENTENCING GUIDELINES MANUAL § 8B2.1(b)(2).
49. Sarbanes-Oxley § 301, 15 U.S.C. § 78f(m)(3)(A).
50. Sarbanes-Oxley § 301, 15 U.S.C. § 78f(m)(4).
51. Sarbanes-Oxley § 302, 15 U.S.C. § 7241; 17 C.F.R. § 229.601.
52. Stephen M. Cutler, Dir., SEC Enf't Div., Speech at Second Annual General Counsel Roundtable, Tone at the Top: Getting It Right (Dec. 3, 2004), www.sec.gov/news/speech/spch120304smc.htm.
53. Andrew Countryman, *Enron Whistleblower Spreads Around Blame*, CHI. TRIB., Jan. 15, 2003.
54. This question-and-answer is based on information from the Institute of Internal Auditors, Altamonte Springs, Florida, and has been reprinted with permission from their website FAQs. *See* www.theiia.org.
55. *Id.*
56. *Id.*
57. *Id.*
58. *See* FAR [48 C.F.R.] §§ 9.406-2, 9.407-2, 52.203-13(b)(3)(i).

3

Assessing and Managing an Ethical Culture

David Gebler

§ 8B2.1. Effective Compliance and Ethics Program

(a) To have an effective compliance and ethics program, . . . an organization shall—

. . .

    (2) otherwise promote an organizational culture that encourages ethical conduct and a commitment to compliance with the law.

U.S. SENTENCING GUIDELINES MANUAL § 8B2.1 (Nov. 2006)

How do you know if your company is effectively promoting "an organizational culture that encourages ethical conduct and a commitment to compliance with the law"? How can you be certain that prosecutors cannot label your compliance efforts as a "paper program"?[1] More importantly, how can you create an environment where your employees sincerely feel that the company is committed to compliance?

Chief Compliance Officers should not be lulled into complacency just because the organization has implemented all of the elements of the Federal Sentencing Guidelines. Despite the deployment of the formal elements of a compliance program:

- Employees will not be *committed* to compliance if the core culture does not support compliance; and
- The organization cannot *encourage* ethical conduct if the underlying culture does not support ethics in its day-to-day activities.

The bottom line is that a company cannot achieve compliance without first addressing the behavioral issues in its culture that impact the ability and the desire to be compliant. The companies that maintain the lowest risk of misconduct have created an environment where employees seek compliance as the most productive way to do their jobs. These companies have created an environment where values such as predictability, accountability, and candor are embedded in the culture.

This chapter explores the factors in the culture that support or detract from compliance and what a company can do to assess and then influence those factors.

The Linkage of Culture and Compliance

Q 3.1   If a company has a compliance program and employees know they must act in accordance with those standards, why does misconduct still occur?

Next time you are driving over the speed limit on the highway, ask yourself: "What would it take to get even an honest person like me to obey the law?" Is it only the fear of being caught that slows you down? We do not want to have a cop at every mile marker, even if we could afford it. So how do you get citizens to willingly observe and obey the law? The situation inside companies is similar. It is one thing to set standards; it is another to get people to follow them. Many compliance officers oversee a multitude of policies and regulations that employees in various positions are expected to follow. Moreover, leadership probably communicates the importance of following the standards. And yet in many companies, misconduct still occurs at an unacceptably high rate.

The simple fact of the matter is that mere awareness of a standard is not enough to compel compliant behavior. In many instances, compliance professionals do not take human factors into enough consideration when programs are implemented and standards enacted. They do not look deeply enough into what drives individual behavior. For the most part, individuals do not engage in unethical behavior inside organizations for personal gain akin to fraud. Most actions that violate company standards occur because employees feel that this behavior is expected of them. Or, employees have rationalized that this activity is the only way to get their job done and meet the expectations of their managers. It is not that employees are

71

dishonest. The vast majority of employees are not only honest, they want to work in a company that values trust and integrity.

So why would any employee ever feel that he or she must engage in unethical activity, especially if senior leadership is on record discouraging such behavior? The evidence points to the culture. While we might like to think of ourselves as autonomous actors and decision-makers, we are deeply affected and influenced by our environment.

Q 3.2 Why should compliance officers focus on culture?

In annual surveys conducted by the Ethics Resource Center, a nonprofit, nonpartisan research organization dedicated to independent research that advances high ethical standards and practices in public and private institutions, research has shown that "culture has a greater impact than a formal ethics and compliance program on outcomes such as observed misconduct, reporting or misconduct, and perceived ability to handle misconduct if faced with such a situation."[2]

The evaluation of culture helps compliance leadership to understand the pressures and frustrations that cause employees to violate compliance standards.

Furthermore, culture pays. Focusing on culture increases the "return on investment" of the ethics and compliance program. Research has shown that integrity-based programs that address ethics and culture are more effective than narrower compliance-based programs in reaching positive outcomes for organizations. One landmark empirical study found that programs that addressed culture issues (discussed below) were more effective in predicting desired compliance outcomes for organizations.[3] For example, in 2007 the Ethics Resource Center found a sixty-one-percentage-point favorable difference in the level of observed misconduct when employees say they work in a strong ethical culture.[4]

Q 3.3 How do we know if our implementation of the elements of the Federal Sentencing Guidelines is sufficient?

Chapter 2 details the elements of a compliance program that are required by the U.S. Sentencing Commission's Federal Sentencing Guidelines. It is true that "[a]n organization can prove it promoted a

"We're moving beyond compliance for a very simple reason: because culture trumps compliance. We're a legalistic society, and we've created a lot of laws. We assume that if you just knew what those laws meant that you would behave properly. Well, guess what? You can't write enough laws to tell us what to do at all times every day of the week in every part of the world. We've got to develop the critical thinking and critical reasoning skills of our people because most of the ethical issues that we deal with are in the ethical gray areas. Virtually every regulatory body in the last year has come out with language that has said in addition to law compliance, businesses are also going to be accountable to ethics standards and a corporate culture that embraces them."

Keith Darcy
President of Ethics and
Compliance Officers Association[5]

culture that encouraged ethical conduct and a commitment to compliance with the law by satisfying the minimum requirements of the Guidelines."[6] However, research has shown that codes of conduct, one example of a required element, are not enough to reduce illegal behavior.[7]

The real answer to determining whether a program is sufficient is based on the company's intent. Is the company sincerely looking to reduce ethics and compliance risks, or is it content with a "paper" program that creates the appearance of good corporate citizenship.[8]

For companies that have a genuine commitment to creating an ethical culture, the Federal Sentencing Guidelines detail the objective elements minimally necessary to maintain a program. However, the elements in the Sentencing Guidelines cannot alone create an ethical culture if additional subjective elements discussed below are not present.

"The culture of compliance is *not* a new concept. Hopefully, everyone here is familiar with the idea. For years, you've been told you need one. We at the SEC have been emphasizing that firms need to create a culture of compliance for many years. You've heard it from Chairmen, from Commissioners, and from the staff, and certainly you've heard it from me. If you've been listening, you know it's *not* enough to have policies. It's *not* enough to have procedures. It's not enough to have good intentions. All of these can help. But to be successful, compliance must be an embedded part of your firm's culture."

Lori A. Richards, Director
Office of Compliance Inspections and Examinations
U.S. Securities and Exchange Commission
April 23, 2003

Q 3.3.1 What do regulators and prosecutors think about culture?

Prosecutors and regulators are looking beyond pro forma adherence to the Federal Sentencing Guidelines as indicators of an ethical culture. Prosecutors consider many factors in deciding how to exercise their discretion on who gets investigated and who gets charged. A key factor is the organization's culture of compliance and how an organization reacts to problems they uncover. A critical indicator of a healthy culture is the organization's stand on self-reporting wrongdoing. Organizations that take the lead and come to the regulators on their own initiative after internally discovering an issue usually come out in a better position at the end than companies that wait until the government comes to them. Generating trust and goodwill is critical, especially in the often lengthy discussions and negotiations that surround an investigation. Prosecutors are interested to know whether an organization has the kind of culture that is inclined to self-report if a violation arises.[9]

Several years ago, when Hewlett-Packard was immersed in a scandal regarding breach of privacy issues and its board, the California Attorney General praised the company for the way it handled the issue: "Fortunately, Hewlett-Packard is not Enron. I commend the firm for cooperating instead of stonewalling, for taking instead of shirking responsibility, and for working with my office to expeditiously craft a creative resolution."[10]

Q 3.3.2   How can an organization evaluate behavior as part of its compliance program?

Introduction of behavioral research into what motivates individual decision-making is changing how compliance officers see the adequacy of their programs. For example, research has shown that two similarly inclined individuals will engage in different behavior related to compliance if faced with different circumstances.[11]

Some ethics researchers are now looking to the behavioral sciences for insights into predicting ethical behavior. For example, research developed by Ajzen and Fishbein in their Theory of Planned Behavior[12] shows that there are three determinants of a person's intentions, which then determine their behavior:

1. Their attitude toward the behavior—that is, do they feel it is right or wrong, and what are the consequences of engaging in that action;
2. The social pressure they feel from others either to perform or refrain from action; and
3. The individual's perceived behavioral control—that is, their estimate of their ability to perform the behavior, considering both their skill and external factors such as getting caught.

For many years companies regarded employees who acted unethically (or even illegally) as inherently different in some way from "normal" employees who would never engage in such behavior. However, research has shown that most individuals who do act unethically likely seem quite normal and unremarkable to their peers and supervisors. These individuals, though, are acutely sensitive to their environments and take cues from the world around them,[13] and it is their perception of what is happening to them that drives their actions. These individuals turn out to be the kind of people that react more strongly to changes in their environment. The specific types

75

situations that trigger different reactions among different types of people are discussed below (*see* Q 3.9).

Research has shown that these external influences are not just broad-based environmental factors such as an individual's socio-economic status, but very specific situations that individuals face. Author Malcolm Gladwell discovers in studies he has collected that "something like honesty isn't a fundamental trait. . . . A trait like honesty . . . is considerably influenced by the situation."[14] Change a few variables to make it easier for students to cheat, for example, and even honest students will fall to the pressure.[15]

Framework of an Ethical Culture

Essential Characteristics

Q 3.4   What are the elements of an ethical culture/a culture of compliance?

There are specific attributes that qualitatively characterize a culture of compliance. Knowledge of the extent to which these elements are present in your organization and what the factors are that deter these elements form the foundation of a culture of compliance.

Since the mid 1990s, researchers and practitioners have made distinctions between compliance-based programs and integrity-based programs.[16]

> A firm using a compliance-based program focuses its efforts on deterrence through threat of detection and punishment for violations of the law or the code of conduct. A firm using an integrity-based approach, on the other hand, focuses its efforts on establishing legitimacy with employees through internally developed organizational values and self-governance.[17]

For example, whereas a compliance-based program focuses on teaching employees the laws and rules they must comply with, an integrity-based program focuses on integrating ethics into employees' decision-making and inspiring them to live up the company's ethical ideals.[18]

The Ethics Resource Center describes an "ethical culture" as having four essential characteristics. These are the visible identifiers that an organization has an ethical culture.

1. **Ethical leadership.** Leaders set the right "tone at the top" and model ethical culture as part of earning the trust of employees.
2. **Supervisor reinforcement.** Employees look to immediate supervisors for signs that the tone at the top is important and is taken seriously.
3. **Peer commitment.** Peers talk about the importance of ethics and support one another in "doing the right thing."
4. **Embedded ethical values.** A sense of "how we do things around here" is integrated into daily activities.[19]

Based on client experience in the ethics and compliance field, there are three core elements that will determine the extent the organization is sustaining an ethical culture.[20] The core elements of the "ethical culture framework" are:

1. **Goals:** *Stated and unstated, individual and organizational*
   In an ethical culture, an individual's goals (whether it is a stated performance goal or an unstated goal, such as wanting to keep one's job) are consistent with the organization's goals. Additionally, individuals need not feel that they have to sacrifice their values in order to meet their goals.
2. **Behaviors:** *Stated standards of behavior and unstated ways in which decisions are made*
   Behaviors reflect the extent to which leaders at all levels demonstrate effective "tone" and engage in actions that positively impact the environment around them. The organization's standards of behavior are consistent with individual and organizational goals as well as the values of the employees.
3. **Values:** *Personal values and the collective values needed for the organization to succeed*
   The extent the organization promulgates shared values and articulates the reasons why certain behaviors are important.

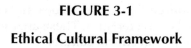

FIGURE 3-1

Ethical Cultural Framework

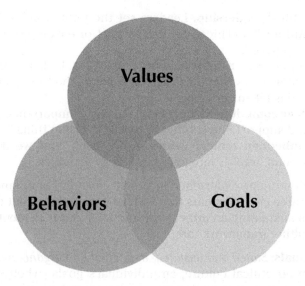

For an organization to have an effective ethical culture, each of these elements must each be fully developed in its own right and must also be in alignment, meaning that each element must complement and support the others. If not, there are likely to be sources of frustration and pressure that can lead to unethical behavior. The tensions that arise both within each of these elements and between and among them that can lead to ethics and compliance risks within an organization.

Organizational and Individual Goals

Q 3.5 How do individual and organizational goals help create an ethical cultural framework?

Employees making the decision between engaging in unethical conduct and reporting or questioning possible misconduct being committed by others are working through a sophisticated decision-making analysis, even if it is done subconsciously. One of the major factors in a decision to act is the employee's determination of whether or not the anticipated action is deemed acceptable in the corporate culture.[21] Setting a positive ethical climate as a goal is important in ensuring that employees' goals are consistent with the organization's goals.

For example, take two employees, one who has a natural inclination to cheat on her timecards and one who does not. There is no certainty that the employee who is more likely to cheat always will, as there is no guarantee that the more honest employee will never cheat. One of the most influential factors in whether or not each individual will cheat is culture.[22] A culture in which there is no respect for such rules makes it very easy for the employee who is inclined to cheat to feel she can get away with adding hours to her timecard. However, if the more honest employee lacks self-confidence and is susceptible to peer pressure, then he may also find it easier to rationalize his behavior in the negative culture, for example, agreeing to punch out a co-worker's timecard two hours after that co-worker has left her shift. Conversely, in a culture where compliance is an accepted norm, the more honest employee will not feel any pressure to violate his norms, and the dishonest employee may feel that cheating is too risky.

Q 3.5.1   How are goals rewarded?

Are employees rewarded only for meeting financial goals? One of the strongest indicators of a company's commitment to ethics is whether it matters where it counts most: in how managers and employees are compensated. Companies committed to maintaining ethical cultures have identified key behaviors required of managers that are included in performance measurement discussions.[23]

Q 3.5.2   How are business goals and ethics linked?

In a true culture of compliance, ethics issues are discussed outside of formal training sessions. A real test of whether ethics is being embedded in the culture is whether or not ethics is being discussed in informal meetings involving difficult issues. It is one thing to attend mandatory ethics or compliance training, another to be thinking of the ethical impact of a decision when someone is under pressure to deliver on time and on budget. When the values of the organization are well understood, employees and managers are comfortable ensuring that all actions and decisions are consistent with agreed-upon principles.[24]

79

Q 3.5.3   Can challenges to business goals be safely raised?

In ethically challenged organizations, employees will not report misconduct they observe. They find it too risky to themselves in terms of fear of retaliation, or they simply do not care.[25] However, even in organizations where employees report on surveys that they would report misconduct, it is not always a sign of a healthy ethical culture.

In an ethical culture the organization often has an opportunity to nip potential trouble in the bud. If management is made aware of issues before they turn into problems, situations can be addressed early. But in many organizations, managers have created a perception that they do not want to be presented with bad news. For managers from this school, employees know what they have to do, and "no" is simply not an answer.

In organizations focused on creating an ethical culture, effort is made to communicate to and train managers in creating an environment where employees can safely raise issues without fear. Better yet, there is an environment of trust where employees can play an active role in solving problems early in the process.

What would your employees say if a prosecutor interviewed them? In a growing number of instances, prosecutors and regulatory investigators are going into the field and asking employees tough questions, like whether they feel comfortable raising issues with management.[26]

Behaviors/Organizational Tone

"[T]he ultimate effectiveness of the new corporate governance rules will be determined by the 'tone at the top.' Adopting a code of ethics means little if the company's chief executive officer or its directors make clear, by conduct or otherwise, that the code's provisions do not apply to them."

SEC Commissioner Cynthia Glassman
April 7, 2003[27]

Q 3.6   What is organizational tone, and what is its role in supporting a culture of ethics and compliance?

Organizational behavior should support and reflect an organizational tone consistent with individual and organizational goals and values. "Behavior" encompasses the formal behaviors sought by the organization (those included in a code of conduct and other policy directives), as well as informal behavior engaged in at all levels of the organization, from top directors and officers, to middle management, to regular staff and employees—that is:

- the "tone at the top,"
- the "mood in the middle," and
- the "buzz at the bottom."

Q 3.6.1   What is the role of top management and organizational leaders in setting the appropriate tone?

It is important that officers and directors adhere to the same standards expected of everyone else; however, "tone at the top" needs to go further than that. Leaders must also model the positive behavior that reduces risks of unethical conduct. Are leaders discussing ethics? Do leaders remind managers of the organization's values when discussing tough issues? Leaders must also be aware of how management policies are perceived when they are deployed into the field. For example, when employees are confused about how to implement a policy, there is a greater risk of engaging in undesired behavior. Are leaders aware of whether a policy is generating confusion? Have they even asked the question?

Q 3.6.2   What is the role of middle management in setting the appropriate tone?

Mid-level managers are often the demographic group within an organization that faces the greatest pressure. They often feel squeezed between carrying out edicts from the top and facing the realities from the field of actually getting the job done. In many organizations, mid-level managers have not had extensive leadership development training. Leadership may not have provided these managers with sufficient tools to both manage the pressure and provide the kind of empathetic reception that employees may need if they have a problem to discuss.

Q 3.6.3   What is the role of regular employees in setting the appropriate tone?

In most organizations, employees spend much of their day outside of the direct view of their supervisor. How do they feel about the ethical climate? If a colleague takes a short-cut, or perhaps violates a code provision, such as unauthorized use of time or resources, will employees say anything? True self-governance means that line employees feel responsible for their actions. They feel emotionally invested in the welfare of the organization. They want to do a good job and want to feel proud of their department and workgroup.

Q 3.6.4   Is the organizational tone always set from the top down?

A powerful influencer of behavior in most organizations—sometimes even more powerful than messages or tone from leadership—is peer pressure.

In the 1990s, an automobile manufacturing facility in the American Southwest touted its Japanese production system as an innovation in quality. Every employee was empowered to pull the andon cord to stop the production line if he saw a defect. But employees were very resistant to pulling the cord. The pressure not to pull was not from leadership or even plant management; it was from the other line employees. Pulling the cord meant the line could be stopped for upwards of ninety minutes to investigate the problem. In times of full production, that delay could mean mandatory Saturday overtime. During bass fishing season, no one wanted to be responsible for keeping people at work on a Saturday.

Organizational, Individual, and Shared Values

Q 3.7   Which values are important to an ethical culture framework?

The values that matter in determining an ethical culture are not the stated core values posted on the website. The organization's unstated values drive behavior. Unstated values may not always even

82

be positive. For example, in some organizations where effective and efficient processes are not actively pursued or implemented, "bureaucracy" and "inconsistency" can be the most common values in the current culture. They are still values because the organization, by default, has created the impression to employees that these values matter because they are so pervasive and nothing has been done to limit them.

The unstated values of an organization are the sum total of the values held by the members of the organization. Assessing these values will help an organization's leadership see whether or not what the organization's members feel is important aligns with the kind of behavior the organization is seeking from its members.

Q 3.7.1   What is the role of collective/shared values in an ethical culture framework?

A landmark study of more than 10,000 employees of six large American companies found that:

> [E]mployees' perception of shared values was a key factor in designing an ethics program. The concept of shared values, as a part of organizational culture has been defined as "the shared set of norms and beliefs that guide individual and organizational behavior. These norms and beliefs are shaped by the leadership of the organization, are often expressed as shared values or guiding principles, and are reinforced by various systems and procedures throughout the organization." "Shared" means that there is consultation with, and "buy-in" from, all the different stakeholders of the organization.[28]

There are numerous models and theories of categorization of values. One model in use in the ethics and compliance field today, known as the Barrett model (after its developer, Richard Barrett),[29] has proven useful in ethics and compliance because, among other things, it breaks down the full range of human beliefs into seven levels of values that are personified in individuals as well as organizations. According to the Barrett model, every individual and organization embodies numerous values, each of which can be placed into one of these seven levels:

83

TABLE 3-2
Seven Levels of Consciousness (The Barrett Model)

Values Level	Characteristics
1. Survival	Financial stability and group member safety
2. Relationship	Harmonious internal relationships that create a sense of belonging
3. Performance	Group order, performance, and effectiveness that engender respect and pride
4. Engagement	Aligning decision-making to the needs of the group members
5. Communal	Aligning around a shared vision, mission, and values
6. Contribution	Cooperating with other groups and caring for group members
7. Service	Caring for humanity, future generations, and the planet

When organizations are surveyed about their values (*see* Q 3.10.3, *infra*), the collective values of the employees reveal the following three key insights about themselves and the organization:

Personal values. The collective personal values of employees are the fuel for change. Employees also want to feel that they can bring their values to work—that there is a shared vision that clarifies the intentions of the organization and gives employees a unifying purpose and direction.

Current culture values. While the organization would never affirmatively state that negative values are important, the fact they persist can reflect a statement of what is important by default. Answering some of the following questions can help determine what values reflect the current work environment and whether some of them are negative:

- Does the current culture permit employees to bring their values to work?
- Does normal pressure to perform become debilitating fear?
- Does a tough boss become manipulative and exploitive?
- Are perceptions of bureaucracy and "firefighting" so pervasive that employees feel not only that they cannot get their work done, but also that there is no point in even raising their concerns?

Desired culture values. What values do employees feel are essential to support an ethical culture? While leadership may have its own list of values—for example, transparency, accountability, and honesty—it is more important to understand whether employees are "on the same page." While in some organizations employees understand how values such as transparency are important for the organization to be high-performance, in most organizations employees do not seeing the world at such a lofty level. In these organizations, more fundamental values such as respect and employee appreciation are as lofty as they can go.

Aligning Goals, Behaviors, and Values

Q 3.8   How do the elements of the ethical culture framework work together?

While each of the three core elements of the ethical culture framework—goals, behaviors, and values—needs to be evaluated on its own, a healthy ethical culture can be sustained only if there is alignment among these elements. An organization's culture is a snapshot in time of how well the organization is creating a sense of balance among goals, behaviors, and values. If any of these areas is not in alignment, tensions and frustrations grow, creating risk.

Q 3.8.1   How do you align goals and values?

Goals must be consistent with values, or they cannot be sustained. For example, goals may reflect short-term or limited objectives that do not reflect the long-term interests of all stakeholders. If this is the case, tensions between the two will arise quickly as people will engage in behavior they do not believe in for only a short period of time. However, the values of the organization must be seen as essential for meeting legitimate business goals. If the values desired by the organization are too vague, there is a risk of them being marginalized and not taken seriously.

Q 3.8.2   ... goals and behaviors?

Lack of alignment means employees underperform or do not have context as to how their efforts matter. If the organization has actual goals that are in tension with stated behavioral standards (such as the code), then employees are caught having to choose between following the rules and doing what is rewarded.

Q 3.8.3   ... behaviors and values?

Behaviors implement values. Employees will not engage in behaviors they do not believe in, and values are not sustainable if people cannot live them. Stated values that are too conceptual may be deemed impractical or unrealistic. Moreover, they will not provide guidance on how to navigate the gray areas outside the "black and white" of the standards of expected behavior.

Barriers to an Ethical Culture

Risk Factors

Q 3.9   What are the barriers to an ethical culture?

Every leader and every employee wants to work in an ethical culture. So what's the problem? The hard reality is that an ethical culture cannot be imposed on an organization. Even if there is sincere commitment from leadership to put into place the elements of an ethical culture, there may be specific risk factors that are preventing an ethical culture from flourishing. These factors could be based on process issues, relationship issues, or a misalignment of goals and incentives.

Ethics and compliance leadership, in order to be able to address these issues, needs to create logical categories of risks that will permit leadership to measure and manage those risks. Since behavior of individuals is derived from our values and beliefs, it is helpful to have a values model that categorizes what we deem important. Again, what is important is determined by what is permitted to occur in the organization, not necessarily what we would like to see. The Barrett values model (*see* Q 3.7.1, *supra*) identifies ethics risks by revealing where employees perceive fears, frustrations, and pressures in the organization.

Q 3.9.1   What risk factors exist, and how should they be addressed?

Experience shows that at each of the first five levels of values listed in the Barrett model[30] there are corresponding ethics-related risks areas:

TABLE 3-3
Risk Areas

Values Level	Related Risks
1. Survival	Fear and uncertainty
2. Relationship	Blame, abusive behavior, information hoarding; pressure to conform
3. Performance	Inability to get one's job done; lack of control
4. Engagement	Lack of accountability
5. Communal	Lack of commitment and context

1.   Survival Values: Fear and Uncertainty

Every organization needs to make financial stability a primary concern. Companies that are all-consumed with just surviving struggle to focus enough attention on how they conduct themselves. This may, in fact, create a negative cycle that makes survival much more difficult.

Employees may be working in an environment of fear. Uncertainty naturally draws people to tighten the circles around them, causing them to have a short-term focus, be self-centered, and only see success as the immediate bottom-line.

At level 1, managers may be exercising excessive control. In these circumstances, unethical or even illegal conduct can be rationalized.

When asked to conform to regulations, organizations may only do the minimum with an attitude of begrudging compliance.

Organizations with challenges at this level need to be confident that managers know and stand within clear ethical boundaries. The type of leader needed to manage a crisis may not be the same one needed to grow the organization.

Researchers have posited[31] that much of WorldCom's unethical behaviors may have been caused by "groupthink." Groupthink is caused when seeking concurrence becomes paramount in team decision-making. Groupthink has been defined as a "mode of thinking that people engage in when they are deeply involved in a cohesive in-group, when the members' strivings for unanimity override their motivation to realistically appraise alternative courses of action."[32]

"In large business organizations, the pressures to conform and the uncertainty surrounding any decision can be significant. . . . Inexperienced managers must rely on local norms for guidance in periods of uncertainty, which can lead to the continuation of wrongful activity. As one employee in a risk-management position at Enron stated:

> If your boss was [fudging], and you have never worked anywhere else, you just assume that everybody fudges earnings. . . . Once you get there and you realized how it was, do you stand up and lose your job? It was scary. It was easy to get into 'Well, everybody else is doing it, so maybe it isn't so bad.'

In the Enron case . . . the individual's thought that the act was wrong was overridden by social pressures to conform to local norms of behavior."[33]

---

2.   Relationship Values: Blame, Abusive Behavior, Information Hoarding; Pressure to Conform

Without good relationships with employees, customers, and suppliers, integrity is compromised. The critical issue at this level is to create a sense of loyalty and belonging among employees and a sense of caring and connection between the organization and its customers.

In many organizations, employees begin to rationalize unethical conduct out of a sense of lack of appreciation. For employees who seek connection and engagement with their company, feeling unappreciated can create a negative sense of entitlement and can validate acts of retribution against the company. The most critical link in the chain is between employees and their direct supervisors. Poor communication makes transparency impossible. Key information may not be disclosed. There is persistent fear of retaliation. Fears about belonging and lack of respect lead to fragmentation, dissension, and disloyalty. When leaders meet behind closed doors or fail to communicate openly, employees suspect the worst. Cliques form, and gossip becomes rife. When leaders are more focused on their own success, rather than the success of the organization, they begin to compete with each other.

3.   Performance Values: Inability to Get One's Job Done; Lack of Control

At this level, the organization is focused on becoming the best it can be operationally, through the adoption of best practices and a focus on quality, productivity, and efficiency. Having a healthy corporate "self-esteem" is important for productivity as well as ensuring that ethics is seen as important for the organization's stability.

Level-3 organizations have succeeded in implementing strong internal controls and have enacted clear standards of conduct. However, organizations need to be alert to resorting to a "check-the-box" attitude that assumes compliance comes naturally from implementing standards and procedures. Organizations need to be mindful both of the risks of hierarchical structures and power-based silos that limit communication and of employee and manager engagement in living ethical principles.

An area of concern is an over-reliance on using "managing by results" or "managing by objectives" metrics to encourage productivity. Research shows that MBO and MBR cultures often misunderstand that the whole is greater than the sum of the parts and that individual goals are often not 100% within the control of each person. Employees can feel trapped in an unfair system that draws them into level-1 uncertainty and self-preservation at the expense of the organization.

A very common ethics risk factor in organizations is a sense of inconsistency and a lack of fairness. Most employees are willing to make personal sacrifices of time, money, and job satisfaction for the good of the group, so long as that sacrifice is not taken advantage of. However, if individual or groups of employees feel that they are being taken advantage of, human nature turns that sense of commitment 180 degrees into a sense of entitlement and perceived self-preservation.

4.   Engagement Values: Lack of Accountability

The focus of level 4 is creating an environment where employees and managers take full responsibility for their own actions. They want to be held accountable, not micro-managed and supervised every moment of every day. For a successful business practices and compliance program, every employee must feel he or she has a personal responsibility for the integrity of the organization. Everyone must feel that his or her voice is being heard. This requires managers and leaders to admit they do not have all the answers and to invite employee participation.

There are strong correlations between ethical cultures and organizations that encourage innovation and creativity. Asking employees to take risks to report what they see and "do the right thing" cannot happen where innovation is inhibited. Data show that in many organizations the majority of employees are not willing to report misconduct. Creating a sense of accountability and responsibility is vital to sustaining an ethical culture.

5.   Communal Values: Lack of Commitment and Context

The critical issue at this level is developing a shared vision of the future and a shared set of values. The shared vision clarifies the intentions of the organization and gives employees a unifying purpose and direction. The shared values provide guidance in decision-making.

Employees enjoy working in an environment where they can be free to express themselves and grow as individuals. The organization develops the ability to align decision-making around a set of shared values. The values and behaviors must be reflected in all of the organization's processes and systems, with appropriate consequences for those who are not willing to "walk the talk." A precondition for success at this level is to build a climate of trust. In an organization that does not maintain values at this level, everyone is out for himself. This lack of engagement also leads to rationalized unethical conduct as a survival mechanism in the organization.

Assessing the Risks

Q 3.10 How do we know if our culture creates ethics and compliance risks?

According to one study, nearly half (49%) of employees observed some type of misconduct taking place in the workplace. This percentage was based on employees' indications that they had observed at least one of fifteen specified behaviors in the prior twelve months. Only 63% of employees who observed misconduct reported it.[34] In any organization with more than several hundred employees, there is likely to be some degree of ethics risk. And no organization is perfect. So the key is for leadership to determine whether the risks are within an acceptable range or whether they are excessive.

COMPLIANCE FACT

Nearly half the workforce observes unethical conduct during the year.

Q 3.10.1   Can't we use our existing employee survey data to assess our compliance risk?

Employee satisfaction surveys often provide some indicators of employee engagement, but such surveys often do not address risk areas. While there is some correlation between overall levels of employee satisfaction and a healthy ethical environment, employee satisfaction survey data usually do not provide sufficient specificity to help a company mitigate culture risks.

In order to better assess, for example, the likelihood of risks at various levels occurring (*see* Q 3.9.1, *supra*) and, if they do occur, how damaging they could be to the organization, a company should perform a culture risk assessment. A culture risk assessment looks at behavior-based factors that create the environment that would allow the undesired activity to occur. This is in contrast to a compliance risk assessment (*see* chapter 4), which looks at the sufficiency of the compliance program and the vulnerability of the organization to violations of standards and laws.

Q 3.10.2   What is the goal of a culture risk assessment?

The assessment instrument or process must get at why employees feel the way they do. Whatever assessment methodology is used, it is important that leadership gain insight into how well the organization is balancing the core elements of the ethical culture framework: goals, behaviors, and values. If any of these areas is not in alignment, tensions and frustrations grow, creating risk.

Leadership must first understand what drives employees' behavior, which values—whether positive or negative—have the most influence in shaping expectations, and how things get done in their organization. In every organization there are unique "break-through behaviors"—a specific set of actions to be engaged in by a specific set of people that will have the most influence in effecting change. Companies that remove these roadblocks (*see* Q 3.9.1, *supra*, discussing these negative behaviors) find employees more willing to be more engaged and take more personal responsibility. They are more trusting and, therefore, willing to speak up and take ownership for their actions.

For example, in one organization employees were hesitant to bring bad news forward to their supervisors. As a result, key information that could reduce the risk of unnecessary pressure to perform at the end of the quarter was not being communicated. The culture risk assessment process revealed that, in this organization's culture, a "cowboy" persona prevailed, where admitting failure or even that there was a risk of not succeeding was unacceptable. The break-through behavior was to establish permission to admit mistakes. In staff meetings, leadership acknowledged that everyone makes mistakes and revealed personal examples of mistakes they had made. For this organization, ensuring that that information was not kept private was key. While mistakes were to be expected, keeping quiet about them was not to be tolerated.

Q 3.10.3   What information are we looking for in a culture risk assessment?

In pulling together the data for the assessment, leadership should gather information from varying sources:

Goals:

- Review of performance management and compensation data: What type of behavior is rewarded in the organization?
- Survey data that reveals how well messages are communicated and received in the field. Do employees have a clear sense of what is expected of them?
- Employee focus groups and manager interviews will reveal gaps in perception and where individual goals are not in alignment with the organization's goals.

Behaviors: Review of survey data as to how well employees understand and follow prescribed standards of behavior. Data from ethics and HR investigations can be helpful. Also, information from periodic performance evaluations can reveal where there are challenges with leaders engaging employees.

Values: A web-based values assessment will provide data about the collective values of the organization and where there are significant variances among key demographic groups. For example, an assessment used with the Barrett values model asks employees to identify their "Top 10" personal values, the "Top 10" values that reflect the current corporate culture, and the "Top 10" values that are essential for the organization to be high-performance.

93

Creating an Ethical Culture

Q 3.11 How do we reduce risks to an ethical culture?

With data in hand revealing insights about the culture, the last stage is to link the culture factors to the ethics risks that the organization faces. Since every organization has its own culture and its own risks, what follows is an example of the approach that could be used to get to the heart of what is challenging your ethical culture.

Identifying Ethics Issues

Q 3.11.1   What are our top ethics issues?

This analysis identifies patterns in the scope of ethics issues your organization faces in order to get at the root causes of the undesired behavior and then identify the best means to rectify the situation. Most large organizations have addressed ethics and compliance issues that fall into one or more of the following categories:

1.   Not following procedures or guidelines (for example, shipping product not to specifications);
2.   Intimidation and abusive behavior;
3.   Improper use of assets (for example, time charging or Internet abuse);
4.   Conflicts of interest (one of the most commonly observed forms of misconduct);[35]
5.   Failure to report to misconduct.

In many organizations these issues are addressed on a "one-off" basis, without definitively looking at the common root causes of the behavior that led to the violations.[36] Evaluating the culture-based risks will help to identify the risk factors and the root causes of the undesired behavior.

Identifying Risk Factors

Q 3.11.2   What are the risk factors?

Risk factors are the values/beliefs, behaviors/policies, and goals/outcomes that can lead to ethics issues. Analogous to looking at diet and smoking as risk factors leading to health issues, this analysis should identify actions inside the organization that, while legal in and of themselves, can lead to undesired behavior.

In order to find common patterns, each of the ethics issues faced by the organization should be looked at in terms of the elements of the ethical culture framework: values, behaviors, and goals:

TABLE 3-4
Identifying Risk Factors in an Ethical Cultural Framework

1. Not following procedures or guidelines	
Values	In many instances, employees do not follow procedures because it is unclear which procedures govern a particular process and no one steps up to resolve the issue. This leads to bottlenecks that create pressure to take shortcuts in order to meet production deadlines. A survey might reveal current culture values such as **confusion** and **inconsistency**. **Blame** and a lack of **accountability** for not meeting deadlines are also common current culture values.
Behaviors	Managers may lack attention to process and detail and may not demonstrate the leadership skills needed to take charge of the situation.
Goals	In demanding results now, senior leadership may be creating pressure to meet the short-term goals without clarifying how to achieve these targets without cutting corners. Employees may not know how to meet the goals without engaging in behavior that contradicts the standards of behavior as well as their own values.
2. Intimidation and abusive behavior	
Values	In many organizations, values such as **respect** and **employee appreciation** are seen as "soft" and not given strategic priority. Yet experience has shown that these are foundational values upon which strategic values such as **innovation** and **customer service** are built.

Behaviors	Ineffective tone at the top and middle: Senior managers may not be seen intervening to demand better interpersonal relations, especially if the organization is perceived to be in crisis.
Goals	The behavior of managers is not incorporated into performance evaluations. **Respect** as a value is not demanded of managers.

3.   Improper use of assets

Values	Values such as **accountability, responsibility, and employee engagement** are likely not to be high. Employees may feel that their organization is a culture where everyone is out for himself or herself. This attitude feeds misguided rationalization of one's actions: "I deserve this." Poor systems and processes—for example, lack of effective controls to deter misconduct and lack of clarity on how to do one's job, giving rise to a sense of alienation and lack of connection to the organization.
Behaviors	Managers have not set a clear sense of what is expected behavior, nor have they established clear consequences for not complying with or conforming to expected standards.
Goals	Employees do not feel connected to organizational goals; there is no sense of "ownership" or incentive to manage the company's assets they can control.

4.   Conflicts of interest

Values	Conflicts of interest, especially potential conflicts of interest, are often the first probing by employees of whether they can get away with something. In many instances, clear and consistent enforcement of standards is sufficient to deter all but those intent on engaging in misconduct.

Behaviors	In many instances, employees engaged in a conflict of interest do not have effective communication in their workplace. People are left to make their own decisions, and raising issues or questions is not encouraged. In some instances, employees engage in conflicts because they perceive that the fastest way to get the job is to work with an insider, such as contracting with a family member.
Goals	Organizational goals are not aligned with individual goals.

5. Failure to report

Values	In some instances, employees do not report observed misconduct because of explicit fear of retaliation or some other form of abusive behavior or humiliation by their supervisor. However, in many circumstances, failure to report is due to a lack of trust in procedures to protect confidentiality or that the organization will act on information reported.
Behaviors	In many instances, there is peer pressure to not report. In an environment where self-interest dominates, reporting misconduct is not acceptable behavior.
Goals	When an employee is not willing to report misconduct, his or her individual "goal" is self-preservation, which is unlikely to be aligned with a broader organizational goal.

Q 3.11.3   Why are these risk factors permitted to flourish?

In looking at the breadth of risk factors linked to the company's ethics issues, compliance leadership should start to see some patterns emerging. There is typically a set of common denominators that underlies a number of the issues. For example:

- Short-term focus. This deters attempts to fix long-term problems; managers feel they have no control to shape their environment, leading to a lack of accountability and personal responsibility.

- Abusive managers. Because abusive managers are not reprimanded, managers with a bias toward personal control are allowed to take advantage of the lack of procedures to create local fiefdoms.
- Poor role modeling. There are no good role models for positive behavior or creating respect for procedures; everyone is looking out only for themselves.
- Lack of accountability. Leaders do not want to lead because it is too risky or "not worth it." Managers see no means to streamline conflicting processes. Employees do not feel safe or engaged enough to step up and do what they know is right.

Developing a Specific Action List

Q 3.11.4   What's needed to address the root cause problem?

Once these common factors are identified, compliance leadership can develop a specific action list that can be focused toward a solution. For example:

- **Short-term focus.** Identify the behaviors that will sustain the business, then reward those behaviors. Leadership can close the gap between meeting quarterly numbers and living the organization's values by identifying specific actions field managers can take to demonstrate how to meet the numbers in a manner consistent with the stated values.
- **Abusive managers.** Create a strategic priority for relationship values such as employee appreciation, respect, and teamwork. Organizations that have evaluated their ethical cultures understand that these relationship values are foundations for generating efficiency, productivity, innovation, as well as honesty and trust.
- **Poor role modeling.** Provide clarity from leadership as to which values are needed, and insist that process improvement be a strategic priority. Leadership needs to ensure that managers are aware of how to implement policies and that they are, in fact, doing it.
- **Lack of accountability.** Ensure that meeting commitments is taken seriously and that there are consequences for not

meeting commitments. Leadership needs to focus on how commitments are made and what is necessary to hold individuals and managers accountable for their actions and their inaction. Leadership must address areas where employees maintain an us-versus-them attitude toward leadership.

Linking Cultural Factors to Ethics Risks

Q 3.11.5   How can we link the solution back to the ethics issues?

Once the underlying root causes are identified, ethics and compliance leadership can link the solutions back to the ethics issues that have been identified:

TABLE 3-5
Linking Solutions to Ethics Issues

1.   *Not following procedures or guidelines*
Instead of merely providing reminder training on the importance of following procedures, leadership can implement strategies that will get at the root cause: • Clear communication. Focus on two-way communication. Are employees able to ask specific questions about the challenges they face in following the procedures? • Accountability. Leadership taking responsibility to set clear standards: will managers and leaders be permitted to not fulfill commitments?
2.   *Intimidation and abusive behavior*
In addition to training on topics such as respect, anti-harassment, and diversity, leadership must be certain that there are clear consequences for managers not demonstrating respect and employee appreciation. Leaders need to help managers and supervisors make the connection between getting critical information and employee perceptions of personal risk in communicating bad news.

3.   *Improper use of assets*
If the root cause is related to employees not feeling connected or engaged, leaders must insist that managers give employees responsibilities for which they can be in control and will be held accountable. Employees need to feel that they have a stake in creating a local work environment that they can take ownership of. Apathy among line employees can be addressed by creating local work groups to build a sense of engagement and camaraderie.
4.   *Conflicts of interest*
Leaders must establish that *how* things get done is as important as *what* gets done. Managers must be able to clearly articulate what are the expected standards of behavior and then enforce those standards in a clear and consistent manner.
5.   *Failure to report*
Leadership must attack the "us-versus-them" attitudes. Leadership must insist that employee appreciation be a metric for evaluating managers. Even minimal "face time" with staff creates basic personal relationships on which to build trust.

Q 3.12 What is the easiest first step in addressing culture issues?

Creating an ethical culture takes time. However, the biggest gains can come in the beginning of the process. Once employees see that leadership is addressing these issues in a serious and ongoing manner, they will increase their levels of engagement and participation.

In most organizations there is usually a person, policy, or experience that encapsulates any frustrations and negativity in the culture. "Everybody knows that we can't do 'X' because of 'Y.'" This is the proverbial "elephant in the room" that must be handled first in order to build credibility for the ethics and compliance program. The best first step to creating ethical culture is to identify these key one or two issues that everyone knows about and that employees perceive management to be slow to respond to. Just acknowledging the issue is a major step. Employees will respond sincerely to openness and transparency. Solving the problem immediately is not essential. Employees know that some issues cannot be fixed overnight. The key is to show genuine progress.

Experience has shown that companies can make the quickest progress by tapping into their employees' natural desire to feel connected and valued. Leaders that have acknowledged their employees' personal values and then acknowledge the issues in the current culture that can create roadblocks have had good success in building the trust needed to create effective ethical cultures.

Notes to Chapter 3

1. *See* Q 1.4.1.
2. David Hess, *A Business Ethics Perspective on Sarbanes-Oxley and the Organizational Sentencing Guidelines*, 105 MICH. L. REV. 1781, 1794–95 (2007).
3. *See* Weaver & Treviño, *Compliance and Values Oriented Ethics Programs: Influences on Employees Attitudes and Behavior*, 9 BUS. ETHICS Q. 315 (1999).
4. ETHICS RESOURCE CENTER, NATIONAL BUSINESS ETHICS SURVEY: AN INSIDE VIEW OF PRIVATE SECTOR ETHICS (2007) [hereinafter 2007 National Business Ethics Survey], at 12, www.ethics.org/files/u5/The_2007_National_Business_Ethics_Survey.pdf ("in companies with little or no ethics and compliance program, 96 percent of employees in companies with weak ethical cultures witnessed at least one incident in the last 12 months, compared to only 35 percent of employees working in strong ethical cultures").
5. Quoted in Andrew Wallmeyer, *Ethics in the Workplace*, CAP. REGION BUS. J., May 2005, www.madison.com/crbj/200505/index.php?ntid=61124.
6. Paul Fiorelli, *Will U.S. Sentencing Commission Amendments Encourage a New Ethical Culture Within Organizations?*, 39 WAKE FOREST L. REV. 565, 581 (2004), http://lawreview.law.wfu.edu/documents/issue.39.565.pdf.
7. Hess, *supra* note 2, at 1790.
8. *Id.* at 1806.
9. Interview with former Massachusetts U.S. Attorney Michael Sullivan, Nov. 15, 2009.
10. Stephen Taub, *HP Settles with California AG*, CFO (Dec. 6, 2006), www.cfo.com/article.cfm/8401015?f=search.
11. Hess, *supra* note 2, at 1785.
12. Icek Ajzen, *The Theory of Planned Behavior*, 50 ORGANIZATIONAL BEHAVIOR & HUMAN DECISION PROCESSES 179 (1991), as cited in Hess, *supra* note 2, at 1785.
13. For an excellent summary of leading research in this area, see MALCOLM GLADWELL, THE TIPPING POINT 133–68 (Little, Brown 2000).
14. *Id.* at 157.
15. *Id.* at 158.
16. The fundamental differences between a compliance-based program and an integrity-based program were articulated by Lynn Sharp Paine, *Managing for Organizational Integrity*, HARV. BUS. REV., Mar.–Apr. 1994, at 106.
17. Hess, *supra* note 2, at 1791.
18. Paine, *supra* note 16, at 113.
19. ETHICS RES. CTR, 2009 NATIONAL BUSINESS ETHICS SURVEY. This survey is available for free download at www.ethics.org.
20. This model was developed by synthesizing the seven elements of organizational effectiveness developed by McKinsey with the three core elements defined by Jim Collins that must be aligned in order for an organization to be

sustainable for the long term. *See Enduring Ideas: The 7-S Framework*, McKINSEY Q., Mar. 2008, www.mckinseyquarterly.com/Strategy/Enduring_ideas_ The_7-S_ Framework_2123; *see also* Jim Collins, *Aligning Action and Values*, 1 LEADER TO LEADER J. (Summer 1996), www.leadertoleader.org/knowledgecenter/ journal.aspx?ArticleID=135.

21. Hess, *supra* note 2, at 1788.

22. *Id.* at 1785.

23. Paine, *supra* note 16, at 143; *see also* Harvey L. Pitt, *Essentials for an Ethical Corporate Culture*, COMPLIANCE WK., July 25, 2006.

24. Linda Klebe Treviño et al., *Managing Ethics and Legal Compliance: What Works and What Hurts*, 41 CAL. MGMT. REV. 131, 143 (1999).

25. 2007 National Business Ethics Survey, *supra* note 4. Client experience using values assessments has shown that in many organizations willingness to report actual misconduct does not necessarily correlate to willingness to raise business issues that could potentially lead to ethics problems if not corrected.

26. Interview with former Massachusetts U.S. Attorney Michael Sullivan, Dec. 2, 2009.

27. Cynthia A. Glassman, SEC Commissioner, SEC Implementation of Sarbanes-Oxley: The New Corporate Governance, Speech to National Economists Club, Washington, D.C. (Apr. 7, 2003), www.sec.gov/news/speech/ spch040703cag.htm.

28. Fiorelli, *supra* note 6, at 581 (citing Linda Klebe Treviño et al., *Managing Ethics and Legal Compliance: What Works and What Hurts*, 41 CAL. MGMT. REV. 131, 131–32 (1999)).

29. RICHARD BARRETT, BUILDING A VALUES-DRIVEN ORGANIZATION: A WHOLE SYSTEM APPROACH TO CULTURAL TRANSFORMATION 16 (Butterworth Heinemann 2006). *See* www.elsevierdirect.com/wps/find/bookdescription.careers/707502/ description#description.

30. *Id.* at 22.

31. M.M. Scharff, *WorldCom: A Failure of Moral and Ethical Values*, J. APPLIED MGMT. & ENTREPRENEURSHIP, July 2005, http://findarticles.com/p/articles/mi_ qa5383/is_200507/ai_n21364331/.

32. Irving Janis articulated this definition of "groupthink" in 1971. *See* M.M. Scharff, *Understanding WorldCom's Accounting Fraud: Did Groupthink Play a Role?*, 11 J. LEADERSHIP & ORG. STUD. 3 (2005).

33. Hess, *supra* note 2, at 1797.

34. 2009 National Business Ethics Survey, *supra* note 19.

35. 2007 National Business Ethics Survey, *supra* note 4.

36. *See generally* Weaver & Treviño, *supra* note 3.

4

Risk Assessment and Gap Analysis

*Kwamina Thomas Williford**

The U.S. Sentencing Commission (the "Commission") in its 1991 Sentencing Guidelines set forth the seven elements of an effective compliance and ethics program.[1] In 2004, the Commission added language that required companies to engage in periodic risk assessments as part of "an essential component of the design, implementation and modification of an effective program."[2] The results of the risk assessment should be used to design, implement, and modify a company's compliance and ethics program with the goal of reducing the risk of criminal or "bad conduct" most likely to occur.

* The author wishes to acknowledge Christopher A. Myers for his contributions to this chapter.

Risk Assessments

The Basics

Q 4.1   What is a risk assessment?

A risk assessment is the identification, evaluation, and prioritization of risks faced by a company.[3]

Q 4.1.1   What are the goals of a risk assessment?

A thorough risk assessment should:

(1)   evaluate the nature, probability, and severity of all potential legal, compliance, and business risks;

(2)   consider the prior history of the company (and similarly situated companies), especially any prior criminal, civil, or regulatory enforcement actions; and

(3)   identify and evaluate reasonable steps the company can take to prevent and detect the specific risks to which the company is exposed.

Q 4.1.2   Why should our company perform a "risk assessment"?

A risk assessment helps a company to understand the nature and likelihood of the risks it faces. It allows a company to tailor its compliance and ethics program and develop controls to mitigate its risks.

Furthermore, section 404 of the Sarbanes-Oxley Act of 2002 requires that public companies file with the Securities and Exchange Commission (SEC) an annual internal controls report that states the responsibilities of management for establishing and maintaining an adequate risk assessment system for the purpose of ensuring regulatory compliance.[4]

Q 4.1.3   What is senior management's role in a risk assessment?

Effective compliance and ethics programs should help demonstrate a commitment to honesty and integrity from the top down. There must be "buy-in" from all sides—not from just the general counsel or compliance officer, but from the management team, board, and committees of the board as well. Thus, the input of senior management is critical not only in implementing a well-designed, comprehensive compliance program, but also in the creation of the program itself, starting with involvement in the risk assessment process.

Senior management often carries a global perspective of a company's operations and can provide valuable input by identifying risk areas, identifying people who can help assess the risk, and facilitating any actions that should be taken in connection with the risks identified in the assessment.

Q 4.1.4   Who should perform the risk assessment?

Risk assessments are typically performed by a company's general counsel, the compliance officer, or outside counsel. Because of the potential privilege and confidentiality issues that might arise during the risk assessment process (many of the risks to be evaluated will be legal and regulatory risks), a company may wish to have its risk assessment conducted through counsel and under the attorney-client privilege. The person(s) responsible for performing the risk assessment should have access to all company business units or functions and be able to gain a full working knowledge of the risks the company faces.

Identifying Risks

Q 4.2　What risk areas should our company be assessing in the first place?

The U.S. Sentencing Guidelines state only that a company "must periodically assess the risk of the occurrence of *criminal conduct*."[5] Nonetheless, companies would be wise not to limit their risk assessments to criminal conduct. Instead, companies should identify and analyze all relevant risks, including legal, compliance, and business risks because the process of assessing risk allows a company to gain perspective into its operations and navigate future pitfalls that may exist.[6]

The risks faced by a company depend on the company's operations and the regulatory schemes that affect those operations. Some risk areas cut across many industries, such as conflicts of interest, unlawful discrimination, fiduciary breaches, employee health and safety, tax infractions, and fraud. Others are more specific to the industry involved. In determining what additional legal and reputational risks your company may face, it may be helpful to consider the following questions:

1. What areas of compliance keep you awake at night?
2. Is your company in a highly regulated industry where companies are the subject of government investigations or settlements? If so, consider the issues being targeted by reported government investigations and enforcement actions.
3. Is your company a public company? If so, consider Securities and Exchange Commission requirements.[7]
4. Is your company in the business of acquiring other companies? If so, consider antitrust implications.[8]
5. Does your company offer products to consumers? If so, consider product liability and consumer protection laws.[9]
6. Does your company advertise its services or products to the public? If so, consider Federal Trade Commission regulations.[10]

7. Does your company collect people's personal information? If so, consider data privacy laws.[11]
8. Does your company conduct business outside the United States? If so, consider the Foreign Corrupt Practices Act (FCPA).[12]
9. Does your company import or export products? If so, consider export control/customs laws.[13]
10. Does your company discharge potentially hazardous chemicals into the air or water? If so, consider the Clean Water Act and the Clean Air Act.[14]
11. Does your company contract with or accept grant funds from the federal, state, or local government? If so, consider the Federal Acquisition Regulation and other government contracting requirements.[15]
12. Does your company make political contributions through a political action committee or otherwise? If so, consider campaign finance laws.[16]

These questions serve as a starting point for a company to use and evaluate the potential risks it faces. The purpose of the exercise would be to cast a broad net to determine what laws and regulations might expose the company to legal, regulatory, or reputational harm.

Gathering Data

Q 4.3   What are the different methods we should use to gather the data?

While there is no standard approach, many companies collect risk assessment data in the same manner that they carry out due diligence in other arenas, such as finance and merger transactions. One-on-one interviews are an excellent way of analyzing a company's risk. Managers and supervisors in different departments should be interviewed. In addition to questioning them about relevant potential risk areas in their departments, counsel should ask what keeps *them* awake at night. Their answers often reveal previously overlooked risk areas.

Other useful techniques include document reviews, written surveys, and focus groups that are diverse both vertically (people at different levels within the organization's structure) and horizontally (people from different departments within the organization).

Q 4.3.1   What documents should we review as part of the risk assessment?

A risk assessment should include a thorough review and analysis of the organization's documents, including:

- the organization's corporate compliance and ethics policies (including the code of conduct);
- any compliance hotline reports (as well as all documentation of any follow-up or investigations);
- internal audit reports;
- the full record of correspondence with oversight bodies and regulatory agencies; and
- any litigation records.

In addition, a risk assessment should take into account industry enforcement trends. The trends would include recent settlement agreements, recent verdicts or judgments involving competitor companies, as well as renewed policy statements or initiatives from enforcement and regulatory authorities. Analyzing these trends helps to shed light on emerging areas that are on the radar screen of enforcement and regulatory authorities. It is prudent for companies to focus on risk mitigation activities in such areas.

Q 4.3.2   How much data is enough? When can we stop gathering data and start using it?

Although companies might be concerned with whether they have enough data, there is no particular requirement regarding the amount of data that must be collected or money that should be spent on a risk assessment. What is required is that companies review the data that is reasonably expected to yield an informed judgment of risk, and *prioritize* their compliance program responses based on what is uncovered in the risk assessment. Obviously, in order to prioritize its risks, an organization must have culled enough information during the data-gathering phase to reach reasonable conclusions as to the organization's greatest potential risks.

Processing the Data; Responding to Assessed Risks

Q 4.4   What should our company do once the data has been gathered?

Once collected, the data should be organized in a manner that will allow the company to prioritize the risks and determine which to address first. When prioritizing a risk, a company should assess the likely occurrence and likely impact of a risk on the company.[17]

Q 4.4.1   What should we consider when assessing "likely occurrence"?

When assessing the likely occurrence, a company should consider the level of the company's activity in that area, the frequency of past occurrences, existing controls in place, whether the controls are effective, and whether industry trends show an emphasis on the conduct. As these areas are considered, identifying a scale with common definitions that works for the company will be important. The key is to set definitions that may be used and understood across business units. There is no one-size-fits-all assessment scale. Every company must define a scale to meet its needs. Table 4-1 sets forth a sample scale that may be helpful in assessing the risk.

Q 4.4.2   What should we consider when assessing likely impact?

When assessing the likely impact, a company should consider and measure various implications that could result if the risk went unaddressed. A company should think about these implications by category and develop a scale with common definitions for the company to utilize in the assessment. Categories to consider may include health and safety, legal/compliance, operational, financial loss, and reputational. Scale definitions will vary by company. The key is to set definitions that may be used and understood across business units. Table 4-2 sets forth an example that may be helpful in assessing the risk.[18]

TABLE 4-1
Sample Likely Occurrence Scale

SCALE	LIKELY OCCURRENCE
1 **Rare**	Aware of the misconduct happening elsewhere; expected to occur once every five years; very effective policies, mandatory training, activities monitored and audited *(which likely detects and/or prevents 90% or more of errors)*.
2 **Unlikely**	Misconduct does occur somewhere from time to time; expected once every three to four years; responsible persons ensure compliance with policies, regular training, internal monitoring, and auditing of activities *(which likely detects and/or prevents 75% or more of errors)*.
3 **Possible**	Misconduct has occurred at least once during your career; expected once every two years; policies are followed and updated, training provided when needed; some informal monitoring *(which may detect and/or prevent major instances of noncompliance)*.
4 **Likely**	Misconduct has occurred several times or more during your career; expected once a year; policies and procedures in place; compliance not enforced or mandated; some on-the-job training and no monitoring *(which may detect and/or prevent only major instances of noncompliance)*.
5 **Almost Certain**	Misconduct has occurred in the last six months; expected more than once a year; no controls in place *(which leads to frequent occurrences of noncompliance)*.

TABLE 4-2
Sample Likely Impact Scale

SCALE	Health & Safety	Legal/Compliance	Operational	Financial Loss	Reputational
1 Incidental	No injuries	Violation with little or no fine/action probable	Very minor, no operational loss	<1% of operating budget	Minor impact to reputation, mention in local news paper
2 Minor	Medical treatment	Civil fines and/or penalties up to $50,000; little risk of exclusion	Impacts one department; possible closure one to two days	>1% of operating budget	Adverse local public attention or complaints
3 Serious	Hospitalization	Serious breach of regulation with investigation or report to authority possible; fines up to $100,000	Impacts more than one department; closes operations for one week	>5% of operating budget	Probably short-term bad press and highlighted concern from community; some constituent fallout
4 Disastrous	Death or permanent injury	Criminal investigation probably, loss of business unit accreditation possible, major litigation, fines up to $1 million	Impacts entire company or business unit and ability to operate for up to two weeks	>10% of operating budget	Substantial adverse national media/public attention, constituent fallout.
5 Catastrophic	Multiple deaths or severe permanent disabilities	Significant prosecution and litigation (e.g., class action); criminal conviction and/or exclusion; fines and penalties in excess of $1 million	Entire company is unable to operate for a month or longer	>25% of operating budget	Prolonged negative press; serious media outcry; sponsors/board question management; substantial constituent fallout

113

Q 4.4.3   How should we prioritize the risks?

Once a company has assessed the likely occurrence and likely impact, it can develop a matrix to help it prioritize the risk level of each risk area. A risk matrix should be used as a tool to help the company work through addressing the risks by addressing those risks with the highest risk level first, then working through to the lower risks identified.

The risk matrix is generated by multiplying the risk's likely occurrence by the risk's likely impact in order to establish a preliminary risk level. These numerical values may be derived from a risk prioritizing scale, such as the one in Table 4-3, and should then be entered into the matrix, as illustrated in Table 4-4.

TABLE 4-3
Sample Risk Prioritizing Scale

Risk Level	Scale
Extreme	17–25
High	14–16
Substantial	10–13
Medium	5–9
Low	1–4

TABLE 4-4
Sample Risk Matrix

Likely Occurrence × Likely Impact = Risk Level

Risk Area	Likely Occurrence	Likely Impact	Risk Level
Data Security	4	4	16
Export Controls	2	3	6
(etc.)	...	...	...
...	...	...	...
...	...	...	...

Gap Analysis

Q 4.5   What is a compliance "gap analysis," and how does it differ from a risk assessment?

While a compliance and ethics gap analysis has some steps in common with a risk assessment, the purposes are different. The purpose of a gap analysis is to determine whether and to what extent your company meets the required elements of an effective compliance and ethics program[19] by revealing any deficiencies within the compliance program.

Q 4.5.1   How do we perform a gap analysis?

Like a risk assessment, a gap analysis can be performed internally by an independent employee (such as the general counsel or the compliance officer) or by a committee, or externally by outside counsel. The compliance and ethics program must be reviewed in light of the required elements of an effective compliance and ethics program. A company should look at the required components and whether the company has those components in place. The appropriate questions to ask include the following:

1. *Standards and procedures.* Does your company have a code of conduct and internal controls reasonably capable of reducing the likelihood of criminal and other improper conduct? Does your company have policies or procedures in place necessary to promote adherence to regulatory obligations?

2. *Organizational leadership and culture.* Is your company's governing authority knowledgeable about the content and operation of the compliance and ethics program, and does it exercise reasonable oversight over the compliance and ethics program's implementation and effectiveness?

3. *Excluding bad actors from managerial ranks.* Does your company take reasonable steps to ensure that individuals with substantial authority have not engaged in illegal activities or conducted themselves in a manner inconsistent with the compliance and ethics program?

4. *Training and education.* Does your company widely promulgate its standards of conduct and policies and procedures

and ensure that its employees are trained on the compliance and ethics program's objectives and relevant policies?

5. *Monitoring and auditing.* Does your company's compliance and ethics program include monitoring and auditing systems that adequately detect criminal and other improper conduct?

6. *Performance incentives and disciplinary measures.* Does your company promote and consistently enforce the compliance and ethics program through incentives and disciplinary actions?

7. *Appropriate remedial action.* If improper conduct has been detected, does your company take reasonable steps both to address it and to prevent further similar misconduct? Are remedial actions being taken to prevent the recurrence of misconduct?

8. *Risk assessment.* Does your company periodically assess the risk of improper conduct within its operations and take appropriate steps to design, implement, or modify each element of the compliance and ethics program to reduce the risk of improper or unethical behavior?

If the answer to any of these questions is no, a gap exists that may be preventing the company's compliance and ethics program from being effective.

Q 4.5.2   What should we do if a gap exists in our compliance and ethics program?

Any gap should be addressed if a company wants to have an effective compliance and ethics program. When addressing a gap, a company should put together a timeline to address each gap and assign someone to be accountable. For information about what is needed in order to have an effective compliance and ethics program component, see chapter 2.

Notes to Chapter 4

1. *See* chapter 2.

2. U.S. Sentencing Comm'n, Amendments to the Sentencing Guidelines 111 (May 10, 2004), www.ussc.gov/sites/default/files/pdf/amendment-process/reader-friendly-amendments/20040430_RF_Amendments.pdf.

3. HOLLAND & KNIGHT, BUILDING & DEVELOPING COMPLIANCE AND ETHICS PROGRAMS: PREPARING AND PROTECTING YOUR ORGANIZATION 45 (Ass'n of Corp. Counsel Sept. 2012). *See generally* U.S. SENTENCING GUIDELINES MANUAL § 8B2.1(c) (U.S. SENTENCING COMM'N 2014).

4. For more on the compliance and ethics requirements of Sarbanes-Oxley, see chapter 30.

5. *Id.* (emphasis added).

6. *See* RONALD E. BERENBEIM, CONFERENCE BD., UNIVERSAL CONDUCT: AN ETHICAL AND COMPLIANCE BENCHMARKING SURVEY 20 (Sept. 2006).

7. *See, e.g.*, Securities Act of 1933, 15 U.S.C. § 77a *et seq.*; Securities Act of 1934, 15 U.S.C. § 78a *et seq.*; Investment Company Act of 1940, 15 U.S.C. § 80-1 *et seq.*; Investment Adviser Act (15 U.S.C. § 80b-1 *et seq.*); *see also The Laws That Govern the Securities Industry*, U.S. SEC. & EXCH. COMM'N, www.sec.gov/about/laws.shtml (last updated Oct. 1, 2013).

8. *See, e.g.*, Sherman Act, 15 U.S.C. §§ 1–7, as amended by the Clayton Act, 15 U.S.C. §§ 12–27.

9. *See, e.g.*, MODEL PROD. LIAB. ACT (for model rules related to product liability); *Product Liability Act*, AM. LEGISLATION EXCH. COUNCIL, www.alec.org/model-legislation/product-liability-act/ (last visited June 30, 2015); Federal Trade Commission Act, 15 U.S.C. §§ 41–58; *see also* chapter 20, *infra* (for key considerations related to consumer products).

10. *See, e.g.*, Federal Trade Commission Act, 15 U.S.C. §§ 41–58.

11. *See, e.g.*, chapter 12, *infra* (for key considerations related to data privacy).

12. *See, e.g.*, chapter 16, *infra* (for key considerations related to corruption).

13. *See* chapter 17, *infra* (for some key considerations related to international trade).

14. *See* chapter 19, *infra* (for key considerations related to environmental discharges).

15. *See* chapter 14, *infra* (for key considerations related to contracting with the government).

16. *See* chapter 18, *infra* (for key considerations related to political contributions).

17. This method has been widely adopted and promulgated in connection with Enterprise Risk Management best practices as a means to help quantify and measure risk. *See* COMM. OF SPONSORING ORGS. OF TREADWAY COMM'N [COSO]: ENTER-

PRISE RISK MANAGEMENT—INTEGRATED FRAMEWORK (Sept. 2004); *see also* PATCHIN CURTIS & MARK CAREY, DELOITTE & TOUCHE LLP, RISK ASSESSMENT IN PRACTICE (COSO Oct. 2012), https://www2.deloitte.com/content/dam/Deloitte/global/Documents/Governance-Risk-Compliance/dttl-grc-riskassessmentinpractice.pdf. COSO is a joint initiative of the five private sector organizations dedicated to providing thought leadership through the development of frameworks and guidance on enterprise risk management.

18. Under this example, the risk should receive the highest scaled number it qualifies for in a particular category. For example, if the risk receives a Health & Safety score of 1, a Legal/Compliance score of 4, and an Operational score of 4, then the risk should be assigned a 4 impact rating.

19. *See* chapter 2.

5

Records Management

*Ieuan G. Mahony**

Records management is a foundational component to any compliance program. As a general rule, a compliance program is designed to assist your organization in meeting legal and regulatory requirements. The program will rely on various internal controls to detect, prevent, and respond to situations that threaten or constitute a breach of these requirements. Central to these internal controls are proper record-keeping requirements. To establish that you have, in fact, complied with your internal controls, your organization will want to rely on a records management system that is rational, documented, and that is itself compliant.

Implementing a new records management policy or updating an existing one certainly may seem as appealing as cleaning the attic; however, a good records management program adds outstanding value to an organization and acts as the foundation for much—if not all—of its compliance efforts. This

* The author wishes to acknowledge Christopher A. Myers and Linda Auerbach Allderdice for their contributions to this chapter.

119

chapter aims to help companies take a considered look at their records management practices and start "cleaning the attic" now.

Records Management Program Basics

Q 5.1   What are the benefits of a records management program?

A reasonable, documented records management program can provide your organization with significant benefits:

- Providing better control over the creation, volume, and content of information;

- Preserving important, useful, and required business records;
- Providing better access to this information, thereby increasing productivity and efficiency;
- Reducing the costs of managing and storing records by periodically "culling" unneeded materials in accordance with the retention schedule;
- Allowing timely and sufficient responses to records requests by regulators and adverse litigants, thereby avoiding their assertions that your organization has engaged in destruction of relevant evidence (referred to as "spoliation of evidence") or other wrongdoing related to disclosure obligations;[1]
- Reducing or eliminating individual exposure of senior management—including liability for both monetary sanctions and imprisonment—for failings in your organization's records management practices;[2]
- Provide a structure that facilitates compliance with various privacy and security law obligations, which generally require that an organization understand the "flow" of certain information through the organization;[3] and
- Allowing your organization to adapt to changed circumstances. For example, new Federal Rules of Civil Procedure recognize that traditional litigation practices, developed primarily for paper-based materials, are not adequate for electronically stored information.[4] Under these new rules, an organization enjoys potentially considerable benefits from having a records management program in place for electronic information. Specifically, under the so-called safe harbor, a court will not impose sanctions for the loss of records if the loss resulted from the routine, good-faith operation of an electronic information system (*see* Q 5.10.3, *infra*).

Q 5.1.1 What are the constituent parts of a records management program?

A records management program includes the following three key components:

1. *A records management policy.* This is the "design" document, structured to:

   - explain the rules for retaining, managing, and destroying records;

- assign responsibility for these tasks to specified managers;
- set applicable sanctions and rewards (where applicable) for compliance; and, most importantly,
- establish procedures for appropriately suspending archiving and destruction rules when the enterprise is presented with actual (or threatened) litigation or government investigation.

2. *A records management schedule.* This schedule should:

- list the categories of records the enterprise generates and relies on;
- identify specific record types within these categories; and
- attach a retention period to each document type.

3. *A set of business rules.* The rules should:

- implement the records management policy;
- incorporate periodic training in the program; and
- provide employees with incentives for compliance and/or sanctions for noncompliance.

Figure 5-1 provides a graphic illustrating these three core components and their subcomponents.

Q 5.1.2   Our organization already has a records "destruction" program; do we still need a records "management" program?

A "records management" program is the same thing as a "records retention" or a "records destruction" program. The difference is one of terminology and emphasis: Referring to the program as a *retention* program suggests that the goal of the program is to retain information. Similarly, referring to the program as a records *destruction* program suggests that the goal of the program is to destroy information. The goal of a properly functioning program is neither to retain nor to destroy information; instead, the program is designed to balance these extremes, to "manage" information, and to serve your organization's business as well as regulatory and compliance goals. Accordingly, the apt descriptive term for the program is records *management*.

Even if your organization already has a program, the discussion that follows is just as pertinent to updating an existing program as it is to creating a new one.

FIGURE 5-1
Core Components of a Records Management Program

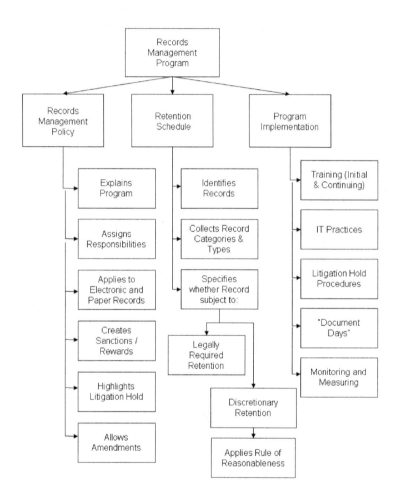

Designing a Program

Q 5.1.3   When it comes to designing a records management program, where should we begin?

1. Select a project "champion." This is the person who will have overall ownership of the process.
2. Assemble an initial project team and assign "seed" resources to the project. This should include legal counsel and your Information Technology Department (IT). Indeed, given the ever-increasing importance of electronic records, your organization will want to involve IT deeply in the planning and implementation process.[5]

TIP: Creating a new records management program or updating an existing one is a collaborative effort that necessarily includes input from representatives in different groups within your organization. The make-up of the initial project team should account for the differing constituencies; the greater the understanding between the various stakeholders in the policy, generally the more efficient the organization's teamwork and compliance.

Q 5.1.4   What role should senior management play?

Records management involves the coordination of people, processes, and technology, and successful management requires employee compliance on all levels. Thus it is important that the project enjoy senior management support from its planning through its implementation. Moreover, both new and updated records management programs will necessarily involve changing existing workplace behaviors and rewriting perhaps comfortable and safe existing business rules. The support and backing of senior management will be required to help employees and managers work through disruptions that new rules and expectations may bring.

Senior management from the outset should encourage key players to participate in the program. The way an organization goes about establishing or updating its policy may well act as a bellwether for later compliance with the policy.[6] The more stakeholders are heard and included in the development process, the more likely the resulting records management program will "attach" to actual processes employed the organization, and thus the more likely the program will be successful, and efficient.

Records

Determining What Your Relevant Records Are

Q 5.2 What is meant by a "record" in "records management"?

A "record" is the fundamental unit or quantum of information on which a records management program operates. In further defining this concept, it is useful to distinguish between the terms "record" and "information." A typical organization generates and relies on a broad range of "information," meaning all data that the organization receives, uses, or creates in the course of operations, whether to meet institutional, operational, legal, or other needs. This information may be intangible—that is, not "captured" on paper, in a computer file, or in some other way that would allow a manager to retrieve and re-use or refer to it later. Thus, the term "record" refers to that subcategory of information that is tangible in form, such as printed on paper, or captured in an employee's notes, or on a network drive. A "record" can be retained and retrieved and is, therefore, appropriate for a records management program.

For example, if the VP of Marketing gives a verbal presentation, the contents of that presentation would be considered "information." But if this unwritten presentation was not captured in a form that later could be replayed—such as video—then it would not be appropriate to consider this information a "record" for inclusion in a records management policy.

IDENTIFYING "RELEVANT RECORDS"

Company X manufactures a device that incorporates a number of component parts. Supplier Y supplies one of these components, and Supplier Y is paid a fixed fee on each sale of the completed device. The contract between Supplier Y and Company X requires Company X to retain "books and records" showing the fees owed to Supplier Y, and gives Supplier Y the right to audit these books and records during the term of the contract and for a two-year period thereafter. Company X will need to account for this audit right and its two-year "tail" in its records management program.

Q 5.2.1 Does our records management program need to apply to all of our records?

Yes, but your program should only attach a retention schedule and apply resources to *relevant records*. As a rule, relevant records fall into one or more of the following three groups of criteria:

- records that have ongoing value for the organization (such as records that your employees continually refer to over time);
- records that applicable statutes and regulations require you to retain; and
- records that your business partners require by contract that you retain, or that nongovernmental standards bodies similarly require your organization to retain.

Email

Q 5.3 How should we handle email?

Because of its volume and ubiquity, email is often viewed by companies addressing records retention issues as different from other types of records. A proper records policy should treat email in the same manner as other records; it is the content of the record and not its form that matters for purposes of records management—whether the record is in paper, electronic, audio, video, or other media, and whether embodied as an email, spreadsheet, word-processing document, or otherwise.

But email does present a unique challenge due to the fact:

(i)   that a significant volume of company email invariably exists;

(ii)   that day-to-day email applications generally are not structured to facilitate long-term storage and targeted, sophisticated search tools;

(iii)   that certain employees will use personal email accounts that reside outside the company's network or will use personal mobile computing devices (such as smart phones) to create and store company email; and

(iv)   most importantly, that email files often contain high-value content and attachments.

In applying records management techniques to the challenges presented by email, many organizations rely on a compliance structure that "delegates" to individual email account holders the real-time responsibility to filter their email for relevant records and appropriately store these records in a manner that permits the records management program to "attach" to the record. The organization will then apply a network rule that will periodically delete the email that has not been so designated by the employee. (See Q 5.5.1 for a further discussion of delegating certain records management compliance responsibilities to individual employees.)

Other Electronically Stored Information (ESI)

Q 5.4   Should our records management program cover electronic information?

Yes. Some of your most valuable information may be stored in electronic format, whether on your computer network, on your employees' laptops and desktop computers, on managers' Personal Digital Assistants, or on other media or storage devices. A proper records management program must cover electronically stored information (ESI). Indeed, a well-drafted records management policy will emphasize that no distinction should be drawn between (a) paper-based and other traditional media, and (b) records in electronic format. As noted above, the importance and prevalence of ESI require that your IT department participate deeply in the planning and implementation of the records management program.

Q 5.4.1   What is metadata and how is it relevant to a records management policy?

Metadata is "data about data." Metadata is created in a variety of ways: a software application might create the metadata automatically (such as a "last modified" field). Users might supply the metadata (adding partially hidden "track changes," for example). Examples of metadata include:

- a file's name;
- the file's location;
- its file format or file type;
- the file size;
- key file dates, such as creation date, date of last modification, date of last access, date of last metadata modification;
- file permissions, which designate who has privileges to read the data, who can write to it, and who can run it; and
- attributes created by the user, such as email subject and addressing.

Metadata is created, modified, and disposed of at many points during the life of electronic information or records. Metadata can be helpful:

- in managing information;
- in effective record retrieval, in that metadata—which "travels" with a record—can be used to store retention information;
- in ensuring that users are accountable for their record keeping, by tracking whether the user is appropriately assisting the record along its lifecycle;
- in proving the authenticity of electronic documents, and in discovering more about their use and provenance in litigation;[7]
- in identifying and managing the relationships that exist between electronic documents, such as multiple versions and drafts; and
- in managing and assisting to enforce security requirements and administrative privileges that have been attached to the

record; for example, privacy concerns, privileged communications or work product, or proprietary interests.

Q 5.4.2 How can ESI be used to support a records management program?

Traditional records management programs were paper-based systems that:

(1) organized documents into categories;
(2) attached a retention period to each document; and
(3) periodically physically searched records within the retention period and disposed of them in accordance with stated policy.

These traditional records management programs were time-consuming, resource-intensive, cumbersome, and—despite the best intentions of the document managers—subject to processing errors. In contrast, the more "modern" records management programs track documents for retention, retrieval, and destruction (in accordance with stated policy) by document profiles and metadata. These programs:

(1) determine categories for retention based on searchable metadata and/or document profiles, using fewer descriptive categories (*e.g.*, "all email" rather than "financial records stored in email");
(2) rely on broader retention periods; and
(3) automate the process of filtering out records subject to a retention period by relying on the system to automatically purge old records—without human intervention or the old physical searching.

While as a general rule metadata is captured automatically based on the specific software applications in use, document profiles are only as accurate as the reliability of the information that has been manually entered to accompany the document. Here, consistent protocols for document identification and data entry are essential for the automated process to work.

In upgrading a records management program, corporate standards may be impacted by standards set for use by government agencies. For example, the National Archives and Records Administration

(NARA) endorsed version 3 of the Department of Defense Electronic Records Management Software Application Design Criteria Standard for use by all federal agencies.[8] A certification process is administered by the Joint Interoperability Test Command Records Management Application (RMA). The impact of the NARA's standards may be particularly noted in the healthcare industry with the intersection of government and private-sector enterprises and use of computerized—or electronically stored information—record keeping. One tool for record management that the NARA has identified is the "big bucket" strategy, which involves using fewer but better-defined categories ("buckets") when managing ESI along with a flexible retention schedule. The goal of this strategy is to enhance consistency and utilization among users, though it may require longer retention periods.

The European Commission has also published a highly regarded and widely adapted set of standards, the Model Requirements for the Management of Electronic Records.[9] Revised in 2008, these standards are commonly known as the "MoReq2" standards and have been translated into twenty-two languages. There are four main components to MoReq2 (specification, a metadata model, a testing framework, and xml schema), plus a change log.

Modernizing a records management program is increasingly important as the regulatory environment covers a wider swath of ESI. Not only is this evident in records management for litigation purposes, it is seen increasingly in the initiatives undertaken by regulatory agencies. For example, in December 2009, the Federal Trade Commission issued new guidelines in determining when email, use of social media, and blogs would be considered a commercial endorsement brought within the enforcement ambit of the agency. In issuing its "Guides Concerning Use of Endorsements and Testimonials in Advertising,"[10] the FTC noted that the issuance by an employer of social media participation policies would "warrant consideration in its decision as to whether law enforcement action would be an appropriate use of agency resources." As the FTC described:

> An online message board designated for discussions of new music download technology is frequented by MP3 player enthusiasts. They exchange information about new products, utilities, and the functionality of numerous playback devices. Unbeknownst to the message board community, an employee of a leading playback device manufacturer has been posting

messages on the discussion board promoting the manufacturer's product. Knowledge of this poster's employment likely
would affect the weight or credibility of her endorsement.
Therefore, the poster should clearly and conspicuously
disclose her relationship to the manufacturer to members and
readers of the message board.[11]

Compliance starts with the proper policy (*see* Q 5.1.1) and must
take into account the use of ESI in a records management program so
as to cover records that may potentially be subject to regulatory
enforcement, such as in the case of the FTC or the healthcare regulatory environment.

Determining the Lifecycle of Relevant Records

Q 5.4.3 For management purposes, should all records be treated the same?

Each record type will have its own optimum lifecycle. The applicable lifecycle of a particular record is tied to the business needs and
legal requirements of the department or business unit that relies on it
and should be determined after identifying the record types associated with a particular department (or business unit). (See the box
below for more on the lifecycle of a record.)

Q 5.4.4 How should we handle duplicate records?

There may be more than one version of any given record. For
example, there are a number of points where copies of a record and
early, superseded drafts of that record may be created. Moreover, a
record may exist both in paper form and in electronic form. An efficient records management policy will define a single "official record."
You should use criteria to determine the form and version for the "official record" that are appropriate for your organization's business and
legal needs. For example, with electronically stored information—
where the concept of "the original" loses its traditional meaning—
version controls and metadata can be used to define the "official"
version of the record. The program may then specify that the retention schedule attaches only to the official record and that all other
copies may (and should) be destroyed. Unless a litigation hold is in
place (discussed below), it is permissible, and it is good practice, to
reduce the volume of retained materials through use of this "official

record" structure. You may, for example, rely on this structure for a determination that "the electronic version of record X" is the official record, and all "record Xs" in paper form should be discarded.

Your organization's policy should also address retention issues concerning drafts of important documents. Where a draft has independent value—for example, where it is a draft of an important contract and it has been exchanged with third parties—you may wish to retain the record.[12]

Creating a Records Management Policy

Q 5.5   What do we do once we have determined the lifecycle for each record type?

Your records management "task force" should begin work on the records management policy. Among other functions, the policy provides a set of rules that spell out how the policy is to be implemented and identifies by position the individuals in your organization that are responsible for compliance with specified rules.

Q 5.5.1   What specific goals should an effective records management policy accomplish?

- Explain the records management program and the retention schedule, including the functions of
  (i) identifying relevant records;
  (ii) determining appropriate retention periods for these records, keyed to their organizational value and to any legally mandated retention periods;
  (iii) providing for the destruction of records at the expiration of their retention period; and
  (iv) suspending this destruction process for records relevant to litigation or a government investigation, immediately on notice.
- Assign responsibilities to various "owners" of record types and other tasks under the policy. Specifically, the policy should identify those positions within each department or business group that are responsible for that group. Individuals in these positions, for purposes of this chapter, are referred to as "Records Coordinators."

THE LIFECYCLE OF A RECORD

First, the record is created, either internally by the organization or externally by a third party. For a third-party-created record, perhaps the organization has an obligation to preserve the confidentiality of the record, based on a nondisclosure agreement with the third party at issue. Perhaps the organization is also obliged to "return or destroy" the record at the end of this relationship. These elements should be considered in assessing the record's lifecycle.

After its creation, the record enjoys a period of active use. "Active use" indicates that employees of the organization refer to the record on a reasonably frequent basis, and the record is stored in an easy-to-access location—for paper records, perhaps in a file cabinet close to the employees working on the matter; and for electronic records, perhaps on a shared network drive, to which team members have immediate access, with full read/write privileges. Figure 5-2 illustrates this "active use" period and also indicates that, as is typical of IT best practices, backup copies of active records are made on a periodic basis (often daily, weekly, monthly, and yearly) and stored in offline locations.

After a period of active use, the record becomes "inactive." The record is not needed for day-to-day or reasonably immediate purposes. Many organizations will migrate such records to lower-cost storage when they are no longer active—such as to offsite locations (for physical records) or network archive locations (for electronic records). Some organizations will rely on backup tapes to store inactive electronic records. Unlike electronic archives—where the records are relatively easy to access—records stored on backup tapes are usually difficult, time-consuming, and expensive to access.[13] Some organizations will leave their inactive records in their active, online systems and incur the added expense of maintaining records of low utility in "high-rent" space. For their inactive records, many organizations rely on a combination of these storage areas—online, near-line archives, and offline backups.

Finally, a record will move from its inactive status to its final disposition, which is either destruction, or permanent retention.

While the concept of "record" sets the broad parameters of a records management program, the concept of "lifecycle" structures the operation of this program. Figure 5-2 provides a simplified example of a record's lifecycle.

FIGURE 5-2
Lifecycle of a Record

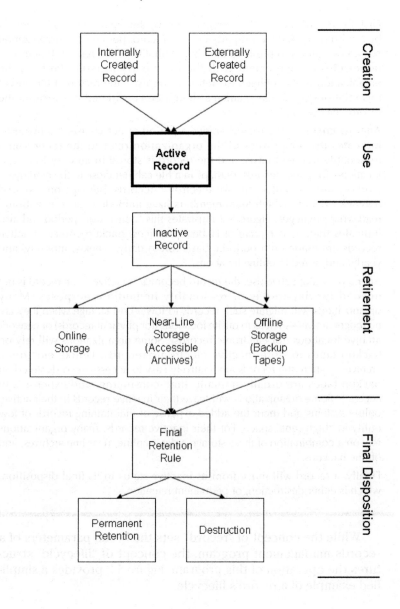

- Emphasize that the policy applies to both paper-based records and electronic records and identifies the positions in the IT department responsible for electronic records management issues.
- Create sanctions and rewards for compliance/noncompliance with the program. Where employees and management see a reasonably direct connection between rewards and compliance, they will be more inclined to undertake the behavioral changes necessary for a new or updated records management program.
- Highlight the importance of the litigation hold process. A good policy provides procedures for implementing a so-called litigation hold. A litigation hold suspends record destruction procedures in order to preserve records that are relevant to the litigation. Perhaps the most visible benefit of a records management program is the avoidance of sanctions in litigation and regulatory proceedings due, in large part, to more effective litigation hold procedures. Issues surrounding litigation holds and the substantial money and other penalties courts have imposed on companies that have failed to meet litigation hold and related records retention obligations are discussed in further detail below.
- Provide a procedure to allow amendments and other changes. An effective compliance program provides for changing future circumstances and establishes procedures for reacting to these changes. A good records management policy similarly allows for further changes. In addition, there may be occasions where a particular record or type of record warrants an exception from an established retention period. The policy should create a procedure for obtaining such exceptions.

What is the optimum compliance structure for your program?

Some organizations prefer to create a centralized function for compliance. Under this structure, resources and staff are specifically assigned to a central records management group or department. This group is then responsible for records management decisions and is involved in records management issues across departments. Other organizations may choose a decentralized or "distributed" structure. Under this structure, records management responsibilities are delegated in a decentralized manner to departments and individual employees. The organization invests in ongoing training of a wide range of employees to ensure these responsibilities are reasonably being met. Still other organizations may structure and rely on automated, technical solutions for records management. These solutions might search content and metadata to identify, maintain, and dispose of records according to predefined retention periods. Your organization should conscientiously determine which of these structures—or which combination of these structures—will fit best with your existing (and desired) culture.

Record Retention Schedules

Q 5.6   What should a retention schedule look like?

A good retention schedule will identify records and place them in convenient groups, such as "insurance policies" or "bylaws and amendments to bylaws." The policy will then place these groups into larger categories by department or other organizational structure. For example, the record groups "insurance policies" and "bylaws and amendments to bylaws" could be grouped into the broader category "General Administrative." Finally, the schedule should attach a retention period to the record type.

Figure 5-3 provides sample entries to a retention schedule:

FIGURE 5-3
Sample Retention Schedule

Record Category	Record	Retention Begins	Duration of Retention Period Thereafter
Finance	Cash disbursements journal	Close of fiscal year when record created	7 years
Finance	Cash receipts journal	Close of fiscal year when record created	7 years
Finance	Subsidiary ledgers: accounts receivables; accounts payable, etc.	Close of fiscal year when record created	7 years
General Administrative Records	Fire inspection reports	Date of record	7 years
Tax Records	Audited financials	Date of record	permanent
Tax Records	Payroll tax records	Close of fiscal year when record created	7 years
Tax Records	Pension/profit sharing information returns	Date of record	permanent

Q 5.6.1   How should we determine retention periods for a particular category of records?

There are three primary sources to consider:

1. Applicable law, either in the form of a statute, an agency regulation,[14] or an enactment of another governmental authority.
2. Standards set by a professional association or other relevant group.
3. The "business rules" and "best practices" of your own organization.

The first—applicable law—is mandatory; your organization must follow retention periods set by law. You may always, if you believe it is warranted, set a retention period that is *greater* than that required by law, but you should not set your retention period at *less* than the legal requirement.

The other two sources for setting your organization's retention periods provide instructive guidance, but are not mandatory. For example, provided your organization has a reasonable basis for its decision, and provided the decision itself is reasonable, then your organization may permissibly set the retention period for "record category XYZ" so that it varies—and is less than—the retention period your industry association advises for the "XYZ record category." For those records that are not subject to a required-by-law retention period, a general rule to follow in determining the appropriate retention period is the so-called Rule of Reasonableness.

Q 5.6.2   Should we retain metadata?

Your organization should identify whether to retain metadata and, if so, which metadata elements to retain. (See Q 5.4.1 for an explanation of metadata.) Work with your IT department and Corporate Compliance Committee to decide whether to employ an automated or a manual system of assigning metadata and whether the metadata should analyze substantive content or formatting document features.

THE RULE OF REASONABLENESS

The "Rule of Reasonableness" governs records that are not covered by a legally required retention period. Where no statute requires a retention period of, say, "seven years from the close of the fiscal year in which the record was created," then your organization can use its discretion in setting the period. This discretion is *not* unregulated, and you need to be reasonable and follow a reasonable process in setting the period. Accordingly, for records not covered by a statutory retention period, you will want to use two tools to set the retention period:

(i)   establish a *reasonable process,* and

(ii) employ this process toward *reasonable results.*

For example:

*   Your organization appoints a few senior managers and relevant department heads to develop draft retention periods for these discretionary retention records.
*   Upon completion, these draft retention periods are circulated for comment to a larger respected group.
*   When the retention periods are finalized, the decision-makers (each in his or her area of focus) can give a reasonable business, operational, or other justification for each retention period.

These justifications do not need to be "right" in the sense that "the majority of experts in this field choose this precise retention period"; rather, these justifications need simply be reasonable. What is "reasonable" here? "Practicality and proportion" should be the guide for the scope, content, costs, and anticipated results of your organization's records management policy for discretionary retention records.[15]

Metadata has a wide range of functions and capabilities. Your organization might choose to retain metadata, therefore, because it serves business needs. In contrast, your organization may determine that some or all metadata is unnecessary and should be disabled. In either situation (or in the wide range of situations between these poles), you will want to ensure that you have made a conscious choice as to the amount, type, and functionality for metadata. As with the Rule of Reasonableness generally, your organization should follow a reasonable process in making decisions concerning metadata and should strive for a result that is similarly reasonable, in light of the business needs and circumstances.

Q 5.6.3   Does the statute of limitations play a role in setting retention periods?

Your organization may wish to consider statutes of limitations in setting the retention period for discretionary retention records, but you may properly determine, under the Rule of Reasonableness, that these statutes do not apply. The Rule of Reasonableness allows a flexible approach. Statutes of limitations generally have a trigger that starts the limitations period running. Many times, a statute of limitations will choose a trigger that is not possible to determine in advance. For example, (i) the statute of limitations on a breach of contract claim might be "six years commencing on the date the contract was breached"; or (ii) the limitations period on a claim for negligence might be "three years from the date the plaintiff first knew or should have known she was injured." These triggers are "indeterminate"—meaning it would be hard for your organization to predict in advance when the contract will be breached or when the plaintiff will know or shall have known of her injuries. These types of triggers make poor bases for a retention period. In sum, your organization should consider statutes of limitation as one factor in setting retention periods for discretionary retention records. This factor need not, and perhaps should not, control the decision.

Q 5.6.4   When a retention period expires for a record, is the record destroyed?

Yes. Where (i) the retention period has expired, and (ii) no litigation holds are in place with respect to the records (see Q 5.11 below for a fuller discussion of litigation holds), then your organization should destroy them in accordance with the retention schedule. Again, unless a statute or regulation otherwise requires, an organization is under no general obligation to retain records generated during the ordinary course of business. Moreover, keeping unneeded and low-value information creates direct costs, indirect costs, and other burdens. At a minimum, the unneeded records increase your records management costs and, by definition, add little to no counterbalancing value. Other records retention and destruction considerations relating to discovery issues are discussed below at Q 5.10.2 to Q 5.11.

Implementing the Policy

Q 5.7 What if we make mistakes here and there in following our records management policy?

No preservation system will be perfect. Courts recognize this fact, particularly where the record holder has acted in good faith, guided by the Rule of Reasonableness.[16] Your organization should make a good-faith effort to implement its unique policy, appoint the necessary personnel to enforce it, and encourage feedback at various levels of the company.

Q 5.7.1 Should we have a training program?

Yes. A training program is important, particularly if you are implementing a new policy or material changes to an existing policy. A reasonable portion of records management can be viewed as "Oh, no, we have to clean the attic over vacation." Most organizations will have an ingrained set of business rules and formal and information practices that drive the records management process essentially by habit. Any changes to this program will require changes in habits, which is difficult. Training is a strong method for beginning this potential sea-change for the revised or new policy.

Q 5.7.2 Should we consider sanctions for noncompliance?

Yes. Your organization's employee handbook, for example, could state that compliance with the records management policy is a required job responsibility and failure to observe the terms could result in corrective measures. Additionally, your organization should explicitly describe its expectations to employees and consider conducting intermittent compliance reviews. You may want to consider attaching some form of sanction to these reviews for failure to comply including, for example, under-retaining, over-retaining, or failing to adhere to legal hold requirements.[17]

If your organization has occasion to defend its policy in litigation or in some other adversarial forum, these types of documented efforts to support the administration and application of the policy will be extremely valuable in demonstrating that the policy is firmly in place and "bears respect."

Employee Use of Personal Devices for Company Business

Q 5.8   How should employers address the issue of employee use of personal devices for company business?

Companies generally recognize that use of various mobile and handheld devices (laptops, smart phones, tablets, etc.) can increase employee efficiency and productivity. Mobile devices present users with considerable flexibility, allowing portable storage and processing of data, and providing access via wireless and cellular networks to company networks. Certain employees might use these personal mobile devices for company purposes. Indeed, any remote device—such as a personal home computer—can present issues involving storage and use of company data on devices that are not within a company's firewall or other security perimeter, if the company's IT department allows remote access to company network resources.

Presented with these issues, a company generally has three options:

(i)   Forbid any use of personal mobile devices (or other devices that exist outside the company's security perimeter) for company business;

(ii)   Permit only certain individuals to engage in these uses, subject to oversight and company policies; or

(iii)   Permit all or the majority of employees to engage in these uses, while maintaining clear policies concerning such uses, requiring strong training regimes, and imposing sanctions for failure to comply.

If a company chooses to allow use of remote mobile devices for a mix of personal and business use, it should consider implementing the following in its mobile and remote computing policy:

(i)   Make clear that the company is the sole and exclusive owner of all business information processed through or stored on the mobile device;

(ii) Impose an ongoing obligation to timely upload to the company's network all relevant company data stored on the mobile device;

(iii) Require the employee to provide the company with open access to company data stored on the device, and to meta-data and other logging information with respect to such data (see Q 5.6.2 concerning metadata);

(iv) Reserve the right to examine the mobile device, requiring the employee to disclose requisite passwords;

(v)   Provide and require the employee to install security applications on the device;

(vi) Consider limiting the number of allowed mobile devices, to reduce the burden on the IT department for supporting security measures on the devices; and

(vii) Require the employee to immediately notify a company-designated manager if the device has been misplaced or stolen, reserving the right to disable or otherwise "brick" the device to prevent or hinder outside parties from accessing company data stored on the device.

A company should strongly consider providing "good-faith and commercially reasonable efforts" to maintain the privacy of personal information resident on the employee's mobile device, and should create structures via its mobile and remote computing policy that allow the employee to "tag" or otherwise identify any personal information on the device again, if the company permits the "co-habitation" of personal and business data on the device.

Backup Systems/Disaster Recovery

Q 5.9   How is our organization's Disaster Recovery Plan different from a records management program?

Most organizations with a computer have—and all should have, unless there is a substantial and stated justification otherwise—a "business continuation plan" or "disaster recovery plan." A disaster recovery plan is designed to allow an organization to resume business operations efficiently in the event of a serious failure in its computer network, communications network, or other mission-critical electronic systems. A central part of these plans is usually a series of system backups that your IT department makes and that essentially copy the information and software stored on your organization's network. A full disaster recovery plan would likely include:

- the definition of what qualifies as a disaster, to trigger the plan;
- what information must be retrieved after disaster;
- what information will be stored in preparation for a possible disaster;
- who is responsible for duplicating and overseeing the information;
- where and how will the information be stored;
- how often will information be updated and refreshed; and
- how long outmoded or duplicate information will be stored.

Q 5.9.1 Can't we just rely on our Disaster Recovery Plan's backup system for records management?

No. You should keep in mind that, although a backup system may be useful for recovering lost or deleted information, it is not a substitute for a formal records and information management policy and system. The process of obtaining information from a backup system is called "restoring." Restoring backup information can be expensive and time-consuming. In order to restore a backup tape, IT personnel must rebuild the tape using the version of the software and related infrastructure that existed at the time the tape was created. Presented with a backup tape from 2000, for example, the IT department would need to recreate and "build" the environment and infrastructure that existed in 2000 in order simply to recover the data before commencing any searches.

In addition, if backups are performed in an incremental manner, it may take a number of individual backup tapes to obtain a full restore of the system sufficient to locate the record at issue. Accordingly, relying on a backup system for records management purposes is generally inadvisable.

Because a disaster recovery plan presents a number of overlaps with a records management policy, an organization should ensure that it coordinates the implementation of a records management policy with IT policies. The champions of a fledgling records management program should understand the backup structure—that is, at a minimum how frequently the system is backed up, what components are backed up, and how long the backup tapes are retained. Many IT departments will "re-cycle" the media used to store the backup information. Each of these re-cycles overwrites the existing data and thus constitutes the "destruction" component of a records management program. As a general rule, cycles for re-use of backup media should be reasonably short and cost-effective.

Litigation Issues/Discovery

Requests for "Not Reasonably Accessible" ESI

Q 5.10 How do ESI rules affect policy?

Federal courts have recently implemented a new set of discovery rules in civil cases designed to accommodate the challenges presented by electronically stored information. Under these rules, a party is *not* required to provide discovery of ESI from sources that are "not reasonably accessible" due to either undue burden or undue cost.[18] The party opposing such discovery bears the initial burden of demonstrating that the requested ESI is not reasonably accessible.[19]

As a general rule, a court will presume that ESI stored on backup tapes qualifies as not reasonably accessible.[20] As discussed above (Q 5.9.1), it can be extremely expensive to restore backup tapes in order to retrieve the information on them, so you will want to avoid having to resort to this source for discovery materials.[21]

In addition to establishing that not-reasonably-accessible ESI is, in fact, not reasonably accessible, your organization will want to be in a position to show that the requesting party has not established good cause to obtain access to the information. The requesting party bears the burden of showing good cause.[22] In determining good cause, courts evaluate a range of factors, including:

- the specificity of the discovery request;
- the importance of the proposed discovery in resolving the issues;

145

- whether the request is unreasonably cumulative or duplica-tive;
- whether the party seeking discovery has had ample oppor-tunity by discovery to obtain the information sought;
- the amount in controversy; and
- whether the burden or expense of the proposed discovery outweighs its likely benefit.[23]

Although these "good cause" factors cannot reasonably be assessed in advance of a specific request, a concept common to the factors is: what is the quality of the discovery the requesting party has obtained independent of the not-reasonably-accessible ESI? Accordingly, to the extent the organization is able to show that it has reasonably complied with ESI discovery requests, independent of recourse to ESI stored on backup tapes, for example, the organization will undermine its adversary's "good cause" arguments.

Responding to a Request for ESI

Q 5.10.1   How can we be best prepared to respond to requests for ESI?

You've been presented with a request: "Produce all files concerning project X ever authored by, emailed to, or opened by Joe." In order to provide an efficient response, you should first assemble a project team with requisite resources and support to compile the necessary information and evaluate your organization's network.

In assembling a response team, you should be able to answer the following questions:

☐ Who is the proper person/team to manage IT functions for records management?

☐ What additional resources are needed to respond to these questions?

☐ Are there existing policies—for example, computer use policies, codes of network conduct, acceptable use poli-cies—that impact practices concerning retention of elec-tronic information?

❏ Do users currently receive any training that impacts on retention practices for ESI?

The response team should understand your organization's current network and files available online:

❏ What operating systems and applications are currently employed?

❏ Where are current user files stored? For example, are they stored on users' hard drives, on shared network drives, on home computers, on thumb drives, on PDAs (like Black-Berry devices)?

❏ What metadata is created with these files?

❏ Where are the servers that host user data located?

❏ Are there size limits on a user's account, for example, size limits with respect to an email inbox?

❏ Are there any automatic deletion features?

❏ Do users have discretion to delete files?

Records Coordinators should also understand the archival "near-line" network structure (if one exists). You should be able to answer the following questions:

❏ Are files archived? If so, is there an automatic archive feature?

❏ How do users obtain files that have been archived?

❏ Is there a de-duplication system in place regarding archived documents?

As the decisive issue in most e-discovery disputes will be access to the responding party's backup systems, a key component in an ESI Response Program is the ability to present a transparent, documented, and rational basis for demonstrating that backup information is not reasonably accessible, thus avoiding or minimizing the extreme burden that discovery of backup information can create.

Your response team should be able to answer the following questions about your organization's backup system:

❏ What systems are backed up?

❐ What is the purpose of the backups? Disaster recovery? Other purposes?

❐ What is the frequency of backups?

❐ What is the backup rotation schedule, that is, how frequently are backup tapes re-cycled?

❐ Are backup tapes encrypted?

❐ Are backup media restored based on user requests? If so, under what circumstances?

❐ What metrics are available to determine the costs of restoring a backup tape? What other resources would be required?

Finally, an organization's IT systems (both automated IT systems and human-driven IT systems) can provide a strong—and perhaps the best—structure for implementing retention schedules and litigation holds. An analysis of your organization's network will mean being able to answer these questions:

❐ Do IT systems incorporate, or are they capable of incorporating, retention schedules?

❐ Is there a litigation hold procedure in place for ESI? If so, how is litigation hold implemented—that is, how is the information preserved?

❐ Does the hold apply across the range of applications, user files, and storage locations identified above?

Q 5.10.2 How should concerns about litigation inform our retention of records?

During actual or reasonably anticipated litigation, government investigation, government audit, or a significant business event like a merger or acquisition,[24] your organization is required to suspend its records management policy and preserve relevant materials. Materials that must be preserved are those that are relevant to the actual or reasonably anticipated litigation, subpoena, government investigation, or significant business event, *regardless* of whether the materials constitute a "record" or "official record" under your policy. For example, assume that, under your policy, only the final version of outgoing correspondence is retained. Once you learn of an actual or threatened proceeding, if earlier versions of outgoing correspondence may be relevant to that proceeding, then they must be retained.

Spoliation of Evidence

Q 5.10.3 What if requested records have already been destroyed in accordance with our retention schedule?

Generally, when the retention period for a record has expired and no litigation holds are in place with respect to that record, your organization should destroy it in accordance with the retention schedule. In fact, storing irrelevant electronic information will increase your organization's discovery burden, potentially by a significant margin. This increased burden may, among other things, prevent timely responses to discovery requests and result in costly sanctions.[25]

If your organization has destroyed records *pursuant to a reasonable records management policy*, then a court—as a rule—will view such destruction as a proper component of conducting business and will not view the conduct as sanctionable spoliation of evidence or obstruction of justice.[26] The new federal rules expressly recognize the safe harbor that a good-faith functioning records management program should provide.

Litigation Holds[27]

Q 5.11 What is a litigation hold?

A litigation hold is a communication issued by Legal as a result of current or anticipated litigation, audit, government investigation, or other matter that warrants suspension of the retention schedule for identified records. A hold is appropriate:

- when the company is involved in litigation;
- when the company reasonably anticipates becoming involved in litigation, such as through receipt of a demand letter, or subpoena;
- when the company is involved in a government investigation or audit; or

- when the company reasonably anticipates becoming involved in a government investigation or audit, such as through receipt of a formal or informal investigation request (each a "Litigation Event").

Upon the occurrence of a Litigation Event, your organization becomes legally required to preserve relevant documents and may face sanctions if it fails to follow this policy and its litigation hold procedures.

OTHER TERMS FOR "LITIGATION HOLD"

- legal hold
- preservation memo
- suspension order
- freeze notice
- hold order
- hold notice

Q 5.11.1   How do we put a litigation hold in place?

To put a hold in place, there first should be a timely *notice* of the litigation hold to your organization's employees and others involved in records management. The following factors are significant with respect to this notice:

- The individual giving the notice should be a senior member of the legal department or separate records management department;
- The notice should include a reasonable description of the relevant documents;[28]
- The notice should be given to those responsible for searching and retaining relevant documents, and may be given in electronic, paper, or other reliable format;[29]

- The organization must commit sufficient attention and resources to meeting its preservation duties in light of the circumstances;[30] and
- The scope and nature of the litigation hold should change over time as the case changes (either contracting or, more importantly, expanding).

The litigation hold needs to apply to all relevant materials, regardless of their format or storage media. At the outset of implementing your records management policy, you should put in place structures to address potential litigation holds. Identify "point persons" responsible for determining when the policy requires suspension. In addition, you may wish to select an individual with strong knowledge of the policy to act as a point person for coordinating the litigation hold. This individual would thereby have knowledge both of the policy and of the litigation hold and could thus act as a knowledgeable, firsthand witness in the proceeding if necessary.

Q 5.11.2   How long should a litigation hold last?

Your litigation hold should be specifically tailored to the situation and should last for the *duration* of the situation giving rise to the hold. Factors to evaluate in considering whether to lift a litigation hold include:

- the form and content of the notice announcing removal of the litigation hold;
- the possible existence of any post-proceeding duty to retain certain records;
- whether records must be retained pursuant to another litigation hold or for some other independent purpose;
- whether the original litigation will lead to subsequent litigation;
- whether third parties associated with your organization may destroy relevant documents; and
- whether to immediately destroy documents or return to a normal destruction schedule.[31]

Notes to Chapter 5

1. *In re* Bank of America Securities LLC, SEC Admin. Proc. File No. 3-11425, Exchange Act Release No. 49,386, 82 SEC Docket 1264 (Mar. 10, 2004), www.sec.gov/litigation/admin/34-49386.htm (regulated entity fined $10 million for allegedly misleading regulators and delaying document production).

2. *See* United States v. Koch Indus., Inc., 197 F.R.D. 463, 483–86 (N.D. Okla. 1998); *In re* Prudential Ins. Co. of Am. Sales Practices Litig., 169 F.R.D. 598, 615 (D.N.J. 1997).

3. Compliance with privacy and security regulations is discussed in chapter 12, *infra*.

4. *See* S. NELSON ET AL., THE ELECTRONIC EVIDENCE AND DISCOVERY HANDBOOK 105 (ABA 2006); *see also* www.uscourts.gov. The new rules became effective December 1, 2006.

5. *See* The Sedona Guidelines: Guidelines & Commentary for Managing Information & Records in the Electronic Age (Sept. 2005) [hereinafter Sedona Guidelines (2005)] at 36–37.

6. *See* Sedona Guidelines (2005), at 13–14.

7. *See* The Sedona Guidelines: Best Practice Recommendations & Principles for Addressing Electronic Document Production 3–4 (June 2007) [hereinafter Sedona Guidelines (2007)].

8. NARA Bulletin 2008-07, Endorsement of DoD Electronic Records Management Software Applications Design Criteria Standard, version 3 (National Archives and Records Administration Sept. 10, 2008), www.archives.gov/records-mgmt/bulletins/2008/2008-07.html.

9. *See* European Commission, MoReq2 Specification: Model Requirements for the Management of Electronic Records (version 1.04) (update and extension 2008), available for download at www.moreq2.eu/moreq2.

10. 16 C.F.R. pt. 255, Guides Concerning Use of Endorsements and Testimonials in Advertising; *see also* www.ftc.gov/os/2009/10/091005endorsementguidesfnnotice.pdf.

11. 16 C.F.R. § 255.5 (Disclosure of Material Connections), ex. 8.

12. *See* Trigon Ins. Co. v. United States, 204 F.R.D. 277, 288–91 (E.D. Va. 2001) (failure to preserve drafts of expert reports led to sanctions); McGuire v. Acufex Microsurgical, Inc., 175 F.R.D. 149, 155–56 (D. Mass. 1997) (an employer may revise documents and discard earlier drafts because "[to] hold otherwise would be to create a new set of affirmative obligations for employers, unheard of in the law—to preserve all drafts of internal memos, perhaps even to record everything no matter how central to the investigation, or gratuitous").

13. Backup copies of electronic documents can present considerable challenges to a records management program. The most common of these challenges are discussed below.

14. A broad range of regulatory structures may be relevant. Consider, for example, the following agencies, each of which has specific records management regulations: Securities and Exchange Commission (SEC), Internal Revenue Service (IRS), Department of Defense (DOD), Department of Labor (DOL), Equal Employment Opportunity Commission (EEOC), and the Environmental Protection Agency (EPA).

15. *See* Sedona Guidelines (2005), at 13.

16. *See* Zubulake v. UBS Warburg LLC, 220 F.R.D. 212, 217 (S.D.N.Y. 2003) (Should an organization "preserve every shred of paper, every e-mail or electronic document, and every backup tape? The answer is clearly 'no.' Such a rule would cripple large corporations . . . that are almost always involved in litigation."); Wiginton v. Ellis, 2003 WL 22439865, at *4, *7 (N.D. Ill. Oct. 27, 2003) (a company need not preserve every paper in its business; the defendant was not obligated to preserve every piece of electronic data in the company).

17. *Cf.* ISO 15489-1 §§ 10–11 (describing possible contours of training and auditing/monitoring programs).

18. Fed. R. Civ. P. 26(b)(2)(B); Zubulake v. UBS Warburg LLC, 217 F.R.D. 309, 320 (S.D.N.Y. 2003).

19. Fed. R. Civ. P. 26(b)(2)(B) ("[T]he party from whom discovery is sought must show that the information is not reasonably accessible because of undue burden or cost.").

20. *See Zubulake*, 217 F.R.D. at 320 ("Backup tapes must be restored . . . fragmented data must be de-fragmented, and erased data must be reconstructed, all before the data is usable. That makes such data *inaccessible*."); Quinby v. WestLB AG, 2005 WL 3453908, at *7 n.8 (S.D.N.Y. Dec. 15, 2005) ("back-up tapes are considered an *inaccessible format* and not readily usable") (emphasis added throughout). "Data on backup tapes used for disaster recovery purposes is usually regarded as inaccessible, because such tapes function to quickly undo catastrophic systems failure, not as a filing cabinet." Grant J. Esposito & Thomas M. Mueller, *Backup Tapes, You Can't Live with Them and You Can't Toss Them; Strategies for Dealing with the Litigation Burdens Associated with Backup Tapes Under the Amended Rules of Civil Procedure*, 13 Rich. J.L. & Tech. 3 (2006); *see also* Rowe Entm't, Inc. v. William Morris Agency, Inc., 205 F.R.D. 421, 429 (S.D.N.Y. 2002) ("Backup tapes, for example, are not archives from which documents may easily be retrieved. The data on backup tapes are not organized for retrieval of individual documents or files, but for wholesale, emergency uploading onto a computer system. Therefore, the organization of the data mirrors the computer's structure, not the human records management structure, if there is one.") (internal citations omitted); Wiginton v. Ellis, 2003 WL 22439865, at *3 (N.D. Ill. Oct. 27, 2003) ("[Defendant's] backup system is not an archiving system that would preserve all information going into [its] computers. Rather, it is a disaster recovery system that takes only snapshots of [the Defendant's] computer files so that if a catastrophic event occurs, the information from the immediately preceding period can be reloaded."); Cache La Poudre Feeds, LLC v. Land O'Lakes, Inc., 244 F.R.D. 614, 628 (D. Colo. 2007) ("One . . . source of [not reasonably accessible] information might be *backup tapes.*"). *See generally* Shira A.

SCHEINDLIN, MOORE'S FEDERAL PRACTICE, E-DISCOVERY: THE NEWLY AMENDED FEDERAL RULES OF CIVIL PROCEDURE 15–16 (2006) ("[E]xamples of [not reasonably accessible] sources, given today's technology, might include *back-up tapes.*").

21. Sedona Guidelines (2007), at 45–49.

22. FED. R. CIV. P. 26(b)(2)(B).

23. *See* FED. R. CIV. P. 26(b)(2)(C)(i)–(iii); FED. R. CIV. P. 26(b)(2)(B) advisory committee note of 2006, subdivision (b)(2).

24. *See* Sedona Guidelines (2005), at 42.

25. *See In re* Prudential Ins. Co. of Am. Sales Practices Litig., 169 F.R.D. 598, 615 (D.N.J. 1997) (although no proof that Prudential intended to hinder discovery through the purposeful destruction of documents, its unorganized approach to document retention denied its opponents access to evidence; because the records at issue were destroyed, the court draws an adverse inference from the absence of the documents).

26. Lewy v. Remington Arms Co., 836 F.2d 1104, 1112 (8th Cir. 1988) (endorsing the following factors regarding a failure to produce evidence: (1) whether the records management policy was reasonable in light of the facts and circumstances surrounding the relevant documents; (2) whether the policy was adopted in bad faith; and (3) whether earlier lawsuits had been filed with such frequency or in such magnitude that it was obvious that certain categories of documents should be retained); *see also* Moore v. Gen. Motors Corp., 558 S.W.2d 720, 735 (Mo. Ct. App. 1977) (destruction of documents was reasonable and permissible where defendant had no knowledge of pending litigation and followed its customary records management practices); Chrysler Corp. v. Blackmon, 841 S.W.2d 844, 847–50, 853 (Tex. 1992) (car manufacturer destroyed crash test reports and other documents pursuant to its document retention policy; court ruled that default judgment sanction was not warranted for document destruction).

27. *See* chapter 7, *infra* (offering Electronic Discovery, for additional discussion of litigation holds).

28. *See* Wiginton v. Ellis, 2003 WL 22439865, at *5 (N.D. Ill. Oct. 27, 2003) (first litigation hold notice did not reflect the proper scope of the preservation obligation).

29. *See In re* Prudential Ins. Co. of Am. Sales Practices Litig., 169 F.R.D. 598, 612–13 (D.N.J. 1997) (emails to employees (i) did not state in bold phrases like "DO NOT DESTROY DOCUMENTS," (ii) did not identify the specific litigation, and (iii) did not explain that failure to comply could create civil or criminal exposure; in addition, not all employees had email access, and complete notices were not circulated in paper format).

30. *See* Danis v. USN Commc'ns, Inc., 2000 WL 1694325, at *39–41 (N.D. Ill. Oct. 20, 2000); *In re* Prudential Ins. Co. of Am. Sales Practices Litig., 169 F.R.D. 598, 612, 615–16 (D.N.J. 1997) (the defendants' earlier litigation hold notices were inadequate; senior management must (i) notify employees of the pending litigation, (ii) give them a copy of the court order, and (iii) inform them of the sanctions for noncompliance).

31. *See* Sedona Guidelines (2005), at 50–51.

6

Internal Investigations

Gregory Baldwin*

An internal investigation is an inquiry conducted by a business into allegations of misconduct by its own employees or agents for the purpose of determining the relevant facts. A properly conducted internal investigation is essential to assisting management or the board in determining whether particular allegations have any merit, who may have been involved, and the level of involvement. An improperly conducted investigation can result in inadvertent waiver of the company's attorney-client privilege, violations of ethical rules, and even criminal exposure for obstructing justice. Properly conducted internal investigations are essential in determining how the facts fit into the appropriate legal and/or regulatory framework; in identifying the appropriate response to allegations of wrongdoing (including appropriate corrective action); and in mitigating the criminal, civil, or regulatory consequences of any actual malfeasance that might be discovered. In the

* The author wishes to acknowledge James Rodio, Christopher A. Myers, Suzanne M. Foster, John S. Irving IV, and Steven D. Gordon for their contributions to this chapter.

context of a compliance program, the internal investigation can be used to document that the company has responded appropriately to allegations of misconduct.

As businesses today face heightened government oversight and enforcement actions, as well as the increasingly severe consequences for criminal, civil, and regulatory violations those activities can impose, internal investigations have become common occurrences. As a result, they have also come to be expected by oversight authorities. While entire books could be (and have been) written on the topic, this chapter focuses on outlining the key considerations and issues related to internal investigations, and the role internal investigations should play in an effective compliance and ethics program.

Pre-Investigation

Allegations of Wrongdoing

Q 6.1   What triggers an internal investigation?

Internal investigations are reactive in nature, in the sense that they are generally triggered by some form of allegation of wrongdoing. These allegations may arise internally or externally. For example, an allegation of wrongdoing may arise *internally* through an effective compliance program, as a report made on a company "hotline" or by an alert employee who notifies the appropriate manager. Questionable conduct that should be investigated may also be discovered internally during a routine financial audit of company finances or during a compliance program audit.

Allegations of wrongdoing may also arise *externally*. For example, a disgruntled current or former employee may report alleged wrongdoing directly to government regulators or to criminal law enforcement authorities, thereby initiating a formal government investigation. Alternatively, disgruntled employees, dissatisfied customers, business competitors, or aggrieved shareholders may initiate a civil lawsuit against the business, which may in turn trigger a formal government civil or criminal investigation of the business.[1] Government agency auditors may also uncover allegedly improper activity by a business in the course of routine agency audits.

> **TIP:** The company's position is measurably improved if potential misconduct is discovered early. Early discovery may lead to a quick investigation and the ability to correct the problem before it becomes difficult to manage and exposes the company to significant sanctions. It also gives the company the opportunity to self-report serious violations before they lead to government investigations. Self-reporting is required under an increasing number of regulatory regimes, and enforcement agencies typically respond to self-reporting more leniently.

Q 6.1.1   What kinds of allegations trigger an investigation?

For our purposes here, there are two types of allegations of wrongdoing: those that present low risk to the company, and those that present high risk to the company. Both may arise either internally or externally.

Low-risk allegations are usually internally reported non-criminal misconduct, as well as civil or regulatory misconduct, that do not expose the company to significant fines, penalties, loss of government business, civil damages, or injury to reputation. These are usually simple "hotline" or other complaints about unfair treatment by a supervisor or co-worker and usually make up the majority of reported misconduct on company "hotlines."

High-risk allegations can arise from internally reported conduct or more commonly from external allegations of criminal, legal, or regulatory misconduct that could expose the company to serious criminal, civil, or administrative fines, penalties, civil damages, or reputational harm. Such allegations can result in expensive "bet-the-company" civil litigation or criminal investigations. The penalties can be crippling if not downright destructive, including not only monetary fines but also loss of government business, revocation of the right to conduct business, damage to reputation, and harm to shareholders.

Q 6.1.2   Are all allegations of wrongdoing subject to investigation?

Senior management and in-house counsel cannot and should not personally address *every* instance of alleged misconduct, although all such allegations, whether low- or high-risk, should be investigated and addressed appropriately. Not every allegation of misconduct requires a full-scale internal investigation. The decision about whether and how to investigate depends on the nature, source, and seriousness of the allegation, as well as on the potential civil, criminal, regulatory, and reputational consequences that may arise from it. The more serious the allegation and the consequences, the more likely it will be that a comprehensive internal investigation should be conducted.

Determining the Type of Investigation

Q 6.2   What determines the type of internal investigation to conduct?

The type of internal investigation basically depends on two factors: the seriousness of the alleged misconduct, and the source of the allegation, such as whether the allegation is internal or external. Low-risk allegations coming from internal sources usually do not require a full-scale internal investigation. Allegations arising from external sources, however, very often call for a thorough internal investigation, especially if the external source is a government agency. The determination of what kind of investigation to conduct requires judgment and experience in understanding the potential ramifications of the alleged misconduct and the impact the source of the allegation has on those ramifications. This determination is an ongoing process, constantly subject to newly discovered information. Be prepared to make periodic reassessments. For example, a limited internal investigation without counsel may initially appear sufficient, but during the course of the investigation additional misconduct may come to light that makes a full-scale internal investigation conducted by outside counsel necessary. Conversely, allegations of misconduct initially may appear more serious than they are, and additional information may allow the internal investigation to be cut short or reduced in scope.

Q 6.2.1   How is the decision about the appropriate type of internal investigation made?

All internal allegations of wrongdoing should be directed to one centralized location for initial review and evaluation as to whether they constitute low- or high-risk allegations. This initial evaluation can be done by the company's compliance officer, in-house counsel, or both working together, to make an initial assessment of the seriousness of the allegation. If the company does not have a compliance officer or in-house counsel, outside legal assistance should be sought. The important point is that, regardless of who conducts the initial evaluation, it should be done by someone who is able to recognize the difference between low-risk and high-risk allegations.

If possible, all internal investigations, whether low- or high-risk, should be initiated and supervised by in-house counsel in order to protect the confidentiality of the investigation through the attorney-client privilege and the attorney-client/work-product doctrine.

In deciding whether to initiate a full-scale internal investigation, a combination of decision makers is called for. As French Premier Georges Clemenceau remarked during World War I, "War is too important to be left to the generals." Allegations of criminal conduct are as close to actual war as any company is ever likely to come, and like war, external criminal allegations are too important to be left to just one group of people to make decisions.

If the company has an independent audit committee, serious allegations of misconduct, especially those potentially involving misconduct by senior management, should be brought to the committee's attention. If the company does not have an independent audit or other board committee, senior management (*excluding* any officers potentially involved in the alleged misconduct) should be involved in the decision. Presumably, senior management constitutes the group that knows the company best and can make reasonably and responsibly balanced decisions regarding internal investigation costs versus the consequences of the alleged misconduct. Whether the independent board committee, senior management, or both are involved in the process, the decision must always include legal counsel, whether in-house, outside, or both.[2] Legal counsel should be in the best position to advise either the board committee or senior management on the range of potential consequences of the alleged misconduct, as well as the most reasonable and responsible reactions to the allegations.

Initiating an Investigation

Determining the Type of Investigation

Q 6.3   How should low-risk allegations of misconduct be investigated?

Investigation of low-risk allegations, while sometimes directed by counsel, may actually be conducted by an independent internal third party, such as the compliance officer, the human resources department, or the appropriate supervisor of the person accused of misconduct (assuming, of course, that the supervisor is independent, not involved in the alleged wrongdoing, and in a position to be objective). The resolution should be reported back to the referring person (that is, the compliance officer or in-house counsel), who can then confirm that the matter has been appropriately resolved. In these instances, the role of in-house counsel is more reactive and includes:

- receiving reports;
- monitoring and ensuring that the investigation is effectively and fairly managed; and
- intervening if the matter becomes so highly sensitive as to potentially involve more serious allegations, adverse publicity, or government intervention.

Q 6.3.1   How should high-risk allegations of misconduct be investigated?

If the initial reviewer concludes that the allegation is a high-risk situation, it should immediately be brought to the attention of senior management or a board of directors committee. Senior management or the board committee should then decide, upon the advice of in-house and/or outside counsel, whether to conduct a full-scale internal investigation.

Once the decision has been made, investigations into serious allegations of wrongdoing must always be initiated and supervised by in-house or outside counsel in order to protect the confidentiality of the investigation through the attorney-client privilege and the attorney-client/work-product doctrine. Beyond providing confidentiality, however, high-risk allegations require direct involvement by in-house counsel, usually with the assistance of outside counsel experienced in conducting internal investigations. (The attorney-client privilege and work-product doctrine are discussed in more detail below, at Q 6.13.1 *et seq.*)

Although these types of internal investigation are expensive, the cost pales when compared to the severity of the consequences of misconduct that is established but not effectively cured or addressed by the company. The cost of failing to recognize and properly investigate high-risk allegations can also be significant, at a minimum by jeopardizing the company's protections under the attorney-client privilege and adversely affecting the company's ability to make timely and proper disclosures to the government.

Q 6.3.2   How do internal allegations affect the investigation?

Internal complaints or reports of misconduct usually come from current and, sometimes, former employees, vendors, or agents. Unless anonymous, they usually provide the company with one or more readily available sources from whom additional information can be obtained. This information assists the company in shaping its investigation.

Some internal complaints, such as those involving minor civil complaints or supervisor mistreatment, may only require a limited inquiry into the conduct of one or only a few employees or managers who are allegedly involved. Moreover, the consequences are limited to relatively minor civil or regulatory damages. Others, however, may involve serious criminal or civil fraud complaints, such as insider trading, financial fraud, or environmental violations. Such complaints must be taken very seriously and addressed promptly. In both cases, however, one or more employees are often available to guide the company with details about the precise nature of the alleged misconduct, or can provide other sources of information, including identifying those persons believed to be involved.

Q 6.3.3   How do external allegations from government authorities affect the investigation?

Allegations of misconduct coming from the government may be much more difficult to pin down and, as such, negatively affect a company's attempt to shape its own internal investigation. In order to respond effectively to a government investigation, the company will need to learn the purpose and scope of that investigation. In other words, the company will want to learn who is investigating it, why it is being investigated, what it is being investigated for, and, if possible, the source of the allegation.

Q 6.3.4   When subject to a government investigation, how does a company determine the scope of the government's inquiry and its own investigative response?

This may be difficult to determine at the outset because most investigations are secret and the government may not be willing to share that information. However, there are frequently clues available. Three good sources of such information are a search warrant, a grand jury subpoena or civil investigative demand (CID), and the government agents or attorneys serving them.

Q 6.3.5   What does the issuance of a search warrant tell us about the government's intentions?

If a company is the subject of a search warrant directed against it, this indicates that the government has reason to believe that there is ongoing criminal activity inside the company and that the company cannot be trusted to fully comply with a records subpoena. Under these circumstances, the government may be unlikely to provide any information about the nature of the underlying investigation. Nevertheless, the issuance of a search warrant[3] itself justifies a much more extensive and rapid inquiry into the underlying circumstances.[4] The records sought in a search warrant provide an indication of the time period, events, and, possibly, individuals who may be involved.

Q 6.3.6   What does the service of a grand jury subpoena or CID say about the intended scope of the government's investigation?

The delivery of a grand jury subpoena or CID to the company can mean several different things, and the company's reaction will depend on the reason for the issuance of the subpoena or CID. The fact that a grand jury has issued a subpoena demonstrates that there is an active criminal investigation. A CID indicates that, at a minimum, there is an ongoing civil fraud investigation, typically involving the civil False Claims Act. Because the Department of Justice often conducts "parallel" or simultaneous civil and criminal fraud investigations, a CID could also be an indicator of a parallel investigation. Learning the company's role in the government's investigation then becomes crucial. The company may only be a "witness," in the sense that it has documents or other information that evidence possible criminal activity by, for example, a customer or a subcontractor. Here, the response may only require efficient document collection and production, or a limited internal review of the customer's account, but not a full-scale internal investigation.

However, a grand jury subpoena or CID may also mean that the company is a target or subject of a criminal or civil fraud investigation.[5] Here, whether target or subject, an immediate and thorough internal investigation is always called for.[6]

The records sought in a subpoena may give the company some information about the time frame for, basis of, and individuals who may be involved in the government investigation.

Q 6.3.7   What information can a government agent or attorney provide?

In some cases, the government agent who served the warrant, subpoena, or CID, or the government attorney involved in the issuance of either, may be willing to provide information about the investigation.

However, contact with the government agent and attorney should be strictly limited to the company's counsel.[7] Neither board committee members nor company management should contact government investigators or counsel. This may cause some delay in determining the basis or substance of the alleged wrongdoing. In-house counsel may be unsuccessful in getting the necessary information.[8] Where information is not provided by the government, the company will have to take the investigation very seriously, plan on a broad internal investigation, and try to determine the basis of the investigation from the limited sources available.[9] An internal investigation promptly begun can always be narrowed or cancelled if justified by new circumstances that come to light. But lost time can rarely, if ever, be recovered.

TIP: Allegations of criminal misconduct against a company must always be considered as particularly serious, regardless of their source, because of the severe consequences that can result to the company itself, as well as to its individual officers, directors, and employees. This is particularly the case where the company becomes aware of allegations of misconduct through a government investigation that has already been initiated. In addition, investigations under the civil False Claims Act, because of their quasi-criminal nature and significant penalties, should be treated in much the same way as criminal investigations.

TIP: In virtually every case in which a company is faced with an ongoing criminal investigation, and in many cases involving only potential civil liability, a full-scale internal investigation is warranted. A properly conducted internal investigation of serious allegations of wrongdoing is often the only way to determine the facts, prepare an effective defense, and minimize or avoid potential criminal punishment, civil or regulatory liability, and reputational damage to the company. In addition, a properly conducted internal investigation can enable a business, under the auspices of its compliance program, to take proper corrective action to halt any ongoing misconduct and prevent it from happening again. This can be crucial in the context of settlement negotiations with the government.

Q 6.3.8   How do allegations from external nongovernment sources affect the type of investigation to be pursued?

Allegations of misconduct may come to a company's attention through a variety of sources, including a civil lawsuit, a pre-litigation demand letter, customer complaints, newspaper reports, or a variety of other sources. As with government-based allegations, these should be closely examined to determine whether an internal investigation is warranted, and if so, what type. Such allegations may involve enormous potential civil or criminal liability that could prove devastating to the company if proven. Moreover, although raised in a civil context and frequently (but not always) involving nongovernmental parties, civil lawsuits and allegations that involve only civil law claims may actually be based upon conduct that could be prosecuted criminally. For example, a shareholder lawsuit may include allegations of securities fraud, which can certainly involve criminal conduct. Since civil lawsuits are public matters, they may come to the attention of government authorities or be brought directly to the attention of government authorities by the complaining parties. A parallel government criminal or regulatory investigation can provide additional leverage against the company in the lawsuit. Allegations of criminal misconduct in a civil complaint may trigger a separate parallel or

165

subsequent criminal investigation based upon the allegations in the civil suit. Thus, the consequences of a civil suit may not be limited only to potential civil damages.

Defining the Purpose of the Investigation

Q 6.4   What steps does the company need to take once a decision to investigate is reached?

Once the company has decided to conduct an internal investigation, the next step is to determine the investigation's timing, scope, staffing, and investigative methods. To accomplish this, there must be a clear understanding of the purpose of the internal investigation.

The purposes of an internal investigation are to determine if the alleged misconduct occurred, stop it if it is ongoing, identify and direct appropriate corrective action to prevent the misconduct from happening again, and provide the company with the information it needs to determine the best approach to external entities, such as enforcement agencies, regulators, potential civil litigants, and the public. In an increasing number of instances, companies that do business with or receive funding from the government are being required to self-report regulatory violations and violations of criminal laws and the civil False Claims Act. One of the considerations at the conclusion of an internal investigation often is whether or not a disclosure is required.

Q 6.4.1   How does the company determine the logistical needs of and methods to be used in an investigation?

Depending on the situation that has given rise to the internal investigation and the type of internal investigation to be conducted, the timing, scope, staffing, and investigative methods will differ.

Allegations arising from external sources, such as criminal law enforcement agencies, government regulators, or competitors, usually call for a broad scope of investigation because they are frequently the prelude to criminal or civil action against the company, and the company will need to know as much as possible to mount an effective defense. On the other hand, allegations arising from internal sources, to the extent they involve isolated non-criminal complaints, are usually narrower in scope.

In the case of an internal complaint alleging sexual harassment, for example, the company will probably know exactly what the allegations are, and it can usually rely on cooperation from the complaining employee. For these investigations, the scope, staffing, and methods will be tailored narrowly.

In a civil lawsuit, the allegations of wrongdoing will be spelled out (to varying degrees) in the complaint initiating the action and can be fleshed out in the discovery process. This tends to provide the company with a map of the alleged wrongdoing and often the identity of the officers or employees allegedly involved. The scope, staffing, and methods used will probably be broader than for one involving an internal complaint of non-criminal misconduct.

A criminal or regulatory fraud investigation will call for the broadest scope, staffing, and investigative methods because of the nature of criminal and civil fraud investigations. The company often will not know how or when the external investigation began, the company's alleged role, the identity of involved officers or employees, the full scope of what the prosecutors, regulators, and investigators are looking at, or when it will end. Frequently, these investigations involve "parallel" proceedings, that is, simultaneous investigations by criminal law enforcement, civil regulatory investigators, and, sometimes, separate state and federal agencies. In addition, such investigations may involve "sources" such as former officers or employees, or even *current* ones. These investigations can be secret in nature and can go in many directions. They can be under way for a significant period of time prior to a company gaining knowledge of the investigation.

Timing

Q 6.5 When should a company initiate an investigation?

Regardless of the type of internal investigation conducted, the decision to initiate an internal investigation should be made as soon as the alleged misconduct has come to the attention of the company.

Similarly, once the decision has been made, the investigation should begin immediately.

The speed with which an internal investigation is conducted will depend upon the basis for the investigation. Obviously, an internal investigation commenced because of an ongoing criminal investigation of the company being conducted by state or federal law enforcement authorities is more urgent than an inquiry into misconduct generated internally, but both require a prompt and diligent response.

Q 6.5.1   Is it beneficial to commence an investigation immediately?

Immediacy has the benefit of stopping any misconduct that may be ongoing. In addition, courts, prosecutors, and regulators generally look more favorably on internal investigations (and the companies that conduct them) that begin immediately upon learning of the alleged wrongdoing, because it indicates that the allegation was taken seriously and that the company's response was reasonable. An immediate response can also be used to demonstrate that the company's compliance program is effective, thereby either avoiding prosecution altogether or substantially reducing the potential penalty for the business.[10]

Scope

Q 6.6   What kinds of inquiries will be involved in an investigation?

Generally, each investigation will, at a minimum, involve some degree of internal document review, a review of electronically stored data, and employee interviews. An investigation may also involve inquiry into information not held or controlled by the company, such as information held by former employees or employees of other companies. Exactly which documents, employees, and non-company-held information must be collected and reviewed will depend on the basis for the investigation. This, in turn, depends upon what the allegation is, as well as the reliability of its source.

Allegations of financial reporting misconduct will normally be very document-intensive and involve forensic accounting. The same is true for allegations of embezzlement or theft, especially because they may also involve inquiry into external matters, such as the alleged perpetrators' lifestyle and spending habits. Allegations of sexual harassment or discrimination will normally be very employee-interview intensive, require little document review, and probably not require forensic accounting. Of course, electronic discovery, including potentially relevant emails, may be important in virtually any investigation. (See chapter 7 on electronic discovery.)

Q 6.6.1   What factors should the company consider in determining the scope of an investigation?

The source of the allegation. Is it an internal report (whose scope may often be reasonably confined to the actual allegation), or is it from an external source (such as a government law enforcement agency)? Government criminal investigations rarely have limits; they tend to follow evidence wherever it takes them. Such investigations require a broad-scope investigation so that the company can get ahead and stay ahead of the curve.

The nature of the allegation. Is it mostly civil, is it clearly criminal, or is it civil with potential criminal implications? Inquiry into many civil allegations may be focused very narrowly on a particular person and act whose consequences, while serious, can be addressed quickly and with little fanfare or external involvement (*e.g.*, an isolated complaint of sexual harassment or discrimination). The consequences of most criminal or financial fraud allegations, on the other hand, are usually so serious in terms of financial and reputational loss that they require not only an internal investigation, but also one whose scope is broad enough to cover the full range of potential misconduct in order to enable the company to respond fully and effectively.[11]

The credibility of the allegation or its source. It is generally accurate to say that some allegations have no credibility and may be safely disregarded (such as the common "nut case" whose allegations are so sweeping and incoherent as to forfeit all credibility). These situations do not call for much, if any, investigation, unless the company is overly cautious or wishes to appear non-judgmental, in which case a cursory inquiry is usually sufficient. Others have only marginal credibility, such as the angry customer with an axe to grind against the company, a disgruntled former employee who was fired for good cause, or a jealous competitor. While these may merit some inquiry, the inquiry may reasonably be narrow, at least initially.[12] In all cases involving a government criminal or regulatory investigation, however, the source should initially be considered the government itself, and highly credible per se, regardless of the actual source used by the government.

Q 6.6.2   When should the scope of the investigation be determined?

To the extent possible, the initial scope of the internal investigation should be determined before the investigation begins, and it should be determined by both senior management or a board committee and legal counsel in consultation together. It is important to bear in mind that the initial decision as to the scope of an investigation cannot be written in stone. It can change, and the company and its counsel should periodically review the scope expressly for that purpose. For example, new wrongdoing not included in the initial allegation may be uncovered. The company must be prepared to deal with that immediately, and resist the temptation to dismiss it out of hand. Similarly, some government-initiated criminal investigations, which generally call for a broad internal investigation, may later be found to have been triggered by a disgruntled ex-employee as an act of retaliation against the company. When this happens the initial breadth of the investigation may be narrowed. In such cases, the scope of the internal investigation should include, but not be limited to, the discovery and disclosure of facts that may discredit the government's source.

TIP: Every internal investigation must be complete and fair. Otherwise, any benefit from having conducted the investigation may be lost at best, and at worst subject the company to litigation. Therefore, determining the tentative scope of the investigation at the outset is crucial.

Leadership

Q 6.7   Who should be in charge of an internal investigation?

Regardless of who *staffs* an internal investigation, the person *in charge* and giving directions should always be *legal counsel*. In any matter involving alleged criminal misconduct, regardless of the source, legal counsel should be used.[13] The counsel selected should be experienced in conducting internal investigations, familiar with the area of law as well as the government agencies involved (and ideally, but not necessarily, even the government personnel involved in the matter), and free from conflicting interests.

Experienced legal counsel will be able to provide the necessary legal analysis, apply the facts learned to the law, conduct the investigation properly, and determine the various legal duties and obligations of the company. The critical reason for legal counsel to be in charge of an internal investigation is the creation and preservation of the attorney-client privilege to preserve communications between the client and counsel, and the work-product doctrine that protects the work product created during the investigation.

Q 6.7.1   How does legal counsel maintain the confidentiality of the investigation?

Proper involvement of legal counsel from the outset will provide the company with the ability to protect the investigation and its results through application of the attorney-client privilege and the work-product doctrine.[14] There may, of course, be instances in which it is in the company's best interests to disclose the results of an internal investigation, particularly to government criminal or regulatory agencies. In instances where this is *not* in the company's best interests, however, parties opposed to the company may attempt to compel disclosure of the internal investigation. In such instances, the attorney-client privilege and the work-product doctrine may be the only protection reasonably available to the company. Even where the ultimate result of an investigation is disclosure to the government, conducting the investigation under privilege gives the company the ability to control the timing and circumstances of any disclosure.

Q 6.7.2   Who is in charge of the investigation—inside counsel or outside counsel?

In selecting counsel, the obvious choices are between the company's in-house counsel (assuming it has inside counsel) and outside counsel. The company must be mindful, however, that use of in-house counsel may cause avoidable problems in preserving the attorney-client privilege, particularly where in-house counsel's duties in the company involve multiple non-legal roles, such as providing business advice in addition to legal advice, or reporting responsibilities to company constituencies that are not part of the internal investigation or to outside third parties such as auditors or governmental regulators. Such non-privileged disclosures and reports may serve as a waiver of the attorney-client privilege, thereby opening the files to the government and/or civil litigants, and potentially making in-house counsel a witness.

Another key consideration is whether in-house counsel has sufficient experience in conducting an internal investigation and dealing with the issues and parties involved in investigating allegations of wrongdoing such as prosecutors, inspectors general, attorneys general, and other regulators.

In addition, if the allegations of wrongdoing involve senior management, it may be particularly awkward for in-house counsel to conduct the investigation and also very difficult for in-house counsel to perform his or her other duties. Consideration must be given to questions of rank and authority within the company, as well as to personal relationships between in-house counsel and members of senior management whose actions may be under investigation. Even the appearance of internal influences on an investigation may fatally compromise its integrity in the eyes of the government and destroy its usefulness. The appearance of internal management influence on counsel conducting the investigation can also result in additional unwanted and avoidable civil litigation.

The company should also keep in mind that government criminal and regulatory authorities often identify in-house counsel as being "with the company" that it alleges has engaged in or permitted the misconduct, and because of that will be more circumspect in dealing with in-house counsel. Government authorities sometimes view in-house counsel as part of the problem and not part of the solution.

With these entrenched views, government authorities tend to believe that an internal investigation conducted by in-house counsel lacks independence and, therefore, lacks credibility. The need for independent outside counsel increases as the seriousness and complexity of the allegations increase. Retaining independent outside counsel is thus the best practice, especially when a criminal investigation is being conducted.

TIP: Decide at the outset who should be in charge of an investigation. Clearly designate one person to be in charge and to make the decisions. It is critical to the success of the investigation. As with any other endeavor, a lack of clear leadership and responsibility can cause confusion, resulting inevitably in conflicting goals and missed opportunities.

Staffing

Q 6.8   How are an investigation's staffing needs determined?

The staffing of an internal investigation is a function of the seriousness of the allegations involved.[15] Minor allegations of misconduct may be handled by the compliance and ethics officer, the human resources department, or an appropriate independent supervisor not involved in the alleged misconduct. More serious allegations may initially require handling by in-house or outside counsel. More complex matters may require the services of outside experts such as professional investigators, forensic accountants, computer forensics experts, or outside counsel who are familiar with the legal and practical issues involved with internal investigations in the particular industry.[16] Where the company is under criminal investigation, it should also seriously consider retaining additional staffing in the form of counsel for officers, directors, or employees who may be interviewed by government agents or served with grand jury subpoenas.

Q 6.8.1   What circumstances warrant the services of professional investigators?

Professional investigators are particularly useful in conducting complex criminal internal investigations, and their use should be carefully considered in the staffing process. Especially useful are former agents from government investigative agencies, who not only have a wealth of experience in conducting fact investigations and witness interviews, but also are skilled in applying the facts to the law. In addition, such investigators may already be familiar with the applicable statutes and regulations involved in the matter, as well as the investigating agency's internal procedures and, most usefully, the government agents conducting the investigation.

Q 6.8.2   Is the work of a professional investigator protected?

Yes, if investigators have been retained by counsel and supervised by counsel in order to bring their work under the umbrella of the attorney-client privilege and work-product doctrine.

Q 6.8.3   What circumstances warrant the services of forensic experts?

The term "forensics" refers to the use of science and technology in investigating and establishing facts. There are two basic categories of forensics experts commonly used in internal investigations.

Forensic accountants. Forensic accountants are particularly helpful in investigations involving allegations of financial irregularities, ranging from allegedly fraudulent reporting of financial information to financial fraud and embezzlement. Forensic accountants are normally employed for the purpose of reviewing and analyzing financial documents that have been seized or subpoenaed by law enforcement agents, or whose production has been demanded in the course of civil litigation. The more complicated the financial issues, the more likely their use will be necessary.

Computer forensics experts. These experts are increasingly important in the age of electronic data ("e-data") storage. It has become increasingly common in both criminal and civil matters for a company to receive broad demands for the retrieval and production of electronically stored data or "e-discovery."[17] Working with the company's IT personnel, computer forensics experts are particularly useful in determining *which* computer files need to be preserved and examined among the possibly thousands of computers and servers in the company, locating and preserving stored e-data, restoring deleted e-data, and efficiently searching e-data for relevant information. They are also extremely useful in ensuring the preservation of existing e-data. Depending on the size of the company, this can be a very complicated, difficult, and expensive task involving the imaging and examination of numerous computer drives and servers for relevant data, and then organizing that data for review and production.[18] In some cases, the company's internal IT department may not have the skills or time required to accomplish the task. Moreover, preservation conducted by an outside expert, as well as a search of e-data conducted by an outside expert, tends to be given greater credibility by government investigators and prosecutors, particularly when data retrieval issues arise, as they frequently do.

In deciding whether to retain forensic experts, the company must balance the cost of such experts against the consequences of the misconduct. The cost can easily reach six or even seven figures, depending on the complexity of the investigation. Balanced against this, however, may be the very survival of the company. Even when survival is not an issue, however, the cost may well be justified.[19]

Q 6.8.4   Is the work of a forensic expert protected?

As with outside professional investigators, forensic experts should be retained only through counsel and for the express purpose of acting in anticipation of litigation and assisting counsel in providing legal advice. Doing so ensures that the confidentiality of their work is protected by the attorney-client privilege and the work-product doctrine to the maximum extent possible.

Gathering Facts

Q 6.9   How are the facts in an investigation determined?

As a general rule, facts will be developed through the following three methods:

- •   Reviewing relevant documents,

- Reviewing relevant e-data, and
- Conducting personal interviews.

Document and Data Preservation and Collection

Q 6.10 How should a company approach its documents and e-data at the initiation of an investigation?

Documents are important in establishing relevant information and an evidentiary trail of information, communication, and knowledge among persons involved in the alleged misconduct. Accordingly, it is crucial at the outset of any investigation to ensure that all potentially relevant documents are preserved, and are not inadvertently or intentionally destroyed. Because of the importance of relevant documents and e-data, it is essential that the company do two things at the very outset of the internal investigation: (1) prevent the destruction of potentially relevant information, and (2) identify what documents and e-data are, or are likely to become, relevant to the investigation.

Q 6.10.1 How does an investigation affect a company's routine document destruction policies?

Since it is more difficult and time-consuming to accurately identify relevant documents and data, and since the definition of what is relevant is likely to change as the investigation progresses, it is generally the best practice—especially when a government subpoena has been issued or litigation has started—to immediately suspend routine document destruction policies until further notice. After the investigation has become more focused and the definition of what is relevant is more certain, some limited routine document destruction policies may be reinstated.

TIP: In a criminal investigation, the government is likely to view the destruction of *any* relevant documents as either criminally reckless or an intentional obstruction of justice.[20]

Q 6.10.2 Is e-data subject to the same ban on destruction?

Yes, but the preservation of e-data is more complicated, largely because the deletion or destruction of e-data usually occurs automatically by operation of other electronic programs. It is therefore essential for the company to clearly convey the suspension of *all* document destruction policies and procedures directly to the company's IT department. This should not be left to merely sending a memo. Counsel in charge of the internal investigation, together with (if necessary) assistants who are well trained in and thoroughly familiar with the storage, retrieval, and preservation of electronically stored data, should meet personally with the head of the IT department and that person's key personnel, in order to ensure that the data preservation message is perfectly clear and that *all* routine electronic data deletion or destruction programs have been turned off. Moreover, such meetings should be followed up periodically to ensure that the directive continues to be followed and that no accidental reinstatement of automatic data destruction software has occurred.

Q 6.10.3 Is the e-data preservation directive confined to the on-site locations?

Another key component in preserving relevant e-data is to identify all locations where electronic data is stored. The number of potential locations is large and growing. Key locations include desktops, servers, backup tapes, laptops, PDAs, cell phones, email (both on the company's system and in individually stored folders), and voice mail. Electronic data, including emails and hard drives, will often establish a record of who created, edited, viewed, and forwarded certain documents or emails.

It is critical to identify all relevant e-data storage locations and take steps to preserve all potentially relevant information stored on them. This may involve imaging hard drives and servers, and should be done in consultation with the IT department, outside e-discovery consultants, or both. Imaging of employees' *home* computers may also be necessary, given the prevalence of many employees who work and communicate with other employees, vendors, or customers from home.

Q 6.10.4   How can documents/data be classified as relevant?

What documents and e-data will be relevant to an internal investigation will depend on the basis for the investigation and its scope.

Internal, non-criminal inquiry. Relevance can be expected to be relatively narrow, focusing on particular individuals, their computers, and documents.

External allegations of misconduct, particularly government-initiated criminal investigations. Relevance is more difficult to determine and more likely to change during the course of the litigation or government investigation.

> **TIP:** Failing to identify accurately what is potentially relevant can, as noted above, have severe consequences for the company, including new charges (such as obstruction of justice) that are not directly related to the original, underlying criminal allegations. Given the severe consequences of failing to adequately identify and preserve relevant documents and data, the best practice is to take an expansive view of relevance at the outset of the internal investigation and to continue to preserve as much material as practicable.

Q 6.10.5   Where can we look for guidance in identifying relevant documents/data in external allegations of criminal misconduct?

Government agent and prosecutor. The government agent and prosecutor involved in serving a search warrant or issuing a subpoena will in many cases be willing to provide useful information regarding the alleged misconduct and the scope of the investigation, and they should never be disregarded as a potential source of information.[21] In fact, a simple telephone call to the prosecutor (whose name and phone number will be on the warrant or the subpoena) can save a great deal of time and often provides accurate information and guidance to the company. Such a call, however, should be made by counsel *only*. During the call, counsel will ask whether the company or any of its officers, directors, or employees are considered targets, subjects, or witnesses in the investigation. Counsel will seek as much information as possible about the investigation, including who else besides the client is involved in the investigation. The information provided can then be used to establish parameters for preservation of data. Often, company counsel can negotiate the terms of the preservation process with a prosecutor or investigator. Such agreements should be reduced to writing so that a different government lawyer or investigator cannot second-guess the failure to preserve certain categories of records.

Court orders and document requests. In most cases, some initial guidance can also be found by careful analysis of document requests, subpoenas, or search warrants (particularly the underlying affidavit of probable cause, although this is usually put under seal by the court issuing the warrant until the government agrees to its disclosure).

Government interview of company employees. In situations where the government has already begun to conduct interviews of company employees, an analysis of the questions asked by the government agents can also provide substantial guidance. In debriefing employees who have been interviewed by government agents, however, great care must be taken to avoid creating the impression that the company is attempting to influence the testimony of its employees or is engaging in any sort of pressure on them. Such tactics will be viewed *very* negatively by the government, can jeopardize the company's credibility with the government, and can even create the impression that the company is attempting to obstruct justice (itself a criminal act). Accordingly, debriefings of company employees who have been interviewed by government agents should be carefully conducted and closely monitored, and then *only* by highly experienced counsel.

Q 6.10.6 What steps should the company take to collect relevant documents for review by counsel?

It is essential in any internal investigation to collect all relevant documents for review by counsel. This is especially the case where the company is responding to a grand jury subpoena or a civil litigation demand for documents, because failure to identify and produce all responsive documents can have extremely adverse consequences to the company.

The first step is to issue a "litigation hold" announcement. The second step is to appoint a "records custodian," who will be in charge of document collection and who will be available to testify if necessary. Because of the possibility of giving testimony, the custodian should *not* be in-house or outside counsel.

Q 6.10.7   What is a "litigation hold"?

A litigation hold is the formal suspension of the company's document retention and destruction policies. It is done to prevent the accidental destruction of documents that may be relevant to a subpoena, a civil lawsuit, or a regulatory summons to produce documents. It should cover all documents arguably relevant to a subpoena or summons, both paper and electronic, both in existence at the time the litigation hold is issued, and also those created afterward. In civil litigation, the litigation hold should cover all documents relevant to the claims or defenses of any party, not just the company. It notifies key employees of document preservation requirements. This particularly includes electronic document destruction policies and procedures, such as routine deletion of emails and recycling of backup tapes (*see also* Q 5.9).

Q 6.10.8   When should a litigation hold be imposed?

A litigation hold should be imposed as soon as the duty to preserve documents arises. For a subpoena or summons, this usually occurs upon service, although if the company has advance notice it arises with the notice itself. In civil litigation, it generally occurs when the company becomes aware of, or is put on notice of, litigation. This can happen when the company is served with a lawsuit complaint, but it can also occur earlier, such as upon the receipt of a demand letter from a potential litigant.

Imposing a "litigation hold" policy is sometimes referred to as the "Zubulake Duty" because it was first and most eloquently expressed by U.S. District Court Judge Scheindlin in *Zubulake v. UBS* (referred to as "*Zubulake V*").[22] *Zubulake V* requires *counsel* to make certain that all potentially relevant electronic data are identified and placed "on hold." This places a heavy duty on counsel. The company and its counsel (in-house or outside) can be severely sanctioned for failure to adequately perform this duty.[23]

Q 6.10.9   What are the responsibilities of the "records custodian"?

In collecting all relevant documents (especially when the company is responding to a subpoena or civil discovery demand), the company should appoint one person to be the company's official records custodian, who will be responsible for searching and collecting responsive documents. That person should work closely with counsel to identify all persons and departments that may have any relevant or responsive documents. The official records custodian should then issue to those persons a written communication (prepared by or under the supervision of counsel) describing the relevant documents and asking each person to respond by a date certain and in writing, stating whether he or she is in possession of such materials. The response, as well as the request, should be in writing, and both should be kept in the record custodian's files. If the responding person has relevant documents, the originals should be forwarded to the records custodian by the responding person. The records custodian should keep a record of exactly which documents were produced by which person and the precise location of the documents when found, because this information may become extremely important. If the documents are to be produced to the government or other third party, they should be reviewed by counsel prior to disclosure in order to identify any attorney-client-privileged material, which should then be either excluded from production or redacted to remove privileged material.

Interviews

Q 6.11 Who must be interviewed?

Depending on the subject matter and scope of the internal investigation, the company may want to interview current and former officers, directors, employees, and agents of the company. It may also necessarily include interviews of other persons not currently or formerly connected with the company.

Q 6.11.1   When should interviews take place?

Whenever practical, the interviews should not take place until after the company has thoroughly reviewed relevant documents and e-data. Accurate information is crucial to the success of the internal investigation, and accuracy will be greatly enhanced if the persons conducting the interview know as much as possible *before* beginning it. Moreover, while the company may request several interviews with its own employees, persons who are not employed by the company might agree to be interviewed only once. Multiple interviews of the same persons may be inevitable in some cases because additional information will be coming in continuously from other interviews. From an efficiency point of view, though, it is generally best to know as much as possible about the company documents and e-data before conducting the *first* interview. While this is generally a best practice, it must be understood that it is not always practically possible because of the speed with which a particular internal investigation must be conducted. The company may not always have the luxury of time on its side.

Q 6.11.2   Who should conduct the interviews?

These interviews can be particularly sensitive, especially in criminal cases, and should only be conducted by experienced counsel.

Whenever possible, two persons should conduct each interview. It need not always be the same two persons, and interviews may be conducted by different teams of interviewers. However, if teams are used, it is very important for each team to always be *fully informed* of all information that other teams have collected.

Preferably, one of the two interviewers should be a lawyer acting on the company's behalf and in anticipation of litigation, in order to provide maximum confidentiality under the attorney-client privilege/work-product doctrine for any notes taken during the interview. The second person can be an investigator, who can serve as a witness to what was said. Having a lawyer as one of the interviewers is not absolutely necessary, however, as long as the interviewers are acting at the direction of legal counsel. Having two persons conduct each interview will help avoid subsequent misunderstanding of what the witness actually said, and in the event that the witness changes his or her story, the company will have a friendly witness to impeach the witness's credibility.

Q 6.11.3   Who do the interviewers represent?

The persons conducting the interview must clearly understand that they represent only the *company* and not the person interviewed, and they must make that clear to the person interviewed, especially when interviewing company officers, directors, and employees. This should be made clear to every witness at the beginning of the interview.

Q 6.11.4   What should the interviewers tell persons who are interviewed?

Especially when interviewing current and former officers, directors, employees, and agents of the company (collectively referred to in this section as the "witness"), the "*Upjohn* warnings" should be given before the interview begins. These warnings are based on the U.S. Supreme Court case of *Upjohn v. United States*, which concerned the scope of the corporate attorney-client privilege.[24] The *Upjohn* warnings should be given to each witness without exception.

Q 6.11.5   How are *Upjohn* warnings given to a witness?

The *Upjohn* warnings are normally given orally; however, they should be based on a prepared written statement to ensure they are given consistently and accurately each time. The fact that the warning was given should be memorialized for each witness interview by either referring to the fact in the handwritten notes of the interview or in a formal memorandum of interview. Some counsel prefer to provide the witness with a written statement of the warnings and have the witness acknowledge them by signing the written statement and keeping it as part of the interview file. This reduces the risk of a witness later claiming that the warnings were not complete or clear. Other counsel prefer to give the warnings orally because they believe a signed written statement is too formal and may have a chilling effect on the witness's cooperation. Whether to give the warning orally or in a written document signed by the witness is a judgment call; the more common practice is to do it orally. However, if the law firm in charge of the internal investigation has ever personally represented a witness for any purpose (whether or not related to the matter under investigation), the warnings should be provided in a written document signed by the witness. This helps to ensure and record that there is no confusion on the part of the witness that the interview is not part of the prior personal attorney-client relationship that counsel had with the witness.[25]

Q 6.11.6   What should be included in the *Upjohn* warnings?

The interviewer should make it clear to the witness, explicitly and unambiguously, that the person conducting the internal investigation is representing the company and not representing the witness.

The purpose of the interview—to gather information for the company in order to provide it with legal advice—should also be made clear.

The interviewer should advise the witness that

- the interview is subject to the company's attorney-client privilege;
- the privilege belongs only to the company, not to the witness;
- it is up to the company alone to decide whether and when the interview should be disclosed to third parties (specifically including federal or state agencies), therefore it is considered to be confidential; and
- the company may make this decision without the consent of the witness.

(The interviewer might also consider telling the witness that any federal or state agencies the company decides to disclose the information to might regard false statements provided by the witness in the interview as a prosecutable criminal offense.)

The witness should be told that he or she may not disclose the questions asked or the answers given to any third parties (whether inside or outside of the company) because that could waive the company's attorney-client privilege. It should be further explained to the witness, however, that, while the interview (that is, the questions asked and the answers given) is subject to the company's attorney-client privilege, and that the privilege belongs only to the company, the *facts* disclosed by the witness are not privileged and may be disclosed to other interviewers (including government agents) without waiving the company's privilege.

The interviewer should ensure that the witness understands his or her relationship with counsel by giving the witness the opportunity to ask questions about the *Upjohn* warnings.

Q 6.11.7 Is there a standard form for *Upjohn* warnings?

A suggested *Upjohn* warning was issued in July 2009 by the Upjohn Warnings Task Force established by the White Collar Crime Committee of the American Bar Association:

> I am a lawyer for or from Corporation A. I represent only Corporation A, and I do not represent you personally.
>
> I am conducting this interview to gather facts in order to provide legal advice for Corporation A. This interview is part of an investigation to determine the facts and circumstances of X in order to advise Corporation A how best to proceed.
>
> Your communications with me are protected by the attorney-client privilege. But the attorney-client privilege belongs solely to Corporation A, not you. That means that Corporation A alone may elect to waive the attorney-client privilege and reveal our discussion to third parties. Corporation A alone may decide to waive the privilege and disclose this discussion to such third parties as federal or state agencies, at its sole discretion, and without notifying you.
>
> In order for this discussion to be subject to the privilege, it must be kept in confidence. In other words, with the exception of your own attorney, you may not disclose the substance of this interview to any third party, including other employees or anyone outside of the company. You may discuss the facts of what happened but you may not discuss *this* discussion.
>
> Do you have any questions?
>
> Are you willing to proceed?[26]

Q 6.11.8   Is a witness allowed to have separate counsel?

A witness may ask the interviewer whether the witness needs separate counsel. This frequently occurs. The interviewer should explain to the witness that the interviewer cannot advise the witness on this issue, but that the witness has a right to have separate counsel. If the company has agreed to provide counsel for witnesses, the interviewer should consider telling the witness so and allowing the witness to consult with that counsel before proceeding with the interview.

> **TIP:** Before engaging in any substantive questioning, the interviewers should tell the witness that:
> * they represent the company only;
> * they do not represent the witness in any capacity;
> * they are conducting the interview as part of an internal investigation being conducted by and for the company;
> * what the witness tells them will not be protected by the attorney-client or any other privilege; and
> * the company reserves the right to disclose any information provided by the witness at any time and to any person or agency, including government law enforcement agencies.[27]

Q 6.11.9   What happens if the witness refuses to cooperate?

If the interviewer is asked what will happen if the witness refuses to cooperate in the internal investigation, the witness should be informed of the company policies (if any) applicable to an internal investigation. Most companies as a matter of policy will discipline employees who refuse to cooperate in internal investigations, up to and including termination of employment.

Q 6.11.10 Is the interview privileged?

The persons conducting the interview must understand that the confidentiality of the interview itself is only protected under the *company's* attorney-client privilege.[28] While the interviewers' mental impressions, interview notes, and subsequent written reports of the interview can be protected as part of the company's attorney-client privilege and the work-product doctrine, it is possible that the person interviewed may inadvertently waive that privilege by disclosing to third parties what was said during the interview. The interviewers represent the company, not the witness, so there is no direct attorney-client privilege between the person interviewed and the interviewer. Instead, the only privilege that attaches to the interview is the *company's*.

Q 6.11.11 Is the witness covered by the privilege?

There is no attorney-client relationship between the interviewer and the witness. However, the content of the interview (that is, the questions asked and the answers given) is covered by the company's attorney-client privilege and the work-product doctrine.

Great care should therefore be taken by the interviewer to ensure that the *company's* privilege attaches, to the greatest extent possible, to the interview. In addition to clearly explaining that the privilege belongs to the *company*, the interviewer should caution the person interviewed that the contents of the interview should not be disclosed to third parties unless specifically authorized by the company in order to avoid an inadvertent waiver of the company's privilege. It should be explained that, while the facts discussed in the interview are not themselves privileged, what the interviewer asks during the interview and the answers given by the witness *are* privileged. Thus, for example, the witness may subsequently be interviewed by government law enforcement agents about the same facts without waiving the company's privilege. Accordingly, the witness should be cautioned that, if asked by any third party (including government agents) what was said by anyone during the internal investigation interview, the witness should assert the company's attorney-client privilege unless otherwise instructed by the company. This should be carefully explained to each witness.

Q 6.11.12 Can the confidentiality of the information disclosed during an interview be waived?

The interviewers should be careful of any remarks they make or any information they disclose to the witness during the interview. Aside from the possibility of inadvertent waiver of the company's privilege by the witness, for all the interviewers know, the witness they are interviewing may be a government source or informant in a criminal case or may be providing information to actual or potential parties opposing the company in civil litigation. Accordingly, the interviewers must keep in mind at all times that anything they say during the course of the interview, any documents they show the witness, and any questions they ask may *not* be treated as privileged or confidential.

> **TIP:** Great care must be taken by the interviewers to avoid creating the impression that they are attempting in any way to influence or intimidate the witness or, in a criminal case, to obstruct justice or prevent a witness from speaking with government agents. Any such impression can easily lead to further civil or criminal charges against the company.

Company Disclosure of the Investigation to Employees

Q 6.12 Should notice be given to the entire company that an internal investigation is under way?

Depending upon the scope of the internal investigation, counsel should consider notifying appropriate employees that the investigation has begun. Internal investigations are generally not a matter that can be effectively conducted in secret. As the investigation proceeds, more and more personnel will become aware of it and, if appropriate action is not taken at the outset, the "rumor mill" will inevitably start to operate. Frequently, unfounded rumors can quickly spread and grow out of control, causing damaging reports to circulate throughout the company and resulting in far more damage to company morale than the truth could ever cause.

Q 6.12.1 Should the notice identify the investigated employees or group of employees?

The notice need not and should not name any particular person or group as the subject of the investigation, nor should it repeat any allegations being made. It is sufficient simply to give notice to employees that an investigation has been commenced.

Q 6.12.2   How should the notice be circulated?

The notice should be sent to the appropriate managers, who should in turn distribute it to the appropriate employees under their supervision. The "appropriate" managers and employees include those who may have any potentially relevant documents, emails or other electronic documents in their possession, custody, or control, and those who may be interviewed during the course of the investigation.

Q 6.12.3   Should a notice include a statement in defense of the company?

If the matter involves a grand jury subpoena or a criminal or regulatory investigation, the notice should briefly and clearly explain in a neutral fashion that the company has received a subpoena or is under criminal or regulatory investigation *without editorializing* on the validity of the investigation or the facts involved. While the company may and should state that it is confident it has not engaged in any wrongdoing, and that it is voluntarily complying with the subpoena or with the government's investigation (as the case may be), it should refrain from any offensive tactics or remarks, such as characterizing the subpoena or investigation as being "politically motivated" or a "witch hunt." Such remarks may appear to be merely defensive; indeed, company management may believe implicitly in the truth of such remarks. Nevertheless, such remarks accomplish nothing, but somehow find their way to the prosecutor or regulator, almost always with adverse consequences for the company.

Q 6.12.4   What information should be included in the notice?

The notice should:

- Inform employees about who is conducting the internal investigation and that the company expects their full and truthful cooperation;
- Remind employees that their first loyalty must be to the company, and not to any particular individuals, colleagues, supervisors, or groups; and

- Warn employees that the existence of the investigation is not a matter to be discussed outside the company or with persons inside the company who have no need to know about it.

Q 6.12.5 What information should be included in a notice if the company is under a criminal investigation?

If the company itself is involved in a criminal investigation, there is a great likelihood that law enforcement agents will either ask the company to make certain employees available for interviews, or that law enforcement agents may on their own directly contact certain employees for interview. Under these circumstances, employees should be warned that either may occur.

In giving such notice, the company should stress that it is imperative that all employees be entirely truthful with law enforcement interviewers and that providing false information may itself be a crime. In addition, employees may be advised by the company, in a *completely neutral fashion*, of their rights if they are approached by law enforcement agents for an interview.

Q 6.12.6 What are an employee's rights if he is approached by law enforcement agents for an interview?

The company may tell their employees that they may:

(1) give an interview if they wish;
(2) refuse to give an interview if they wish; or
(3) request that they be interviewed only in the presence of an attorney.

TIP: A company must consult carefully with counsel before providing employees any explanation of their rights. It is imperative that the company not appear to be advising its employees *not* to agree to an interview by law enforcement. This will create the impression that the company is attempting to impede or obstruct the government's investigation, which may itself constitute a criminal act and will have very adverse consequences for the company.

Q 6.12.7 Should the company obtain and pay for legal representation for officers, directors, or employees who may be interviewed by law enforcement agents?

Many employees are understandably intimidated by the prospect of being interviewed by law enforcement agents, so it is generally the best practice to offer to provide an attorney for them to consult with before such an interview and to attend the interview with them. If the company does this, it should tell its employees (as part of the information discussed above) that counsel will be made available for them on the employee's request, that the company will select the lawyer who will represent them, and that the lawyer will be made available at the company's expense but will be representing the employee and not the company. As a cost-control measure, however, it should be made clear that employees may retain *any* lawyer of their choice, but that, if an employee retains a lawyer other than the one selected by the company, that employee will be solely responsible for the legal fees incurred. The lawyer retained by the company should be someone who understands that he or she is representing the employee(s) and not the company, but who will be willing to work cooperatively with the company's counsel.

The same is true for officers and directors as well. Here, however, it is generally best practice to allow them to select their own counsel, subject to approval of the fee arrangement by the company.

Neither the company's in-house counsel nor its outside counsel should represent individual officers, directors, or employees as well as the company because of the possibility that potential conflicts will arise between the company and the individuals, which could result in the disqualification of the company's counsel from representing the company.

Q 6.12.8 If the company obtains counsel for officers, directors, or employees, should it enter into a joint defense agreement with that counsel?

A joint defense agreement is an agreement among individually represented parties that extends the attorney-client privilege among the participants so as to form a common "joint defense privilege." Joint defense agreements are available in both criminal and civil matters litigation, and they may be oral, although many practitioners and some courts prefer them to be in writing.

The chief benefit to having a joint defense privilege is that it protects the confidentiality of communications passing from one party to the attorney for another party. However, the decision to enter into a joint defense agreement should be carefully considered by counsel for the company, especially in a criminal investigation, because the benefits of protected information-sharing may be outweighed by the complications caused if the company decides it wants to waive its attorney-client privilege and cooperate with the government. A written joint defense agreement should be very carefully drafted by experienced counsel to minimize risks to the company.

Q 6.12.9 What if an officer, director, or employee is named as a subject or target of a criminal investigation?

Officers, directors, or employees who are named as subjects or targets of a criminal investigation should necessarily be segregated completely from every aspect of the company's internal investigation. In regard to retaining counsel for them, the government, until 2008, considered this to indicate a lack of cooperation on the part of the company. Since then, however, the government no longer takes that position.[29] In some cases, state law requires the company to indemnify officers and directors for their legal expenses arising from their activities as officers or directors. In other cases, the company's governing documents (such as articles of incorporation or bylaws) require or authorize such indemnification. And often the company has an insurance policy that covers these legal expenses incurred by officers and directors. In deciding whether to pay for legal representation for these persons, the company should always check state law, its governing documents, and its D&O insurance policy as part of the decision-making process.

Q 6.12.10 What other information should be contained in the notice to employees?

Employees should be warned:

(1)   Do not engage in "coffee room" or "water cooler" gossip;

(2)   Do not discuss the existence of the investigation, or any matter related to it, with any persons (especially media) outside the company;

(3)   Do not discuss any aspect of the investigation with other persons *within* the company, except those who need to know (such as their supervisors) and, of course, the persons conducting the investigation;

(4)   Do not send any emails or memos about the investigation to anyone unless expressly told to do so by counsel or the persons conducting the investigation (such unauthorized emails will probably not be protected by the attorney-client privilege or the work-product doctrine from subsequent forced disclosure, and may be very damaging to the company);

(5)   Do not engage in any document or e-data destruction, alteration, or deletion, especially at the early stages. It is often unclear what documents may prove to be relevant, particularly where the investigation was prompted by a grand jury subpoena or civil demand for documents, and the destruction or alteration of relevant, responsive documents and e-data may have extremely serious, adverse consequences;

(6)   Do not prepare any "defensive" memos or emails, even those addressed "to the file" or to the author, because they will not be protected by the attorney-client privilege or work-product doctrine and may be very damaging to the company, other employees, or even the author;

(7)   Do not make any verbal or written remarks (including emails) that are intended as jokes and that may come across later as serious communications (*e.g.*, "Hey, they finally caught you. Ha-ha!"). Judges, juries, and opposing civil litigants have notoriously poor senses of humor.

Employees should be warned that they *should*:

(a)   Cooperate fully and truthfully with the persons conducting the internal investigation;

(b)   Preserve all documents and e-data, and immediately suspend all document and e-data destruction or deletion policies and procedures until further notice;

(c)   Know who the company media spokesperson is, if the company has appointed one (together with his or her contact information), and refer *all* outside inquiries regarding the investigation or anything related directly or indirectly to it to that person; and

(d) Immediately report any outside inquiries (especially including, but not limited to, media or press inquiries) to either the employee's immediate supervisor or the company spokesperson (every supervisor should be instructed to immediately refer such inquiries directly to counsel).

TIP: Have company counsel review any notice to employees before issuing it, especially if it includes any discussion of employees' rights in regard to interviews by government agents. If the matter already is, or may become, a matter of public interest, the company should consider appointing one or more persons to act as its media spokesperson, and if this is done, all employees should be advised of who those persons are and that they should refer all outside inquiries to them. Finally, depending upon the nature of the matter under investigation, the company should consider retaining a media relations specialist. In this regard, care should be taken to take the appropriate steps to preserve, to the extent possible, the company's attorney-client privilege and the attorney work-product protection.

Privileged Information

Privileges

Q 6.13 Should internal investigations be kept confidential?

Yes. Protection of the internal investigation from disclosure to third parties is essential for a company. The internal investigation may contain extremely sensitive or damaging information that can be used by the government in a prosecution of the company (or its officers, employees, or directors) or by hostile parties suing, or seeking grounds to sue, the company. Frequently, the internal investigation will contain damaging information that may actually provide a road map of wrongdoing to parties hostile to the company. It is therefore essential that the investigation be conducted at every step in such a manner as to ensure, to the maximum extent possible, all available legal protections against forced disclosure, particularly including the attorney-client privilege and the work-product doctrine. This means that the disclosure of any reports regarding the investigation should be limited only to those in the company with a real "need to know." It may be the case, especially in a criminal or regulatory investigation, that it is in the company's best interests to disclose the results of an internal investigation to the government. But this should be the company's decision; *forced* disclosure by subpoena or civil discovery demands should be avoided at all costs.

Q 6.13.1   How are internal investigations protected?

The attorney-client privilege and the work-product doctrine are the primary legally recognized means by which the internal investigation can be protected from disclosure.[30] Care must be taken at every step of the internal investigation to safeguard these privileges to the extent they are applicable.

Attorney-Client Privilege

Q 6.14 When does the attorney-client privilege attach?

Every company has an attorney-client privilege, but like the attorney-client privilege between individuals and their lawyers, it will apply only under certain conditions, and it may be waived inadvertently.

Generally, corporate communications, including internal investigation discussions and witness interviews, will be protected by the attorney-client privilege when:

(1) the communication is made for the purpose of securing legal advice for the company;

(2) the employee making the communication does so at the request or direction of a company supervisor (for the purpose of the company securing legal advice);[31]

(3) the subject of the communication is within the scope of the employee's employment; and

195

(4)   the communication is not disclosed beyond those within the company who need to know it.[32]

TIP: The essential element in establishing attorney-client privilege is that the communication is made *for the purpose of the company securing legal advice*. So, take care to ensure in every step of an internal investigation that there is a record of the purpose of an internal investigation activity and that the specific purpose is to enable counsel to gather the necessary information to provide legal advice to the company concerning the events that gave rise to the internal investigation.

Q 6.14.1   Does the privilege apply to communications with former employees?

Not all courts have applied the privilege to *former* employees. Therefore, before engaging in any such communications, counsel should first determine the law of the jurisdiction involved. Further, the question may not necessarily arise in the jurisdiction in which the interview is conducted or the company is located. For example, a third party may try to compel disclosure in Illinois of an interview conducted in Virginia. For these reasons, even if it appears that the interview of a former employee *may* be protected, consideration must be given to whether it is necessary for a complete internal investigation, and if the interview is conducted, the interviewer should keep in mind that it may *not* be privileged.

Q 6.14.2   Does the privilege apply to communications with third parties?

Interviews with third parties are almost certainly *not* protected by the privilege. For example, take an internal investigation of employee embezzlement in which the employee set up a mail drop for diverted company funds. An interview with the persons involved in the mail drop will not be privileged (although it may receive limited protection under the work-product doctrine). This raises the question of how to treat third parties such as outside consultants, that is, forensic accountants, computer forensics experts, and media relations consultants. Generally, if a third-party consultant has been retained through counsel for the express purpose of providing legal advice, then the communications are expressly confidential; and if the consultant is necessary for effective communication between counsel and the company, then the privilege may apply.[33]

Q 6.14.3   Is the attorney-client privilege absolute?

No. The attorney-client privilege will not be applied to prevent a forced disclosure of communications with counsel when the attorney has been consulted "to further a continuing or contemplated criminal or fraudulent scheme."[34] This exception to the privilege is known as the crime-fraud exception. If a client consults an attorney for the purpose of furthering a *continuing or ongoing* crime or fraudulent scheme, then the privilege will not apply, regardless of the party to whom it ostensibly belongs. The burden of establishing the crime-fraud exception to the privilege is on the party seeking to overcome an asserted privilege and compel disclosure.

Q 6.14.4   Does the crime-fraud exception apply to all disclosures of criminal activity?

No. The crime-fraud exception does not apply to disclosures of past wrongdoing made by a client to counsel for the purpose of seeking legal advice. Thus, a disclosure (or admission) of past criminal activity to one's lawyer will be protected by the privilege. Similarly, disclosures of past criminal conduct by an officer, director, or employee to the *company's* attorney will be protected from disclosure by the *company's* privilege.

Q 6.14.5   May a disclosing witness prevent a company from disclosing their admission of past criminal conduct?

Since the privilege belongs to the *company* in an internal investigation, it is up to the *company*, not to the *disclosing witness*, to decide whether to waive the privilege and disclose the communication.

Work-Product Doctrine

Q 6.15 What is protected under the work-product doctrine?

The work-product doctrine protects documents—such as memos and reports of interviews, notes of interviews, and written reports— that were prepared in anticipation of litigation or trial, unless the party seeking them demonstrates "substantial need" and "undue hardship." The doctrine is expressly recognized by Federal Rule of Civil Procedure 26(b)(3) and is applied by virtually every jurisdiction. However, the "crime fraud" exception to the attorney-client privilege also applies to the work-product doctrine.

Q 6.15.1 How does the scope of the work-product doctrine compare to that of the attorney-client privilege?

The scope of the work-product doctrine is broader than that of the attorney-client privilege in that it can cover the work product that results from even *non-privileged* communications. As in the earlier example of an internal investigation of employee embezzlement in which the employee set up a mail drop for diverted company funds, although the communications exchanged in the interview with the "mail drop" third party are not protected by the attorney-client privilege, the notes or report of that interview may still be protected from disclosure under the work-product doctrine as long as they were prepared in anticipation of litigation.

> **TIP:** In order to establish that the materials were prepared in anticipation of litigation, it is the better practice for the work product to have been prepared at the direction of counsel.

Q 6.15.2 Must a company release its entire work product upon a third party's showing of substantial need and undue hardship?

The mental impressions, conclusions, or opinions of counsel will not be subject to disclosure even if a party can demonstrate "substantial need" and "undue hardship." This includes purely factual data, such as company documents that have been compiled by or at the direction of counsel in anticipation of litigation, although the documents themselves are not privileged. Thus, the written interim or final reports of an internal investigation, including underlying memos of witness interviews, are generally not subject to forced disclosure by third parties as long as they are prepared in anticipation of litigation, by or at the direction of counsel, and contain the authors' mental impressions or conclusions.

Waiver of the Attorney-Client Privilege and Work-Product Protection

Q 6.16 Can the attorney-client privilege and work-product protection be waived?

The attorney-client privilege and the work-product protection can be waived either intentionally or inadvertently. An intentional waiver will occur if the company decides to make a voluntary disclosure of the privileged or protected information to any third party, including the government. An inadvertent waiver may occur if the company unwittingly discloses the privileged or protected information in response to a civil litigation discovery request or in response to a government subpoena, although in September 2008, the Federal Rules of Evidence were amended to limit the scope of subject matter waiver and the impact of inadvertent disclosure of privileged material.

Q 6.16.1 What motivates companies to waive their privileges?

Companies often make voluntary disclosures in an attempt to quickly resolve wrongdoing and avoid harsher penalties that may be imposed after a full investigation by the government.

Under the Federal Sentencing Guidelines, a voluntary disclosure of pertinent information and cooperation with the government reduces the corporation's offense level in the guideline calculation, thereby reducing the potential sentence under the Guidelines.[35]

Q 6.16.2   What is required under a voluntary disclosure?[36]

A voluntary disclosure typically requires complete, full, and truthful disclosure of the alleged improper conduct. This principle often means that, before deciding to trust the disclosing party, the government may expect a waiver of the privileges and disclosure of all relevant information developed during the internal investigation—although, as explained below, the extent to which the government can seek a waiver is a complicated and controversial topic. Regardless of whether the government formally requests a waiver, full disclosure will frequently include information gained during the course of the internal investigation and might well require at least a limited waiver of the privileges.

Q 6.16.3   What is the scope of a waiver of the attorney-client privilege or work-product protection?

Voluntary production of privileged or protected information to the government, or to any third party, may effect a *general* waiver of the privilege and protection as to all the world. This leaves documents such as interview notes and memoranda, as well as attorney-opinion analyses, subject to discovery in *civil* litigation if the information is relevant to it. Most courts have been hostile to attempts by companies to engage in "limited waivers" of privileged or protected information.[37] Companies should generally expect that a voluntary disclosure of otherwise privileged and protected information to one party, including the government, will be considered to be a waiver as to all the world, and that hostile civil litigants will use the waiver as grounds for disclosure in the civil litigation. Also be aware of the possibility that waiver of the privilege by disclosure can also result in a waiver of the privilege as to the entire subject matter at issue, depending on the jurisdiction.

Federal Prosecutorial Guidelines on Waiver

Q 6.17 What guidelines do federal prosecutors follow when seeking a waiver of the attorney-client privilege and the attorney work-product protection?

In order to understand the guidelines followed by federal prosecutors in regard to a company's attorney-client privilege and attorney work-product protection, it is necessary to understand the changing history of the Department of Justice guidelines for charging businesses with criminal conduct. This is reflected in a series of Department of Justice memoranda issued between 1999 and 2008 and referred to as the Holder Memorandum, the Thompson Memorandum, the McNulty Memorandum, and the Filip Memorandum.

Q 6.17.1   What is the Holder Memorandum?

This memorandum contained guidelines that instructed federal prosecutors evaluating the level of a company's cooperation to consider, among other things, its willingness to waive its attorney-client and work-product protections.[38] This policy was reiterated in January 2003 by its successor, the Thompson Memorandum.

Q 6.17.2   What is the Thompson Memorandum?

The Thompson Memorandum updated the guidelines but continued the waiver considerations included in the Holder Memorandum.[39] Based on the guidelines in these memoranda, federal prosecutors routinely required companies to waive the privilege in order to either avoid criminal prosecution or secure cooperation status for sentencing credit.

The Justice Department's policy on waiver was subject to severe and continuing criticism, which culminated in a U.S. district court opinion severely critical of the Thompson Memorandum guidelines, and in the introduction of proposed remedial federal legislation designed to overturn a number of its key provisions, including the policy regarding waiver of the privilege. The district court opinion, issued in June 2006 by District Court Judge Kaplan in *United States v. Stein*,[40] held that the use of the Thompson Memorandum to pressure KPMG to refuse to indemnify its employees' legal fees incurred in their defense against the criminal charges violated the Fifth and Sixth Amendments, and criminal charges against thirteen KPMG officers and directors were dismissed. The *Stein* opinion was later upheld in August 2008 by the Second Circuit.[41]

Six months after the district court's opinion in *Stein*, the Attorney-Client Privilege Protection Act of 2006 was introduced in Congress.[42] Although this proposed legislation was not passed, it would have prohibited government prosecutors from considering a company's willingness to waive its attorney-client privilege as a factor in determining whether the company had cooperated with the government. The bill would also have prohibited government prosecutors from considering whether the company had agreed to indemnify its employees' legal fees in the investigation or had entered into a joint defense agreement.

Largely in response to both the *Stein* opinion and the proposed legislation, Deputy Attorney General Paul J. McNulty issued a new memorandum to Justice Department prosecutors in December 2006.[43]

Q 6.17.3   What is the McNulty Memorandum?

The McNulty Memorandum outlined new guidelines for federal prosecutors to follow when seeking a privilege waiver from a company. The McNulty Memorandum allowed federal prosecutors to seek a waiver only where there was a "legitimate need" for the privileged information, and then only after they had first obtained supervisory-level approval. Even with such approval, however, prosecutors were permitted to seek only what the McNulty Memorandum referred to as "Category I" information, which consisted of purely factual information relating to the underlying misconduct. Another classification of privileged information, referred to as "Category II" information, included actual attorney-client communications and non-factual work product, and could be sought only when the Category I information was insufficient. Requests for Category II information required an even higher level of advance supervisory approval. Although prosecutors were allowed to consider a company's refusal to waive privilege over Category I information in assessing cooperation, the refusal to provide Category II information could not be considered—although a company's *agreement* to waive privilege could be favorably considered favorably in the prosecutor's assessment.[44]

Criticism of the government's policies nevertheless continued, and in June 2007 the Attorney-Client Privilege Protection Act of 2006 was re-introduced in the 110th Congress as the Attorney-Client Privilege Protection Act of 2007.[45] Within weeks, in an apparent effort to avoid the passage of this bill, Deputy Attorney General Mark R. Filip issued the Filip Memorandum, which contains current Justice Department policy regarding corporate privilege waiver.[46]

Q 6.17.4   What is the Filip Memorandum?

The Filip Memorandum states the current Justice Department policy on privilege waiver (as well as indemnification of employees' legal defense costs and joining joint defense agreements).

The Filip Memorandum recognizes that the attorney-client privilege and the attorney work-product protection serve an extremely important function in the American legal system. It further recognizes that a company may freely waive its own privileges if it chooses to do so and that such waivers occur routinely when companies conduct an internal investigation and then disclose the details of that investigation to law enforcement officials in an effort to seek prosecution of the offenders.

The policy states, however, that what the government needs to advance its investigations is not *waiver* of the privilege, but instead the disclosure of *facts* known to the corporation about the criminal misconduct under review. Thus, "while a company remains free to convey non-factual or 'core' attorney-client communications or work product—if and only if the company voluntarily chooses to do so—*prosecutors should not ask for such waivers and are directed not to do so*. The critical factor is whether the corporation has provided the *facts* about the events"[47] under investigation, and not a formal waiver of the company's privilege.

The policy further states that, "so long as the corporation timely discloses relevant facts about the putative misconduct, the corporation may receive due credit for such cooperation, regardless of whether it chooses to waive privilege or work product protection in the process."[48] Further, recognizing that internal investigations typically involve employee interviews, the policy states that

> [t]o receive cooperation credit for providing factual information, the corporation need not produce, and prosecutors may not request, protected notes and memoranda generated by the lawyers' interviews. To earn such credit, however, the corporation does need to produce, and prosecutors may request, relevant factual information—including relevant factual information acquired through those interviews, unless the identical information has otherwise been provided—as well as relevant non-privileged evidence such as accounting and busi-

ness records and emails between non-attorney employees or agents.[49]

The policy also provides that, in evaluating cooperation, prosecutors should not take into account whether a company has advanced or reimbursed attorney fees or provided counsel to employees, officers, or directors under investigation or indictment, and prosecutors may not ask the company to refrain from doing so. Similarly, the mere participation by the company in a joint defense agreement does not render the company ineligible to receive cooperation credit, and prosecutors may not ask the company to refrain from entering such agreements.[50]

Q 6.17.5   What is the current policy?

In effect, what the current policy means is this: Company officers, directors, and employees are usually interviewed in the course of an internal investigation. If those interviews are done by counsel for the company, counsel's notes and memoranda of the interviews are usually protected by the attorney-client privilege and/or as attorney work product. But now, in order to receive cooperation credit for providing the *factual* information that the government needs, the corporation need *not* produce, and prosecutors may *not* request, protected notes or memoranda generated by the lawyers' interviews. Further, non-factual or core attorney work product, such as counsel's mental impressions or legal theories, need not be disclosed, and prosecutors may not request the disclosure of such attorney work product as a condition for cooperation credit. However, to earn cooperation credit, the company *does* need to produce, and prosecutors *may* request, relevant factual information, including relevant factual information acquired through those interviews (unless the identical information has otherwise been provided), as well as relevant non-privileged evidence such as accounting and business records and emails between non-attorney employees or agents. Also, companies may provide counsel for employees, officers, and directors during and after the government's investigation and may advance or reimburse those attorney fees. Finally, the company may enter into joint defense agreements without forfeiting its eligibility for cooperation credit. If, however, either of these actions is done for the purpose of obstructing the government's investigation, it may be used to deprive the company of any cooperation credit and may also constitute a separate criminal offense.

Counsel for companies who believe that prosecutors are violating these policies are encouraged by the guidelines to raise their concerns with the prosecutor's supervisors, such as the appropriate U.S. attorney or assistant attorney general.[51]

Notes to Chapter 6

1.   These same classes of people are frequently the source of whistleblower suits (qui tam actions) under federal or state civil false claims acts. Private citizens may file complaints under these acts on behalf of government programs they allege have been defrauded. The complaints are served on the Department of Justice or state attorneys general, who are then required to conduct an investigation into the merits of the cases. See chapter 11 for more information on the False Claims Act.

2.   The audit committee and management may sometimes constitute separate groups, and need separate legal representation, even though it is the company paying for the legal representation in either case. Counsel must, therefore, always take care to clearly identify exactly who is being represented, and act accordingly. *See* Q 6.11.3, *infra*.

3.   The government must submit an affidavit to the court for the court to determine whether the warrant should be issued. The affidavit is normally submitted under seal. The affidavit is usually not unsealed until some time after criminal charges are brought.

4.   Like a devastating fire or natural disaster, the issuance of a search warrant can be very disruptive to a company, since it too can involve the loss of key files, records, and even entire computers containing crucial customer and financial information necessary for the company's day-to-day operations. Although the government will eventually provide copies of seized files, this can take months to arrange and accomplish. Meanwhile, the company's obligation to its customers, agents, and employees continues. For this reason, every company should always maintain backup files and records of its important documents.

5.   The *U.S. Attorneys' Manual* defines a "target" as "a person as to whom the prosecutor or the grand jury has substantial evidence linking him or her to the commission of a crime and who, in the judgment of the prosecutor, is a putative defendant. An officer or employee of an organization which is a target is not automatically considered a target even if such officer's or employee's conduct contributed to the commission of the crime by the target organization. The same lack of automatic target status holds true for organizations which employ, or employed, an officer or employee who is a target." The *U.S. Attorneys' Manual* defines a "subject" of an investigation as "a person whose conduct is within the scope of the grand jury's investigation." U.S. ATTORNEYS' MANUAL § 9-11.151 (1997).

6.   Regardless of whether an internal investigation is triggered by a subpoena, a subpoena served on a company should always immediately be delivered to counsel. The subpoena must be carefully reviewed, and steps must be taken immediately to ensure that responsive documents that are potentially relevant to the inquiry are not altered or destroyed. The full request must be thor-

oughly understood, including the items sought, the date they are due, the issuing authority, and the requirements involved in production.

7. See Q 6.10.5 for a discussion of whether it is more appropriate for inside counsel or outside counsel to contact government attorneys.

8. Prosecutors will sometimes divulge information to outside counsel but not internal lawyers, in part because of their view that internal lawyers sometimes wear multiple hats, serving as both legal advisors and business advisors.

9. As discussed earlier (*see* Q 6.3.5, *supra*), when a company is served a search warrant, it implies that the company is probably the subject or target of a criminal investigation and should initiate a broad internal investigation immediately.

10. *See* U.S. Sentencing Guidelines Manual § 8C2.5 (2008).

11. Many matters that appear to be criminal on their face are ultimately resolved civilly. Bank Secrecy Act and Securities Act violations are good examples of these situations. Other criminal matters may initially involve one specific issue, but ultimately result in completely different, albeit related, criminal charges (such as perjury and obstruction of justice).

12. It is worth keeping in mind an old adage: "Even a blind squirrel eventually finds a nut." Some attention should be paid even to allegations of marginal credibility, particularly if they involve a matter where the source of information is one whose position would make the source privy to inside information. For example, a competitor who loses a government contract bid and then accuses the winning bidder of bribery is in a better position to have some evidence of wrongdoing, even though the initial reaction may be that the accusation is just a matter of "sour grapes."

13. In-house counsel may be involved. However, because many in-house counsel are assigned non-legal as well as legal duties, great care must be taken to ensure that in-house counsel, when conducting an internal investigation, is acting *only* in his or her *legal* capacity. Otherwise, the protections afforded by the attorney-client privilege and the work-product doctrine may be lost to the company. Moreover, conducting an internal investigation can be extremely time-consuming and seriously interfere with in-house counsel's day-to-day duties, as well as undermine key relationships with senior management. Because of these considerations, the best practice, particularly in complicated criminal investigations, is to retain experienced outside counsel.

14. *See* Q 6.13.1 *et seq.*, *infra* (for a more detailed discussion of the attorney-client privilege/work-product doctrine).

15. The initial question in staffing is the determination of who is *in charge of* the internal investigation, which is discussed in Q 6.7, *supra*.

16. Non-legal outside assistance should always be retained through counsel, not through company management, and for the express purpose of acting in anticipation of litigation to ensure that the confidentiality of their work is protected by the attorney-client privilege and work-product doctrine to the maximum extent possible.

17. On December 1, 2015, amended Federal Rules of Civil Procedure governing handling of electronically stored data by companies involved in federal

civil litigation or that are on notice that litigation may commence went into effect. These amended rules govern federal civil cases, but they also establish an unofficial standard for the handling and production of electronically stored data in criminal cases. *See* chapter 7, Electronic Discovery, for a discussion of key issues to consider when responding to a request that seeks e-discovery.

18.   In conducting an internal investigation, attention should be given to identifying *all* electronic data storage facilities, including employees' home computers. Many employees and officers routinely work from home using either personal computers or computers assigned to them by the company. A thorough review of the company's electronic data must include these as well as the relevant office computers.

19.   For example, in an internal embezzlement scheme, forensic experts may be essential not only to proving the misconduct against the embezzler, but also in locating and recovering carefully hidden stolen funds or secreted assets of the wrongdoer.

20.   Companies must keep in mind the example of Arthur Andersen and the destruction of Enron-related internal documents. Arthur Andersen was never charged with fraud in connection with its Enron work; it was charged with obstruction of justice arising from its destruction of relevant documents. Although ultimately exonerated by the U.S. Supreme Court, Arthur Andersen was destroyed in the process.

21.   See Q 6.3.7, *supra*, for a similar discussion on the value of government agents in providing information in determining the scope of the government's investigation, and a company's subsequent use of such information in formulating its own investigation.

22.   Zubulake v. UBS Warburg LLC, 229 F.R.D. 422 (S.D.N.Y. 2004).

23.   *See, e.g.*, Phx. Four, Inc. v. Strategic Res. Corp., 2006 WL 1409413, 2006 U.S. Dist. LEXIS 32211 (S.D.N.Y. May 22, 2006).

24.   Upjohn v. United States, 449 U.S. 383 (1981). *Upjohn* did not itself address the issue of warnings, but issues arose from it as to who held the privilege regarding interviews and who could waive it. These issues have taken on substantial significance for corporations under regulatory or criminal investigation because of the likelihood that a corporation may want to disclose information learned in the internal investigation in order to gain credit for cooperation with the government. The resolution of these collective issues arising from *Upjohn* has coalesced into the "*Upjohn* warnings."

25.   *See, e.g.*, United States v. Nicholas, 606 F. Supp. 2d 1109 (C.D. Cal.), *rev'd sub nom.* United States v. Ruehle, 583 F.3d 600 (9th Cir. 2009).

26.   *See* www.acc.com/education/webcasts/upload/Upjohn-Warnings.pdf.

27.   In Upjohn v. United States, 449 U.S. 383 (1981), the U.S. Supreme Court ruled that communications with low-level employees, as well as with officers and directors, could be protected, provided: (1) the communication was made at the direction of corporate officials to obtain legal advice; (2) the matters communicated fell within the scope of the employee's duties and were not available from upper level employees; (3) employees were aware that the purpose of the inquiry was to help in obtaining legal advice; and (4) the communications were intended

to be kept confidential. Since individuals are not clients for the purpose of the privilege, the individual employee may not exercise the privilege to protect himself.

28. If the witness is a *former* employee, then the interview may not be protected from disclosure even by the company's attorney-client privilege. While virtually all jurisdictions recognize that internal interviews conducted *with current employees* for the purpose of providing the company legal advice are protected by the company's privilege, not all jurisdictions recognize that interviews with *former* employees are privileged.

29. *See* QQ 6.17–6.17.5.

30. Other potentially applicable protections are the self-evaluation privilege and the joint defense agreements. The self-evaluation privilege has been recognized by only a few courts, and then under very limited circumstances. This privilege has generally been rejected by the federal courts, and no court has applied it as a bar to disclosure to government agencies.

31. Note that this refers to an *employee* communication. Communications with parties outside the company may or may not be privileged. The application of the privilege to communications (including interviews) with *former* employees depends on the jurisdiction. Some jurisdictions extend the privilege to communications with former employees, and some limit it only to current employees. Communications with third parties who are not and never were employed by the company will *not* be privileged (although notes and memos of such interviews may be protected by the work-product doctrine).

32. *See* Upjohn v. United States, 449 U.S. 383 (1981).

33. In regard specifically to media relations consultants, see FTC v. GlaxoSmithKline, 294 F.3d 141 (D.C. Cir. 2002) (holding that where legal counsel worked with the media expert in the same manner as with full-time employees and the expert acted as part of a team with full-time employees so as to have been completely intertwined with the company's litigation strategy, the privilege applied).

34. *In re* Berkley & Co., 629 F.2d 548, 553 (8th Cir. 1980); SEC v. Herman, 2004 WL 964104 (S.D.N.Y. May 5, 2004).

35. *See* U.S. SENTENCING GUIDELINES MANUAL § 8C2.5(g) (2008).

36. See chapter 8 for a complete discussion of voluntary disclosures.

37. *See, e.g., In re* Qwest Commc'ns Int'l, 450 F.3d 1179 (10th Cir. 2006). *But see* Diversified Indus. v. Meredith, 572 F.2d 596 (8th Cir. 1977) (recognizing a limited waiver when disclosure was made under compulsion of a government subpoena); *In re* Steinhardt Partners, 9 F.3d 230 (2d Cir. 1993).

38. Named for Deputy Attorney General Eric H. Holder Jr., the memorandum was entitled "Principles of Federal Prosecution of Business Organizations" and was issued to Justice Department prosecutors in June 1999. Other considerations in addition to waiver of the privilege included whether the corporation had agreed to indemnify its officers, directors, or employees for their investigation-related attorney fees, and whether it had agreed to participate in a joint defense agreement, both of which were considered to be indicative of a company's *lack* of cooperation with the government.

39. The Thompson Memorandum was named for Deputy Attorney General Larry D. Thompson and was issued in January 2003.

40. United States v. Stein, 435 F. Supp. 2d 330 (S.D.N.Y. 2006).

41. United States v. Stein, 541 F.3d 130 (2d Cir. 2008).

42. The Attorney-Client Privilege Protection Act of 2006, S. 30, 109th Cong. (2006).

43. Principles of Federal Prosecution of Business Organizations, Memorandum from Paul J. McNulty, Deputy Attorney Gen., to Heads of Department Components and U.S. Attorneys (Dec. 12, 2006), www.usdoj.gov/dag/speeches/2006/mcnulty_memo.pdf.

44. The McNulty Memorandum also prohibited prosecutors from considering whether a company indemnified its employees' attorney fees, unless the circumstances indicated that the indemnification was intended to impede a criminal investigation. A company's joining a joint defense agreement, however, continued to be a valid factor for consideration by prosecutors.

45. H.R. 3013, 110th Cong. (2007).

46. The guidelines are found in Principles of Federal Prosecution of Business Organizations § 9-28.000 (Aug. 2008), www.usdoj.gov/opa/documents/corp-charging-guidelines.pdf [hereinafter Filip Memorandum].

47. Filip Memorandum § 9-28.710 (Aug. 2008) (emphasis added).

48. Id. § 9-28.720(a).

49. Id. § 9-28.720(a) n.3.

50. Id. § 9.28.730. These policies do not apply, however, to situations in which the payment of attorney fees was made for the purpose of obstructing the government's investigation.

51. Id. § 9-28.760.

7

Electronic Discovery

*Sonya Strnad**

Thanks to technological advances and software development, the realm of electronic documents is ever increasing and has become the dominant form of communication for many companies and individuals. Virtually every one of us today creates electronically stored information (ESI) on a daily basis without even thinking about it. ESI can be created by using word-processing or spreadsheet programs, email, text messages, blogs, social media, surfing the Internet, electronic calendar entries, PDAs, specialized databases, GPS data, CDs, DVDs, hard drives, backup tapes, etc.

Because ESI is frequently unstable and susceptible to corruption or deletion, and because of the many different types of ESI storage and format, it is particularly important that your company thoroughly document its efforts to preserve, collect, and produce ESI in the litigation context. Careful and detailed record keeping can help to avoid sanctions and other adverse results while reducing overall costs.

*   The author wishes to acknowledge Tracy Nichols for her contributions to this chapter.

Overview

Q 7.1   Why is electronic data so significant?

As technology develops, businesses and individuals communicate more frequently using electronic means rather than paper. Use of electronic forms of communication such as email, text messaging, social media, and instant messaging provides much easier and more immediate delivery of information than the old-fashioned way of sending a piece of paper in the mail, receiving a written response, and filing paper documents into a file cabinet for future reference. Because of the ease of electronic communication, 93% of all information is now generated in electronic form, and 70% of these documents are never reduced to hard copy.[1]

Electronic data is also much more easily stored and accessed than paper files. One gigabyte of data can equal roughly 100,000 pages of documents. Nowadays, the typical computer hard drive stores between 160 to 500 gigabytes of data—that's a potential of 16 million to 50 million pages of documents. Even if individuals who use a computer had enough file cabinet space to store all of the data from their computer in hard copy, locating a single document from those millions of pages by performing a manual search would be incredibly cumbersome compared to the speed and ease of electronically locating documents, most of which are text-searchable.

Additionally, electronically stored information may be stored in many locations, ranging from company servers to employee smartphones, like BlackBerry devices and iPhones, to third-party locations, such as archiving solutions, cloud or virtual storage, social media platforms, etc.

Q 7.2 What is e-discovery?

E-discovery refers to the processes of **preserving, collecting, processing**, and **producing** electronically stored information during litigation or other investigations. Typically e-discovery is limited to active and archived data. Deleted data is generally not preserved and collected unless the specific facts of the case necessitate that deleted data also be included. Each step of this process is described briefly here and treated in more detail below.

Preservation. The purpose of preserving electronic data is to ensure that relevant data is available to be produced in litigation or other investigations and is not intentionally or inadvertently deleted.

Collection. Once preserved, data may need to be harvested. This too can be a simple or more involved process depending on the circumstances creating a need for collection.

For example, it can be as easy as creating a copy of an email folder (called a .pst if using an Outlook email account) or more sophisticated if a forensic copy must be made by an outside forensic vendor. (See Q 7.8 for more about e-discovery vendors.) A forensic collection of data will ensure that no data, including deleted files and metadata,[2] has been altered.

Processing. In many instances, it is necessary to preserve and collect sources of electronic data without knowing exactly which documents will be needed. The next step in e-discovery—processing

213

electronic data—refers to the technical procedures used to determine which of the collected electronic data should be reviewed and in what format it will be reviewed.

For example, processing ESI will often include running various search terms and time frames against the collected body of data to quickly locate the most relevant and useful documents to review. In other instances, data may be processed using advanced conceptual searching tools to locate relevant documents. Processing data also includes more technical processes to exclude certain types of data, such as non-relevant system files or programs, and de-duplication of documents that appear more than once within a data set (such as an email to fifty people).

Production. Once documents have been processed and reviewed, it may be necessary to produce certain documents to another party. Productions to other parties may include native file format productions[3] or productions of documents converted to .tiff or .pdf images. Depending on the production format, this may involve Bates stamping[4] and creating an index or "load file" to assist the recipient in loading the production into a particular database for review.

Q 7.2.1   In what context does e-discovery usually occur?

E-discovery typically occurs when it becomes necessary to evaluate and review bodies of electronic documents related to a particular topic, whether it be in a civil or criminal litigation, arbitration, internal investigation, regulatory or other government investigation, or perhaps in response to a non-party document request or subpoena. Often an entity that has documents relevant to litigation or an investigation is also asked to preserve documents even if it is not party to the litigation. For example, a company involved in litigation may require their accountants, lawyers, banks, financial advisors, or subsidiaries to preserve electronic data related to their relationship with that company.

Records Management[5]

Q 7.3 What can our company do now so that we are in a better position if we are ever sued?

Every company should evaluate its current document retention policy (or records management program), examine whether it is being followed, and train employees to comply with it.

If a company has such a policy, it should review the policy to make sure it adequately covers electronic documents that are generated, used, and received by the company. If the company doesn't have a document retention policy, it should consider implementing one. The policy should contain a litigation hold process that provides guidance to employees (including the company's IT staff) as to what procedures should be followed once litigation is anticipated.

Next, a company should take steps to make sure that its employees consistently comply with the document retention policy. Having a retention policy that is honored more in the breach than in compliance will not help to protect a company involved in litigation or an investigation. Sometimes this may entail additional training for employees, as well as a system of monitoring compliance with the policy and taking steps to further train or reprimand those who are not in compliance.

In addition to providing training on compliance with the document retention policy, employees should also be trained on what kind of documents to create and what kind of documents not to create. Because email and other forms of electronic communication are so common and easy to use, they often contain informal, ambiguous, loose, or colorful language that could easily be misconstrued later during the course of litigation. It is better to counsel employees that they should write emails in a way that will not cause future embarrassment or unwarranted liability for them or the company, and to leave colorful or humorous language for a phone call or face-to-face meeting.

If your company uses social media platforms, it should consider adopting a social media policy if it has not done so already. From an e-discovery perspective, the policy should clearly address whether personal employee social media accounts created and/or used for work purposes are considered to be company property or whether the company has the right to access them. Should the company need to implement a legal hold, such social media policies will help the company and its employees determine whether such social media accounts fall within the custody or control of the company, or if the company has the legal right or practical ability to access them.

Finally, a company should evaluate whether it is needlessly warehousing data, such as old backup tapes or other archival media. The company should also know the exact location of its backup tapes and other archival media and what they contain. Companies involved in litigation are often forced to needlessly pay additional costs to restore backup tapes or other archival media because they were improperly catalogued, or not catalogued at all.

Preservation

Q 7.4   What data should be preserved?

A party must take reasonable steps to retain all documents within its control that are potentially relevant to the anticipated litigation. This obligation also applies to relevant documents that may not be within a party's direct control, but to which a party has the legal right or practical ability to access, such as documents maintained by vendors (like accountants) or affiliated entities.[6] This obligation does not require that every document within the company be preserved, as long as reasonable steps are taken to preserve relevant documents.[7] For federal civil matters, preservation may be limited to the documents or data that is relevant to a claim or defense and is proportional to the needs of the case.[8]

Q 7.4.1   How is ESI preserved?

Preservation may be as simple as refraining from opening, changing, or deleting a document. However, electronic data can be destroyed easily by the stroke of a key, either intentionally or inadvertently, or by letting automatic functions run. While it may be possible to restore deleted data, it can often be a costly and time-consuming process, and there are no guarantees that data will be recovered. So it is important to take affirmative steps to prevent deletion or alteration of ESI.

One of the most reliable ways to preserve data is to engage a reputable e-discovery vendor to copy any potentially relevant data. A vendor will lend credibility to your preservation efforts and will document the process. This is particularly important if it is necessary to preserve deleted data. Another method for preserving data is for a company's IT department to merely copy relevant data, although this method should only be considered if the parties know that document metadata and/or deleted data are not important to the litigation. Often this kind of do-it-yourself data preservation may not capture certain metadata or deleted data (for example, when copying a Word document, often the "create date" shows as the date of preservation, not the original creation date of the document). As with any preservation effort, it is important to document each step taken to preserve documents.

Avoiding Inadvertent Deletion or Alteration of Data

Q 7.4.2   How do we prevent data from being unintentionally deleted or altered?

Examples of routine tasks that result in data destruction include:

- automatically deleting sent or received email after a certain period of time;
- changing a record's transaction date (and last user field) by opening a document with an "automatic update" date field;
- recycling and overwriting backup tapes after a specified time; or
- updating master files or spreadsheets with current information (such as pricing sheets, quarterly forecasting, etc.).

Preventing such data from being deleted or altered can mean disengaging automatic delete maintenance functions, rerouting data into a "data hotel" created for the express purpose of preserving data, or pulling backup tapes out of a recycling rotation.

Litigation Holds

Q 7.5   When is the duty to preserve or issue a "litigation hold" triggered?

There are various events that trigger the duty to preserve electronic documents (as well as paper documents).[9] Some events are more obvious than others, such as the filing of a complaint in civil litigation, the receipt of a preservation notice or letter from another party, receipt of a subpoena or document request from a government entity or third party, a preservation order, and certain business-related events (mergers or acquisitions, technology reviews, etc.). A party is also under an obligation to preserve documents that are relevant to pending or reasonably foreseeable litigation.[10] While this last category can be more difficult to determine, consider whether attorney work product has been generated or a noteworthy or striking event (such as the termination of a disgruntled employee) has taken place. These events may also trigger the duty to preserve documents—even before an EEOC complaint or lawsuit is filed.

Q 7.5.1   In what format should a litigation hold be issued?

Although there are no rules or statutes regarding the form of a litigation hold, courts increasingly expect litigants to issue written legal holds and may find parties who fail to do so negligent.[11] Should a party's preservation efforts be called into question, it is often difficult to show that appropriate steps were taken and that a litigation hold was timely implemented if the hold is issued orally. Therefore, it is prudent to issue written legal holds, even if the jurisdiction in which you anticipate litigation does not require it.

Q 7.5.2   Who should receive the litigation hold notice?

All of the "key players" (and their support staff) who were involved in the matter and might have relevant documents should receive the litigation hold. Keep in mind that key players may also include individuals who may not have email accounts, employees who may no longer be employed with the company, or board members.

The company's IT department should always receive a copy of the litigation hold and understand that, even if they are not considered a key player in the litigation, they are nevertheless a crucial part of the litigation hold because they have access to the largest amount of data and data sources within the company.

Q 7.5.3   How do we determine who the "key players" are?

In order to determine who should receive a litigation hold notice, it is first necessary to identify the universe of potentially relevant data. If litigation is reasonably foreseeable but has not yet begun, evaluate the facts surrounding the triggering event to determine what universe of data may be relevant. If a complaint has been filed or a subpoena issued, the company and its outside counsel should review it as a starting point in order to identify what kind of data is relevant to the matter. Once this universe has been identified, identify a point person in each department that generated or handled relevant data to help draft the list of key players.

Likewise, a party is under an obligation to preserve all documents within its control or documents for which it has the legal right or practical ability to access; so consider whether outside parties may have documents relevant to the litigation. This often comes up where vendors perform outsourced work such as payroll, billing, customer service, administration of employee benefits (including stock option programs), manufacturing, legal work, and accounting. Vendors may also be used to host or archive company data (including cloud storage and social media). Affiliated company entities or individuals may also have relevant documents. These entities may include corporate parents, subsidiaries, joint ventures, and current and former directors, officers, employees, or consultants.

Q 7.5.4   What should the litigation hold cover?

A litigation hold should cover all sources of potentially relevant documents within a party's control (as described above). Keep in mind that in federal civil cases, the hold may be limited to relevant data or documents that are relevant to the claims or defenses in the matter that are proportional to the needs of the case.[12] This involves understanding the company's electronic data architecture and interviewing all key players to determine which kinds of electronic documents they would have created, accessed, or received. Some examples are:

- company-supported email accounts;
- desktop computers, laptops, notebooks, iPads, or other similar tablet devices;
- file servers housing shared or personal drives;
- smartphones/PDAs such as BlackBerry devices, iPhones, etc.;
- social media accounts;
- cell phones;

- specialized databases;
- backup tapes;
- portable storage media (CDs, DVDs, USB drives, jump drives, backup drives, memory sticks, flash drives, iPods, other external hard drives, etc.);
- instant messaging;
- text messaging;
- voice mail;
- abandoned or decommissioned servers;
- Internet usage; and
- GPS data.

A litigation hold may also extend to systems not supported by the company but that are used by key players and contain relevant data. These may include:

- personal or home computers;
- laptops, notebooks, iPads, or other similar tablet devices;
- personal email accounts through Internet service providers (Gmail, Yahoo!, MSN, etc.);
- personal portable storage media;
- social media accounts;
- personal cell phones and text messages; or
- instant messaging through an Internet service provider.

Even less-accessible records, such as backup tapes or outdated legacy data,[13] may be covered under the litigation hold if it is possible that they contain relevant data. Lastly, the litigation hold may cover sources of data held by agents or other third parties that may contain relevant information.[14]

Litigation Hold/Data Preservation Obligations

Q 7.5.5   What are in-house counsel's or upper management's obligations with respect to implementing and maintaining a litigation hold?

The obligation to preserve potentially relevant documents is an affirmative one that rests squarely on the shoulders of senior corporate officers, and corporate leadership can be held responsible (and personally liable) for document retention problems, including e-discovery mistakes.[15] Should in-house counsel or senior management of a company not have the expertise to be able to implement and maintain a litigation hold, they are under an obligation to retain the legal and technical expertise to be able to do so.[16] Courts will look to see who is ultimately responsible for the enforcement of a litigation hold, which is often the CEO or general counsel of a company; delegating such tasks to someone like a paralegal or an in-house attorney with no litigation experience will not satisfy senior management's obligation for enforcing a litigation hold. Ultimately, senior management, including in-house counsel, are tasked with informing the company and its records custodians (including key players) of pending litigation and their responsibilities for complying with their obligation to preserve documents potentially relevant to the dispute, including drafts and non-identical copies of the document.[17] Further, the obligation to enforce a litigation hold starts with ensuring that the litigation hold covers all *sources* of relevant information, not just specific documents.[18]

Q 7.5.6   What are outside counsel's obligations?

Like in-house counsel, outside counsel is obligated to search for all sources of potentially relevant documents and ensure that they are preserved. This includes conducting a methodical survey of the company's sources of data during the relevant time frame and may require further inquiry about whether sources of ESI that were employed at the time but are no longer in service contain relevant data, such as outdated or discontinued computer systems, computer workstations (like desktops or laptops), computer or email accounts, backup tapes or servers. If unable to determine this information, counsel or upper management may need to employ a vendor or technician to assist in making this determination.[19] Another part of the process of identifying relevant sources of data is for counsel to interview each employee who may know of potentially relevant documents. Courts have opined that unless this step is taken, counsel has not fulfilled its preservation obligations.[20]

While counsel may need assistance in performing these duties, it is clear that attorney participation is vital to the preservation process, and preservation duties may not be wholly delegated to personnel within the company that do not have an appreciation for what is required without adequate supervision.[21]

Once a litigation hold has been implemented, counsel (either in-house or outside) must also take steps to remind the company of the scope of the litigation hold and affirmatively monitor compliance.[22] This obligation persists until the litigation hold has been lifted, even if the corporate identity changes, such as through mergers, de-mergers, acquisitions, and bankruptcy.[23]

Pitfalls in Data Preservation/Consequences of Failure to Preserve Data

Q 7.6   What can happen if I fail to take reasonable steps to preserve data?

If relevant data is deleted or altered—intentionally or inadvertently—after the duty to preserve has been triggered, the company and individuals may be subject to sanctions for spoliation. As a result, the court may allow an adverse inference instruction, allowing a jury to assume that a party's failure to produce documents means that the party destroyed documents that would have supported their adversary's claims, or the court may impose monetary sanctions against the party and its counsel. The court may even dismiss a party's claim(s) as sanction for spoliation of data.

Q 7.6.1   What is spoliation?

Spoliation is the destruction or significant alteration of evidence or the failure to preserve property for another's use as evidence in pending or reasonable foreseeable litigation.[24]

Q 7.6.2   What are some of the hazards to be aware of in trying to implement a litigation hold?

The stage at which most sanctionable errors are made is the document preservation stage, chiefly because a large number of judgment calls must be made early on when you may not have a full understanding of the issues at hand and do not have the ability to consult with a judge or adversary to make sure your preservation efforts and decisions are reasonable. Additionally, there are no "do-overs" if you get it wrong and relevant documents are deleted or otherwise lost.

Therefore, how well you have instituted and complied with litigation hold obligations is paramount. Often litigation hold decisions will not be scrutinized until later stages of litigation. With the benefit of hindsight, you will be judged on whether you adequately preserved documents, whether they came from the right sources, and whether you implemented the hold when you should have known the litigation was foreseeable. With this in mind, it is best to err on the side of caution and invest the time and resources to protect yourself at the outset from potential spoliation issues.

Q 7.6.3   What kinds of sanctions can result from a failure to preserve data?

Developing case law shows that litigants are not expected to preserve every bit of data and hinder a company's day-to-day business; however, courts do expect that reasonable efforts be made to preserve relevant data. The case law on the facing page provides concrete examples of errors that have merited sanctions.

Q 7.6.4   When can we lift the litigation hold?

A litigation hold may be lifted once the litigation has been completely resolved, including any appeals that may be pursued. Depending on the circumstances, it may be advisable to seek agreement from an adversary should you wish to lift a litigation hold prior to this time. However, if there is additional foreseeable litigation on the horizon, such as civil litigation following a criminal or government investigation, the litigation hold should remain intact.

Where reasonably foreseeable litigation does not result in litigation, it is safe to lift the litigation hold if the matter is settled without litigation, once the statute of limitations for the anticipated claims has passed, or when circumstances have changed so that litigation is no longer reasonably foreseeable.

Should your company have multiple litigation holds, it is important to ascertain that there are no common sources of documents subject to another litigation hold before lifting your hold.

CASE STUDIES:
Phx. Four, Inc. v. Strategic Res. Corp.[25]

The abandonment of computer workstations and servers without first determining whether they contained relevant ESI.

Sanctions: Outside counsel and client ordered to reimburse plaintiff equally for costs and fees associated with bringing sanctions motion, for which they could not look to insurers to pay their share. Additionally, client and counsel ordered to pay $10,000 for re-depositions of certain defendants.

 United States v. Philip Morris USA, Inc.[26]

Failure to suspend automatic deletion of emails and instruct employees not to delete emails after a preservation order was in place.

Sanctions: Defendant ordered to pay monetary sanction in the amount of $2,750,000; eleven key employees precluded from testifying.

 Metro. Opera Ass'n v. Local 100, Hotel Emps. & Rest. Emps. Int'l Union[27]

Lack of attorney participation in determining that all sources of documents had been preserved, including non-identical copies of documents.

Sanctions: Default judgment entered against defendants for various egregious discovery violations deemed to rise to the level of willfulness and bad faith (as well as sanctions in the form of attorney fees).

In re NTL, Inc. Sec. Litig.[28]

Failure to keep a litigation hold in place through the change of the company's identity for documents within the company's practical ability to control.

Sanctions: Magistrate Judge recommended adverse inference be granted against defendant and ordered defendant to pay attorney fees and costs.

 Qualcomm, Inc. v. Broadcom Corp.[29]

After trial it was discovered that Qualcomm failed to produce 46,000 relevant emails and documents.

Sanctions: Qualcomm ordered to pay Broadcom $8.5 million in attorney fees and costs; six attorneys (outside counsel) referred to the State Bar of California for investigation into possible ethical violations.

Perhaps most notorious of all:

 ***Coleman (Parent) Holding, Inc. v.
Morgan Stanley & Co.***[30]

Banking institution failed to locate 1,423 backup tapes until after discovery had closed, which resulted in a $1.58 billion judgment.

Sanctions: After adverse inference granted for various e-discovery violations, jury awarded plaintiff $1.58 billion judgment, which included punitive damages of $850 million.

Collection

Q 7.7   How soon after preservation will we need to start collecting documents?

In the ordinary case, collection of documents should not start until counsel has conferred on the format of production and the scope of the information that will be at issue in the case. Under the Federal Rules of Civil Procedure, the parties to a lawsuit are required to confer at the beginning of the lawsuit to discuss the scope of discovery.[31] Until that conference occurs it will be difficult to determine which of the documents that have been preserved under the litigation hold will actually need to be collected.

However, the company should be aware that preservation of documents may require some measure of collection (such as forensic imaging of a hard drive) in order to avoid changing or deleting data associated with a particular electronic document,[32] such as metadata.[33]

Q 7.7.1   How should we begin collecting the internal documents that our litigation counsel will need?

The collection of internal documents should begin in much the same manner as the process for determining the proper distribution and enforcement of the litigation hold. The collection of documents will usually start with a defined list of topics, persons involved, and date ranges. The company should seek to understand the universe of the documents that will need to be collected, which will include understanding the data creation and storage practices of the users (employees) involved in creating or storing relevant information. Collection methods may include keyword searching and imaging.

Keyword Searching

Q 7.7.2   Is keyword searching an effective way to collect ESI?

Yes and no. Collection of documents is frequently accomplished using keyword searching. But you should be aware of the potential dangers of over-reliance on keyword searching.

In many cases, searching within one data set created using a certain application will not identify documents created using other applications that are embedded or linked to the data set being searched. The classic example is keyword searching within an email application; such a search may be effective at identifying responsive information within the emails itself, but be ineffective at identifying responsive information in the attachments to the emails.

In many cases, the most efficient choice is to have the data processed into an application that is capable of searching across all application types. This processing is usually done by an outside vendor. However, the technology of data searching is continually evolving, and the company should inquire of its counsel and vendors about the most efficient method for culling potentially responsive data.

Problems also arise when a keyword search does not reach all of the intended data. For example, hard drives may be partitioned into separate sectors. So, in some cases, it might be necessary to conduct two or more searches to reach all of the data on a single hard drive. A company should also be aware that collection of documents may require collection of metadata, which often requires the use of specialized software and processes.

Aside from the technical aspects of keyword searching, a company and its counsel should consider whether the use of keyword searching is likely to locate relevant documents that contain loose or informal language.

While running keyword searches is a useful technique for locating documents, it is by no means a fail-proof tool. Inadequate or unreliable search terms pose additional risks to the data collection process.[34] As technology evolves, alternative search methods may be used to replace or supplement the use of keyword searching, including, but not limited to, data clustering and other analytical and conceptual searching tools.

Keyword searching is discussed in relation to further, substantive culling of collected documents below at Q 7.10.1.

Imaging

Q 7.7.3   What is "imaging"?

Frequently, the most efficient and forensically effective method of collecting data is to "image" (make an exact bit-for-bit copy, or mirror image, of) the entire piece of storage media on which the relevant information is contained and extract data from the copy. The company should consult with counsel and vendors about the advantages of this process.

E-Discovery Vendors

Q 7.8   What is an e-discovery vendor?

In response to the increasing role of ESI in litigation and the level of technical expertise that is required, many new companies are setting themselves up as "e-discovery vendors." E-discovery vendors assist clients in collecting and retrieving electronic data. They generally have access to software, personnel, and expertise that law firms and corporations do not.

Q 7.8.1   When should I consider hiring one?

As mentioned above, hiring an e-discovery vendor may be necessary and advisable, depending on the scope, nature, and difficulty of ESI collection. Frequently a company's IT department may not be capable of effectively identifying and collecting relevant information because of time demands, lack of expertise, or because the company lacks the technology to perform the necessary tasks. Vendors also provide a repeatable and verifiable process. If needed, they can later be called upon to testify to the defensibility of data preservation and collection efforts.

Consider using an e-discovery vendor when litigation involves forensic issues. Reputable vendors employ certified professionals who are trained to find, preserve, and collect data that has been lost, destroyed, or otherwise manipulated.

Finally, even if the performance of a specific e-discovery task does not strictly require the use of a vendor, engaging one may save you time and money.

Q 7.8.2   Are there any special concerns with regard to using an e-discovery vendor for data collection?

The quality of a vendor's work is difficult to predict and can change rapidly, because a vendor's overall ability depends largely on the talent and experience of the individuals working for it at any given time. You should ask a potential vendor about its ability to audit its own work and the methods used to ensure quality control. Quality control is particularly important when the work to be performed is forensic in nature or involves data analysis of any kind. You should ask for references and make inquiries of prior customers who would be willing to discuss (in general terms) the vendor's work. Finally, the proposed vendor should be asked to give estimates or forecasts of what the scope of work may be for the specific task, the specific time frames for completing various key points, and the estimated costs.

Backup Tapes

Q 7.8.3   Do I have to collect data from backup tapes?

Backup tapes and other types of disaster-recovery media are a bugaboo in the world of e-discovery. The Federal Rules of Civil Procedure themselves do not specifically address backup tapes, but do give some guidance about the circumstances under which data from such tapes may be required to be collected. Under the Federal Rules of Civil Procedure, a party can object to producing ESI that is not proportional to the needs of the case.[35] Additionally, they can object on the basis that the sources of data are "not reasonably accessible because of undue burden or cost."[36] However, the requesting party may ask the court to compel the production of such data on a showing of "good cause," meaning that the benefits of obtaining the data outweigh the costs.[37] A court receiving such a request is directed to consider a number of factors in determining whether to order that sources of data that are "not reasonably accessible" be searched.[38]

The costs of retrieving data from backup tapes are invariably higher than the costs of retrieving active data (that is, data that is on a live server). Therefore, many litigants argue that they should not be compelled to search backup media for relevant information. The requesting party will frequently argue that it is impossible to know what benefit may be gained from a search of the backup data source until the search is complete. In such situations, courts frequently order (or the parties agree to) some form of sampling or preliminary investigation into the contents of the backup media.[39] If the requesting party can make a showing of good cause and the court orders the searching of the backup media, frequently the court will attempt to lessen the burden on the producing party by, for example, ordering the requesting party to pay some of the costs of retrieving the data.[40]

Pitfalls, Potential Hazards, and Other Considerations

Q 7.9   What are some of the document collection hazards I should be aware of?

In order to prevent later claims of alteration or spoliation, it is advisable to keep track of the chain of custody of any documents collected or any media storage device that is imaged. If forensic issues are anticipated in the case, the company should consult with counsel and vendors about the most effective method for maintaining control over and documentation of the chain of custody.

Also, the company should be sensitive to the fact that collecting documents may, in some cases, alter the document itself. For example, printing a document, sending a document as an attachment in an email or forwarding an email to a specified account or folder may change the metadata of the document. For that reason it is often advisable to simply make a mirror image of the storage media (for example, an email user's account on an email server) and extract the data from the copy using specialized software.

Q 7.9.1   What can happen if data that the other side wants in the litigation was destroyed?

The Federal Rules of Civil Procedure recognize that ESI is frequently subject to automated protocols that may result in the destruction or alteration of potentially relevant evidence. In many cases, evidence is destroyed or altered despite the best efforts of the company to preserve relevant evidence. The Rules provide that the court will not sanction a party when information is destroyed due to the routine operation of an information system, so long as the party took reasonable efforts to preserve it.[41] The Committee Notes to the

2015 Amendment to Rule 37(e) of the Federal Rules of Civil Procedure point out that whether a party took reasonable steps is a fact-intensive inquiry that involves determining the extent to which a party knew of risks to preservation and protected against them.

Q 7.9.2   Are there special considerations for collecting data outside the United States?

Collecting data from outside the United States can often be a thorny issue, depending on the country from which data is sought. Some countries, like those in the European Union, have data privacy laws that may prohibit the collection of personal data. What is considered to be personal data in such countries is often construed much more broadly than in the United States. Despite such protection, U.S. courts often insist that a party must collect and produce relevant data from foreign locations.[42] In some instances, this may require obtaining consent from the individuals or employees whose data must be collected and the use of an e-discovery vendor that has certified its compliance with the U.S.-EU Privacy Shield, among other considerations. In such instances, it is advisable to obtain legal advice regarding data privacy issues from local counsel, who can provide the necessary information regarding data collection matters.

Processing and Production

Narrowing the Dataset; Technology-Assisted Review

Q 7.10 How do I determine what documents to review and/or produce?

The goal of collection is to ensure that relevant information needed for the matter at hand is preserved and available. However, not all collected data is necessarily produced. Once data has been collected, it is necessary to determine what will need to be reviewed and produced. This may involve identifying a certain source of data or subset of custodians' data for processing and review. Once this narrower dataset has been identified, the data is processed (typically by a vendor) to remove duplicates and program (executable) files. It may also involve filtering data within a certain time frame. Although this technical processing typically reduces the amount of data significantly, the resulting data set usually requires further, substantive culling to identify those documents most likely to be relevant.

Q 7.10.1   What tools are useful in further review of collected documents?

For some time, parties have relied on traditional keyword searching as a means to cull data further, if this was not already employed during the data collection phase (*see* Q 7.7.2). As previously discussed, the use of keyword search terms can be helpful in reducing the amount of data to be processed and reviewed, but it is not fool-proof. As technology has developed, parties have increasingly used other tools to either supplement or replace keyword searching. The variety of technology-assisted review tools (TAR) abound, all with different monikers such as "predictive coding," "intelligent prioritization," and "data clustering," to name a few. Some analytical tools are based on language or numerical logarithms, while others are based on more technical relationships, like email threads or near duplicates. Until recently, however, parties were loath to shift away completely from the use of traditional keyword searching because it was unclear whether courts would view these tools favorably. This is no longer the case. Starting with *Monique Da Silva Moore v. Publicis Group & MSL Group*, courts have embraced TAR as a means for significantly reducing costs of review and time needed to produce documents.[43] In one instance, the court ordered parties sua sponte to use predictive coding even though it had not been requested by either party.[44]

Although case law on these types of tools continues to develop, the trends in case law and legal scholarship suggest that TAR may be a more accurate, timely, and cost-effective means for locating and reviewing documents than traditional keyword searching and linear review, when properly employed. However, there is no "one-size-fits-all" approach to searching and reviewing. Depending on the case and the kinds of documents, certain predictive coding tools may not be as effective as traditional keyword searching. This is often the case when there are very few documents that meet the necessary criteria on which the technology will train its decision-making process. Therefore, decisions as to how to substantively cull data for review and production should be based on an evaluation of the kind of data, issues, and technologies available, and may also include a sampling of the data to further validate the process.

Format

Q 7.11 In what format should my data be produced?

Under the Federal Rules of Civil Procedure, the requesting party may designate the format for production of ESI.[45] If no format is designated, the producing party must deliver the information as it is "ordinarily maintained" or in a "reasonably usable" form.[46] Because the processing and production of ESI will vary from case to case depending on, among other things, the type and volume of the ESI, the Rules also provide that the production of ESI be the subject of discussion between litigation counsel.[47]

Q 7.11.1 What are my options regarding data production format?

In general, ESI can be produced electronically in three ways:

(1) *native format*—the form in which it was stored or maintained on the electronic storage media from which it came.
(2) *image format*—such as TIFF or PDF.[48]
(3) *processed format*—often a combination of an image of the document with additional data (such as the complete text of the document and its metadata) in a searchable, indexed table. Production in a "processed" format often is done to enable the receiving party to load the data (including the image) into a software application that can search, index, and otherwise manipulate the data.

Each of these production formats has its advantages and disadvantages. For example, some forms of production allow for the routine production of metadata, while with other forms production of metadata may be more difficult. Some forms of production allow for the efficient application of Bates or other unique, visible identification numbers, while with other forms such application is all but impossible. Similarly, some forms of production allow for easy redaction of privileged, confidential, or irrelevant information, while with other formats redaction may be much more difficult and expensive. Finally, you should consider the time frames within which collection, processing, review, and production must take place. Some formats of production take longer than others to accomplish with the necessary quality control or auditing of results.

Cost

Q 7.12 How much does it all cost?

The marketplace for e-discovery services is highly competitive and dynamic. In addition, unexpected changes in the scope or difficulty of electronic discovery are common. Estimating the cost of electronic discovery for any particular case is difficult for even the most experienced attorney or vendor. In general, the costs associated with electronic discovery can be broken into two components: vendor costs and attorney review costs.[49]

Vendor costs: Although pricing models vary greatly from vendor to vendor, electronic discovery vendors commonly charge on a per-hour basis for collection of data, and on a per-gigabyte basis for culling data (culling can include, for example, removing duplicate documents, referred to as "de-duping") and processing data into a usable format. Higher or different rates may be charged for specialized services, such as recovery of data from backup tapes or deleted data. Some vendors may also provide advanced searching and culling technology, such as conceptual searching and predictive coding, which provide greater early case assessment and help to significantly reduce attorney review time.[50] Therefore, the vendor costs associated with electronic discovery on a specific case will vary with the size and complexity of the data to be recovered.

Although vendor costs may seem significant at the outset of a matter, they are typically much lower than attorney review costs. Therefore, it is often most cost-effective to utilize ever-evolving vendor technology to further cull and search a data set in order to minimize attorney review costs and manage the overall case budget.

Attorney review costs: Attorney review occurs after processing has taken place and the universe of data has been reduced to those documents most likely to contain relevant data. Attorney review includes searching or reviewing data that has been processed and selecting documents based on relevance, privilege, and other factors.

The company should also consider the intangible costs of electronic discovery in terms of disruption to the business and IT functions. In many cases employing a vendor or otherwise "out-sourcing" e-discovery tasks can reduce these intangible costs.

Notes to Chapter 7

1. *The Proposed Rules of Civil Procedure: An Overview by Judge Shira A. Scheindlin, Author of the Zubulake Opinions* (Fios, Inc. webcast Feb. 8, 2006).
2. Metadata has been described as "data about data" or data automatically added to a document beyond the user's control. For example, in a Word document, metadata may include information showing the author of the document, the dates on which it was created and modified, and who else may have seen or edited the document.
3. Native file format refers to the format of a document in its original form as it was generated and used, such as a Word document (.doc) or Excel spreadsheet (.xls).
4. "Bates stamping" is named for the automatic numbering machine patented by the Bates Manufacturing Company and is now a generic term for any process whereby a unique reference number is marked on each page of a document for ease in later identifying and locating a document.
5. *See* chapter 5, *supra* (offering in-depth coverage of all of the aspects of records management policy, procedure, and compliance).
6. *See* FED. R. CIV. P. 34(a); *In re* NTL, Inc. Sec. Litig., 244 F.R.D. 179 (S.D.N.Y. 2007).
7. *See* Zubulake v. UBS Warburg LLC (*Zubulake IV*), 220 F.R.D. 212, 217–18 (S.D.N.Y. 2003) (a corporation need not preserve every document, because such a rule "would cripple large corporations . . . that are almost always involved in litigation"); Rimkus Consulting Grp., Inc. v. Cammarata, 688 F. Supp. 2d 598, 613 (S.D. Tex. 2010) ("[w]hether preservation or discovery conduct is acceptable in a case depends on what is *reasonable*, and that in turn depends on whether what was done—or not done—was *proportional* to that case and consistent with clearly established applicable standards") (emphasis in original).
8. FED. R. CIV. P. 26(b)(1).
9. *See* chapter 5, *supra* (discussing litigation holds in the context of a records management program).
10. Kronisch v. United States, 150 F.3d 112, 126 (2d Cir. 1998).
11. *See, e.g.*, Pension Comm. v. Banc of Am. Sec., LLC, 685 F. Supp. 2d 456, 464 (S.D.N.Y. 2010) (the failure to issue a written litigation hold after July 2004 "constitutes gross negligence because that failure is likely to result in the destruction of relevant information"); Point Blank Sols., Inc. v. Toyobo Am., Inc., 2011 WL 1448137 (S.D. Fla. Apr. 5, 2011).
12. FED. R. CIV. P. 26(b)(1).
13. Legacy data refers to data still maintained by a company for which it no longer has the hardware or software to access.
14. *See* Silvestri v. Gen. Motors Corp., 271 F.3d 583, 591 (4th Cir. 2001).

15. *See* Danis v. USN Commc'ns, 2000 WL 1694325, 2000 U.S. Dist. LEXIS 16900 (N.D. Ill. Oct. 20, 2000); Swofford v. Elsinger, 671 F. Supp. 2d 1274 (M.D. Fla. 2009).

16. *Id.*

17. *See* Metro. Opera Ass'n v. Local 100, Hotel Emps. & Rest. Emps. Int'l Union, 212 F.R.D. 178, 222 (S.D.N.Y. 2003).

18. *See* Phx. Four, Inc. v. Strategic Res. Corp., 2006 WL 1409413 (S.D.N.Y. May 23, 2006).

19. *See id.*

20. *See* Zubulake v. UBS Warburg LLC (*Zubulake V*), 229 F.R.D. 422 (S.D.N.Y. 2004).

21. *See Metro. Opera Ass'n*, 212 F.R.D. at 222.

22. *See Zubulake V, supra* note 20.

23. *See In re* NTL, Inc. Sec. Litig., 244 F.R.D. 179 (S.D.N.Y. 2007).

24. West v. Goodyear Tire & Rubber Co., 167 F.3d 776, 779 (2d Cir. 1999).

25. *See Phx. Four, Inc.*, 2006 WL 1409413.

26. *See* United States v. Philip Morris USA, Inc., 327 F. Supp. 2d 21 (D.D.C. 2004).

27. *See Metro. Opera Ass'n*, 212 F.R.D. at 178.

28. *See In re* NTL, Inc. Sec. Litig., 244 F.R.D. 179 (S.D.N.Y. 2007).

29. Qualcomm, Inc. v. Broadcom Corp., 2008 WL 66932 (S.D. Cal. Jan. 7, 2008).

30. *See* Coleman (Parent) Holding, Inc. v. Morgan Stanley & Co., 2005 WL 679071 (Fla. Cir. Ct. Mar. 1, 2005); Coleman (Parent) Holding, Inc. v. Morgan Stanley & Co., No. CA 03-50-45 Al (Fla. Cir. Ct. Mar. 23, 2005), *rev'd on other grounds*, 955 So. 2d 1124 (Fla. 4th Dist. Ct. App. 2007).

31. FED. R. CIV. P. 26(f).

32. *See* Q 7.6, *supra* (for more on inadvertent deletion or alteration of data).

33. *See* note 2, *supra* (defining "metadata"). Metadata is also discussed in chapter 5.

34. *See* Victor Stanley, Inc. v. Creative Pipe, Inc., 250 F.R.D. 251 (D. Md. 2008); United States v. O'Keefe, 537 F. Supp. 2d 14, 24 (D.D.C. 2008); William A. Gross Constr. Assocs., Inc. v. Am. Mfrs. Mut. Ins. Co., 256 F.R.D. 134 (S.D.N.Y. 2009).

35. FED. R. CIV. P. 26(b)(1).

36. FED. R. CIV. P. 26(b)(2)(B).

37. *Id.*

38. FED. R. CIV. P. 26(b)(2)(C).

39. *See, e.g.*, Barrera v. Boughton, 2010 WL 3926070, at *3 (D. Conn. Sept. 30, 2010) (the "concept of sampling to test both the cost and the yield is now part of the mainstream approach to electronic discovery"); Phillip M. Adams & Assocs., LLC v. Fujitsu Ltd., 2010 WL 1901776, at *4 (D. Utah May 10, 2010) (ordering data sampling and allowing requesting party to move for additional discovery if "sampling yields something significant").

40. *See, e.g.*, Zubulake v. UBS Warburg, LLC, 217 F.R.D. 309 (S.D.N.Y. 2003); Quinby v. WestLB, AG, No. 04 Civ. 7406 (S.D.N.Y. Sept. 22, 2006).

41. FED. R. CIV. P. 37(e).

42. *See, e.g., In re* Air Cargo Shipping Servs. Antitrust Litig., 2010 WL 2976220, at *2–3 (E.D.N.Y. July 23, 2010) (granting motion to compel granted because U.S. interest in enforcing antitrust laws outweighed South African interest in enforcing blocking statute, where prospect of criminal prosecution for violating South African statute was "speculative at best").

43. Monique Da Silva Moore v. Publicis Groupe & MSL Grp., 2012 WL 607412 (S.D.N.Y. Feb. 24, 2012).

44. *See* EORHB, Inc. v. HOA Holdings, LLC, No. 7409 (Del. Ch. Oct. 15, 2012) ("This seems to me to be an ideal non-expedited case in which the parties would benefit from using predictive coding. I would like you all, if you do not want to use predictive coding, to show cause why this is not a case where predictive coding is the way to go.").

45. FED. R. CIV. P. 34(b).

46. FED. R. CIV. P. 34(b)(ii).

47. *See* FED. R. CIV. P. 26(f), 37(a)(2)(B).

48. The company should, in general, avoid production in an imaged format that is not searchable. Many courts have held that production of non-searchable image documents does not meet a party's obligations under the rules. *See, e.g., In re* Verisign, Inc. Sec. Litig., 2004 WL 2445243 (N.D. Cal. Mar. 10, 2004).

49. *See, e.g.,* Jay Yurkiw, *Top 10 E-Discovery Developments and Trends in 2012,* TECH. L. SOURCE (Jan. 31, 2013) (vendor costs accounted for roughly 27% of e-discovery costs—8% for collection and 19% for processing—while document review accounted for the remaining 73%).

50. *See, e.g.,* Monique Da Silva Moore v. Publicis Groupe SA, Case No. 1:11-CV-01279 (S.D.N.Y. Apr. 25, 2012) (affirming magistrate judge's February 24, 2012, order that the use of predictive coding software to reduce the costs of document review was more appropriate than keyword searching).

8

Voluntary Disclosure of Wrongdoing

*Michael Manthei**

Whether to make a voluntary disclosure is a very serious decision that should not be undertaken lightly or without the advice
of qualified counsel. It will expose the company and its officers
and directors to public scrutiny and can result in significant
penalties. There is no formula or blanket rule that can be
applied to the decision whether to make a voluntary disclosure; each case turns on its own facts and on a balancing of
the advantages that might be gained against the losses that
will accrue. A voluntary disclosure is appropriate only when
the company has a reasonable basis to believe that there has
been a criminal, civil, or administrative violation. If there is a
concern that a disclosure to the government of the situation by
another source may be imminent, consideration should be
given to making an expedited voluntary disclosure. On the
other hand, if the government already has the information, the
benefits of disclosure can be significantly reduced.

* The author wishes to acknowledge Chistopher A. Myers, Suzanne M. Foster,
  and Andrew Namkung for their contributions to this chapter.

239

The Basics

Q 8.1   What is a voluntary disclosure of wrongdoing?

A voluntary disclosure is a formal or informal process whereby a corporation "confesses" compliance violations or other wrongdoing to a government enforcement entity *before* the government learns of the conduct from other sources or conducts its own investigation.

Benefits and Risks

Q 8.1.1   Why would a corporation disclose wrongdoing rather than simply fix the problem?

The principal reason corporations make voluntary disclosures is the anticipation of reduced penalties and the hope that the government will forego criminal prosecution or civil False Claims Act actions against the company.[1]

Consider the following government departments and agencies and their policies regarding voluntary disclosure:

HHS	Department of Health and Human Services' Provider Self-Disclosure Protocol holds out the prospect of reduced penalties for entities that disclose healthcare fraud and other violations of federal healthcare program guidelines.[2]
DOD	Department of Defense's voluntary disclosure program offers reduced penalties, enhanced confidentiality, and the opportunity to control the ensuing investigation.[3]
DOJ/ Antitrust Division	Antitrust Division's Corporate Leniency Policy reduces or eliminates civil penalties, and it will not bring criminal charges against entities that voluntarily disclose wrongdoing.[4]
OSHA	U.S. Occupational Safety and Health Administration allocates nearly one-third of its budget to "cooperative compliance programs."[5]
DOJ	Department of Justice's policy for environmental violations encourages self-auditing and disclosure by offering leniency, up to and including declining to prosecute.[6]
EPA	Environmental Protection Agency's "Voluntary Audit Policy" promotes disclosure of environmental violations by significantly reducing or eliminating certain penalties, and provides that EPA generally will not recommend criminal prosecution of the disclosing company.[7]
SEC	The SEC's Enforcement Cooperation Program and 2001 Report of Investigation and Statement (the "Seaboard Report") incentivize voluntary disclosures to the SEC and highlight thirteen factors that the SEC will consider in deciding the level of leniency.
IRS	The IRS's Voluntary Disclosure Practice incentivizes voluntary disclosure by broadly allowing taxpayers to timely disclose any noncompliance relating to tax obligations. Voluntary disclosures may result in the IRS not recommending prosecution.

Q 8.1.2 Does voluntary disclosure of wrongdoing preclude criminal prosecution?

No. The government still may bring criminal charges after a voluntary disclosure. However, as noted above, the various protocols for voluntary disclosures all hold out the possibility that criminal prosecution either will not be recommended or may be declined. Further, DOJ "Principles for the Prosecution of Business Organizations" identifies the corporation's "timely and voluntary disclosure of wrongdoing and its willingness to cooperat[e] in the investigation" as one of the factors that must be evaluated when determining whether to prosecute a corporation.[8]

Making a Voluntary Disclosure

Contents of the Disclosure

Q 8.2 What are the basic elements of a voluntary disclosure?

Though the programs of the various governmental agencies described above vary slightly in some of their details, they all share the same basic structural requirements:

- Internal recognition of potential wrongdoing.
- Preliminary evaluation/investigation.
- Consideration of an initial disclosure of the wrongdoing to the appropriate agency or to DOJ.
- Conduct of a thorough internal investigation.
- Full disclosure of investigation results to the government.
- Cooperation in any follow-up investigation or verification process by the government.[9]
- Agreement to a negotiated resolution.
- In some instances, agreement to undertake specific ongoing compliance efforts (*e.g.*, a "corporate integrity agreement").

Q 8.2.1 What information should be included in the initial disclosure?[10]

The initial disclosure must be written and should include:

- the name, address, agency identification number (if any), and tax identification number of the disclosing entity;
- a description or diagram of the pertinent relationships among the entities involved in the wrongdoing and making the disclosure;
- the name and address of the disclosing entity's designated representative for purposes of the disclosure;
- an indication of whether the entity has knowledge that the matter being disclosed is under investigation or inquiry by the government;
- a full description of the nature of the matter being disclosed;
- the names of entities and individuals who were involved in the conduct and an explanation of their roles;
- the period of time during which the conduct occurred;
- the names of the programs that have been affected, including a calculation of any damages to the government programs;
- the reasons why the disclosing entity believes that a violation of federal criminal, civil, or administrative law may have occurred;
- a certification by an authorized representative of the provider that the disclosure submission contains truthful information and is based on a good-faith effort to bring the matter to the government's attention for the purpose of resolving any potential liabilities.

After the Voluntary Disclosure

Internal Investigation/Self-Assessment

Q 8.3   What happens after the initial disclosure?

Generally, after the corporation has made its initial disclosure, it will be expected to conduct an internal investigation and self-assessment and to report those findings to the relevant agency or to the DOJ. While the internal investigation is being conducted, the agency generally will agree to forego its own investigation. Depending on the nature and complexity of the conduct involved, it may be possible to conduct the internal investigation prior to making the initial disclosure. In that case, the company would submit its self-assessment report with the initial disclosure.

Q 8.3.1   What should an internal investigation cover?

The company usually will address three areas in its investigation:

(1)   The scope and nature of the improper activity;
(2)   The steps taken to discover and respond to the problem; and
(3)   The financial impact of the improper activity.

A discussion of these will be included in the written report of the investigation.

Internal Investigation Report

Q 8.3.2   What information should be reported regarding the scope of the activity?

The coverage of the scope of the activity should include:

* the potential causes of the incident or practice (*e.g.*, lack of internal controls, circumvention of procedures, etc.);
* details about the incident or practice;
* the identity of the division, department, branches, or related entities that were involved or affected;
* an assessment of the impact of the practice (*e.g.*, in a regulated industry, an assessment of the impact on the affected government program on the health, safety, and welfare of the public generally or of program participants);
* a description of the time period during which the activity occurred;
* the identity of any corporate officials, employees, or agents who knew of or participated in the practice;
* the identity of corporate officials, employees, or agents who—based on their job responsibilities—should have known about, but failed to detect, the improper practices;
* a description of the monetary impact of the activity.

Q 8.3.3 What information should be reported regarding the discovery and response to the problem?

The internal investigation report should also describe the circumstances under which the activity was discovered and document the steps taken to address the problem and prevent future abuses, including:

- a description of how the incident or practice was identified and the origin of the information that led to the discovery;
- a description of the entity's efforts to investigate and document the incident or practice;
- a chronology of the investigative steps taken in the entity's internal investigation, including:
  - a list of individuals interviewed and pertinent information about them (*e.g.*, name, address, title), along with the dates and subject matter of each interview;
  - a description of files, documents, and records reviewed;
  - a summary of the auditing activity and the documents relied upon in estimating financial impact;
- a description of the actions taken to stop and/or correct the inappropriate conduct;
- the identity of any related businesses that may be affected by the conduct, and steps taken to prevent a recurrence of the incident (*e.g.*, new accounting or control measures, increased audit efforts, increased supervision);
- a description of any disciplinary action taken against corporate officials, employees, or agents as a result of the improper activity;
- a description of all notices or disclosures provided to other affected government agencies.

Typically, disclosure protocol guidelines will require that an authorized representative of the disclosing entity sign and submit a certification that the internal investigation report contains truthful information and is based on a good-faith effort to uncover the facts relevant to the wrongdoing.

Q 8.3.4   How does the company assess the financial impact of the disclosed activities?

The method of calculating financial impact will vary depending on the industry, the nature of the conduct, and whether direct payments from the government are involved. Where direct payments are involved, the entity must employ a methodology that is statistically valid and consistent with generally accepted audit principles. If the entity is a healthcare company disclosing under the Health and Human Services' Provider Self-Disclosure Protocol, it must follow one of the methodologies approved by the HHS Office of Inspector General in the Protocol—that is, a review of all affected claims for federal healthcare program reimbursement or review of a statistically valid random sample of claims that is then extrapolated across the universe of claims affected by the disclosed conduct.[11]

Generally, where there is a financial impact—*i.e.*, where the disclosed conduct resulted in the expenditure of government funds that must be returned—the disclosure should include a work plan that describes the assessment procedure. The work plan should address:

- the objectives of the review and how the proposed procedures will meet those objectives;
- the population of claims that will be studied and an explanation of the methodology used to arrive at that population;
- the sources of data that will be used, including any legal standards that will be applied and the documents that will be relied upon;
- the identity of the personnel who will be conducting the review and their qualifications for conducting the self-assessment.

The results of the assessment will be disclosed to the government in a self-assessment report. Typically, the self-assessment report must include a certification signed by an authorized representative of the disclosing entity that verifies the truthfulness of the information in the report and that the entity proceeded in good faith.

Government's Verification Investigation

Q 8.3.5   What happens after the company submits its disclosure and self-assessment reports?

Upon receipt of the Voluntary Disclosure Report and the Self-Assessment Report (if any), the affected agency typically will set about to verify the disclosed information. The nature and extent of the government's verification investigation will depend entirely upon the quality and thoroughness of the internal investigation and self-assessment reports. During the verification process, the entity must continue to cooperate with the government by making all work papers and supporting documentation available to the government. Usually, the more comprehensive and thorough the company's internal investigation, the less extensive will be the government's confirmation activities.

Privilege Concerns

Q 8.4   How does voluntary disclosure affect the attorney-client and work-product privileges?

Self-disclosure necessarily brings into question the possible waiver of the attorney-client privilege and of the work-product doctrine. When internal investigations are undertaken by company counsel and result in a voluntary disclosure, the facts discovered during the investigation must be disclosed to the government. Careful consideration must be given to the intentional or inadvertent waiver of privileges that may result from the submission of the Self-Assessment and of the Voluntary Disclosure Report. The issues related to the attorney-client privilege and work-product doctrine are dealt with extensively in chapter 6, Internal Investigations. While the facts, and, in many instances, legal conclusions developed by counsel during the course of an internal investigation, are usually disclosed, less typical is the disclosure of the actual communications between counsel and representatives of the company. However, disclosure of this type of privileged information may permit the government to expedite its investigation. In addition, the disclosure of this type of privileged information, in some circumstances, may be important in enabling the government to evaluate the accuracy and completeness of the company's voluntary disclosure. Careful consideration of whether to disclose this type of privileged information is imperative, as waiver of privileges can have serious collateral consequences.

Waiving Attorney-Client and Work-Product Protections

Q 8.5   When are requests for privileged information permitted?

In order to understand the guidelines followed by federal prosecutors in regard to a company's attorney-client privilege and attorney work-product protection, it is necessary to understand the changing history of the DOJ guidelines for charging businesses with criminal conduct.

In 1999, the Justice Department issued what was generally referred to as the Holder Memorandum.

Q 8.5.1   What is the Holder Memorandum?

This memorandum contained guidelines that instructed federal prosecutors evaluating the level of a company's cooperation to consider, among other things, its willingness to waive its attorney-client and work-product protections.[12] This policy was reiterated in January 2003 by its successor, the Thompson Memorandum.

Q 8.5.2   What is the Thompson Memorandum?

The Thompson Memorandum updated the guidelines but continued the waiver considerations included in the Holder Memorandum.[13] Based on the guidelines in these memoranda, federal prosecutors routinely required companies to waive the privilege in order to either avoid criminal prosecution or secure cooperation status for sentencing credit.

The DOJ's policy on waiver was subject to severe and continuing criticism, which culminated in a U.S. district court opinion severely critical of the Thompson Memorandum guidelines, and in the introduction of proposed remedial federal legislation designed to overturn a number of its key provisions, including the policy regarding waiver of the privilege. The district court opinion, issued in June 2006 by district court Judge Kaplan in *United States v. Stein*,[14] held that the use of the Thompson Memo to pressure KPMG to refuse to indemnify its employees' legal fees incurred in their defense against the criminal charges violated the Fifth and Sixth Amendments, and criminal charges against thirteen KPMG officers and directors were dismissed. The *Stein* opinion was later upheld in August 2008 by the Second Circuit.[15]

Six months after the district court's opinion in *Stein*, the Attorney-Client Privilege Protection Act of 2006 was introduced in Congress.[16] This proposed legislation would have prohibited government prosecutors from considering a company's willingness to waive its attorney-client privilege as a factor in determining whether the company had cooperated with the government. The bill would also have prohibited government prosecutors from considering whether the company had agreed to indemnify its employees' legal fees in the investigation or had entered into a joint defense agreement.

Largely in response to both the *Stein* opinion and the proposed legislation, Deputy Attorney General Paul J. McNulty issued a new memorandum to Justice Department prosecutors in December 2006.[17]

Q 8.5.3 What is the McNulty Memorandum?

The McNulty Memorandum outlined new guidelines for federal prosecutors to follow when seeking a privilege waiver from a company. The McNulty Memorandum allowed federal prosecutors to seek a waiver only where there was a "legitimate need" for the privileged information, and then only after they had first obtained supervisory-level approval. Even with such approval, however, prosecutors were permitted to seek only what the McNulty Memorandum referred to as "Category I" information, which consisted of purely factual information relating to the underlying misconduct. Another classification of privileged information, referred to as "Category II" information, included actual attorney-client communications and non-factual work product, and could be sought only when the Category I information was insufficient. Requests for Category II information required an even higher level of advance supervisory approval. Although prosecutors were allowed to consider a company's refusal to waive privilege over Category I information in assessing cooperation, the refusal to provide Category II information could not be considered—although a company's *agreement* to waive privilege could be considered favorably in the prosecutor's assessment.[18]

249

Criticism of the government's policies nevertheless continued, and in June 2007 the Attorney-Client Privilege Protection Act of 2006 was re-introduced in the 110th Congress as the Attorney-Client Privilege Protection Act of 2007.[19] Within weeks, in an apparent effort to avoid the passage of this bill, Deputy Attorney General Mark R. Filip issued the Filip Memorandum, which contains current Justice Department policy regarding corporate privilege waiver.[20]

Q 8.5.4   What is the Filip Memorandum?

The Filip Memorandum states the current Justice Department policy on privilege waiver (as well as indemnification of employees' legal defense costs and joining joint defense agreements).

The Filip Memorandum recognizes that the attorney-client privilege and the attorney work-product protection serve an extremely important function in the U.S. legal system. It further recognizes that a company may freely waive its own privileges if it chooses to do so and that such waivers occur routinely when companies conduct an internal investigation and then disclosed the details of that investigation to law enforcement officials in an effort to seek prosecution of the offenders.

The policy states, however, that what the government needs to advance its investigations is not *waiver* of the privilege, but instead the disclosure of *facts* known to the corporation about the criminal misconduct under review. Thus, "while a company remains free to convey non-factual or 'core' attorney-client communications or work product—if and only if the company voluntarily chooses to do so—*prosecutors should not ask for such waivers and are directed not to do so.*"[21] The critical factor is whether the corporation has provided the *facts* about the events under investigation, and not a formal waiver of the company's privilege.

Q 8.5.5   What is the current policy?

In effect, what the current policy means is this: Company officers, directors, and employees are usually interviewed in the course of an internal investigation. If those interviews are done by counsel for the company, counsel's notes and memoranda of the interviews are usually protected by the attorney-client privilege and/or as attorney work product. But now, in order to receive cooperation credit for providing the *factual* information that the government needs, the corporation need *not* produce, and prosecutors may *not* request, protected notes or memoranda generated by the lawyers' interviews.[22] Further, non-factual or core attorney work product, such as counsel's mental impressions or legal theories, need not be disclosed, and prosecutors may not request the disclosure of such attorney work product as a condition for cooperation credit. However, to earn cooperation credit, the company *does* need to produce, and prosecutors *may* request, relevant factual information, including relevant factual information acquired through those interviews (unless the identical information has otherwise been provided), as well as relevant non-privileged evidence such as accounting and business records and emails between non-attorney employees or agents.[23]

Counsel for companies who believe that prosecutors are violating such guidance are encouraged by the guidelines to raise their concerns with the prosecutor's supervisors, such as the appropriate U.S. attorney or assistant attorney general.[24]

Resolving the Investigation

Cooperation

Q 8.6   What happens if I change my mind after disclosure?

Once a disclosure is made, it is too late to start over. The government expects disclosing entities to act diligently and to cooperate throughout the voluntary disclosure process. If an entity fails to cooperate or to act in good faith to resolve the disclosed matter, the government will consider it an aggravating factor when determining an appropriate resolution to the matter. The government also may remove the entity from the voluntary disclosure protocol and seek to conduct its own full-blown investigation of the company. Failure to cooperate fully after making a voluntary disclosure also increases the likelihood that the government will file criminal charges if the disclosure involves criminal conduct.

Settlements/Corporate Integrity Agreements

Q 8.7   How are voluntary disclosures finally resolved?

Voluntary disclosures typically will result in the entity paying back any money owed to the government. Civil fines or monetary penalties may be imposed, but under the protocols of various agencies these fines may be reduced substantially or eliminated altogether. In rare instances, the agency receiving the voluntary disclosure may refer the company to the DOJ for criminal prosecution, notwithstanding that the disclosure was voluntary. This could happen in a situation where the government, unknown to the entity, was already far along in its own investigation.

Under various agencies' protocols, particularly the HHS OIG Provider Self-Disclosure Protocol, the government may seek or require an agreement by the disclosing entity to implement future compliance measures as a prerequisite for settlement or for declining or deferring criminal prosecution. Sometimes called "corporate integrity agreements," these settlement arrangements incorporate the requirement that the entity establish (or maintain an existing) effective compliance program and that such program included certain specific elements to address the disclosed wrongdoing and to prevent recurrence. These agreements can be quite onerous in that they usually require that the entity retain outside auditors to conduct periodic compliance audits. For this reason, we usually recommend that companies considering or involved in voluntary disclosures take all necessary measures to enhance their compliance programs and, in particular, implement measures to correct any wrongdoing discovered and prevent reoccurences.

Under most settlements, the entity also will have to certify its continued compliance with relevant statutes and regulations. Any failure of compliance could result in additional fines or withdrawal of the government's agreement to decline or to defer prosecution. In many cases, the settlement agreement contains a confession of judgment or a waiver of indictment that, respectively, sets a liquidated damages amount or allows the government to bring criminal charges simply by filing an information, which is a statement of the criminal charges filed with the court.

Notes to Chapter 8

1.   Companies with compliance programs based on the Federal Sentencing Guidelines or similar standards will also emphasize ethical behavior, or "doing the right thing." This ethical commitment will often include a component that requires disclosure of compliance violations to appropriate authorities.

2.   63 Fed. Reg. 58,399 (Oct. 30, 1998).

3.   Department of Defense Voluntary Disclosure Program (July 1986); *see also* The Department of Defense Voluntary Disclosure Program—A Description of the Process (Apr. 1990), www.dodig.osd.mil/IGInformation/archives/vdguide-lines.pdf. The DOD Voluntary Disclosure Program should be considered, in many respects, superceded by recent changes to the Federal Acquisition Regulation (FAR), which require mandatory self-reporting of criminal violations, civil False Claims Act violations, and significant overpayments by many federal government contractors and subcontractors. These new FAR requirements are outlined in detail in chapter 14, Government Contractors.

4.   Corporate Leniency Policy (Aug. 10, 1993); *see also* www.usdoj.gov/atr/public/guidelines/0091.pdf.

5.   Orly Lobel, *Interlocking Regulatory and Industrial Relations: The Governance of Workplace Safety*, 57 ADMIN. L. REV. 1071 (2005).

6.   U.S. Dep't of Justice, Factors in Decisions on Criminal Prosecutions for Environmental Violations in the Context of Significant Voluntary Compliance or Disclosure by the Violator, 4 DOJ MANUAL § 5-11.104A.

7.   Final Policy Statement, Incentives for Self-Policing: Discovery, Disclosure, Correction and Prevention of Violations, www.epa.gov/compliance/resources/policies/incentives/auditing/finalpolstate.pdf.

8.   The most current version of these guidelines is referred to as the "Filip Memorandum," after Deputy Attorney General Mark R. Filip. They are found in Principles of Federal Prosecution of Business Organizations §§ 9-28.300(A)(4), 9-28.700 (Aug. 2008), www.usdoj.gov/opa/documents/corp-charging-guide-lines.pdf.

9.   One of the significant benefits that usually flows from a voluntary disclosure is that the government agency will typically allow the company to complete its own investigation and evaluate the results before undertaking any government investigation. As long as the company's investigation is thorough and the results are disclosed in a manner that satisfies the government, it is unlikely that the government will carry on a separate, extensive investigation of its own. As should be obvious, a government investigation can be significantly more disruptive and more expensive for companies than their own internal investigations.

10.   This question and the succeeding questions describing the voluntary disclosure process represent a composite of the requirements of the various programs mentioned earlier in this chapter and provide basic guidance. The indi-

253

vidual protocols should be consulted to determine the exact requirements applicable to a particular contemplated disclosure.

11. *See* 63 Fed. Reg. at 58,402–03.

12. Named for Deputy Attorney General Eric H. Holder Jr., the Memorandum was entitled "Principles of Federal Prosecution of Business Organizations" and was issued to Justice Department prosecutors in June 1999. Other considerations in addition to waiver of the privilege included whether the corporation had agreed to indemnify its officers, directors, or employees for their investigation-related attorney fees, and whether it had agreed to participate in a joint defense agreement, both of which were considered to be indicative of a company's *lack* of cooperation with the government.

13. The Thompson Memorandum was named for Deputy Attorney General Larry D. Thompson and was issued in January 2003.

14. United States v. Stein, 435 F. Supp. 2d 330 (S.D.N.Y. 2006).

15. United States v. Stein, 541 F.3d 130 (2d Cir. 2008).

16. The Attorney-Client Privilege Protection Act of 2006, S. 30, 109th Cong. (2006).

17. Principles of Federal Prosecution of Business Organizations, Memorandum from Paul J. McNulty, Deputy Attorney Gen., to Heads of Department Components and U.S. Attorneys (Dec. 12, 2006), www.usdoj.gov/dag/speeches/2006/mcnulty_memo.pdf.

18. The McNulty Memorandum also prohibited prosecutors from considering whether a company indemnified its employees' attorney fees, unless the circumstances indicated that the indemnification was intended to impede a criminal investigation. A company's joining a joint defense agreement, however, continued to be a valid factor for consideration by prosecutors.

19. H.R. 3013, 110th Cong. (2007). In 2009, the Attorney-Client Privilege Act of 2009 was introduced into Congress but died in committee. This act would have disallowed federal prosecutors and investigators from demanding or requesting waiver of the attorney-client privilege and attorney work-product protection. *See* S. 445, 111th Cong. (2009); H.R. 4326, 111th Cong. (2009).

20. The guidelines are found in Principles of Federal Prosecution of Business Organizations § 9-28.000 (Aug. 2008), www.usdoj.gov/opa/documents/corp-charging-guidelines.pdf [hereinafter Filip Memorandum].

21. Filip Memorandum § 9-28.710 (Aug. 2008) (emphasis added).

22. *Id.* § 9-28.720 n.3.

23. Further, under current DOJ policy, prosecutors should not take into account whether a corporation is advancing or reimbursing attorney fees or providing counsel to employees, officers or directors under investigation or under indictment, and prosecutors may not request that a company refrain from taking such action, as long as such payments are not intended to obstruct the government's investigation or prosecution. Similarly, participation in a joint defense agreement does not render the company ineligible to receive cooperation credit, and prosecutors may not request that a company refrain from entering into such agreements.

24. Filip Memorandum § 9-28.760.

9

Witness Preparation

*Daniel I. Small**

Not so long ago, persuading corporate executives that they needed extensive preparation before testifying in a legal proceeding was a battle. Many confident, articulate executives were convinced they could just "go in and tell my story," and they were insulted by the notion that they needed some lawyer to prepare them. Too many experienced lawyers did not push back.

Then came an explosion of high-profile lawsuits and investigations, and with them a parade of highly successful executives and others who proved to be very bad witnesses. Gates, Stewart, Libby, Kozlowski, Lay—the list goes on. Now executives faced with the prospect of being a witness may wonder if there is some reason this happened and if it could happen to them. The answers are "yes" and "yes."

* The author would like to acknowledge Jonathan E. Anderman and Christopher A. Myers for their contributions to this chapter.

255

Like so much else in the law, true witness preparation is a narrow area that requires years of experience and expertise. Many excellent lawyers, including litigators, have not focused on this critical part of the process enough to understand how difficult it can be for executives and others to succeed in a witness environment and how challenging effective witness preparation can be. This chapter outlines the basics of witness preparation, provides steps for readying a witness for testifying, and spells out important techniques that can make the process significantly fairer and more productive and significantly less dangerous for the employee *and* the employer.

Importance of Witness Preparation

Q 9.1   Why is witness preparation important?

When someone is called as a witness in any kind of legal matter, it is usually a new and disturbing experience. Still, few people understand at the outset just how unnatural and difficult testifying as a witness really is. *It is not a conversation.* It does not look like one or feel like one, so no one should expect it to be like one. Testifying is very different from anything we do in our normal lives. It has its own language and rhythm. Question, pause, answer, stop. It is a narrow and artificial world where every word is taken down under oath and may be picked apart. Learning to communicate effectively in the question-and-answer format is one of the key goals of effective witness preparation.

Executives sometimes fail to understand that, when confronted with a lawsuit or investigation, they are entering a different and dangerous world. In this world, it is not just about experience and intelligence; it is about preparation and about understanding the audience, the rules, and the core themes of the case. Executives who have already spent years mastering the corporate world must nonetheless understand it takes commitment, time, and effort. Still, in this day and age of high-profile witnesses, it is surprising how often witnesses hear from counsel the old refrain, "Meet me half an hour before your deposition, and we'll prepare." In most litigation today, for most substantive witnesses, that is *not* meaningful preparation. Witness preparation is a multi-step process—extensive and intensive—that requires a commitment of time and energy from both lawyer and witness. Anything less puts the witness—and his or her employer—at risk.

Unprepared witnesses, through mistakes, gossip, and guesses—or worse—can badly damage a company and at the very least send an investigation in unnecessary directions that cost dearly in time, money, anxiety, and possibly even the company's reputation. The efforts of even the best-intentioned employee to "help" the company, or to "help" the investigators, can backfire badly. The unprepared employee is unlikely to understand the issues, the law, and (most importantly) the very precise and unnatural witness environment.

Q 9.1.1   Is witness preparation unethical?

This might make sense if every lawyer, investigator, and witness walked into the interview with the same lack of preparation and the same risks. But they do not.

Witness preparation is all about leveling the playing field.

The questioner is experienced in the witness interview process, skilled in turning every careless word to his or her advantage, familiar with the case, and (perhaps most importantly) infallible. No matter how many mistakes the questioner makes, it does not matter. The questioner is not under oath. Yet just one mistake by a witness can severely damage his credibility, or his case, and live on forever. What could be more unfair?

How can lawyers fulfill their obligation to represent clients "zealously within the bounds of the law"[1] and allow this to happen? They cannot. The great Wigmore recognized the "absolute necessity of such a [witness preparation] conference for legitimate purposes."[2]

The challenge, then, is not whether to prepare witnesses, but how (*see* Q 9.7.1, *infra*).

"A lawyer who did not prepare his or her witness for testimony, having had an opportunity to do so, would not be doing his or her professional job properly."[3]

Q 9.1.2   Isn't witness preparation expensive?

Many people in your company may say that thorough witness preparation costs too much, both in terms of money and time. They are right: it is expensive. Witness preparation takes a lot of time, and legal fees today are extraordinarily high. But this is the wrong time and place to save. The real issue with cost is always relative. What is the alternative? Saving time and money up front by leaving a witness without counsel or without preparation can cost dearly later in time, money, and heartache. Investing money in managing and preparing for the litigation process can pay off in money, results, and morale.

Initial Planning

Q 9.2   What can a company do in advance?

Unfortunately, the government will rarely send you an engraved invitation to an investigation. Investigators may take complaints from disgruntled employees, visit employees at their homes at night, or appear unannounced with a search warrant. So the more you plan ahead, the more you can limit the confusion, fear, and damage of the unknown.

Given that an investigation is complex, confusing, and fraught with hazards for all involved, employers must guide employees about what to do when confronted with an investigation. First, employers should generally advise employees to cooperate with and tell the truth in a government investigation. Second, companies must help their employees understand that—whether at home or at the office—

they do not *have* to speak with investigators without an attorney, and they would be ill-advised to do so.

Employees can politely but firmly take the questioners' cards and say they will have a lawyer get in touch. In order to facilitate this process, the company needs to have a point person and a process for employees to report any government contact. In addition, the company needs to decide in advance when and how it will provide counsel to represent and prepare employee witnesses.

Counsel for Company Employees

Q 9.3 Why do our own employees need counsel for an internal investigation?

Suppose an employee "agrees" to be interviewed without counsel, and down the road things go badly for him. Who is he going to blame for his lack of representation and resulting "confusion" and "coercion"? Himself? Human nature says he will blame others—the company or company counsel. Whatever you might gain in efficiency or cost savings up front by allowing an employee not to have representation pales in comparison to the cost and damage down the road.

Nor is the common wisdom correct that you get "better" answers from unrepresented employees. Bad answers often stem from executive and employee confusion. They wonder how much truth helps their company, their co-workers, and themselves. Bad testimony and bad decisions can cause problems on many levels long after you have forgotten why you let the interview go forward without counsel in the first place. The answers to those questions are not always so clear for company counsel either. For example, we have seen cases where unrepresented and unprepared employees, eager to please and assuming company counsel is *their* counsel, "confidentially" unload everything they can think of—gossip, innuendo, speculation—"garbage" that a lawyer representing *them* could help them wade through and sort out *before* any interview takes place. Then, to the employee's surprise and anger, company counsel decides that enough questions are raised by all that garbage to require further investigation or disclosure to others.

Q 9.4   Is it more efficient for in-house counsel to represent company employees?

Using in-house counsel to represent company employees is a common temptation in both internal and external investigations, but it is usually a mistake—sometimes a very dangerous one. Two of the main problems are expertise and privilege.

As to expertise, most in-house counsel are not experienced in the methods and challenges of witness preparation. Consequently, preparation is often inadequate, and all parties (the employee and the company) are put at unnecessary risk.

Privilege creates an even more dangerous situation. In most cases, the company wants to know any negative evidence a witness may have. After all, that is the point of internal investigations, and an essential part of responding to external investigations. But suppose such information exists; suppose Employee *A* has information about something Employee *B* did that may also put the company at risk. If you, as in-house counsel, attempt to represent Employee *A*, one of a number of things may happen (all of them bad). For example:

(1)   Employee *A* may not believe that as company counsel you really represent her interests, so she may not tell you the negative information. Now a bad situation has been made worse. You have the false comfort that there is nothing wrong *and* an interview memo that may include false statements by Employee *A*. Your chances of uncovering the facts have decreased, and the chances have increased that you will be called as a witness down the road when someone else discovers the facts and alleges "cover-up." You know that you did not encourage the witness to lie to protect your company, but will everyone else believe you? Will the employee, when confronted, stand by you?

(2)   Suppose you are persuasive enough to get Employee *A* to tell you what she knows. What then? If you truly represent her, you cannot breach her confidence and tell the company, which you also represent (and get paid by). Nor can you tell Employee *B*, who would reasonably expect that his own company's counsel *would* tell him. You are badly conflicted in several directions. If you ask Employee *A* to waive her

privilege, will anyone believe it was truly a voluntary waiver since her employer requested it? Unlikely.

Upjohn *Warnings*

Q 9.4.1   Don't the *Upjohn* warnings protect company counsel?

More than three decades ago, in *Upjohn v. United States*,[4] the Supreme Court addressed what the Ninth Circuit has recently described as the "treacherous path which corporate counsel must tread . . . when conducting an internal investigation."[5] And so were born "*Upjohn* warnings."

Every day in internal investigations across the country, employees are told that counsel represents the company, not the individual; that counsel is conducting an investigation for the company; and that what is said should be covered by the company's privilege, controlled by the company alone. It has become increasingly clear that these warnings can be inadequate in the real world. Two principal problems have emerged: conflicts and comprehension.

The environment in which *Upjohn* was decided years ago seems almost quaint compared to today. Company counsel and employees were interested mostly in future policies and tax implications. The words "bribery" and "jail" never appeared. It was a kinder, gentler world for corporate wrongdoing. White collar investigations today, and the risks to all concerned, are very different. One result is that the relationship between employer and employee has in many cases gone from caring to cutthroat. Corporations go to considerable lengths to sacrifice employees to save themselves, and vice versa. These increasing conflicts also make the issues of who represents whom far more challenging.

As for the problem of comprehension, simply put, the *Upjohn* warnings are largely legalese to most normal people. When an employee sits down with their employer's lawyer to discuss issues related to their employment, they naturally assume that the conversation is privileged, and not only at the company's whim. The resulting confusion can harm both employer and employee. The days when we could pretend that a short oral warning was adequate to apprise a corporate employee of his or her rights are long gone. It's a jungle out there, one that requires clear advice and counsel. Exercising caution at this critical stage can help protect the integrity of the investigation, protect the company, and protect the employee.

Q 9.5   What is the process for obtaining outside counsel for witnesses in an internal investigation?

First, assess the needs based on the types of individuals involved. How many witnesses, and at what levels? The Department of Justice puts witnesses into three basic categories: witnesses, subjects, and targets. While their definitions are not realistic or useful, the idea of three general categories is a helpful one.

The mere "witnesses," or ministerial witnesses, are the record keepers, IT people, and other company employees who were not directly involved in the actions under investigation. For those folks, it may be appropriate to have them represented, if at all, by company counsel.

On the other extreme are the targets—employees, particularly decision makers, whose conduct is at the heart of the issue and who were really responsible. Targets will likely need individual counsel to avoid conflicts and disqualification down the road.

In the middle are the "subjects"—people who may have known about or played some role in the matter under investigation but were not the central figures. For those folks, if they consent, it may be appropriate, and to everyone's benefit, to have one lawyer represent that entire group. In a larger matter, there may really be several different groupings within this middle layer, and each group may need separate counsel.

Preparing the Witness for Testimony

Q 9.6   What is the difference between witness preparation and witness coaching?

The witness is the author, the creator of the material. The lawyer is the translator, helping the witness to communicate in a strange language, rhythm, and environment, but not creating new material. As Chief Justice Burger observed when considering the dynamics of witness preparation, "an attorney must respect the important distinction between discussing testimony and seeking to improperly influence it."[6]

The key is to emphasize to the witness right from the start the importance of "tell the truth." Disciplinary Rule 7-102(A) of the ABA's Model Code of Professional Responsibility states that a lawyer "shall not . . . participate in the creation or preservation of evidence when he knows or it is obvious that the evidence is false" or "counsel or assist his client in conduct that the lawyer knows to be illegal or fraudulent." The witness needs to clearly and unequivocally understand that counsel seeks no more—and no less—than the truth. Still, "tell the truth" is only the beginning of the preparation. As Oscar Wilde said, "The plain and simple truth is rarely plain and never simple."

Q 9.7 What is "real" witness preparation?

Real witness preparation is an intensive, interactive, evolving process from both the lawyer's and client's perspectives. There are seven basic steps:

1. **Introductions.** Imagine sitting down on a park bench and having a total stranger ask you about your most troubling secrets. You would not feel comfortable doing that, so why should anyone think a witness would feel comfortable doing the same thing just because the other person is a lawyer? A witness and his lawyer should take the time to learn about each other and establish trust and communication.
2. **Reviewing the facts.** Going through the who, what, when, why, where, and how one time is rarely enough. In a football game on TV, a play is repeated in slow-motion because in real time it happens too fast for most viewers to follow and explain. The same is true for witnesses.
3. **Reviewing the process.** Do not assume that any witness really knows or understands this bizarre process. Every witness needs to hear and understand the process, so apologize, if you feel you must, for erring on the side of too much information, but then do precisely that.
4. **Putting it together.** The facts do not change, but the method of communicating effectively in a question-and-answer

format is something that takes a lot of getting used to. Explore the rules for being an effective witness.

5. **Anticipating problems.** Now is the time to identify potential problems and prepare accordingly. What are the witness's fears about the process, his abilities, his job, his reputation? Finally, prepare him for questions *about the preparation.* Be sure the witness understands that the first, last, and fundamental message is: "Always tell the truth."

6. **Doing a dry run.** No amount of discussion can fully explain the question-and-answer process. Like anything difficult and unnatural, doing it right takes practice. The best approach is to do some kind of dry run with your witness so that he or she can experience the process firsthand. It does not need to be formal or cover all the possible topics, so long as it gives a sense of the process. The dry run should be as realistic and extensive as possible. Do a dry run with every witness.

7. **Reviewing the dry-run transcript.** Another great benefit of doing a dry run is to generate and review a transcript or video. Depending on the case, the privilege issues, and the resources, this can mean anything from a full videotaped session with a court reporter to a simple tape-recording that can be transcribed for review. Reviewing a videotape and/or transcript is the best way for both lawyer and client to see and understand how and why the rules work, and what the witness can do better.

Q 9.7.1   How can effective witness preparation help "level the playing field"?

In the world of a witness examination, the questioner appears to be in control. However, this is an illusion even the most accomplished executive can fall victim to. The reality is that the witness has the right and the responsibility to take control, not necessarily in an adversarial way. Most executives know that, when it comes to meetings or other interactions, the way to take control of the situation is not by shouting the loudest, but by utilizing some clearly established techniques or rules. So it is with testimony.

Q 9.8 What are the ten most important rules for witnesses?

Most of the following rules are difficult for executives and others. They are contrary to what executives and others are used to, and often counterintuitive. But if they are practiced, these rules can impose a degree of discipline and control on the process that makes it significantly fairer and more productive and significantly less dangerous for employees *and* their employers.

1. **Take your time.** Slow it down, think it through, and control the pace. Lawyers want rapid-fire Q&A, but if the lawyer makes a mistake, no one cares. If the witness makes a mistake, it can live on forever. From the very first question, pause before you answer.

2. **Remember you are making a record.** You are dictating the first and final draft of a very important document, with no rewind button and no second draft, so think about your language. Certain words can take on special meanings— jargon, legalese, slang, etc. Learn what those words are in your case, remembering that words can have different meanings to different people.

3. **Tell the truth.** A formal witness (and even in an "informal" interview, think of the witness as a formal witness) takes an oath in three parts. Consider all three. "The truth" means honest answers and honest mistakes—the real story, not red herrings or robotic answers. "The whole truth" means a responsibility to bring out both the bad stuff *and* the good stuff. "Nothing but the truth," reflects a very narrow concept. It is what you saw, heard, or did. Everything else is a guess.

4. **Be relentlessly polite.** They are attacking you, so it is natural to want to respond in kind. But remember that a witness who is angry or defensive is not thinking clearly and is not in control of the language or the pace. Lawyers know that. A few garbage questions, and off we go! Don't fall for it. Be relentlessly polite, positive, and focused.

5.   **Don't answer a question you don't understand.** Is it vague language, strange phrasing, or distorted assumptions? Is it just too long to be clear? Don't answer it. Just say, "Please, rephrase the question" and wait for a clear, fair question.

6.   **If you don't remember, say so.** Life is long; memories are short. Make clear what you *don't* know. Just say, "I don't recall" and stop.

7.   **Do not guess.** Much of what makes people good conversationalists involves guessing. But guessing is inappropriate and dangerous for a witness, whether it is details, inferences, or hypotheticals.

8.   **Do not volunteer.** "Question, pause, answer, stop." It is not your job to help the questioner fill in the blanks. A witness must become comfortable with the silence of waiting for the next question.

9.   **Be careful with documents.** Take the magic out of documents—it is just paper. There is a simple, unvarying protocol witnesses should follow:

   (a) If you are asked a question that relates in any way to a document, ask to see the document. Don't allow anyone to draw you into a debate with a document that is not in front of you. You cannot win.
   (b) Read all of it, slowly and carefully.
   (c) Ask for the question again. It is basic fairness.

10.   **Use your counsel.** Listen to everything that is said, think carefully about objections, ask questions when you can, and take breaks before you need them (not long after).

Notes to Chapter 9

1. MODEL CODE OF PROF'L RESPONSIBILITY EC 7-1.
2. 3 WIGMORE ON EVIDENCE § 788 (4th ed. Aspen 2000).
3. District of Columbia Bar, Ethics Op. No. 79, at 139 (1979).
4. Upjohn Co. v. United States, 449 U.S. 383 (1981).
5. United States v. Ruehle, 583 F.3d 600 (9th Cir. 2009).
6. Geders v. United States, 425 U.S. 80, 89 n.3 (1976).

10

Settling with the Government

Mark A. Flessner & Simon B. Auerbach *

An organization that can demonstrate its commitment to preventing, detecting, and correcting problems and mistakes frequently can persuade the government that settlement is an appropriate resolution to a particular violation, whether that organization is the subject of criminal, civil, or administrative actions, and regardless of the governmental entity pursuing the charge, claim, or sanction. Such organizations also may be able to negotiate more favorable settlement terms than entities that do not have existing, demonstrably effective compliance programs.

* This chapter is adapted from a previous version originally prepared by Jennifer A. Short, Suzanne M. Foster, and Christopher A. Myers.

The Role of Compliance in Settlements

Prior Compliance Efforts

Q 10.1   What role does compliance play in settling with the government?

In seeking a settlement, an entity that can demonstrate robust compliance efforts has significant advantages. A criminal investigation, for instance, often evolves into a civil settlement if the company's good-faith compliance efforts could affect the government's ability to prove criminal intent. And even if a criminal charge is unavoidable, an investigation that begins with the potential for multiple felony counts might instead result in a deferred prosecution agreement or a plea agreement with fewer and lower-level charges if the violation was an isolated event or a circumstance that can be addressed through a company's compliance structure.

In civil enforcement actions, the existence of an effective compliance program can limit the damages and penalties that the government seeks to recover.

Finally, the enforcement divisions of many administrative agencies (for example, the Offices of the Inspector General at the Department of Health and Human Services, the Department of Defense, the Enforcement Division of the Securities and Exchange Commission, etc.) will consider whether a company has an effective compliance program when deciding if they should impose penalties and sanctions.

Q 10.2   Can settlement agreements impose additional compliance provisions on an already effective compliance program?

Yes. A settlement with the government is often conditioned upon the company's accepting compliance provisions in the settlement agreement itself. Having post-settlement monitoring is now commonplace. Even a company with an existing compliance structure is likely to find that the government insists on increased oversight of the company's business for the duration of the settlement agreement. For example, as a condition of settlement, a company may have to:

- designate or hire an employee to be responsible for overseeing and managing the implementation of the new compliance provisions;
- appoint a committee to ensure the new compliance provisions are maintained;
- adopt new policies and institute additional employee training;
- conduct performance reviews of the employees subject to the new training; and
- provide periodic, for example annual or semi-annual, reports to the government on the status of compliance.

Many of these provisions can be found in a 2014 consent decree entered into by H&R Block.[1] Not only can the government impose such requirements, but the settlement agreement often will provide specific contractual as well as administrative remedies that the government can pursue if the company fails to comply with its compliance obligations. The agreement may also require a company to give up some of the rights it would otherwise enjoy in an administrative proceeding if it is found to have breached the provisions of the settlement agreement. For instance, the settlement may provide that the enforcing agency has the right to unilaterally determine a "material breach" and institute suspension or exclusion proceedings without giving the company an opportunity to object to the agency's declaration of a breach.

Ongoing Compliance Monitoring

Q 10.2.1   How does the government ensure ongoing compliance monitoring?

Depending on the terms of a settlement agreement or court order, a company may be required to have its post-settlement compliance monitored by an "independent compliance monitor" or "independent review organization." (The individual or organization performing this function may also be referred to as an "independent examiner," "independent reviewer," or "Special Master," among other terms.) In 2014, as part of a civil settlement, the Department of Justice required H&R Block to retain an independent consultant who had to be approved by all the parties. The consultant was required to provide an annual written evaluation, and H&R Block had to incorporate recommendations within the evaluation within a certain period of time.[2] This scenario is not unusual as a monitor typically prepares a written report of its findings and makes recommendations for improving corporate controls. The report is submitted to the company, to the government, and sometimes to a court, in accordance with the terms of the settlement agreement or court order. Other standard evaluations may include a claims or records audit, a review of the company's books and records, and interviews with employees.

Q 10.2.2   Who selects the monitor and who pays for it?

As in the H&R Block case, the government usually will want to approve the person or company being proposed as the independent monitor.[3] The settling company, however, generally bears full responsibility for the monitor's compensation and other expenses. In a criminal matter, including a deferred prosecution agreement (discussed below), an independent monitor may also be appointed or approved by the court. In that case, the monitor will submit reports to the court as ordered.

Independent monitors and their activities can be and usually are very expensive.[4] Recognizing that a monitor may be an unnecessary expense for a company with a good, pre-existing compliance structure, agencies like HHS-OIG have attempted to tailor their agreements to fit the circumstances of the case. Conversely, a company that has failed to implement its own compliance measures may be required to accept the recommendations of an independent monitor or else explain to the government why those recommendations are being rejected.

Parallel Proceedings and Global Resolutions

Q 10.3   How are settlements affected by parallel proceedings?

An organization that has been investigated by the government is often the subject of parallel proceedings—criminal, civil, and administrative—all of which need to be resolved. In many instances, the company will find itself negotiating settlements with several different governmental entities, each of which has independent enforcement powers.

For example, a criminal prosecutor with the Department of Justice or local U.S. attorney's office is responsible for pursuing violations of federal criminal statutes such as the mail fraud and wire fraud statutes. The same conduct might also give rise to civil liability under the False Claims Act, the Health Care Fraud statute, and other laws that are enforced by the government's civil authorities at the Department of Justice. A conviction, plea, admission of liability, or settlement of either a criminal or civil violation might also trigger or provide a basis for liability in another area, with adverse consequences including civil monetary penalties, exclusion, suspension, or debarment from federal programs administered and enforced by administrative authorities. Resolution of allegations at the federal level can also give rise to further charges by state authorities, where a similar division of criminal, civil, and administrative enforcement authority may be found.[5]

Q 10.3.1   What is a global resolution?

Cooperation between civil enforcement and administrative agencies is fairly typical, and increasingly, criminal prosecutors are becoming more open to working out so-called global settlements, where enforcement authorities and agencies coordinate their investigative and settlement efforts so that all interested governmental parties are represented.[6]

Because of the risks inherent in parallel proceedings, companies must be aware of the consequences of a settlement or other resolution with one government entity. For example, certain criminal convictions and civil judgments (*e.g.*, fraud) trigger an administrative agency's power to suspend, debar, or exclude the company from participating in government programs.[7] However, each agency has independent authority to enforce the laws or regulations for which it is responsible, and the government's collective interests may diverge at certain points during the negotiation process. Sometimes, for example, a criminal prosecutor will refuse to wait for a target company to resolve parallel civil or administrative investigations. This can expose a company to significant risks. If at all possible, it is usually in a company's best interest to push hard for a global resolution with all relevant government agencies.

Settling with the SEC

Q 10.4   How are settlements with the SEC different from those with other administrative agencies?

Settlements with the Securities and Exchange Commission (SEC) are procedurally distinct from other administrative settlements. Although the SEC maintains an Enforcement Division, the SEC staff does not have independent authority to enter into settlements. "Settlements" must be accepted and approved by the SEC.[8]

Q 10.4.1   What are the mechanisms for settling with the SEC?

After conducting an investigation, the SEC Enforcement Division may make an enforcement recommendation to the SEC to bring charges against the company. In many cases, the company is notified of the staff's intention to make such a recommendation through a "Wells Notice" letter or phone call. In those instances, the company may choose to make a "Wells Submission" in response to the proposed charges.

SEC staff may discuss settlement with the company during its investigation, after a Wells Submission, or even after the SEC has instituted an enforcement proceeding. A company's ability to negotiate a reduction in charges or fines, however, is greater before an enforcement proceeding has begun.

After terms of a settlement are agreed upon, SEC staff must obtain the approval of the commission. The matter is presented as a commission order instituting administrative proceedings or cease-and-desist proceedings. The order will note that the responding company has submitted an offer of settlement that the commission has determined to accept.

Q 10.4.2   What kinds of sanctions may be imposed?

The SEC is statutorily authorized only to enjoin companies from disobeying the law in the future, to require companies to provide an accounting, and to assess monetary payments in the form of equitable disgorgements or civil monetary penalties.[9] The monetary payments can be quite large. For example, in 2010, Goldman, Sachs & Company entered into a consent decree with the SEC and agreed to disgorge $15 million and to pay a civil penalty in excess of $500 million.[10] While the commission does not have statutory or regulatory authority to impose compliance provisions on a company, in the context of negotiating a settlement agreement the SEC can insist upon including compliance terms as a contractual matter. Similar to what has already been discussed, these terms may include hiring an independent consultant to review the company's policies and procedures and submit a written report to both the company and the SEC. The company may then be required to implement any changes that the consultant recommends and certify its compliance to the SEC. The company may also be obligated to cooperate with the SEC's ongoing investigations related to the practices at issue (for example, investigations of individuals, including former company employees).

Similarly, an order instituting cease-and-desist proceedings upon an offer of settlement may include compliance undertakings and other sanctions. In addition, the company is ordered to cease and desist from committing or causing any future violations of the securities laws.

In an order for an administrative proceeding, the SEC makes findings of fact and conclusions of law. The settling party usually does not admit or deny the SEC's findings. The company may be required to disgorge certain funds and/or pay a civil monetary penalty. In addition, the company may agree to certain undertakings, or compliance terms.

Settling in Civil Actions

Compliance and Reporting Provisions

Q 10.5   Can a civil settlement agreement include compliance and reporting provisions?

Yes. As a condition of settlement, the government may require a company to institute a comprehensive compliance program that contains all the elements described in the Federal Sentencing Guidelines. A company will likely need to adopt new, specific procedures or controls to address the conduct at issue. In addition, the company may be required to hire an outside auditor or monitor to review its adherence to its compliance program and submit reports to the government. In some cases, the government may insist that it (or even the court, in a court-approved settlement) appoint the compliance auditor or monitor. As with administrative settlement agreements, civil settlements often require the company to make periodic reports for a specified period of time. In a 2012 case, a company had to pay for an independent expert to conduct inspections and provide three reports to the FDA.[11] Each report had specific certification requirements that the expert had to make. Other settlement agreements require that these reports be provided to the civil enforcement authorities, to the responsible administrative agencies, and to the court.

A civil settlement agreement typically will also empower the government to pursue specified contractual remedies for a failure to comply with the compliance (or other) provisions of the agreement. These remedies can include the right to seek specific performance or the ability to refer the company to the appropriate administrative enforcement agency for suspension, debarment, or exclusion. Administrative agencies that join in these settlement agreements may provide that a material breach of the agreement constitutes independent grounds for suspension or debarment. The agency may also negotiate terms that, in the event of a material breach and a notice of suspension, debarment, or exclusion, the settling company is limited in its rights of review and the arguments that it can present for review.[12]

When an Agency Joins

Q 10.5.1   What happens when an agency joins a civil settlement agreement?

In some instances, an administrative agency may join in a civil settlement agreement rather than pursuing a stand-alone agreement with an errant company. The agency's interests in monitoring the company's compliance efforts may then be incorporated directly into the civil settlement agreement. If the agreement requires the settling company to make periodic reports regarding its compliance efforts, those reports are likely to be made to the oversight agency (although the civil enforcement authorities may also receive a copy of any reports). As a general rule, civil settlement agreements in which the regulating agency joins tend to be more streamlined and contain fewer compliance provisions than a stand-alone administrative agreement; however, the terms may still be burdensome and expensive for the settling company.

These settlement agreements are considered to be Department of Justice documents rather than administrative agency documents.[13] HHS-OIG refers to such agreements as Settlement Agreements with Integrity Provisions.

Q 10.5.2   Will an administrative agency always join in a civil settlement agreement?

No. A regulatory agency may decline to participate in a settlement if, for example, it believes that the activity at issue does not trigger its administrative enforcement powers. In order to resolve and release "claims" in a settlement, the agency must consider the subject behavior to be a violation of a regulation that the agency has the power to enforce. An agency might also conclude that its interests are best served by negotiating a separate settlement agreement. This circumstance can arise where the civil enforcement authorities have not coordinated with the administrative agency in conducting their investigation and the regulators wish to have more time to conduct an independent investigation.

Settling in Criminal Procedures

Plea Agreements

Q 10.6   Do plea agreements contain compliance and reporting provisions?

Law enforcement authorities generally do not seek to impose compliance terms as part of a criminal plea agreement. Criminal prosecutors are concerned primarily with addressing past wrongdoing and obtaining, where appropriate, restitution for those harmed by the conduct at issue. The existence of a compliance plan during the period of wrongful activity (or even after) may impact a prosecutor's assessment of criminal intent.

Compliance elements *are* likely to be incorporated as part of the civil or administrative settlement arrangements where prosecutors participate in a global resolution of criminal, civil, and administrative charges, as discussed above.

Likewise, compliance measures can be imposed as a condition for probation by the court when sentencing a company on a plea agreement. The court may appoint an independent monitor or special master to review the company's internal controls and compliance structures, with reports due to the court on a periodic basis.[14] The court's orders on conditions for probation may be anticipated and referenced in the criminal plea agreement.

Deferred Prosecution Agreements and Non-Prosecution Agreements

Q 10.6.1   What are deferred prosecution agreements and non-prosecution agreements?

A deferred prosecution is an agreement that establishes a probationary period during which the Department of Justice will hold criminal charges in abeyance while the company reforms its systems and cooperates with the government in pursuing individuals who participated in the alleged criminal activity. At the end of the probationary period, if the company has met the terms of the agreement, the government will dismiss the proposed criminal charges. A criminal matter is filed with the court and a case number assigned. The criminal complaint or indictment may be attached to the agreement, or the parties may attach a stipulation of facts that would support an indictment.

A non-prosecution agreement (NPA) is a contract not to prosecute a target company while that company reforms its systems and cooperates with the government in pursuing individuals who participated in the alleged criminal activity. An NPA is an agreement establishing a period of probation wherein if the company has met the terms of the agreement, no formal charges will be filed. The advantage of the NPA verses the DPA is that NPAs are not necessarily made public.

Q 10.6.2   What are the advantages of a deferred prosecution agreement?

For some companies, a deferred prosecution agreement avoids the stigma of a high-profile criminal indictment and the penalties that could follow a conviction. It also provides a mechanism for companies to reassure their shareholders that any systemic weaknesses that allowed the wrongful activity to occur are being corrected.

Q 10.6.3   What are the drawbacks of a deferred prosecution agreement?

Deferred prosecution agreements often contain rather onerous terms. The company will be required either to acknowledge that the government can prove its case or to admit to the facts alleged and outlined in the agreement.[15] The company may also be required to

279

institute significant reforms that may include replacing the existing management structure, hiring outside auditors, implementing new governance procedures, working with an independent monitor,[16] and making regular reports to the government. The company may also be obligated to pay fines or monetary penalties, disgorge profits resulting from its criminal activity, and create a fund to compensate shareholders harmed by the wrongdoing. If there is a breach of the deferred prosecution agreement, the company may be exposed to additional fines.[17]

In addition, a deferred prosecution agreement will require the company to cooperate fully with the government as it continues to investigate and prosecute the individuals involved in criminal activity. Cooperation includes making the company's books and records available to the government, allowing prosecutors and regulatory enforcement authorities to share confidential information about the company with each other, making employees available for interview, and waiving the company's attorney-client privilege and work-product protection.

Settling with Administrative Agencies

Q 10.7   How do settlements with an administrative agency differ from those with an enforcement agency?

An administrative settlement agreement can be prompted by the agency's own investigation, or it may follow a civil or criminal enforcement action that presents administrative consequences. While criminal and civil enforcement authorities may be concerned primarily with redressing past wrongdoing, agencies responsible for ongoing regulatory oversight are particularly interested in ensuring that improper conduct will not recur. For this reason, administrative settlement agreements routinely impose compliance obligations for a specified period of time, usually three to five years. More and more frequently, however, criminal and civil enforcement authorities also emphasize compliance measures in their plea and settlement agreements as a means to preserve and protect the integrity of government programs. In some cases, the responsible administrative agency will join in such a settlement; in other cases, the settling company will need to resolve any administrative compliance requirements in a separate agreement.

Q 10.7.1   What compliance-related provisions might an administrative agency seek to include in a settlement agreement?

Typical provisions include reporting obligations, a requirement to conduct periodic audits, a certification of compliance, and an agreement to provide open access to the company's books and records. In addition, if the settling company does not have a comprehensive compliance program in place, the agency likely will require that one be implemented. The settlement agreement prescribes the structure of the program in detail, thus eliminating the company's flexibility to determine for itself how to incorporate the elements of an effective compliance program as outlined broadly in the Federal Sentencing Guidelines.

Q 10.7.2   What are some common types of settlement agreements?

Different agencies use different nomenclature for their administrative settlement agreements. Some common administrative agreements include:

- corporate integrity agreements,
- certificate of compliance agreements, and
- administrative compliance agreements.

Corporate Integrity Agreements

Q 10.7.3   What is a corporate integrity agreement?

A corporate integrity agreement (CIA) is an administrative agreement between a healthcare provider and the Department of Health and Human Services Office of Inspector General (HHS-OIG) that is often negotiated in conjunction with the settlement of civil fraud claims. The CIA is in addition to the civil settlement with the Department of Justice and specifically imposes compliance obligations on the provider. HHS-OIG's ability to enter into CIAs is based on its authority to exclude providers who have submitted false claims in violation of the False Claims Act[18] or the civil monetary penalties law[19] from participating in federally funded healthcare programs.[20] In exchange for the OIG's agreement not to seek to exclude a provider, the provider consents to the obligations contained in the CIA.

A CIA typically extends for either three or five years, depending on the nature and circumstances of the violation being addressed. Although the OIG will take into account and recognize a provider's existing compliance structures, the agency can impose fairly significant requirements. Recent examples of CIAs are available on HHS-OIG's website.

Q 10.7.4   What compliance-related provisions can a CIA mandate?

Under a comprehensive CIA, a settling company can be required to, among other things:

- hire a compliance officer and/or appoint a compliance committee;
- develop written standards, procedures, and policies;
- implement a comprehensive employee training program;
- review and/or audit claims submitted to federal healthcare programs;
- establish a confidential disclosure program, or "hotline";
- restrict employment of ineligible persons;
- retain an independent review organization (described further below) to conduct audits; and
- submit a variety of reports to the OIG on a periodic basis for the duration of the CIA.

If a provider has a pre-existing compliance program, a CIA is likely to require that the program remain in place and that any missing elements be established.[21] If a provider does not have a compliance program in place, the CIA will impose one, typically one much more expensive to operate than one the company might design on its own. In either case, the OIG will monitor the provider's compliance efforts for the duration of the CIA to ensure the integrity of claims being submitted to federal healthcare programs.

A CIA also allows the OIG to take immediate action against a provider who is deemed to violate the terms of the agreement. In some cases, the OIG can initiate exclusion proceedings based on a breach of the CIA terms while limiting the provider's ability to challenge the proceedings. A CIA also might include specified monetary penalties for non-compliance; these penalties can accrue daily until the deficiency is corrected. A March 2014 CIA provides a list of "stipulated penalties" that result in, for example, a $2,500 fee for each day of non-compliance. This CIA also has a $50,000 stipulated penalty for each false certification relating to the requirements in the CIA.[22]

The OIG thus adds to its usual arsenal of regulatory remedies a layer of contractual rights to enforce provider compliance.

Certificate of Compliance Agreements

Q 10.7.5   What is a certification of compliance agreement?

In certain circumstances, HHS-OIG may negotiate a Certificate of Compliance Agreement (CCA) in lieu of a CIA. Like a CIA, a CCA is an agreement between HHS-OIG and a healthcare organization that resolves the organization's administrative exclusion liability. The CCA, however, recognizes that, in some cases, a comprehensive CIA may not be appropriate or necessary to ensure the integrity of the federal healthcare programs. The OIG has outlined the criteria to be considered in establishing either a CIA or CCA.[23]

A CCA is typically used when the organization already has a compliance program in place. It requires the organization to maintain its existing compliance program and to certify (in a declaration attached to the CCA itself) that such compliance measures are in place. In addition, the CCA can impose reporting requirements similar to those found in a CIA for the duration of the CCA. Generally speaking, a CCA imposes fewer obligations than a CIA and thus can reduce the costs of complying with the agreement.[24]

Administrative Compliance Agreements

Q 10.7.6   What is an administrative compliance agreement?

An administrative compliance agreement is the vehicle used by the Department of Defense (DOD) suspension and debarment officials to address concerns about a government contractor's responsibility. The Federal Acquisition Regulation (FAR) subpart 9.4 describes the DOD's authority and procedures for suspension and debarment of contractors.[25]

The Army's Suspension and Debarment Office notes that the term "compliance agreement" is used instead of "settlement agreement" to reflect the emphasis on changing contractor behavior in order to "improv[e] the overall integrity and efficiency of the Government procurement process."[26]

Q 10.7.7   What does an administrative compliance agreement specifically require?

Although administrative compliance agreements vary according to the circumstances at issue, they typically require the subject contractor to establish a contractor responsibility program (CRP). A CRP contains the same elements found in a comprehensive compliance program under the Federal Sentencing Guidelines, including

- a code of conduct,
- written policies and procedures,
- a training program,
- a compliance officer and/or committee,
- an open, non-retaliatory reporting phone number,
- periodic reviews and audits, and
- reports to the company's board.

In addition, for the duration of the administrative compliance agreement, the contractor may be required to make periodic reports to suspension and debarment officials. Often, these reports are to be made by the company's compliance officer, or ethics program director (EPD). A contractor may need to seek approval from suspension and debarment officials for any individual that it proposes as an EPD.

Administrative compliance agreements often remain in effect for five years, but the duration of the agreement will vary according to the circumstances of each case. Suspension and debarment officials can reserve the right to unilaterally extend the term of the agreement until they are comfortable that the company is appropriately deemed a "responsible contractor."

Violations of an administrative compliance agreement can provide independent grounds for suspension and debarment.

TIP: Before entering into a deferred prosecution agreement, consider the potential collateral effects. By acknowledging criminal wrongdoing, you may be estopped from denying or defending your behavior in civil litigation or administrative proceedings. Similarly, you may not be able to limit your waiver of attorney-client privilege to the government alone, and could find yourself compelled to produce privileged material to civil litigants. In addition, by agreeing to cooperate with government investigators to pursue individuals, your company may create discomfort and unrest among its employees.

Notes to Chapter 10

1. *See* Consent Decree, Nat'l Fed'n of Blind v. HRB Dig. LLC & HRB Tax Grp., Inc., Case No. 1:13-cv-10799 (D. Mass. Mar. 6, 2014), www.ada.gov/hrb-cd.htm.

2. *See id.*

3. *Id.* at 23.

4. According to one report, the appointment of former U.S. Attorney General John Ashcroft as the independent monitor for Zimmer Holdings is expected to cost the company between $28 million and $52 million. Philip Shenon, *Ashcroft Deal Brings Scrutiny in Justice Dept.*, N.Y. TIMES, Jan. 10, 2008, at A1.

5. The information in this chapter focuses on the federal enforcement system. Counsel should be consulted regarding the potential for state involvement as particular matters arise.

6. Where both federal and state interests are implicated, it is not uncommon for agencies in both systems to coordinate efforts (*e.g.*, a state Medicaid Fraud Control Unit will work closely with enforcement authorities representing the interests of the federal healthcare programs). A "global settlement" with federal authorities may reference and/or provide remedies to certain interests of the states. For example, in a healthcare fraud settlement that impacts federal dollars for both Medicare and state-run Medicaid programs, a settlement is likely to require the company to make payments to both the U.S. Treasury and to the states affected by the conduct at issue. *See, e.g.*, 2006 Schering-Plough Corp. Settlement Agreement and Release, www.usdoj.gov/ usao/ma/Press%20Office%20-%20Press%20Release%20Files/Schering-Plough/SettlementAgreement.pdf.

7. *See, e.g.*, 48 C.F.R. § 9.406.2 (causes for debarment of government contractors); 42 C.F.R. § 1001.101 (mandatory exclusion from federally funded healthcare programs); 42 C.F.R. § 1001.201 (permissive exclusion).

8. *See* chapter 34, *infra*.

9. *See, e.g.*, 15 U.S.C. §§ 77h-1, 78u-2, 78u-3.

10. Consent Decree, SEC v. Goldman, Sachs & Co., No. 1:10-cv-3229 (S.D.N.Y. July 20, 2010), ECF No. 25.

11. Consent Decree, United States v. Invacare Corp., No. 1:12-cv-03086 (N.D. Ohio Dec. 21, 2012), ECF No. 4.

12. For example, a settlement with HHS-OIG might include a dispute resolution provision that limits the issues for administrative law judge review to whether the provider company was in material breach of the agreement, and if so, whether the company can cure the breach.

13. Therefore, HHS-OIG lists active "Settlement Agreements with Integrity Provisions" on its website, but does not link to a copy of those agreements, which must be obtained through a request to the Department of Justice. *See* www.oig.hhs.gov/fraud/cias.asp.

14. *See, e.g.,* 1999 BP Plea Agreement, www.usdoj.gov/opa/pr/1999/September/437enr.htm.

15. *See, e.g.,* Deferred Prosecution Agreement, United States v. Total, S.A., No. 1:13-cr-239 (E.D. Va. May 29, 2013), ECF No. 2.

16. The use of independent monitors in cases with deferred prosecution agreements is increasing. *See* Vincent L. DiCianni, *New Principles Can Help Advance Independent Corporate Monitoring*, AHLA HEALTH LAW. WKLY., July 2008, at 1.

17. *See* Deferred Prosecution Agreement ¶ 6, United States v. Total, S.A., *supra* note 15.

18. 31 U.S.C. § 3729.

19. 42 U.S.C. § 320a-7a.

20. *See id.* § 1001.201.

21. *See* chapter 2, *supra.*

22. *See* Corporate Integrity Agreement Between the Office of Inspector General of the Department of Health and Human Services and Alliance Rehabilitation LLC, Active Physical Therapy Services, LLC, Rajeev Gupta, Geeta Trehan, and Thomas Bray, at 22–23 (Mar. 7, 2014), https://oig.hhs.gov/compliance/corporate-integrity-agreements/cia-documents.asp (follow "Alliance Rehabilitation LLC" hyperlink).

23. An Open Letter to Health Care Providers from Janet Rehnquist, Dep't of Health and Human Services Inspector General (Nov. 20, 2001), http://oig.hhs.gov/fraud/docs/openletters/openletter111901.htm.

24. HHS-OIG posts its current CIAs and CCAs on its website at www.oig.hhs.gov.

25. The various DoD component agencies have promulgated regulations to supplement the FAR. Some of these supplemental regulations address suspension and debarment proceedings within a particular component agency. *See generally* chapter 14, Government Contractors.

26. *See Automatic Suspensions: A Solution in Need of a Problem,* at n.19, LAW360 (May 11, 2012) (quoting Comments on Administrative Compliance Agreements), www.law360.com/articles/338114/automatic-suspensions-a-solution-in-need-of-a-problem; *see also Contract and Fiscal Law: Army Procurement Fraud Branch Frequently Asked Questions*, JAGCNET, www.jagcnet.army.mil/Sites/contractandfiscallaw.nsf/homeContent.xsp?open&documentId=B32C891A1B3C0CA385257CD1004B6460 (last visited July 29, 2014).

11

The False Claims Act

Lynne M. Halbrooks & Timothy J. Taylor [*]

The False Claims Act (FCA) is a civil statute that permits the U.S. Department of Justice (DOJ) to sue in federal court to recover government money paid on false or fraudulent claims. It also allows private individuals to sue in federal court in the name of the U.S. government. These private lawsuits are called "qui tam"[1] or "whistleblower" cases.

The original False Claims Act was enacted by Congress in 1863 to fight fraud in the sale of supplies and provisions to the Union during the Civil War. Congress has substantially amended the statute five times since: in 1943, 1986, 2009, and twice in 2010.[2] With each amendment, the FCA's scope has expanded. The District of Columbia and nearly thirty states have also enacted FCA-type statutes.[3] The FCA has been described as "the government's premier tool to recover government money lost to fraud and abuse."[4]

---

[*] Trisha M. Rich updated this chapter for the 2014–2016 publications. Lynne M. Halbrooks and Timothy J. Taylor substantially revised this chapter for the 2017 publication. Earlier editions of this chapter were written with contributions from Michael Manthei, Christopher A. Myers, and Richard O. Duvall.

289

The FCA has become an extraordinarily popular—and powerful—weapon in the government's enforcement arsenal. Recent years have seen a rapid increase in the number of qui tam suits filed, which now average over 650 per year—almost two per day. FCA recoveries have also increased. Until 2009, recoveries were typically around $1 billion per year. Since then, recoveries have ranged from $2.5 billion to $5.7 billion per year.[5]

In reaction to the FCA's strict penalties and long reach, many organizations have implemented sophisticated compliance programs and made extraordinary efforts to comply with the law. This shift in corporate culture demonstrates the power of the FCA and its lasting impact.

Basics of the False Claims Act

Q 11.1 What kinds of actions are typically brought under the False Claims Act?

FCA claims may arise in conjunction with any federally funded program, project, or contract. These actions have arisen most frequently in connection with programs run by the U.S. Department of Health and Human Services (HHS) or the Department of Defense (DOD). From 1987 through 2013, approximately $26 billion of total FCA settlements and judgments involved HHS programs, while DOD-related cases accounted for approximately $5.7 billion of the total. Cases involving all other federal programs combined yielded roughly $6.4 billion.[6] That trend changed in FY 2014 when the largest recoveries ($3.3 billion) came from financial institutions "in the wake of the housing and mortgage crisis. . . ."[7] FCA actions against organizations and individuals involved in federal healthcare programs like Medicare and Medicaid accounted for another $2.4 billion.[8]

The FCA's reach beyond HHS and DOD programs was further extended in May 2009 when the statute was amended pursuant to the Fraud Enforcement and Recovery Act of 2009 (FERA).[9] Under the previous version of the law, a "claim" eligible for coverage under the FCA referred to requests or demands for payment that were presented directly to the U.S. government. With the 2009 amendments, "claims" now include requests for money or property that are made to a contractor, grantee, or other recipient if the money being requested is to be spent or used on the government's behalf or to advance a government program or interest and the government is providing or will reimburse any portion of the money.[10] Consequently, subcontractors, subgrantees, and other participants in any contract or program that is—even in part—supported with federal funds can be held accountable for "false claims" under the FCA. This includes, for example, companies working on state contracts that receive federal funding, such as road work and construction projects being funded through the 2009 economic stimulus package.

291

Provisions of the FCA

Q 11.2   What specifically does the FCA prohibit?

The 2009 amendments to the FCA broadened the liability provisions to the act. The 2009 changes to these provisions are noted in **bold** below.

The False Claims Act imposes civil liability on any person who:

1. knowingly presents, or causes to be presented, a false or fraudulent claim for payment or approval;[11]
2. knowingly makes, uses, or causes to be made or used, a false record or statement **material to** a false or fraudulent claim;[12]
3. conspires to commit a violation of **any other provision of the act that gives rise to liability;**[13]
4. has possession, custody, or control of property or money used by the government and **knowingly** delivers less than **all of that money or property;**[14]
5. is authorized to make or deliver a document certifying receipt of property used, or to be used, by the government and, intending to defraud the government, makes or delivers the receipt without completely knowing that the information on the receipt is true;[15]
6. knowingly buys, or receives as a pledge of an obligation or debt, public property from an officer or employee of the government, or a member of the armed forces, who lawfully may not sell or pledge property;[16] or
7. knowingly makes, uses, or causes to be made or used, a false record or statement **material** to an obligation to pay or transmit money or property to the government, **or knowingly conceals or knowingly and improperly avoids or decreases an obligation to pay or transmit money or property to the government.**[17]

Q 11.2.1   What is a "claim" for purposes of the FCA?

The 2009 amendments broadened the FCA's definition of a "claim,"[18] which now includes:

any request or demand, whether under a contract or otherwise, for money or property **and whether or not the United States has title to the money or property, that—**

(i) is presented to an officer, employee, or agent of the United States; or

(ii) is made to a contractor, grantee, or other recipient, **if the money or property is to be spent or used on the Government's behalf or to advance a Government program or interest, and** if the United States Government—

    (I) provides **or has provided** any portion of the money or property requested or demanded; or

    (II) will reimburse such contractor, grantee, or other recipient for any portion of the money or property which is requested or demanded . . . .

As applied, "claims" under the FCA include specific demands for payment that are made to the federal government, such as invoices submitted pursuant to a federal government contract or claims for medical services rendered when submitted to Medicare. The 2009 revisions to the definition of claim make clear that the statute also encompasses claims submitted by subcontractors and subgrantees when the funding comes from or will be reimbursed by the federal government, even though the claim is not submitted directly to a government agency.

Q 11.2.2   What is a false claim?

A claim is "false" when it is objectively untrue—for example, when it affirmatively misrepresents the services, goods, or fees for which payment is claimed, or where the claim does not meet the requirements of the statute, regulation, or contract that authorizes payment.

Q 11.3   What does it mean to present a false claim "knowingly"?

The FCA penalizes only the "knowing" submission of false claims. The word "knowing" has a broader meaning under the FCA than might be expected using the common understanding of the word. Under the statute, the submission of a false claim is "knowing" when the defendant:

1.   has *actual knowledge* that the claim is false;
2.   acts with *deliberate ignorance* as to the truth or falsity of the claim; or
3.   makes the claim in *reckless disregard* of its truth or falsity.[19]

The "deliberate ignorance" standard was intended to "preclude 'ostrich' type situations, where an individual has 'buried his head in the sand' and failed to make an inquiry that would have revealed the false claim."[20] One congressional sponsor of the 1986 amendments to the FCA explained the knowledge requirement: "While the Act was not intended to apply to mere negligence, it is intended to apply in situations that could be considered gross negligence where the submitted claims to the government are prepared in such a sloppy or unsupervised fashion that resulted in overcharges to the government. . . ."[21]

The "reckless disregard" standard is probably the most frequently used during whistleblower litigation. It generally is viewed as the equivalent of gross negligence.[22] To engage in a "reckless disregard of the truth or falsity" of a claim means that the defendant ignored or failed to check the accuracy of the claim being made, or that policies, procedures, or training were inadequate to ensure submission of accurate claims.

Penalties for False Claims

Q 11.4   What are the penalties for violating the FCA?

• *Civil penalties*: Fines now range from $5,500 to $11,000 per false claim but will likely soon double.[23]
• *Treble damages*: In addition to civil penalties, the FCA provides that the government can recover "3 times the amount of damages which the Government sustains because of [the violation.]"[24]
• *Attorney fees and costs*: The court can require the defendant to pay the costs incurred by the government and attorney fees incurred by a whistleblower, if applicable.[25]

Another potential repercussion for those liable under the FCA is the threat of suspension or debarment from doing business with the government, or exclusion from participation in federally funded healthcare programs.[26] The so-called corporate death penalty is the threat of debarment or exclusion that prompts most FCA cases to settle out of court.

Additionally, the DOJ has recently emphasized its commitment to holding individual wrongdoers accountable. FCA liability may not only be a problem for a company, but for the individuals involved in the conduct—possibly including corporate leaders who recklessly allowed the fraud to occur.[27]

FCA penalties and damages add up quickly because each "claim" is considered an independent violation.

 CASE STUDY[28]

An office products supply company brought qui tam actions against several of its competitors, alleging that the defendant companies had submitted false claims by selling office products manufactured in countries that do not have reciprocal trade agreements with the United States. The defendants' federal contracts prohibited them from selling such items to U.S. government agencies.

The defendants faced enormous penalties (*e.g.*, 1,000 invoices for paperclips manufactured in Taiwan could yield $10 million or more in penalties), plus treble damages. Not surprisingly, the defendants negotiated settlements.

Conduct That Gives Rise to False Claims Liability

Q 11.5   What conduct most commonly leads to FCA liability?

As outlined above, there are seven ways to violate the FCA. Four are most common:

1. A person knowingly submits a false or fraudulent claim for payment from government funds.

This often involves someone submitting bills for work that was not performed or for goods that were not delivered. For instance, in the context of healthcare programs, an unscrupulous person might obtain a Medicare "provider number" that allows him or her to supply some type of medical equipment—such as a wheelchair—that is reimbursable under Medicare or Medicaid. Then the provider bills the Medicare program for wheelchairs that were not actually provided to beneficiaries, or provides them to beneficiaries who do not actually need them.

In addition, the Affordable Care Act codifies the DOJ's long-held position that requests for payment that violate the anti-kickback statute are also false claims under the FCA.[29] The Affordable Care Act also extends FCA coverage to payments on state-run health-insurance "exchanges," if those payments include federal funds.[30]

2. A person knowingly makes, uses, or causes to be made or used a false record or statement that is material to getting a false or fraudulent claim paid.

This type of violation occurs, for example, where a contractor issues a false certification needed to support a claim. For instance, a physician's order generally is necessary to dispense medical equipment to patients. Falsifying the physician's certification to support a claim for reimbursement would fall into this category.

 CASE STUDY[31]

In March 2016, a corporation paid $5 million to settle allegations that it had won government contracts set aside for service-disabled, veteran-owned small businesses, when its certifications that it was eligible were not true.

---

3.   A person conspires to violate the FCA.

The FCA originally only applied to conspiracies "to defraud the government" by getting a false or fraudulent claim allowed or paid. The 2009 FCA amendments changed the FCA, so there is now liability for any conspiracy to violate any other provision of the act.

 CASE STUDY[32]

In 2009, two German moving companies settled allegations that they had conspired together and with other companies to inflate and set the rates they charged to U.S. freight forwarding companies for services rendered in Germany. In turn, the freight forwarders bid and won federal contracts at inflated prices. The government recovered nearly $14 million from the conspirators.

4.   A person knowingly makes or uses a false record or statement that is material to an obligation to pay or transmit money or property to the government, or knowingly conceals or knowingly and improperly avoids or decreases an obligation to pay or transmit money or property to the government.

This is usually called a "reverse false claim," because, rather than presenting an affirmative claim for payment, a violator essentially withholds funds that it owes to the government while falsely reporting that it owes less.

The 2009 FCA amendments changed the reverse false claim provision in two ways. First, the amendments added language to create liability for concealing, avoiding, or decreasing an obligation to pay money owed to the government. Second, they added a definition for "obligation," to mean "an established duty, whether or not fixed," including the "retention of any overpayment."[33] The Affordable Care Act mandates that any overpayments must be both reported and returned within sixty days of discovery. Unreturned overpayments are considered "obligations" under the reverse false claim provision.[34]

   CASE STUDY[35]

Shell Oil Company paid $49 million in 2003 to settle allegations that, among other things, it underreported and underpaid royalties it owed to the government under its leases with the Department of the Interior.

Qui Tam/Whistleblower Actions

Q 11.6   What is a "whistleblower" or "relator"?

The FCA contains a qui tam, or whistleblower, provision that allows a private party to file an FCA lawsuit on behalf of the government. The private party is known as a "relator." By including the qui tam provision in the FCA, Congress intended to encourage citizens to act as "private attorneys general" in addressing frauds upon the government. To this end, the relator may be rewarded a share of any money recovered as a result of the lawsuit.[36]

Q 11.7   Who can be a whistleblower?

Private individuals can bring an FCA action unless the information underlying their suit has already been publicly disclosed—the idea being that plaintiffs should be rewarded for bringing secret frauds to light, not for capitalizing on frauds already publicly known. Plaintiffs can avoid this "public-disclosure bar" by showing that they are an "original source" of the information about the fraud.[37] What constitutes an "original source" has changed over time and depends on the facts.[38] Since the Affordable Care Act's amendments to the FCA in 2010, an "original source" has been defined as anyone who either (i) voluntary disclosed to the government the facts underlying their FCA action before they were publicized, or (ii) has knowledge that is "independent of and materially adds to" the public disclosure and who provided that information to the government before filing their FCA action.[39]

Q 11.8   How much can the whistleblower make?

The relator shares in any recovery that is obtained in the case, whether by judgment or by settlement. If the government intervenes, the relator receives between 15% and 25% of the recovery. If the government declines to intervene, then the relator may proceed with the lawsuit and may be awarded 25% to 30% of any recovery, plus costs and attorney fees.[40] Relators' shares of the proceeds have grown in recent years, hitting a new high of nearly $600 million in FY 2015.[41]

 CASE STUDY

The DOJ declined to intervene in a qui tam suit brought by a former employee of a pharmaceutical provider. The relator pursued the case on her own and in 2014 received $17 million of the $124 million settlement.[42]

Filing a Claim

Q 11.9   What is the procedure for filing a qui tam action?

A relator typically files an FCA complaint in the federal district court where the fraudulent conduct allegedly occurred.[43] The complaint is filed under seal and does not become public until the government has had the opportunity to investigate or until the court orders that the seal be lifted. The relator serves a copy of the complaint on the U.S. attorney general and the U.S. attorney for the district in which the suit is filed, but is specifically prohibited from serving the defendant in the action.[44] Along with the complaint, the relator must provide the government with all material evidence and information that the relator possesses relating to the defendant's fraud.[45]

Q 11.9.1   How long does the complaint remain under seal?

The complaint remains under seal for at least sixty days, and the government may petition the court for additional time to continue the seal.[46] This allows the government time to investigate the allegations and to determine whether to intervene in the action. FCA complaints can remain under seal for many months, or even years.[47]

Q 11.9.2   How and when does the government become involved in the prosecution of a qui tam action?

Following its investigation, the DOJ determines whether to intervene in the lawsuit. If it intervenes, the DOJ takes control of the prosecution. The government may choose to file its own complaint or amend a qui tam relator's complaint "to clarify or add detail" to the claims on which it is intervening and "to add any additional claims."[48] The FCA provides that, for statute of limitations purposes, the government's pleading "shall relate back to the filing date" of the qui tam complaint to the extent that it involves the same conduct.[49]

If the government intervenes, the relator remains a party to the case and, unless the government imposes limitations on the relator's participation, he or she can play a role in the case.[50] If DOJ declines to intervene, the relator may proceed with the lawsuit on his or her own.[51] The government also has the authority to seek to dismiss the case.[52] In practice, it is difficult to persuade the government to take this step instead of simply allowing the relator to proceed on his or her own. Frequently, the government attempts to settle the case while the complaint remains under seal, thus avoiding the decision on whether to intervene. Indeed, many qui tam actions are never unsealed.[53]

Q 11.9.3   How does a defendant learn that an FCA action is pending?

An FCA action brought by the government (rather than by a private relator) is filed and served on the defendant in the same manner as any other civil lawsuit. By contrast, when a qui tam (relator) action is filed, it can remain under seal for months or even years without the public becoming aware of the case and without the defendant being served. Until the government determines whether it will intervene in the case, the defendant may very well be unaware that a lawsuit is pending against it.

More frequently, though, companies learn that they are the subject of an FCA investigation or claim when they receive a subpoena or civil investigative demand (CID) that requests the production of documents and materials, interrogatories, or even deposition testimony, related to the qui tam claims. These requests are part of the government's investigative efforts required under the FCA.[54] Subpoenas may come from an investigative agency, like the FBI or an office of inspector general. The DOJ often enlists such agencies in its FCA work. The service of a subpoena or CID often leads to a conversation with the investigating authority, and in many cases, the informal communication confirms that an FCA claim has been filed or at least likely has been filed. Government attorneys may specifically solicit the company's cooperation and generally are willing to listen to the company's perspective on the matter, including presentations of evidence that the company deems relevant.[55]

Sometimes the defendant might learn of the complaint in a letter from the government seeking the defendant's voluntary cooperation in the government's investigation of the allegations. This occurs when the government needs the defendant's assistance to obtain information necessary to complete the government's investigation, but for tactical or other reasons does not want to use a subpoena or CID. To disclose the existence of the FCA claim while it remains under seal, government counsel must move the court, in secret, for permission to disclose the existence of the lawsuit and the allegations in the complaint to the defendant. This is a standard procedure, and the court typically will defer to the government's request for a partial unsealing.

The Lifecycle of an FCA Case

Q 11.10 What happens after the defendant learns that an FCA case has been filed?

The lifecycle of an FCA case typically lasts several years, from the time the relator raises the claim to its final resolution. In that time, a number of things will happen. The major events are discussed below.

Document Production

Q 11.11   Our company has just received a subpoena that indicates the government is investigating a potential FCA violation; what should we do?

Contact the government attorney to try to arrange a meeting or phone call during which the substance of the allegations may be revealed. Typically, the subpoena or CID will give a strong indication of the focus of the government's investigation and hence the nature of the allegations. Nevertheless, in a meeting, the government may be more specific about its concerns.

Additionally, subpoenas and CIDs are likely to be very broad. At the initial meeting with the government, it is often possible to negotiate limits on the scope, timing, and methodology of initial document production. In many cases, the government will agree to narrow its requests. In so doing, the government will necessarily indicate its primary areas of concern.[56]

Q 11.11.1   The government refuses to narrow the scope of its broad requests; what can we do?

You can seek a protective order from the court, as you would in any other civil case. You face an uphill battle. Whether you have received an FCA CID or a subpoena, a court will likely apply the same standard, which is essentially that the request be within the agency's power and not an "abuse of the court's process."[57]

Q 11.11.2   The government has narrowed the scope of its requests; what do we do?

Once the scope of the response is determined, either by negotiation or motion for protective order, you must respond to the subpoena or demand by producing the requested documents. (See chapter 7 for a complete discussion of the associated compliance issues.)

Q 11.11.3 What use can the government make of our documents once produced?

The DOJ can share information obtained under a CID with a relator if it determines that "it is necessary as part of any false claims act investigation."[58] The DOJ may also use the documents for "any use that is consistent with the law," which is virtually any legal, investigative, or governmental purpose.[59]

Parallel Internal Investigation[60]

Q 11.12 Why should we conduct an internal investigation?

Very often, the resources of government attorneys are spread thinly, and they may not have a chance to review documents until months after they are produced.[61] This generally provides a company time to conduct its own investigation to determine whether an FCA violation has occurred. With this information in hand, you will have a chance to frame the story for the government and will be better situated to negotiate a declination, dismissal, or a settlement, or to prepare for a trial.

Q 11.12.1 Would we ever choose to disclose our findings to the government attorneys?

In many instances, yes. Though it may be counterintuitive, disclosing the findings of your internal investigation may help to resolve the case on terms more favorable to you than if you did not disclose your findings. The government will take your cooperation into account when determining whether and on what allegations to intervene. Disclosure also gives you the opportunity to cast in the best light any potentially inappropriate conduct. Finally, it allows an opportunity to foreshadow and impress upon the government attorneys the merit of any defenses. Often the government will offer its most advantageous settlement proposals before the decision on intervention has been made.[62]

TIP: Whether or not to disclose the results of an internal investigation is perhaps the most significant decision you will make in the course of an FCA investigation. You will want to consider the potential impact of disclosure on your ability to maintain the attorney-client privilege and work-product protection.[63]

Interviewing Witnesses

Q 11.13 Who should be interviewed during an internal investigation?

Internal investigation interviews typically focus on employees and former employees, although that pool may expand to include outside vendors, consultants, or customers.

Internal interviews must be handled appropriately, by an attorney, in order not only to preserve the company's privileges, but to apprise the person being interviewed that the company may decide to waive its privileges or share information from the interview with the government. In addition, the attorney conducting the interview must make clear that he or she represents the company and not the interviewee. The awkwardness of these disclaimers can be diminished by attorneys who have experience in handling sensitive investigations and who understand the nuances of the employee interview situation.

Q 11.13.1 What should we do if, during the course of our investigation, we discover that an employee has engaged in illegal or unethical conduct?

Normally, you would take appropriate disciplinary action. Decisions on termination must be carefully balanced against the necessity of the employee's cooperation in the investigation. It might be appropriate to delay any disciplinary action until the facts known to the employee are completely investigated. At some point, however, you will want to consider how to discipline employees who are believed to have engaged in illegal or unethical conduct. You must take care to ensure that your standards for imposition of discipline are consistently applied to all employees; otherwise, you open yourself to a number of employment-related claims and also claims for retaliation, which are discussed below.

Getting Information from the Government

Q 11.14 What kind of information can we get from the government, and how should we go about getting it?

It is imperative to get as much information as possible from the government so that your internal investigation may be targeted (and cost-effective). Even though the complaint is under seal, the government can give you information about the relator's case. Ideally, the government will agree to give you a copy of the sealed complaint (with restrictions on further disclosure) and a copy of the relator's statement of material facts that he or she must present to the government when filing the complaint.

The government, of course, is not required to provide these documents. But because these documents will be discoverable once the case is unsealed, the government may agree to your request. In any event, you should try to obtain them as soon as possible.

You should also request any other factual material used in preparing the complaint or exchanged between the government and the relator. Requests for factual information should include the results of any government agency investigations. Again, the basis is that these materials will be discoverable in any event once the complaint is unsealed, and having them provided early may expedite resolution of the case. Finally, you should ask the government to identify any witnesses that possess knowledge of the facts.

Typically, the government will not agree to provide all this information. However, one can argue that an early exchange of key information will benefit both parties. As noted, all this material will be discoverable after the government makes its intervention decision and the case is unsealed. Early exchange will help to focus both parties, will speed the investigative process, and may provide the bases for an early resolution.

Pre-Intervention Presentations

Q 11.15   When is it in our interest to share information with the government?

It is common for the defendant to make a pre-intervention presentation to the government. Its primary purpose is to attempt to persuade the government not to intervene in the case at all. A secondary purpose is to advocate for an early settlement.

The timing of the pre-intervention presentation is very important. The defendant typically will want to make the presentation early, before the government has made a large investment of time and manpower. This gives the defendant the opportunity to create the narrative and focus the issues in the case.

Often, the government wants to delay the presentation until after it has had time to fully investigate the relator's allegations. However, the government may be persuaded that an early presentation benefits the government, at least to the extent that it saves the government time and resources. Sometimes, if trust can be established, the government will defer some portions of its investigation to allow the company to fully investigate and present findings on the issues.

As noted, the government may not agree to share documents or information early in the case. Because there is risk associated with disclosing facts to the government, it may not be in the defendant's best interest to make any pre-intervention presentation if the government will not share information. The purpose of a pre-intervention presentation is to benefit both parties through the exchange of information. If the exchange is one-sided and the presentation becomes "free discovery" for the government, the defendant should consider not making a presentation.

Motions Practice

Q 11.16   What happens once the complaint is unsealed?

The case proceeds like any other civil case. There likely will be disagreements over discovery, which will lead to the filing of various motions. A defendant may consider filing motions to dismiss, and ultimately both sides may file motions for summary judgment. In this respect, the FCA case will present the same tribulations as any other litigation.

Negotiating Damages

Q 11.17 How are damages and penalties calculated under the FCA?

As noted above, potential fines can add up quickly in an FCA case, since statutory penalties are assessed for each violation (for example, number of claims) committed.[64] In some instances, there may be many thousands of claims that are alleged to be false.

A violator can also be found liable for treble the damages incurred by the government. Though "speculation and guesswork should not be the basis for ascertaining damages, damages need not be calculated by mathematical precision."[65] Accordingly, the appropriate measure of damages is a somewhat amorphous concept in the context of the FCA, and the government frequently seeks to recover triple the amount it actually paid.[66] While in some circumstances, "amounts paid" may be the best measure of the actual damages the government sustained because of the submission of the false claims,[67] as a general rule, single damages are the amount it paid minus the amount it would have paid had the claim not been false.[68]

Q 11.17.1 How should we approach damages in the context of settlement?

Because FCA damages are so malleable, the appropriate amount to be paid in an FCA settlement is likely to be a heavily negotiated issue. One strategy is to try to limit the number of claims under consideration. You can do this through both factual and legal arguments. Factually, there may be weaknesses or holes in the government's evidence. Legally, there may be arguments of varying strength that the claims were not "false," or if technically false, that they were not submitted "knowingly." (Defenses are discussed in more detail below.) Ultimately, each party must weigh the strengths and weaknesses of its case in arriving at the final settlement.

Settlements

Q 11.18   Is the process of negotiating a settlement in an FCA case different from that in any other litigation?

Yes and no. Most FCA cases settle before trial, as is typical in civil litigation. Ideally, the settlement agreement will be filed together with the government's complaint in intervention, and the case thus will be settled simultaneously with its unsealing. This typically will decrease the amount of publicity that the case draws, although the DOJ will also usually post a press release announcing the settlement.

The settlement calculus changes, however, if there is a parallel criminal investigation of the conduct underlying the FCA claim. In that case, both the civil claims and the criminal charges typically are settled together, but the process may be more drawn out. Negotiations often are complicated by the fact that a criminal settlement could lead to the defendant's exclusion or debarment from government programs. Where there is a possibility of mandatory exclusion, the government may agree to allow a non-operational subsidiary or related entity to take the criminal guilty plea. This arrangement insulates the main corporate defendant from the risk of mandatory exclusion.[69]

Retaliation

Q 11.19   What should we do if we learn that the whistleblower is a current employee of our company?

It is often quite frustrating for a company facing a qui tam action to realize that the very person who filed the lawsuit may be a current employee who is using his or her existing position to aid in a matter adverse to the company. However, you must be cautious not to respond to that frustration by retaliating against an employee who is suspected of being a whistleblower.

The FCA provides that an employee may file an FCA retaliation claim in the event that he or she is discharged, demoted, suspended, threatened, harassed, or in any other manner discriminated against in the terms and conditions of his or her employment as the result of the employee filing, assisting in the investigation of, or testifying in an

FCA matter. Aggrieved whistleblowers may seek to recover all relief necessary to make them whole, including reinstatement with the same seniority status, two times the amount of any backpay lost as a result of the retaliation, attorney fees, and costs.[70]

Q 11.19.1 What should we do if we learn that the whistleblower works for one of our contracting partners?

The FCA prohibits retaliation—discharge, demotion, suspension, threats, harassment, or any other discrimination—against any employee, contractor, or agent because of their pursuit, or any "associated others[']" pursuit, of (i) an FCA claim or (ii) other efforts to stop an FCA violation.[71] People retaliated-against have three years to bring a retaliation claim and are entitled to "all relief necessary to make [them] whole," including two-times backpay, special damages, and attorney fees.[72] Because the anti-retaliation provisions cover contractors and agents, if you learn that the whistleblower is an employee of one of your company's contracting partners, then take care to ensure that the person's employment status is not affected because of his or her efforts to prevent or report false claims by, for example, a request that the person be transferred to a different project or a sudden termination of the contracting partner. Such actions could be perceived as retaliation.[73]

Defending an FCA Claim

Q 11.20 What are the most common defenses to an FCA claim?

1. The claims in question were not "false." In other words, the claim met all the requirements imposed by law or by contract, and all the information it contained was true. It is important to remember that many statutory and regulatory provisions are complicated, confusing, and subject to multiple interpretations. The mere fact that a defendant selected the interpretation most favorable to its position when submitting a claim does not make the claim "false."[74]

If the alleged false claim is based upon a violation of a statute, it also might be argued that compliance with the statute was not a condition of payment.[75] The FCA was not intended to provide a universal remedy for every statutory or regulatory violation. Standing alone, therefore, the violation of laws, rules, and regulations will not necessarily support an FCA claim.[76]

Even if a statute or rule on its face does not make compliance a prerequisite to payment, relators often assert that the claim form itself included either an express or implied certification of compliance, for example, by including words under a signature line such as "I certify that this claim complies with all applicable requirements for its payment." The failure of compliance makes the certification, and thus the claim, "false." In cases based on a "false certification," the defendant will try to show that there was substantial compliance with the underlying statutes and rules and therefore that the certification was true.[77]

2.   *If false, the claims were not submitted with knowledge of the falsity.* In other words, the defendant submitted the false claim accidentally or merely negligently.[78]

Lack of intent can be shown by establishing that the government had knowledge of the facts and circumstances surrounding the claim. For example, a company that contracted with the Environmental Protection Agency (EPA) successfully defended an FCA action by showing that the corporation had communicated with the EPA about its problems under the contract and that it had worked closely with the EPA to solve those problems. Based on the government's knowledge of the circumstances, the court threw out an FCA claim alleging that the company had submitted claims that did not comply with the contract.[79] Lack of intent can also be shown by demonstrating that the company reasonably, but perhaps mistakenly, interpreted a complex statute, regulation, or contract. A party relying in good faith on a reasonable interpretation of the law is not subject to liability "because the good faith nature of his or her action forecloses the possibility that the knowledge requirement is met."[80]

3.   *If false, the claim was not "materially" false.* This argument posits that the falsity, even if known by the defendant, was not material to the government's decision to pay the claim. In other words, the government did not rely on the false information in making the payment and would have paid the claim regardless of the falsity.[81] The term "material" is a simple one—"having a natural tendency to influence, or be capable of influencing, the payment or receipt of

money or property"[82]—but its application in court has not been, often turning on contractual interpretation or contested facts.[83]

4.   The government suffered no damages. The majority of courts has held that damages is not a required element of an FCA claim and that the penalty provisions apply regardless of whether the government lost any money.[84] Nevertheless, with certain kinds of false claims—where the violation was tied to getting claims paid—the courts have debated over whether damages is a required element.[85] Unfortunately for defendants to whom the amended FCA applies, those provisions have eliminated the link between the violation and payment.

Nonetheless, in light of the ongoing debate and murkiness over the proper measure of FCA damages, a defendant can still argue for a zero-damages award.

5.   The defendant relied on the advice of counsel. A defendant's good-faith reliance on the advice of counsel and/or of an accountant also may negate any inference that a claim is knowingly false.[86] Notwithstanding its common use in tax cases (where a defendant will claim that he or she relied on the advice of an accountant or lawyer in preparing his or her tax return), the "advice of counsel" defense can be used in any case involving complex or technical regulations with respect to which a person typically would turn to counsel for advice. Good examples are the Medicare and Medicaid programs.[87] Program rules, particularly those involving payment for goods and services provided to program beneficiaries, can be so complicated that healthcare providers typically will consult with and rely on the advice of attorneys, accountants, and other consultants.

To establish a defense of good-faith reliance on professional advice, a defendant must prove the following:

- the advice was sought and received before taking action;
- the defendant in good faith sought the advice of the professional;
- the defendant's purpose in seeking advice was to determine the lawfulness of future conduct;
- the defendant made a full and accurate report to the professional of all material facts that the defendant knew; and
- the defendant acted strictly in accordance with the advice of the professional who had been consulted.[88]

Of course, a defendant cannot hide behind its attorney or other consultant if, despite the advice, the defendant knew that the claim is false.[89] This might occur, for instance, if the defendant withheld information or otherwise misled the consultant.[90]

Statute of Limitations

Q 11.21   What is the statute of limitations for an FCA violation?

An FCA case must be filed either (1) within six years after the FCA violation is committed; or (2) within three years after an "official of the United States charged with the responsibility to act in the circumstances" either knew about or should have known about the facts giving rise to the FCA violation.[91] Regardless of when the fraud is or should have been discovered, FCA claims are barred if not brought within ten years after the date on which the violation is committed.[92]

FCA retaliation cases are governed by the most closely analogous state limitations period in the state where the retaliation claim is brought.[93]

FCA Compliance Programs

Q 11.22   Can a compliance program prevent FCA claims?

Minimizing the risk of an FCA lawsuit is one of the best business reasons for a compliance program. A compliance program should lower the risk of FCA liability by setting affirmative policies and procedures, providing training and monitoring, and establishing a means for employees to bring potentially inappropriate billing and marketing practices to management's attention. When companies have an effective compliance program—including audits and billing spot checks—they can also argue more convincingly that they did not knowingly submit false claims, but rather that any problematic conduct was caused by innocent mistakes or rogue employees. By contrast, a weak compliance program alone can satisfy the FCA's element of "reckless disregard."[94]

The government likewise weighs the effectiveness of an organization's compliance program when deciding whether to intervene in an

FCA action. Under DOJ guidance applicable expressly to criminal cases but also, by analogy, to the FCA, DOJ asks: "Is the corporation's compliance program well designed?" and "Does the corporation's compliance program work?"[95] Affirmative answers improve the likelihood that the DOJ will decline intervention.

Regulating Compliance

Q 11.23   What is the Deficit Reduction Act of 2005 and how does it affect the FCA and compliance programs?

In 2006, Congress passed the Deficit Reduction Act of 2005 (DRA).[96] Section 6032 of the DRA requires that, as of January 1, 2007, healthcare providers who receive $5 million or more in Medicaid reimbursement must educate their employees about the FCA and whistleblower protections. Specifically, the DRA mandates that covered Medicaid providers develop written policies for their employees, management, and contractors that address in detail:

- the FCA and comparable state anti-fraud statutes, including the whistleblower provisions in those laws;
- the company's policies and procedures for preventing and detecting fraud, waste, and abuse; and
- an employee's right to whistleblower protection and the importance of such whistleblower and qui tam laws in detecting and preventing fraud, waste, and abuse.

COMPLIANCE FACT

Legal Mandates for Compliance and Compliance Programs. In New York, Medicaid providers are required to develop, adopt, and implement effective compliance programs aimed at detecting fraud, waste, and abuse in the Medicaid program.[97] The Affordable Care Act requires providers and suppliers enrolled in federal healthcare programs to create and maintain compliance programs as a condition of their continued participation.[98]

The DRA also encourages states to enact FCA-type statutes: those that do receive a 10% increase in their share of Medicaid false claim recoveries.[99]

COMPLIANCE FACT

State False Claim Statutes. A number of state FCA-type statutes are limited specifically to Medicaid claims.[100] States with generally applicable FCA-type statutes include:

California	Cal. Gov't Code §§ 12650–56
Delaware	Del. Code Ann. tit. 6, §§ 1201–09
District of Columbia	D.C. Code §§ 2-308.03 to -308.21
Florida	Fla. Stat. §§ 68.081 to 68.09
Hawaii	Haw. Rev. Stat. §§ 661-21 to -29
Illinois	740 Ill. Comp. Stat. 175/1 to 175/8
Indiana	Ind. Code §§ 5-11-5.5-1 to 55-11-5.5-18
Kansas	Kan. Stat. Ann. §§ 75-7501 to -7511
Massachusetts	Mass. Gen. Laws ch. 12, § 5A(A)–(O)
Minnesota	Minn. Stat. § 15C.01 *et seq.* (effective July 1, 2010)
Montana	Mont. Code Ann. §§ 17-8-401 to -412
Nevada	Nev. Rev. Stat. §§ 357.010 to 357.250
New Hampshire	N.H. Rev. Stat. Ann. §§ 167:61-b to 167:61-e
New Jersey	N.J. Stat. §§ 2A:32C-1 to -15, -17, and -18
New Mexico	N.M. Stat. §§ 44-9-1 to 44-9-14
New York	N.Y. State Fin. Law §§ 187–94
North Carolina	N.C. Gen. Stat. §§ 1-605 to -618
Rhode Island	R.I. Gen. Laws §§ 9.1.1-1 to 9.1.1-8
Tennessee	Tenn. Code §§ 4-18.101 to .108
Vermont	Vt. Stat. tit. 32, §§ 630–42
Virginia	Va. Code Ann. §§ 8.01-216.1 to 8.01-216.19

Notes to Chapter 11

1.   "Qui tam" is an abbreviation of the Latin phrase *qui tam pro domino rege quam pro se ipso in hac parte sequitur*, meaning "he who sues in this matter for the king as well as for himself."

2.   In early 2010, the Patient Protection and Affordable Care Act (Affordable Care Act), Pub. L. No. 111-148, 124 Stat. 119 (Mar. 23, 2010), substantially amended the FCA. Later in 2010, the Dodd-Frank Wall Street Reform and Consumer Protection Act (Dodd-Frank), Pub. L. No. 111-203, 124 Stat. 1376 (July 21, 2010), expanded whistleblower protections.

3.   So have the cities of Chicago and New York. *See* Mun. Code of Chi., ch. 1-22; N.Y.C. Admin. Code, tit. 7, ch. 8. See the table preceding these endnotes for the current list of state FCA-type statutes.

4.   Press Release, Sen. Chuck Grassley, False Claims Act and Fraud Enforcement (Apr. 20, 2009), http://grassley.senate.gov/news/press_ releases.cfm (search press releases by date).

5.   Civil Div., U.S. DOJ, Fraud Statistics - Overview, www.justice.gov/opa/file/796866/download (Nov. 23, 2015).

6.   *See* U.S. DEP'T OF JUSTICE, CIVIL DIV., FRAUD STATISTICS—OVERVIEW: OCTOBER 1, 1987—SEPTEMBER 30, 2013, www.justice.gov/civil_docs_forms/C-Frauds_FCA_statistics.pdf.

7.   Press Release No. 14-1300, U.S. Dep't of Justice, Justice Department Recovers Nearly $6 Billion from False Claims Act Cases in Fiscal Year 2014 (Nov. 20, 2014), www.justice.gov/opa/pr/justice-department-recovers-nearly-6-billion-false-claims-act-cases-fiscal-year-2014.

8.   Fraud Statistics, *supra* note 5.

9.   Fraud Enforcement and Recovery Act of 2009 (FERA), Pub. L. No. 111-21.

10.   FERA § 4(a)(2) (definition of "claim").

11.   31 U.S.C. § 3729(a)(1)(A). This provision eliminates the requirement under the previous version of the act that the claim be presented "to an officer or employee of the U.S. government or a member of the armed forces of the United States." Note that all of the basic liability provisions under the act were renumbered under the 2009 amendments.

12.   *Id.* § 3729(a)(1)(B). This provision replaces language requiring that the false record or statement be made "to get a false or fraudulent claim paid or approved by the government" in response to the U.S. Supreme Court's decision in Allison Engine Co. v. U.S. *ex rel.* Sanders, 553 U.S. 662 (2008), which held that the "false statement" provision of the FCA contained an intent requirement because of the "to get" language. *See* S. REP. NO. 111-10, Fraud Enforcement and Recovery Act of 2009 (Mar. 23, 2009) [hereinafter FERA Senate Report].

13.   *Id.* § 3729(a)(1)(C). Previously, the conspiracy provision only applied where a person conspired to defraud the government by "getting a false or fraud-

ulent claim allowed or paid." *See, e.g.*, U.S. *ex rel.* Huangyan Imp. & Exp. Corp. v. Nature's Farm Prods., Inc., 370 F. Supp. 2d 993 (N.D. Cal. 2005) (previous conspiracy provision did not extend to conspiracies to violate "reverse false claims" section).

14. *Id.* § 3729(a)(1)(D). This provision allows the government to recover for conversion of government property; the 2009 amendment eliminated technical language that required the alleged violator to have received a receipt for the government property.

15. *Id.* § 3729(a)(1)(E). The 2009 amendments did not change this provision.

16. *Id.* § 3729(a)(1)(F). The 2009 amendments made no substantive changes to this provision.

17. *Id.* § 3729(a)(1)(G). The added language of this section creates liability for actions to conceal, avoid, or decrease an obligation to the government. This provision is sometimes referred to as the "reverse false claims" provision.

18. The text in bold indicates changes to the statutory language from the 2009 amendments. *See* 31 U.S.C. § 3729(b)(2).

19. *See* 31 U.S.C. § 3729(b)(1)(A). Note that the last substantive changes to the "knowing" standard of the FCA were made in the 1986 amendments to the statute; the 2009 amendments merely renumbered the definitions section of the act, which contains the definition of "knowing."

20. United States v. Entin, 750 F. Supp. 512, 518 (S.D. Fla. 1990).

21. *Id.* at 518 (quoting 132 CONG. REC. H9389 (daily ed. Oct. 7, 1986) (statement of Rep. Berman)).

22. *See, e.g.*, United States v. Krizek, 111 F.3d 934, 942 (D.C. Cir. 1997) ("[T]he best reading of the [False Claims] Act defined reckless disregard as an extension of gross negligence."); *see also* U.S. *ex rel.* Williams v. Renal Care Grp., Inc., 696 F.3d 518, 530 (6th Cir. 2012) ("Only those who act in 'gross negligence' . . . will be found liable under the False Claims Act.") (quoting S. REP. NO. 99-345, at 20 (1986)).

23. *See* 31 U.S.C. § 3729(a)(1) (statutory penalty range of $5,000 to $10,000 per claim, "as adjusted by the Federal Civil Penalties Inflation Adjustment Act of 1990"); 28 C.F.R. § 85.3(a)(9) (increasing the penalties for FCA violations, effective September 29, 1999). FCA penalties are slated to nearly double on August 1, 2016, to $10,781–$21,563, per new legislation requiring agencies to adjust their civil penalties for inflation. *See* Bipartisan Budget Act of 2015, Pub. L. No. 114-74 § 701; 81 Fed. Reg. 26,127 (implementing the legislation). However, practitioners should take note of U.S. *ex rel.* Bunk v. Birkart Globistics GmbH & Co., 2012 WL 488256 (E.D. Va. Feb. 14, 2012), where the district court reduced a $50 million penalty as unconstitutionally excessive. In contrast, a recent case from the Fourth Circuit found that a $24 million penalty was not constitutionally excessive where damages were not proven at trial and where the government had paid only $3.3 million for the services at issue. U.S. *ex rel.* Bunk v. Gosselin World Wide Moving, N.V., 741 F.3d 390 (4th Cir. 2013), *cert. denied*, 135 S. Ct. 83 (2014).

24. A defendant may reduce its liability, however, if it self-reports to the government within thirty days of discovering an FCA violation and fully cooperates in

any government investigation. In this circumstance, a court may assess "not less than" two times the amount of damages. *See* 31 U.S.C. § 3729(a)(2)(A)–(C).

25.   *See* 31 U.S.C. §§ 3729(a)(3), 3730(d)(1), (2).

26.   *See, e.g.*, 48 C.F.R. § 9.400 (suspension and debarment procedures for government contractors); 42 U.S.C. § 1320a-7 (exclusion from Medicare and state health programs).

27   *See* Memorandum from Sally Quillian Yates, Deputy Att'y Gen., U.S. Dep't of Justice, Individual Accountability for Corporate Wrongdoing (Sept. 9, 2015) [hereinafter Yates Memo].

28.   Press Release No. 5-549, U.S. Dep't of Justice, Staples Pays United States $7.4 Million to Resolve False Claims Act Allegations (Oct. 18, 2005), www.justice.gov/opa/pr/2005/October/05_civ_549.html.

29.   42 U.S.C. § 1320a-7b(g). For further discussion of the anti-kickback statute, see chapter 21.

30.   42 U.S.C. § 18033. This section became effective January 1, 2014.

31.   Press Release, U.S. Dep't of Justice, The Hayner Hoyt Corporation to Pay $5 Million to Resolve False Claims Act Liability (Mar. 14, 2016), www.justice.gov/opa/pr/hayner-hoyt-corporation-pay-5-million-resolve-false-claims-act-liability.

32.   Press Release No. 09-618, U.S. Dep't of Justice, United States Settles Claims Alleging Bid Rigging Conspiracy with Two German Moving Companies (June 23, 2009), www.justice.gov/criminal/npftf/pr/press_ releases/2009/jun/06-23-09_2grmn-comp-bid-riging-consp.pdf.

33.   31 U.S.C. § 3729(b)(3); *see also* FERA Senate Report at 14 ("an 'obligation' arises across the spectrum of possibilities from the fixed amount debt obligation where all particulars are defined to the instance where there is a relationship between the Government and a person that 'results in a duty to pay the Government money, whether or not the amount owed is yet fixed'") (citations omitted). The breadth of "obligation" under the FCA has left healthcare providers, in particular, concerned about how the amended FCA will be applied to overpayments from Medicare or Medicaid, which are often the subject of disputes between providers and government administrators.

34.   42 U.S.C. § 1320a-7k(d). The final rule implementing this provision was published recently. *See* 81 Fed. Reg. 7654–84 (Feb. 12, 2016).

35.   Press Release No. 03-613, U.S. Dep't of Justice, Civil Fraud Recoveries Total $2.1 Billion for FY 2003 (Nov. 10, 2003), www.usdoj.gov/opa/pr/2003/November/03_civ_613.htm [hereinafter 2003 DOJ Press Release].

36.   31 U.S.C. § 3730(b), (d).

37.   31 U.S.C. § 3730(e)(4).

38.   *See, e.g.*, U.S. *ex rel.* Advocates for Basic Legal Equality v. U.S. Bank, No. 15-3654, slip op. (6th Cir. Mar. 14, 2016) (public disclosure barred claims covered in earlier consent order); U.S. *ex rel.* Mateski v. Raytheon Co., No 13-55341, slip op. (9th Cir. Mar. 7, 2016) (public studies disclosing generalized fraud did not bar specific claims); U.S. *ex rel.* Beauchamp v. Academic Training Ctr., No. 15-1148, slip op. (4th Cir. Feb. 25, 2016) (allegations raised prior to news article not subject to public-disclosure bar).

39.   31 U.S.C. § 3730(e)(4)(B).

40. *Id.* § 3730(d)(1), (2).

41. Fraud Statistics, *supra* note 5.

42. Brian Mahoney, *DOJ Signs on to $124M Omnicare FCA Kickback Settlement*, LAW360 (June 25, 2014), www.law360.com/articles/551726/doj-signs-on-to-124m-omnicare-fca-kickback-settlement. The relator did have to pay back $4.2 million to resolve the company's allegations of sanctionable conduct. *See id.*

43. 31 U.S.C. § 3732(a). Note that the 2009 amendments added a subsection (c) to this provision to allow service of the complaint on a state or local government that is named as a co-plaintiff with the United States. The state and local government enforcement authorities are then authorized to conduct their own investigation and prosecution of the action, consistent with the sealing provisions of the FCA. *See* 31 U.S.C. § 3732(c).

44. *Id.* § 3730(b)(2).

45. A number of federal courts have held that FCA complaints must meet the more stringent pleading requirements of Rule 9(b) of the Federal Rules of Civil Procedure. *See, e.g.,* U.S. *ex rel.* Hopper v. Solvay Pharm., Inc., 588 F.3d 1318 (11th Cir. 2009); U.S. *ex rel.* Folliard v. CDW Tech. Serv., Inc., 722 F. Supp. 2d 20 (D.D.C. 2010). The U.S. Supreme Court recently denied certiorari in a case presenting this issue. U.S. *ex rel.* Nathan v. Takeda Pharm. N.A., Inc., 707 F.3d 451 (4th Cir. 2013), *cert. denied,* 134 S. Ct. 1759 (2014).

46. *Id.* § 3730(b)(2), (3).

47. *See, e.g.,* Press Release, U.S. Attorney's Office, Dist. of Mass., Nation's Largest Nursing Home Pharmacy and Pharmaceutical Manufacturer Pay $112 Million to Settle False Claims Act Cases (Nov. 3, 2009), www.justice.gov/usao/ma/press.html. The qui tam action was originally filed in 2006, and the government filed its complaint in intervention in 2009. *See* U.S. *ex rel.* Resnick v. Omnicare, Inc., No. 06-10149 (D. Mass. Mar. 3, 2009).

48. 31 U.S.C. § 3731(c).

49. *Id.* This provision was added as part of the 2009 amendments, primarily to address the relation-back and statute-of-limitations issue that had been the subject of litigation.

50. *Id.* § 3730(b)(4), (c)(1), (2).

51. *Id.* § 3730(c)(3).

52. *Id.* § 3730(c)(2)(A).

53. *Id.* § 3730(c)(2)(B). This provision authorizes the government to settle an FCA case after intervening. In practice, however, the government will try to settle the case before it intervenes, and the relator typically joins in the settlement.

54. *Id.* § 3733(a)(1). The CID provisions were expanded with the 2009 amendments to allow the attorney general to delegate authority to issue CIDs.

55. *Id.* § 3730(a) ("The Attorney General diligently shall investigate a violation under section 3729.").

56. When companies discover they are being investigated for possible FCA violations, usually they should engage outside counsel experienced in handling such investigations and dealing with the DOJ.

57.   United States v. Markwood, 48 F.3d 969, 979 (6th Cir. 1995); *see also* Coronado v. Bank Atl. Bankcorp., 222 F.3d 1315, 1320 (11th Cir. 2000) ("unreasonable or oppressive"). The FCA's CID provision states that the standards governing discovery under the Federal Rules of Civil Procedure apply, but only "to the extent that the application of such standards to any [CID] is appropriate and consistent with the provisions and purposes of this section." 31 U.S.C. § 3733(b)(1)(B). No court has interpreted this provision, but it is unlikely that it significantly restricts the government's authority.

58.   *Id.* § 3733(a)(1).

59.   *Id.* § 3733(*l*)(8); *see id.* § 3733(i)(3).

60.   Internal investigation procedures are discussed at length in chapter 6, Internal Investigations.

61.   Of course, as discussed above, the 2009 amendments to the FCA now allow the government to expand its resources by making responses to CIDs available to relators and their counsel—persons who are both interested and financially motivated to find support for the claims asserted.

62.   In addition, sometimes a civil FCA investigation by the government is accompanied by a "parallel" criminal investigation into the same or related behavior. Conducting a thorough internal investigation and presenting your findings to the government can sometimes be instrumental in persuading the government that the matter should be handled civilly, rather than through a criminal prosecution.

63.   The DOJ used to weigh a company's willingness to disclose privileged and work product materials as an element of "cooperation" in criminal investigations (and by extension, civil investigations also). The DOJ later clarified that waiver of privileged materials is not a factor in determining "cooperation"— although a company's willingness to share factual information is a consideration. More recent DOJ guidance has raised the cooperation bar, requiring companies to disclose all relevant facts to receive any cooperation credit. *See* Yates Memo, *supra* note 27. The DOJ has made clear, however, that this demand for cooperation must respect the "bounds of the law and legal privileges." *Id.* at 4. Time will tell how and if DOJ will honor that provision.

64.   United States v. Bornstein, 423 U.S. 303 (1976).

65.   United States v. Collver Insulated Wire Co., 94 F. Supp. 493, 498–99 (D.R.I. 1950).

66.   *See, e.g.*, United States v. Sci. Applications Int'l Corp., 653 F. Supp. 2d 87 (D.D.C. 2009), *aff'd in part, vacated in part, remanded by* 626 F.3d 1257 (D.C. Cir. 2010). The D.C. Circuit held on appeal that when assessing damages, the fact finder should consider the value of the goods and services received by the government, adopting a "benefit of the bargain" approach. *Id.*, 626 F.3d at 1278–79; *see also Bunk*, 2012 WL 488256, at *11 (refusing to impose a civil penalty of $50,248,000 because it was "grossly disproportional to the harm caused" by the defendants, and would thus result "in the imposition of an excessive fine in violation of the Eighth Amendment").

67. *See, e.g.*, United States v. Rogan, 517 F.3d 449 (7th Cir. 2008) (defendant who submitted Medicare claims while in violation of the anti-kickback statute was not entitled to receive any payment on those claims, per the terms of the statute).

68. *Bornstein*, 423 U.S. 303; *see also* U.S. *ex rel.* Harrison v. Westinghouse Savannah River Co., 352 F.3d 908 (4th Cir. 2003); United States v. TDC Mgmt. Corp., 288 F.3d 421 (D.C. Cir. 2002).

69. Depending on how the plea and settlement are structured, however, the defendant could still be at risk for permissive exclusion (in the context of federally funded healthcare programs) or for suspension and debarment (for government contractors). *See, e.g.*, 42 U.S.C. § 1320a-7(b); FAR 9.406.

70. 31 U.S.C. § 3730(h)(1). For the elements required to successfully show a retaliation claim, see U.S. *ex rel.* Glynn v. Edo Corp., 710 F.3d 209, 214 (4th Cir. 2013).

71. 31 U.S.C. § 3730(h)(1).

72. *Id.; see id.* § 3730(h)(2)–(3).

73. The First Circuit has examined the retaliation claims of former employees who had previously filed a qui tam FCA action against their employer. *See* Harrington v. Aggregate Indus.-Ne. Region, Inc., 668 F.3d 25 (1st Cir. 2012). The court held that a plaintiff must first set forth a prima facie case of retaliation, and then the burden shifts to the employer to articulate a legitimate, non-retaliatory reason for the adverse employment action, which imposes merely a burden of production, not one of proof.

74. *See* U.S. *ex rel.* Costner v. URS Consultants, Inc., 317 F.3d 883 (8th Cir. 2003); *see also* Q 11.3, *supra*.

75. *See* Mikes v. Straus, 274 F.3d 687 (2d Cir. 2001); U.S. *ex rel.* Hopper v. Anton, 91 F.3d 1261 (9th Cir. 1996).

76. *See Anton*, 91 F.3d at 1266.

77. Recent judicial decisions demonstrate a split among the federal circuits regarding the limits of the implied certification theory. *See* U.S. *ex rel.* Hutcheson v. Blackstone Med., Inc., 647 F.3d 377 (1st Cir. 2011) (recognizing the implied false certification theory and finding the court's inquiry to be fact-intensive rather than a bright-line test); Chesbrough v. VPA, P.C., 655 F.3d 461, 468 (6th Cir. 2011) (holding that a "relator cannot merely allege that a defendant violated a[n] [industry] standard—he or she must allege that compliance with the standard was required to obtain payment"); U.S. *ex rel.* Pilecki-Simko v. Chubb Inst., 443 F. App'x 754, 757–58 (3d Cir. 2011) (recognizing the validity of the implied certification theory but dismissing the plaintiff's complaint for failure to adequately allege scienter). The Supreme Court recently took up a case to decide whether the FCA actually does allow "false certification" liability and, if so, just how far that theory goes. *See* Universal Health Servs. Inc. v. U.S. *ex rel.* Escobar, No. 15-7 (U.S. June 30, 2015).

78. *See* Q 11.3, *supra*, discussing the "reckless disregard" standard and simple negligence; *see also Renal Care Grp.*, 696 F.3d at 530–31, discussing the "reckless disregard" standard and other circuit courts' interpretations of that standard.

79. *Costner*, 317 F.3d at 883.

80. U.S. *ex rel.* Oliver v. Parson Co., 195 F.3d 457, 464 (9th Cir. 1999); *see also* U.S. *ex rel.* K&R Ltd. P'ship v. Mass. Hous. Fin. Agency, 530 F.3d 980 (D.C. Cir. 2008).

81. *See* U.S. *ex rel.* Berge v. Bd. of Trs. of Univ. of Ala., 104 F.3d 1453, 1460 (4th Cir. 1997).

82. 31 U.S.C. § 3729(b)(4).

83. *See, e.g.*, United States v. Triple Canopy, Inc., 775 F.3d 628, 637 (4th Cir. 2015) ("Express contractual language may constitute dispositive evidence of materiality, but materiality may be established in other ways, such as through testimony demonstrating that both parties to the contract understood that payment was conditional on compliance with the requirement at issue." (internal quotation marks and citations omitted)), *petition for cert. docketed*, No. 14-1440 (U.S. June 8, 2015).

84. *See, e.g.*, U.S. *ex rel.* Schwedt v. Planning Research Corp., 59 F.3d 196 (D.C. Cir. 1995).

85. *See, e.g.*, United States v. Bouchey, 860 F. Supp. 890, 893–94 (D.D.C. 1994); Blusal Meats v. United States, 638 F. Supp. 824 (S.D.N.Y. 1986), *aff'd*, 817 F.2d 1007 (2d Cir. 1987). Note that the statutory language that tied the violation at issue to actual *payment* of the claim was eliminated with the 2009 amendments to the FCA, likely ending the debate that damages are a necessary element of some FCA violations.

86. *See, e.g., Renal Care Grp.*, 696 F.3d at 531 (Medicare reimbursements); United States v. Fawaz, 881 F.2d 259, 265 (6th Cir. 1989) (tax evasion); United States v. Brimberry, 961 F.2d 1286, 1290 (7th Cir. 1992) (tax perjury).

87. *See generally Renal Care Grp.*, 696 F.3d at 531.

88. United States v. O'Conner, 158 F. Supp. 2d 697, 728 (E.D. Va. 2001).

89. *See, e.g.*, United States v. Mutuc, 349 F.3d 930, 936 (7th Cir. 2003) (advice by attorney to client to lie under oath cannot support a defense to perjury); United States v. Olbres, 61 F.3d 967, 970–71 (1st Cir. 1995) (reliance on the advice of an accountant depends on "whether the defendants *knew* when they signed the return that it understated their income"); United States v. Whyte, 699 F.2d 375, 380 (7th Cir. 1983) (valid defense to charge of filing false tax return if defendant adopts and files the returns as prepared without having reason to believe they are incorrect).

90. United States v. Claiborne, 765 F.2d 784, 798 (9th Cir. 1985), *abrogated on other grounds*, Ross v. Oklahoma, 487 U.S. 81 (1988).

91. *See* Kellogg, Brown & Root Servs., Inc. v. U.S. *ex rel.* Carter, 135 S. Ct. 1970 (2015) (reversing decision holding that the Wartime Suspension of Limitations Act tolled the FCA's statute of limitations).

92. 31 U.S.C. § 3731(b).

93. *See* Graham Cty. Soil & Water Conservation Dist. v. U.S. *ex rel.* Wilson, 545 U.S. 409 (2005).

94. United States v. Merck-Medco Managed Care, LLC, 336 F. Supp. 2d 430, 440–41 (E.D. Pa. 2004).

95. Memorandum from Eric B. Holder, Deputy Att'y Gen., Bringing Criminal Charges Against Corporations (June 16, 1999) [hereinafter Holder Memo], www.justice.gov/criminai/fraud/documents/reports/1999/charging-corps.pdf. The

Holder Memo's discussion of compliance plans has carried through subsequent revisions of DOJ policy (*e.g.*, the "Thompson Memo" and the "McNulty Memo"), and in August 2008, was officially included in the U.S. Attorneys' Manual, which guides all federal prosecutors within the DOJ. *See* Press Release No. 08-757, U.S. Dep't of Justice, Justice Department Revises Charging Guidelines for Prosecuting Corporate Fraud (Aug. 28, 2008), www.justice.gov/archive/opa/pr/2008/August/08-odag-757.html; U.S. Attorneys' Manual § 9-28.800.

   96.   Deficit Reduction Act of 2005 (DRA), Pub. L. No. 109-171. DRA § 6032 is codified at 42 U.S.C. § 1396a(a)(68).

   97.   N.Y. SOC. SERV. LAW § 363-d.

   98.   42 U.S.C. § 1395cc(j)(8).

   99.   DRA § 6031.

   100.   *See, e.g.*, ARK. CODE ANN. §§ 20-77-901 to 20-77-911; COLO. REV. STAT. §§ 25.5-4-304 to 25.5-4-306; CONN. GEN. STAT. §§ 176-301a to 176-301p; GA. CODE ANN. §§ 49-4-168 to 49-4-168.8; LA. REV. STAT. ANN. §§ 46:437.1 to 46:440.3; MD. CODE ANN. §§ 2-601 to 2-611; MICH. COMP. LAWS §§ 400.601 to 400.613; MO. REV. STAT. §§ 191.900 to 191.910; OHIO REV. CODE ANN. §§ 5111.03, 5111.101; OKLA. STAT. tit. 63 §§ 5053.1 to 5053.7; TENN. CODE ANN. §§ 71-5-181 to 71-5-185; TEX. HUM. RES. CODE §§ 32.039, 36-001 to 36-132; UTAH CODE ANN. §§ 26-20-1 to 26-20-15; WASH. REV. CODE §§ 48.80.010 to 48.80.900; WIS. STAT. § 20.931 *et seq.*

12

Privacy and Security of Personal Information

Ieuan G. Mahony & Maximillian J. Bodoin*

An individual's interest in privacy can be viewed as the right simply "to be let alone by other people."[1] This right can also include the right to engage anonymously in public debate.[2] Recently, the right as applied to personal information has taken on renewed importance due to the prevalence and threat of "identity theft." Generally, under the legal structures outlined below, an organization that collects information that is "personal" to a natural person—such that he or she can be identified through the information—is obligated to maintain the privacy of the information. Moreover, it is not simply an obligation to keep the information private; the Federal Trade Commission (FTC), for example, is increasingly interested in whether a data controller has employed proper "security" to its systems to maintain this privacy[3] and prevent identity theft.[4]

*   The authors wish to acknowledge Christopher A. Myers for his contributions to this chapter.

323

Unfortunately, U.S. law does not provide a unified framework regulating the gathering and use of personal information.[5] Instead of being "collected" into a single statute, U.S. protections for privacy in personal information have resided in discrete federal and state legislation governing particular industries and practices, or in the common law, with practices varying from sector to sector.[6]

This chapter outlines the wide range of laws and regulations that may apply to your organization's data security and privacy obligations—a system that has been referred to as a "patchwork" of laws[7]—and offers guidance on corporate compliance issues relating to privacy and security of personal information.

Data Privacy Laws

An Overview

Q 12.1   What are the particular concerns that drive privacy law?

- **Identity theft.** Forty-seven states currently have data breach notification laws in place designed to protect personal information from identity theft.[8] These laws are generally structured to require an organization to notify data subjects if there has been unauthorized access to, or acquisition of, their personal information in unencrypted form.[9] In addition, several states require an organization to notify the attorney general or other governmental entity in the event of a data breach, and many also require notification to consumer reporting agencies if the number of involved data subjects surpasses a defined threshold. To further guard against identity theft, the Federal Trade Commission and five other governmental agencies jointly issued the so-called Red Flag Rules. Under these rules, financial institutions and creditors that maintain certain kinds of "covered accounts" must develop and implement written programs to prevent, detect, and respond to possible incidents of identity theft. The Red Flag Rules apply not only to consumer accounts, but also to business accounts, where there is a reasonably foreseeable risk of identity theft with respect to the account. Although the Red Flag Rules thus apply to a potentially broad group of businesses, the rules are relatively flexible and allow each organization to tailor its red flags program to reflect the size, scope, and sophistication of its operations.[10]
- **Financial information.** The Gramm-Leach-Bliley (GLB) Act requires financial institutions to maintain reasonable protections for personal information they collect from their customers.[11]
- **Protected health information.** HIPAA requires covered entities to protect "protected health information."[12]
- **Online privacy of children.** The Children's Online Privacy Protection Act of 1998 (COPPA)[13] requires that hosts of commercial websites obtain "verifiable" parental consent before collecting personal information from children under

325

the age of thirteen. COPPA also requires that the host disclose what information is sought and how that information will be used.

- **Cross-border transfer of personal information.** The European Union has comprehensive data protection legislation in place designed to protect the personal data of persons located in the EU. The legislation, known as the EU Data Protection Directive 95/46/EC,[14] expressly prohibits the transfer of personal information from the EU to non-EU countries that do not provide an adequate level of protection for personal information except under limited circumstances. Under this regime, the United States does not provide "adequate protection" for EU-sourced personal information. Accordingly, an entity in the United States "importing" personal information from the EU must either (a) certify to the Department of Commerce's "Safe Harbor,"[15] or (b) sign one of the Commission's "standard contractual clauses" to provide the requisite protections.
- **Credit reports.** The Fair Credit Reporting Act[16] restricts access to consumer reports and imposes safe disposal requirements, among other requirements.[17]
- **Identity verification.** Section 326 of the Uniting and Strengthening America by Providing Appropriate Tools Required to Intercept and Obstruct Terrorism (USA PATRIOT) Act,[18] requires verification of the identity of persons opening accounts with financial institutions.
- **Drivers' information.** The Driver's Privacy Protection Act of 1994 (DPPA), for example, prohibits most disclosures of drivers' personal information.[19]
- **"Catch-All" protections.** Section 5 of the Federal Trade Commission Act prohibits unfair or deceptive practices.[20] This is the basis on which the FTC relies in bringing actions to enforce and police conduct in the online business-to-consumer world.[21]

Definitions of "Personal Information" (State Statutes)

California:

"For purposes of this section, 'personal information' means an individual's first name or first initial and last name in combination with any one or more of the following data elements, when either the name or the data elements are not encrypted:

(1) Social security number.

(2) Driver's license number or California Identification Card number.

(3) Account number, credit or debit card number, in combination with any required security code, access code, or password that would permit access to an individual's financial account.

(4) Medical information.

(5) Health insurance information."[22]

Florida:

"For purposes of this section, the term "personal information" means an individual's first name, first initial and last name, or any middle name and last name, in combination with any one or more of the following data elements when the data elements are not encrypted:

(a) Social security number.

(b) Driver's license number or Florida Identification Card number.

(c) Account number, credit card number, or debit card number, in combination with any required security code, access code, or password that would permit access to an individual's financial account."[23]

Definitions

Q 12.1.1   What is the legal definition of "personal information"?

Each of the legal regimes presents a slightly different definition of "personal information." The following provides a sense of these variations.

Standard Online Definition. In the context of an online privacy policy, "personal information" is often defined as any information that could reasonably be used to identify a data subject including, for example, a data subject's name, age, address, email address, photograph, Social Security number, or any combination of this or similar information.

State Definitions. State statutes typically define "personal information" as a state resident's name in combination with any one or more of the following data elements: (i) Social Security number; (ii) driver's license number or other government identification number; or (iii) account number, credit card number, or debit card number, in combination with any required security code, access code, or password that would permit access to an individual's financial account.

State definitions of personal information often vary. The box on page 335 offers two such examples—one typical, and one atypical.

Federal Definition. The following are examples of some federal laws' broad definitions of the term (and its functional equivalents).

- **Children's Online Privacy Protection Act:**

   The term "personal information" means individually identifiable information about an individual collected online, including—

   (A) a first and last name;
   (B) a home or other physical address including street name and name of a city or town;
   (C) an e-mail address;
   (D) a telephone number;
   (E) a Social Security number;
   (F) persistent identifiers that can be used to recognize a user over time and across different sites such as a cookie, an IP address, or a unique device identifier;

(G) a photo, video, or audio file containing the child's image or voice;

(H) any other identifier that the Commission determines permits the physical or online contacting of a specific individual; or

(I) information concerning the child or the parents of that child that the website collects online from the child and combines with an identifier described in this paragraph.[24]

• **Gramm-Leach-Bliley Act.** GLBA incorporates definitions for both "nonpublic personal information" and "personally identifiable financial information":

Nonpublic personal information. (A) The term "nonpublic personal information" means personally identifiable financial information—

(i) provided by a consumer to a financial institution;

(ii) resulting from any transaction with the consumer or any service performed for the consumer; or

(iii) otherwise obtained by the financial institution.[25]

* * *

"Personally identifiable financial information" means any information:

(i) A consumer provides to you to obtain a financial product or service from you;

(ii) About a consumer resulting from any transaction involving a financial product or service between you and a consumer; or

(iii) You otherwise obtain about a consumer in connection with providing a financial product or service to that consumer.[26]

• **HIPAA.** HIPAA incorporates definitions for both "protected health information" and "individually identifiable health information":

"Protected health information" means individually identifiable health information:

(1) Except as provided in paragraph (2) of this definition, that is:

(i) Transmitted by electronic media;

329

          (ii) Maintained in electronic media; or

          (iii) Transmitted or maintained in any other form or medium.

    (2) Protected health information excludes individually identifiable health information in:

          (i)   Education records covered by the Family Educational Rights and Privacy Act, as amended, 20 U.S.C. § 1232g;

          (ii) Records described at 20 U.S.C. § 1232g(a)(4)(B)(iv); and

          (iii) Employment records held by a covered entity in its role as employer.[27]

* * *

"Individually identifiable health information" is information that is a subset of health information, including demographic information collected from an individual, and: (1) Is created or received by a health care provider, health plan, employer, or health care clearinghouse; and (2) Relates to the past, present, or future physical or mental health or condition of an individual; the provision of health care to an individual; or the past, present, or future payment for the provision of health care to an individual; and (i) That identifies the individual; or (ii) With respect to which there is a reasonable basis to believe the information can be used to identify the individual.[28]

Compliance

Q 12.1.2   What steps should our organization take to ensure compliance with data protection laws?

1. Determine what personal information, if any, your organization collects. This first step is key.

2. Examine the means your organization uses to collect personal information, which may include:

    •   online forms;

    •   purchasing of marketing and other databases;

    •   publicly available sources;

    •   receipt of personal information from business partners;

- call centers;
- receipt of personal information from customers in person or over the phone.

3. Examine your organization's use of personal information.

These uses may be wholly internal to your organization (and thereby raise considerably fewer data protection issues), or they may involve sharing personal information with others (which as a rule will raise more privacy and security issues).

4. Examine your organization's storage of personal information.

- Where does your organization store personal information that it collects or receives?
- Does your organization take reasonable steps to ensure that personal information it collects is protected from unauthorized access?
- Does your organization implement a record retention policy? How long is personal information retained?
- Who has access to stored personal information?
- Are security mechanisms (both physical and electronic) in place to protect stored personal information from unauthorized access or disclosure?
- Has your organization implemented a Disaster Recovery Plan?
- Does your organization have an Electronic Discovery Response Plan in place?
- Does your organization take measures to verify the accuracy of personal information it receives?

FIGURE 12-1
Personal Information Checklist

You should be able to answer these important questions regarding your company's use of personal information:

❏ Who within your organization has access to personal information?

- Customer Service personnel?
- Human Resources personnel?
- IT personnel?
- Outside consultants?
- Other personnel?

❏ For what purposes is your organization using personal information?

❏ Do any third parties have access to, or are they entitled to use of, personal information?

- Affiliates?
- Marketing firms?
- Advertising agencies?
- Other related third parties?
- Third-party service providers or outsourcing partners?

❏ Has your organization entered into any advertising, co-branding, or other relationship that is inconsistent with your privacy policy practices and procedures?

❏ Under what circumstances does your organization release personal information or provide it upon request?

- Pursuant to law enforcement requests?
- Pursuant to private investigator requests?
- With knowledge of imminent harm to an individual?
- With knowledge of a substantial financial loss?
- Pursuant to a judicial order?

❑   What exposure does your organization have for unauthorized access to, or dissemination of, personal information?

- Employee misuse?
- Databases?
- Security glitches?
- Identity theft scams?

❑   What measures does your organization take to check or confirm the credentials of the person providing or requesting personal information?

❑   Has your organization experienced a data breach or incident of identity theft in the past? If so, what has your organization done to address any identified security vulnerabilities that contributed to the breach?

Your Company's Privacy Policy

Q 12.2   Should we implement a privacy policy?

Yes; and while you may have an existing privacy policy, determine if it is applicable only to personal information collected online. The FTC, for example, will assume that, unless stated otherwise, online privacy policies cover information that is collected offline. It is good practice to have a privacy policy in place and available to consumers in particular.

Q 12.2.1   Where should our organization place its privacy policy?

An online privacy policy is meant to be a type of "contract" between a site visitor and the site. The policy states what the host will do (and commits the host to these statements), and then elicits from the site visitor a "consent." It is unlikely that a judge would conclude that a privacy policy does in fact constitute a binding agreement if it is hidden on the site. Accordingly, a host should post links to the policy on the home page, and prominently on all other pages. Moreover, hosts seeking to maximize the likelihood that their policies will be enforced as contracts will have the user click an "I accept" button referring to the privacy policy before the site processes personal data submitted by the visitor.

The FTC's Final Rule under COPPA adopts a similar approach. This Rule, and guidelines published surrounding implementation of the Rule, provide that a host must post on its homepage a clear and prominent link (the FTC suggests using larger font or different color with a contrasting background) to a notice of its privacy and information practices.[29] In addition, such a notice must be placed at each page on which personal information is collected from children. An operator of a general audience site with a separate area for children users must post a link to its notice on the children's homepage.[30]

Q 12.2.2   What principles should inform our privacy policy?

"Fair information practices" of privacy advocates follow five core principles:[31]

1. **Notice.** Consumers should be given notice when they enter a site concerning the site's information-gathering practices. This notice should identify:

   (a) the entity that is collecting the information;
   (b) the uses to which the information will be put;[32]
   (c) the entities who will potentially receive the information;
   (d) the type of information that will be collected and how it will be collected (by cookies, for example);
   (e) whether the consumer has a choice about providing the information; and
   (f) how the collector will safeguard the information.

2. **Choice/Consent.** Consumers should be given a choice, after being informed as to the site's information-gathering practices, as to whether they wish to participate, or instead wish to opt out. This opt-out right takes on increased importance where so-called secondary uses of the information are at issue, namely, uses beyond those necessary to complete the contemplated transaction. This principle encompasses choice both as to internal secondary uses (such as marketing back to consumers) and external secondary uses (such as disclosing data to third parties).

Under the FTC's new COPPA regulations, special consent rules apply to children. Acceptable methods for obtaining the required "verifiable consent" from the child's parent include having the parent:

- sign a consent form and send it back to you via fax, mail, or electronic scan;
- use a credit card, debit card, or other online payment system that provides notification of each separate transaction to the account holder;
- call a toll-free number staffed by trained personnel;
- connect to trained personnel via a video conference; or
- provide a copy of a form of government-issued ID that the website host must check against a database, and then must delete the identification from its records when the verification process is completed.

3. **Access.** Consumers should be given the ability to access the data the site has collected, and the ability to contest the accuracy and completeness of that data.[33]

4. **Security.** The data must be accurate and secure, and the site must take reasonable steps to protect against unauthorized access, loss, or use of the data.[34]

5. **Redress.** There must be at the site a mechanism to enforce the site's privacy principles.[35]

Q 12.2.3   What types of choices should data subjects be allowed?

A privacy policy that is consistent with fair information practices principles will generally implement a model that provides data subjects with the ability to determine how the organization uses their personal information. Two available models include:

- Opt-in. Data subjects are *excluded* from the participant group unless they affirmatively "opt in." This structure generally results in significantly smaller participant groups.
- Opt-out. Data subjects are *included* in the participant group unless they affirmatively request an exit. This structure generally results in significantly larger participant groups.

Q 12.2.4   How should my organization administer its privacy policy?

- Has the organization appointed someone to oversee the implementation and compliance with the privacy policy?
- Do the various departments within the organization have a uniform process for handling personal information that comports with the established privacy policy?
- Does the organization employ a process for amending the privacy policy, and does said process include a means of implementing any amendments?

Q 12.2.5   What happens if we modify the privacy policy?

An organization should have a method for informing data subjects that the privacy policy has been modified or amended. Often, this can be accomplished by requiring a website user, for example, to click an "I accept" button referencing the revised policy. It is good practice in a privacy policy to anticipate changes and to allow a simple mechanism for the policy's owner to implement these changes.

Q 12.2.6   Should our organization display any third-party seals of approval?

There is a range of programs that will "certify" your privacy policy and procedures. In these programs, the third party will review your privacy policy and provide a channel for your site visitors to use if they have privacy-related complaints. The program owner will allow an organization that has passed the program standards to display the program logo on the site.[36]

Your Employees' Privacy

Q 12.3   What privacy rules apply to our organization's employees?

The Electronic Communications Privacy Act (ECPA) affords the primary federal protection for private online communications. The ECPA's purpose is to address the "problem of unauthorized persons deliberately gaining access to, and sometimes tampering with, electronic or wire communications that are not intended to be available to the public."[37]

Q 12.3.1   What criminal sanctions does the ECPA provide for?

The ECPA includes fines or imprisonment of up to five years for violations.[38] In addition, a person whose email, for example, has been intercepted has the right to recover civil damages, including punitive damages and attorney fees, against the interceptor.[39]

Monitoring Employee Email

Q 12.3.2   Are we allowed to monitor our employees' email?

Yes; the ECPA allows the monitoring of email where one of the parties to the email consents to the monitoring.[40] Note, however, that state law may be more restrictive.[41]

To obtain authorization to monitor their employees' email under this provision, employers often institute written email policies in which employees acknowledge that the email system belongs to their employer and in which the employees grant consent to their employer to review email on the system for various business purposes (as further described, below).

Q 12.3.3   Do we need a written email policy?

It is strongly recommended. Irrespective of your potential willingness or desire to monitor your employees' email, you should strongly consider a written email policy. In addition to notifying employees that email may be monitored, you should consider including email usage guidelines in a written email policy. For example, you may want to prohibit the use of email to harass or threaten others. See Figure 12-4, below, for examples of clauses you might consider including in a written policy regarding employee/company email.

Data Security

Identity Theft

Q 12.4   What is identity theft?

Identity theft is a fraud that involves pretending to be someone else in order to steal money or get other benefits. Identity theft affects nine million Americans each year.[42] One study found that identity theft rose 13% in 2011, noting that more than 11.6 million adults became a victim of identity theft in the United States.[43]

Although identity theft can take many forms, a classic example is credit identity theft. It occurs when a criminal obtains goods or services by impersonating someone else. The criminal steals personal and/or financial information from a victim and then pretends to be the victim by presenting those stolen credentials to a merchant. The merchant provides the goods or services to the criminal and then charges the victim's credit card (or sends the bill to the victim's address, provided by the criminal).

FIGURE 12-2
Credit Identity Theft

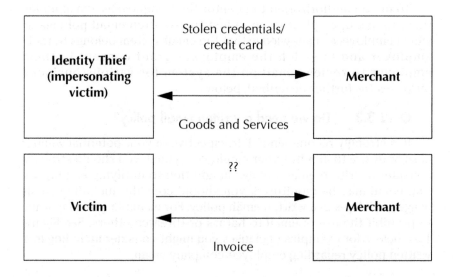

Q 12.4.1   Are states taking actions to require organizations to protect individuals against identity theft?

Efforts have begun on the state level to extend protections against identity theft beyond the original "notice of security breach" statutes. For example, Massachusetts introduced the Massachusetts Identity Theft Regulation ("Regulation 201") in order to establish standards for the protection of personal information of Massachusetts residents.[44] Regulation 201 applies to any entity possessing "personal information" about a Massachusetts resident, which is roughly defined as a resident's name in combination with a Social Security number, driver's license number or financial account number. Regulation 201 requires covered entities to take a variety of actions including, but not limited to:

(i)   developing a written information security program;

(ii) designating personnel with responsibility for the program;

(iii) assessing security measures currently in place (for both paper and electronic records), and revising measures as necessary;

(iv) obtaining contractual assurance from third party services providers that have access to personal information;

(v)   providing employee training; and

(vi) regularly reviewing and updating the written program as necessary.

Q 12.4.2   Are there federal regulations that require organizations to protect individuals against identity theft?

The FTC and five other governmental agencies jointly issued the Identity Theft Red Flags and Address Discrepancy Rules[45] to "detect, prevent, and mitigate identity theft in connection with the opening of certain accounts or certain existing accounts."[46] The regulations went into effect on January 1, 2011.

The Red Flag Rules apply to financial institutions and creditors that maintain "covered accounts." The law covers creditors who regularly, and in the ordinary course of business, meet one of three general criteria. They must:

(1)   obtain or use consumer reports in connection with a credit transaction;

(2)   furnish information to consumer reporting agencies in connection with a credit transaction; or

(3)   advance funds to—or on behalf of—someone, except for funds for expenses incidental to a service provided by the creditor to that person.[47]

339

Q 12.4.3 What should our identity theft prevention program include?

As a general rule, your identity theft prevention program should be appropriate to the size and complexity of your organization and the nature and scope of its activities. Your program should include reasonable policies and procedures to:

1. identify relevant security vulnerabilities and incorporate them in the compliance program;
2. detect security vulnerabilities that have been incorporated into the compliance program;
3. respond appropriately to any security vulnerabilities that are detected to prevent and mitigate identity theft; and
4. update the compliance program periodically to reflect changes in identity theft risks to the entity and its customers.

In addition, the program should be written, and it should be approved by your board of directors. Appoint an individual to administer the program and provide training for staff.

COMPLIANCE TIP

In addition to stealing personal information, identity thieves are increasingly interested in stealing corporate identifying information in order to commit business-to-business (B2B) identity theft. In determining whether you face a risk from B2B identity theft, consider the following ways identity thieves use corporate information to commit fraud:

1. **Imposter poses as a current customer.** An individual steals the identity of one of your corporate customers. The individual, posing as the corporate customer, contacts you and attempts to access, acquire, or change information associated with the account or to obtain goods or services through the account.

---

2. **Imposter poses as a new customer.** An individual steals the identifying information of an employee of an actual company that is not one of your current clients. The individual, posing as a representative of the potential new client, attempts to acquire goods or services from you.

3. **Imposter poses as your company.** An individual steals the identity of one of your employees. The individual, posing as a representative of your company, contacts actual or potential customers and attempts to acquire their billing or other identifying information.

FIGURE 12-3
Examples of Red Flags[48]

Documents provided for identification appear to have been altered or forged.

Personal identifying information provided by the customer is not consistent with other personal identifying information provided by the customer.

The Social Security number provided is the same as that submitted by other persons opening an account or other customers.

Mail sent to the customer is returned repeatedly as undeliverable although transactions continue to be conducted in connection with the customer's covered account.

Notification is received from a customer that he or she is the victim of identity theft.

Q 12.4.4   Do we need an identity theft prevention program for our service providers?

You should take steps to ensure that your service providers follow reasonable policies and procedures designed to detect, prevent, and mitigate the risk of identity theft. If you are a service provider, you may be asked to implement an identity theft prevention program or agree to follow the covered entity's program.

Third-Party Security Audits

Q 12.5   What security protections should we have in place?

If your organization handles sensitive information routinely, you should consider engaging a third party to perform a security audit. This provides requisite "comfort" to those of your business partners who rely on your security practices.

For example, the Statement on Standards for Attestation Engagements No. 16 ("SSAE 16"), which is an enhancement to the Statement on Auditing Standards No. 70: Service Organizations ("SAS 70"), is an auditing statement of the Auditing Standards Board of the American Institute of Certified Public Accountants (AICPA) that defines the professional standards used by a service auditor to assess the internal controls of a service organization and issue a service auditor's report. Service organizations that may have an SSAE 16 or SAS 70 report include processors of insurance and medical claims, hosted data centers, application service providers (ASPs), and credit processing organizations.

FIGURE 12-4
Recommended Clauses for Your
Company's Email Policy

❏   A statement that, as between the company and the employee, the company owns the computer network, all software and hardware, and all business records;

❑ A statement that the company will monitor use, for maintenance purposes, for network performance purposes, to ensure compliance with this policy, and for other purposes in the employer's discretion;

❑ A statement establishing that there is no expectation of privacy in email sent or received on the employee's work account or that stores work email;

❑ A statement identifying uses of the system that are prohibited;

❑ A statement reinforcing the company's confidential information policy, as it applies to email and digital information;

❑ A statement that a violation of the policy will subject the employee to discipline; and

❑ Where possible, arranging to have each employee acknowledge that he or she has read and understands the policy.

FIGURE 12-5
Data Security Checklist

Your organization should be in a position to answer "yes" to each of these questions, and to verify this answer:

❑ Have you implemented firewalls and other technical protections to your computer networks to prevent unauthorized access to personal information?

❑ Have you implemented encryption technology, particularly on laptops and other portable electronic devices capable of storing data?

❏ Have you implemented physical security measures to protect against the unauthorized access to personal information contained in physical files?

❏ If your organization relies on third parties for the processing or other handling of its personal information:

   (a) does the contract provide sufficient security protections to your organization; and

   (b) has your organization obtained a security audit, showing due diligence as to this third party's security practices?

❏ Have you implemented an "incident response plan" for potential security breaches?

❏ Are employees trained to properly protect the security of personal information?

❏ Is intrusion detection software in place?

❏ Are log files in place that would allow the tracing of an intruder?

Compliance Programs

Q 12.6   What should our privacy and security program look like?

It should include compliance and auditing procedures. This program should include training for employees in the privacy policy and applicable privacy protection procedures. Training records should be maintained to verify attendance and proper training. Preferably, those employees with broader access to sensitive personal information will have heightened training, commensurate with the sensitivity of data. Moreover, an organization should consider revising employment agreements to reflect additional responsibilities that employees may have placed on them due to the implementation of new privacy and security programs. As with any compliance program, there should be benefits and penalties associated with employee compliance/noncompliance with the privacy policy.

COMPLIANCE TIP

In assessing your organization's privacy and security programs, keep in mind that a corporate reorganization (such as a merger or acquisition) may have "thrown together" inharmonious policies. As the operations are integrated, you will want to harmonize these documents and procedures.

Q 12.7   Are public companies required to take additional steps in terms of compliance with privacy obligations?

Yes. Regulatory and legislative interest in these areas continues to grow. For example, the FTC issued a key report in March 2012, entitled "Protecting Consumer Privacy in an Era of Rapid Change: Recommendations for Businesses and Policymakers."[49] This report focuses on:

- the importance of a privacy policy and related procedures, as the baseline for protecting personal information, and with attention to reasonable collection limits, sound retention practices, and data accuracy;
- so-called privacy by design, which is the requirement that privacy protections be built into products and services from the outset;
- meaningful privacy choices for data subjects; and
- greater transparency in data privacy and security practices, including more robust, frequent, and meaningful consumer privacy notices and disclosures.

Q 12.8   Do we need to be concerned in our compliance program about class action cases seeking to enforce privacy obligations?

Initially, class action plaintiffs experienced a lack of success in the data privacy and security area, and courts rejected claims that plaintiffs had suffered an increased risk of identity theft, or that their personal data had inherent value that was lost by disclosure.[50] Certain courts, however, are beginning to accept plaintiffs' class action arguments, relying on FTC statements to show that personal information has a monetary value, among identity thieves in particular.[51] The risk of potential class action exposure gives compliance programs increased importance.

Cybersecurity Insurance

Q 12.9   Is coverage available to insure against risks associated with data privacy and security?

Yes. This insurance goes by several names, including "cybersecurity," "cyber liability," and "cyber risk," and is generally designed to cover financial losses to an insured resulting from damages caused by a computer or network-based incident.[52] Commentators generally view the current cybersecurity insurance market as small, with the exception of the market for third-party coverage for data breaches, where a relatively wide range of policies are available. These policies insure against losses that the insured causes to its customers and others, and generally cover direct losses from a security breach involving personal information. These losses consist of "clean-up" costs from the breach, including:

(i)   preparing and sending out security breach notifications;
(ii) forensic analyses; and
(iii) credit monitoring for the data subjects impacted by the breach.

Notes to Chapter 12

1. Katz v. United States, 389 U.S. 347, 350 (1967).
2. McIntyre v. Ohio Elections Comm'n, 514 U.S. 334, 34–42 (1995) (the First Amendment protects the right to speak anonymously).
3. *Consumer Information*, FED. TRADE COMM'N, www.ftc.gov/bcp/conline/pubs/buspubs/security.shtm (last visited June 18, 2015).
4. *See Red Flags Rule*, FED. TRADE COMM'N, www.ftc.gov/redflagsrule (last visited June 18, 2015).
5. Although U.S. law does not currently provide a unified framework to address the protection of personal information, the issue has not been ignored by legislatures. The House of Representatives has introduced H.R. 580, the Data Accountability and Trust Act, which is intended to protect consumers by requiring reasonable security policies and procedures to protect data containing personal information, as well as a national notification procedure in the event of a data breach.
6. J. Thomas Rosch, Comm'r, Fed. Trade Comm'n, Remarks before the ABA Section of Antitrust Law Consumer Protection Conference Georgetown University Law Center, Washington, D.C.: Where Do We Go from Here?—Some Thoughts on the Future of the Consumer Protection Mission, at 2 (Jan. 29, 2007), www.ftc.gov/speeches/rosch/070129RoschABAconsprotconf.pdf.
7. *See* Dep't of Health & Human Servs., Standards for Privacy of Individually Identifiable Health Information, 64 Fed. Reg. 59,918, 59,920 (Nov. 3, 1999), www.access.gpo.gov/su_docs/aces/aces140.html.
8. *See* www.ncsl.org/programs/lis/cip/priv/breachlaws.htm; *see also* www.ftc.gov/infosecurity/. Such laws are also in place in the District of Columbia, Puerto Rico, and the Virgin Islands. The only states that lack these types of security breach laws are Alabama, New Mexico, and South Dakota.
9. *See generally* THE PRESIDENT'S IDENTITY THEFT TASK FORCE REPORT (Sept. 2008), www.ftc.gov/os/2008/10/081021taskforcereport.pdf.
10. 16 C.F.R. § 681.2. The FTC's enforcement date for the Red Flag Rules is May 2009. *See* www.ftc.gov/opa/2008/10/redflags.shtm.
11. 15 U.S.C. §§ 6801–09; 16 C.F.R. pt. 313 (FTC); 12 C.F.R. pt. 30, app. B (OCC, national banks); *id.* pt. 208, app. D-2 and pt. 225, app. F (FRB, state member banks and holding companies); *id.* pt. 364, app. B (FDIC, state non-member banks); *id.* pt. 570, app. B (OTS, savings associations); *id.* pt. 748, app. A (NCUA, credit unions); 16 C.F.R. pt. 314 (FTC, financial institutions that are not regulated by the FRB, FDIC, OCC, OTS, NCUA, CFTC, or SEC); 17 C.F.R. pt. 248.30 (SEC); *id.* pt. 160.30 (CFTC).
12. 42 U.S.C. § 1320d *et seq.*
13. 15 U.S.C. § 6501 *et seq.*

14. Directive 95/46/EC of the European Parliament and of the Council of 24 October 1995 on the protection of individuals with regards to the processing of personal data and the free movement of such data, 1995 O.J. (L281) 0031-0050.

15. *See* www.export.gov/safeharbor/.

16. 15 U.S.C. §§ 1681–1681x, as amended.

17. Pub. L. No. 108-159, 117 Stat. 1952.

18. 31 U.S.C. § 5318(1).

19. 18 U.S.C. § 2721 *et seq.*

20. 15 U.S.C. § 45(a). Further, the federal bank regulatory agencies have authority to enforce section 5 of the FTC Act against entities over which they have jurisdiction. *See* 15 U.S.C. §§ 6801–09.

21. For example, the FTC recently brought an action against Wyndham Worldwide Corporation seeking permanent injunctive relief and other equitable relief in connection with Wyndham's alleged failure to maintain reasonable and appropriate data security for consumers' sensitive personal information. *See* Fed. Trade Comm'n v. Wyndham Worldwide Corp., No. 2:12-cv-01365-SPL (D. Ariz. 2012).

22. CAL. CIV. CODE § 1798.82(h).

23. FLA. STAT. § 817.5681(5).

24. *See* 15 U.S.C. § 6501(8); 16 C.F.R. § 312.2.

25. 15 U.S.C. § 6809(4)(A).

26. 16 C.F.R. § 313.3(o)(1).

27. 45 C.F.R. § 160.103.

28. *Id.*

29. This suggestion is made in a November 1999 compliance publication that also indicates "A link in small print at the bottom of the page—or a link that is indistinguishable from other links on your site—is not considered clear and prominent." *See* www.ftc.gov/bcp/conline/pubs/buspubs/coppa.htm; 64 Fed. Reg. at 59,894 (final rule).

30. 16 C.F.R. § 312.4(b)(1)(iii).

31. *See, e.g.*, Dep't of Health, Educ., & Welfare, Records, Computers, and the Rights of Citizens (1973); FED. TRADE COMM'N, PRIVACY ONLINE: A REPORT TO CONGRESS 7–11 (June 1988), www.ftc.gov/reports/privacy3/ index.htm.

32. The FTC is taking a more exacting approach to privacy policies and website terms of use. Under a September 9, 2009, consent order, the FTC sanctioned a company for deceptive trade practices based on its online business activities where, even though the business followed its terms for data collection and online tracking, the "overall impression" of the website contradicted those terms. *See In re* Sears Holdings Mgmt. Corp., 2009 WL 2979770 (F.T.C. Aug. 31, 2009). Greater attention to specific practices, therefore, is required.

33. An Advisory Committee to the FTC issued a detailed report discussing whether online consumers should be given access, and the nature of this access, to personal information collected about them at online sites. *See* FINAL REPORT OF THE FTC ADVISORY COMMITTEE ON ONLINE ACCESS AND SECURITY (May 15, 2000), www.ftc.gov/acoas/papers/finalreport.htm#I.

34. *See* Privacy Online: Fair Information Practices in the Electronic Marketplace: A Report to Congress, at iii (May 2000), www.ftc.gov/os/2000/05/index.htm#22.

35. *See* FED. TRADE COMM'N, PRIVACY ONLINE: A REPORT TO CONGRESS 7–10 (1998), www.ftc.gov/sites/default/files/documents/reports/privacy-online-report-congress/priv-23a.pdf; *see also* Implementing the OECD "Privacy Guidelines" In the Electronic Environment: Focus on the Internet, at 7–8 (Sept. 1998), http://oecd.org/dsti/sti/it/secur/index.htm.

36. *See* www.truste.com; www.bbbonline.org.

37. *See* S. REP. NO. 99-541, at 1 (1986), *reprinted in* 1986 U.S.C.C.A.N. 3589, 3590.

38. 18 U.S.C. § 2511(4).

39. *Id.* § 2520.

40. *Id.* § 2511(2)(d).

41. *See, e.g.*, MASS. GEN. LAWS ch. 272, § 99 (allowing monitoring of communications only where both parties to the communication consent).

42. *Fighting Identity Theft with the Red Flags Rule: A How-To Guide for Business*, FED. TRADE COMM'N, www.ftc.gov/tips-advice/business-center/guidance/fighting-identity-theft-red-flags-rule-how-guide-business (last visited June 25, 2015).

43. JAVELIN STRATEGY & RESEARCH, THE 2012 IDENTITY FRAUD REPORT: SOCIAL MEDIA AND MOBILE FORMING THE NEW FRAUD FRONTIER. For an overview of this report, see Press Release, Javelin Strategy & Research, Identity Fraud Rose 13 Percent in 2011 According to New Javelin Strategy & Research Report (Feb. 20, 2012), https://www.javelinstrategy.com/news/1314/92/Identity-Fraud-Rose-13-Percent-in-2011-According-to-New-Javelin-Strategy-Research-Report/d,pressRoomDetail.

44. *See* 201 MASS. CODE REGS. §§ 17.01–17.05, Standards for the Protection of Personal Information of Residents of the Commonwealth.

45. 16 C.F.R. pt. 681 [hereinafter Red Flag Rules]; *see also* 72 Fed. Reg. 63,718 (Nov. 9, 2007), www.ftc.gov/sites/default/files/documents/federal_register_notices/identity-theft-red-flags-and-address-discrepancies-under-fair-and-accurate-credit-transactions-act/071109redflags.pdf.

46. 16 C.F.R. § 681.1(d)(1).

47. *See Fighting Identity Theft with the Red Flags Rule: A How-To Guide for Business*, FED. TRADE COMM'N, www.ftc.gov/tips-advice/business-center/guidance/fighting-identity-theft-red-flags-rule-how-guide-business (last visited June 25, 2015).

48. Additional examples of potential red flags are listed at 16 C.F.R. pt. 681 app. A, supp. A.

49. FED. TRADE COMM'N, PROTECTING CONSUMER PRIVACY IN AN ERA OF RAPID CHANGE: RECOMMENDATIONS FOR BUSINESSES AND POLICYMAKERS (Mar. 2012), www.ftc.gov/sites/default/files/documents/reports/federal-trade-commission-report-protecting-consumer-privacy-era-rapid-change-recommendations/120326privacyreport.pdf.

50. *E.g.*, *In re* iPhone Application Litig., 2011 WL 4403963, at *4 (N.D. Cal. Sept. 20, 2011); LaCourt v. Specific Media, Inc., 2011 WL 1661532, at *3–4 (C.D. Cal.

Apr. 28, 2011). These courts, and others, generally held that unless plaintiffs could allege current, non-speculative out-of-pocket losses, no "case or controversy" existed, and accordingly ruled that the plaintiffs lacked standing.

51. *See* Anderson v. Hannaford Bros. Co., 659 F.3d 151 (1st Cir. 2011); Claridge v. RockYou, Inc., 785 F. Supp. 2d 855 (N.D. Cal. 2011).

52. *See* U.S. DEP'T OF HOMELAND SEC., CYBERSECURITY INSURANCE WORKSHOP READOUT REPORT (Nov. 2012), www.dhs.gov/sites/default/files/publications/cyber-security-insurance-read-out-report.pdf.

13

Procuring Computing Resources:

IP Licensing, Outsourcing, and Cloud Computing

Ieuan G. Mahony

As with nearly all assets, an organization has two fundamental choices: "buy" or "build." Under the "traditional"
approach, an organization would "build" its own network and
computing infrastructure, license software, purchase ongoing
maintenance for that software, and "build" its own integrated
software environment. There are significant new developments
in how your organization can obtain these computing
resources—such as via cloud computing—and these developments, coupled with more traditional licensing, maintenance,
and outsourcing methods, present key choices for your organization. These choices, moreover, may significantly impact your
compliance obligations, and these obligations (and risks) must
be weighed against the potential cost savings and increased
efficiencies that these new developments promise.

This chapter provides you with tools to assist you in (a) assessing licensing, outsourcing, and cloud computing structures for procuring your computing resources; (b) focusing on the "soft spots" and compliance risks of these structures; and (c) comparing and evaluating the employment of these structures for some, or all, of your organization's computing resources.

Procuring Computing Resources

The Basics

Q 13.1   What are "computing resources"?

The term "computing resources" refers generally to the resources that an organization employs for its computing needs. The term thus includes

(1)   an organization's infrastructure, including network hard-ware, servers, routers, and other network components;

(2)   the organization's information technology (IT) personnel and outside IT vendors;

(3)   the organization's software platforms, including operating systems and back-end databases; and

(4)   the organization's software applications, including word processing, spreadsheet, and other applications used by the organization's non-IT employees.

It is possible for your organization to shift to a service provider for each of these "layers" of computing resources, or to retain some or all of this responsibility in-house. In shifting layers of computing resources to a third party, your organization can also seek to transfer the risk of these functions to the service provider. Yet it is not possible to transfer full risks to another, and your organization will under all circumstances remain accountable for the most severe risks: damage to its reputation through the service provider's failure, permanent loss of data, a failure of regulatory compliance, or (most dramatically) a failure of the organization as a whole. Accordingly, your organization is well advised to carefully consider the structure and details of its procurement and use of computing resources.

Procurement Models

Q 13.2   What alternatives are generally available to my organization for procuring computing resources?

Your organization has essentially three options:

(1)   *The "in-house model."* Obtain and provide computing resources in-house, procuring hardware and licensing software for use on its own network.

(2)   *The "outsourcing model."* Outsource some or all of these functions to a third party under a "dedicated" structure, where your organization uses the outsourcing service provider's resources in a "private" manner and does not share the service provider's resources with others.

(3)   *The "cloud computing model."* Share the service provider's resources, with "logical" (but not physical) walls between your organization's data and computing resources and those of other customers of the service provider, all as detailed further below.[1]

Q 13.2.1   What is the "in-house model" for obtaining computing resources?

With the in-house model, your organization generally owns its infrastructure and licenses its operating system and application software. With its software licenses, the organization pays for ongoing maintenance and support to keep the software up-to-date and "healthy." The expenses of these computing resources are generally longer-term, capital expenses.

Q 13.2.2   What is the "outsourcing model" for obtaining computing resources?

With the outsourcing model, your organization shifts some or all of its capital costs to a third-party service provider, and this third party supplies the resources month by month, yearly, or according to some other time increment, in exchange for a subscription payment. The organization thus obtains "access" to resources held by another, does not "license" these resources, and possess the resources itself. Specifically, in an outsourcing model software is not installed on your organization's network; instead the "software bits"—the code itself— physically reside on servers controlled by the service provider. The data associated with these outsourced software applications generally is also resident on the service provider's servers. The service provider provides dedicated computing resources to your organization, so that no other third parties will share these resources. Outsourcing models range from enterprise-wide agreements, where an organization outsources the majority of its computing functions to the third-party service provider, to an application service provider structure (ASP), where the organization outsources a targeted application or suite of applications.

Due to the service provider's control over the computing resources that house the organization's applications and associated data, the organization generally negotiates a service level agreement (SLA) with the service provider, under which the service provider agrees to express benchmarks ("service levels"), providing the organization with measurable assurance that its access to these computing resources will be robust and essentially without interruption.[2] For example, some service providers agree to make computing resources available to the organization on a "five nines" basis—that is, 99.999% —excluding scheduled downtime. (SLAs are discussed in more detail at Q 13.8.)

Q 13.2.3 How does "cloud computing" relate to my organization's computing resources?

A cloud computing model shares certain similarities with the outsourcing model. In the cloud computing model, your organization tasks a third party with providing computing resources; in turn, this third party agrees to control, provide, and make available these resources. As in the outsourcing model, the cloud service provider hosts your organization's data. Beyond these similarities, the cloud computing model presents significant differences.

First, the cloud computing model can be structure in a variety of way and allows an organization to select the level of services it wishes to obtain from the cloud. Specifically, the structures the organization might choose include:

(a) *infrastructure-as-a-service* (IaaS), where the organization simply obtains infrastructure services from the cloud service provider to house the organization's computing resources and generally retains control over its operating systems, storage, and software applications;

(b) *platform-as-a-service* (PaaS), a computing platform where the service provider offers IaaS services and also provides software operating system platforms, which the organization uses to house applications the organization creates using the platform and tools supplied by the provider; and

(c)   *software-as-a-service* (SaaS), a full "stack" of services, where the organization obtains IaaS services and PaaS services and also obtains access to the service provider's software applications; the organization can access the service provider's software applications from various devices through a thin client interface such as a web browser software.[3]

Second, the cloud computing model moves away from the "dedicated resources" structure of the outsourcing model to shared use of computing resources. For example, the cloud computing model relies on a "multi-tenant" structure, where a range of customers shares the same computing resources of the service provider. In addition, the model is designed for rapid scaling, allowing your organization's utilization of the service provider's resources to "spike" up and down, with your organization paying for only the resources it uses. The cloud thus is designed to "abstract" the infrastructure complexities of servers, applications, data, and computing platforms, and present your organization with a simple, scalable, and unified set of computing resources, for a periodic fee.

Finally, in evaluating a cloud computing model, your company should consider issues surrounding company data. These include the following elements:

(1)   Verify how your company data will be erased at the close of the relationship, or upon your request;

(2)   Ensure that your cloud service provider has a documented process for securely disposing of data storage hardware, to prevent insufficiently deleted company data from "traveling" with legacy hardware; and

(3)   Require the cloud service provider to administer access controls over data (albeit tied to your company's enforcement of policies concerning employees' proper treatment and protection of cloud services passwords).

Choosing the Appropriate Model

Q 13.3 What are the key considerations when comparing the options for obtaining computing resources?

What are your organization's core competencies? If your organization provides data management and data mining services, outsourcing its databases or moving these elements to the cloud may be inadvisable.

What is the sensitivity of functions your organization will perform based on the computing resources? If these functions are less sensitive and not mission-critical, your organization will have greater flexibility in allowing a third party to control them through either an outsourcing or cloud computing model.[4] In contrast, if your organization has high privacy and security compliance requirements, it will need to take more care in moving from an in-house model and in obtaining specific protections against associated risks presented by the outsourcing and cloud computing models.

Are there existing downstream contractual obligations that moving away from an in-house model may upset? An organization contemplating giving a service provider control over some or all of its computing resources must consider these contractual obligations and ensure that the relevant assurances and warranties it obtains from its service provider are at least as strong as those same assurances and warranties it provides in turn to its customers and other contracting parties.

Each of these considerations, as well as other key considerations with regard to procuring and using computing resources, is addressed in further detail below.

Intellectual Property Rights

Q 13.4 In these transactions, what vendor intellectual property rights, if any, should my organization be concerned with?

Intellectual property rights come in various "flavors": patent rights, rights under copyright law, and rights in trade secrets and confidential information. Each of these is based on an underlying legal structure and generally is invoked by specific language in a grant of rights. For example, a standard "patent invocation" in the grant of rights would read:

> During the term, LICENSOR[5] hereby grants to LICENSEE a royalty-bearing, non-exclusive, non-sublicensable, non-transferable license to make, have made, use, sell, offer to sell, and import LICENSED PRODUCTS.

In contrast, a standard "copyright invocation" in the grant of rights would read:

> During the term, LICENSOR hereby grants to LICENSEE a royalty-bearing, non-exclusive, non-sublicensable, non-transferable license to copy, modify, distribute, publicly perform, and publicly display the LICENSED WORKS.

Presented with these different flavors of intellectual property rights and the differing standard grant language, your organization has two broad options: (1) employ descriptive language to capture the details of the asset; or (2) use functional language to broadly capture the goals or function of the asset.

With descriptive language, the approach is to track and detail each intellectual property flavor impacted by the transaction at a granular level. With this approach, your organization might structure its agreements, for example, so that there are separate provisions addressing (a) assets protected by copyright, and (b) assets protected by patent (and addressing possible overlaps between the categories).

With a functional approach, your organization would structure its agreements (a) to provide a broad definition of "intellectual property rights," encompassing all rights under patent law, copyright law, and trade secret law (for example), and (b) so that the grant of rights language is abstracted from the specific intellectual property flavors involved, reading, for example:

> During the term, LICENSOR under its intellectual property rights hereby grants to LICENSEE a royalty-bearing, non-

exclusive, non-sublicensable, non-transferable license to use, copy, modify, distribute, and otherwise exploit the LICENSED PRODUCTS.

As a general rule, functional language is more favorable to the party seeking to enjoy the intellectual property rights at issue, while descriptive language is more favorable to the party providing the rights and seeking to "meter" these rights in small, granular increments.

Q 13.5 Should my organization be concerned about its own intellectual property rights?

Yes. Your organization should attend carefully to its own intellectual property rights. In any material licensor-licensee relationship, information and value can flow in both directions. Value flows from the licensor in the form of licensed software or access to software services; but value can also flow from the licensee in the form of data, feedback, and ideas provided to the licensor. Your organization should attend to this outbound flow of intellectual property value.

For example, in many structures the licensor will request that it shall own all feedback, suggested improvements, and other ideas from the licensee. Assume your organization is negotiating with a licensor for in-house computing components, and the licensor makes such an ownership request. The licensor will justify this request by stating that allowing your organization to retain ownership of these "contributions" will potentially taint its software, by allowing your organization to control—through its ownership rights—at least some components of the licensor's core intellectual property asset.

Although this point is reasonable, in making this request the licensor ignores the potentially significant "blocking" effect that an ownership transfer may have on your organization. Assume your organization suggests a new workflow structure that (1) significantly streamlines and simplifies the licensor's software application, and (2) provides your organization with significant benefits independent of the licensor's software. If your organization has transferred ownership of the intellectual property assets embodied in this workflow, then your organization would be precluded from practicing or implementing this workflow—even independent of the software—without permission of the licensor.

A solution to this "blocking" threat is for your organization to retain sufficient rights to enjoy its invention or other idea, either through:

- retaining ownership of the asset (and associated intellectual property), while licensing this asset to the licensor on a non-exclusive basis; or
- transferring ownership of the asset to the licensor, but retaining a non-exclusive, royalty-free, perpetual grant-back of rights, allowing your organization to continue to practice the invention.

In sum, your organization should pay close attention to outbound intellectual property rights to ensure that, at a minimum, the structure does not prevent your organization from exploiting intellectual property assets that it generates in connection with its relationship with the licensor.[6]

Q 13.5.1   My organization engages a range of other vendors in connection with its computing resources. Do we need to address system access by these third parties?

Yes, your organization should assess its requirements for the computing resource at issue and ensure that it obtains necessary intellectual property rights. For example, a common licensing- and subscription-based restriction on licensees is the requirement that the licensee employ the resource for its "internal uses only." This limitation is generally intended to prevent the licensee from providing the benefits of the resource to additional downstream users, outside the control of the licensor. Yet this common restriction can be read to preclude your organization, for example, from giving its other vendors access to the licensed resource for purposes of integrating the resource with other components of your network. Moreover, there may be situations where your organization will rely on a third party to maintain the software at issue in the event the licensor is unable or unwilling to meet maintenance obligations.[7]

One solution to this limitation is to negotiate a structure whereby your organization is entitled to provide vendors access to the computing resource, provided these vendors are bound by non-disclosure obligations that prevent their use of the software outside their relationship with your organization. In any event, your organization should ensure that it has considered whether it expects to give third parties access to the computing resource provided by the licensor, and should negotiate appropriate sublicensing or related access rights.

"Agile Development" Model

Q 13.5.2   A vendor proposes to develop software for my organization using an "agile development" methodology. What does this mean for us?

Under a traditional development model:

(1)   the parties agree upon a comprehensive set of requirements for the software;

(2)   the developer fashions the commissioned software to comply with these requirements;

(3)   warranties, other performance requirements, and fixed-fee obligations (if any) are all keyed to these requirements and the scope of work these requirements represent; and

(4)   the licensee is provided a relatively extensive testing and acceptance period, whereby the software is tested against these requirements.

This traditional approach—sometimes referred to as a "waterfall" development model, because it proceeds like a waterfall from one phase to another within "the banks of a river channel"—can present a somewhat rigid structure. Moreover, because requirements often evolve and change during the course of development, requiring resort to a formal change order procedure, the waterfall approach can result in higher costs, formalities, and paperwork.

An "agile" development model significantly softens the formalities involved with the traditional waterfall approach. An agile development model does not rely on detailed, up-front specifications and requirements, recognizing that these "rules" may well change over the course of the development. Instead, the vendor commits to working closely with the hiring party to align development work with the hiring party's needs and goals in a flexible and agile manner, providing frequent iterations of deliverables to allow considerable feedback from—and thus, in effect, "real-time" requirements development with—the hiring party.

An agile development model can present drawbacks. For example, the combination of a fixed fee for the work and the absence of detailed specifications allows parties potentially to "game" the relationship by taking competing positions on the specific requirements of a scope of work. For example, the hiring party (1) might take the position that general directions in the scope of work require extensive and detailed work by the developer on elements that are not needed to accomplish the "spirit" of the scope of work, while (2) refusing to modify the fixed contract amount, thus prejudicing the developer. Similarly, the developer (1) might take the position that the general language of the scope of work does not sufficiently describe elements needed to accomplish the "spirit" of the scope of work, while (2) demanding that the hiring party pay additional amounts—above the fixed contract amount—to include these elements, thus prejudicing the hiring party. One solution to these drawbacks is to include specific obligations concerning communications, mutual commitments to timing and efforts in refining the development process, and a schedule for the vendor's providing iterations of the deliverables, as the development progresses.

The formalities provided by a waterfall's more traditional development structure may benefit your organization significantly in certain projects, while the more flexible and generally less-expensive agile development approach may provide strong value in other circumstances. In any event, your organization should consider available alternatives when seeking to procure custom development work.

Cloud Deployment Models

Q 13.6   My company is considering migrating certain network services to the cloud. Are there particular deployment models that we should consider?

There are a variety of cloud deployments, consisting generally of the following:

(1)   in a *private cloud* deployment, where the cloud computing resources are hosted privately on the premises of the cloud

customer, or in a data center, controlled by the cloud services provider, but with resources dedicated to the customer;

(2)   in a *community cloud* deployment, where the cloud computing system is shared among a limited number of trusted partners (such as, for example, an industry group), and hosted either across these entities, or on servers controlled by the cloud services provider;

(3)   in a *public cloud* deployment, where the cloud computing resources are shared among members of the public, without limit; or

(4)   in a *hybrid cloud*, where different components of the customer's computing requirements are hosted in different cloud deployments.

The nature of the deployment will drive the resources available to your company. For example, a private cloud deployment will generally provide more limited, localized resources, and a public cloud will provide access to significant remotely accessed resources.[8] The deployment models will determine the nature of your company's control over its resources, and the scale, cost, and availability of these resources, as further described in this chapter.

Integrating New Computing Resources into Existing Systems

Q 13.7   Are there any special considerations our organization should be aware of when integrating the new computing resource within our existing systems?

Yes. Assuming, for example, that the new software must inter-operate with other components within your computing ecosystem, your organization will want to consider three fundamental points:

1.   whether your organization already holds rights in the application programming interfaces (APIs) needed to allow the new software and your existing systems to inter-operate;

2.   whether open-source software will "touch" your existing systems in a material way; and

3.   whether the integration will require work with your organization's "legacy data" generated by the system that the new software will replace or that the new software will otherwise process.

Q 13.7.1   What are "rights in interfaces"?

For the integration to take place, your organization must have rights to the interfaces—the APIs or "connection points"—that will allow the new software and the existing system to work together. The transaction with the licensor of the new software will invariably include these rights; it is generally the rights in existing system components that can raise issues. Moreover, to the extent your organization is writing code or engaging a third party to write code to allow this inter-operability, ownership of and right in this new asset—as described above—must be addressed.

Open-Source Software

Q 13.7.2   What is open-source software?

Broadly speaking, software falls into two categories: proprietary or open-source. Proprietary software is software that is licensed such that the licensee is given access only to object code—the 1's and 0's that a machine reads—but that humans, without more, cannot read. Open-source software is licensed under an "open-source" model, whereby the licensor gives the licensee access to, and rights to modify, the source code of the application, which is software in a form humans can read and understand without more.

Q 13.7.3   What open-source software considerations may affect our system?

Open-source software takes on increasing importance in any software transaction. Access to the source code for a software application may provide significant value to a licensee, whether through the increased security and hardening that proponents of open-source models claim, or through decreased development costs: A developer can avoid the expense of developing software that is already available in open-source form.

Open-source software can, however, present significant draw-backs. Certain flavors of open-source software are provided under so-called copyleft or (less complementary) "viral" licenses. These licenses—such as the general public license (GPL)—require the licensee, in certain circumstances, to open-source its own propri-etary software as a condition to enjoying certain rights in the soft-ware. In sum, your organization should not reactively accept or reject use of open-source, but instead should consider:

- the circumstances of the development and your organiza-tion's planned uses for the open-source software;
- the open-source licenses involved; and
- the architecture of the new code, and its relationship to the existing proprietary code base.

Many organizations reject in an outright manner any use of open-source (unless specific exceptions are negotiated). The following is an illustrative clause showing this approach:

> "Open Source Software" means any software, documentation, or other material that contains, or is derived (in whole or in part) from, any software, documentation, or other material that is distributed as free software, open source software (*e.g.*, Linux), or similar licensing or distribution models, including, but not limited to, software, documentation, or other material licensed or distributed under any of the following licenses or distribution models, or licenses or distribution models similar to any of the following: (i) GNU's General Public License (GPL), GNU's or Lesser/Library GPL (LGPL), or the Mozilla Public License (MPL). You represent and warrant that you will not use, and will not authorize any third party to use, any Open Source Software in connection with the development services in any manner that requires that any licensee assets or services be (a) disclosed or distributed in source code form, (b) made available free of charge to recipients, or (c) modifiable without restriction by recipients.

Legacy Data

Q 13.7.4   What concerns are raised by legacy data?

The presence of legacy data can present considerable challenges to integration. The format of the legacy data may well be incompatible with the new system, requiring a migration path and a mapping of old data formats—or schema—to the new formats/schema. Moreover, the legacy data may well have been generated through various manual processes and may contain a range of inconsistencies. Such artifacts in your organization's legacy data may prevent your vendor from using purely automated means to "port" the data to the new system, instead, requiring the vendor to employ considerably more expensive (and time-consuming) manual processes.

Maintaining Computing Resources

Service Level Agreements and Service Level Objectives

Q 13.8   What factors affect maintenance of our computing resource assets and monitoring of performance?

Once new computing resources have been procured, installed, and integrated with your existing systems and business rules, the organization should ensure that the new system is maintained, bugs and defects that might arise are repaired, and the system is generally updated. In addition, your organization will want these services provided on a timely basis, with the immediacy of the vendor's response keyed to the severity of the impact on your organization. Key to obtaining these types of maintenance services—as well as assurances of system performance—are service level agreements (SLAs) and service level objectives (SLOs).

Q 13.8.1   What role do SLAs and SLOs play in maintaining computing resources?

An SLA generally provides performance metrics by which to gauge—on a reasonably objective manner—the service provider's fulfillment of obligations. An SLO generally includes the same provisions, but characterizes these performance metrics as "goals" or "targets," rather than fixed standards. SLAs and SLOs generally apply to an outsourcing or cloud computing model, where the vendor controls the application and network environment, and do not generally apply in an in-house model, where the customer controls these assets.

SLAs and SLOs typically include the following provisions:

- An uptime obligation, where the service provider commits to keeping the system available for a set period of time, excepting downtime scheduled during announced periods and for maintenance purposes;
- A through-put requirement that sets standards for the speed and capacity of the vendor's systems;
- A response time and remediation time provision that sets standards for how quickly the vendor must respond to a failure or other defect in the system, and the time frame within which the vendor commits to remediating the defect (response and remediation times are generally calibrated to the severity of the problem, with faster response and remediation times set for more severe system issues);
- A system for reporting, addressing, and tracking problems;
- A structure for benchmarking the performance of key software applications, and from these benchmarking figures, establishing key system performance requirements;
- A set of disaster recovery procedures (also referred to as "business continuity procedures") that specifies how and when the system will be restored after a service interruption, and that might include, for example, a co-location facility (data center that leases space and infrastructure to others) that is located in a geographically distinct location and that replicates the primary data center;
- Support for forensics examination, if your company retains an audit trail, log files, or other information concerning access, use, or other treatment or aspects of its data set;
- A set of security specifications addressing physical system security, as well as technical security, such as firewall protection, access controls, and related protections; and
- Penalties for non-compliance with the standards, generally in the form of performance credits against future fees—a

remedy for SLA non-performance that is less dramatic than outright termination of the agreement.

Your organization should not underestimate the importance of maintenance and service level requirements (as reflected in SLAs and SLOs). These requirements perform the function, in many ways, of ongoing warranties that set the boundaries, in a fundamental way, of the computing resources in which your organization has invested.

Audit Requirements

Q 13.8.2   How can we use audit requirements to enhance maintenance of our system?

Assuring good vendor practices and proper maintenance can also be accomplished by negotiating procedures for periodic audits. The organization may decide to mandate periodic audits to be performed by a third party and according to a standards structure negotiated by your organization, or audits may be conducted directly by your organization or its representatives. Given compliance requirements that hold your organization responsible for its service provider's conduct—particularly with respect to privacy and security protections—including an audit procedure in your relationship with vendors provides strong value.

Employee Policies

Q 13.8.3   Can company policies enhance system maintenance?

Yes. As a component of maintaining its computing resources, your organization should consider implementing policies that ensure that your computing resources goals are transparent, and that guide employees and hold them accountable for compliance on an "on the ground and in the trenches" basis. In developing such policies, the following should be taken into consideration:

- Due to the potentially disruptive copyleft, viral nature of certain flavors of open-source software, your organization should consider a policy requiring oversight, and management approval of the use of open-source software;

- Employees increasingly install applications—such as iPhone applications—on handheld devices that may interface with your organization's computing resources. These applications often are attached to click-through agreements that may purport to bind your organization. These applications, in addition, may present security and "virus introduction" threats. Accordingly, your organization should consider a policy for filtering and allowing only approved applications (if any) that might impact the organization's own computing resources;
- Your organization should also consider addressing situations where an employee uses such a mobile device not simply for your company's business purposes, but also for his or her personal purposes. The "bring your own device" (or BYOD) phenomenon, which recognizes the dual-use nature (business and personal) of many mobile devices, is increasing present in corporate settings. Your company should consider adopting policies that also address this aspect of mobile device use (*see* Q 5.8); and
- A general acceptable use policy (AUP) that broadly sets standards for employee behavior with respect to computing resources, system passwords, and other key system components and conduct.

Managing Risk

Q 13.9 As we expand access to our computing resources, how should we approach risks arising from this expansion?

There are four general approaches to managing risk in a computing environment:

(i) risk avoidance, consisting of removing the conditions that create the risk;

(ii) risk mitigation, consisting of identifying and taking steps to contain and minimize anticipated losses arising from the risk;

(iii) risk acceptance, consisting of bearing the risk and budgeting for associated potential losses; and

(iv) risk transfer, consisting of obtaining insurance to cover the risk.[9]

Of these approaches, risk avoidance and risk mitigation are generally the optimal priorities.

To evaluate the optimal approach to risk in your company ecosystem, the first step is to undertake a risk assessment, with the goal to

(a) identify sensitive information, including company intellectual property and trade secrets, as well as protected personal information;

(b) determine the location of this information (stored digitally, in paper form, or other form);

(c) identify the current information security protections for the information, including physical protections, technical protections, and personnel-based protections; and

(d) assess the risks of unauthorized access to the information, and the potential impact of such access on the company.

In evaluating your computing resources and associated information security, you should generally include considerations concerning the following:

(i) *organizational and administrative controls*, which determine which employees are authorized to perform data-related operations such as creation, access, disclosure, transport, and destruction of information;

(ii) *physical controls,* designed to protect storage media on which company information resides, and the facilities that house these storage devices; and

(iii) *technical controls* that will likely include identity and access management (IAM) technologies, encryption of data-at-rest and data-in-motion, and auditing and tracking functions for company data.

Where your company is publicly traded, under SEC disclosure guidance, you are instructed to disclose your company's material cybersecurity risks, cyber incidents, and the nature of insurance coverage (if any) for these risks.[10]

Compliance Issues

Q 13.10   How do computing resources relate to our compliance obligations?

Your organization's computing systems and procurement processes impact your compliance obligations, including:

- responsibility for service provider's compliance with regulations, and obligations to select appropriate service providers and monitor their compliance;
- potentially conflicting regulatory obligations arising from cross-border operations; and
- e-discovery and data retention obligations, where your organization's data is resident on third-party servers, as in outsourcing and cloud computing models.

Responsibility for Third Party

Q 13.10.1   Can an organization procuring computing resources be held responsible for actions of a service provider?

Numerous regulatory structures require that your organization vet service providers to ensure that they provide adequate security and privacy to the data they may access that is sourced from your organization. These regulatory structures include HIPAA, GLBA, new written information security program regulations, and proposed FTC Red Flags regulations.[11] Moreover, your organization will generally remain responsible for the actions of its service providers, or "data processors." Recent regulatory guidance under the EU Data Protection Directive,[12] for example, confirms this fundamental responsibility of covered organizations—the "data controller"—for its data, whether or not this data is held by a processor.[13]

Multiple Jurisdictions/Regulatory Regimes

Q 13.10.2   How do we address conflicting regulatory requirements for cross-border operations?

Regulatory structures are based on the geographical location of your organization's operations, data, and computing resources.

Where these operations and assets span a number of jurisdictions, they may be subject to a range of regulatory regimes, and these regimes may conflict. Multi-tenancy and shared resources are two of the defining characteristics of cloud computing environments. Computing capacity, storage, and network are shared among multiple users.

For example, in the outsourcing model and particularly in the cloud computing model, data may be stored offsite and under the control of your service provider, with web-based access managed by this service provider. The "physical location" of this data may be unclear. In the United States, state laws governing security breaches[14] may impose a range of obligations on your organization. In cross-border transactions, this risk can significantly increase, as one foreign government agency, for example, may demand access to the data in a manner that conflicts with your organization's obligations to other regulatory authorities or to the data subjects whose personal information your organization holds. These obligations, coupled with the unclear location of the data, present compliance risk.

To seek to address these concerns, service providers in both outsourcing and cloud computing models offer "segregated" facilities that seek to minimize the risk that unexpected regulatory authorities will claim jurisdiction over your organization's data and operations.

If your company requires a level of visibility into and control over the geographic location of its data, you should consider a private cloud deployment. This "flavor" of cloud services provides the platform best suited for maintaining control over the location of the servers that process and store your company's data. (Private cloud deployments are discussed in Q 13.6.)

Special Considerations for Electronically Stored Information

Q 13.11   What compliance risks are raised by storing data with a third party?

A cloud computing model relies on multi-tenancy and other shared resources among customers. One customer's "space" is separated from other customers' spaces, for example, by logical barriers (created software) among partitions on a single server, and not through separate, physically isolated servers. There are risks that these logical isolations might fail, thus commingling the spaces and the data of the multiple tenants sharing the overall resource. This potential "isolation failure" presents compliance risks, as well as contractual and other risks.

In both the outsourcing and the cloud computing models, the service provider generally hosts and controls access to your organization's data, including documents, spreadsheets, financial information, and other communications. In the event of U.S.-based litigation, this data likely will be relevant, and your organization's litigation opponent will seek discovery of this information, referred to under Federal Rules of Civil Procedure as electronically stored information (ESI). To comply with these discovery obligations, your organization will need the cooperation of its service providers.

In addition, a range of regulatory structures require specific retention periods for certain documents.[15] Here again, your organization will require the assistance of its service providers to meet this regulatory obligation. Your organization, therefore, is well advised, at the outset of the relationship, to obtain contractual commitments from its service providers to provide needed cooperation in these regards.

Q 13.11.1   What data security protections should be in place?

With an outsourcing or cloud computing model, your organization may have little or no control over the security of its data. Moreover, if a security incident or security breach occurs, your organization may not obtain notice of the event sufficient to allow an appropriate regulatory response. To provide protections to your organization in this regard, you may seek to negotiate specific, detailed security and privacy obligations on a contract-by-contract basis with your service providers.

As an alternative to this potentially costly and time-consuming process, your organization could consider referring to certain security standards that are increasingly accepted, particularly by larger service provider players in this space, and requiring service providers to comply with these standards.

One standard is the Statement on Auditing Standards No. 70: Service Organizations (SAS 70). This is an auditing statement of the Auditing Standards Board of the American Institute of Certified Public

Accountants that defines the professional standards used by a service auditor to assess the internal controls of a service organization and issue a service auditor's report. Service organizations that may have an SAS 70 report include processors of insurance and medical claims, hosted data centers, application service providers (ASPs), and credit processing organizations.[16]

Another available standard is ISO/IEC 27001, which specifies a formal management system designed: (a) to establish management control over security issues; and (b) to provide a certification process, to allow interested parties a level of assurance that the security controls have been assessed by an independent third party.[17]

A final illustrative method for obtaining assurances as to security is to obtain so-called trust services from oversight organizations such as SysTrust and WebTrust.[18] An advantage to a report from these organizations over an SAS 70 report is that these reports can generally be circulated in an unrestricted manner to others, while an SAS 70 report has restricted circulation.

Disengaging from a Licensor or Service Provider

Vendor Lock-In

Q 13.12   How do we disengage from a licensor or service provider?

Upon expiration or termination of the vendor relationship, an organization must consider an exit strategy and methods of preserving its independence from the vendor. Many vendors will make it difficult for your organization to migrate its computing resources to another vendor, seeking to structure the relationship to maximize "vendor lock-in." If your vendor obtains some level of vendor lock-in, the vendor isolates itself to a degree from competition from alternative vendors and, thus, may become able to extract higher-than-competitive pricing and other concessions from your organization.

What follows are possible exit strategies and methods for avoiding or reducing the threat of vendor lock-in.

Q 13.13   How can an organization seeking to terminate its relationship with a vendor reduce the threat of vendor lock-in?

There are three things an organization can do:

1. Ensure that it has unconditional access to data in readily portable formats.
2. Obtain transition assistance.
3. Negotiate a source code escrow agreement.

Q 13.13.1   How do we get unconditional access to portable data?

A key point of leverage for a vendor that is unscrupulous or merely hard-bargaining is its control over your data. This control can take various forms. For example, a licensor or service provider might store the data in a proprietary format or with use of claimed proprietary database schema so that you are hindered from efficiently migrating the data to an alternative platform both by the proprietary formatting and the cost. Or a service provider might, upon termination of the relationship, limit your access to data by relying upon provisions it negotiated that allow the provider to deny access if it asserts that your organization in some manner has acted improperly or is in breach of the agreement.

These mechanisms can provide a vendor with powerful leverage. Accordingly, your organization should demand:

(a) that it retain unconditional access to its data under all circumstances, whether or not the vendor claims a breach;
(b) that the data be stored in a readily portable format (preferably specifying the format); and
(c) reserving the right upon request to obtain a full download of the data set, with no charge, or at reduced charges (depending on the frequency of the download requests).

Transition Assistance

Q 13.13.2   What is transition assistance?

Your organization should also consider negotiating the general right to "transition assistance" from its vendors, which can include working with the new vendor on integration projects, working to migrate data, transferring third-party software licenses needed by your organization to continue using aspects of the system, and similar services. Generally, the obligation to provide transition assistance will be time-limited, ranging from, for example, sixty to ninety days.

Transition assistance, given its potentially broad scope, is usually provided on a "time and materials" basis, and your organization can consider negotiating an hourly rate for these services at the time of executing the parties' master agreement. If the vendor complains that transition assistance is inappropriate where your organization is in breach of the agreement (particularly its payment terms), the parties can agree that such assistance is conditioned on pre-payment of the estimated costs and your organization's payment of undisputed amounts under pre-termination invoices.

Source Code Escrow Agreements

Q 13.13.3   What are escrow agreements?

A source code escrow agreement is generally structured as follows:

- The licensor agrees to deposit up-to-date copies of the source code for the license software applications with a third-party escrow agent;
- The agent is instructed to release this source code upon the occurrence of certain trigger events, such as the licensor's breach of the agreement, a failure of maintenance, or other such events that threaten the licensee's ability to continue to enjoy use of the software; and
- The licensee is given rights to use, copy, and modify this source code in order to maintain and update the software application.

A company should consider negotiating a source code escrow agreement with a vendor (assuming the relationship is not solely an open-source relationship, where no such agreement is necessary) with suitable triggers for release of code needed to maintain and improve its system. Holding the right to obtain source code provides an organization with added comfort that, if its vendor fails in its performance, the organization has some ability to employ "self-help" by using the source code to repair and keep in working order the software it has licensed. This right supplements the licensee's rights under the Bankruptcy Code to continue its use of the software, even in the event of the licensor's bankruptcy, on certain enumerated conditions.[19]

Notes to Chapter 13

1.   The structure has been simplified. For example, it is possible for an organization to commission a "private cloud," to host this private cloud within the organization's data center or co-location facility, and to operate this private cloud with the organization's own IT department. *See, e.g.*, T. MATHER, S. KUMARASWAMY & S. LATIF, CLOUD SECURITY AND PRIVACY 24 (O'Reilly 2009). Accordingly, at the margins, the various structures overlap. To capture overall concepts, this chapter focuses on central, paradigm structures and does not address issues at the margin.

2.   Some service providers, for example, agree to make their computing resources available to the organization on a "five nines" basis—or 99.999%—excluding scheduled downtime. SLAs are discussed in more detail at Q 13.8.

3.   *See* Nat'l Inst. of Standards & Tech. (NIST), Cloud Computing, http://csrc.nist.gov/groups/SNS/cloud-computing/; *see also* European Network & Info. Sec. Agency, Cloud Computing Risk Assessment, www.enisa.europa.eu/act/rm/files/deliverables/cloud-computing-risk-assessment (defining cloud computing). GoogleApps is an example of a SaaS offering. *See* www.google.com/apps/intl/en/business/faq.html.

4.   For example, based on similar reasoning, the U.S. government relies on a cloud computing model for certain less sensitive governmental functions and provides a governance and oversight structure for agencies "moving to the cloud." *See* http://csrc.nist.gov/groups/SMA/ispab/documents/minutes/2009-12/cloud-computing-government-tic.pdf.

5.   For convenience, the party providing licensing rights or access rights, in any of the models discussed, will be referred to as the "licensor."

6.   These potential "joint development" structures present a number of additional issues, such as (i) which party bears the burden of prosecuting and maintaining (and paying for) any patents that may arise from the joint development; (ii) which party has the right (or the obligation) to enforce the jointly developed and owned rights; and (iii) the compensation structure (if any) for each party's use of the rights.

7.   An example of this "failure of maintenance" situation and its effects are addressed below. *See* Q 13.13.3, *infra* (discussing software escrow agreements).

8.   *See* MARK L. BADGER, TIMOTHY GRANCE, ROBERT PATT-CORNER & JEFFREY M. VOAS, NAT'L INST. OF STANDARDS & TECH., SPECIAL PUB. NO. 800-146, CLOUD COMPUTING SYNOPSIS AND RECOMMENDATIONS (May 29, 2012), www.nist.gov/customcf/get_pdf.cfm?pub_id=911075.

9.   Chapter 12 discusses cybersecurity insurance. *See* Q 12.9.

10.   *See* SEC CF Disclosure Guidance: Topic No. 2 on Cybersecurity (Oct. 13, 2011), www.sec.gov/divisions/corpfin/guidance/cfguidance-topic2.htm.

11.   These regulations are discussed in chapter 12 and chapter 26.

12.   Council Directive 95/46/EC, On the protection of individuals with regard to the processing of personal data and on the free movement of such data, 1995 O.J. (L 281) 31, http://ec.europa.eu/justice_home/fsj/privacy/docs/95-46-ce/dir1995-46_part1_en.pdf.

13.   *See Article 29 Data Protection Working Party, Opinion 1/2010 on the concepts of "controller" and "processor,"* 00264/10/EN, WP 169 (Feb. 16, 2010), http://ec.europa.eu/justice_home/fsj/privacy/docs/wpdocs/2010/wp169_en.pdf.

14.   These laws and regulations are referenced in chapter 12.

15.   Records management and records retention issues are discussed in detail in chapter 5.

16.   SAS 70 has been enhanced by the Statement on Standards for Attestation Engagements No. 16 ("SSAE No. 16").

17.   *See* www.iso.org/iso/catalogue_detail?csnumber=42103.

18.   *See WebTrust/SysTrust Licensing,* WEBTRUST, www.webtrust.org/homepage-documents/item27834.aspx (last visited July 13, 2015).

19.   *See* 11 U.S.C. § 365(n).

14

Government Contractors

David S. Black, Thomas M. Brownell &
William M. Pannier *

It is imperative that government contractors have effective compliance programs. Government contractors are especially vulnerable to civil or criminal liability for misconduct arising from government auditor and investigator scrutiny and "whistleblower" employee actions. Unlike commercial contracts, federal contracts require compliance with a maze of statutes, regulations, and contract clauses that impose controls on doing business with the government.[1] For example, a government contractor must open its books to any number of government agencies for audits authorized under the law. Prudent government contractors implement robust compliance programs in order to adhere to the often complex regulatory requirements to detect early in the process any failures of compliance. In addition, as explained below, new government regulations require that many government contractors have compliance and ethics programs.

* The authors wish to acknowledge John S. Irving IV and Christopher A. Myers for their contributions to this chapter.

A contractor that violates procurement laws and regulations may incur statutory and regulatory penalties, possible suspension and debarment from continuing to work for the government, and accusations of fraud. In the event of violations, audits, and/or enforcement actions, an effective compliance program may demonstrate the company's good faith and lack of fraudulent intent. This can be crucial in reaching a fair, appropriate, and cost-effective resolution and settlement with a government agency. Effective compliance programs may also help avoid suspension, debarment, or exclusion from participation in government programs and future contracts. In light of the tremendous costs of defense and investigation, damage to reputation, harm to shareholders or owners, and settlement costs, an effective compliance and ethics program is essential to a government contractor's success.

Overview

Q 14.1   What are the benefits to contractors of developing, implementing, and maintaining a compliance program?

Effective compliance programs help contractors to navigate the often complex regulatory procedures governing the performance of and payments received under contracts. Effective compliance and ethics programs will help to ensure compliance with regulatory requirements and to detect early in the process any failures of compliance. In the event of violations, government audits, investigations, and/or enforcement actions, compliance programs can help to demonstrate the company's commitment to corporate integrity, good faith, and lack of fraudulent intent. This can be crucial in reaching fair, appropriate, and cost-effective resolutions and settlements with government agencies. Good programs can also help to avoid suspension, debarment, or exclusion from participation in government programs and future contracts. In light of the tremendous costs of defense and investigation, damage to reputation, harm to shareholders or owners, and settlement costs, an effective compliance and ethics program is essential to help a government contractor:

1. recognize activities and contracting practices that are prohibited when contracting with the government;
2. recognize what situations may create an opportunity for these prohibited activities;
3. establish policies and procedures to avoid such activities;
4. train employees to understand the company's policies and procedures; and
5. enforce policies and procedures—for example, the company might implement supervision and monitoring of employee performance, or internal audit systems.

Q 14.2   Generally speaking, what should a government contractor's compliance program aim to do?

At a minimum, it must establish a written code of conduct that describes standards of behavior that ensures adherence to federal procurement laws and regulations. A contractor must train employees in corporate policies and procedures. To ensure that all employees comply with all procurement requirements, a contractor should develop an internal auditing and monitoring system to identify violations. A contractor's compliance program should also include a mechanism for reporting and investigating suspected violations. A contractor should also maintain procedures for disciplining employees who violate corporate policies. Systematic reviews to compare policies with corporate practices and procedures will help a contractor avoid procurement pitfalls, especially as business grows over the years.

Any compliance program must allow for modification to accommodate changes in procurement laws and regulations. A contractor should monitor changes in laws and regulations and update its compliance plan accordingly.

Although compliance costs are generally allowable, a contractor must take care in distinguishing any unallowable costs, such as those incurred in defending any fraud proceedings instituted against the contractor. This requires establishing procedures for separately charging unallowable costs arising from compliance issues. In the end, a compliance and ethics program is not just a cost center, but a proven method for protecting and enhancing the value of a government contractor's business.

Compliance Programs and the FAR

Q 14.3 Does the Federal Acquisition Regulation (FAR) include provisions requiring compliance programs?

Yes. The FAR codifies and publishes uniform policies and procedures for all executive agency acquisitions.[2] Each agency may also have separate acquisition regulations that implement or supplement the FAR.[3] FAR 3.10, implemented in contract clauses, including 52.203-13 and 52.203-14, requires certain contractors to:

- Have a code of business ethics and conduct within thirty days of contract award;
- Develop internal controls to support the code within ninety days of contract award;
- Implement a formal "awareness" or training program on the code within ninety days of contract award;
- Exercise "due diligence" to prevent and detect improper conduct;
- Promote an organizational culture that encourages ethical conduct and a commitment to compliance with the law;[4]
- Display a hotline poster;[5]
- Report "credible evidence" of any violation of federal criminal law involving fraud, conflict of interest, bribery, or gratuity violations found in title 18 of the U.S. Code, or of a violation of the civil False Claims Act;[6] and
- "Fully cooperate" in government audits, investigations, or corrective actions relating to contract fraud and corruption.[7]

The FAR rules also provide that a contractor or subcontractor may be suspended or debarred for "knowing" failure by one of its "principals"[8] to disclose a violation (as described above) or to disclose significant overpayment(s) on the contract, other than over-payments resulting from contract financing payments[9] (*see* Q 14.6.1 *et seq.*, *infra*[10]). "Principal" means "an officer, director, owner, partner, or a person having primary management or supervisory responsibilities within a business entity (*e.g.*, general manager; plant manager; head of a subsidiary, division, or business segment and similar positions)."[11]

Q 14.3.1   Who is subject to these rules?

These aspects of the FAR rules and the contract clauses regarding business ethics and conduct apply to contracts, and subcontracts with all agencies exceeding $5 million (including options), with a performance period of 120 days or more. All contractors, regardless of size, must:

(1)   have a code of business ethics and conduct and make this code available to all employees engaged in performance of the contract;

(2)   exercise some form of "due diligence" to prevent and detect criminal conduct and promote an ethical organizational culture; and

(3)   comply with the mandatory disclosure obligation.[12]

However, the requirement to have an ongoing business ethics aware-ness and compliance program and an internal control system set forth in FAR 52.203-13(c) *does not apply* to contracts for commercial items or to non-commercial item contracts in which the contractor represented itself as a "small business concern" pursuant to the award of the contract.[13]

The disclosure requirement, and the related potential for suspension or debarment, applies to all contracts and subcontracts, regardless of whether the clause is included in the contract and regardless of the contract value or duration.[14] According to the rule, it applies to all existing contracts and subcontracts, including completed contracts and subcontracts within three years after final payment.

Code of Business Ethics and Conduct

Q 14.3.2   How must contractors fulfill the code of conduct requirement?

Contractors with qualifying contracts are required to have a code of business ethics and conduct within thirty days of award.[15] The code should address ethical business practices, conflicts of interest, and expected standards of ethical and moral behavior. The code should cover dealings with customers, suppliers, employees, and other parties. Contractors also must make the code available to all employees involved in performance of the contract.[16]

Internal Controls System/Training Program

Q 14.3.3   What is required in an internal controls system and training program?

Contractors must develop and implement an internal controls system to support the code and implement a training program within ninety days of award.[17] The business ethics and compliance training program as well as the internal control system should suit the size of the company and the extent of its government contracting business, as well as ensure that corrective measures are promptly instituted and carried out.[18]

The FAR's minimum requirements for the internal control system and training program are based on the Federal Sentencing Guidelines and include:

- Taking reasonable steps to communicate the contractor's standards and procedures and other aspects of the ethics and compliance program through effective training programs and other dissemination of information appropriate to an individual's roles and responsibilities;
- Establishing procedures to "facilitate timely discovery of improper conduct in connection with government contracts." This includes at a minimum:
  - Assigning responsibility for oversight of the program at a sufficiently high level and providing adequate resources to ensure the effectiveness of the program;

387

- Making reasonable efforts to exclude individuals as principals who have engaged in conduct that violates the contractor's code (*i.e.*, do not employ violators as managers or supervisors);
- Conducting periodic reviews of company practices, policies, procedures, and internal controls for compliance with the code and the requirements of government contracting. This includes:
  - monitoring and auditing to detect improper conduct;
  - periodic evaluation of the effectiveness of the program and internal control system;
  - periodic assessment of the risks of improper conduct and implementation of appropriate steps to address the risks identified;
- Establishing an internal reporting system that provides for anonymous or confidential reporting (when desired) of suspected improper conduct (*e.g.*, hotline/helpline);
- Imposing a consistent system of disciplinary action for engaging in or failing to take reasonable steps to detect and prevent improper conduct, as well as incentives to encourage compliant behavior; and
- Making timely disclosure of violations of federal criminal law involving fraud, conflict of interest, bribery, or gratuity violations, or violations of the civil False Claims Act (described further below).[19]

Q 14.3.4   Who should participate in a training program?

Training requirements apply to the contractor's principals, employees, and, when appropriate, to its agents and subcontractors. All principals and employees should receive training on the contractor's code as well as other aspects of the company's business ethics awareness and compliance program and internal control system. All principals and employees should periodically receive copies of the code and reminders about the company's internal control system and internal reporting obligations. In addition, it is appropriate for a contractor to train or otherwise disseminate information regarding specific compliance risks and related policies and procedures to individuals based on their respective roles and responsibilities with the company.

TIP: In most instances, ninety days is not a sufficient period of time to develop and implement an internal controls system and training program. Contractors bidding on qualifying contracts are well-advised to begin work on internal controls and training programs before they receive a qualifying award.

Internal Reporting and Hotline Posters

Q 14.3.5 What is required for an internal reporting system and hotline poster?

A contractor must have an internal reporting mechanism, such as a hotline or helpline, that allows employees to make anonymous or confidential reports of suspected instances of improper conduct.[20] Employees must receive instructions that encourage them to make such reports.[21]

Unless a contract is for the acquisition of a commercial item or will be performed entirely outside the United States, contractors must post fraud hotline posters.[22] Fraud hotline posters may be supplied by a contractor with a compliance program or by the contracting agency; however, the contractor may still be required to post any required DHS fraud posters.[23] A contractor must also display an electronic version of the poster on its website if the website is used to provide information to employees.[24]

Reporting of Violations

Q 14.3.6 What are the mandatory disclosure requirements?

All contractors and subcontractors are required to disclose to the agency credible evidence of violations of federal criminal law involving fraud, conflict of interest, bribery or gratuities, or violations of the civil False Claims Act.[25]

389

Disclosure must be made when any "principal" of a contractor or subcontractor has "credible evidence" that a principal, employee, agent, or subcontractor has committed a violation of federal criminal laws or the civil False Claims Act in connection with the award, performance, or closeout of a contract or subcontract.

In order to avoid grounds for suspension or debarment, contractors and subcontractors are required to report credible evidence of violations in relation to any government contract awarded to the contractor or any subcontract thereunder, even if FAR 52.203-13 was not included in the contract.[26]

The disclosure requirement for an individual contract or subcontract continues until at least three years after final payment on the contract.[27]

Q 14.3.7   What is the time frame for disclosure?

A contractor must make "timely" disclosure. There is no set time period for what constitutes "timely" reporting.

Although the FAR does not impose any strict deadline for disclosure, the civil False Claims Act provides a financial incentive to disclose within thirty days. A civil False Claims Act defendant's liability will be limited to double damages (rather than treble damages) if the defendant "furnished officials of the United States responsible for investigating false claims violations with all information known to such person about the violation within 30 days after the date on which the defendant first obtained the information" and such disclosure is made prior to the commencement of any criminal prosecution, civil action, or administrative action.[28]

Time for an investigation by the contractor is permitted. The FAR Council states that the term "credible evidence" implies that a contractor will undertake a "preliminary examination of the evidence to determine its credibility before deciding to disclose to the Government."[29] Timeliness is generally measured from the date of determination that credible evidence exists. This raises issues for contractors or subcontractors who may already have credible evidence of prior violations. Failure to timely disclose such violations is grounds for suspension and debarment.

Q 14.3.8   How is disclosure made?

In writing.

Q 14.3.9   To whom is disclosure made?

Disclosures should be made to the agency OIG with a copy to the contracting officer.[30] Contracts used by multiple agencies, such as the Federal Supply Schedules, require making disclosure to the OIG for the ordering agency and the OIG of the agency responsible for administering the contract.[31]

Q 14.3.10   What must be disclosed?

Credible evidence of violations of federal criminal law involving fraud, conflicts of interest, bribery or gratuities prohibited in title 18 of the U.S. Code, and violations of the civil False Claims Act.[32]

Q 14.3.11   What is "knowing" failure to disclose?

"Knowing" failure means actual knowledge of the violation on the part of one or more of the contractor's or subcontractor's principals, as defined in FAR 2.101. In other words, contractors must make written disclosures when a principal of the company has knowledge of a violation. Under the definition of "principal," this could include compliance officers or directors of internal audits, as well as persons in other positions of responsibility.[33] "Until the contractor has determined the evidence to be credible, there can be no 'knowing failure to timely disclose.'"[34]

Note that the government must, to the extent permitted by law, safeguard and treat information obtained pursuant to the disclosure requirement as confidential when the information has been marked "confidential" or "proprietary" by the company.[35] This makes it important for contractors to ensure that all information being submitted to the government, at any time, is properly marked.

Full Cooperation with the Government

Q 14.3.12   What is required for "full cooperation"?

The FAR requires contractors and subcontractors to "fully cooperate" with the government in the government's efforts to audit, investigate, or take corrective action relating to violations that must be disclosed. "Full cooperation" means

> disclosure to the Government of information sufficient for law enforcement to identify the nature and extent of the offense and the individuals responsible for the conduct. It includes providing timely and complete response to Government auditors' and investigators' requests for documents and access to employees with information.[36]

Full cooperation does *not* require:

- that a contractor disclose information covered by the attorney-client privilege or work-product doctrine (however, contractors are advised that facts are not protected and must be disclosed); or
- that any officer, director, owner, or employee waive his or her Fifth Amendment rights.[37]

Contractors may conduct a thorough internal investigation and defend proceedings or disputes relating to potential or disclosed violations and still "fully cooperate."[38]

Knowing Failure to Disclose Violations

Q 14.3.13 What are the implications of suspension and debarment for knowing failure to make mandatory disclosures?

The FAR suspension and debarment provisions include an additional ground for suspension or debarment. This permits the government to suspend or debar a contractor or subcontractor for "knowing" failure by a principal to make the mandatory disclosures identified above, as well as failure to disclose significant overpayment(s) on the contract (other than overpayments resulting from contract financing payments as defined in FAR 32.001). *This applies to all existing contracts and subcontracts (and those within three years after final payment), regardless of whether the compliance program clause is included in the contract and regardless of the contract value or duration.*[39]

Q 14.3.14 What constitutes failure to report "significant overpayments"?

The rule does not define this term. The FAR Council indicated that this new ground for suspension or debarment may not be based on monetary value alone, and what constitutes a "significant overpayment" will be determined by the suspension and debarment official.[40] (Contractors are already obligated to report and return overpayments under the payments clauses.)[41]

Practical Considerations

Subcontractors

Q 14.4 Are contractors required to flow-down the clauses into subcontracts?

Yes. The government requires prime contractors to flow-down the compliance clauses in all subcontracts expected to exceed $5 million and with a performance period of 120 days or more.[42] This includes commercial item contracts and contracts performed outside the United States. Prime contractors must only verify the existence of the subcontractor's code, compliance program, and internal controls, and need not review the program for adequacy.[43]

Performance Evaluations

Q 14.5 Will a contractor's compliance program be considered in performance evaluations?

Yes. Under FAR 42.1501, a contractor's performance information includes compliance with contract requirements, cooperation with the government, and the contractor's record of integrity and business ethics. Contractors can expect to see performance evaluations to include consideration of the contractor's compliance with FAR 52.203-13.

Noncompliance

Potential Liability

Q 14.6   What does a government contractor risk by not having a compliance program?

In addition to statutory, regulatory, and administrative penalties, government contractors are exposed to an especially high risk of being accused of perpetrating fraud on the government due to the highly regulated nature of doing business with the government. Fraud can take many forms, including false claims, false statements, racketeering, mail fraud, and wire fraud, among others. Accusations of fraud expose government contractors, including many of the individuals employed by these contractors, to criminal, civil, administrative, and contractual remedies. As discussed above at Q 14.3.13, the government may suspend or debar a contractor, or subcontractor, for "knowing" failure by one of the company's "principals" to disclose a violation of federal criminal law involving fraud, conflict of interest, bribery, or gratuity violations found in title 18 of the U.S. Code; a violation of the civil False Claims Act, or a significant overpayment(s) on the contract, other than overpayments resulting from contract financing payments, as defined in FAR 32.001. An effective compliance program will help contractors detect potential violations, permit contractors some time to complete an internal investigation to determine whether "credible evidence" of a violation exists, and finally, disclose violations as required under the FAR. (Chapter 2 discusses the Federal Sentencing Guidelines and provides additional information on the types of penalties a contractor may face for criminal activities.)

Q 14.6.1   Can a contractor be found liable for the acts of its employees?

Yes. Under certain circumstances, the fraudulent, criminal, or other seriously improper conduct of agents of a contractor may be imputed to the contractor when the agent's conduct occurred during performance of his/her duties or in order to further the contractor's business.[44] Again, under the FAR, a contractor may be suspended or debarred for the "knowing" failure by one of the company's "principals" to make a required disclosure. In addition, improper conduct of persons associated with a company (including a joint venture) may be imputed to the company, especially where the conduct occurs in connection with the duties of the person or if the conduct is known, approved by, or acquiesced by the company.

Q 14.6.2 What types of liability might government contractors incur?

The government may seek criminal, civil, administrative (*e.g.*, suspension and debarment), and contractual remedies (*e.g.*, damages, default, termination) against government contractors that violate any of the statutes, regulations, or contractual clauses governing business conducted with the government.

The liability under the civil False Claims Act is particularly noteworthy: The contractor may be liable for three times the amount of damages that the government sustains because of the false claim, plus a civil penalty of between $5,500 and $11,000 per violation.[45]

Criminal and Civil Penalties

Q 14.7 What criminal and civil penalties may government contractors face?

The government can bring enforcement actions under a number of civil and criminal statutes. The primary criminal and civil penalty statutes are:

- the False Claims Acts,[46]
- false statements,[47]
- mail fraud,[48]
- wire fraud,[49]
- major fraud,[50]
- conspiracy,[51]
- the Racketeer Influenced and Corrupt Organizations Act (RICO),[52]
- obstruction of justice,[53]
- Truth in Negotiations Act,
- Program Fraud Civil Remedies Act, and
- Foreign Assistance Act of 1988.

Sometimes, as in the case of the False Claims Act and RICO, there are both civil and criminal sanctions available to the government.

Q 14.7.1   What makes a case criminal rather than civil?

The primary factors that the government considers in deciding whether to proceed with criminal or civil enforcement actions are the degree to which a violation is knowingly committed (the intent, or *mens rea* of the person or entity that commits the violation) and the degree to which the government can prove guilt in a criminal case "beyond a reasonable doubt," compared to the lesser civil standard, "by a preponderance of the evidence." Other factors include:

- the degree to which civil statutes are better suited to the facts of a case;
- which forum is most likely to make the government whole;
- the need for deterrence; and
- the nature of the investigating agency and its relationships with civil and criminal enforcement authorities.

Q 14.7.2   How are criminal fines determined?

The amounts of criminal fines are typically the product of the possible statutory range (noted below where applicable) and calculations under the Sentencing Guidelines. Fines can be agreed to by the parties in the context of a guilty plea—often with some flexibility to designate funds to purposes other than the fine itself, such as community service. Fines are otherwise determined by the court. Keep in mind, however, that the government might seek an "alternative fine" above the statutory maximum in a criminal case. An alternative fine is the greater of twice the gain to the defendant or twice the loss to the victim.[54] Complicating matters is the fact that determining the gain or loss can be difficult.

Q 14.7.3   How can contractors be held liable under the False Claims Act?

The False Claims Act[55] provides for both civil and criminal penalties for submitting false claims to the government. The vast majority of False Claims Act enforcement cases are civil. The act permits not only the government but private citizens acting on its behalf to bring civil enforcement actions. The act, along with the civil and criminal penalties for its violation, is described in detail in chapter 11.

Q 14.7.4   What constitutes a false statement violation?

It is a criminal offense to knowingly and willfully make a false statement to a government agency,[56] to include:

(1)   falsifying, concealing, or covering up a material fact using any trick, scheme, or device;

(2)   making any materially false, fictitious, or fraudulent statements or representation; or

(3)   making or using a false writing or document knowing that it contains a materially false, fictitious, or fraudulent statement or entry.

Typical questions that arise are whether the false statement was material and whether it was made in a matter that was within the jurisdiction of the relevant government entity. Violations are punishable by up to five years in prison (eight years if terrorism-related), and statutory maximum fines of up to $250,000 for individuals and $500,000 for organizations.

Q 14.7.5   What constitutes a criminal mail fraud violation?

Mail fraud occurs when the mails are used to further a scheme to defraud.[57] A government contractor must take care not to cause the use of the U.S. mails or any private commercial interstate carrier to:

•   defraud another;

•   obtain money or property by means of false or fraudulent pretenses, representations, or promises; or

•   deprive another of honest services.[58]

Mail fraud allegations often accompany other charges when the mails are used to perpetrate offenses such as bribery, illegal gratuities, kickbacks, or illegal contingent fees. Below, this chapter describes these offenses as they present compliance issues for government contractors.

Violations of the mail fraud statute are punishable by fine under the Sentence of Fine statute (below) or imprisonment of not more than twenty years, or both.[59] If the violation affects a financial institution, violations are punishable by fines of not more than $1 million or imprisonment of not more than thirty years, or both.[60]

Q 14.7.6   What constitutes a wire fraud violation?

Wire fraud occurs when wire, radio, or television communication are used in interstate or foreign commerce to further a scheme to defraud.[61] A government contractor must take care not to cause the use of wire, radio, or television to transmit writings, signs, signals, pictures, or sounds for the purpose of executing a fraudulent scheme.[62]

Wire fraud allegations often accompany other charges when the mails are used to perpetrate offenses such as bribery, illegal gratuities, kickbacks, or illegal contingent fees. Below, this chapter describes these offenses as they present compliance issues for government contractors.

Violations of the wire fraud statute are the same as those for mail fraud. Wire fraud is punishable by fine under the Sentence of Fine statute (below) or imprisonment of not more than twenty years, or both.[63] If the violation affects a financial institution, such person shall be fined not more than $1 million or imprisoned not more than thirty years, or both.[64]

Q 14.7.7   What constitutes a major fraud violation?

A contractor, subcontractor, or supplier on a government contract may commit "major fraud" where it knowingly executes or attempts to execute a scheme to defraud the government or to obtain money or property by false pretenses, representations, or promises involving a contract valued at $1 million or more.[65]

Penalties include fines of $1 million and ten years' imprisonment.[66] The fine may increase to $5 million if the gross loss to the government or gross gain to the defendant is $500,000 or greater or if the offense involves a conscious or reckless risk of serious personal injury.[67] The maximum fine imposed is $10 million.[68]

In addition, a whistleblower may obtain a payment of up to $250,000 for information relating to a possible prosecution for a major fraud.[69] A court may order the person convicted to reimburse the Department of Justice for this payment.

Q 14.7.8 How can the conspiracy statute affect government contractors?

It is a criminal offense to conspire with others to violate a federal law.[70] Conspiracy requires agreement to violate a law and an act by at least one of the conspirators in furtherance of that agreement. It is often charged along with the substantive offense, that is, whatever violation the conspirators planned to commit. Charging conspiracy has tactical advantages for the government. For example, the government can combine the cases of a less culpable person with a more culpable one, and more easily use the statements of one conspirator against the other. Conspiracy is punishable by up to five years in prison and statutory maximum fines of up to $250,000 for individuals and $500,000 for organizations.[71]

Q 14.7.9 What behaviors can subject a government contractor to obstruction of justice liability?

Obstruction of justice is a criminal offense that comes in a number of forms. The most typical in the current context are obstruction of pending agency proceedings;[72] obstruction of federal audits;[73] falsification of records to obstruct government investigations;[74] and destruction of corporate audit records.[75] Criminal penalties range from five to twenty years in prison and statutory maximum fines of up to $250,000 for individuals and $500,000 for organizations.

Obstruction of justice pertains to efforts taken to avoid detection after another law may have been violated. Contractors need to be particularly careful in dealing with government investigations to ensure not only that purposeful obstruction does not occur, but also that records potentially relevant to government audits or investigations are properly preserved to avoid their purposeful or inadvertent destruction.

Q 14.7.10 What is required to avoid liability under the Truth in Negotiations Act?

The Truth in Negotiations Act (TINA) requires offerors, contractors, and subcontractors to provide the government with cost or pricing data when negotiating contracts or contract modifications over a specified threshold—currently $700,000.[76] Cost or pricing data must be accurate, complete, and current.

Q 14.7.11   What are "cost or pricing data"?

Cost or pricing data include "all facts that . . . prudent buyers and sellers would reasonably expect to affect price negotiations significantly."[77] This data may include vendor quotations, nonrecurring costs, information on changes in production methods, information on production or purchasing volume, data supporting business productions, data supporting operations costs, unit-cost trends, make-or-buy decisions, estimated resources to attain business goals, and information on management decisions that could have a significant bearing on costs.[78] Although cost or pricing data do not require judgmental information, they do require the factual information from which the judgment was derived.

Q 14.7.12   What are the requirements for providing cost or pricing data to the government?

The contractor must submit all cost or pricing data reasonably available as of the date of agreement as to contract price or another time agreed upon between the contractor and the contracting officer.[79]

Under limited circumstances, the government does not require a contractor to provide cost or pricing data when the government:

- awards a contract at or below $150,000;
- determines that agreed prices are based on prices set by law or regulation or adequate price competition;
- acquires a commercial item;
- grants a waiver;
- modifies a contract or subcontract for commercial items;
- exercises an option at the price established at contract award or initial negotiation;
- uses the proposal solely for overrun or interim billing price adjustments.[80]

In addition, the contracting officer may require information other than cost or pricing data to support a price reasonableness determination.[81] Contractors do not need to certify information other than cost or pricing data.

Remember, the government has the right to audit a contractor's books, records, documents, and other data related to contract negotiation, pricing, or performance for three years after final payment on the contract.[82] This audit right does not extend to data other than cost or pricing data.

Q 14.7.13 How might a contractor incur liability?

Offerors, contractors, and subcontractors must certify that the cost or pricing data provided are "accurate, complete, and current" as of the date on which the parties agreed upon a price.[83] When a contractor submits information that is inaccurate, incomplete, or noncurrent, the government may assert a defective pricing claim against the contractor, demanding a reduction in the contract's price to compensate for the effect of the undisclosed or inaccurate data.[84] Failure to submit a signed certificate does not provide a contractor with a defense to a defective pricing claim.[85]

Q 14.7.14 What civil remedies can the government seek for such violations?

Damages for a defective pricing claim after payment include recovery of the price adjustment, interest on overpayments made by the government, and penalties up to the amount of the overpayments if the contractor knowingly submitted defective data.[86]

TIP: To ensure compliance with requirements to provide cost or pricing data, a contractor should make all employees aware of the liabilities that arise from defective pricing. The highest risk arises from the actions of personnel in upper management, contract managers, financial managers, negotiators, sales representatives, and in-house attorneys. The contractor should make these groups of employees especially aware of actions or inactions for which the contractor may incur liability.

Q 14.7.15 What are the civil penalties for violations of the Program Fraud Civil Remedies Act?

Although the Program Fraud Civil Remedies Act involves the assessment of civil penalties, these small-dollar fraud cases are handled in administrative hearings and discussed under the section below regarding administrative penalties.

Q 14.7.16   What are the civil penalties for violations of the Foreign Assistance Act?

A government contractor that submits false claims under the banner of foreign aid shall forfeit or refund the claim payment plus 25%. In addition, the contractor will pay the greater of $2,200 and double the damages or 50% of the payment for each fraudulent act together with the costs of the lawsuit.[87]

Support for claims, such as certifications, statements, contracts, abstracts, bills of lading, government or commercial invoices, or government forms, may subject a contractor to liability.

Q 14.7.17   What other civil penalties might government contractors be subject to?

Under the Forfeiture of Claim statute, applicable only in the Court of Federal Claims, if a government contractor practices any fraud against the government in proving, stating, establishing, or allowing a claim, the contractor will forfeit the claim to the United States.[88]

Administrative Penalties

Q 14.8   What administrative penalties may government contractors face?

The FAR provides for suspension[89] and/or debarment[90] of contractors that engage in improper acts.

Q 14.8.1   What are the implications of suspension?

In order to protect the government from improper acts of contractors, an agency may temporarily suspend a contractor's work for the executive branch pending the completion of an investigation and any ensuing legal proceedings.[91] A suspension may not exceed eighteen months, unless legal proceedings have been initiated within that period.[92]

Q 14.8.2 What are the implications of debarment?

A contractor may be debarred for any improper act of any employee furthering the contractor's business. To be debarred, the contractor's improper act must affect the present responsibility of the contractor or subcontractor. An agency will generally debar a contractor from working for the executive branch for no more than three years, depending on the nature of the violation.[93] However, the government has discretion to extend debarment for an additional period.[94] It is important to note that the government may also seek to debar a contractor's employees and affiliates.[95]

Q 14.8.3 What kinds of contractor acts can result in suspension and/or debarment?

- Committing fraud or a criminal offense in obtaining, attempting to obtain, or performing a public contract or subcontract;
- Violating a federal or state antitrust statute in the submission of an offer;
- Committing embezzlement, theft, forgery, bribery, falsification or destruction of records, making false statements, tax evasion, or receiving stolen property;
- Intentionally mislabeling a product as "Made in America" when it was not made in the United States;
- Committing any other offense indicating a lack of business integrity or honesty;
- Violating the terms of a government contract or subcontract by willful failure to perform, historically failing to perform, or unsatisfactory performance;
- Violating the Drug-Free Workplace Act of 1988;
- Violating the Immigration and Nationality Act employment provisions;
- Committing an unfair trade practice;
- "Knowing" failure by one of a contractor's (or subcontractor's) "principals" to disclose a violation of federal criminal law involving fraud, conflict of interest, bribery, or gratuity violations found in title 18 of the U.S. Code, or a violation of the civil False Claims Act, or a significant overpayment(s) on the contract, other than overpayments

resulting from contract financing payments, as defined in FAR 32.001.[96]

Q 14.8.4   What administrative penalties are available under the Program Fraud Civil Remedies Act?

Cases involving false claims or false statements under $150,000 that the Department of Justice declines to prosecute are handled in administrative hearings and may subject a contractor to penalties under the Program Fraud Civil Remedies Act. Civil penalties of up to $5,500 for each *certified written* false statement and false claim may be imposed under this act.[97] A court may also assess damages of twice the amount of the false claim in cases where the government has already paid the contractor's claim.

The act requires that agencies have implementing regulations that specify the identity of investigating and reviewing officials for that agency, as well as the procedures for conducting administrative hearings. This act has not been widely used to combat fraud. However, government contractors should be aware that the Program Fraud Civil Remedies Act provides the government an additional means of imposing penalties for fraudulent behavior, even when large sums of money are not available as remedies.

Contractual Remedies

Q 14.9   What other contractual clauses might trigger penalties in government contracts?

Certain contracts may include a clause assessing penalties for unallowable costs. Likewise, certain government contracts allow for price reduction for defective cost or pricing data.

Q 14.9.1   What penalties are triggered by "unallowable costs"?

Contracts in excess of $700,000 include a clause assessing penalties for unallowable costs.[98] Unallowable costs include any cost that cannot be included in prices, cost-reimbursements, or settlements under a government contract to which it is allocable.[99] The government will assess these penalties when a government contractor includes unallowable indirect costs in its final indirect cost rate

Q 14.10

proposals or the final statement of costs incurred or estimated to be incurred under a fixed-price incentive contract.[100]

If the contractor includes an indirect cost that is expressly unallowable under the FAR cost principles (or an agency FAR supplement), the penalty equals the amount of the disallowed costs allocated to the contract plus interest on any paid portion of the disallowance.[101] If the contractor includes an indirect cost that was determined to be unallowable before the contractor submitted its proposal, the penalty equals two times the amount of the disallowed costs allocated to the contract.[102] Other criminal, civil, and administrative penalties may also apply.

Q 14.9.2   How can defective cost or pricing data result in price reduction?

Negotiated contracts requiring government contractors to provide cost or pricing data include a clause allowing for a price reduction for the submission of defective data. This clause implements the requirements set forth in TINA as described above. Where a contractor submits cost or pricing data that is not complete, accurate, and current, the government will reduce the cost accordingly and modify the contract. The contractor must also reimburse the government for any overpayment plus interest on the amount overpaid.[103]

Obtaining Government Contracts

Compliance Concerns for Offerors

Q 14.10   What compliance issues may arise when preparing bids on government contracts?

While preparing a bid on work for the government, contractors must comply with certain statutes and regulations requiring contractors to make particular certifications. Contractors must also comply with requirements affecting issues such as eligibility of contractors to bid on work, submission of cost accounting information, and participation in anticompetitive behavior. As a result, many government contractors should implement compliance regimes and systems that

better prepare them for responding to certification and documentation requirements in proposals.

Q 14.10.1   What kinds of certifications might contractors be required to make?

Solicitations for government contracts often require offerors and
awardees to certify the accuracy of certain information. Agencies
may include agency-specific requirements and/or those included in
the FAR, such as:

- verification of representations and certifications currently
  posted electronically on the Online Representations and
  Certifications Application website;[104]
- debarment, suspension, proposed debarment, and other
  responsibility matters;[105]
- the existence (or nonexistence) of organizational conflicts of
  interest;
- compliance with Cost Accounting Standards;[106]
- allowability of final indirect costs;[107]
- certification that the contractor reached its prices independently, without agreement or consultation with other
  bidders and that the contractor's offer will not be disclosed
  to other bidders before bidding opens;[108]
- small business program eligibility;[109]
- certification that end products will comply with the country-
  of-origin requirements of the Buy American Act[110] or the
  Trade Agreements Act;[111]
- a representation that an institution is or is not a historically
  black college or university or a minority institution;[112]
- for contracts with an estimated value of $500,000 or more, a
  representation that the information about the contractor in
  the Federal Awardee Performance and Integrity Information
  System (FAPIIS) is current, accurate, and complete;[113]
- compliance with labor laws.[114]

Generally, the certifications required for a particular government
contract are set forth in the request for proposals issued by the
agency for that contract.

One of the e-government initiatives requires any bidder or offeror
that must register in the System Award Management (www.sam.gov)

database to also provide electronic representations and certifications into the Online Representations and Certifications Application website. Contractors must verify these representations and certifications at least annually.

TIP: Government contractors should seek to implement policies and procedures for ensuring that they make accurate representations and certifications to the government at all times. The civil False Claims Act, for example, allows the government to seek *treble damages* and penalties for each false statement or certification presented to the government. This means that *each communication* to the government has the potential to subject a contractor to liability. (See chapter 11 for more information on the False Claims Act.)

Q 14.10.2 When is a contractor eligible to bid on a government contract?

In general, agencies will only solicit offers from, award contracts to, and consent to subcontracts with contractors that are:

- "responsible," and
- free from organizational conflicts of interest.

Q 14.10.3 What makes a contractor "responsible"?

To be determined "responsible," a prospective awardee must have the ability and capacity to perform the contract.[115] To assist with a determination of the offeror's responsibility, each solicitation includes a provision requiring the offeror to certify as to its status regarding:

(1) debarment, suspension, proposed debarment, or proposed ineligibility for award;
(2) any convictions or civil judgments rendered against the contractor for:
  (a) committing fraud or a criminal offense in obtaining, attempting to obtain, or performing a public contract or subcontract;

407

    (b) violating a federal or state antitrust statute in the submission of an offer;

    (c) committing embezzlement, theft, forgery, bribery, falsification or destruction of records, making false statements, tax evasion, or receiving stolen property;

(3) present criminal or civil charges for the above-listed offenses;

(4) any contracts that the government terminated for default within the preceding three years.[116]

Failure to furnish such a certification may render the offeror "nonresponsible" and therefore ineligible for award of the contract.[117] As discussed elsewhere, false statements in any certification may subject a contractor to liability.

The government maintains a list of contractors generally excluded from working for executive agencies due to their status as "nonresponsible." This publicly available list is known as the "Excluded Parties List."[118] The Excluded Parties List System includes contractors that have been debarred, suspended, proposed for debarment, declared ineligible, or otherwise excluded or disqualified from working as either a prime contractor or subcontractor for the government.[119]

Organizational Conflicts of Interest

Q 14.10.4 What are "organizational conflicts of interest"?

An organizational conflict of interest (OCI) occurs when:

> because of other activities or relationships with other persons, a person is unable or potentially unable to render impartial assistance or advice to the Government, or the person's objectivity in performing the contract work is or might be otherwise impaired, or a person has an unfair competitive advantage.[120]

The government prescribes limitations on contracting to prevent the existence of conflicting roles that might bias a contractor's judgment or give a contractor an unfair competitive advantage.[121]

Solicitations often require offerors to certify that they have disclosed all facts—or that they are not aware of any facts—that could give rise to an OCI. An offeror's failure to provide a complete and accurate OCI certification could result in serious consequences, including liability under the False Claims Act.[122]

In general, agencies will not award a contract to a successful offeror if an OCI exists that cannot be avoided or mitigated.[123] An agency has the discretion to waive the general rules regarding OCIs under certain circumstances when it is in the government's interest to do so.[124]

Q 14.10.5 Under what circumstances might an OCI arise?

An OCI may result from an actual or potential conflict of interest existing on a current contract or on a future acquisition.[125] The three types of OCIs addressed in FAR 9.5 are:

(1)   biased ground rules OCI;
(2)   unequal access to nonpublic information OCI; and
(3)   impaired objectivity OCI.[126]

The "biased ground rules" OCI arises where a firm, as part of its performance of one government contract, sets the ground rules for another government contract by, for example, writing the statement of work or the specifications. In reviewing allegations of "biased ground rules" OCIs, GAO's primary concern is whether a firm is in a position to skew the competition, intentionally or unintentionally, in its own favor.[127] A separate concern arising in this context is that a firm, by virtue of its special knowledge of the agency's future requirements, enjoys an unfair advantage in the competition for those requirements.[128] In reviewing protests brought on the basis of a "biased ground rules" OCI, GAO will generally presume that setting the ground rules gives the contractor an actual benefit and competitive advantage. Absent an approved mitigation plan that resolves the conflict, the contractor is usually disqualified from later source selection.

An "unequal access to nonpublic information" OCI arises when, as part of its performance of a government contract, a firm gains access to competitively useful nonpublic information that may provide a competitive advantage in a subsequent competition for a government contract.[129] Examples of nonpublic information include proprietary information, source-selection information, or other competitively useful nonpublic information. Generally, there is no issue of bias in these cases; thus, the concern in the "unequal access to nonpublic information" OCI is limited to the issue of competitive advantage.[130]

An "impaired objectivity" OCI occurs when a firm's work under one government contract could require the firm to evaluate either itself or a competing contractor, such as through a performance assessment or proposal evaluation.[131] The concern in an "impaired objectivity" OCI is that a firm's ability to render impartial advice to the government could be, or appear to be, undermined by its relationship with the entity whose work product is being evaluated.[132]

Q 14.10.6   What can a government contractor do to identify OCIs?

By taking into consideration certain fundamental principles, a contractor can determine whether any of the three types of OCIs is an active or potential issue:

1. To determine whether a "biased ground rules" OCI is an active or potential issue, analyze whether the contractor or any of its affiliates or subcontractors provided to the government, or to a prime contractor working for the government, services under a separate contract that establish the need for the instant procurement, or drafts of specifications or work statements.

2. To determine whether an "unequal access to nonpublic information" OCI is an active or potential issue, consider whether the contractor or any of its affiliates or subcontractors obtained information from the government while in performance of another contract and whether this gives the contractor an unfair competitive advantage in the present procurement because other contractors do not possess the information.

3. To determine whether an "impaired objectivity" OCI is an active or potential issue, analyze whether the contractor, by virtue of its other contracts or business relationships, has an incentive to provide biased advice under the instant contract.

Government contractors must maintain good records regarding the nature of each contract and the work they perform. Contractors should pay special attention to contracts where OCIs are more likely to occur, such as contracts involving

(1) management support services;

(2) consultant or other professional services;

(3) contractor performance of or assistance in technical evaluations; or

(4) systems engineering and technical direction work performed by a contractor that does not have overall contractual responsibility for development or production.[133]

To detect OCIs, contractors may want to focus on reviewing their research and development work and the development of specifications for future solicitations, especially when performed for the same agency. In addition, contractors should pay attention to contracts under which they have access to the proprietary information of other contractors or the agency's source selection information. The FAR, as well as many agency-specific regulations, provides examples to illustrate situations in which OCI questions arise.[134]

TIP: To ensure compliance with the regulations, a contractor might establish a company-wide contracts database to aid in tracking work and alerting managers and contract personnel to potential OCIs.

Q 14.10.7 How can the impact of organizational conflicts of interest be mitigated?

The principal objective of any mitigation plan is to eliminate the effect of an existing or potential OCI so that the offeror can avoid disqualification. Once an OCI arises, it can be difficult to mitigate its impact.

Generally, strategies for mitigating an OCI involve creating a firewall that provides for the organizational, physical, and electronic separation of personnel involved in the activities that give rise to the OCI. To be effective, such a firewall must be enforced and should be combined with supplemental efforts, including training, nondisclosure agreements, document control, and audits. In the case of unequal access to information OCIs where the offeror has already benefited from access to the nonpublic information, an alternative mitigation strategy is for the government to disclose the competitively useful nonpublic information to the other competitors. Effective strategies for mitigating a "biased ground roles" or "impaired objectivity" OCI may include implementation of effective OCI detection mechanisms, consistent agency oversight, and recusal of the conflicted contractor that possesses the OCI.

A contractor is not permitted to self-mitigate an actual or potential OCI. Instead, the FAR requires disclosure of the OCI to the contracting officer. Only the contracting officer is authorized to assess whether an OCI can be mitigated and whether a proposed mitigation plan sufficiently addresses and resolves the issue.

Cost Accounting

Q 14.10.8 What are a federal contractor's compliance responsibilities regarding accounting for costs?

Government contracts generally require the implementation of specialized accounting and data collection systems prior to entering into a cost reimbursement type of federal contract. This results from mandated compliance with the FAR's "cost principles," the Cost Accounting Standards (CAS), and TINA.

Q 14.10.9 How must a contractor comply with the FAR's "cost principles"?

The FAR's cost principles generally define when and to what extent a government contractor's costs can be recovered under a cost reimbursement type of government contract.[135] In order to recover a particular cost, that cost must be

(1) allowable,
(2) reasonable, and
(3) allocable.[136]

If a particular cost does not meet these criteria, the FAR provides that the government may recover from the contractor any of these costs initially paid.[137]

Q 14.10.10 How must a contractor comply with the FAR's Cost Accounting Standards?

The FAR's CAS were designed to achieve uniformity and consistency in cost accounting practices used by contractors and subcontractors. The complex CAS rules apply only to cost reimbursement–type government contracts and subcontracts over $500,000.[138] A limited number of contracts are exempt from the CAS.[139] A contractor must comply with all the CAS if it receives a single CAS-covered (nonexempt) contract or a net CAS-covered contract award of $50 million or more during the accounting period (usually the fiscal year).

In certain cases, the CAS requires the contractor to submit a disclosure statement regarding the cost accounting practices that it follows. The contractor must strictly adhere to the practices in the statement and amend the statement whenever the contractor makes any changes to these practices. A contractor must include complete and accurate information in its disclosure statement because falsifying or concealing information may subject the contractor to fines and/or imprisonment under criminal and civil fraud statutes.

It is important to note that the Code of Federal Regulations, the FAR, and the Defense Contract Audit Agency's *DCAA Contractor Audit Manual*[140] all make clear that the CAS do not apply to small business concerns. The Code of Federal Regulations establishes CAS applicability[141] and, in relevant part, directs that contracts and subcontracts with small businesses are exempt from all CAS requirements.[142] FAR part 30, in turn, prescribes the policies and procedures for applying the CAS rules and regulations to negotiated procurements (contracts and subcontracts), also making clear that it does not apply to small businesses.[143] Lastly, section 8-103.2 of the *DCAA Contract Audit Manual* expressly recognizes that contracts and subcontracts with small businesses are exempt from all CAS requirements. In section 8-103.3 of the manual, the DCAA explains that, when a subcontract is awarded under a CAS-covered prime contract, the subcontract's CAS coverage is determined in the same manner as prime contracts awarded to the subcontractor's business unit in that it must be first determined if any of the CAS exemptions found in the Code of Federal Regulations[144] apply to the subcontract. The DCAA's manual also directs that a CAS-covered prime contractor could not place the requirement for CAS compliance on a subcontract with a small business because 48 C.F.R. § 903.201-1(b)(3) specifically exempts

413

contracts and subcontracts with small businesses from CAS requirements. Thus, all of the applicable rules and regulations make clear that contracts and subcontracts with small businesses are exempt from CAS compliance. While small business contractors must have an accounting system that is operable (even if not technically CAS-compliant), *prime contractors* have the responsibility to manage their subcontracts.[145]

The FAR has also added a requirement that all major system acquisitions, including land, structures, equipment, intellectual property (*e.g.*, software), and information technology (including IT service contracts), require contractors and subcontractors to have or to develop an Earned Value Management System (EVMS).[146] Agencies have the discretion to require an EVMS for other acquisitions. An EVMS is a "project management tool that effectively integrates the project scope of work with cost, schedule, and performance elements for optimum project planning and control."[147] The agency must review and accept the proposed system and any subsequent revisions to the system to determine if it complies with the thirty-two criteria set forth in American National Standards Institute/Electronics Industries Alliance (ANSI/EIA) Standard-748 (current version at the time of award).[148] As part of the EVMS, a contractor will need to develop robust internal controls, including detailed policies and procedures for implementing the EVMS.

Although an EVMS could be seen as a burdensome requirement, a validated EVMS generally has the potential to facilitate compliance with accounting and financial reporting requirements and maximizing profits on contracts.

Q 14.10.11 What are the compliance requirements of the Truth in Negotiations Act for government contractors?

TINA requires offerors, contractors, and subcontractors to submit "cost or pricing data" when a negotiated contract, subcontract, or modification is expected to exceed $700,000.[149] The contractor must certify that the data submitted is accurate, complete, and current.[150] If a contractor submits data that is not accurate, current, and complete, as certified, the government may reduce the contract price accordingly.[151] Thus, contractors must know what data fall within the definition of "cost or pricing data," how the contractor may submit data, what constitutes "complete" data, and how "current" the data must be. In essence, the government uses TINA to level the playing field for negotiating contracts and contract modifications by ensuring that the government has the same factual data as the contractor at the time of price negotiations. If the government discovers that a contractor improperly withheld data, the government is entitled to seek a price reduction.[152]

Q 14.10.12 What requirements regarding anticompetitive behavior must a contractor comply with?

Combinations and conspiracies in restraint of trade are illegal.[153] Activities that violate laws prohibiting such anticompetitive behavior include bid-rigging, collusive bidding, and price-fixing. Such antitrust violations are serious crimes that can subject contractors and their employees to criminal penalties and civil damages; also, both companies and individuals may face suspension and debarment from contracting with the government.

Price-fixing, bid-rigging, and other collusive agreements can be established either by direct evidence, such as the testimony of a participant, or by circumstantial evidence, such as suspicious bid patterns, joint actions, and communications between competitors. Price-fixing occurs where competitors agree to raise, fix, or otherwise maintain the price at which their goods or services are sold. Contractors are also prohibited from entering into agreements with their competitors to skew the competition in favor of a particular contractor by way of:

- bid suppression, where contractors agree not to bid or to withdraw their bids;
- subcontracting schemes, where contractors agree not to bid or to submit a losing bid in exchange for a subcontract on the project;
- complementary bidding, where a designated winner tells the other contractors of its bid plans or tells the other contractors how they should bid;
- bid rotation, where contractors take turns as the low bidder in a series of contracts; and
- market division, where contractors agree to somehow divide the market between themselves (for example, contractors may divide the market into geographic regions).

Participation in any such anticompetitive behavior will subject a contractor and its employees to criminal and civil suits. Conviction of a felony based on the above behavior may result in a fine (up to $10 million for a corporation and up to $1 million for an individual), imprisonment up to ten years, or both.[154] Civil suits may result in injunctive relief requiring a contractor and its employees to stop all anticompetitive behavior and/or civil damages including treble damages and penalties of up to $10,000 for each violation.[155]

Any actions that amount to collusive bidding will subject a contractor to liability under a multitude of other statutes as well, including the False Claims Act, the false statements statute, and RICO, as well as statutes regarding wire fraud, mail fraud, and conspiracy. Contractors, and the individuals, engaging in improper behavior may also be suspended or debarred. Liability arising under these statutes is described elsewhere in this chapter.

Compliance Issues Arising During Contract Performance

Q 14.11   What potential improper business practice violations occur during contract performance?

Contractors and prospective contractors must ensure that all employees comply with ethics-related statutes and regulations. Some of these statutes and regulations address business practices that are universally discouraged; others address activities that a contractor might undertake with its commercial customers, but that are prohibited activities with federal employees. Such statutes and regulations cover:

- procurement integrity;
- bribery and illegal gratuities;
- contingent fees;
- kickbacks;
- foreign corrupt practices;
- lobbying restrictions;
- personal conflicts of interest;
- false claims; and
- false statements.

These kinds of violations undermine the integrity and competitive nature of the procurement process, and an effective compliance program is one way of preventing or at least discovering them. Contractors that violate any of these statutes and regulations may face civil, administrative, and/or criminal sanctions.

Disclosure of Procurement Information and Documents

Q 14.11.1 What are the statutes/regulations dealing with disclosure of procurement information with which a government contractor must comply?

The Procurement Integrity Act.[156] This act protects procurement information and documents from unauthorized disclosure. It generally prohibits disclosure of contractor bid or proposal information or source selection information obtained by virtue of his/her position on a federal procurement.[157] A person may not abuse his/her position as a present or former U.S. official, or present or former contractor acting on behalf of or advising the government on a federal procurement. Of significance to contractors, the Procurement Integrity Act prohibits a person from knowingly *obtaining* source selection information or contractor bid and proposal information and subjects violators to up to five years' imprisonment or criminal fines.[158]

Theft of Government Property Statute.[159] Procurement information or documents containing information may also be protected as "things of value" under this statute, which penalizes for theft, conversion, and conveyance of government property.

The Espionage Act.[160] Government contractors with security clearances should also be aware of criminal espionage statutes that govern communication of national security information, especially classified information. Personnel with security clearances are effectively prohibited from disseminating classified documents to other people with security clearances when the dissemination is not pursuant to the performance of official duties. Contractors should note that these statutes also impose penalties for mishandling national security information in a grossly negligent manner.

Bribes/Illegal Gratuities

Q 14.11.2   What compliance issues does gift-giving raise?

The line between an acceptable gift and an illegal gratuity/bribe is not always easily identified, and making mistakes can result in criminal liability. In order to prevent liability, contractors must train employees who deal with the federal government to observe the statutes and regulations that prohibit contractors from providing anything of monetary value to personally benefit federal employees, such as gifts and entertainment. Criminal statutes and regulations prohibit individuals and contractors from giving bribes, gratuities, or gifts to public officials, witnesses, or government officials.[161]

Q 14.11.3   What is the difference between a bribe and a gratuity?

The offeror's intent. Depending on the intent the offeror possesses when giving it, the same "thing of value" could qualify as a bribe or a gratuity.

A bribe is anything of value given to a public official *with the specific intent* to influence an official act (or failure to act) or to induce the public official to violate an official duty or to commit fraud.[162]

For example, a contractor that gives something of value to a public official with the expectation of favorable treatment under a contract would be guilty of bribery. The public official would also face criminal charges for asking for or accepting a bribe. The thing of value does not need to be actually offered, but it is sufficient that the bribe be offered, promised, asked for, or requested in connection with the official act.[163]

In comparison, an illegal gratuity is something of value given as a reward *for or because of an act the official performs as part of his/her duties.*[164]

For example, a contractor that treats a public official to a meal in exchange for, or because of, an official act may be guilty of a bribe. In contrast, paying for a meal or drinks only for the purpose of creating good feelings is likely to be viewed as a gratuity.

Q 14.11.4 What are acceptable gifts?

The Office of Government Ethics has provided guidance on what "things of value" a government employee can accept without violating the criminal statutes and regulations regarding bribery and illegal gratuities. Acceptable gifts to public officials include:

- modest items of food and refreshments offered other than as part of a meal (*e.g.*, soft drinks, coffee, or cookies);
- greeting cards and items with little intrinsic value intended purely for presentation (*e.g.*, plaques, certificates, and trophies);
- gifts of $20 or less, provided that the gifts do not exceed $50 per calendar year;
- an honorary degree of less than $200 if it is offered to the public on a regular basis.[165]

Q 14.11.5 What are the penalties for illegal giving of "things of value"?

In addition to imprisonment of up to fifteen years, criminal penalties for bribery include a fine of the greater of either three times the monetary value of the bribe or the set penalty of $500,000 for an organization or $250,000 for an individual. The public official may also be disqualified from holding a federal office.[166]

Criminal penalties for illegal gratuities include imprisonment of up to two years and/or a fine of $500,000 for organizations or $250,000 for individuals.[167]

Government contracts of over $150,000 also include the FAR's "Gratuities clause." This clause prohibits a contractor from offering or giving an illegal gratuity or a bribe to a public official in order to obtain a contract award or receive favorable treatment under a contract.[168] Where a contractor violates the "Gratuities clause," the contractor may be terminated for default, suspended, or debarred from contracting with the government. Where the contract uses funds appropriated to the Department of Defense, the contractor may be assessed damages of up to ten times the value of the gratuity or bribe.[169]

Kickbacks

Q 14.11.6   What are a federal contractor's compliance obligations regarding kickbacks?

Contractors must properly train employees to not offer or accept kickbacks. Like bribes and gratuities, a kickback may also include any "thing of value," such as money, fees, commissions, credits, gifts, or gratuities.[170] Statutes and contract provisions prohibit contractors from giving or receiving a kickback for the purpose of improperly obtaining or rewarding favorable treatment in connection with a government contract or subcontract.[171] Favorable treatment may include obtaining unwarranted waivers of deadlines or acceptance of non-conforming goods.

The FAR implements the Anti-Kickback Act of 1986,[172] which authorizes criminal and civil penalties to deter behavior having the purpose of improperly obtaining or rewarding favorable treatment in connection with federal contracts and subcontracts.[173] The FAR requires a contractor to have in place and follow reasonable procedures designed to prevent and detect possible kickbacks.[174] The FAR also requires contractors to establish and follow reasonable procedures to prevent and deter violations from occurring during operations and in its direct business relationships.[175] Contractors must also report possible violations and cooperate fully with any federal agency investigation.[176] Agencies may have agency-specific regulations that further supplement the FAR requirements.

Violating the Anti-Kickback Act will result in harsh criminal, civil, and administrative penalties, including up to ten years' imprisonment for individuals, damages of twice the amount of each kickback, and up to a $10,000 civil penalty for each occurrence.[177] In addition, an agency may offset the amount of the kickback against money owed to the contractor on the related contract, withhold fees, or terminate the contract.[178]

Contingent Fees

Q 14.11.7   What is a contingent fee?

A "contingent fee" is any commission, percentage, brokerage, or other fee that is contingent upon the success that an individual or contractor has in securing a government contract.[179]

Q 14.11.8   What compliance considerations regarding contingent fees should a federal contractor be aware of?

All government contracts over $150,000 require the contractor to warrant that the contractor has not retained any person or organization to seek the contract for a commission, percentage, brokerage, or contingent fee.[180] The law provides that a "bona fide agency" or a "bona fide employee" may be employed in such a manner as long as no improper influence is exerted to obtain any government contract.[181] Improper influence includes actions regarding a government contract on any basis other than the merits of the matter.[182]

Under the Foreign Military Sales (FMS) program (see below), a foreign government may appoint an agent for the legitimate purpose of accomplishing the FMS transaction. The Security Assistance Management Manual (SAMM) includes a form letter to be used for this purpose. This letter should be signed at the Minister or Deputy Minister of Defense level. This agent must also not propose to exert or exert improper influence in obtaining government contracts.

The law requires government personnel to promptly report any violations.[183] Agencies must also preserve any specific evidence and pertinent data, including a record of all actions taken.[184] A contractor should also preserve evidence that may support its defense.

For a violation of the warranty against contingent fees, the government may reject the bid or proposal (when violation discovered before award), void the contract without liability or recover the full amount of the commission, percentage, brokerage, or contingent fee, initiate suspension and debarment, and refer the matter to the Department of Justice.[185]

Payments to Foreign Officials

Q 14.11.9   What compliance issues should contractors engaging in foreign business activities be aware of?

The Foreign Corrupt Practices Act (FCPA) extends the above anti-corruption principles relating to U.S. public officials to foreign officials.[186] American companies and individuals may not bribe a foreign government official to obtain or keep business.[187] The FCPA also prohibits payment to any third person knowing that any portion of the payment is a bribe to be given to a foreign official.[188] For example, a contractor could be liable if it gives a payment to any agent or intermediary if it knew of the bribe. A contractor would face liability for "knowing" about a bribe if the contractor consciously disregarded or willfully blinded itself to a situation where its agent bribes a foreign official.

Issuers of securities, under the Securities Exchange Act of 1934, must also (1) maintain books and records that accurately and fairly reflect the company's transactions, and (2) design adequate internal accounting controls sufficient to provide reasonable assurances that management has authorized all transactions and that all transactions are recorded.[189] Subsidiaries and affiliates must comply with these requirements as well.[190] Implementing adequate accounting procedures may protect contractors from criminal liability, which requires that the contractor know of its failure to meet these requirements or falsify its records.[191]

Q 14.11.10 Are there any kinds of payments to officials that are permitted?

Yes; the FCPA does permit payments to officials to expedite or facilitate performance of a routine government action, such as:

- obtaining proper official documentation to do business in a foreign country (but not including discretionary approval of said documents);
- processing governmental papers (*e.g.*, a visa);
- providing police protection, mail services, or inspections related to the contract;

- providing utilities, protecting products from deterioration, or loading and/or unloading products.[192]

Q 14.11.11 What are the penalties for violations?

Penalties for violating the FCPA include:

- criminal fines of up to $2 million for each contractor's "willful" violation of the FCPA and individual fines of up to $100,000 for company officials (the company may not pay fines on behalf of the officials);
- imprisonment of company officials for up to five years, according to the Federal Sentencing Guidelines (see chapter 2 for a discussion of the Federal Sentencing Guidelines);
- a civil fine of $10,000.[193]

The general civil and criminal penalties of the Securities Exchange Act of 1934 apply where violations of the accounting requirements occur.[194] Civil penalties include fines of up to $100,000 for individuals and $500,000 for companies, in addition to any other action that the SEC or the attorney general is entitled to bring.[195]

Personal Conflicts of Interest

Q 14.11.12 What kinds of relationships may create personal conflicts of interest?

In general, statutes and regulations restrict three types of "revolving door" issues:

(1) current government employees seeking future employment with contractors;
(2) former government employees working for or on behalf of contractors; and
(3) former contractor employees now working in the government.

Many situations that may create an appearance of a personal conflict of interest expose a contractor to liability. Therefore, contractors should establish a system for conflict avoidance to adhere to the following restrictions. In addition, compliance policies and procedures must reflect the FAR's integrity reporting requirement to timely disclose to the government credible evidence of the criminal personal conflict of interest statutes in title 18 of the U.S. Code, which are discussed below.[196]

Q 14.11.13 What are the restrictions on current government employees seeking employment from government contractors?

Government employees may not participate personally and substantially in a matter affecting the financial interest of any person or organization with whom the employee is negotiating employment opportunities or has any arrangement concerning prospective employment.[197] Government employees and contractor employees who knowingly violate this law may face civil and criminal penalties.[198] Moreover, it is grounds for suspension and debarment if a contractor fails to timely disclose knowledge of credible evidence of violations of the statutes in title 18 of the U.S. Code criminalizing certain personal conflicts of interest.[199]

Criminal liability arises where a current government employee participates in any particular government matter that would affect the financial interests of any contractor with which the employee is negotiating, or has an arrangement, for future employment.[200] The employee must recuse him/herself from working on the matter even if merely discussing potential employment with a government contractor.[201]

A contractor may also be exposed to criminal and civil liability, in addition to administrative remedies such as contract rescission, when an employee "personally and substantially" participates in a procurement in certain specific functions involving:

- the specification or statement of work;
- the solicitation;
- the evaluation of bids or proposals, or selecting a source;
- negotiation of price terms and conditions of the contract; or
- the review or approval of the award of a contract.[202]

A government employee participating in such a manner must report the contact with the contractor and reject the prospective employment or recuse him/herself from the procurement.[203] The employee must also submit a notice disqualifying him/herself from further participation.[204]

Q 14.11.14 What are the restrictions on former government employees currently working for government contractors?

A former government employee who served in specific contracting roles or performed specific contracting functions on certain contract matters over $10 million generally may not receive compensation from the contractor for service as an employee, officer, director, or consultant for one year.[205] However, an employee may work for a division or affiliate of the contractor that does not produce the same or similar products or services as those involved in the $10 million procurement.[206]

A former government employee who personally and substantially participates in a competitive procurement in excess of $150,000 must follow specific procedures outlined in the Procurement Integrity Act if s/he receives an offer of non-federal employment from an offeror.[207] The official must immediately report the contact to the agency and must either reject the employment offer or disqualify him/herself from further participation in the federal procurement.[208]

A former government employee is also subject to criminal liability if s/he violates other restrictions regarding communications with the government. These restrictions vary in duration and depend on the type of position held while working for the government.[209] A former government employee is subject to the following, among other restrictions:

- a lifetime ban on the same "particular matter involving specific parties";
- a two-year ban on the same contract or matter that was pending and in the employee's chain of supervision;
- for senior employees a one-year prohibition against working on any matter involving the employee's former agency.[210]

The following table demonstrates the restrictions imposed upon a federal employee's future activities as a government contractor's employee.

TABLE 14-1
Restrictions on a Federal Employee's
Future Activities As a Contractor's Employee

Position	Restriction	Duration
Executive Branch Employee	No communicating or appearing before any department, agency, court, or court martial about matters in which employee participated personally and substantially as an executive branch employee.	permanent[211]
	No communicating or appearing before any department, agency, court, or court martial about matters that employee should know were pending under his/her official responsibility within one year before the termination of his/her federal employment.	two years after termination of federal employment[212]
Senior Executive Branch Employee	No communicating or appearing before *the department or agency in which the senior executive branch employee served* in connection with *any matter.* Employee shall not *represent, aid, or advise a foreign entity* with the intent to influence a decision of officer or employee of the United States in carrying out his/her official duties.	one year after termination of federal employment[213]

Position	Restriction	Duration
Very Senior Executive Branch Employee	No communicating or appearing before *the department or agency in which the very senior executive branch employee served.* Employee shall not *represent, aid, or advise a foreign entity* with the intent to influence a decision of officer or employee of the United States in carrying out his/her official duties.	one year after termination of federal employment[214]
Federal Procurement Personnel	If contacted by bidder or offeror regarding non-federal employment, employee must promptly report contact in writing to supervisor and designated agency ethics official; must reject possibility of non-federal employment or disqualify him/herself.	Agency must retain reports of employment contacts for two years from report submission.
	Employee shall not disclose contractor bid or proposal information or source selection information.	permanent[215]
Certain Federal Contracting Officials	Employee shall not accept compensation from a contractor as an employee, officer, director, or consultant of the contractor.	one year after a covered contracting action involving the company[216]

Q 14.11.15 What are the restrictions on government employees who previously worked for government contractors?

A government employee must recuse him/herself from any particular matter in which s/he has a financial interest. This may occur where a former employee of a government contractor has a continuing financial interest in his/her former employer, including situations where the employee receives benefits such as stock, stock options, pensions, or deferred compensation arrangements.[217] A contractor may not supplement a government employee's federal salary as compensation for serving the government.[218] A contractor may not compensate a government employee for doing his government job, rather than to compensate the person for past services.

On any contract or matter involving the former employer, a government employee must recuse him/herself:

- for one year after leaving a contractor's employment;
- for two years after receiving a payment from a former employer that was:
  (1) in excess of $10,000,
  (2) determined after the former employer knew that the individual was considered for government employment, and
  (3) not pursuant to the former employer's established compensation system;
- as long as circumstances create concerns about the employee's impartiality.[219]

Q 14.11.16 What can a contractor considering hiring a government employee do to avoid liability?

A contractor considering hiring a government employee should consider requesting that the employee obtain an ethics opinion before hiring the employee. A government employee has a right to obtain an ethics opinion from a duly authorized ethics counselor.[220] A government employee who in good faith relies on that advisory opinion in accepting compensation from a particular contractor will not be found to have knowingly violated the Procurement Integrity Act, unless the government employee has actual knowledge or reason to believe that the opinion is based upon fraudulent, misleading, or otherwise incorrect information.[221] It is important to note that, while this opinion is sufficient to protect the former government employee, it may not be sufficient to protect a contractor from an OCI allegation under FAR 9.5.

Organizational Conflicts of Interest

Q 14.11.17 Under what circumstances might organizational conflicts of interest arise during the performance of a government contract?

As described above, a contractor seeking a government contract should follow procedures for detecting organizational conflicts of interest and for disclosing known OCIs in offers, bids, and proposals for contracts. Although agencies make OCI determinations prior to awarding contracts, OCIs may also arise after award, for example, as a result of a merger and acquisition. As a result, a contractor may find that it has an OCI that it must disclose to the agency. This makes it imperative that the contractor know the OCI disclosure requirements for each agency for which it performs. In the event of a merger and acquisition, a contractor must review and analyze past and current contracts of all business units to ensure that its certification as to the existence of OCIs remains accurate. By not checking for any OCIs, a contractor may face civil and/or criminal penalties for making false claims and statements to the government.

Lobbying

Q 14.11.18 What kinds of lobbying activities are restricted?

Government contractors may not use appropriated funds to attempt to influence the award or modification of a contract.[222] Appropriated funds include funds provided to a federal agency pursuant to an annual appropriations act or permanent law for the purpose of making payments out of the U.S. Treasury for specified purposes.

Pursuant to the statute, each person who requests or receives a federal contract, grant, loan, or cooperative agreement in excess of $100,000 must furnish a declaration consisting of both a certification and a disclosure.[223] (Lobbying disclosure requirements are discussed further in the next section.) The FAR also requires that suspected violations must be reported to an agency appointed official.[224]

Civil penalties include fines ranging from $10,000 to $100,000 in addition to other civil remedies.[225] To avoid liability, contractors should establish a policy against hiring lobbyists or adjust their accounting systems to prevent charging the government for unallowable costs associated with lobbyists.

Lobbying Disclosures

Q 14.11.19 What kinds of lobbying requirements must federal contractors comply with?

The Lobbying Disclosure Act of 1995[226] requires (with a few exceptions) that certain individuals and organizations register with the Clerk of the House and the Secretary of the Senate within forty-five days after making a lobbying contact or being employed to initiate a lobbying contact with a covered legislative or executive branch official (including staff).[227] Individuals who must register include those spending at least 20% of their time on lobbying activities. Any organization employing at least one lobbyist must also register.

Lobbying contacts include oral or written communications made to officials on behalf of a client with regard to the administration or execution of a federal program of policy, including negotiation, award, or administration of a federal contract.[228]

Each registrant must file semiannual reports with the Clerk of the House and the Secretary of the Senate that disclose the specific issues being lobbied, his/her clients, estimates of lobbying income and expenses, and interests of foreign entities.[229]

Penalties include a civil fine of up to $50,000.[230] The most difficult situation occurs where a contractor hires outside individuals or firms to perform some lobbying services while employees also provide some of the same services.

Unreasonable Restrictions on Subcontractor Sales

Q 14.12 What are a contractor's ethical obligations in relation to subcontractors?

In contracts over $150,000, the prime contractor may not unreasonably restrict a subcontractor's ability to make direct sales to the United States of any supplies or services made or furnished under a contract.[231]

Employment/Wage-and-Hour Compliance Issues

Q 14.13 What wage-and-hour statutes and regulations should a compliance program account for?

Contractor compliance plans should include policies and procedures to ensure compliance with the following statutes and regulations:

1. Davis-Bacon Act;
2. Service Contract Act;
3. Walsh-Healey Public Contracts Act;
4. Equal Employment Opportunity;
5. Drug-Free Workplace Act;
6. employment eligibility verification rules; and
7. recent executive orders.

Although many of these issues are discussed elsewhere in this book, the following questions and answers discuss the relevance of these statutes and regulations in the context of government contract regulations. Violating these regulations may subject government contractors to criminal, civil, administrative, and/or contractual liability, as discussed elsewhere in this chapter.

Q 14.13.1 Is a contractor required to report its company's compliance with labor and employment laws?

Yes. Executive Order 13673[232] requires, for contracts and subcontracts over $500,000, that contractors and subcontractors self-report whether there has been a decision rendered against the contractor within the previous three years for violation of any of a number of state and federal labor laws.[233] The FAR Council released a proposed FAR amendment on May 28, 2015, implementing Executive Order 13673.[234] The propose rule, if finally implemented, would add a new FAR subpart 22.20 and related sections in parts 9 and 52. These include the Fair Labor Standards Act, OSHA, the National Labor Relations Act, the Davis-Bacon Act, the Service Contract Act, the Equal Employment Opportunity regulations, the Family and Medical Leave Act, and the Americans with Disabilities Act. The contracting officer must provide the contractor an opportunity to make a disclosure prior to the award of a covered contract and at six-month intervals

431

during the course of contract performance. That opportunity must include an opportunity for the contractor to disclose any steps it has taken to correct the violations of or to improve compliance with any laws it has violated. Prime contractors are required to flow down these requirements to their subcontractors and certify to the contracting officer that they have done so.

Q 14.13.2   What is the information a contractor supplies in the labor law disclosures used for?

Executive Order 13673 requires that the contracting officer consider the disclosures pre-award in determining whether the contractor is a "responsible source that has a satisfactory record of integrity and business ethics" and thus whether it should receive an award. During contract performance, the contracting officer is instructed to use the information, in consultation with the agency's labor compliance officer, to determine whether action is necessary to require appropriate remedial measures to avoid further violations, as well as remedies such as decisions not to exercise an option on a contract, contract termination, or referral to the agency suspending and debarring official. Prime contractors are required to use disclosures received from their subcontractors in making similar decisions about subcontracts and in making disclosures to the contracting officer.

Q 14.13.3   Is an employer's right to arbitrate employment disputes limited?

Yes. Pursuant to Executive Order 13673, in contracts with estimated values in excess of $1 million, contractors are prohibited from requiring an employee to arbitrate title VII claims or claims arising out of sexual assault or harassment, except upon the voluntary consent of employees and independent contractors obtained after the dispute arises. This limitation does not apply where the employees are covered by a valid collective bargaining agreement.

Q 14.13.4   What are a government contractor's obligations regarding compliance with the Davis-Bacon Act?

Solicitations for construction within the United States valued in excess of $2,000 include a contract clause implementing Davis-Bacon

Act requirements.[235] In general, a government construction contractor must:

- unconditionally pay all laborers and mechanics the full amount of wages and fringe benefits due at time of payment at least once per week;[236]
- pay rates not less than those contained in the Secretary of Labor's wage determination attached to the solicitation (or contract) for the classification of work actually performed;[237]
- post the wage determination and the Davis-Bacon poster at its worksites for the contract at all times.[238]

Related contract clauses also require that construction contractors:

- submit weekly payroll including accurate and complete information on rates accompanied by a certification;[239]
- certify that the payroll is correct and complete and that the contractor has paid its employees the full weekly wages earned.[240]

Failure to provide records or make records available may result in suspension and debarment.[241] Noncompliance or false certifications may subject the contractor and its employees to criminal penalties, civil liability, and administrative and/or contractual remedies as described above.

Q 14.13.5   ... with the Service Contract Act?

Service contracts over $2,500 contain mandatory provisions regarding:

- minimum wages and fringe benefits;
- safe and sanitary working conditions;
- notification to employees of the minimum allowable compensation; and
- equivalent federal employee classifications and wage rates.[242]

Service contracts may not exceed five years.[243] Many exemptions to the Service Contract Act exist.[244] For example, the Service Contract Act does not apply to contracts with the United States for construction, alteration, or repair of public buildings or public works, including painting and decorating. The contract will include any applicable Service Contract Act clauses absent contractor certification that an exemption applies.

By entering the contract, the contractor and its officials certify that the contractor is eligible for award and complies with the Service Contract Act.[245] Signing a contract when not in compliance constitutes a false statement that may subject the contractor and its employees to criminal penalties, civil liability, administrative, and/or contractual remedies as described above.[246]

Q 14.13.6   ... with the Walsh-Healey Public Contracts Act?

In contracts with the United States for the manufacture or furnishing of materials, supplies, articles, and equipment in excess of $10,000, government contractors must represent and stipulate that:

- all employees will be paid at least minimum wage;
- employees will not be required to work in excess of forty hours per week;
- no male person under sixteen years of age, female person under eighteen years of age, or convict labor will be employed; and
- working conditions will not be unsanitary, hazardous, or dangerous to the health and safety of employees.[247]

Indefinite-delivery contracts, basic ordering agreements, and subcontracts under section 8(a) of the Small Business Act are subject to these requirements. Statutory and regulatory exemptions exist.[248] For example, the Walsh-Healey Act does not apply to perishables, agricultural or farm products, or public utility services.

Compliance with the safety, sanitary, and factory inspection laws of the state in which the work or part thereof is to be performed demonstrates compliance with the Walsh-Healey Public Contract Act.[249] Noncompliance or false certifications may subject the contractor and its employees to criminal penalties, civil liability, administrative and/or contractual remedies as described above.

Q 14.13.7   ... with Equal Employment Opportunity requirements?

All government contracts require compliance with the Equal Opportunity clause in Executive Order 11246, unless exempt.[250]

Government contractors, not construction contractors, with fifty or more employees and a contract of at least $50,000 (or bills of lading expected to total at least $50,000 in a twelve-month period) must develop a written affirmative action program for each of its establishments within 120 days of the commencement of its work.[251] For contracts of at least $10 million, contractors must obtain pre-award clearance from the Office of Federal Contract Compliance Programs to confirm that the contractor complies with the requirements of Executive Order 11246.[252]

All or part of the requirements may not apply for contracts involving national security and for specific contracts where the Deputy Assistant Secretary of the Department of Labor determines that the national interest requires an exemption.[253] In limited circumstances, even though a contract includes the Equal Opportunity clause, exemptions apply for:

(1) transactions for $10,000 or less;
(2) work outside the United States;
(3) contracts with a state or local government;
(4) work on or near Indian reservations;
(5) facilities not connected with contracts;
(6) an indefinite-quantity contract;
(7) contracts with religious entities.[254]

The FAR requires that contracts include the Equal Opportunity clause, as well as other related clauses. The Equal Opportunity clause generally requires that all government contractors treat all employees and potential employees without engaging in any discriminatory practices.[255] Related clauses also prohibit the use of segregated facilities[256] and require representations regarding equal opportunity obligations in previous contracts and submission of compliance reports.[257] Construction contracts have similar requirements under separate clauses.[258]

A contractor must also submit forms and permit review of its records during agency compliance evaluations. Noncompliance or falsification of records may subject the contractor to criminal penalties, civil liability, administrative remedies, and contractual remedies, as described above.

In addition to criminal penalties, civil liability, administrative remedies, and contractual remedies, government contractors in violation of the Equal Opportunity clause may face penalties including publication of the names of the contractor or its unions; cancellation, termination, or suspension of contracts; and/or debarment.[259]

Q 14.13.8   ... with the Drug-Free Workplace Act?

Government contractors must agree to provide a drug-free workplace.[260] Violations of the Drug-Free Workplace Act subject government contractors to suspension of payments, termination of the contract, debarment for a period of up to five years, and/or other remedies as available.[261]

Q 14.13.9   ... under other recent executive orders?

Because government contractors are subject to executive-branch control to an extent that most other employers are not, President Obama has issued a number of executive orders that regulate employment practices in the government contracting industry. As with Executive Order 13673, discussed above, these executive orders, and their implementing regulations not only contain their own enforcement mechanisms, fines, and penalties, but also potentially impact a finding that the contractor is "responsible," for purposes of obtaining government contracts. These executive orders include:

- Executive Order 13495, which requires successor contractors to make job offers to certain employees of the incumbent contractor who would otherwise lose their jobs as a result of the transition from one contract to another;[262]
- Executive Order 13496, which requires government contractors to post notice of employees' rights under federal labor laws;[263]
- Executive Order 13658, which requires most government contractors to pay an enhanced minimum wage, amounting to $10.15 per hour for the period beginning January 1, 2016;[264]
- Executive Order 13665, which protects employees' rights to discuss their own and others' pay and benefits with other employees, so long as the employees obtain that information through ordinary means, and not as part of their essential job functions—that is, not from confidential official compensation files;[265]

- Executive Order 13706, which requires government contractors to offer up to fifty-six hours of paid sick leave per year to employees to cover the employee's own illness and medical care, care of sick spouses or family members, and attention to counseling and legal issues arising out of domestic violence, sexual assault, or stalking.[266]

Q 14.14 Are government contractors subject to any special employment verification requirements?

Yes. Most federal contracts with a period of performance greater than 120 days and valued over $150,000[267] contain FAR 52.222-54 (Employment Eligibility Verification), which requires contractors and subcontractors to use the E-Verify system to verify the employment eligibility of:

- all new employees hired to work in the United States during the contract term after they complete Form I-9, Employee Eligibility Verification Form;
- all existing employees who are "assigned to the contract" (for example, these employees generally work directly on the government contract within the United States; this would not include an employee in a support role such as an indirect or overhead function who does not perform any substantial duties on the contract).

However, contracts for commercially available off-the-shelf items are not required to include this clause. When included in a prime contract, this clause must also be flowed down to subcontracts for services or construction valued over $3,000 to be performed in the United States.

Q 14.15 What is E-Verify?

E-Verify is a free, government-run, web-based system that electronically verifies the employment eligibility of employees. Participating employers register online and use the system to electronically compare information from an individual's I-9 Form against more than 425 million records in the Social Security Administration's database and more than 60 million records in Department of Homeland Security databases. E-Verify only establishes employment eligibility—it does not verify an individual's immigration status.[268]

Q 14.15.1   Are there E-Verify exemptions?

Contractors do not generally need to verify an employee if the contractor has already verified his/her employment through E-Verify, if the employee holds certain active U.S. government security clearances, or if the employee has been issued certain credentials after completing a background investigation.[269]

Q 14.15.2   Must a contractor verify its entire workforce?

No. However, a contractor may elect to verify all of its existing employees (hired after November 6, 1986), rather than verify those employees assigned to the contract. A contractor electing to verify its entire workforce is required to initiate verification for each employee within 180 days of enrollment in E-Verify or notification to E-Verify Operations of the contractor's decision to verify its entire workforce.[270]

Q 14.15.3   When must a contractor enroll and use E-Verify?

If a contractor is not enrolled in E-Verify at the time of the contract award, the contractor must enroll in E-Verify within thirty calendar days of contract award.[271] Once enrolled, the contractor has ninety calendar days to begin using E-Verify to verify the employment eligibility of *all* new hires, whether or not assigned to the contract, within three business days after the date of hire.[272] The contractor must verify the employment eligibility of each employee assigned to the contract within ninety calendar days after the date of enrollment or within thirty calendar days of the employee's assignment to the contract—whichever date is later.[273]

If a contractor is already enrolled in E-Verify at the time of contract award, the contractor must verify all new employees within three business days after the date of hire if the contractor has already been enrolled for ninety calendar days or more.[274] If the contractor has been enrolled for less than ninety days, the contractor has a ninety-day window after enrollment to begin verification of all new hires within three business days after the hire date. For each employee assigned to the government contract, the contractor must begin using E-Verify within ninety calendar days after the contract award or within thirty calendar days of the employee's assignment to the contract—whichever date is later.[275]

Intellectual Property Compliance Issues

Q 14.16   What proprietary intellectual property concerns should a compliance program account for?

Statutes and regulations protect both contractor and government rights in intellectual property use and ownership. The FAR includes clauses that cover rights in:

1. technical data and computer software;
2. copyrighted works; and
3. patented inventions.

These clauses as well as the rights in and licenses for use of intellectual property can be quite complicated.

Q 14.16.1   What technical data and computer software rights should a government contractor be concerned with?

A government contractor should be concerned about any data or computer software delivered to the government under a government contract in which the contractor desires to retain intellectual property rights. Such retained intellectual property rights are necessary to allow the contractor to modify, copy, create derivative works, license, sell, or otherwise transfer the data or software after the government contract is completed.

Data generally includes any recorded information, regardless of form or the media on which it may be recorded, including computer software.[276] Computer software includes source code listings, design details, algorithms, processes, flow charts, formulas, and related material that would enable the computer program to be produced, created, or compiled.[277]

Generally, the rights a contractor grants to the government and is allowed to retain in data and software is determined by the policies of FAR subpart 27.4 (for defense contracts, DFARS subparts 227.71 and

227.72), the related contract clauses that are specifically incorporated into the contract, and the circumstances under which the contractor developed or created the data or software. However, retaining intellectual property rights in data and software requires the contractor to take specific affirmative steps to assert and protect its rights, which are set forth in the contract clauses.

Generally, in regard to data or computer software that is *first produced in the performance of a government contract*, a contractor grants to the government "unlimited rights."[278] In this situation, the government acquires unlimited rights in the data or software to use, disclose, reproduce, prepare derivative works, distribute copies to the public, and perform publicly and display publicly, in any manner and for any purpose, and to have or permit others to do so.[279] Subject to the unlimited rights granted to the government, the rights retained by the contractor in data or software first produced in the performance of a government contract include (1) the right to assert copyright in such data or software; and (2) the right to use, release to others, reproduce, distribute, or publish such data or software, unless prohibited by law, express terms of the contract, or restrictive markings on data received by the contractor that was necessary for the performance of the contract.[280]

As a general matter, for computer software that the contractor *develops entirely at private expense* and that is a trade secret, is commercial or financial and confidential or privileged, or is copyrighted, a contractor grants only "*restricted rights*" to the government and retains all other rights.[281] Generally, restricted software may not be used, reproduced, or disclosed by the government, except restricted software may be:

- used or copied for use with the computer(s) for which it was acquired, including use at any government installation to which the computer(s) may be transferred;
- used or copied for use with a backup computer if any computer for which it was acquired is inoperative or with a replacement computer;
- reproduced for safekeeping (archives) or backup purposes;
- modified, adapted, or combined with other computer software, *provided* that the modified, adapted, or combined portions of the derivative software incorporating any of the

delivered, restricted computer software shall be subject to the same restricted rights; and

- disclosed to and reproduced for use by support service contractors or their subcontractors subject to certain restrictions.[282]

For data (other than software) that pertain to items, components, or processes *developed at private expense* that embody trade secrets or are commercial or financial and confidential or privileged, a contractor grants only "*limited rights*" to the government and retains all other rights.[283] Generally, limited rights data may be reproduced and used by the government with the express limitation that they will not, without written permission of the contractor, be used for purposes of manufacture nor disclosed outside the government— except that the government may disclose the data outside the government for specific purposes, provided that the government makes such disclosure subject to the prohibition against further use and disclosure.[284]

A key compliance issue for contractors seeking to protect data or computer software delivered to the government under a contract is to take the steps required to assert and preserve whatever rights they may retain in such data or software. The applicable clauses set forth specific requirements and procedures that a contractor *must follow* to avoid waiving their intellectual property rights in data and computer software. Such mandatory requirements include affixing a "limited rights notice" on limited rights data or a "restricted rights notice" on restricted software *prior to delivery* to the government.[285] In addition, the applicable clauses set forth procedures that a contractor must follow in order to assert copyright in data and computer software first produced in the performance of a contract, including when a contractor is required to obtain the prior written consent of the government to assert copyright in such data or software.[286] Compliance with all applicable procedural requirements is important to asserting and preserving a contractor's rights to prevent the unauthorized disclosure and use of intellectual property by the government and other third parties.

A contractor must be prepared to justify and defend any restrictive markings placed on limited rights data or restricted software.[287] A contracting officer may inspect data at the contractor's facility pursuant to a contract clause granting the right to inspect. The contracting officer or designee may inspect the data to verify the contractor's assertion of the limited rights status of data or restricted rights status of computer software, or for evaluating work performance under the contract.[288] If the asserted restriction is found not to be substantially justified, the contractor must pay the costs incurred by the government for reviewing the asserted restriction as well as fees and other expenses.[289]

Contractor compliance plans should also include policies and procedures to ensure compliance with statutes and regulations requiring the contractor to furnish written assurances at the time when the data is delivered or is made available that the data is complete and accurate and satisfies the requirements of the contract.[290]

During performance of a government contract, a contractor may also obtain proprietary data from another contractor in limited circumstances. For example, a contractor may obtain proprietary data to make repairs. In these circumstances, the contractor would receive this data from the government with strict prohibition against further use and disclosure of the data.[291] Compliance plans should include procedures for ensuring proper use and nondisclosure of this data.

Q 14.16.2   What copyright protections should a government contractor be concerned with?

A government contractor should be concerned about asserting and protecting the copyright in all data and computer software delivered to the government under a government contract. The policies and procedures applicable to contractor assertions of copyright are generally set forth in the FAR and applicable contract clauses.[292]

In general, a contractor may obtain a copyright in data first produced in the performance of a government contract.[293] However, in situations where a contractor is forced to incorporate data already under another company's copyright protection into the data it is delivering under its contract, the contractor should first obtain necessary copyright license rights for the copyrighted work from the government.[294] The contract may include a clause requiring the contractor to indemnify the government and agents against any liability incurred as the result of the violation of copyright or any libelous or other unlawful matter contained in such data.[295] Compliance programs should include procedures for tracking ownership and disclosure of data protected by copyright.

Q 14.16.3 What rights in patented inventions should a government contractor be concerned with?

With regard to patented inventions under the FAR, contractors agree to protect the government's interest in the inventions by disclosing all patented inventions made under both prime contracts and subcontracts, as well as by providing reports regarding subject inventions.[296] Further, contractors must establish and maintain active and effective procedures to assure prompt identification and disclosure of patented inventions to contractor personnel responsible for patent matters.[297] Contractor procedures must include maintenance of laboratory notebooks and other records as are reasonably necessary to document the conception and/or the first actual reduction to practice of subject inventions, and records that show compliance with the procedures for identifying and disclosing patented inventions.[298] The contracting officer may withhold payment for failure to establish, maintain, and follow effective procedures for identifying and disclosing subject inventions, to disclose any subject invention, to deliver acceptable reports, or to provide information regarding subcontracts.[299]

Violating statutory and regulatory requirements regarding required disclosures, representations, and communications with the government may subject government contractors to criminal, civil, administrative, and/or contractual liability, as discussed elsewhere in this chapter.

Domestic and Foreign Preferences

Q 14.17 What are a government contractor's obligations regarding the products/ components and services it uses?

A contractor must take care to comply with procurement laws relating to the country of origin of any goods procured by the government. Understanding the rules that impose the government's preferences and limitations on the national origin of products and services acquired from domestic and foreign sources may help a contractor avoid potentially severe penalties or losing a contract award.

Violating statutes and regulations regarding domestic and foreign preference requirements may subject government contractors to criminal, civil, administrative, and/or contractual liability, as discussed elsewhere in this chapter.

During the performance of a government contract, a contractor must comply with its certification (usually made in its offer) that it will supply end products that comply with the applicable domestic preference requirement. As discussed elsewhere, violating such a certification may expose a contractor to liability, including under the False Claims Act. In order to avoid such liability, a compliance program should include a procedure to adequately screen the country of origin of end products supplied to the government.

Q 14.17.1 What domestic and foreign preference statutes and regulations should a compliance program account for?

Contractor compliance plans should include policies and procedures to ensure compliance with, among others:

1. Buy American Act;
2. Trade Agreements Act;
3. Berry Amendment;
4. Fly American Act;
5. Arms Export Control Act; and
6. Foreign Military Sales Program.

Q 14.17.2 What are a government contractor's obligations regarding compliance with the Buy American Act?

In procurements valued above $3,000 and below $203,000, the Buy American Act restricts the purchase of supplies that are not domestic end products.[300] A "domestic end product" is either an unmanufactured end product mined or produced in the United States, or an end product manufactured in the United States where the cost of the end product's domestic components exceeds 50% of the total component cost.[301] For manufactured items, the 50% "component test" does not apply to commercial off-the-shelf (COTS) items, as that term is defined in FAR 2.101.[302] The Buy American Act requires contractors to certify that products are domestic end products.[303]

In addition to the Buy American Act, transactions involving certain foreign countries or situations are prohibited.[304] The Office of Foreign Assets Control (OFAC) maintains a list of Specially Designated Nationals and Blocked Persons at www.treas.gov/offices/enforcement/ofac/sdn.

The Buy American Act (as implemented in FAR part 25) is one of the main vehicles through which domestic preferences are enforced, but there are many other statutes that include "Buy American" provisions. Many of these requirements are similar, but not identical, to the Buy American Act. For example, the American Reinvestment and Recovery Act (the "Recovery Act")[305] and the implementing regulations in the FAR prohibit the use of Recovery Act funds for any project for the construction, alteration, maintenance, or repair of a public building or a public work unless all of the iron, steel, and manufactured goods used in the project are produced in the United States. This means that the Recovery Act, as implemented by the FAR, requires that contractors "use only domestic construction material" in performing construction contracts that use Recovery Act funds. There is no cost of components requirement for the Recovery Act.

This section describes the general requirements and exceptions to the Buy American Act; this does not represent the entire analysis that must be performed to determine compliance with the Buy American Act. There is a maze of statutes and regulations that include various "Buy American" provisions, complicating the determination of which "Buy American" requirements apply, how to comply with the applicable requirements, and what information is needed in order to make an accurate certification.

Q 14.17.3 Are there any exemptions to the Buy American Act?

The Buy American Act does not apply to:

- end products or materials procured for use outside the United States;[306]
- items procured that are not mined, manufactured, or produced in sufficient commercial quantities or satisfactory quality in the United States;[307]
- end products purchased specifically for commissary resale;[308]

- cases where the head of the agency determines that domestic preference is not in the public interest;[309]
- cases where the contracting officer determines that the cost of a domestic end product would be unreasonable;[310]
- the acquisition of information technology that is a commercial item, when using fiscal year 2004 or subsequent fiscal year funds;[311]
- cases where the contracting officer, after evaluating offers of foreign construction material, concludes that the cost of domestic construction material is unreasonable.[312]

Department of Defense acquisitions are subject to slightly different requirements. Acquisitions of end products in designated Federal Supply Groups are covered by trade agreements if the value of the acquisition is at or above the applicable trade agreement threshold and no exception applies.[313] If an end product is not in one of the listed groups, the trade agreements do not apply. In general, where end products are not included in the Federal Supply Groups, the solicitation will be subject to the Department of Defense's Buy American Act requirements.

Department of Transportation (DOT) grants for construction projects are subject to the Buy *America* Act, which is distinct from the Buy *American* Act. Under the Buy America Act, DOT requires grant recipients to use domestic steel, iron, and manufactured products in DOT construction projects, including those funded by the Recovery Act. However, an analysis of what constitutes compliance with these agency-specific requirements is further complicated by differing interpretations of the various agencies, such as the Federal Highway Administration (FHWA) and Federal Transit Administration (FTA), whose regulations implement the same Buy America Act requirements differently. For example:

TABLE 14-2
Comparison of Agency Interpretations of Buy America Act

FHWA	FTA
Grant recipients are required to use domestic steel and iron materials that are to be permanently incorporated in a federal aid project.	Grant recipients are required to use only domestic items (not just those including iron and steel).
Grant recipients are not required to use domestically manufactured products other than those including iron and steel.	All of the components included in the item must be manufactured in the United States.

These examples demonstrate that complying with Buy American requirements can be complicated.

The government has waived Buy American Act restrictions with regard to products from certain countries that have signed an international trade agreement with the United States.[314] Trade agreements generally permit the government to procure from other countries end products that meet certain criteria. For example, the government may acquire end products from "designated" countries that have signed an international trade agreement with the United States, such as a World Trade Organization Government Procurement Agreement (WTO/GPA) country, a Caribbean Basin country, or a least-developed country.[315]

Q 14.17.4 What remedies may be sought for violations of the Buy American Act?

In addition to contractor liability and/or penalties as described elsewhere, a violation of the Buy American Act may result in additional liability for contracts involving construction or construction materials. For example, a contractor may bear costs of furnishing domestically made construction materials to replace improperly supplied foreign-made construction materials.[316] The government may also reduce the contract price, even if the government permits continued supply of the foreign construction materials.[317]

The government may also suspend a contractor for up to three years from any public construction contract if the contractor or its subcontractors, materialmen, or affiliated suppliers fail to comply with the Buy American Act.[318]

Customs laws also impose monetary fines up to $250,000 and allow for imprisonment of up to one year for any intent to conceal the actual country of origin for end products.[319] The Customs Service has published detailed regulations for obtaining a final determination or an advisory ruling regarding the country of origin of a contractor's foreign product.[320]

Q 14.17.5 What are a government contractor's obligations regarding compliance with the Trade Agreements Act?

For procurements meeting the WTO/GPA threshold, the government will generally exempt products from over 100 countries from any evaluation penalties. These countries include qualifying countries, designated countries, least-developed countries, and countries designated under the Caribbean Basin Trade Initiative.[321] However, certain key manufacturing countries, such as China, Malaysia, India, and the Philippines, are not exempt.

Contractors must pay close attention to what is permitted on each contract. Because signatories to trade agreements may change, the applicable contract clause for each contract must be checked to determine which countries qualify as designated countries for that contract.

For procurements under this threshold, the government does not consider whether the product was manufactured in a designated or nondesignated country. Rather, these procurements treat all products manufactured in foreign countries as foreign end products. However, these procurements are still subject to the lower dollar threshold requirements of the North American Free Trade Agreement (NAFTA) and the Israeli Trade Act (also known as the U.S.–Israel Free Trade Area Agreement).[322]

Q 14.17.6 ... with the Berry Amendment?

When procurements use Department of Defense funding, the Berry Amendment requires that certain items be grown, reprocessed, reused, or produced in the United States:

- food;
- clothing;
- tents, tarpaulins, or covers;
- cotton and other natural fiber products, woven silk or woven silk blends, spun silk yarn for cartridge cloth, synthetic fabric or coated synthetic fabric (including all textile fibers and yarns that are for use in such fabrics), canvas products, or wool;
- any item of individual equipment manufactured from or containing such fibers, yarns, fabrics, or materials;
- hand or measuring tools.[323]

Items not grown, reprocessed, reused, or produced in the United States may qualify for one of the limited exemptions from the Berry Amendment.[324]

The original Berry Amendment excluded Department of Defense specialty metals and applied generally to textile materials. However, contracts entered after July 2009 may include a clause that places restrictions on the acquisition of certain articles that contain specialty metals.[325] Each contract should be checked to determine whether the July 2009 version of the DFARS clause is included. This clause requires that specialty metals incorporated into items delivered under certain contracts be melted or produced in the United States, its outlying areas, or a "qualifying country." This clause has limited exemptions for certain acquisitions and may be waived by a written determination that acceptance of the item is necessary to the national security interests of the United States. If the contract includes a prior version of this clause, different requirements apply. As such, it is imperative to understand the requirements of the clause included in each contract.

Q 14.17.7 ... with the Fly American Act?

The Fly American Act creates certain preferences for U.S. air carriers. It requires all federal agencies, government contractors, and subcontractors to use available U.S.-flag air carriers for U.S. government-financed international air transportation of personnel (and their personal effects) or property.[326] The FAR also includes implementing provisions. However, these provisions do not apply to contracts using the simplified acquisition procedures for FAR part 13 or contracts for commercial items.[327] Contractors should see the FAR clause in contracts where this act applies.

Q 14.17.8   ... with the Arms Export Control Act?

The Arms Export Control Act (AECA) sets forth a broad framework for controlling the export of "defense articles and defense services" by requiring mandatory licensing to "friendly" countries under certain circumstances.[328] The AECA requires that all manufacturers, exporters, and importers of defense articles or defense services register with the Department of State and obtain a license issued by the Directorate of Defense Trade Controls in order to sell or transfer any item on the U.S. Munitions List to the control or possession of a "foreign person" or a person acting on behalf of a foreign person.[329] Persons engaging in brokering activities relating to the manufacture, export, import, or transfer of defense articles or defense services also must register.

Relevant terms, export licensing requirements, and the U.S. Munitions List are defined and set forth in the International Traffic in Arms Regulations (ITAR), pursuant to the AECA. For example, ITAR defines "defense article" as "any item or technical data" designated on the U.S. Munitions List, which contains twenty-one categories of items.[330] "Defense services" include providing assistance or training to "foreign persons," whether in the United States or abroad.[331] A "foreign person" includes *any* "natural person who is not a lawful permanent resident."[332] A "foreign person" also generally includes any entity or group not incorporated or organized to do business in the United States.[333] Contractors are often surprised to learn that under the ITAR, the contractor has "exported" technical data merely by "disclosing (including oral or visual disclosure) or transferring technical data to a foreign person, *whether in the United States or abroad.*"[334]

Q 14.17.9   What are the Arms Export Control Act's licensing requirements?

To obtain an export license, a contractor must meet certain eligibility requirements, such as not having been convicted of violating certain criminal statutes, debarred, or the subject of an indictment of certain criminal statutes.[335] A "foreign person" may *not* obtain a license to export an item on the U.S. Munitions List.[336] Some exemptions to obtaining a license exist. However, contractors exporting defense articles—including technical data—that are exempt from the license requirement must still adhere to other export requirements set forth in the regulations, such as notification letters, declarations, record maintenance, certifications, non-transfer and use assurances, and other reporting requirements.[337]

Contractors that hire foreign national employees must obtain a license from the Department of State's Directorate of Defense Trade Controls to allow the employee access to technical data or defense services required for performing his or her responsibilities. Also, certain technologies, such as the Missile Technology Control Regime Annex, are subject to stringent export restrictions that require consideration during the hiring process. As part of its compliance program, a contractor with foreign national employees should also consider implementing a technology control plan that would set forth procedures to control access to technical data by all employees regardless of job description. These procedures might include controlled access to areas containing technical data and password protection for accessing technical data. At a minimum, implementing a technology control plan may document a contractor's good-faith effort to comply with the ITAR.

Limited exceptions for the export of technical data and defense services exist. The Canadian exemption allows certain transfers of technical data and defense services to persons registered in Canada as "crown companies."[338] Generally, this exception only applies to registered companies and not to Canadian nationals employed in the United States.

Q 14.17.10 What are the penalties for violations of the Arms Export Control Act?

Violating the Arms Export Control Act may result in criminal penalties up to $1 million per violation and up to ten years' imprisonment or civil penalties up to $500,000 per violation.[339] A contractor who violates the AECA may also lose the ability to apply for export licenses and face suspension and debarment.[340] Willful violations of the AECA or the rules or regulations issued under the AECA may incur criminal penalties of up to $1 million or imprisonment of up to ten years, or both.[341] Making false statements or omitting material facts may result in the same criminal penalties.[342] Violations of the AECA or implementing regulations may also result in civil penalties of up to $500,000.[343]

Q 14.17.11 What are a government contractor's obligations regarding compliance with the Foreign Military Sales Program?

The AECA authorized the Foreign Military Sales (FMS) Program, which authorizes the Department of Defense to enter into contracts for resale to foreign countries or international organizations.[344] The FMS Program uses formal contracts or agreements, known as Letters of Offer and Acceptance, between the United States and an authorized foreign purchaser.[345] These contracts provide for the sale of defense articles and/or defense services, including training. FMS acquisitions are conducted under the same acquisition and contract management procedures used for other defense acquisitions.[346]

Pursuant to the AECA, a contractor must obtain prior approval to sell or lease defense articles, defense services, or training to eligible foreign purchasers. Certain items may not be purchased using the FMS Program.

Counterfeit Electronic Parts

Q 14.18 What obligation does a government contractor have to ensure that the products it delivers to the government do not contain "counterfeit electronic parts"?

All government contractors have an obligation to comply with the specific requirements of their contracts concerning the origin and quality of their products. These requirements are typically detailed in specification requirements that materials meet "brand name or equal" requirements or that they be new and not refurbished, unless otherwise indicated. Contractors may also be required to indemnify the government if the products they deliver infringe the patents, trademarks, and other intellectual property rights of third parties.[347]

Effective May 6, 2014, defense contractors have a new and separate obligation to inspect for and detect "counterfeit electronic parts" and to prevent their introduction into equipment delivered to the government.[348]

Q 14.18.1   What is a "counterfeit electronic part"?

A "counterfeit electronic part" is

- an electronic component, integrated circuit, or assembly
- that is an unlawful or unauthorized reproduction, substitution, or alteration
- that has been knowingly mismarked, misidentified, or otherwise misrepresented to be
- an "authentic electronic part" manufactured either by (a) the original manufacturer; or (b) a source with the express written authority of the original manufacturer, including an authorized aftermarket manufacturer.[349]

Q 14.18.2   What does DFARS require to prevent incorporation of counterfeit electronic parts into equipment delivered to the government?

DFARS requires contractors subject to CAS and most contractors and subcontractors engaged in supplying electronic parts or equipment to the Department of Defense to establish and maintain procurement systems for the detection and avoidance of counterfeit electronic parts.[350] A proposed rule released September 21, 2015, would require contractors to obtain electronic parts only from "trusted suppliers," unless it would be impossible to do so.[351] "Trusted suppliers" include original equipment manufacturers (OEMs), authorized dealers of OEMs, and any other suppliers identified as "trustworthy" pursuant to yet-to-be defined Department of Defense standards and processes.

Q 14.18.3   What is an acceptable counterfeit electronic parts detection and avoidance system?

The criteria for an acceptable counterfeit electronic parts detection and avoidance system are detailed in DFARS 252.246-7007(c) and must include provisions for: training of personnel, testing and inspecting incoming parts, maintaining electronic part traceability, using only trusted suppliers, reporting to the government, and quarantining counterfeit or suspected counterfeit parts.

Q 14.18.4   Are there any exemptions to this rule?

Yes. DFARS 252.246-7007, Contractor Counterfeit Electronic Part Detection and Avoidance System, is not required to be included in Small Business Administration set-aside solicitations and contracts.[352]

Q 14.18.5   Is a contractor required to flow down these requirements to its subcontractors?

Yes. The clause is required to be flowed down to subcontractors and suppliers at any tier "that are responsible for buying or selling electronic parts or assemblies containing electronic parts, or for performing authentication testing."[353]

Q 14.18.6   Is a contractor required to report to the government information concerning suspected or confirmed counterfeit electronic parts?

Yes. The contractor must report to the contracting officer and to the Government-Industry Data Exchange Program (GIDEP) whenever it suspects or becomes aware that any parts purchased by or for it for delivery to the government contain counterfeit electronic parts. The counterfeit electronic parts may not be returned to the seller or otherwise returned to the supply chain until or unless they are determined in fact to be authentic.[354] The notification is required to be made within sixty days.[355]

Q 14.18.7   Are the costs of dealing with counterfeit electronic parts and any required rework or corrective action allowable?

Possibly. The costs of counterfeit electronic parts and the cost of rework or corrective action resulting from the use of such parts are unallowable unless:

(1)   the contractor has an operational system to detect counterfeit electronic parts that has been approved by the Department of Defense;

(2)   the counterfeit electronic parts are government-furnished property; and

(3)   the contractor gives timely notice to the government.[356]

Special Considerations

Compliance Issues Arising Under Particular Types of Contracts

Q 14.19   What particular types of government contracts raise special compliance issues?

Violating statutes and regulations regarding small business contracts, U.S. General Services Administration (GSA) schedule contracts, and foreign military sales contracts may subject government contractors to criminal, civil, administrative, and/or contractual liability, as discussed elsewhere in this chapter. Thus, contractor compliance plans should include policies and procedures to ensure compliance with the statutes and regulations set forth below, among others.

Q 14.19.1   What special issues should a small business compliance plan address?

Under the FAR's December 2008 compliance requirements, a small business does not need to implement internal controls system and training requirements under contracts for which it has certified its status as small. However, small businesses should remain alert to the fact that they must adhere to *all* compliance requirements on contracts for which it is other than small. Thus, small businesses should plan to implement and maintain internal controls and training if they have at least one contract for which they are other than small.

A small business contracting with the government should include procedures for tracking and recertifying the size status of the company in its compliance program. As of June 30, 2007, the U.S. Small Business Association requires that a small business performing contracts with a duration (including options) of more than five years recertify its small business size status prior to the sixth year of performance.[357] Thereafter, a contractor is required to recertify its size status prior to the exercise of an option under a long-term contract.[358] This rule does not apply to orders issued under a multiple-award contract, a blanket purchase agreement, or a subcontract.[359] For contracts with durations in excess of five years, the contracting officer must request recertification no more than 120 days prior to the end of the contract (or option).[360]

For a small business performing any set-aside contract (long-term or a traditional contract with a base year and four option years) that is subject to an approved novation, the contractor must recertify its small business size status to the procuring agency within thirty days of the novation or inform the agency that it is other than small.[361] In addition, within thirty days after a merger or acquisition that *does not require* a novation, the contractor must re-represent its size status.[362]

If the contractor certifies that it is other than small, the agency cannot count the options or orders issued under the contract toward its small business prime contracting goals.[363] When the size status changes, the government may decide not to exercise the option and resolicit the work to a small business. The government may also decide to terminate the contract for convenience if it can no longer claim small business credit for the contract.

Q 14.19.2   What issues may arise in GSA contracts?

GSA contracting officers work hard to ensure that all Multiple Award Schedule (MAS) contracts are awarded at a fair and reasonable price. To achieve this goal, GSA regulations require prospective contractors to disclose during contract negotiations key information regarding their commercial sales practices and discounting policies. Access to this information enables GSA to determine whether the prospective contractor's proposed price compares to the price the contractor extends to its category of customers that are most aligned with the government (known as the "basis of award customer(s)"). During negotiations, GSA will attempt to negotiate equal or better prices, terms, and conditions than the contractor provides to the basis of award customer(s).

Contractors disclose their commercial sales practices in tables that identify customer types and corresponding discounts extended to each. A company has many types of customers and determining which customer or category of customers is most aligned with the government requires consideration of both commercial end users and partners (authorized resellers, distributors, etc.). The commercial sales practices disclosure is fairly comprehensive, requiring sales information pertaining to all classes of non-federal customers, the terms and conditions extended to each class, any concessions, and any discounts (discretionary and exceptional) extended to each class. In preparing an offer, contractors certify that their commercial sales practices are current, accurate, and complete. Furthermore, all of this information is subject to audit. Contractors should have policies and procedures for ensuring that all sales practices, including standard and non-standard discounting and concessions in terms and conditions, are completely and accurately captured and reflected in its disclosure. At the conclusion of negotiations, GSA and the contractor will agree on the customer or category of customers that will serve as the basis of award customer(s) for the purpose of discount(s) offered to federal customers under the MAS contract.[364]

During contract performance, schedule contract holders must monitor sales to their basis of award customer(s)—with a special focus on any price discount or concession in terms—to ensure they continue to simultaneously grant the same favorable terms and conditions to the government.[365] If the contractor makes a deal with basis of award customer(s) that disturbs the price-discount relationship the contractor agreed to maintain vis-à-vis the federal customer for the same type of deal, then the contractor must extend the same price reduction or concession in terms to the government.[366] The contractor may even be required to refund money to the government.[367] Even a single transaction can trigger a reduction in the price extended to the government in the future. Thus, schedule contract holders must have compliance plans that include policies and procedures for monitoring the discount(s) provided to basis of award customer(s), so that any disturbance in that price-discount relationship results in a report to the government.

Throughout contract performance and, in particular, during pre- and post-award audits, prudent contractors will consider the following regarding their commercial sales practices:

- What are the contractor's standard discounting practices? For example, does the contractor maintain discounts for volume or duration?

- What are the contractor's non-standard discounting practices, such as competitive reasons or customer-specific circumstances?
- Has the contractor defined different customer types and do these differences adequately explain corresponding discounting practices?
- Does the contractor review and cross-reference basis of award customer sales, federal customer sales, price discounts, and concessions in terms?
- What are the contractor's procedures for ensuring that its commercial sales practices disclosures are current, accurate, and complete?

Additionally, throughout the contract period and, in particular, during post-award audits, prudent contractors will consider the following regarding the company's price reduction monitoring and reporting requirements:

- What customer or category of customers serves as the basis of award customer(s)?
- What is the price-discount relationship between the basis of award customer and the federal customer?
- Is the price-discount relationship articulated in the contract? Is it clear when the price-discount relationship might be disturbed, prompting the contractor to report the better deal to the government?
- Does the contractor have a mechanism for monitoring and recording when the price-discount relationship is disturbed? Does the mechanism distinguish between standard and non-standard discounts, those that need to be reported and those that do not?
- Does the contractor's price reduction clause compliance mechanism allow the contractor to timely report the disturbance to the government?
- If the price-discount relationship has been disturbed, has the contractor been filing price reduction modifications in a timely manner?
- Does the contractor monitor its sales for discount trends or patterns in concessions that can change non-standard discounts into standard discounts?

Another post-award requirement is the tracking and quarterly reporting of sales and payment of the Industrial Funding Fee (IFF). The IFF covers the cost of operating the MAS program and is a 0.75% user fee imposed on MAS contract holders. The IFF is built into a contractor's prices, collected from customer agencies, and paid to GSA on a quarterly basis. Contractors should have a defined and documented system for identifying sales subject to the fee. Additional post-award compliance issues include managing partner relationships by documenting agreements, notifying the government of partner relationships, timely reporting sales when partner agreements require paying the IFF where necessary, and validating/ auditing partner reported sales.

Other document management compliance issues include keeping records of all official documents, including award documents, price lists, contract modifications, and orders. All price lists, current and archived, must be maintained. There must be a process for implementing timely updates to product and price lists and, in turn, processing contract modifications. Other compliance obligations arising out of the Trade Agreements Act and small business subcontracting must be considered.

Compliance Issues Arising Under the Sarbanes-Oxley Act

Q 14.20 How does the Sarbanes-Oxley Act affect government contractors?

The Sarbanes-Oxley Act[368] focuses primarily on the conduct of publicly traded firms (and firms about to go public), their officers and directors, and their accountants and advisers. Some of the provisions and reporting standards included in Sarbanes-Oxley affect government contractors, as outlined below. However, government contractors have an advantage beyond other publicly traded firms as a result of certain controls placed upon companies contracting with the federal government. (See chapter 30 for a detailed explanation of the Sarbanes-Oxley Act requirements.)

Q 14.20.1 What advantages do government contractors have in dealing with Sarbanes-Oxley?

Statutes, regulations, and contracts already impose certain controls on government contractors. Government contractors generally have existing, extensive compliance regimes and systems that better prepare them for responding to the certification and documentation requirements of Sarbanes-Oxley. For example, government contractors already possess a certain level of documentation and compliance with CAS or the cost principles of the FAR. Government contractors can potentially adapt existing compliance mechanisms to reconcile existing controls and systems with those required under Sarbanes-Oxley.

Q 14.20.2   What obligations do officers of government contractors have under Sarbanes-Oxley?

Signing officers, CEOs, and CFOs must certify certain listed matters in the company's reports filed with the SEC. For example, certifications include, among other issues, that:

- there are no untrue statements or omissions;
- the financial statements and other information are accurate;
- they have responsibility for establishing, maintaining, and evaluating the effectiveness of disclosure controls, procedures, and internal control over financial reporting; and
- they have disclosed any changes in internal controls, significant deficiencies, and material weaknesses in design or operation of internal control over financial reports, or any fraud.[369]

The CEO and CFO must also accompany each periodic report containing financial statements with a written certification. The officer must certify that the period report "fully complies" with securities law requirements and that the information fairly presents the company's financial condition and results of operations. The maximum penalty for an officer who certifies a nonconforming report is a $1 million fine or a ten-year term in prison. The maximum penalty for an officer who makes a "willful" certification is a $5 million fine or a twenty-year term in prison.[370]

Q 14.20.3   What obligations do program managers and product line executives have?

Individuals working "under the direction" of officers and directors must be precise and accurate in communications with auditors. These individuals could be held accountable for misleading communications about program status if these communications are provided in reports expected to be disclosed to auditors.[371]

Q 14.20.4   What are in-house lawyers' obligations?

In-house lawyers must report credible evidence of any material violation of federal or state law "up the ladder." In addition to reporting violations of federal or state securities laws and any material breach of a fiduciary duty arising under federal or state law, in-house lawyers must identify and assess violations of federal and state procurement laws. This may include high-risk areas such as defective pricing, collusive pricing, mischarging, false reporting of costs, violations of export control laws, product substitution, latent defects, or crimes listed throughout this chapter.[372]

Compliance Issues Arising Under the Freedom of Information Act

Q 14.21   What compliance issues may arise under the Freedom of Information Act?

Agencies may receive requests for contractor documents under the Freedom of Information Act (FOIA). Each agency has rules governing releases of information under FOIA. These rules set forth the time, place, fees (if any), and procedures to follow when submitting a FOIA request. FOIA requires each agency to promptly make available for public inspection and copying those records reasonably described by any individual in a request that has been properly submitted to the agency.[373] When withholding documents, the agency must specify the exemption under which it retains the documents, such as:

- matters related to national security;
- matters specifically exempted under statutes;
- trade secrets and commercial or financial information.[374]

For example, a particular FOIA request may specifically seek contractor documents related to a contract. A separate statute prohibits agencies from disclosing contractor proposals, except that an agency may disclose the portion of the proposal incorporated into the contract awarded.[375] An agency will generally work with the contractor and withhold the contractor's trade secrets and commercial or financial information. However, if the FOIA requestor fights the withholding of information, the agency or possibly a court would determine what information is ultimately released. A court may enjoin the agency from withholding records. Contractors should implement a process for handling FOIA requests. In addition, contractors should implement procedures and train employees to mark all documents submitted to the government believed to be subject to the exemption applying to confidential commercial or financial information with the following legend: "Contains Proprietary Information of [XYZ, Inc.] Subject to FOIA Exemption (B)(4) Not to Be Disclosed Outside the Government." Contractors should similarly mark documents containing information subject to other FOIA exemptions.

Combating Trafficking in Persons

Q 14.22   What are a government contractor's responsibilities with respect to eliminating human trafficking from the supply chain?

Effective March 2, 2015, all government contractors are obligated to comply with federal efforts to combat the trafficking in persons and to comply with the specific requirements of their contracts in this regard. These requirements are typically imposed by certain FAR and DFARS provisions.[376] Chapter 38 of this book discusses anti-human trafficking and forced labor and provides additional information on the principal federal and state anti-human trafficking efforts, as well as the responsibilities of individual companies in eliminating human trafficking from their supply chains and in managing their enforcement risks.

Q 14.22.1   What are the human trafficking activities that are required to be prevented?

U.S. government solicitations and contracts are to prohibit contractors, contractor employees, subcontractors, subcontractor employees, and their agents from:

- engaging in severe forms of trafficking in persons during the period of performance of the contract;
- procuring commercial sex acts during the period of performance of the contract;
- using forced labor in the performance of the contract;

- destroying, concealing, confiscating, or otherwise denying access by an employee to the employee's identity or immigration documents, such as passports or driver's licenses, regardless of issuing authority;
- using misleading or fraudulent practices during the recruitment of employees or offering of employment;
- using recruiters that do not comply with local labor laws of the country in which the recruiting takes place;
- charging employees recruitment fees;
- failing to provide return transportation or pay for the cost of return transportation upon the end of employment, for an employee who is not a national of the country in which the work is taking place and who was brought into that country for the purpose of working on a U.S. government contract or subcontract;
- providing or arranging housing that fails to meet the host country's housing and safety standards; or
- failing, if required by law or contract, to provide an employment contract, recruitment agreement, or other required work document in writing (such written document shall be in a language the employee understands).[377]

Q 14.22.2 Under what circumstances must a government contractor notify the government about human trafficking activities it learns of?

A contractor must immediately inform the contracting officer and the agency inspector general of any credible information it receives from any source (including host-country law enforcement) that alleges a contractor employee, subcontractor, subcontractor employee, or an agent thereof has engaged in human trafficking.[378] Information sufficient to identify the nature and extent of the offense and the individuals responsible for the conduct must be provided. The contractor must also provide notice of any actions taken against a contractor employee, subcontractor, subcontractor employee, or agent as a result. If more than one contract is involved, the contractor must inform the contracting officer for the contract with the highest dollar value.

Q 14.22.3   What must a government contractor do if the agency inspector general undertakes an investigation concerning human trafficking?

A contractor must cooperate fully in providing reasonable access to its facilities and staff (both inside and outside the United States) to allow contracting agencies and other responsible federal agencies to conduct audits, investigations, or other actions to ascertain compliance with applicable legal authority.[379] Likewise, it must provide timely and complete responses to government auditors' and investigators' requests for documents. Finally, the contractor must protect all employees suspected of being victims of or witnesses to prohibited activities, and shall not prevent or hinder the ability of these employees from cooperating fully with government authorities.

Q 14.22.4   What are the possible consequences a government contractor might face for failing to fulfill the anti-human trafficking requirements?

A contractor that fails to satisfy the anti-human trafficking requirements is subject to a range of potential consequences. For example, the government may:

- require the contractor to remove an employee or employees from the performance of the contract;
- require the contractor to terminate a subcontract;
- suspend contract payments until the contractor has taken appropriate remedial action;
- withhold or deny an award fee, consistent with the award fee plan, for the performance period in which the government determined contractor non-compliance;
- decline to exercise available options under the contract;
- terminate the contract for default or cause, in accordance with the termination clause of this contract; or
- suspend or debar the contractor.[380]

Q 14.22.5   Should a government contractor's compliance program be revised to account for anti-human trafficking requirements?

Yes, and it is absolutely required where a contractor has a contract with an estimated value over $500,000 for (i) supplies, other than commercially available off-the-shelf items, that are acquired outside the United States, or (ii) services to be performed outside the United States.[381] The anti-human trafficking aspects of the compliance program should be tailored and appropriate to the size and complexity of the contract and the nature and scope of the contractor's contract activities. At a minimum, it should include:

- an awareness program to inform contractor employees about the government's policy prohibiting trafficking-related activities, the activities prohibited, and the actions that will be taken against the employee for violations;
- a process for employees to report, without fear of retaliation, activity inconsistent with the policy prohibiting trafficking in persons, including a means to make available to all employees the hotline phone number of the Global Human Trafficking Hotline (1-844-888-FREE) and its email address (help@befree.org);
- a recruitment and wage plan that only permits the use of recruitment companies with trained employees, prohibits charging recruitment fees to the employee, and ensures that wages meet applicable host-country legal requirements or explains any variance;
- a housing plan, if the contractor or subcontractor intends to provide or arrange housing, that ensures that the housing meets host-country housing and safety standards;
- procedures to prevent agents and subcontractors at any tier and at any dollar value from engaging in trafficking in persons and to monitor, detect, and terminate any agents, subcontracts, or subcontractor employees that have engaged in such activities.

Finally, the contractor shall post the relevant contents of the compliance plan, no later than the initiation of contract performance, at the workplace and on the contractor's website (if it has one); if posting at the workplace or on the website is impracticable, the contractor shall provide the relevant contents of the compliance plan to each worker in writing.

Q 14.22.6   Are there certification requirements concerning compliance with anti-human trafficking requirements?

Yes; annually after receiving an award, a contractor must submit a certification to the contracting officer that it has implemented a compliance plan to prevent human trafficking and to monitor, detect, and terminate any agent, subcontract, or subcontractor employee engaging in prohibited activities. Also, the contractor must certify that, after having conducted due diligence, to the best of the contractor's knowledge and belief, neither it nor any of its agents, subcontractors, or their agents is engaged in any such activities; or if human trafficking abuses have been found, that the contractor or subcontractor has taken the appropriate remedial and referral actions.[382] The DFARS similarly requires a representation from offerors that it will not engage in human trafficking.[383]

Q 14.22.7   Is a government contractor required to flow down these requirements to its subcontractors?

Yes. A contractor is required to include the substance of the FAR clause in all subcontracts and in all contracts with agents for supplies, other than commercially available off-the-shelf items, acquired outside the United States, or services to be performed outside the United States.[384]

TIP: Government contractors are subject to a complex web of regulations when competing for and performing federal contracts and subcontracts. These laws present numerous tripwires that can expose an unwary contractor and its employees to civil and criminal liability and debarment from future business with the government.

To manage their legal risks, contractors should implement an effective compliance program that includes reasonable internal controls and training. Such a compliance program should include a periodic assessment of the contractor's most essential

---

risk areas and the development of policies and procedures to implement business processes to promote compliance. The compliance program must also include internal reporting mechanisms and procedures to investigate and respond to problems when they arise.

Although it is easy to view compliance as an obligatory box to check, government contractors should think of their compliance program as a useful management tool to promote business practices that are both ethical and smart. Ultimately, an effective compliance program is a key to maximizing profitability in the federal marketplace.

Notes to Chapter 14

1. Although this chapter highlights many of the key areas that an effective compliance program will address for contractors doing business with the government, it does not address all government contracting issues comprehensively. A government contractor should seek legal counsel to adequately address the company's individual issues and situation.

Furthermore, some of the issues that arise under government contracts also have implications for other organizations receiving funds from the government (*e.g.*, grant recipients).

2. The Federal Acquisition Regulation (FAR) is codified at 48 C.F.R. pts. 1–53.

3. For example, the Department of Defense has its own supplement known as the Defense Federal Acquisition Regulation Supplement (DFARS), found at 48 C.F.R. pts. 201–53.

4. The FAR requirements were modeled specifically on U.S. Sentencing Commission guidance contained in the commission's *Sentencing Guidelines Manual* on "effective" compliance and ethics programs. The requirements to exercise "due diligence" and to promote an ethical culture are taken directly from this manual. U.S. SENTENCING GUIDELINES MANUAL § 8B2.1(b). These terms of art are well understood in the context of the commission's sentencing guidelines, and contractors should look to the *Sentencing Guidelines Manual* for guidance on their meaning. *See also* chapter 2 (providing significant detail on the requirements of the federal sentencing guidelines).

5. FAR 52.203-14.

6. 31 U.S.C. § 3729 *et seq.*

7. FAR 52.203-13, 52.203-14.

8. "*Principal* means an officer, director, owner, partner, or a person having primary management or supervisory responsibilities within a business entity (*e.g.*, general manager; plant manager; head of a subsidiary, division, or business segment and similar positions)." 73 Fed. Reg. at 67,090; FAR 2.101; FAR 52.203-13(a).

9. Contract financing payments are defined in FAR 32.001, Definitions.

10. *See also* ABA, SECTION OF PUBLIC CONTRACT LAW, GUIDE TO THE MANDATORY DISCLOSURE RULE: ISSUES, GUIDELINES, AND BEST PRACTICES (Huffman & Levy eds., 2010). This informative guide, published in January 2010, provides approximately 400 pages of information regarding interpreting many of the broad and undefined terms used in the mandatory disclosure rule.

11. FAR 2.101.

12. *Id.* 52.203-13(b).

13. *Id.* 52.203-13(c).

14. 73 Fed. Reg. 67,085.

15. FAR 52.203-13(b).

16. *Id.*
17. *Id.* 52.203-13(c).
18. *Id.* 3.1002(b).
19. The training and internal control systems are not required on contracts with small businesses or for commercial items, as defined in FAR 2.101. *See* FAR 52.203-13(c).
20. *Id.* 52.203-13(c)(2)(ii)(D).
21. *Id.*
22. *Id.* 3.1004(b); FAR 52.203-14.
23. *Id.* 52.203-14(c).
24. *Id.* 52.203-14(b)(2).
25. *Id.* 52.203-13(b)(3).
26. *Id.* 9.406-2(b)(1)(vi).
27. *Id.* 59.406-2(b)(1)(vi), 9.407-2(a)(8), 52.203-13(b)(2)(ii)(F)(3).
28. 31 U.S.C. § 3729(a)(2).
29. 73 Fed. Reg. 67,073.
30. *Id.* 52.203-13(b)(3)(i).
31. *Id.* 52.203-13(b)(3)(iii).
32. *Id.* 9.406-2(b)(1), 9.407-2(a)(8), 52.203-13(b)(3)(i).
33. *See* 73 Fed. Reg. 67,079.
34. 73 Fed. Reg. 67,074.
35. FAR 52.203-13(b)(3)(ii).
36. *Id.* 52.203-13(a)(1).
37. *Id.* 52.203-13(a)(2).
38. *Id.* 52.203-13(a)(3).
39. 73 Fed. Reg. 67,085.
40. 73 Fed. Reg. 67,080.
41. *See, e.g.*, FAR 52.232-25, 52.232-26, 52.232-27, and 52.212-4(i)(5).
42. FAR 52.203-13(d).
43. 73 Fed. Reg. 67,084.
44. *See* FAR 9.406-5.
45. 31 U.S.C. § 3729(a)(1).
46. See chapter 11 for a more thorough discussion of the False Claims Act.
47. 18 U.S.C. § 1001.
48. *Id.* § 1341.
49. *Id.* § 1343.
50. *Id.* § 1031.
51. *Id.* § 371.
52. *Id.* § 1961 *et seq.*
53. *Id.* §§ 1505, 1516, 1519.
54. *Id.* § 3571(d).
55. 31 U.S.C. §§ 3729–33; 18 U.S.C. § 287.
56. *See* 18 U.S.C. § 1001.
57. *Id.* §§ 1341, 1346.
58. *Id.* § 1346.
59. *Id.*

60. *Id.*
61. *Id.* § 1343.
62. *Id.*
63. *Id.* § 1343.
64. *Id.*
65. *Id.* § 1031(a).
66. *Id.*
67. *Id.* § 1031(b).
68. *Id.* § 1031(c).
69. *Id.* § 1031(g). Limited groups of individuals are not eligible for this payment.
70. *Id.* § 371.
71. Punishment is less where conspirators plan to commit a misdemeanor, rather than a felony. As a practical matter, most violations of federal law are felonies.
72. 18 U.S.C. § 1505.
73. *Id.* § 1516.
74. *Id.* § 1519.
75. *Id.* § 1520.
76. FAR 15.403-4; 10 U.S.C. § 2306a; 41 U.S.C. § 254b.
77. 10 U.S.C. § 2306a(h)(1); FAR 2.101.
78. FAR 2.101.
79. *See id.* 15.406-2.
80. 10 U.S.C. § 2306a(b) and (c); FAR 15.403-1 and -2.
81. 10 U.S.C. § 2306a(d); FAR 15.403-1 and -3.
82. FAR 15.209(b), 52.215-2(f).
83. 10 U.S.C. § 2306a(a); FAR 15.403-4(b)(2).
84. 10 U.S.C. § 2306a(e).
85. *Id.*
86. 10 U.S.C. § 2306a; 41 U.S.C. § 254b; FAR 15.407-1(b)(7), 52.215-10(d)(2).
87. 22 U.S.C. § 2399b.
88. 28 U.S.C. § 2514.
89. FAR 9.407 discusses suspension.
90. *Id.* 9.406 discusses debarment.
91. *Id.* 9.407-4(a).
92. *Id.* 9.407-4(b).
93. *Id.* 9.406-4(a).
94. *Id.* 9.406-4(b).
95. *Id.* 9.403 (defining "affiliates").
96. *Id.* 9.406-2, 9.407-2.
97. 31 U.S.C. §§ 3801, 3802.
98. FAR 42.709-6, 52.242-3 ("Penalties for Unallowable Costs" clause).
99. *Id.* 2.101.
100. 10 U.S.C. § 2324; FAR 42.709, 52.242-3.
101. FAR 42.709-1(a)(1).
102. 41 U.S.C. § 256(b); FAR 42.709-1(a)(2).

103. FAR 52.215-10(d).

104. *Id.* 52.204-8.

105. *Id.* 52.209-5.

106. *Id.* 52.230-1.

107. *Id.* 52.242-4.

108. *Id.* 52.203-2 (Independent Price Determination).

109. *Id.* 52.219-1, 52.212-3 (commercial items).

110. *Id.* 52.212-3, 52.225-2 to -4.

111. *Id.* 52.225-6.

112. *Id.* 52.226-2.

113. *Id.* 9.104-7; 52.209-7(c).

114. *See* 80 Fed. Reg. 30,548 (May 28, 2015) (discussion of Exec. Order No. 13,673 and implementing regulations).

115. *See* FAR 9.104-1 (listing the general standards a contractor must meet to be deemed "responsible").

116. *Id.* 52.209-5(a) ("Certification Regarding Responsibility Matters").

117. *Id.* 52.209-5(c).

118. *See id.* 9.404, 9.405.

119. *Id.* 9.404(b); *see* QQ 14.8.1 and 14.8.2 (discussing the implications of suspension and debarment).

120. FAR 2.101.

121. *Id.* 9.505.

122. *See* U.S. *ex rel.* Harrison v. Westinghouse Savannah River Co., 352 F.3d 908 (4th Cir. 2003) (affirming FCA judgment against a contractor based upon its failure to disclose a proposed subcontractor's OCI).

123. FAR 9.504(c). This chapter limits the discussion of OCI provisions to those included in the FAR. Some agencies have established additional criteria, not described in this chapter.

124. *Id.* 9.503.

125. *Id.* 9.502(c).

126. *See* Aetna Gov't Health Plans, Inc., Found. Health Fed. Servs., Inc., B-254397 et al., 1995 WL 449806, 95-2 CPD ¶ 129, at 12–13 (Comp. Gen. July 27, 1995).

127. Aetna Gov't Health Plans, Inc., Found. Health Fed. Servs., Inc., B-254397 et al., 1995 WL 449806, 95-2 CPD ¶ 129 at 8–10 (Comp. Gen. July 27, 1995); FAR §§ 9.505-1, 9.505-2.

128. *Aetna*, 95-2 CPD ¶ 129 at 8–10.

129. FAR 9.505-4.

130. *Actna*, 95-2 CPD ¶ 129 at 8–10.

131. FAR 9.505-3.

132. *Aetna*, 95-2 CPD ¶ 129 at 8–10.

133. *See* FAR 9.502(b).

134. *See, e.g., id.* 9.508.

135. The discussion in this chapter is limited to contracts with commercial organizations. This chapter does not address, for example, contracts with educational or not-for-profit institutions. *See generally* FAR 31.2.

136. *See* FAR 31.201-2, -3, and -4, 31.204.
137. *Id.* 31.201-5 and -6.
138. 41 U.S.C. § 422(f)(2)(A).
139. 48 C.F.R. §§ 9903.201-1(b), 9903.301.
140. DEFENSE CONTRACT AUDIT AGENCY, DCAA CONTRACT AUDIT MANUAL (Dec. 2009), www.dcaa.mil/cam.htm.
141. 48 C.F.R. § 9903.201-1.
142. *Id.* § 9903.201-1(b)(3).
143. FAR 30.000 ("This part does not apply to sealed bid contracts or to any contract with a small business concern").
144. 48 C.F.R. § 9903.201-1.
145. FAR 42.202(e)(2).
146. *See id.* 34.2.
147. *Id.* 2.101.
148. *Id.*
149. *Id.* 15.403-4(a)(1). Note that FAR 15.403-1 includes a limited number of exceptions from coverage under TINA.
150. 10 U.S.C. § 2306a(a)(2); 41 U.S.C. § 254b(a)(2).
151. *See* FAR 31.201-5 and -6.
152. *See id.* 52.215-10 and -11.
153. 15 U.S.C. § 1.
154. Sherman Antitrust Act, 15 U.S.C. §§ 1–7; *see also* Federal Trade Commission Act, 15 U.S.C. § 45(a).
155. Federal Trade Commission Act, 15 U.S.C. § 45(*l*).
156. 41 U.S.C. § 423.
157. *Id.* § 423(a)–(b); FAR 3.104-3.
158. *Id.* § 423(b), (e).
159. *Id.* § 641.
160. *Id.* §§ 792–99.
161. *Id.* § 201.
162. *Id.* § 201(b).
163. *Id.* § 201.
164. *Id.* § 201(c).
165. 5 C.F.R. §§ 2635.203, 2635.204.
166. 18 U.S.C. §§ 201(b), 3559(a)(5), 3571.
167. *Id.* §§ 201(c), 3559(a)(5), 3571.
168. *See* FAR 3.202, 52.203-3 (implementing 10 U.S.C. § 2207).
169. *Id.* 3.204(c), 52.203-3.
170. *Id.* 52.203-7(a).
171. 41 U.S.C. §§ 51–58; FAR 3.502-2, 52.203-7.
172. 41 U.S.C. §§ 51–58; *see* FAR 3.502-2, 52.203-7.
173. *See* FAR 3.502, 52.203-7.
174. *Id.* 52.203-7(c).
175. *Id.* 3.502-2(i), 52.203-7(c).
176. *Id.* 52.203-7(c).
177. 41 U.S.C. § 54.

178. *Id.* §§ 55–56.
179. FAR 3.401.
180. 10 U.S.C. § 2306(b); 41 U.S.C. § 254(a); FAR 3.401, 3.403, 3.404.
181. FAR 3.401, 3.402, 3.403, 52.203-5(b).
182. *Id.* 3.401.
183. *Id.* 3.405(a).
184. *Id.* 3.406.
185. *Id.* 3.405(b), 52.203-5(a).
186. *See* 15 U.S.C. §§ 78dd, 78dd-1, 78dd-2, 78dd-3, 78ff.
187. *Id.* §§ 78dd-1, 78dd-2, 78dd-3.
188. *Id.* §§ 78dd-1(a)(3), 78dd-2(a)(3), 78dd-3(a)(3).
189. *Id.* § 78m(b).
190. *Id.*
191. *Id.*
192. *Id.* §§ 78dd-1(f)(3), 78dd-2(h)(4), 78dd-3(f)(4).
193. *Id.* § 78ff(c), 78dd-2(g), 78dd-3(e).
194. *Id.* § 78u.
195. *Id.* § 78u(d) and (e).
196 FAR 52.203-13.
197. 18 U.S.C. §§ 203, 205, 208.
198. *Id.* § 216; 28 C.F.R. § 85.3(c).
199. FAR 9.406-2(b)(1)(vi).
200. 18 U.S.C. § 208.
201. *See* 5 C.F.R. §§ 2635.601 to .606.
202. FAR 3.104-1.
203. *Id.* 3.104-5(a).
204. *Id.* 3.104-5(b).
205. 41 U.S.C. § 423(d)(1); FAR 3.104-3(d)(1).
206. 41 U.S.C. § 423(d)(2); FAR 3.104-3(d)(3).
207. 41 U.S.C. § 423(c)(1); FAR 3.104-3(c).
208. 41 U.S.C. § 423(c)(1); FAR 3.104-3(c).
209. *See* 18 U.S.C. § 207.
210 *Id.*
211. *Id.* § 207(a)(1); 5 C.F.R. § 2641.201(a).
212. 18 U.S.C. § 207(a)(2); 5 C.F.R. § 2641.202(a).
213. 18 U.S.C. § 207(c); 5 C.F.R. § 2641.204(a).
214. 18 U.S.C. § 207(d); 5 C.F.R. § 2641.205(a).
215. 41 U.S.C. § 423(a); FAR 3.104-3(a).
216. 41 U.S.C. § 423(d); FAR 3.104 3(d).
217. 18 U.S.C. § 208; 5 C.F.R. § 2635.403.
218. 18 U.S.C. § 209.
219 5 C.F.R. §§ 2635.502, 2653.503.
220. FAR 3.104-6.
221. *Id.* 3.104-6(d).
222. 31 U.S.C. § 1352; FAR 3.802, 52.203-11, 52.203-12.
223. *Id.*

224. FAR 3.806.

225. 31 U.S.C. § 1352(c); FAR 3.807 (stating that agencies "shall impose and collect civil penalties pursuant to the provisions of the Program Fraud and Civil Remedies Act, 31 U.S.C. 3803 (except subsection (c)), 3804–3808, and 3812").

226. 2 U.S.C. §§ 1601–12.

227. *Id.* § 1603.

228. *Id.* §§ 1602(8), 1603.

229. *Id.* § 1604.

230. *Id.* § 1606.

231. 41 U.S.C. § 253g; 10 U.S.C. § 2402; FAR 3.503, 52.203-6.

232. Exec. Order No. 13,673, 79 Fed. Reg. 45,309 (July 31, 2014).

233. A proposed rule implementing the executive order was published in the *Federal Register* on May 28, 2015. *See* 80 Fed. Reg. 30,548 (May 28, 2015). Comments were due on July 27, 2015. The contractor should check to determine when or if a final rule is issued.

234. 80 Fed. Reg. 30,548 (May 28, 2015).

235. FAR 22.407(h), 52.222-5, 52.222-6.

236. *Id.* 52.222-6(b).

237. *Id.*

238. *Id.*

239. *Id.* 52.222-9(b).

240. *Id.* 52.222-9(b)(2).

241. *Id.* 52.222-9(c).

242. 41 U.S.C. § 351; FAR 22.1002, 52.222-41.

243. FAR 22.1002-1.

244. *Id.* 22.1003.

245. *Id.* 52.222-41(p).

246. *See id.* 52.222-41(p)(3) (18 U.S.C. § 1001 provides the criminal penalties for making false statements).

247. 41 U.S.C. §§ 35–45; FAR 22.610, 52.222-20.

248. 41 U.S.C. § 36; 41 C.F.R. § 50-201.603; FAR 22.604-1, -2.

249. 41 U.S.C. § 35.

250. *See* FAR pt. 22.8.

251. *Id.* 22.804-1, 52.222-25 (construction contractors must meet different requirements of FAR, such as 22.804-2 and 52.222-23).

252. *Id.* 22.805. Exemptions appear in 22.807, 52.222-24.

253. *Id.* 22.807(a).

254. *Id.* 22.807(b).

255. *Id.* 52.222-26. The government may include other pertinent clauses in certain circumstances. *See* FAR 52.222-21, -22, -23, -24, -25, -27, -29.

256. *Id.* 52.222-21.

257. *Id.* 52.222-22.

258. *See id.* 22.804-2, 52.222-23, 52.222-27.

259. *Id.* 22.809.

260. *See id.* pt. 23.5; *see also* 52.223-6.

261. *Id.* 23.506.

262. Exec. Order No. 13,495 (Jan. 30, 2009); *see* FAR 52.222-17.

263. Exec. Order No. 13,496 (Jan. 30, 2009); *see* 29 C.F.R. pt. 471; Nat'l Ass'n of Mfrs. v. Perez, 103 F. Supp. 3d 7 (D.D.C. 2015) (upholding presidential authority to issue rule).

264. Exec. Order No. 13,658 (Feb. 12, 2014); *see* 80 Fed. Reg. 55,646 (Sept. 16, 2015).

265. Exec. Order No. 13,665 (Apr. 8, 2014); *see* Final Rule, 80 Fed. Reg. 54,934 (Sept. 11, 2015).

266. Exec. Order No. 13,706, 80 Fed. Reg. 54,697 (Sept. 7, 2015) (effective only after January 1, 2017).

267. FAR 22.1803.

268. 8 U.S.C. § 1324a; *see* www.dhs.gov/E-Verify.

269. FAR 52.222-54(d).

270. *Id.* 52.222-54(b)(4).

271. *Id.* 52.222-54(b)(1)(i).

272. *Id.* 52.222-54(b)(1)(ii).

273. *Id.*

274. *Id.* 52.222-54(b)(2)(i)(A).

275. *Id.* 52.222-54(b)(2)(i)(B).

276. *Id.* 27.401 (defining "data"); for contracts with the Department of Defense, refer to DFARS 227.71, 252.227-2013.

277. FAR 52.224-14 (defining "computer software"); for contracts with the Department of Defense, refer to DFARS 227.72 *et seq.*, 252.227-2014.

278. FAR 52.227-14(b); for contracts with the Department of Defense, refer to DFARS 227.71, 252.227-2013.

279. *Id.* 52.227-14(a) (defining "unlimited rights").

280. *Id.* 52.227-14(b)(2).

281. *Id.* 52.227-14(a) (defining "restricted computer software"); for contracts with the Department of Defense, refer to DFARS 227.72 *et seq.*, 252.227-2014.

282. *Id.* 52.227-14(a) (defining "restricted rights"), 52.227-14(g).

283. *Id.* 52.227-14(a) (defining "limited rights data").

284. *Id..* 52.227-14(a) (defining "limited rights"), 52.227-14(g).

285. *Id.* 52.227-14(g).

286. *Id.* 52.227-14(c).

287. 41 U.S.C. § 253d(a).

288. FAR 27.404-6.

289. 41 U.S.C. § 253d(f).

290. 41 U.S.C. § 418a(d)(7); FAR 27.406(d), 52.227-21.

291. FAR 27.404-2(c)(1).

292. FAR 27.404-3, 52.227-14(c); DFARS 227.7103-9, 227.7203-9, 252.227-7013, 252.227-7014.

293. FAR 27.404-3, 52.227-17(c); *see also id.* 52.227-20(c) (copyright protection for data first produced in the performance of this SBIR contract).

294. *Id.*

295. *Id.* 52.227-18(b).

296. *Id.* 52.227-13.

297. *Id.* 52.227-13(e)–(f).

298. *Id.*

299. *Id.* 52.227-13(g).

300. *Id.* 25.100. Contractors should note that similar rules apply to Department of Defense procurements. *See* 10 U.S.C. § 2534(a); DFARS 225.70.

301. FAR 25.003.

302 *Id.* 25.101(a)(2) (citing 41 U.S.C. § 431).

303. *Id.* 25.1101.

304. *See id.* 25.701, 52.225-13.

305. American Recovery and Reinvestment Act of 2009, Pub. L. No. 111-5, 123 Stat. 115.

306. 41 U.S.C. § 10a; FAR 25.100, 25.200.

307. FAR 25.103(b), 25.104 (including a list of over 100 exempt items), 25.202(a)(2).

308. *Id.* 25.103(d).

309. *Id.* 25.103(a), 25.202(a)(1).

310. *Id.* 25.103(c), 25.202(a)(3).

311. *Id.* 25.103(e).

312. *See id.* 25.202(a)(3).

313. *Id.* 225.401-70.

314. DFARS 25.402(a)(1); *see* Q 14.17.5 (for a more detailed explanation of the Trade Agreements Act).

315. FAR 25.400 *et seq.*

316. *See id.* 25.206(c).

317. *See id.*

318. *See id.* 25.206(c)(4).

319. *See* 19 U.S.C. § 1304(*l*).

320. *See* 19 C.F.R. § 177.

321. 19 U.S.C. §§ 2511(b), 2512(a), 2701 *et seq.*; *see also* FAR 25.403 to .407.

322. *See* FAR 25.402.

323. 10 U.S.C. § 2533a(b); DFARS 225.7002-1.

324. 10 U.S.C. § 2533a(c)–(h); 48 C.F.R. § 225.7002-2.

325. DFARS 242.225-7009 (July 2009).

326. 49 U.S.C. § 40118.

327. FAR 47.405.

328. 22 U.S.C. § 2778(a)(1); *id.* § 2751.

329. *Id.* § 2778(b), (g)(6); 22 C.F.R. § 122.

330. 22 C.F.R. § 120.6; *see* 22 C.F.R. § 120.10 (defining "technical data").

331. *Id.* § 120.9(a).

332. *Id.* § 120.16.

333. *Id.*

334. *Id.* § 120.17(a)(4) (emphasis added).

335. *Id.* § 120.1(c).

336. *Id.*; 22 U.S.C. § 2778(g)(5).

337. *See, e.g.,* 22 C.F.R. §§ 123.16, 126.5, 120.30; 22 U.S.C. § 2778(i).

338. 22 C.F.R. § 126.5.

339. 22 U.S.C. § 2778(c), (e).

340. *Id.* § 2778(g)(4); 22 C.F.R. § 127.7; FAR 9.407-2.

341. *Id.* § 2778(c).

342. *Id.*

343. *Id.* § 2278(e).

344. DFARS 225.7300.

345. *Id.* 225.7301(a).

346. *Id.* 225.7301(b).

347. *See, e.g.*, FAR 52.227-3, -4.

348. 79 Fed. Reg. 26,092 (May 6, 2014).

349. DFARS 202.101.

350. *Id.* 246.870-2, 246.870-3.

351. 80 Fed. Reg. 56,939 (Sept. 21, 2015).

352. DFARS 246.870-3(b).

353. *Id.* 252.246-7007(c)(9), (e).

354. *Id.* 252.246-7007(c)(6).

355. *Id.* 231.205-71.

356. *Id.* 231.205-71(b).

357 *See* 13 C.F.R. § 121.404.

358. *Id.*

359. *Id.*

360. *Id.* § 121.404(g)(3).

361. *Id.*

362. FAR 52.219-28(b)(2).

363. 13 C.F.R. § 121.404(g)(3).

364. GENERAL SERVICES ADMINISTRATION ACQUISITION MANUAL (GSAM) §§ 538.271(c), 552.238-75(a).

365. *Id.* §§ 538.272(a), 552.238-75.

366. *Id.* § 552.238-75.

367. *See id.* § 552.238-75(g).

368. Pub. L. No. 107-204, 116 Stat. 745.

369. The civil certification provision of the act, section 302, is codified at 15 U.S.C. § 7241.

370. The criminal certification provision of the act, section 906, is codified at 18 U.S.C. § 1350.

371. Pub. L. No. 107-204, § 303, 116 Stat. 745.

372. *Id.* § 307.

373. 5 U.S.C. § 552(a).

374. *Id.* § 552(b).

375. 10 U.S.C. § 2305(g).

376. *See, e.g.*, FAR 22.17, 52.222-50; DFARS 252.222-7007.

377. FAR 22.1703(a)(1)–(9), 52.222-50(b)(1)–(9).

378. *Id.* 52.222-50(d).

379. *Id.* 52.222-50(g).

380. *Id.* 52.222-50(e).

381. *Id.* 22.1703(c), 52.222-50(f)(1), (h)(1)–(5).

382. *Id.* 52.222-50(h)(5).
383. DFARS 252.222-7007.
384. FAR 52.222-50(i).

15

International Investigations

*Steven D. Gordon**

If counsel thinks that his or her practice and clients are completely domestic, it is important to take a careful second look for unnoticed international risk elements. As a function of globalization, international investigations are increasing in frequency and importance in many areas of the law. This chapter examines the issues typical in international investigations and discusses some popular practice areas where these issues may arise. While the steps necessary to conduct a successful international investigation are similar to those needed for domestic internal investigations,[1] this chapter provides additional suggestions.

*   The author wishes to acknowledge Ronald A. Oleynik for his contributions to this chapter.

479

The Basics

Q 15.1   What is an international investigation?

International investigations come in myriad forms and contexts, and any investigation or prosecution may become global at any time. Generally, an investigation can be identified as "international" in nature based on any of the following elements:

(1) the parties,
(2) the overseas territorial or "cyber" scope,
(3) the legal issues (including elements of foreign law or procedure),
(4) the relevant agency involved.

Special Issues

Q 15.2   What are some of the special issues raised by international investigations?

Among the challenges a company should anticipate are the difficulties it may encounter in the coordination of:

- foreign evidence,
- foreign computer forensics,
- foreign witnesses,
- foreign counsel,
- a parallel domestic investigation, and/or
- responding to foreign government action.

Furthermore, counsel must be aware that different or conflicting legal procedures, privileges, and immunities may impact how an investigation is conducted and may affect a company's "rush to the prosecutor" in multiple jurisdictions to benefit from amnesty programs or leniency under the Federal Sentencing Guidelines.

TIP: Difficulties in international investigations suggest the need for international counsel on the investigative team. The international counsel recruited must be sensitive to the specific cultural, linguistic, and substantive issues likely to arise in a specific case.

Document Collection/Review

Q 15.3   What kinds of considerations are raised by special issues related to document collection and review?

There are both legal and practical issues.

Foreign laws may affect how documents are collected, transported, and/or analyzed. For example, the European Union (EU) has strict limits on transmitting personal data outside of Europe, including *intra-company* data transfers.[2] Other nations have comparable restrictions.[3] EU laws will not allow documents containing personal data to be brought into the United States without government permission or individual consent (measured by a stringent standard). Alternatively, the personal data can be redacted so that the identity of the person cannot be ascertained. But this may render the documents useless for investigative purposes.

Thus, arrangements may have to be made to review documents only in overseas locations. Documents may require redaction of any information that could disclose personal data such as names, positions, locations, and responsibilities.

Further, in searching for relevant documents, keyword search terms must take into account both English and relevant foreign languages. Depending on the country, it may be difficult to obtain forensic assistance to handle tasks such as scanning of documents. The necessary equipment and personnel may need to be brought into the country.

Witness Interviews

Q 15.4   What special issues exist relating to witness interviews?

Once again, there are legal and practical issues.

Local laws may govern how the interviews are conducted, who is present, and what documents can be shown to a witness. The labor and employment laws or privacy laws of many countries allow employees to refuse to submit to questioning by company counsel who are conducting internal investigations.

Language and cultural differences also must be considered. An interpreter often will be necessary. Will an independent interpreter be obtained or will reliance be placed on a bilingual company employee or on local counsel? If possible, all documents relevant to a particular witness should be obtained, analyzed, and translated beforehand, as there may be only one opportunity to conduct the interview. The assistance of local counsel may be essential to ensure that local law issues, language barriers, and cultural sensitivities are taken into account and managed.

Sometimes, it may be impossible to interview witnesses on-site due to local security concerns. Or it may be prudent for other reasons to conduct interviews away from the worksite.

The logistics almost certainly will be more challenging than for domestic investigations: travel arrangements must be made; passports, visas, and permits obtained; interviews scheduled; locations arranged; and an interpreter(s) engaged. Unless the client already has local counsel who is capable of assisting in the investigation, such counsel may need to be identified and retained. Time may be restricted and interviews may be one-shot opportunities. These concerns place a premium on careful planning of—and preparation for—witness interviews abroad.

Q 15.4.1   Can telephone interviews be used?

On-site visits and interviews often are crucial to understanding the conduct of a company and its employees in context. Moreover, they may be required for a credible presentation to the U.S. government. And on-site visits and interviews frequently yield more information than telephone interviews do. It is difficult to question a witness about multiple documents over the telephone, or to gauge the witness's reaction to various questions.

Still, interviews by telephone or video conference can have a role in an international investigation. They may be a necessary part of a preliminary inquiry to determine whether a problem exists that requires further investigation and in-person interviews. Telephone interviews can be used as follow-up interviews of witnesses who already have been questioned in person or to interview secondary witnesses. And if the issue at stake is sufficiently modest, cost considerations may mandate "long-distance" rather than on-site interviews.

Attorney-Client Privilege

Q 15.5   Does the attorney-client privilege apply in an international investigation?

Most countries recognize some form of the attorney-client privilege, but the scope of the privilege varies greatly. Most foreign jurisdictions do *not* recognize any attorney-client privilege for *in-house* counsel, and where it is recognized, it is not absolute. In a 2008 survey, only thirteen out of thirty-nine European countries recognized the attorney-client privilege for in-house counsel.[4] The European Union does not.[5] Thus, in a number of jurisdictions, interviews conducted by in-house counsel may be subject to disclosure.

Jurisdiction

Q 15.6   When do U.S. courts have jurisdiction over a company's foreign activities?

Jurisdiction issues are important where a foreign subsidiary may have acted unlawfully and the U.S. government and/or a private litigant seek to impose liability on the U.S. parent corporation. Even where U.S. courts lack jurisdiction over the subsidiary, they have sanctioned the U.S. parent for failure to comply with court orders issued to the subsidiary.[6]

Q 15.6.1   Do U.S. laws apply to conduct outside the United States?

Some important U.S. laws apply to conduct outside the United States, sometimes even when conducted by foreign companies or individuals. These include the following examples:

- *Foreign Corrupt Practices Act.*[7] The FCPA makes it unlawful for any U.S. company or any officer, director, employee, agent, or stockholder to offer or pay anything of value to a foreign official in order to obtain or retain business. The law applies to illicit payments made by U.S. citizens or companies that take place wholly outside the United States. It covers U.S. citizens, nationals, or residents who work for foreign companies (or subsidiaries). It also applies to foreign companies (and subsidiaries) who commit an act in furtherance of a bribe within the territory of the United States.
- *Travel Act.*[8] The federal Travel Act has been used to prosecute bribes paid overseas to private parties. The act applies to anyone who travels abroad or uses the mail with intent to promote or carry on an unlawful activity, including violations of state law. Many states have laws forbidding commercial bribery,[9] and so, if a foreign bribe would violate applicable state law, it potentially can be prosecuted as a federal offense under the Travel Act.

- *Sarbanes-Oxley Act of 2002.*[10] SOX imposes on corporations listed on a U.S. exchange, including companies located completely outside the United States, an audit committee requirement, expanded disclosure requirements, and a certification requirement, among other things.
- *Sherman Act.*[11] The antitrust provisions of the Sherman Act cover anticompetitive activities outside the United States that harm imports, domestic commerce, or U.S. exports. (The Foreign Trade Antitrust Improvements Act excludes from the Sherman Act's reach most anticompetitive conduct that causes only foreign injury.)[12]
- *U.S. export control laws.* These laws, by their nature, cover actions that have a foreign component. The U.S. export control laws apply to U.S. companies and individuals, as well as to foreign companies and individuals who have possession or control over export controlled items of U.S. origin, regardless of where the transaction takes place. Targeted transactions include exports from the United States, re-exports or re-transfers of U.S.-origin controlled items, brokering of defense items, dealing with embargoed countries or individuals. (For a detailed discussion on export controls, see chapter 17.)

Travel

Q 15.7 Does travel to the United States by foreign officers raise any special issues?

An investigation by the U.S. government may impact the travel plans of foreign officers or employees of the company or its subsidiary. The Department of Justice, particularly the Antitrust Division, has increased its use of border watches to detect the entry of foreign witnesses and subjects of investigation into the United States. Thus, travel to the United States could result in an individual being served with a grand jury subpoena or even an arrest warrant. Further, the Antitrust Division places fugitive criminal defendants (that is, individuals who have been charged) on a "Red Notice" list maintained by Interpol. This is essentially an international wanted notice that many of Interpol's member countries recognize as the basis for a provisional arrest, with a view toward extradition. The Antitrust Division will seek to extradite any fugitive defendant apprehended through the Interpol Red Notice watch.[13]

Affected Practice Areas

Q 15.8   What are some of the major practice areas where international investigations typically occur?

Affected practice areas include:

- cartel anticompetitive and unfair business practices,
- noncartel anticompetitive and unfair business practices,
- anti-bribery,
- export controls,
- corporate governance,
- intellectual property.

Cartel Anticompetitive and Unfair Business Practices

Q 15.8.1   How frequent and significant are government investigations of suspected international cartels?

The investigation and prosecution of international cartels is one of the highest priorities—if not *the* highest priority—of the Antitrust Division. International cartels tend to be more complex, broader in geographic scope, and larger in terms of affected volumes of commerce than domestic antitrust conspiracies.[14] Criminal fines at the $10 million level have become commonplace, with top-end penalties in excess of $100 million for single companies and fines exceeding the $1 billion level for single industries.[15]

The Antitrust Division has prosecuted international cartels operating in a number of sectors, including vitamins, textiles, construction, food and feed additives, food preservatives, chemicals, graphite electrodes (used in making steel), fine arts auctions, ocean tanker shipping, marine construction, marine transportation services, rubber chemicals, synthetic rubber, dynamic random access memory used in computers and servers, marine hose, and air transportation.[16]

Q 15.8.2   Does the government face special problems in investigating and prosecuting international cartels?

The Antitrust Division reports that its most typical problem is that key documents and witnesses are located abroad—out of the reach of U.S. subpoena power and search-and-seizure authority. But foreign countries increasingly are cooperating with U.S. antitrust investigations and are starting to conduct their own investigations and prosecutions of anticompetitive activities.

Obtaining jurisdiction over foreign corporate defendants has not been a significant problem for the Antitrust Division. It is usually able to show that a company has a sufficient presence in the United States, through its own activities and/or its management and control of its U.S. subsidiaries, to justify the exercise of jurisdiction over it.[17]

Q 15.8.3   Why has the government been so successful in prosecuting international cartels?

The Corporate Leniency Program is the Antitrust Division's most effective investigative tool in prosecuting domestic and foreign cartels. Under this program, the first company to come forward and cooperate with the division automatically receives leniency (that is, is not prosecuted) if there is no pre-existing investigation. Leniency may still be available even if cooperation begins after a government investigation is underway. Further, all officers, directors, and employees who come forward with the company and cooperate are protected from criminal prosecution.

The effectiveness of this program was enhanced by 2004 legislation that (i) significantly increased the criminal penalties for cartel activities, and (ii) sweetened the deal for companies who come forward and cooperate by providing that, while they remain liable civilly for damages caused to their customers, their liability is limited to single damages rather than treble damages.[18] Moreover, the Antitrust Division program has served as a model for similar corporate leniency programs that have been adopted by other antitrust authorities around the world in recent years.

Noncartel Anticompetitive and Unfair Business Practices

Q 15.8.4 What are investigation "triggers" in the area of noncartel anticompetitive and unfair business practices?

1. *Pre-merger notification and review.* Pre-merger notification and review have become standard practice worldwide and require experience in managing the complexities of parallel pre-merger proceedings by two or more competition authorities.

2. *Worldwide marketing programs.* International marketing campaigns may raise issues of deceptive and unfair practices, whose definitions are often different from those used in the United States.

3. *Dominant positions.* A company's mere dominance in foreign or world markets increases the risk of an antimonopoly investigation.

Anti-Bribery

Q 15.8.5 What laws address bribery in an international context?

The Foreign Corrupt Practices Act[19] (FCPA) aims to prevent the bribery of foreign government officials, either directly or through an intermediary such as a joint venture partner or agent, in order to obtain or retain business. The FCPA also requires publicly traded companies to maintain records that accurately and fairly represent the company's transactions through an adequate system of internal accounting controls.

Q 15.8.6 Who is subject to the Foreign Corrupt Practices Act?

The FCPA applies to all publicly traded and private businesses in the United States, as well as to foreign subsidiaries, agents, distributors, advisors, and individuals.

Q 15.8.7   Is there an international consensus on anti-bribery regulation?

In recent years, a number of foreign countries have enacted or stepped up enforcement of their own anti-bribery statutes. Thirty-seven countries, including the United States, have ratified the Organization of Economic Cooperation and Development (OECD) Convention on Combating Bribery of Foreign Public Officials in International Business Transactions.[20]

Export Controls

Q 15.8.8   Why do export controls trigger international investigations?

International compliance programs and investigations are implicit in cases involving all aspects of U.S. export controls under the Department of Commerce, Department of State, and other national security regimes such as that of the Nuclear Regulatory Commission.

Q 15.8.9   Is there a particular industry significantly affected by U.S. export controls?

International investigations in the area of technology will increase as companies extend their presence globally, outsource their operations abroad, and maintain a diverse international workforce. Technology companies' corporate compliance and risk management rely on a clear understanding of national security concerns, proliferation of sensitive technologies, and counter-terrorism strategies as reflected in U.S. and foreign export control regimes.

Q 15.8.10   What sorts of issues commonly arise in international investigations of export control issues?

Most, if not all, international investigations require interviews, document collection, and analyses that extend to actions taken by foreign subsidiaries, affiliates, parties, or employees. The following are among the issues that commonly arise:

- Are there restrictions on collecting personal information related to foreign employees' export activities?

- How should export violations be discussed with foreign employees without violating U.S. export laws?
- Are export licenses needed to conduct an internal investigation? If so, how many?
- When should investigators obtain export licenses from foreign governments to transfer U.S.-/foreign-origin combined data back to the United States?
- Can an investigator collect export-related information involving foreign-person violations and forward that data to the U.S. government without additional authorizations?

Corporate Governance

Q 15.8.11   What failures in corporate governance trigger an investigation?

The possibilities for transnational corporate governance investigations are myriad. Some of the most common reasons to initiate an investigation include:

- securities fraud and unauthorized trading,
- commodities fraud and unauthorized trading,
- bank fraud,
- mail and wire fraud,
- government contract fraud,
- tax fraud, and
- related directors and officers litigation.

In addition, product liability and environmental, health, and safety violations are unfortunate and compelling reasons for the immediate initiation of an investigation. One need only consider the legal, financial, and humanitarian impact of the disaster in Bhopal, India for a reminder of the need for internal corporate vigilance.[21] Relaxing that vigilance when operating overseas can be a "bet the company" decision with devastating consequences.

Q 15.8.12   Are there external triggers for a corporate governance investigation?

Compliance with a number of statutes requires initiating a corporate governance investigation. These special statutes include the USA PATRIOT Act, the Bank Secrecy Act, money-laundering statutes, whistleblower claims, and Sarbanes-Oxley.

Intellectual Property

Q 15.8.13   What industries are vulnerable to international intellectual property rights infringement?

Traditionally, international intellectual property (IP) investigations involved patent infringement and the theft of trade secrets. Today IP investigations with a global reach can arise in virtually every sector of industry, especially in telecommunications, pharmaceuticals, biotechnology, chemicals, book publishing, film, music, or with respect to any trademark or other corporate identity worth stealing and exploiting worldwide in a host of formats and languages.

Many companies conduct worldwide investigations of stolen IP rights, counterfeit goods, services offered worldwide on the Internet, or related fraud on a continuing basis.

Q 15.8.14   What legal actions are available to a party whose IP rights are being infringed abroad?

In the past, the only practical methods of defending a company's IP in the United States and abroad seemed to be litigation in the courts or a section 337 investigation[22] conducted by the U.S. International Trade Commission. The primary remedies were: (1) seeking an exclusion order that directed Customs to stop infringing imports from entering the United States, or (2) a cease-and-desist order against a named importer or other person engaged in unfair acts that violated section 337.

Today, many foreign countries have improved their IP laws and have made it possible to attack infringers in their own home markets and extend effective IP rights into those markets. It has become increasingly possible to reach foreign conspirators and thieves through their own countries' criminal laws. To do so, however, it is necessary to conduct an international investigation on a cost-efficient and effective basis.

> **TIP:** In IP and many other areas, it is not only the compliance-based *defensive* investigation but also the rights-based *offensive* international investigation that must be considered in exercising responsible corporate leadership.

Conducting an Effective International Investigation

Initial Steps

Q 15.9   What preliminary considerations are necessary prior to carrying out an international investigation?

1. Establishing objectives and priorities with the client. In almost every investigation there are potential tradeoffs between the

    (a)   time schedule,
    (b)   resources expended, and
    (c)   results sought.

It is ultimately the client that has to set the priorities for the investigation. When conditions are optimal, these considerations may not conflict with each other, but when conditions are not perfect, the client must be willing to prioritize and stick to those priorities.

2. Issue spotting. Effective and comprehensive issue spotting at the outset of the investigation is critical.

- What (potential) violations are at stake?
- What are the legal elements of the violation(s)?
- Are there legal privileges or other limitations that may constrain the investigation?
- Are there time limits?

Additional issues may well arise as the investigation proceeds, but there is no substitute for foresight.

3. Knowing your client. Familiarity with the client's business, personnel, and organization is important to structuring an internal investigation that is efficient and thorough. To the extent that counsel lacks such knowledge, assistance should be obtained from executives or supervisors who can provide it.

4. Establishing a plan. After establishing the objectives and priorities of the investigation, spotting the issues, and assessing the lay of the land, an investigative plan should be developed that estab-

lishes, at least preliminarily, who will be interviewed, what topics will be covered, and what documents will be reviewed. This plan may be formal or informal, and it should be subject to review and adjustment as the investigation proceeds.

Conducting the Investigation

Q 15.9.1   Who will conduct the investigation?

Assembling the right team to staff the investigation and any ensuing litigation, mediation, or negotiation is critical to its success. As discussed above, it is essential to recruit counsel and staff who are sensitive to the specific cultural, linguistic, and substantive issues that are likely to arise in a specific case.

The investigation may be conducted by attorneys, outside investigators, internal audit staff, other company employees, or some combination thereof. The actual composition of a particular team will depend on the nature and significance of the issue(s), the need for specialized expertise, cost concerns, and time deadlines. If the company wants to obtain the protections of the attorney-client privilege and the attorney work-product doctrine, then the investigation must be conducted under the supervision of counsel. And, in most cases, it will be necessary to secure the assistance of the company's information technology personnel who can access and copy the computers or email of relevant employees.

The time and expense involved in transporting the investigative team to the locale of the investigation can make international investigations quite costly. Sometimes cost savings can be achieved by using local counsel or investigators. On the other hand, if the issue is serious and ultimately the company—through counsel—will have to disclose it to and resolve it with the U.S. government or a foreign government, then it is very much preferable that the investigation have been conducted by this same counsel. The credibility of the investigation is paramount to its cost.

Notes to Chapter 15

1. Much of this chapter's discussion of international investigations assumes a basic understanding of internal investigations. You may find it helpful to read this chapter in conjunction with chapter 6, which provides detailed coverage of domestic internal investigations.

2. Council Directive 95/46/EC, on the protection of individuals with regard to the processing of personal data and on the free movement of such data, 1995 O.J. (L 281) 31, http://ec.europa.eu/justice_home/fsj/privacy/docs/95-46-ce/dir1995-46_part1_en.pdf.

3. An international survey of privacy laws can be found on the Global Internet Liberty Campaign's website. *Privacy and Human Rights: An International Survey of Privacy Laws and Practice*, GLOB. INTERNET LIBERTY CAMPAIGN, http://gilc.org/privacy/survey/ (last visited July 13, 2015).

4. Robert G. Morvillo & Robert J. Anello, *Attorney-Client Privilege in International Investigations*, N.Y.L.J., Aug. 7, 2008.

5. Case C-550/07 P, Akzo Nobel Chems. Ltd. & Akcros Chems. Ltd. v. European Comm'n (Grand Chamber Apr. 29, 2010), www.acc.com/advocacy/upload/AG-Opinion-AKZO-042910.pdf.

6. *See, e.g.*, Cooper Indus., Inc. v. British Aerospace, Inc., 102 F.R.D. 918 (S.D.N.Y. 1984); Marc Rich & Co., A.G. v. United States, 707 F.2d 663 (2d Cir. 1983).

7. Foreign Corrupt Practices Act of 1977 (FCPA), 15 U.S.C. § 78dd-1 *et seq.*

8. Travel Act, 18 U.S.C. § 1952.

9. *See* United States v. Parise, 159 F.3d 790, 804 & n.1 (3d Cir. 1998) (Garth, J., dissenting) (collecting state commercial bribery statutes).

10. Sarbanes-Oxley Act of 2002 (SOX), Pub. L. No. 107-204, 116 Stat. 745.

11. Sherman Act, ch. 647, 26 Stat. 209 (July 2, 1890), 15 U.S.C. §§ 1–7.

12. *See* F. Hoffmann-La Roche Ltd. v. Empagran S.A., 542 U.S. 155, 158 (2004).

13. Thomas O. Barnett, Assistant Attorney Gen., Dep't of Justice, Antitrust Div., Presentation at Georgetown Law Global Antitrust Enforcement Symposium (Sept. 26, 2007), www.justice.gov/atr/public/speeches/speech_2007.htm.

14. Gary R. Spratling, Deputy Assistant Attorney Gen., U.S. Dep't of Justice, Antitrust Div., Criminal Antitrust Enforcement Against International Cartels, Presentation at Advanced Criminal Antitrust Workshop: A Practical Approach to Criminal Investigations (Feb. 21, 1997), www.justice.gov/atr/public/speeches/1056.pdf.

15. Scott D. Hammond, Deputy Assistant Attorney Gen. for Criminal Enf't, U.S. Dep't of Justice, Antitrust Div., Recent Developments, Trends, and Milestones in the Antitrust Division's Criminal Enforcement Program, Speech before the ABA Section of Antitrust Law Spring Meeting, at 10–12 (Mar. 26, 2008), www.justice.gov/atr/public/speeches/232716.pdf.

16. *Id.* at 17.

17.   Spratling, *supra* note 14, at 9–12.

18.   On November 19, 2008, the Antitrust Division issued a policy paper entitled Frequently Asked Questions Regarding the Antitrust Division's Leniency Program and Model Leniency Letters (FAQs), www.justice.gov/atr/public/criminal/239583.pdf.

19.   For a more detailed discussion of the FCPA, see chapter 16.

20.   For a more detailed discussion of the OECD, see www.oecd.org/department/0,3355,en_2649_34859_1_1_1 _1_1,00.html.

21.   For more information on the Bhopal Union Carbide gas leak disaster that took place on December 3, 1984, see http://news.bbc.co.uk/1/hi/programmes/bhopal/default.stm.

22.   19 U.S.C. § 1337.

16

Foreign Corrupt Practices Act

Don Zarin & Timothy D. Belevetz*

The Foreign Corrupt Practices Act (FCPA) presents one of the most significant compliance risks for U.S. companies engaged in international business activities. It has two substantive parts: the anti-bribery provisions, which make it illegal to bribe a foreign official for any improper advantage, and the accounting provisions, which impose certain accounting and record-keeping requirements upon companies that have registered securities with the SEC.

Part I of this chapter addresses the FCPA's bribery provisions, and Part II addresses the accounting provisions.

---

*   Don Zarin is the author of Part I of this chapter; Timothy D. Belevetz is the author of Part II.

PART I
FCPA's Anti-Bribery Provisions

PART II
FCPA's Accounting Provisions

PART I
FCPA's Anti-Bribery Provisions*

Prohibition on Bribery

Q 16.1   What do the anti-bribery provisions of the FCPA prohibit?

Under the anti-bribery provisions of the FCPA,[1] it is unlawful for issuers, domestic concerns, or any officer, director, employee, agent, or stockholder acting on behalf of such entity, to offer, promise, pay, or authorize the payment, directly or indirectly through any other person or firm, of anything of value to a foreign official in order to obtain or retain business or any other improper advantage. In addition, foreign companies and foreign nationals may be subject to prosecution under the FCPA if they commit any act in furtherance of the bribery of a foreign official "while in the territory of the United States."

Specifically, the FCPA prohibits:

(i)   issuers, domestic concerns, and certain foreign entities, and any officer, director, employee, agent, or stockholder acting on behalf of such entities from

(ii)   using an instrumentality of interstate commerce or doing any act while in the territory of the United States

(iii)   corruptly

(iv)   in furtherance of an offer, payment, promise to pay, or authorization of payment of

(v)   anything of value

(vi)   to a foreign official, foreign political party or official thereof, or any candidate for foreign political office, or

(vii)   to any person while knowing that all or a portion of such money or thing of value will be offered, given, or promised, directly or indirectly to a foreign official

---

*   Part I of this chapter is authored by Don Zarin, who would like to acknowledge John S. Irving IV for his contributions to Part I.

(viii) for purposes of influencing any act or decision of such foreign official, inducing such official to do or omit to do some action, inducing such official to influence any act or decision of such government, or securing any improper advantage

(ix) in order to assist in obtaining or retaining business, or directing business to any person.

Q 16.2   Who is subject to prosecution under the FCPA?

The FCPA applies to:

(1) issuers;[2]

(2) domestic concerns;[3]

(3) foreign persons and foreign non-issuer entities who commit an act in furtherance of a corrupt payment while in the territory of the United States;[4] or

(4) any officer, director, employee or agent of such issuer, domestic concern, or non-issuer foreign entity (acting within the territory of the United States) or any stockholder acting on behalf of such entity.

Jurisdictional Prerequisites

"Issuers"

Q 16.3   What are the meaning and scope of "issuers"?

Issuers[5] that have a class of securities registered pursuant to section 12 of the Exchange Act or that are required to file reports under section 15(d) of the Exchange Act[6] are subject to the FCPA. This includes several subsets of entities:

- issuers with a class of securities registered on a national securities exchange pursuant to section 12(b) of the Exchange Act;

- issuers with a class of equity securities listed on the National Association of Securities Dealers Automated Quotation (NASDAQ) system;

- issuers that have $10 million or more in assets on the last day of their most recent fiscal year and that have a class of equity securities held by 500 or more persons, with the exception of issuers specifically exempt under section 12 or the rules thereunder, or that have received an exemption from the SEC;[7]
- foreign private issuers whose securities are registered under the Exchange Act;[8]
- banks and other financial institutions that file Exchange Act reports with the Office of the Comptroller of the Currency (OCC) or other appropriate financial institution agency, also known as "section 12(i) companies";[9] and
- issuers that offered securities to the public using the vehicle of a registration statement and prospectus pursuant to the Securities Act of 1933—but only during the one-year "duty to update" period following the offering ("section 15(d) registrants").[10]

"Domestic Concerns"

Q 16.4 What are the meaning and scope of "domestic concerns"?

The term "domestic concerns" means:

(A) any individual who is a citizen, national, or resident of the United States; and
(B) any corporation, partnership, association, joint-stock company, business trust, unincorporated organization, or sole proprietorship that has its principal place of business in the United States, or that is organized under the laws of a state of the United States or a territory, possession, or commonwealth of the United States.[11]

The application of the FCPA was originally limited to business enterprises organized in the United States or that have their principal place of business there. It did not cover foreign companies, including foreign subsidiaries of U.S. companies. The legislative history confirms that only U.S. (and not foreign) companies were covered by the FCPA.[12] But U.S. citizens, nationals, and residents, even those employed by foreign companies, were and are subject to the FCPA's jurisdiction if they engage in illicit payments abroad.[13]

"Officer, Director, Employee, Agent, or Stockholder"

Q 16.5   What are the scope and application of "officer, director, employee, agent, or stockholder"?

The application of the FCPA extends to the officers, directors, employees, or agents of issuers, domestic concerns, or non-issuer foreign entities that commit an act in furtherance of a bribe while in the territory of the United States, or stockholders acting on behalf of such entities. This may include non-U.S. nationals and foreign companies.

An employee or agent of a U.S. company can be held liable under the FCPA even if the U.S. company is acquitted or never charged with an offense.[14] Presumably, this also applies to foreign nationals who are employees or agents of a U.S. company.[15] All employees or agents of U.S. businesses are subject to both civil and criminal penalties.[16] In addition, if a foreign corporation is an issuer (that is, its securities are listed on a U.S. stock exchange), its foreign national employees may be subject to the jurisdiction of the FCPA as well.[17]

Q 16.5.1   What is the scope of an agency relationship and the application of principles of agency in determining FCPA liability?

In DOJ and SEC enforcement actions, foreign companies that served as *agents* of issuers or domestic concerns have been charged with violating the FCPA.[18] The DOJ has also brought several recent FCPA enforcement actions against foreign subsidiaries of domestic concerns or issuers on the grounds that the foreign subsidiaries acted as agents of their parent companies. The legal basis for this position appears to be tenuous, at best. (See the case studies that follow.)

In their Resource Guide to the FCPA,[19] the DOJ and SEC assert that a parent company may be liable for its subsidiary's conduct under traditional agency principles and that the fundamental characteristic of agency is "control."[20] The Resource Guide further indicates that under principles of respondeat superior, if an agency relationship exists, the parent company would be liable for the acts committed by the subsidiary's employees.[21]

The term "agent" has several different meanings and applications.[22] It is often used interchangeably with employee in a master-

CASE STUDY: *SEC v. Panalpina, Inc.*[23]

The SEC charged Panalpina, Inc., a non-issuer, with aiding and abetting and acting as an "agent" of its U.S. issuer customers in the bribery of foreign officials. Panalpina, the U.S. subsidiary of a global freight forwarder and logistics service provider, bribed foreign officials to obtain preferential Customs and import treatment for its customers. In charging Panalpina, the SEC acknowledged that Panalpina was not an issuer under the FCPA, but nevertheless charged it with assisting its issuer customers.

 CASE STUDY: *United States v. DPC (Tianjin) Co.*[24]

In a plea agreement that arose from a voluntary disclosure, DPC (Tianjin) Co., a wholly owned Chinese subsidiary of Diagnostics Products Corporation ("Diagnostics"), pled guilty to one count of a violation of the FCPA. DPC produces and sells diagnostic medical equipment. It made payments to physicians and laboratory personnel employed by a government-owned hospital in China to influence their decisions to purchase the company's products. Diagnostics had no knowledge of and did not authorize the improper conduct.

The plea agreement charged the Chinese subsidiary with being an "agent" of Diagnostics.[25] The plea agreement specified the use of an instrumentality of interstate commerce—that is, the Chinese subsidiary caused a proposed budget to be sent from Los Angeles to China by phone, facsimile, and email, and sent an email message from China to Diagnostics in California, which attached a monthly report that included payments to laboratory personnel and doctors. But there is no support or justification for determining that the foreign subsidiary acted as an "agent" of its parent company.

CASE STUDY: *SEC v. ENI, S.p.A. & Snamprogetti Netherlands B.V.*[26]

The SEC charged Snamprogetti Netherlands B.V., a Dutch company, with a violation of the anti-bribery provisions, when it acted as "an agent of a U.S. issuer," for its part in a decades-long scheme to bribe Nigerian officials to obtain engineering, procurement, and construction contracts. Snamprogetti was an indirect wholly owned subsidiary of ENI, S.p.A., an Italian company and an issuer under the FCPA. The complaint asserted that ENI exercised control and supervision over Snamprogetti, but provided no factual support for the assertion that Snamprogetti acted as an agent of ENI.

servant relationship.[27] In this case, the principal may be liable for the actions of its servants employed to perform service in his affairs and who controls or has the right to control the conduct of the services.[28] But for this type of agency relationship to occur between a parent and its subsidiary, the parent must exercise control over all of the day-to-day affairs and direct all of the operations of the subsidiary and its employees.[29] This type of situation is rare.[30]

In *Pacific Can Co. v. Hewes*,[31] cited in the Resource Guide,[32] the court stated that if one corporation controls and operates another, it may be liable under agency principles. But the court also noted that ownership of all of the stock of the subsidiary and common officers and directors was insufficient to establish an agency relationship.[33]

While there is some legal support for the assertion that a subsidiary may be an agent of the parent company, the standards and requirements to establish such a relationship are far more rigorous than the issue of control.[34] In most wholly owned parent-subsidiary relationships, the parent company exercises considerable control over the operations of its subsidiary.

While the term "agent" is not defined in the FCPA, the legislative history suggests that the term was intended to mean a foreign sales agent or other similar type of intermediary. The law of agency generally refers to an intermediary-type relationship. The *Restatement of the Law of Agency, Third*[35] indicates that an agency is a fiduciary relationship that arises when the principal manifests assent to the agent to act on its behalf and the agent agrees to do so.[36] While there may be instances where a subsidiary acts as a true intermediary for its parent, such instances are likely to be rare.

Moreover, Congress did not intend to impute liability to the U.S. corporation for the illicit conduct of its foreign sales agent, without the knowledge and/or authorization of the U.S. company. Rather, liability under the FCPA of the parent company for the illicit conduct of its agent/subsidiary is based on the parent company's knowledge and/or authorization of the actions of its agent/subsidiary.[37]

Foreign Persons, Foreign Non-Issuer Entities

Q 16.6   To what extent does the FCPA apply to foreign natural and legal persons?

To conform the FCPA to the OECD Convention, which calls on each member state to establish jurisdiction over the bribery of a foreign official committed by "any person" in whole or in part in the territory of the member state,[38] the 1998 amendments expanded the scope of the FCPA to cover foreign natural and legal persons, but required, as a jurisdictional nexus, that such foreign persons commit an act in furtherance of the bribery of a foreign officials "while in the territory of the United States."[39] As a result of this amendment, the FCPA now applies to "any person," but contains differing jurisdictional standards for different categories of persons.

The jurisdictional standards under which foreign companies and foreign nationals can be prosecuted under the FCPA include:

(i) foreign companies that are issuers;[40]
(ii) foreign nationals who are officers, directors, employees, or stockholders acting on behalf of a domestic concern or an issuer;
(iii) foreign persons (natural and legal) who act as agents of a domestic concern or an issuer;

CASE STUDY: *Japan Petroleum Co. v. Ashland Oil*[41]

The standards and requirements set forth in *Japan Petroleum Co. v. Ashland Oil* provide useful guidance on the issue of whether a subsidiary is an agent of the parent company. In that case, involving a breach of contract, the court considered whether Ashland Oil (Nigeria) Company (AON), a wholly owned subsidiary of Ashland Oil, Inc.,[42] was an agent of its parent company. The subsidiary was organized solely to act as an operating vehicle for the parent; all crude oil accrued to the parent; the parent company signed the production agreement; most of the officers and directors of the subsidiary were affiliated with the parent (or a division of the parent); the officer of the subsidiary received no separate or additional compensation beyond what he received as an officer of the parent; the subsidiary submitted its budget to the parent for review; any expenditures above certain limits were approved by the person who was an officer of both the parent and subsidiary, and by the management committee of the parent if the expenditures exceeded another limit; the parent advanced funds to and guaranteed bank loans extended to the subsidiary; and the parent represented to shareholders that the subsidiary's operations were in fact the parent's operations.

The court held that the subsidiary was *not* an agent of the parent company. Instead, the court determined that the subsidiary was not a shell company, but rather an operating company with obligations and rights of its own. Under local law, it possessed corporate powers that the parent did not have; the foreign government had some control over determining the well locations; the foreign subsidiary maintained its own bank accounts and prepared profit and loss statements; employed local auditors; and employed some local staff. Accordingly, the court found that the subsidiary "possess[ed] sufficient indicia of a separate corporate existence that it [could not] be viewed as a mere agent or instrumentality" of the parent company.

(iv) foreign persons (natural and legal) who commit an act in furtherance of a prohibited payment while in the territory of the United States, or whose agent does so;

(v) foreign persons (natural and legal) whose co-conspirator commits an act in furtherance of a prohibited payment while in the territory of the United States;[43]

(vi) foreign persons (natural and legal) who aid and abet a domestic concern or issuer.[44]

In the Resource Guide, the DOJ asserts that subject matter jurisdiction exists over foreign nationals and foreign companies if they engage, either directly or through an agent, in any act in furtherance of a corrupt act while in the territory of the United States.[45] Moreover, in the Resource Guide, the DOJ/SEC assert jurisdiction over a foreign national or a foreign company if it "causes" its agent to carry out an act in furtherance of the bribe within the territory of the United States.[46] Under this statutory provision, foreign persons (natural and legal) are not required to also utilize the mails or other instrumentality of interstate commerce (see the discussion of an instrumentality of interstate commerce at Q 16.7, *infra*). Rather, any act within the territory of the United States in furtherance of the bribe suffices.[47]

In addition, however, the DOJ continues to bring enforcement actions against and assert jurisdiction over foreign companies that only "cause" conduct (by non-agents) to take place within the territory of the United States in furtherance of a bribe.

Q 16.6.1   What does "territory of the United States" encompass?

The term "territory of the United States," is given a broad interpretation to encompass all areas over which the United States asserts territorial jurisdiction.[48] This includes not only the actual territorial boundaries of the fifty states, as well as territories, possessions, and commonwealths, but also includes airplanes flying under its flag, and persons aboard aircraft en route to the United States.[49] Under this broad interpretation, a telephone call made by a foreign national on a U.S. airline flying over Europe could arguably be deemed to be an act within the territory of the United States.

Q 16.6.2   Would a person physically outside the United States who causes an act to be done within the territory of the United States fall under FCPA jurisdiction?

In an indication of potentially broad enforcement intentions, a Department of Justice official, at a conference on the FCPA shortly after enactment of the 1998 amendments, suggested that the DOJ might consider an act physically done outside the territory of the United States (for example, email sent by foreign national from abroad) that triggers/causes an act to be done within the territory of the United States to be sufficient to meet this jurisdictional requirement.[50] Such an interpretation would effectively bring the jurisdictional requirement close to the "instrumentality of interstate commerce" test (*see* Q 16.7, *infra*). This approach had been rejected by the administration in its internal deliberations. But this concept of asserting jurisdiction over foreign persons that "cause" an act to be done within the territory of the United States continues to rear its head from time to time in DOJ enforcement actions.[51]

Q 16.6.3   Is a U.S. parent company necessarily liable under the FCPA's anti-bribery provision for improper conduct of its foreign subsidiary?

Under the 1998 amendments, foreign corporations, particularly foreign subsidiaries of U.S. companies, and foreign national employees of foreign subsidiaries, may now be independently liable under the FCPA.[52] This can occur even though the U.S. parent company had no knowledge of or involvement with such conduct. While the U.S. parent company may not be liable under the anti-bribery provision of FCPA for the improper conduct engaged in by its foreign subsidiary, the press reports of the indictment of a U.S. company's foreign subsidiary are unlikely to make such a fine distinction. Accordingly, this amendment constituted a significant expansion of the FCPA.

CASE STUDY: *SEC v. Sharef* [53]

In addition to the requirements of subject matter jurisdiction, the court recently addressed the issue of whether a foreign national has sufficient minimum contacts for a court to exercise personal jurisdiction. In *SEC v. Sharef*, the SEC charged Herbert Stefan, a former executive at Siemens AG with bribery involving Argentine officials. Stefan, a German citizen, encouraged the bribery payments to Argentine officials and participated in a phone call in furtherance of the bribe, which was initiated from the United States by a co-defendant. The court found that Stefan's actions were too attenuated to establish minimum contacts with the United States. The exercise of personal jurisdiction, therefore, exceeded the limits of due process.[54]

It would appear, therefore, that while the jurisdictional reach of the FCPA is exceedingly broad, it is nevertheless not without its limitations.

"Instrumentality of Interstate Commerce"

Q 16.7　What are the meaning and scope of "instrumentality of interstate commerce"?

An additional jurisdictional prerequisite to liability under the FCPA is the requirement that the U.S. company "make use of the mails or any means or instrumentality of interstate commerce in further-ance of" an illicit payment.[55] The term "interstate commerce" covers trade, commerce, transportation, or communication among the states or between any foreign country and any state, or between any state and any place outside the United States. It also includes the intrastate use of a telephone or other interstate means of communi-cation or any other interstate instrumentality.[56]

The inclusion of the phrase "in furtherance of" as part of this jurisdictional standard was intended to make clear that for liability to attach, the use of interstate commerce need only be in furtherance of making a prohibited payment.[57] This clause significantly broadened the jurisdictional scope of the FCPA, making it easier to meet this requirement. Under this standard, the use of an interstate facility need only be "incident to an essential part of the scheme."[58]

As a practical matter, the interstate commerce nexus will generally be an easy element to meet.[59] A telephone call or trip to the United States by the agent or employee of the foreign subsidiary to discuss the matter would suffice. So too would the transnational use of computers, the repatriation of earnings, or the consolidation of the books and records.[60] Moreover, the use of an instrumentality of interstate commerce does not have to be made by the defendant himself. When the use of an instrumentality of interstate commerce was the foreseeable result of the defendant's action, the jurisdictional requirement would be met, even if it was done by a third party. (See the *SEC v. Straub* case study below.)

Q 16.7.1   What is nationality jurisdiction?

The 1998 amendments to the FCPA expanded the jurisdictional basis for the prosecution of U.S. companies and U.S. citizens by adding an alternative basis for jurisdiction—the nationality principle.[61] Under this alternative standard, the FCPA would apply the nationality principle of jurisdiction to illicit payments made by U.S. citizens and U.S. companies that take place wholly outside the United States, without any use of an "instrumentality of interstate commerce" in furtherance of the illicit conduct.

The alternative nationality principle of jurisdiction would apply to:

(1)   "issuers" organized under the laws of the United States, or a state, territory, possession or commonwealth of the United States or a political subdivision thereof;[62]

(2)   any officer, director, employee, agent, or stockholder of such issuer that is a U.S. citizen or national,[63] acting on behalf of such issuer;[64]

(3)   any corporation, partnership, association, joint stock company, business trust, unincorporated organization, or self-proprietorship organized under the laws of the United States or any state, territory, possession, or commonwealth of the United States, or any political subdivision;[65]

CASE STUDY: *Schmuck v. United States*[66]

In *Schmuck v. United States*, the defendant was charged with mail fraud for rolling back odometers of used cars and then selling the automobiles to unknowing retail dealers for inflated prices due to low-mileage readings. The dealers in turn resold the cars to their customers. To complete the resale transaction, the dealer mailed a title-application form to the state Department of Transportation. The Court was called upon to decide whether the mailing of the title application form by the automobile dealers (who were not involved in the fraudulent scheme) was "in furtherance" of the fraudulent scheme. In affirming the conviction, the Court stated that "[i]t is sufficient for the mailing to be 'incident to an essential part of the scheme,' . . . or 'a step in the plot.'"[67] The Court distinguished several cases in which the mailing occurred after the defendant's scheme had already reached fruition[68] and concluded that in those instances, the use of the mail was not "in furtherance" of the scheme to defraud.[69] The Court also stated that innocent or routine use of an instrumentality of interstate commerce, as well as use of an instrumentality of commerce that may have been counterproductive to the scheme, was sufficient.[70]

(4)   any individual who is a citizen or national[71] of the United States.[72]

A foreign national employee of a U.S. company who resides abroad would not be subject to the alternative jurisdictional standard. Rather, the regular jurisdictional requirement—use of an instrumentality of interstate commerce—would apply. However, a foreign national employee of a U.S. company who makes an illicit payment outside the United States would subject the U.S. company to liability under the alternative nationality standard of jurisdiction, under principles of respondeat superior.

511

CASE STUDY: *SEC v. Straub*[73]

In *SEC v. Straub*, the SEC charged senior executives of Magyar Telekom, Plc (a foreign issuer) with violations of the FCPA in connection with a bribery scheme in Macedonia. The defendants' use of an instrumentality of interstate commerce involved the sending of email messages from outside the United States that were nevertheless routed through and/or stored on network servers located within the United States. The defendants, in a motion to dismiss, asserted that they did not meet the jurisdictional requirement, as they did not know about the use of servers located in the United States and did not intend to use an instrumentality of interstate commerce in a corrupt manner. The court rejected these arguments, stating that it was foreseeable that Internet usage might involve U.S. network servers and that corrupt intent was not required.[74]

The application of the alternative nationality principle of jurisdiction effectively replaces/vitiates the "instrumentality of interstate commerce" standard for U.S. citizens and U.S. companies. However, as a practical matter, this change is unlikely to have a significant effect. The "instrumentality of interstate commerce" standard has been very broadly interpreted. It would be a rare factual situation, indeed, where a U.S. company or U.S. citizen engaged in the bribery of a foreign official without otherwise using an instrumentality of interstate commerce in furtherance of the illicit conduct.[75]

"Corruptly"

Q 16.8   **What are the meaning and scope of "corruptly"?**

In order to be in violation of the FCPA, a payment must be made "corruptly." The term "corruptly" connotes an evil motive or purpose, an attempt to wrongfully influence the recipient. In the legislative history, the "corruptly" requirement makes clear that in order to violate the FCPA, a payment must be intended to influence the recipient to "misuse his official position" in order to wrongfully direct or obtain business.[76] It encompasses a quid pro quo element: a nexus between the illicit payment and the expected conduct of the foreign official.

The FCPA thus applies to payments made for a corrupt purpose, but it does not require that the violative action be fully consummated or succeed in producing the desired outcome.[77] A willful attempt to influence a foreign official through an offer or promise (or authorization of the offer or promise) of anything of value suffices. The prohibition against "corrupt" payments also applies to payments made by third parties, where the corporation pays the third party knowing that the payment will be passed on in whole or in part to a foreign official for a proscribed purpose.[78] On the other hand, an employee who makes an illicit payment at the behest and direction of his supervisor may not be acting corruptly under the FCPA.[79] The payment of money to a foreign official in true extortion situations, such as to keep an oil rig from being dynamited, would also not constitute a corrupt payment.[80]

Q 16.8.1   What constitutes corrupt intent, and how important is intent in establishing the "corruptly" standard?

Congress intended the "corruptly" standard under the FCPA to conform with the "corruptly" requirement under the domestic bribery law.[81] To establish the crime of bribery under the domestic bribery statute, the money or value must be knowingly offered or given to an official with the intent and expectation that, *in exchange for the money*, some act of the official would be influenced.[82] The money must be offered or given with more than some generalized hope or expectation of ultimate benefit on the part of the donor.[83] This distinction between a payment in consideration for[84] some conduct by the official and a payment with "some generalized expectation" of ultimate benefit (for example, goodwill) can be most clearly understood in the comparison between an unlawful bribe and lawful business entertainment. It is the quid pro quo aspect of the payment that distinguishes between the lawfulness or illegality of the expenditure.[85]

The focus is upon the subjective intent of the briber—the defendant's intention in making the payment, rather than the recipient's intent in carrying out official acts.[86] A party can be convicted of bribery despite the fact that the recipient had no intention of altering his official activities, or even lacked the power to do so.[87] It is neither material nor a defense to bribery that the official might lawfully and properly make the very recommendation or take the very action that the briber wanted the official to make without the bribe.[88] Evidence of an awareness of the illegality of the transaction may also be sufficient to prove corrupt intent.[89] Moreover, a person who authorizes an illicit payment does not need to know the specific official who will receive the payment.[90]

In the context of the FCPA, a payment to a foreign official with the intent to influence his decision, induce him to do or omit to do any act, or induce him to use his influence with a foreign government entity *in exchange for the payment* constitutes corrupt intent.

While the criminal conviction of a company requires proof that the defendant acted corruptly, the criminal conviction of an individual under the FCPA requires proof that the defendant acted not only "corruptly," but also "willfully."[91] In *United States v. Kozeny*,[92] the court held that willfulness meant that the defendant's conduct was unlawful, and not that the defendant in fact knew that his conduct violated the FCPA.[93] In *United States v. Kay*,[94] the court stated that "willfully" requires that the defendant knows he is committing the act itself and knows that it is in some way wrong. It does *not* require that the defendant knows he was violating the specific provisions of a law.[95]

Q 16.8.2   Does the FCPA apply to payments involving duress or extortion?

U.S. companies operate in many high-risk countries where the health and safety of their employees may be at risk. Persons that are compelled to provide payments to avoid imminent harm generally lack corrupt intent.[96] The Resource Guide indicates that payments involving extortion or duress are not made with the requisite corrupt intent.[97] However, these situations are very narrow and very limited in scope. The Resource Guide draws a distinction between the imminent threat of health or bodily injury versus economic coercion. The latter threat would not amount to extortion.[98]

In *SEC v. NATCO Group, Inc.*,[99] immigration prosecutors in Kazakhstan claimed that workers at Natco's subsidiary in Kazakhstan did not have the proper immigration documents. The Kazakh prosecutors threatened to fine, jail, or deport the workers if the company did not pay cash fines. Believing the threats to be genuine, the company paid the monies, but inaccurately described and improperly booked the transaction. Explicitly acknowledging that extortion was a valid defense, the SEC only charged NATCO with a violation of the books and records and internal accounting control provisions of the FCPA.[100]

"Foreign Official"

Q 16.9   What is the meaning and scope of "foreign official"?

The FCPA proscribes only illicit payments made to a foreign official, foreign political party or official thereof, or a candidate for foreign political office.[101] It was not intended to, and does not, address bribes or kickbacks paid to employees of private, nongovernmental entities.[102] Nor does the FCPA proscribe payments (for example, discounts or donations) made directly to a government department or agency that are not for the personal use or benefit of a foreign official.[103]

The FCPA defines the term "foreign official" as meaning:

> any officer or employee of a foreign government or any department, agency, or instrumentality thereof, or of a public international organization, or any person acting in an official capacity for or on behalf of any such government or department, agency, or instrumentality, or for or on behalf of any such public international organization.[104]

The scope of the elements of this definition are described below.

Q 16.9.1   What is the meaning and scope of "officer or employee" as used in the definition of "foreign official"?

Neither the FCPA nor its legislative history contains any guidance on the scope of the terms "officer" or "employee."[105] There are no cases under the FCPA that further define these terms. Nor is it clear whether the scope of these terms should be determined with reference to foreign local law.[106] The domestic bribery statute[107] and the

515

Federal Tort Claims Act (FTCA),[108] and the cases decided thereunder, offer the most instructive guidance in delineating the scope of these terms under the FCPA.

Based upon these statutes and cases, an "officer" of a foreign government would include individuals appointed by the head of state or by heads of executive departments and individuals who hold positions authorized by statute. An "employee" of a foreign government would include individuals whose day-to-day performance is supervised by the governmental authority.

Under the domestic bribery statute, the term "public official" is defined to mean, among other things, "an officer or employee or person acting for or on behalf of the United States . . . in any official function."[109] This language is similar to the FCPA definition of "foreign official." In interpreting the meaning of "officer" under this statute, the court in *United States v. Bordonaro*[110] held that the term includes members of draft boards whose positions are authorized by federal statute and who are appointed by the president. In *Felder v. United States*,[111] the circuit court ruled that "officers" include "persons acting under appointments 'embracing the idea of tenure, duration, emolument, and duties.'" Based on this definition, the court went on to hold that the attorney general and the U.S. attorney would be considered "officers" of the United States.[112]

The scope and meaning of the term "employee" of the United States often arises in cases under the FTCA.[113] In such cases, the court is frequently asked to discern whether an alleged tortfeasor is an employee of the United States, rather than an independent contractor. The U.S. Supreme Court addressed this question in *United States v. Orleans*[114] and *Logue v. United States*[115] and indicated that the determination turns on whether the government has the authority to supervise the alleged tortfeasor's day-to-day operations.

In *Resendez v. United States*,[116] the Ninth Circuit elaborated on the "control test" established by the Supreme Court, noting noted that there are additional factors that "traditionally determine the existence of the common-law relationship of master and servant" that should also be examined to "determine whether the wrongdoer is an employee of the Government for whose torts the United States must respond." They include:

the extent of control which the master may exercise over the details of the work; whether or not the one employed is engaged in a distinct occupation or business; the nature of the occupation, with reference to whether the work is usually done under the direction of the employer or by a specialist without supervision; the skill required in the particular occupation; whether the employer or the workman supplies the tools, equipment, and the place of work for the person doing the work; the length of time for which the person is employed; the method of payment, that is, whether by time or by the job; whether or not the parties believe they are creating the relation of master and servant, etc.[117]

Q 16.9.2   What is the meaning and scope of "agency or instrumentality" of a foreign government as used in the definition of "foreign official"?

The breadth and scope of the term "agency or instrumentality" of a foreign government are not delineated in the FCPA or in its legislative history. Enforcement authorities have long taken the position that the phrase includes state-owned or state-controlled commercial enterprises and that the provision of commercial services does not necessarily preclude an entity from being an instrumentality of a foreign government. The Resource Guide indicates that determining whether a state-owned or -controlled entity constitutes an instrumentality requires a fact-specific analysis of the entity's ownership, control, status, and function.[118] Thus, a state trading corporation,[119] a mining enterprise, a transport organization such as a shipping line[120] or an airline,[121] or a steel company could have come within the definition of an agency or instrumentality in enforcement actions.[122]

In May 2014, the U.S. Court of Appeals for the Eleventh Circuit largely agreed with the government's position in holding that an "instrumentality" is an entity that (1) is controlled by a foreign government and (2) performs a function that the controlling government treats as its own.[123] The question in that case was whether a Haitian telecommunications company that supplied phone time to Esquanazi's Florida company was an "instrumentality" of the Haitian government, where there was no law specifically designating the recently privatized Haitian telecommunications company as a public entity, but where there was a history of governmental involvement in the management and financing of that entity. The court listed the following non-exclusive factors to weigh in determining whether an entity is controlled by a foreign government:[124]

1.   The foreign government's formal designation of that entity;
2.   Whether the government has a majority interest in the entity;
3.   The government's ability to hire and fire the entity's principals;
4.   The extent to which the entity's profits, if any, go directly into the governmental fisc;
5.   The extent to which the government funds the entity if it fails to break even; and
6.   The length of time these indicia have existed.

In determining whether an entity performs a function that the foreign government treats as its own, the court listed the following factors that, again, are not exclusive:[125]

1.   Whether the entity has a monopoly over the function it exists to carry out;
2.   Whether the government subsidizes the costs associated with the entity providing services;
3.   Whether the entity provides services to the public at large in the foreign country; and
4.   Whether the public and the government of that foreign country generally perceive the entity to be performing a governmental function.

There have been several other fairly recent enforcement actions where partially government-owned entities have been deemed to be "instrumentalities" of foreign governments, including:

*   *United States v. Aguilar*[126] (U.S. District Court for the Central District of California, 2011): Lindsey Manufacturing Co. and several executives were charged with funneling bribes to officials of Mexico's state-owned electrical utility company. Although the court ultimately dismissed the indictment for prosecutorial misconduct, it denied a defense motion to dismiss the indictment and found that the Mexican utility company could be an "instrumentality" under the FCPA where: electricity is solely a government function under the Mexican Constitution, the language of the statute creating the utility stated that it was "a decentralized public entity,"

and the utility's board was composed of government officials. The court listed characteristics tending to suggest that
an entity is an "instrumentality," including:

- whether the entity provides a service to citizens;
- whether the key officials are appointed by the government;
- whether the entity is financed by the government; and
- whether the entity is perceived to be performing
  governmental functions.

- *United States v. Alcatel-Lucent*[127] (U.S. District Court for the
  Southern District of Florida, 2010). In this settled enforcement
  case, the government alleged that Telekom Malaysia, an entity
  of which the Malaysian Ministry of Finance owned 43%, was an
  "instrumentality," and highlighted a combination of ownership and control factors, including that the Ministry of
  Finance held a special shareholder position with veto power
  over all expenditures and operational decisions for Telekom,
  and that it appointed senior officers of the company.

- *United States v. Kellogg Brown & Root (KBR)*[128] (Southern
  District of Texas, 2009): KBR pled guilty in February 2009 to
  conspiracy and substantive FCPA violations. At issue were
  bribes paid to officials of Nigeria LNG Ltd. (NLNG) in connection with a natural gas project on Bonny Island. The charging
  document that KBR agreed with as part of the plea agreement asserted that NLNG was an entity and instrumentality
  of the Nigerian government because it was responsible for
  developing and regulating Nigeria's oil and gas industry and
  because a Nigerian government-owned entity was NLNG's
  largest shareholder, owning 49%. The remaining 51% was
  owned by several multinational oil companies. The charging
  document explained that the Nigerian government exercised
  control over NLNG—including the ability to block the
  awarding of engineering, procurement, and construction
  contracts—through the members appointed to NLNG's
  board.

Q 16.9.3   What is the meaning and scope of "acting for or on behalf of" as used in the definition of "foreign official"?

The FCPA and its legislative history provide no guidance on the meaning of the term "acting for or on behalf of."[129] It is therefore necessary once again to look to the domestic bribery statute and the FTCA, and cases thereunder, for some guidance on the meaning and scope of this term.

These statutes and cases suggest that the term "acting in an official capacity for or on behalf of," under the FCPA, would likely include individuals whose activities are controlled by the foreign government or who occupy a position of public trust and have official governmental responsibilities.

CASE STUDY: *Dixson v. United States*[130]

The leading decision addressing the meaning of the term "acting for or on behalf" in the domestic bribery statute is *Dixson v. United States*. In *Dixson*, the Supreme Court ruled that whether an individual acted for or on behalf of the United States does not depend upon the existence of a "direct contractual bond" with the government, but rather turns on whether the person occupies a position of public trust with official federal responsibilities.[131] The Court then went on to hold that the defendants, who were responsible for administering federal community development grants, were "public officials," given their operational roles in administering a social service program administered by Congress and the fact that they were charged with abiding by federal regulations.[132]

Q 16.9.4   What is the meaning and scope of "public international organization" as used in the definition of "foreign official"?

The OECD Convention included officials of a "public international organization" within the definition of a foreign public official.[133] Accordingly, to conform the FCPA to the OECD Convention, the 1998 amendments to the FCPA expanded the definition of a foreign official to include any official or employee of a public international organization, or any person acting on behalf of a public international organization.[134]

The "public international organizations" covered by the FCPA are those organizations designated by executive order pursuant to the International Organizations Immunities Act,[135] or any other international organization designated by the president by executive order.[136] This includes such organizations as the Organization of American States, the European Space Agency, the Hong Kong Economic and Trade Offices, the World Bank,[137] and the United Nations.[138]

Foreign Political Party; Candidate for Foreign Political Office

Q 16.10   Why does the FCPA prohibit offers or payments to a foreign political party or official thereof or any candidate for foreign political office?

The FCPA proscribes illicit payments not only to foreign officials, but also to a foreign political party, an official of a foreign political party, or a candidate for foreign political office.[139] The inclusion of this class of individuals in the FCPA is a recognition that such persons may be influential in the award of government business.

Q 16.10.1   How does the FCPA determine whether a payment to a foreign political party/candidate is legitimate or corrupt?

The FCPA recognizes that "corrupt" payments are not intended to include legitimate and lawful campaign contributions made in the course of legitimate lobbying and other normal representations to foreign government officials.[140] Generally, political contributions are not tied to the support of any particular transaction and are therefore not intended as a quid pro quo. However, reliance on the absence of corrupt intent does not provide an adequate comfort level in defending oneself under the FCPA.

In some instances, campaign contributions may be lawful under the written laws of a foreign country.[141] Such a situation may constitute a rare instance in which the affirmative defense (for payments that are lawful under the written laws of a foreign country) may be applicable. However, in many countries, such payments may not be impermissible, although not expressly permitted under the written laws of that country.[142] It is preferable for U.S. companies to avoid making any campaign contributions that are not expressly permitted under the written laws of the foreign country.

Q 16.10.2 Can the foreign agent of a U.S. company make contributions to a foreign political party/candidate?

A more difficult practical issue arises in this situation. Where the foreign agent of a U.S. company makes political campaign contributions, it may be difficult, as a practical matter, to know whether such payments are provided for legitimate reasons or are improperly proffered as a quid pro quo. If the foreign country's laws do not require disclosure of such contributions, the possibility for abuse is further increased. If the "campaign contributions" of the foreign agent in fact constitute illicit payments (that is, are intended as a quid pro quo), the U.S. company could be subject to scrutiny by enforcement authorities to determine whether it authorized such payments to be made, or whether it intended to utilize the foreign agent as an intermediary for illicit political contributions.

To minimize this possibility, the U.S. company may want to prohibit the foreign agent from making any campaign contribution. If this is not practical, then the U.S. company should require disclosure of the contributions. In addition, the agency agreement should contain, in addition to other appropriate representations, the following additional representation:

- that any campaign contribution will, at all times, be in compliance with local law;
- that no campaign contributions shall be made in exchange for any specific benefits related to any transaction; and

- that the foreign sales agent will keep accurate books and records of all campaign contributions and such contributions shall be subject to audit by the U.S. company or its designee.

"Anything of Value"

Q 16.11   What is the meaning and scope of "anything of value"?

The FCPA prohibits payments and gifts or the giving of "anything of value" to influence the receiving foreign official.[143] The phrase "anything of value" is not defined in the FCPA or in its legislative history. The term is, however, contained in many other U.S. criminal statutes, and it has been broadly construed to encompass both tangible and intangible benefits that an official subjectively believes to be of value.[144]

Courts have construed the phrase "thing of value" broadly to also include intangible items, such as information,[145] sex,[146] the testimony of a witness,[147] and assistance in arranging for the merger of two unions.[148]

The Model Penal Code uses terms such as "benefit" and "pecuniary benefit" in its anti-bribery provisions.[149] The term "benefit" is defined as "gain or advantage, or anything regarded by the beneficiary as gain or advantage, including benefit to any other person or entity in whose welfare he is interested."[150] According to the Model Penal Code Commentary, the purpose of defining the term so broadly is "to reach every kind of offer to influence official or political action by extraneous incentives."[151] Under this standard, the giving of a benefit, not to the beneficiary himself (that is, the official), but rather to a third person or entity whose well-being the beneficiary is interested in, would constitute a benefit. For example, an offer to admit the child of an official to college in exchange for favorable action by the official would constitute a "benefit" under this standard.[152]

CASE STUDY: *United States v. Williams*[153]

In *United States v. Williams*, the U.S. Court of Appeals for the Second Circuit considered the meaning of the phrase "anything of value" contained in the domestic bribery statute[154] and the unlawful gratuity statute.[155] In *Williams*, a U.S. Senator received shares of stock in several corporations in return for his help in obtaining government contracts. Although the stock had no commercial value, the senator expected that the shares would have commercial value when he received them. The court affirmed the lower court's jury instruction that construed the statute to focus on the value the defendant subjectively attached to the items received.[156] The court further stated that "[t]he phrase 'anything of value' in bribery and related statutes has consistently been given a broad meaning . . . to carry out the congressional purpose of punishing misuse of public office."[157]

Q 16.11.1 Does "anything of value" under the FCPA extend to payments given to a third party in whose welfare the beneficiary is interested?

It is unclear. While the U.S. domestic bribery statute[158] explicitly forbids the payment of anything of value by which a public official himself will not benefit but that will be of advantage to "any other person or entity,"[159] the FCPA does not contain a comparable provision.[160] The FCPA instead appears to focus on whether there is any intent or expectation that the official will personally benefit from the thing of value.[161] Some Department of Justice Review Procedure Releases further indicate that U.S. enforcement authorities consider payments to other persons in whose well-being an official is interested (for example, relatives) constitute the giving of something of value to an official.[162]

CASE STUDY: *United States v. Liebo*[163]

The U.S. Court of Appeals for the Eighth Circuit has suggested the possibility of a more expansive view of the extent of the giving of "anything of value." In *Liebo*, the defendant was convicted of providing airplane tickets for the honeymoon of an official in the Niger Embassy in order to influence another official who was the relative and friend of the embassy official. The indictment made clear that the recipient (the Embassy employee) was himself a foreign official.[164] Nevertheless, the court commented that the relationship between the two relatives/friends was such that a jury could infer that the gift provided to the Embassy official was intended to buy the influential official's help in getting the contract award.[165]

Q 16.11.2   Can charitable contributions be construed as "anything of value" for purposes of FCPA liability?

As the Resource Guide explains, "The FCPA does not prohibit charitable contributions or prevent corporations from acting as good corporate citizens. Companies, however, cannot use the pretense of charitable contributions as a way to funnel bribes to government officials."[166] Companies should exercise due diligence and controls to mitigate FCPA risks in making charitable contributions.[167]

Influencing a Foreign Official

Q 16.12   Is the FCPA limited to payments designed to influence a foreign official's acts or decisions?

The scope of the FCPA is limited to a prohibition of an offer, promise, authorization or payment for purposes of:

- influencing any act or decision of a foreign official in his official capacity, or

CASE STUDY: *SEC v. Schering-Plough*[168]

The SEC initiated an enforcement action against Schering-Plough for the violation of the books and records and internal control provisions of the FCPA arising from the conduct of its subsidiary. The Polish office of the subsidiary made a series of donations to a charitable organization in Poland that restores castles and other historical sites in the Silesian region of Poland. The founder and president of the foundation was also the Director of the Silesian Health Fund, a government body that provides money to purchase pharmaceutical products and influences purchases by hospitals. The SEC took the position that, while the payments were made to a bona fide charity, they were in fact bribes intended to influence the director to purchase the company's products. In effect, the payments to the foundation constituted "value" to the official.

- inducing such foreign official to do or omit to do any act in violation of the lawful duty of such official,[169] or
- inducing such foreign official to use his influence with a foreign government or instrumentality thereof to affect or influence any act or decision of such government or instrumentality,[170] or
- securing any improper advantage.[171]

Thus, the FCPA applies to payments designed to influence an act or decision of a foreign official (including a decision not to act) or to induce such an official to use his influence to affect a governmental act or decision.[172] Payments to influence the enactment or promulgation of legislation or of regulations[173] or to induce an official to misuse his official position[174] also come within the scope of this prohibition.

Business Purpose Test

Q 16.13   What is the business purpose test under the FCPA?

The FCPA applies only to payments intended to influence an official's acts or decisions "in order to assist . . . in obtaining or retaining business for or with, or directing business to, any person."[175] This so-called business purpose test is meant to limit the scope of the prohibition by requiring that the illicit payment be made with the purpose of directing business to any person, maintaining an established business relationship, or diverting a business opportunity from any person.[176] Under this standard, payments made to an official with the purpose of inducing the official to take an action that assists the U.S. company in carrying out its existing business would violate the FCPA, even though the payments were not related to the underlying transaction.[177] For instance, payments to officials to reduce or eliminate customs duties,[178] to change the classification of a product, or to circumvent a quota or licensing system would violate the FCPA.[179]

Q 16.13.1   What are some examples of actions taken to obtain or retain business?

The Resource Guide provides illustrative examples of actions taken to obtain or retain business, including

- (i)   winning a contract,
- (ii)   influencing the procurement process,
- (iii)   gaining access to nonpublic bid tender information,
- (iv)   evading taxes or penalties,
- (v)   influencing lawsuits or enforcement actions,
- (vi)   obtaining exceptions to regulations, and
- (vii)   avoiding contract termination.[180]

Payments Through a Third Party

Q 16.14   What liability is there under the FCPA for bribery payments made through third parties?

Foreign sales agents were responsible for many of the questionable foreign payments disclosed during the 1970s. As a result, the FCPA included a provision delineating the circumstances under which a U.S. company or its officers and employees would be held accountable for illicit payments made indirectly through intermediary third parties.[181] Under the FCPA, a U.S. company may be subject to potential liability with regard to improper payments made by a third party, when:

(1) the U.S. company pays *"any person*, while *knowing* that all or a portion of such money or thing of value will be offered, given, or promised, directly or indirectly, to any foreign official, to any foreign political party or official thereof, or to any candidate for foreign political office"[182] in connection with the sale of the U.S. company's product or service; or

(2) the U.S. company *authorizes* any improper payment made or to be made by a third party (for example, foreign subsidiary) in connection with the sale of the U.S. company's equipment or services.[183]

A person's state of mind with respect to "knowing" is discussed at Q 16.15. The standard for authorizing improper payments is discussed at Q 16.16.

The U.S. domestic bribery statute[184] does not contain a special standard for illicit payments made through intermediary third parties. Rather, criminal liability generally depends upon a person's involvement as an accomplice, such as aiding and abetting.[185] In contrast, the FCPA may hold a U.S. company directly responsible for the conduct of a third party if the U.S. company "knew" that the money or thing of value given to the third party would be used, directly or indirectly, to make an illicit payment. Interestingly, however, the foreign intermediary engaging in the illicit conduct may be outside the scope of, and therefore not subject to, liability under the FCPA.[186]

Q 16.14.1   Who falls within the scope of "any person . . ." for purposes of third-party payments?

While "any person" would include the agent (that is, foreign sales representative) of a U.S. company, the third-party payment provision applies to *any* entity or individual, in the United States or abroad. Thus, a marketing consultant, distributor, joint venture partner, foreign subsidiary, contractor, or subcontractor would be included within the scope of this provision.

Knowledge Standard

Q 16.15   Are individuals and businesses still subject to FCPA liability if a bribe is paid by a third party without their actual knowing?

The FCPA, as amended,[187] makes it very clear that proof of actual knowledge is not required:

> (2) (A) A person's state of mind is "knowing" with respect to conduct, a circumstance, or a result if—
>   (i)   such person is aware that such person is engaging in such conduct, that such circumstance exists, or that such result is substantially certain to occur; or
>   (ii) such person has a firm belief that such circumstance exists or that such result is substantially certain to occur.
>   (B) When knowledge of the existence of a particular circumstance is required for an offense, such knowledge is established if a person is aware of a high probability of the existence of such circumstance, unless the person actually believes that such circumstance does not exist.[188]

The legislative history explains that this standard is intended to encompass concepts of "conscious disregard" or "deliberate ignorance" of circumstances:

> The Conferees intend that the requisite "state of mind" for this category of offense include a "conscious purpose to avoid learning the truth." Thus, the "knowing" standard adopted covers both prohibited actions that are taken with "actual

knowledge" of intended results, as well as other actions that, while falling short of what the law terms "positive knowledge," nevertheless evidence a conscious disregard or deliberate ignorance of known circumstances that should reasonably alert one to the high probability of violations of the Act.

. . . [T]he Conferees also agreed that the so-called "head-in-the-sand" problem—variously described in the pertinent authorities as "conscious disregard," "willful blindness" or "deliberate ignorance"—should be covered so that management officials could not take refuge from the Act's prohibitions by their unwarranted obliviousness to any action (or inaction), language or other "signaling device" that should reasonably alert them of the "high probability" of an FCPA violation.

. . . As such, it covers any instance where "any reasonable person would have realized" the existence of the circumstances or result and the defendant has "consciously chose[n] not to ask about what he had 'reason to believe' he would discover."[189]

The FCPA thus imputes knowledge where factual information possessed by a U.S. company indicates a "high probability" that conduct prohibited by the statute may result.[190] Moreover, if a company consciously disregards or deliberately ignores circumstances that should reasonably have alerted it to a high probability of a violation, the standard will be satisfied.[191] This standard appears to apply both to past conduct (that is, a high probability that a bribe has already been made) and to future conduct (that is, a high probability of a future illicit payment) (*see Kozeny* case study, *infra*).

The requirement of only an awareness of a high probability of prohibited conduct, combined with the imputation of knowledge to one who consciously disregards or deliberately ignores information, creates a standard of knowledge considerably looser than *actual* knowledge. In effect, one can be deemed to have knowledge that a payment to a third party will result in an illicit payment if one consciously disregarded or deliberately ignored information that indicated a high probability that the third party would make an illicit payment. Such a standard is akin to a "recklessness" standard.[192] Indeed, one DOJ official stated that the department applies a standard of "reckless disregard" or "willful blindness" to the knowledge requirement.[193]

Congress intended that the "knowing" standard contained in the FCPA be consistent with the knowledge standard for criminal liability as developed by existing case law. There is ample precedent for imputing criminal liability under the knowledge standard to those who act in conscious disregard or deliberate ignorance of the incriminating facts.[194]

CASE STUDY: *United States v. Kozeny*[195]

In *United States v. Kozeny*, the defendant, a businessman, was convicted of conspiring to violate the FCPA's anti-bribery provisions after agreeing to pay Azeri officials in a scheme to encourage the privatization of the state oil company of the Azerbaijan Republic. The court affirmed the jury instruction that knowledge may be established by showing a person consciously avoided learning the truth.

The district court admitted expert testimony on corruption in Azerbaijan generally to prove that "a person of [the defendant's] means, who was considering making a large investment in a venture in Azerbaijan, would have at least been aware of the high probability that bribes were being paid." The evidence allowed by the court included "[t]hat Azerbaijan was known to be a corrupt nation, that the post-Communist privatization processes in other countries have been tainted by corrupt practices, that the [state-owned oil company] was a strategic asset of Azerbaijan, and that a [co-conspirator] was notorious as the 'Pirate of Prague'" for his prior corrupt dealings in the Czech Republic. Also, the court was satisfied that third parties' knowledge of the bribes could be introduced at trial because the close business relationships between these individuals and the defendant created "a fair basis to infer that the knowledge of these third parties can be imputed to [the defendant]."

While instructing the jury on the knowledge standard, however, the judge cautioned that "while a finding that the person was aware of the high probability of the existence of a fact is enough to prove that this person possessed knowledge, it is not sufficient in order to determine that the person acted 'willfully' or 'corruptly' which is a separate and distinct element of the offense."[196]

 CASE STUDY: *United States v. Jewell*[197]

In *United States v. Jewell*, the U.S. Court of Appeals for the Ninth Circuit held that the term "knowingly" as used in criminal statutes is not limited to positive knowledge, but includes the state of mind of one who does not possess positive knowledge only because he consciously avoided it.[198]

> [T]he rule is that if a party has his suspicion aroused but then deliberately omits to make further enquiries, because he wishes to remain in ignorance, he is deemed to have knowledge. . . . The rule that willful blindness is equivalent to knowledge is essential, and is found throughout the criminal law.[199]

Q 16.15.1   What should a company do if it suspects possible wrongdoing by a foreign agent or other third party?

Frequently, a U.S. company not directly involved in an illicit payment discovers that a third party with which it has a commercial relationship—be it a sales representative, distributor, contractor/ subcontractor, or joint venture partner—has made an illicit payment with regard to a contract award involving the sale of the U.S. company's goods or services. Moreover, it is infrequent that the U.S.

company would know for certain that the third party in fact made a prohibited payment. More frequently, suspicions or concerns are raised when allegations or inconclusive information comes to its attention. The allegations of wrongdoing are generally vehemently denied by the third party. The third party may also have important contacts and ties with government officials, thereby making it difficult and commercially damaging to disengage from the relationship. It is in this kind of commercial setting that the potential liability of a U.S. company for actions of a third party is most murky, making the actions required of the U.S. company unclear.

Because it there is little practical difference between the current "knowledge" standard and the prior "reason to know" standard[200] (the 1988 amendments in effect only eliminated the negligence standard as a basis for liability),[201] the necessity under the "reason to know" standard to inquire about and to follow up on information that comes to the attention of a U.S. company and that indicates possible wrongdoing remains unchanged.[202] Accordingly, when suspicious information comes to the attention of a U.S. company regarding the activities of its foreign sales agent/distributor or other third party, the knowledge standard under the FCPA requires that the company undertake a due diligence inquiry into the suspicious activity. Otherwise, it could be deemed to have consciously disregarded or deliberately ignored information that would have alerted it to the likelihood of a violation. The failure to inquire, if significant, could result in the imputation to the U.S. company of knowledge regarding the illicit conduct. Furthermore, a business's compliance program should include due diligence of any prospective foreign agents.[203]

Q 16.15.2 What are some examples of "red flags" associated with third parties?

While there are no specific instances of "red flags" identified in the FCPA, the Resource Guide identifies a number of circumstances that should alert a U.S. company to the likelihood that a third party may be engaged in illicit conduct:

- excessive commissions to third-party agents or consultants;
- unreasonably large discounts to third-party distributors;
- third-party "consulting agreements" that include only vaguely described services;

CASE STUDY: *United States v. Jacobs*[204]

In *United States v. Jacobs*, the defendant, charged with dealing in stolen U.S. Treasury Bills, responded that he did not know the bills were stolen. The court of appeals affirmed the lower court's charge to the jury with respect to guilty knowledge:

> [K]nowledge is established if the defendant was aware of a high probability that the bills were stolen, unless the defendant actually believed that the bills were not stolen.
>
> Knowledge that the goods have been stolen may be inferred from circumstances that would convince a man of ordinary intelligence that this is the fact. The element of knowledge may be satisfied by proof that a defendant deliberately closed his eyes to what otherwise could have been obvious to him.
>
> Thus, if you find that a defendant acted with reckless disregard of whether the bills were stolen and with a conscious purpose to avoid learning the truth the requirement of knowledge would be satisfied, unless the defendant actually believed they were not stolen.[205]

- the third-party consultant is in a different line of business than that for which it has been engaged;
- the third party is related to or closely associated with the foreign official;
- the third party became part of the transaction at the express request or insistence of the foreign official;
- the third party is merely a shell company incorporated in an offshore jurisdiction; and
- the third party requests payment to offshore bank accounts.[206]

Other examples include negative reference checks, press reports of improprieties, and midstream requests for additional compensation.

Standard of Authorization

Q 16.16   What is the standard for authorization of illicit payments under the FCPA?

The FCPA not only prohibits the payment, offer, or promise of payment to a foreign official, but also proscribes the "authorization" of an illicit payment to be made by another.[207] Thus, if a U.S. company "authorizes" its sales representative, consultant, or controlled foreign subsidiary to make an illicit payment, the U.S. company will be in violation of the FCPA.[208] The FCPA also would apply in cases where a U.S. company "authorizes" its controlled foreign subsidiary to make an illicit payment indirectly through an intermediary, such as an agent of the foreign subsidiary.[209]

The standard for authorization is not defined in the FCPA. However, legislative history makes it clear that authorization can be either explicit or implicit.[210] To "authorize" conduct, in the context of the FCPA, appears to mean to manifest assent or direction, either explicitly or implicitly, to carry out the conduct.

Q 16.16.1   What constitutes implicit authorization?

This is not always easy to ascertain in the complicated commercial setting of international transactions. In interpreting whether or not authorization was granted, courts generally consider all of the surrounding circumstances, such as the relationship of the parties, the business in which they are engaged, the subject matter of the authorization, and the legality or illegality of the issue.

Q 16.16.2   Does passive acquiescence constitute authorization?

Whether mere passive acquiescence, by itself, could constitute authorization depends upon the nature of the relationship between the U.S. company and its agent or the third party and upon the surrounding circumstances.[211] Acquiescence, combined with some further manifestation of assent, would likely constitute authorization. Indeed, conscious acquiescence in a series of unauthorized acts may be interpreted as a manifestation of authorization to engage in similar acts in the future.[212] Moreover, while mere acquiescence to an illicit activity may not be sufficient to evidence an intent and agreement to engage in the illicit conduct,[213] this acquiescence when combined with other overt acts could provide the basis for allegations of conspiracy to violate the FCPA.[214]

CASE STUDY: *Pattis v. United States*[215]

In *Pattis v. United States*, the defendant sold materials and appliances to parties knowing that the materials would be used to make illegal liquor. The U.S. Court of Appeals for the Ninth Circuit held that by making it possible for the parties to carry out the unlawful objective of the conspiracy, the defendant became a co-conspirator.

CASE STUDY: *Deacon v. United States*[216]

In *Deacon v. United States*, the defendant, even after he learned that the facilities he had provided were being used in a conspiracy to sell and transfer lottery tickets in interstate commerce, continued to permit the use of the facilities. The U.S. Court of Appeals for the First Circuit in affirming the conviction rejected the defendant's argument that it was illogical to hold that he became a conspirator by reason of his failure to withdraw from a conspiracy in which he was never a participant. The court found that the defendant's failure to disavow his connection with the conspirators within a reasonable time after becoming aware of the conspiracy and his permitting the conspirators to continue to use the facilities warranted the inference that he elected to associate himself with the criminal enterprise. The court expressed the view that the defendant was under a "duty," after learning the facts, to take some definite, decisive, and positive step to withdraw from the venture.

Q 16.16.3   What should a company do if it suspects that a payment it did not authorize has been made?

In view of the circumstantial nature of implicit authorization, it is particularly important, when a U.S. company becomes aware of possible illicit payments made by its agent or other third party, to establish a clear record that the U.S. company did not and does not authorize such conduct. Since people ordinarily express some dissent or objection to acts done on their behalf that they did not authorize and do not approve, it is important to repudiate and, where appropriate, disassociate from such conduct.

Similarly, it is important that a U.S. company not remain passive when confronted with possible illicit conduct. Rather, it should unequivocally express its disapproval and repudiation of such conduct. The nature of the relationship between the company and its agent or the third party and the surrounding circumstances will dictate the manner in which the disapproval should be voiced. The jury instruction provided by the court in *Deacon* provides a useful framework to consider:

> [I]f the jury find[s] that [the defendant] went into this enterprise believing that it was a legal one, . . . and did not know any [illegal] enterprise was to be engaged in . . . until he was informed . . . that [an illegal enterprise] was going on, you should find the defendant not guilty as charged, if you find that at the time that he first became acquainted with or had knowledge that the illegal acts were being done that he repudiated them instantly.
>
> . . . [W]hen one seeks to disassociate himself from an illegal enterprise, his disassociation must be full, decisive and complete . . . .[217]

PART II
FCPA's ACCOUNTING PROVISIONS*

Prohibition on Off-the-Books Accounting

Q 16.17   What do the accounting provisions of the FCPA prohibit?

In addition to the anti-bribery provisions, the FCPA includes accounting provisions that make off-the-books accounting by public companies illegal. The scope of the accounting provisions is extensive. Unlike the anti-bribery provisions, which pertain exclusively to bribes to foreign public officials, the accounting provisions cover all of the financial transactions of a public company, or "issuer."[218] The requirements reflect the fact that companies often try to conceal the payment of bribes by recording them as something else in their books and records. Payments can be disguised as consulting fees, supplier and vendor payments, travel and entertainment expenses, rebates, discounts, sales and marketing expenses, commissions, royalties, write-offs, or miscellaneous expenses.

The accounting provisions consist of two basic components. The "books and records" requirements mandate that issuers create and maintain accurate records reflecting transactions and the disposition of assets.[219] The "internal controls" component requires issuers to have a system of internal accounting controls sufficient to provide an accurate recording of transactions.[220] Together, they are intended to ensure "that the assets of the issuer are used for proper corporate purpose[s]."[221]

Unlike the anti-bribery provisions, which require a corrupt purpose, violations of the accounting provisions can lead to civil sanctions under a strict liability standard. In other words, an issuer may violate the accounting provisions where no bribe has been offered or paid and even where the underlying transaction is completely legal. The accounting provisions also serve to extend the

---

* Part II of this chapter is authored by Timothy D. Belevetz.

FCPA's reach to commercial bribes paid by an issuer along with other violations of U.S. and local law.[222]

Books and Records

Q 16.18   What does the "books and records" provision require?

Under the "books and records" provision, issuers must "make and keep books, records, and accounts, which, in reasonable detail, accurately and fairly reflect the transactions and disposition of the assets of the issuer."[223]

Q 16.18.1   What constitutes "records" covered by the books-and-records provision?

Because the Exchange Act defines records broadly, most of a company's records are considered its "books, records, and accounts."[224] They are not limited to publicly filed financial statements, but are also deemed to include underlying documents maintained in the normal and ordinary course of business such as purchase orders, invoices, expense reports, and receipts used to support reimbursement requests.

Q 16.18.2   What constitutes "in reasonable detail"?

The "in reasonable detail" requirement means the level of detail that would "satisfy prudent officials in the conduct of their own affairs."[225] In adopting this definition, Congress observed that "[t]he concept of reasonableness of necessity contemplates the weighing of a number of relevant factors, including the costs of compliance."[226]

Q 16.18.3   What constitutes "accurately and fairly"?

As noted in the legislative history, "an issuer's records should reflect transactions in conformity with accepted methods of recording economic events."[227] There is no materiality threshold. In theory, any transaction, even a small one, can lead to liability under the books-and-records provision. The reality, however, is that an issuer's records need not be free of any errors. In making enforcement decisions, the SEC staff typically will take into account the proportionality and purpose of the inaccuracies.[228]

Q 16.18.4   How many years of records must an issuer keep?

While there is no defined amount of time an issuer is required to "keep" the records, given that most public companies must report summary financial data for a historical five-year period, issuers should maintain records for at least six years.[229]

Internal Controls

Q 16.19   What does the "internal controls" provision cover?

In recognition of the fact that bribes are often paid in instances where internal controls over financial reporting are weak, the FCPA's accounting provisions include a requirement to devise and maintain effective internal controls. Specifically, the internal controls provision says that issuers must:

> devise and maintain a system of internal accounting controls sufficient to provide reasonable assurances that—
>
> (i)   transactions are executed in accordance with management's general or specific authorization;
>
> (ii) transactions are recorded as necessary (I) to permit preparation of financial statements in conformity with generally accepted accounting principles or any other criteria applicable to such statements, and (II) to maintain accountability for assets;
>
> (iii) access to assets is permitted only in accordance with management's general or specific authorization; and
>
> (iv) the recorded accountability for assets is compared with the existing assets at reasonable intervals and appropriate action is taken with respect to any differences.[230]

The SEC and DOJ have defined internal controls over financial reporting as "the processes used by companies to provide reasonable assurances regarding the reliability of financial reporting and the preparation of financial statements."[231] The primary objective is to have in place a system designed to prevent an individual from using corporate funds to pay a bribe to a foreign official. Good internal controls, however, will also decrease the likelihood of embezzlement, self-dealing by an employee, commercial bribery, and export control violations.

Q 16.19.1   What is the standard for assessing an issuer's internal controls?

The standard is not accuracy, material or otherwise, but rather reasonableness. Issuers must provide "reasonable assurances" that transactions and access to corporate assets are properly authorized and recorded. In conformity with the books-and-records provision's "reasonable detail" condition, "reasonable assurances" means "such level of detail and degree of assurance as would satisfy prudent officials in the conduct of their own affairs."[232] A company's internal controls may be inadequate whether or not its financial reporting is inaccurate.

Q 16.19.2   Are there specific internal controls that an issuer is required to adopt?

No, there are no particular internal controls a company is required to adopt. Instead, issuers are expected to implement and use a system that works for them given their size, market, product, and billing and payment processes and the regulatory environment and geographic locations in which they do business.

Management should continually monitor the internal controls and modify them as conditions change. For example, a company that expands the sale of its products or services to a country with a reputation for official corruption should make changes to its internal controls to mitigate the risk of a bribe being paid to a public official in that country.

Q 16.20   Who is subject to civil exposure under the accounting provisions?

The accounting provisions of the FCPA apply only to issuers. Issuers, however, are accountable for not only their own books and records, but also, under certain circumstances, those of consolidated subsidiaries (including foreign subsidiaries), affiliates, and joint ventures under its control. Because an issuer may not be able to exercise the same level of control over minority-owned subsidiaries and affiliates that it can over wholly or majority-owned entities, parent companies owning 50% or less of a subsidiary or affiliate are required merely to use good-faith efforts to cause the entity to implement a

CASE STUDY: *In re BHP Billiton Ltd.*
& BHP Billiton Plc[233]

In a settled SEC administrative action brought in May 2015, the SEC charged BHP Billiton, an Australia-based metal resources company, with failing to maintain internal controls. The SEC accused the company, whose American depositary shares were traded on the New York Stock Exchange, with paying travel and entertainment expenses for sixty government officials and employees of state-owned businesses, along with some of their spouses, at the 2008 Olympic Games in Beijing. The company sponsored the games and provided raw materials to make the Olympic medals. Most of the guests were from African and Asian nations with well-established reputations for corruption. In addition, many were involved in the negotiations for then-pending government contracts with Billiton, although there were no allegations of actual bribery. The SEC asserted that Billiton had identified the risks of hosting the foreign officials at the Olympics, but failed to create and implement internal controls sufficient to prevent the company from inviting them and paying their travel expenses. The company agreed to settle the action with a $25 million fine.

system of internal accounting controls consistent with its own obligations.[234]

Companies, including subsidiaries and affiliates, and individuals may also be held civilly liable for aiding and abetting or causing an issuer's violations of the accounting provisions.[235] Individuals and organizations can face civil exposure for falsifying the books and records of an issuer or evading its internal controls.[236] Corporate officers may have civil liability as control persons for an issuer's violations of the accounting provisions,[237] and both officers and directors may have to face civil liability for making false statements to auditors.[238]

In addition, under Sarbanes-Oxley, an issuer's "principal officers," usually the chief executive officer and chief financial officer, may be liable for signing false certifications in an issuer's quarterly and annual financial reports.[239]

Q 16.20.1   Is there criminal exposure for violations of the accounting provisions?

Although the accounting provisions are usually enforced through civil actions brought by the SEC, in certain cases violations can form the basis of criminal charges. Both entities and individuals can face criminal exposure for knowingly and willfully violating the accounting provisions.[240]

Q 16.20.2   What constitutes "knowingly and willfully" violating the accounting provisions?

The FCPA does not define "knowingly" with regard to the accounting provisions, nor does it define "willfully" with regard to either the anti-bribery or accounting provisions. Because few litigated cases have addressed the criminal accounting provisions, the DOJ and courts will look to general case law for a definition of "knowingly." The legislative history of the statute demonstrates that Congress intended that criminal penalties would not be imposed for merely failing to comply with the accounting provisions, but would apply "where acts of commission or omission in keeping books and records or administering accounting controls have the purpose of falsifying books, records, or accounts or of circumventing the accounting controls."[241] Knowledge of illegality is not necessary.[242] Generally, deliberate falsification will satisfy the knowledge requirement.

Notes to Chapter 16

1.   For a thorough understanding of all aspects of the FCPA, see DON ZARIN, DOING BUSINESS UNDER THE FOREIGN CORRUPT PRACTICES ACT (PLI, 2d ed. 2013 & Supp. 2015).

2.   15 U.S.C. § 78dd-1. An issuer is defined as "any person who issues or proposes to issue any security . . . ." Exchange Act § 3(a)(8), 15 U.S.C. § 78c(a)(8).

3.   *Id.* § 78dd-2.

4.   *Id.* § 78dd-3. *See* Q 16.6.1, *infra.* In enacting the FCPA, Congress limited its jurisdictional scope principally to U.S. entities. During its deliberations, the conference committee, recognizing the jurisdictional, enforcement, and diplomatic difficulties inherent in extending U.S. law to foreign entities such as subsidiaries of U.S. companies, opted against the application of the FCPA to such foreign entities. H.R. REP. NO. 94-831, at 14 (1977) (Conf. Rep.). However, in 1998, Congress amended the FCPA to conform to the Convention on Combating Bribery of Foreign Public Officials in International Business Transactions. These amendments expanded the jurisdictional reach of the FCPA to include foreign persons or entities who commit any act in furtherance of a prohibited payment while in the territory of the United States. On December 17, 1997, members of the Organization for Economic Co-Operation and Development signed the Convention. It entered into force on February 15, 1999. Organization for Economic Co-Operation & Development, Convention on Combating Bribery of Foreign Public Officials in International Business Transactions, Nov. 21, 1997, 37 I.L.M. 1, www.oecd.org/corruption/oecdantibriberyconvention.htm [hereinafter OECD Convention].

5.   15 U.S.C. § 78dd-1.

6.   *Id.* § 78m(b)(2); *see also id.* §§ 78l, 78o(d).

7.   *Id.* § 78l(g); 17 C.F.R. § 240.12g-1 (2012). A foreign corporation can become subject to the registration requirements of the Exchange Act without actively intending to sell or trade its securities in the United States or to U.S. residents, if such securities are widely held in the United States. Pursuant to Exchange Act § 12(g) and Rules 12g-1 and 12g3-2(a) thereunder, a foreign private issuer that has $10 million or more in assets at the end of its most recent fiscal year is required to register any class of equity securities if any such class is held of record by 500 or more persons worldwide, including 300 or more in the United States. 15 U.S.C. § 78l(g); 17 C.F.R. §§ 240.12g-1, 240.12g3-2(a) (2012). A foreign issuer can avoid this registration requirement by applying for an exemption with the SEC under Rule 12g3-2(b) of the Exchange Act, 17 C.F.R. § 240.12g3-2(b) (2012).

8.   Foreign stocks may be sold in the United States in the form of American Depositary Receipts (ADRs). To facilitate trade in foreign securities, the Exchange Act provides an exemption from the registration and filing requirements for these types of foreign issuers. Exchange Act Rule 12g3-2(b), 17 C.F.R. § 240.12g3-2(b) (2012). These foreign issuers are therefore outside the scope of the FCPA. Never-

theless, numerous foreign issuers have entered the U.S. public market directly—companies like Daimler-Chrysler, Shanghai Petrochemical, Enterprise Oil, and Alcatel Alsthom. *See* James R. Silkenat, *Overview of U.S. Securities Markets and Foreign Issuers*, 17 FORDHAM INT'L L.J. 4, 5 (1994). In addition, ADRs that are listed on national securities exchanges such as the New York Stock Exchange or are quoted on NASDAQ are also subject to the requirements of the Exchange Act. In such an instance, the foreign company *would* be subject to the application of the FCPA. As of December 31, 2011, 965 foreign companies were registered with the SEC. *See* U.S. Dep't of Justice, Criminal Div. & U.S. Sec. & Exch. Comm'n, Enforcement Div., A Resource Guide to the U.S. Foreign Corrupt Practices Act, at 11 (Nov. 14, 2012), www.justice.gov/criminal/fraud/fcpa/guide.pdf. In fact, many of the largest penalties imposed by the DOJ/SEC for FCPA violations were imposed against foreign issuers. These companies include Siemens A.G. ($800 million); BAE ($400 million); Total S.A. ($398 million); Snamprogetti Netherlands B.V. ($365 million); Technip S.A. ($338 million); JGC ($218.8 million); and Daimler A.G. ($185 million). *See* Richard L. Cassin, *Alcoa Lands 5th on Our Top Ten List*, FCPA BLOG (Jan. 10, 2014), www.fcpablog.com/blog/2014/1/10/alcoa-lands-5th-on-our-top-ten-list.html. Several companies, including Technip S.A., Deutsche Telekom and its subsidiary Magya Telekom Plc, Akzo Nobel N.V., and Allianz SE, delisted its ADRs from a U.S. stock exchange or terminated its SEC registration in part due to FCPA enforcement actions.

    9.   15 U.S.C. § 78*l*(i).

    10.   *Id.* § 78o(d). However, if an issuer, in any fiscal year subsequent to the year in which it registered its securities, has 300 or more recordholders of a class of publicly held securities during any fiscal year, such issuer is subject to the reporting requirements of § 15(d) of the Exchange Act as to that fiscal year. *Id.*

    11.   *Id.* § 78dd-2(h)(1).

    12.   *See* S. REP. NO. 95-114, at 11 (1977); *see also* Dooley v. United Techs. Corp., 803 F. Supp. 428, 439 (D.D.C. 1992). However, the legislative history makes clear that any U.S. company that engages in bribery of foreign officials "indirectly through any other person or entity" would itself be liable under the act. H.R. REP. NO. 94-831, at 14; *see also* discussion *infra* section Q 16.8.

    13.   H.R. REP. NO. 94-831, at 14.

    14.   *See, e.g.*, Dooley v. United Techs., Inc., 803 F. Supp. 428 (D.D.C. 1992).

    15.   United States v. Morton, Cr. No. 3-90-061-H (N.D. Tex. 1990), *reprinted in* 2 FOREIGN CORRUPT PRAC. ACT REP. (Bus. Laws, Inc.) 698.62 to .67 (Canadian agent of U.S. bus company was charged with and pleaded guilty to bribing Canadian officials to secure a bus contract); *see also* Motion to Dismiss the Second Superseding Indictment (Docket No. 149), United States Opposition (Docket No. 161), Defendant's Reply (Docket No. 174), and Order Denying Motion to Dismiss (Docket No. 190), United States v. Hoskins, No. 3:12-CR-00238 (D. Conn. 2013).

    16.   *See, e.g.*, Press Release No. 10-747, U.S. Dep't of Justice, Innospec Agent Pleads Guilty to Bribing Iraqi Officials and Paying Kickbacks Under the Oil for Food Program (June 25, 2010), www.justice.gov/opa/pr/2010/June/10-crm-747.html (the former agent of Innospec, Inc. pled guilty to conspiracy to commit wire fraud, violating the FCPA and falsifying books and records, and to a violation

of the FCPA); Litigation Release No. 21,615 (Aug. 5, 2010) (SEC filed a settled enforcement action against the same agent); *see also* SEC v. Cantor, No. 03-CV-2488, ¶ 78 (S.D.N.Y. 2003) (noting that anti-bribery provisions of FCPA apply to any employee of company).

17. *See* SEC v. Straub, 921 F. Supp. 2d 244 (S.D.N.Y. 2013) (prosecution of executives of Hungarian telecommunications company listed on the New York Stock Exchange, an issuer under the FCPA); United States v. Sapsizian, 1:06-CR-20797-PAS (S.D. Fla. Mar. 20, 2007) (a French citizen employed by Alcatel, a French telecommunications company whose ADRs were listed on the New York Stock Exchange, pled guilty to a conspiracy to violate the FCPA and violating the FCPA) (jurisdiction based on use of any means of instrumentality of interstate commerce in furtherance of an illicit payment); *see also* Press Release No. 07-411, U.S. Dep't of Justice, Former Alcatel Executive Pleads Guilty to Participating in Payment of $2.5 Million in Bribes to Senior Costa Rican Officials to Obtain a Mobile Telephone Contract (June 7, 2007), www.justice.gov/opa/pr/2007/June/07_crm_411.html.

18. As an agent, the jurisdictional nexus required for liability is the use of an instrumentality of interstate commerce. *See* Q 16.6.

19. U.S. DEP'T JUSTICE, CRIMINAL DIV. & U.S. SEC. & EXCH. COMM'N, ENF'T DIV., A RESOURCE GUIDE TO THE U.S. FOREIGN CORRUPT PRACTICES ACT (Nov. 14, 2012) [hereinafter Resource Guide], www.sec.gov/spotlight/fcpa/fcpa-resource-guide.pdf.

20. Resource Guide at 27–28 (citing Pac. Can Co. v. Hewes, 95 F.2d 42 (9th Cir. 1938)). See the discussion of parent-subsidiary liability under agency principles in PHILLIP I. BLUMBERG, BLUMBERG ON CORPORATE GROUPS § 63.03[c] (Supp. 2013), indicating that courts often confuse agency concepts with piercing the corporate veil principles. It is important to distinguish situations in which liability may be imposed on a parent company because of the agency relationship from cases in which the corporate veil of the subsidiary is pierced. *See* RESTATEMENT (SECOND) OF AGENCY app. § 14M (1957).

21. *Id.*

22. *See* RESTATEMENT (SECOND) OF AGENCY § 1 (Agency; Principal; Agent), § 2 (Master; Servant; Independent Contractor) (1957); RESTATEMENT (THIRD) OF AGENCY § 1.01 (Agency Defined), § 2.04 (Respondeat Superior) (2005).

23. SEC v. Panalpina, Inc., No. 4:10-CV-4334, ¶ 6 (S.D. Tex. Nov. 4, 2010).

24. Plea Agreement, United States v. DPC (Tianjin) Co., No. CR 05-482 (C.D. Cal. May 20, 2005), and Information, No. CR 05-482 (C.D. Cal. May 20, 2005). The SEC also entered a cease-and-desist order against Diagnostics, charging Diagnostics with a violation of the FCPA, as well as the books and records and internal controls provision of the FCPA. *In re* Diagnostics Prods. Corp., Accounting and Auditing Enforcement Release No. 2249 (May 20, 2005).

25. The prohibition of the FCPA applies to any "issuer" or "domestic concern," and to "any officer, director, employee or *agent* of such [issuer or] domestic concern or any stockholder thereof acting on behalf of such [issuer or] domestic concern." 15 U.S.C. § 78dd-2(a) (emphasis added).

26.   SEC v. ENI, S.p.A. & Snamprogetti Netherlands B.V., No. 4:10-cv-2414 (S.D. Tex. July 7, 2010). *See* Accounting and Auditing Enforcement Release No. 3205 (Nov. 4, 2010).

27.   RESTATEMENT (SECOND) OF AGENCY § 2; RESTATEMENT (THIRD) OF AGENCY § 2.04.

28.   *Id. See* BLUMBERG, *supra* note 20, § 63.03[A].

29.   *See* RESTATEMENT (SECOND) OF AGENCY, App. § 14M (1957), citing Judge Cardozo in Berkey v. Third Ave. Ry. Co., 155 N.E. 58 (1926), *motion denied*, 155 N.E. 914 (1926) ("stock ownership, common executive officers, and nearly identical boards of directors" insufficient to establish agency); *see also* BLUMBERG, *supra* note 20, § 63.03[A].

30.   *Id.*

31.   Pac. Can Co. v. Hewes, 95 F.2d 42 (9th Cir. 1938). The Resource Guide also cites United States v. Nynex Corp., 788 F. Supp. 16, 18 n.3 (D.D.C. 1992), in support of its assertion that a corporation can be held criminally liable for the acts of its agents. However, in the *Nynex* case, the indictment for criminal contempt was based on the violation of a court decree, which specifically applied to Nynex acting directly or through any affiliated enterprise. Moreover, Nynex had a duty under the decree to ensure that its subsidiaries carried out the terms of the decree.

32.   Resource Guide at 27 n.178.

33.   *Pac. Can Co.*, 95 F.2d 42.

34.   But the SEC has effectively disregarded the separate legal status of a public company's foreign subsidiary in imposing civil liability under the accounting provisions of the FCPA.

35.   RESTATEMENT (THIRD) OF AGENCY § 1.01.

36.   *Id.* § 1.01.

37.   *Id.*

38.   OECD Convention, *supra* note 4, art. 4, ¶ 1.

39.   International Anti-Bribery and Fair Competition Act of 1998, Pub. L. No. 105-366, § 4, 112 Stat. 3302, 3306; 15 U.S.C. § 78dd-3(a).

40.   Provided such companies meet the jurisdictional requirement to use the mails or other instrumentality of interstate commerce. 15 U.S.C. § 78dd-1(a).

41.   Japan Petroleum Co. v. Ashland Oil, 456 F. Supp. 831 (D. Del. 1978).

42.   AON was owned by two Nigerian subsidiaries of Ashland Oil.

43.   *See* Resource Guide at 12.

44.   *See* United States v. Marubeni Corp., 12 CR 022 (S.D. Tex. Jan. 17, 2012) (Marubeni aided and abetted a domestic concern in violating the FCPA); *see also* Resource Guide at 12. Foreign persons may also be subject to liability under other U.S. laws, such as money laundering, for corruption-related conduct.

45.   Resource Guide at 11.

46.   *Id.* at 11 n.55.

47.   15 U.S.C. § 78dd-3; *see also* Resource Guide at 12.

48.   Resource Guide at 22; S. REP. NO. 105-277, at 6 (1998).

49.   S. REP. NO. 105-277, at 4; *see also* Response of the United States to the Phase I Questionnaire, First Self-Evaluation and Mutual Review, submitted by the

U.S. government to the OECD, art. 4.1 (Oct. 30, 1998), www.justice.gov/criminal/fraud/fcpa/docs/response1.pdf.

50. Comments made by the Deputy Chief of the Fraud Section, Dep't of Justice, at the American Bar Association Conference on the Foreign Corrupt Practices Act (Feb. 19, 1999).

51. *See, e.g.*, SEC v. Panalpina World Transp. (Holding) Ltd., No. 10-769 (S.D. Tex. Nov. 4, 2010) (*see* case study, *supra*); Press Release No. 10-360, U.S. Dep't of Justice, Daimler AG and Three Subsidiaries Resolve Foreign Corrupt Practices Act Investigation and Agree to Pay $93.6 Million in Criminal Penalties (Apr. 1, 2010), www.justice.gov/opa/pr/2010/April/10-crm-360.html; Information, United States v. SSI Int'l Far East, Ltd., 3:06-CR-00398-KI (D. Or. 2006) (plea agreement arising from voluntary disclosure; improper payments had been made to managers of government-owned customers in South Korea and China in exchange for the purchase of scrap metal); United States v. Vetco Gray Controls, Inc., No. H-07-004 (S.D. Tex. Feb. 6, 2007) (plea agreement arising from voluntary disclosure; several British companies and their U.S. affiliate pled guilty to a violation of the FCPA and conspiracy to violate the FCPA for improper payments made to Customs officials in Nigeria).

52. *See* Plea Agreement, United States v. Vetco Gray UK Ltd. & Vetco Gray Controls, Ltd., CR H-07-004 (S.D. Tex. Feb. 6, 2007); Plea Agreement, United States v. Syncor Taiwan, Inc., No. 02-CR-1244-SVW (C.D. Cal. 2002); United States v. ABB Vetco Gray, Inc. & ABB Vetco Gray UM Ltd., No. CR H-04-279 (S.D. Tex. June 22, 2004).

53. Opinion and Order, SEC v. Sharef, No. 11 Civ. 9073 (S.D.N.Y. Feb. 19, 2013). According to the court, the due process analysis consists of two components: the minimum contacts analysis and a reasonableness inquiry.

54. *Id. But cf.* SEC v. Straub, 921 F. Supp. 2d 244 (S.D.N.Y. 2013) (court upheld exercise of personal jurisdiction of individuals involving bribery scheme in Macedonia, where the individual signed off on misleading management representations to the company's auditors and signed false SEC filings).

55. 15 U.S.C. §§ 78dd-1(a), 78dd-2(a).

56. *Id.* § 78dd-2(h)(5).

57. H.R. REP. No. 94-831, at 12. The Senate bill originally contained the "in furtherance" clause. S. 305, 95th Cong. (1977). The bill passed by the House required that interstate commerce be "directly used" to offer or make the prohibited payment. H.R. 3815, 95th Cong. (1977). The Department of Justice expressed the view that the "directly used" language in the House bill was unduly restrictive and narrow, and recommended inclusion of the "in furtherance" clause contained in the Senate bill. *See* H.R. REP. No. 95-640, at 18 (1977) (Conf. Rep.).

58. *See* SEC v. Straub, 921 F. Supp. 2d 244 (S.D.N.Y. 2013) (memorandum and order) (allegations that defendant sent Protocols and Letter of Intent, which were essentially bribe offers, via email satisfies "in furtherance" language); United States v. Kay, 513 F.3d 432 (5th Cir. 2007) (allegedly false documents used to calculate bribes sent in interstate commerce met "in furtherance" requirement); *see also* United States v. Draiman, 784 F.2d 248, 251 (7th Cir. 1986) (quoting United States v. Lea, 518 F.2d 426, 430 (7th Cir.)), *cert. denied*, 449 U.S. 823 (1980). *See*

generally KATHLEEN BRICKEY, CORPORATE CRIMINAL LIABILITY § 8.53 (2d ed. 1992) (discussion of the use of the mails for the purpose of executing a scheme or artifice to defraud).

59. *See* Response of the United States, *supra* note 49, art. 4.4.

60. Note that conduct that does not meet the jurisdictional requirements under the foreign payments provisions may nevertheless be subject to liability under the accounting provisions. *See* SEC v. Montedison, S.p.A., Civ. Action No. 1:96 CV02631 (HHG) (D.D.C. Nov. 21, 1996).

61. While the United States has traditionally followed the territorial principle of jurisdiction in the application of its criminal laws, there is some limited precedent for the application of the nationality principle of jurisdiction. *See, e.g.,* Economic Espionage Act of 1996, 18 U.S.C. §§ 1831–39, 1837 (the statute "applies to conduct outside the United States if . . . the offender is a natural person who is a citizen or permanent resident alien of the United States, or an organization organized under the laws of the United States"); Laundering of Monetary Instruments, 18 U.S.C. § 1956(f) ("There is extraterritorial jurisdiction over the conduct prohibited . . . if . . . the conduct is by a U.S. citizen."); *id.* § 1957(d) ("the offense . . . takes places outside the United States . . . but the defendant is a United States person"); *see also* Foreign Assets Control Regulations, 31 C.F.R. pt. 500 (2013).

62. International Anti-Bribery and Fair Competition Act of 1998, § 2(c). Foreign corporations that are "issuers" (*i.e.,* that have ADRs listed on the New York Stock Exchange) would only be subject to the regular jurisdictional requirement of "use of an instrumentality of interstate commerce."

63. The alternative jurisdiction applies to a "U.S. person," which is defined as a "national" of the United States, as specified in 8 U.S.C. § 1101(a)(22). This would not include a permanent resident of the United States.

64. International Anti-Bribery and Fair Competition Act of 1998, § 2(c).

65. *Id.* § 3(d).

66. Schmuck v. United States, 489 U.S. 705, *reh'g denied*, 490 U.S. 1076 (1989).

67. *Id.* at 710–11 (quoting Badders v. United States, 240 U.S. 391, 394 (1916)); *see also* Pereira v. United States, 347 U.S. 1, 8 (1954) ("not necessary that the scheme contemplate the use of the mails as an essential element").

68. *Schmuck*, 489 U.S. at 711–15 (referring to Kann v. United States, 323 U.S. 88 (1944); Parr v. United States, 363 U.S. 370 (1960); and United States v. Maze, 414 U.S. 395 (1974)). *But cf. id.* at 722 (dissenting opinion).

69. *Id.* at 713–14. Similarly, the use of an instrumentality of interstate commerce that occurs before the inception of the crime would not meet the "in furtherance" requirement. *See* United States v. Beall, 126 F. Supp. 363, 366 (N.D. Cal. 1954). On the other hand, the use of an instrumentality of commerce which occurred subsequent to the criminal acts may be "in furtherance" of the scheme if it promotes the scheme, relates to acceptance of the proceeds of the scheme, or facilitates concealment of the scheme. *See* United States v. Rauhoff, 525 F.2d 1170, 1176 (7th Cir. 1975).

70. *Schmuck*, 489 U.S. at 715; United States v. Biesiadecki, 933 F.2d 539, 545 (7th Cir. 1991).

71. International Anti-Bribery and Fair Competition Act of 1998 § 4.

72. *Id.*

73. Complaint, SEC v. Straub, No. 11 Civ. 9645 (S.D.N.Y. Dec. 29, 2011).

74. SEC v. Straub, 921 F. Supp. 2d 244, 262–64 (S.D.N.Y. 2013).

75. *See* Response of the United States, *supra* note 49, arts. 4.2, 4.4. In 2006, the DOJ announced that a U.S. citizen who served as a translator in Iraq pled guilty to offering a bribe to a senior Iraqi police officer to facilitate the police department's purchase of armored vests and other equipment. Jurisdiction was based on the nationality principle. *See* Press Release No. 06-500, U.S. Dep't of Justice, U.S. Civilian Translator Pleads Guilty to Offering Bribe to Iraqi Police Official (Aug. 4, 2006), www.justice.gov/opa/pr/2006/August/06_crm_500.html.

76. H.R. REP. NO. 95-640, at 7–8; S. REP. NO. 95-114, at 10–11. In United States v. Liebo, 923 F.2d 1308, 1312 (8th Cir. 1991), involving a violation of the FCPA, the court affirmed the following jury instruction of the term "corruptly":

> [T]he offer, promise to pay, payment or authorization of payment, must be intended to induce the recipient to misuse his official position or to influence someone else to do so. . . . [A]n act is corruptly done if done voluntarily and intentionally, and with a bad purpose of accomplishing either an unlawful end or result, or a lawful end or result by some unlawful method or means.

77. H.R. REP. NO. 95-640, at 8; S. REP. NO. 95-114, at 10. *See* Press Release No. 06-171, U.S. Dep't of Justice, U.S. Civilian Translator Arrested for Offering Bribe to Iraqi Police Official (Mar. 24, 2006), www.justice.gov/opa/pr/2006/March/06_crm_171.html. A U.S. citizen who served as a translator in Iraq was arrested for offering a bribe to an Iraqi police official (charge brought for an *offer to bribe*, though no bribe was ever executed). *See* Press Release No. 06-500, *supra* note 75, announcing a guilty plea for a violation of the FCPA; *see also* Press Release No. 08-1020, U.S. Dep't of Justice, Virginia Physicist Pleads Guilty to Illegally Exporting Space Launch Data to China and Offering Bribes to Chinese Officials (Nov. 17, 2008), www.justice.gov/opa/pr/2008/November/08-nsd-1020.html (Shu Quan-Sheng, a U.S. citizen, pled guilty to charge that he offered money to Chinese officials to secure a hydrogen tank system contract).

78. S. REP. NO. 95-114, at 11. *See* United States v. Bistrong, No. 1:10-CR-00021 (D.D.C. Jan. 21, 2010) (Bistrong pled guilty to violating the FCPA in making an estimated $4.4 million in payments to intermediaries and agents knowing the money would be passed to procurement officers.).

79. *See Liebo*, 923 F.2d at 1314.

80. S. REP. NO. 95-114, at 10–11; *see* United States v. Kozeny, 582 F. Supp. 2d 535, 540–41 (S.D.N.Y. 2008) (consistent with legislative intent, an individual in the situation of "true extortion" would negate the corrupt intent of "having an improper motive or purpose" and a payment designed to "induce the recipient to misuse his official position").

81. H.R. REP. No. 95-640, at 8 (the word "corruptly" connotes anevil motive or purpose such as that required under 18 U.S.C. § 201(b) which prohibits domestic bribery). *See generally* Gary M. Elden & Mark S. Sablemann, *Negligence*

Is Not Corruptive: The Scienter Requirement of the Foreign Corrupt Practices Act, 49 GEO. WASH. L. REV. 819, 826–28 (1981) (an instructive review of cases interpreting the "corruptly" standard). Numerous other statutes also contain a "corruptly" requirement. One law review article states that there are sixty-four federal statutory provisions that contain the word "corruptly" or a variant thereof. *Id.* at 824.

82. United States v. Traitz, 871 F.2d 368, 396 (3d Cir.), *cert. denied*, 493 U.S. 821 (1989); United States v. Johnson, 621 F.2d 1073, 1076 (10th Cir. 1980); United States v. Arthur, 544 F.2d 730, 734 (4th Cir. 1976); United States v. Brewster, 506 F.2d 62 (D.C. Cir. 1974). A defendant need not know that he is violating the FCPA by bribing the official—only that he intends to wrongfully influence that official. SEC v. Straub, 921 F. Supp. 2d 244 (S.D.N.Y. 2013); *see also infra* notes 92–95 and accompanying discussion.

83. *Brewster*, 506 F.2d at 80–82.

84. Because of the ambiguity of the "corruptly" standard, criminal law reformers had proposed to replace this requirement in the domestic bribery statute with "as consideration for," to emphasize the importance of the quid pro quo aspect of bribery. *See* OBERMAIER & MORVILLO, WHITE COLLAR CRIME: BUSINESS & REGULATORY OFFENSES § 3.03[1] (citing S. REP. NO. 96-553, at 398 (1979)); W. VA. CODE ANN. § 61-5A-3 (1966 & Supp. 1994) (West Virginia bribery statute).

85. *See Brewster*, 506 F.2d at 71, 72.

86. United States v. Kozeny, 582 F. Supp. 2d 535, 541 (S.D.N.Y. 2008) (jury charge for possessing corrupt intent under the FCPA will emphasize that the "proper focus is on [defendant's] intent").

87. *Id.*; *see also* United States v. Anderson, 509 F.2d 312, 332 (D.C. Cir. 1974), *cert. denied*, 420 U.S. 991 (1975); United States v. Hall, 245 F.2d 338 (2d Cir. 1957); United States v. Troop, 235 F.2d 123, 124–25 (7th Cir. 1956).

88. United States v. Jannotti, 673 F.2d 578, 601 (3d Cir.), *cert. denied*, 457 U.S. 1106 (1982). *But cf.* United States v. Campbell, 684 F.2d 141, 148 (D.C. Cir. 1982) (payments to any official for acts that would have been performed in any event are probably illegal gratuities rather than bribes).

89. *See* United States v. Hsieh Hui Mei Chen, 754 F.2d 817, 822 (9th Cir.), *cert. denied*, 471 U.S. 1139 (1985); *see also* WALTER S. SURREY & RICHARD A. POPKIN, A LAWYER'S GUIDE TO INTERNATIONAL BUSINESS TRANSACTIONS: THE UNITED STATES RESPONSE TO FOREIGN CORRUPT PRACTICES 44 (2d ed. 1982) (suggesting that a violation of foreign law meets the corrupt intent requirement).

90. SEC v. Straub, 921 F. Supp. 2d 244 (S.D.N.Y. 2013); *see also* Resource Guide at 14.

91. To obtain a criminal penalty against an individual, 15 U.S.C. § 78dd-1 provides:

> Any officer, director, employee or agent of an issuer, or stockholder acting on behalf of such issuer, who *willfully* violates subsection (a) or (g) of Section 78dd-f of the title shall be fined not more than $100,000 or imprisoned not more than 5 years, or both.

92. United States v. Kozeny, 493 F. Supp. 2d 693 (S.D.N.Y. 2007), *aff'd*, 541 F.3d 166 (2d Cir. 2008).

93. *See also* SEC v. Straub, 921 F. Supp. 2d 244 (S.D.N.Y. 2013).

94. United States v. Kay, 513 F.3d 432 (5th Cir. 2007).

95. *See also* Resource Guide at 14.

96. *See* United States v. Kozeny, 582 F. Supp. 2d 535 (S.D.N.Y. 2008) (evidence of extortion goes to the issue of corrupt intent).

97. Resource Guide at 27.

98. *Id.*; *Kozeny*, 582 F. Supp. 2d at 535.

99. SEC v. NATCO Grp., Inc., Civil Action No. 4210-cv-98 (S.D. Tex. Jan. 11, 2010); Accounting and Auditing Enforcement Release No. 3102 (Jan. 11, 2010).

100. *Id.*

101. 15 U.S.C. §§ 78dd-1(a), 78dd-2(a). In contrast to the FCPA, the OECD Convention does not extend to political parties or political candidates.

102. Commercial bribery may, however, be a violation of the Travel Act. *See* Perrin v. United States, 444 U.S. 37 (1979); United States v. Mead, Cr. No. 98-240-01 (D.N.J. 1998).

103. In a U.S. Department of Justice Opinion Procedure Release, the Department of Justice expressed its intention not to bring enforcement proceedings against a company that sought to contribute $25,000 directly to a local customs agency in an African nation. The company intended the contribution to be used to establish a program that would provide financial incentives to local customs officials in order to improve enforcement of anti-counterfeiting laws. Noting that the contribution went directly to the agency (and not to individual officials), that the company lacked control over the distribution of funds, and the existence of certain procedural safeguards, the DOJ implicitly concluded that the program would not contravene the FCPA. Foreign Corrupt Practices Act Opinion Procedure Release No. 06-01 (Oct. 16, 2006), www.justice.gov/criminal/fraud/fcpa/opinion/2006/0601.pdf. *See* Foreign Corrupt Practices Act Opinion Procedure Release No. 07-03 (Dec. 21, 2007) (advance payment to cover administrative costs in a court proceeding will be made to a government entity rather than a foreign official), www.justice.gov/criminal/fraud/fcpa/opinion/2007/0703.pdf. *But cf.* SEC v. Gen. Elec. Co.; Ionics, Inc.; and Amersham plc, Accounting and Auditing Enforcement Release No. 3159 (July 27, 2010) (enforcement action for violations of the books and records and internal control provisions where GE failed to properly account for kickbacks to the Iraqi Health Ministry in the form of computer equipment, medical supplies and services).

104. 15 U.S.C. § 78dd-2(h)(2). The 1998 amendments, to conform the FCPA to the OECD Convention, added "public international organizations" to the definition of a foreign official. International Anti-Bribery and Fair Competition Act of 1998, *supra* note 39, § 2(b). Prior to the 1988 amendments, the term "foreign official" did not include employees of a foreign government whose duties were essentially ministerial or clerical. 91 Stat. 1498 (1977). This exclusion provided the basis for permitting so-called facilitating payments, and was replaced in the 1988 Amendments by an explicit exception for facilitating payments. 15 U.S.C. §§ 78dd-1(b), 78dd-2(b).

105. *But see* United States v. Aguilar, 783 F. Supp. 2d 1108 (C.D. Cal. 2011), and cases cited therein for cases holding that officers and employees of state-owned entities are foreign officials under the FCPA.

106. *Cf.* SEC v. Ashland Oil, Inc., 2 FOREIGN CORRUPT PRAC. ACT REP. (Bus. Laws, Inc.) 696.95, involving an SEC civil injunctive action for a payment to an Omani official, in violation of the anti-bribery provisions of the FCPA. In that case, the SEC referred to an Omani Decree for reference in defining a "government official" in its Complaint for Permanent Injunction (¶ 10). *But cf.* Department of Justice Opinion Procedure Release No. 94-1 (May 13, 1994) (DOJ rejects any consideration of local law in determining whether the general director of a state-owned enterprise is a foreign official under the FCPA).

107. 18 U.S.C. § 201(a)(1).

108. 28 U.S.C. § 2671 *et seq.* The FTCA is a vehicle pursuant to which private plaintiffs may sue the U.S. government for injury caused by the negligent conduct of its employees.

109. 18 U.S.C. § 201(a)(1); *see also* Jay M. Zitter, Annot., *Who Is Public Official Within Meaning of Federal Statute Punishing Bribery of Public Official*, 161 A.L.R. FED. 491 (2000).

110. United States v. Bordonaro, 253 F. 477 (W.D.N.Y. 1918).

111. Felder v. United States, 9 F.2d 872, 873 (2d Cir. 1925), *cert. denied*, 270 U.S. 648 (1926).

112. *See also* United States v. Marcus, 166 F.2d 497, 503 (3d Cir. 1948). *Marcus* involved the alleged bribery of the District Enforcement Supervisor in the Office of Price Administration. This individual was appointed by the head of the Office of Price Administration, an emergency executive department. The circuit court, in affirming the status of this individual as an "officer," held that an officer is one "appointed by the President by and with advice and consent of the Senate, or by the President alone, the courts of law or the head of some executive department of the government." *Id.* (citing United States v. Germaine, 99 U.S. 508 (1879)); *see also* McGrath v. United States, 275 F. 294 (2d Cir. 1921) (looking to definition of officer in Constitution to determine whether income tax inspectors appointed by the Commissioner of Internal Revenue with the approval of the Secretary of the Treasury could be considered "officers" of the United States). There is also little doubt that members of the military are "officers" of the government. *See* United States v. Kidd, 734 F.2d 409 (9th Cir. 1984) (U.S. Army private); United States v. Apex Distrib. Co., 148 F. Supp. 365 (D.R.I. 1957) (U.S. Naval officer); *see also* 28 U.S.C. § 2671.

113. "Employee" of the government under the FTCA includes . . . "employees of any federal agency, member of the military . . . forces of the United States . . . and persons acting on behalf of a federal agency in an official capacity." *See* 28 U.S.C. § 2671.

114. United States v. Orleans, 425 U.S. 807, 815 (1976).

115. Logue v. United States, 412 U.S. 521, 528–29 (1973); *see also* Rodriguez v. Sarabyn, 129 F.3d 760 (5th Cir. 1997).

116. Resendez v. United States, 993 F.2d 884 (9th Cir. 1993).

117. *Id.* (citation omitted). The Tenth Circuit in Woodruff v. Covington, 389 F.3d 1117, 1126 (10th Cir. 2004), applied similar factors. The control test has been applied in numerous other cases. *See, e.g.*, Kirchmann v. United States, 8 F.3d 1273, 1274–75 (8th Cir. 1993), involving alleged groundwater contamination caused during construction of a missile site. The Eighth Circuit held that employees of General Dynamics who had contracted with the U.S. Air Force to build the missile facility were not government employees for purposes of the FTCA. The basis for the court's decision was that the U.S. Air Force did not exercise day-to-day control over their physical performance in the disposal of hazardous waste at the missile site. *Id.* at 1275; *see also* Cazales v. Lecon, Inc., 994 F. Supp. 765 (S.D. Tex. 1997); Berkman v. United States, 957 F.2d 108 (4th Cir. 1992).

118. Resource Guide at 20, listing the non-exclusive factors that the courts considered, as follows:

- the foreign state's extent of ownership of the entity;
- the foreign state's degree of control over the entity (including whether key officers and directors of the entity are, or are appointed by, government officials);
- the foreign state's characterization of the entity and its employees;
- the circumstances surrounding the entity's creation;
- the purpose of the entity's activities;
- the entity's obligations and privileges under the foreign state's law;
- the exclusive or controlling power vested in the entity to administer its designated functions;
- the level of financial support by the foreign state (including subsidies, special tax treatment, government-mandated fees, and loans);
- the entity's provision of services to the jurisdiction's residents;
- whether the governmental end or purpose sought to be achieved is expressed in the policies of the foreign government; and
- the general perception that the entity is performing official or governmental functions.

119. *See* Lucent Techs., Inc., Civil Action No. 07-CV-02301 (D.D.C. 2007); Press Release No. 07-1028, U.S. Dep't of Justice, Lucent Technologies Inc. Agrees to Pay $1 Million Fine to Resolve FCPA Allegations (Dec. 21, 2007) (excessive travel expenditures to employees of Chinese state-owned entities); *see also In re* Elecs. Data Sys. Corp., Accounting and Auditing Enforcement Release No. 2725 (Sept. 25, 2007) (payments to employees of Indian state-owned entities to prevent cancellation of contracts); United States v. Baker Hughes Servs. Int'l, Inc., No. H-07-129 (S.D. Tex. Apr. 11, 2007) (improper payments to employees of state-owned oil company).

120. *See, e.g.*, SEC v. Westinghouse Air Brake Techs. Corp., Civil Action No. 08-CV-706 (E.D. Pa. Feb. 14, 2008); Press Release No. 08-116, U.S. Dep't of Justice, Westinghouse Air Brake Technologies Corporation Agrees to Pay $300,000 Penalty to Resolve Foreign Bribery Violations in India (Feb. 14, 2008) (payments to member of Indian Railway Board); O'Connell Mach. Co. v. M.V. Americana, 734 F.2d 115 (2d Cir.), *cert. denied*, 469 U.S. 1086 (1984).

121. SEC v. Con-way, Inc., Accounting and Auditing Enforcement Release No. 2866 (Aug. 27, 2008) (payments to employees of state-owned airlines); Ofikuru v. Nigerian Airlines Ltd., 670 F. Supp. 89 (S.D.N.Y. 1987).

122. H.R. REP. NO. 94-1487, at 14–16 (1976), *reprinted in* 1976 U.S.C.C.A.N. 6604, 6613–14. *See* Press Release No. 08-491, U.S. Dep't of Justice, AGA Medical Corporation Agrees to Pay $2 Million Penalty and Enter Deferred Prosecution Agreement for FCPA Violations, (June 3, 2008) (deferred prosecution; payments to physicians at state-owned hospitals to induce them to purchase products); Plea Agreement, United States v. Syncor Taiwan, Inc., No. 02-CR-1244-SVW (C.D. Cal. 2002) (involving a conviction under the FCPA for improper payments made to physicians of government-owned hospitals); *see also* U.S. Dep't of Justice Opinion Procedure Release No. 94-1 (May 13, 1994) (employee of state-owned entity going through privatization not yet completed is a foreign official); Cargill Int'l S.A. v. M/T Pavel Dybenko, 991 F.2d 1012, 1016 (2d Cir. 1993) ("[A]fter the first shares are distributed [under privatization], nearly half the shares will remain with the Russian State Property Fund for a period of three years. We consider an entity at such an early stage of privatization to be sovereign under the Foreign Sovereign Immunities Act."). The SEC seems to have partly relied on a similar rationale in a complaint filed against former executives of ITXC Corp., an international telecommunications carrier. The complaint alleges that Steven Ott and Michael Young violated the FCPA by, inter alia, bribing officials of Sonatel, a Senegalese telecommunications company partly owned by the Senegalese government. Complaint, SEC v. Ott, No. 06-4195 (D.N.J. 2006). However, at the time of the alleged bribery, the Senegalese government no longer owned a majority stake in *Sonatel*, having sold off 61% of the company in 1997 as part of a privatization plan. *See* Int'l Monetary Fund, Senegal: Enhanced Structural Adjustment Facility Policy Framework Paper, 1998–2000, at 3–4 (Feb. 27, 1998), www.imf.org/external/NP/PFP/Senegal/seneg.pdf; *see also* SEC v. Siemens AG, Civil Action No. 1:08-CV-02167 (D.D.C. Dec. 12, 2008) (alleging that illicit payments to a technical consultant working for the Moscow Project Implementation Unit, a quasi-governmental unit responsible for the Moscow Third Ring project, were made to a government official).

123. United States v. Esquenazi, 752 F.3d 912, 925 (11th Cir.), *cert. denied*, 135 S. Ct. 293 (2014).

124. *Id.*

125. *Id.* at 926.

126. United States v. Aguilar, 783 F. Supp. 2d 1108 (C.D. Cal. 2011) (denying the defendants' motion to dismiss the indictment).

127. The criminal case is United States v. Alcatel-Lucent S.A., No. 1:10-CR-20906 (S.D. Fla. 2010). The companion SEC civil case is SEC v. Alcatel-Lucent, No. 1:10-CV-24620 (S.D. Fla. 2010).

128. United States v. Kellogg Brown & Root LLC, No. 4:09-CR-00071 (S.D. Tex. 2009).

129. *But see* U.S. Dep't of Justice Opinion Procedure Release (Sept. 1, 2010) (consultant will not be acting on behalf of the foreign government in performing the consulting contract).

130. Dixson v. United States, 465 U.S. 482 (1984).

131. *Id.* at 496.

132. *Id.* at 497; *accord* United States v. Strissel, 920 F.2d 1162, 1166 (4th Cir. 1990) (defendant, who was not employed by federal government, was still "public official" within meaning of domestic bribery statute because he administered federal funds in a federal program and his responsibilities were "federal" in nature); *see also* United States v. Gelb, 881 F.2d 1155, 1163 (2d Cir.), *cert. denied*, 493 U.S. 994 (1989) (relying on *Dixson* and holding that certain postal employees were "public officials" for purposes of the bribery statute because they held "'positions of public trust'" and were "acting for the United States in an official capacity"); Guccione v. United States, 847 F.2d 1031, 1037 (2d Cir. 1988), *cert. denied*, 493 U.S. 1020 (1990) (holding that although a former con man turned FBI informant and operative was "not technically a federal 'employee,'" he was acting on the government's behalf as an undercover operative because he rendered his services while under the control and supervision of the FBI and its special agents); Thompson v. Dilger, 696 F. Supp. 1071, 1074 (E.D. Va. 1988) (holding that "a person does not act on behalf of a federal agency in an official capacity where . . . there is no governmental authority to supervise the person's daily activities" and applying the control test adopted in *Logue* and *Orleans*); United States v. Griffin, 401 F. Supp. 1222, 1230 (S.D. Ind. 1975), *aff'd mem.*, 541 F.2d 284 (7th Cir. 1976) (holding that defendants, who were empowered to conduct a competitive bidding system in connection with the solicitation and awarding of bids for a federal program, were "acting for or on behalf of the United States").

133. OECD Convention, *supra* note 4, art. 1, ¶ 4a.

134. International Anti-Bribery and Fair Competition Act of 1998 § 2(b).

135. 22 U.S.C. § 288 (1998).

136. International Anti-Bribery and Fair Competition Act of 1998 § 2(b).

137. *See* SEC v. Titan Corp., Civil Action No. 05-0411 (D.D.C. Mar. 1, 2005) (Titan paid an employee of the World Bank, a "foreign official" under the FCPA, to assist in obtaining local investors for a project).

138. *See* United States v. Bistrong, No. 1:10-CR-0021 (D.D.C. Jan. 21, 2010) (the United Nations was a public international organization and thus its officials were foreign officials under the FCPA).

139. 15 U.S.C. §§ 78dd-1(a)(2), 78dd-2(a)(2). In contrast to the FCPA, the OECD Convention does not apply to political parties. *See* George J. Wallance, *Major Victory for U.S. As Foreign Corrupt Practices Act Goes Global*, BUS. CRIMES BULL.: COMPLIANCE & LITIG. 1, 3 (Feb. 1998).

140. H.R. REP. NO. 100-576, at 918–19 (1988) (Conf. Rep.), *reprinted in* 1988 U.S.C.C.A.N. 1547, 1951–52.

141. *See* 15 U.S.C. §§ 78dd-1(c)(1), 78dd-2(c)(1).

142. For example, in Nepal, which has had a democratic system for only a short period, there is no Nepalese law regulating contributions to political parties or candidates for political office. It is therefore not prohibited for companies or individuals to make such contributions.

143. 15 U.S.C. § 78dd-2(a).

144. *See* United States v. Schwartz, 785 F.2d 673, 679 (9th Cir.), *cert. denied*, 479 U.S. 890 (1986) (interpreting "thing of value" under 18 U.S.C. § 1954 broadly to include tangible and intangible items).

145. United States v. Sheker, 618 F.2d 607, 609 (9th Cir. 1980) (information concerning location of a witness was a "thing of value" under 18 U.S.C. § 912); United States v. Girard, 601 F.2d 69, 71 (2d Cir. 1979) (statute making it unlawful to sell without authority any record or thing of value of the United States was violated by sale of information).

146. *See* McDonald v. Alabama, 329 So. 2d 583, 587–88 (Ala. Crim. Ct. App. 1975) (sexual intercourse, or the promise of sexual intercourse, is a thing of value under a bribery statute), *cert. denied*, 429 U.S. 834 (1976).

147. United States v. Zouras, 497 F.2d 1115, 1121 (7th Cir. 1974) (holding the testimony of a witness to be a "thing of value" when construing 18 U.S.C. § 876, which prohibits extortion of "money or other thing of value").

148. United States v. Schwartz, 785 F.2d 673, 680–81 (9th Cir.), *cert. denied*, 499 U.S. 890 (1986) (holding that "thing of value" includes the intangible of providing assistance in arranging a merger when interpreting 18 U.S.C. § 1954, which prohibited offering "anything of value" with intent to influence actions of union benefit plan trustees).

149. MODEL PENAL CODE § 240.0 (Proposed Official Draft 1962). The Model Penal Code was approved by the American Law Institute by resolution dated May 24, 1962. Many of its provisions have been followed, in varying degrees, by numerous states. *See* MODEL PENAL CODE AND COMMENTARIES (ALI 1980) [hereinafter Model Penal Code Commentary].

150. *Id.* § 240.0(1).

151. Model Penal Code Commentary, *supra* note 149, § 240.1 commentary at 24.

152. *Id.*

153. United States v. Williams, 705 F.2d 603, 622–23 (2d Cir.), *cert. denied*, 464 U.S. 1007 (1983).

154. 18 U.S.C. § 201(c).

155. *Id.* § 201(g).

156. *Williams*, 705 F.2d at 623.

157. *Id.* (quoting United States v. Girard, 601 F.2d 69, 71 (2d Cir.), *cert. denied*, 444 U.S. 871 (1979)). Similarly, in United States v. Gorman, 807 F.2d 1299, 1305 (6th Cir. 1986), *cert. denied*, 484 U.S. 815 (1987), the Sixth Circuit held that loans and promises of future employment to public officials constituted a "thing of value" under the unlawful gratuity statute. The court stated that in order to put the underlying policy of the statute into effect, the term "thing of value" should be broadly construed. The focus therefore was placed on the value that the official subjectively attaches to the gift. *See also* United States v. Crozier, 987 F.2d 893, 901 (2d Cir.), *cert. denied*, 510 U.S. 880 (1993) (holding that "any payment that the defendant subjectively believes has value, including a loan, constitutes a thing 'of value' within the meaning" of a statute prohibiting corrupt payments to officials who dispense federal funds).

158. 18 U.S.C. § 201.

159. *Id.* § 201(b)(1). The domestic bribery law was expanded by Congress in 1962 to forbid the offer or promise of something of value from which a public official himself will not benefit but which will be of advantage to another person in whose well-being he is interested. *See* S. REP. NO. 87-2213 (1962), *reprinted in* 1962 U.S.C.C.A.N. 3852, 3857.

160. The OECD Convention clearly proscribes payments made to a foreign official, "for that official or for a third party." OECD Convention, *supra* note 4, art. I, ¶ 1.

161. *See* FCPA Review Procedure Release No. 83-01 (May 12, 1983), in which a U.S. company retained a Sudanese government corporation as its agent. Commissions were to be paid directly to the Sudanese corporation, and not to any individual, for deposit in an authorized financial institution in Sudan. The DOJ declined to take any enforcement action, commenting that "[t]here is no expectation that any individual Sudanese government official will personally benefit from the proposed agency relationship." *See also* FCPA Review Procedure Release No. 82-03 (Apr. 22, 1982) (no enforcement action taken where there was no expectation that any individual government official would personally benefit from arrangement where commissions were to be paid to a government-controlled trade organization).

162. *See, e.g.*, FCPA Review Procedure Release No. 80-01 (Oct. 29, 1980), in which the DOJ declined to take any enforcement action with respect to a fund for the American education and support of the adopted children of a foreign official who was elderly and semi-invalid and whose duties were only ceremonial and did not involve substantive decision-making responsibilities. This release implicitly suggests that something of value given to the children of an official may constitute value given to the official. *See also* FCPA Review Procedure Release No. 83-02 (July 26, 1983) (declining to take enforcement action against a firm that was to pay the travel and lodging expenses of an official and his spouse for a proposed promotional tour).

163. United States v. Liebo, 923 F.2d 1308 (8th Cir. 1991).

164. Indictment, United States v. Liebo, Criminal No. 4-89-76 (D. Minn. 1988), www.justice.gov/criminal/fraud/fcpa/cases/liebor/1989-05-04-liebo-indict.pdf.

165. *Liebo*, 923 F.2d at 1311. The Resource Guide at 16 cites this case as an example of payments to third parties that violated the FCPA. *See also* SEC v. Bell-South, Civil Action No. 1:02-cv-0113 (N.D. Ga. Jan. 15, 2002). (The SEC initiated an action against BellSouth for a violation of the accounting provisions of the FCPA in part for the alleged improper payments made by its Nicaraguan subsidiary to the wife of a Nicaraguan legislator. The legislator chaired a key legislative committee responsible for the repeal of a law restricting foreign ownership of telecommunications companies. The payments to the wife were booked as consulting services. By asserting that the payments were improperly recorded, the SEC is implicitly asserting either that the payments to the wife were indirect payments made to the legislator; or that the monies provided to a person in whose well-being the official was interested (*i.e.*, the wife) was intended as a quid pro quo for the legislator's assistance in repealing the law restricting foreign ownership); United States v. Siemens Bangl. Ltd., No. 1:08-CR-00369 (D.D.C. Dec. 12, 2008) (alleging the

hiring of the son of a high-level official of the Bangladeshi executive branch who had influence over the award decision, the hiring of the nephew of a senior official in the Ministry of Posts and Telecommunications, and payments to the daughter of an official in the government-owned telecommunications regulatory entity ostensibly to work as an engineer); *In re* Avery Dennison Corp., Accounting and Auditing Enforcement Release No. 3021 (July 28, 2009) (hired the spouse of a foreign official in charge of projects the company wanted to pursue); United States v. DaimlerChrysler China Ltd., No. 1:10-cr-00066-RJL (D.D.C. 2010) (Daimler-Chrysler China Ltd. and Daimler provided the following things of value, among others, to the son of a Chinese government official who made purchasing decisions in order to assist in securing business: internships at Daimler for him and his girlfriend; letters from a former Daimler employee to German immigration officials to assist him and his girlfriend with their efforts to obtain student visas; €2,233 in expenses to attend a truck race in July 2004 for him, the Chinese government official, and others; use of a Mercedes passenger car for a period of time; and employment at Daimler from January–April 2005 with a monthly salary of €600); United States v. Control Components, Inc. No. 09-00162 (C.D. Cal. 2009) (CCI paid college tuition of the children of at least two executives at CCI's state-owned customers for the purpose of securing business); SEC v. UTStarcom, Inc., No. 09-cv-6094 (N.D. Cal. Dec. 31, 2009) (UTStarcom "provided foreign government customers or their family members with work visas and purportedly hired them to work for [UTStarcom] in the U.S., when in reality they did no work for the company"); SEC v. Tyson Foods, Inc., Litigation Release No. 21,851 (Feb. 10, 2011) (official's wife put on payroll even though she performed no services); a non-prosecution agreement entered into between the DOJ and RAE Sys., Inc., dated December 10, 2010, included charges that a notebook computer was given as a gift to the son of an official to obtain business, www.justice.gov/criminal/fraud/cases/rae-systems/12-10-10rae-systems-pdf; SEC v. Universal Corp., Case No. 1:10-cv-01318 (D.D.C. Aug. 6, 2010) (payments made to the wife of an official and the brother of an official).

166. Resource Guide at 16.

167. *See id.* at 16–19.

168. SEC v. Schering-Plough Corp., Case No. 1:04CV00945 (D.D.C. June 9, 2004); *In re* Schering-Plough Corp., Admin. Proc. File No. 3-11517, Exchange Act Release No. 49,838 (June 9, 2004).

169. The 1988 amendments added this clause to the existing law.

170. 15 U.S.C. §§ 78dd-1(a)(1), 78dd-2(a)(2).

171. *Id.*

172. H.R. REP. NO. 94-831, at 11–12.

173. *Id.* at 12; *see also* United States v. Siemens S.A. (Arg.), No. 1:08-CR-00368 (D.D.C. Dec. 12, 2008). In this conspiracy charge, Siemens S.A. (Argentina), a Siemens-controlled subsidiary, was initially awarded a national identity card project in Argentina, but this project was put on hold when a new Argentine government came to power. In exchange for a "national decree" requiring new identity cards for Argentine citizens, Siemens (Argentina) paid millions of U.S.

dollars to a senior official of the new Argentine government to influence or induce action. The promised national decree was never issued.

174. H.R. Rep. No. 95-640, at 8; *see also* Non-Prosecution Agreement between U.S. Department of Justice and Armor Holdings, Inc. (July 13, 2011), Press Release No. 11-911, U.S. Dep't of Justice (July 11, 2011) (payments made to U.N. official to induce that official to provide nonpublic, inside information and to cause the U.N. to award a contract to the company).

175. 15 U.S.C. §§ 78dd-1(a), 78dd-2(a).

176. H.R. Rep. No. 94-831, at 12.

177. *See* SEC v. Jackson, 4:12-cv-00563 (S.D. Tex. 2012) (SEC charged three oil services executives of participating in a bribery scheme to obtain illicit permits for oil rigs in Nigeria in order to retain business under oil drilling contracts); United States v. Saybolt, Inc., 98 Cr. 10266 WGY (D. Mass. 1998); United States v. Mead, Cr. 98-240-01 (D.N.J. 1998) (plea agreement and conviction for conspiracy to violate the FCPA and violation of the FCPA arising from a payment to Panamanian officials to obtain a favorable lease in the Panama Canal Zone); *see also* SEC v. Summers, No. 4:10-cv-02786 (S.D. Tex. Aug. 5, 2010) (Country manager of Pride International, Inc. settled charges that he authorized improper payments in exchange for obtaining receivables owed to the company); discussion in Q 16.11, *supra*.

178. United States v. Aibel Grp. Ltd., No. H-07-005 (S.D. Tex. Nov. 7, 2008) (plea agreement related to corrupt payments to Nigerian customs officials for preferential treatment during the customs process); *In re* Con-way Inc., Accounting and Auditing Enforcement Release No. 2867 (Aug. 27, 2008) (allegations that Con-way's foreign subsidiary induced foreign officials to violate customs regulations, improperly settle customs disputes, and reduce or not enforce legitimate fines); *see also* United States v. Kay, 359 F.3d 738 (5th Cir. 2004), *cert. denied*, 555 U.S. 813 (2008) (holding that payments allegedly made to Haitian government officials for purpose of reducing corporation's customs duties and taxes were potentially within FCPA's prohibition against payments to foreign officials to "obtain or retain" business).

179. Panalpina World Transport (Holding) Ltd., a global freight forwarding and logistics services firm based in Basel, Switzerland, and five other oil and gas services companies and subsidiaries bribed foreign officials in various countries to circumvent local rules and regulations relating to importing goods and materials. *See, e.g.*, United States v. Panalpina, Inc., No. 4:10-CR-00765 (S.D. Tex. Nov. 4, 2010); United States v. Tidewater Marine Int'l Inc., No. 4:10-CR-00770 (S.D. Tex. Nov. 4, 2010); United States v. Shell Nigeria Expl. & Prod. Co., No. 4:10-CR-00767 (S.D. Tex. Nov. 4, 2011); United States v. Pride Int'l Inc., No. 4:10-CR-00766 (S.D. Tex. Nov. 4, 2010); United States v. Transocean, Inc., No. 4:10-CR-00768 (S.D. Tex. Nov. 4, 2010). The 1988 Conference Report refers to the *United Brands* case as an example of prohibited conduct. United States v. United Brands Co., Cr. No. 78-538 (S.D.N.Y. 1978); SEC v. United Brands Co., Civil No. 75-0509 (D.D.C. 1976) (an SEC action was followed by a criminal charge from the DOJ alleging a conspiracy to commit mail fraud). That case involved bribes paid by United Brands to the President of Honduras in order to obtain a lower export tax on bananas and an exten-

sion of favorable commercial terms on its Honduran properties. The Conference Report distinguishes these activities from lobbying or conducting other normal representations with government officials. In FCPA Opinion Procedure Release No. 04-01 (Jan. 6, 2004), the DOJ declined to take enforcement action against a U.S. law firm planning to hold a comparative law seminar on labor and employment law in Beijing, China where the firm had agreed to pay the travel and accommodation costs of Chinese government officials wishing to attend the seminar. In reaching this opinion, the DOJ relied on a number of facts, including that the firm "ha[d] no business before the entities that may send officials to the seminar" and that it "[was] unaware of any pending or anticipated business between the clients who will be invited to the seminar and the Chinese officials who will attend."

180. Resource Guide at 13.

181. 15 U.S.C. §§ 78dd1(a)(3), 78dd-2(a)(3); S. REP. NO. 99-486 (1986).

182. 15 U.S.C. §§ 78dd-1(a)(3), 78dd-2(a)(3) (emphasis added).

183. *Id.* §§ 78dd-1(a), 78dd-2(a) (prohibits "authorization of the payment of any money, or . . . authorization of the giving of anything of value"). *See* Q 16.16 *et seq., infra.*

184. 18 U.S.C. § 201; *see also supra* note 158 and accompanying text.

185. To be liable as an accomplice, a person must act with intent that the offense be committed. *See, e.g.,* United States v. Medina, 887 F.2d 528, 532 (5th Cir. 1989) (to be convicted of aiding and abetting, defendant must share the principal's criminal intent and engage in some affirmative conduct to aid the venture); United States v. Pearlstein, 576 F.2d 531, 546 (3d Cir. 1978) ("[I]t is necessary that the alleged aider and abettor associate himself with the unlawful venture and participate in it with the intent that its illegal objective be obtained.").

186. *See* QQ 16.2 & 16.3, *supra.*

187. Prior to the 1988 amendments, a U.S. company could be liable for a payment made to an intermediary party, while knowing or *having reason to know* that the payment would be given to a foreign official. 91 Stat. at 1495, 1497. The 1988 amendments deleted the "reason to know" standard relating to payments to third parties. The "reason to know" standard created significant uncertainties for U.S. companies regarding their potential liability under the FCPA with respect to operations abroad. This standard appeared to encompass the situation where a U.S. company negligently disregarded the risk that a sales agent may use payments made to it by the U.S. company to bribe a foreign official. *See Business Accounting and Foreign Trade Simplification Act: Joint Hearings on S. 414 Before the Subcomm. on Int'l Fin. & Monetary Pol'y and the Subcomm. on Sec. of the S. Comm. on Banking, Hous., & Urban Affairs,* 98th Cong., 1st Sess. (1983) (Memorandum from Deputy Attorney Gen. Edward C. Schmults) [hereinafter Schmults Memorandum]. In actuality, however, the requirement that a payment be made "corruptly" made it difficult to prosecute anyone under a negligence standard. Moreover, the Department of Justice had indicated that, as a matter of enforcement policy, it would not prosecute anyone under a negligence standard. *See* S. REP. NO. 99-486, at 25. In clarifying the bribery standard through the deletion of "reason to know," Congress in effect eliminated only the possibility that simple *negligence* could be a basis for criminal liability. At the same time, Congress made

it clear that the knowledge standard extended beyond actual knowledge, to cover a *conscious disregard, willful blindness,* or *deliberate ignorance* of circumstances that should alert one to the likelihood of an FCPA violation. H.R. REP. NO. 100-576, *reprinted in* 1988 U.S.C.C.A.N. 1949, 1952–54. In practical terms, the distinction may not be very significant. The blurring of this distinction is best exemplified in the criminal trial and conviction of Frederic Bourke (United States v. Kozeny, No. 1:05-CR-00518-SAS-2), wherein the judge provided jury instructions on the conscious avoidance standard of knowledge. The jury foreman was quoted as saying "We thought he knew and he definitely should have known." Ellen Podgor, *Year & a Day in FCPA Case—But Will It Hold on Appeal?,* WHITE COLLAR CRIME PROF BLOG (Nov. 12, 2009), http://lawprofessors.typepad.com/whitecollarcrime_blog/2009/11/year-a-day-in-fcpa-case.html. *See* discussion at *Kozeny* case study below.

188. 15 U.S.C. §§ 78dd-1(f)(2), 78dd-2(h)(3).

189. H.R. REP. NO. 100-576, at 919–21, *reprinted in* 1988 U.S.C.C.A.N. 1953–54 (citations omitted); *see also* discussion in Resource Guide at 22.

190. MODEL PENAL CODE § 2.02(d)(7) contains a similar standard:

> *Requirement of Knowledge Satisfied by Knowledge of High Probability.* When knowledge of the existence of a particular fact is an element of an offense, such knowledge is established if a person is aware of a high probability of its existence, unless he actually believes that it does not exist.

However, the Code provision applies only when what is involved is a matter of an existing fact, not circumstances. Model Penal Code Commentary, *supra* note 149, § 2.02 cmt. 9. In contrast, the FCPA would impute knowledge not just of a particular fact, but of the criminal act itself.

191. *See* United States v. King, 351 F.3d 859 (8th Cir. 2002), wherein the court gave a deliberate ignorance instruction to the jury where the defendant was on notice of possible bribery activity and deliberately declined to investigate; *see also* Information, United States v. Baker Hughes Servs. Int'l, Inc., No. CR H-07-0219 (S.D. Tex. Apr. 11, 2007) (alleging that the defendant's conduct was "knowing" when the defendant was instructed by a foreign, state-owned oil company to retain a certain "consultant," the defendant did retain the consultant even though it performed no legitimate services, and the defendant's employee stated that if the consultant were not retained "we can say goodbye to this and future business"); Plea Agreement, United States v. Vetco Gray UK Ltd. & Vetco Gray Controls Ltd., No. CR H-07-004 (S.D. Tex. Feb. 6, 2007) (alleging the defendants' conduct was "knowing" within the meaning of the FCPA when the company's employees had been informed that they did "not want to know" what a foreign agent has to do to make deliveries clear customs, and when employees admitted that payments to the agent "likely lined customs' officials pockets").

192. *See, e.g.,* the definition of "recklessly" in the Model Penal Code:

> A person acts recklessly with respect to a material element of an offense when he consciously disregards a substantial and

unjustifiable risk that the material element exists or will result
from his conduct . . . .

MODEL PENAL CODE § 2.02(2)(c).

193. Statement of Deputy Chief of the Fraud Section, U.S. Dep't of Justice,
Criminal Div., in an address before the Foreign Trade Council (Apr. 21, 1994). *But
cf.* H.R. REP. NO. 100-40, at 76 (1987) (indicating that reckless disregard will not
give rise to a criminal prosecution under the FCPA). *See* SEC v. El Paso Corp., Civil
Action No. 07CV00899 (S.D.N.Y. Feb. 7, 2007) (claiming that the company was
"reckless in not knowing" of illicit payments).

194. *See, e.g.,* United States v. Puente, 982 F.2d 156 (5th Cir.), *cert. denied,* 508
U.S. 962 (1993) (reckless indifference shown by defendant in failing to read form
was sufficient to establish scienter requirement for the crime of fraud); United
States v. White, 765 F.2d 1469 (11th Cir. 1985); United States v. Dick, 744 F.2d 546
(7th Cir. 1984).

195. United States v. Kozeny, 664 F. Supp. 2d 369 (S.D.N.Y. May 29, 2009), *aff'd,*
667 F.3d 122 (2d Cir. 2011).

196. *Id.,* Jury Charge S2 05 Cr. 518 (SAS); *see also* Resource Guide at 23.

197. United States v. Jewell, 532 F.2d 697 (9th Cir.) (en banc), *cert. denied,* 426
U.S. 951 (1976); *see also* United States v. Shannon, 137 F.3d 1112, 1115 (9th Cir.),
cert. denied, 524 U.S. 962 (1998) (upholding the use of a *Jewell* instruction).

198. *Jewell,* 532 F.2d at 702, *cited with approval in* H.R. REP. NO. 100-576, at 920,
reprinted in 1988 U.S.C.C.A.N. at 1953.

199. *Id.* at 700 (quoting GLANVILLE WILLIAMS, CRIMINAL LAW: THE GENERAL PART
§ 57, at 157, 159 (2d ed. 1961)).

200. *See supra* note 187, discussing the "reason to know" standard.

201. The DOJ never prosecuted a company or individual under the FCPA on
the basis of "reason to know." *See* S. REP. NO. 99-486, at 25.

202. DOJ officials have remarked that the deletion of "reason to know" has
changed neither the prosecution standard nor counsel's advice. This is, in fact,
the case.

203. Resource Guide at 23.

204. United States v. Jacobs, 475 F.2d 270 (2d Cir.), *cert. denied,* 414 U.S. 821
(1973).

205. *Id.* at 287, *quoted with approval in* H.R. REP. NO. 100-576, at 920, *reprinted
in* 1988 U.S.C.C.A.N. 1953. Similarly, in United States v. Manriquez Arbizo, 833 F.2d
244, 248 (10th Cir. 1987), the court upheld a conviction for possession of mari-
juana despite the defendant's claim that he lacked the requisite knowledge. The
court approved the following jury instruction as an appropriate interpretation of
"knowing": "The element of knowledge may be satisfied by inferences drawn from
proof that a defendant deliberately closed his eyes to what would otherwise have
been obvious to him. A finding beyond a reasonable doubt of a conscious
purpose to avoid enlightenment would permit an inference of knowledge."

206. Resource Guide at 22.

207. 15 U.S.C. §§ 78dd-1(a), 78dd-2(a) ("*authorization* of the payment of any
money, or . . . authorization of the giving of anything of value").

208. *See* SEC v. Veraz Networks, Inc. No. 5:10-CV-2849 (N.D. Cal. 2010) (Veraz supervisor authorized consultant to provide gifts to Vietnamese officials); United States v. Kellogg Brown & Root LLC, No. H-09-071 (S.D. Tex. Feb. 6, 2009) (KBR authorized consultants to make illicit payments to Nigerian government officials on its behalf); SEC v. Eric L. Mattson & James W. Harris, Accounting and Auditing Enforcement Release No. 1444 (Sept. 12, 2001); Exchange Act Release No. 44,784 (Sept. 12, 2001); Accounting and Auditing Enforcement Release No. 1447 (Sept. 12, 2001) (Baker and Hughes authorized its accountant/agent to pay a $75,000 bribe to an Indonesian tax official to reduce the tax assessment against its wholly owned Indonesian subsidiary); *see also* discussion of third-party payments, *supra* Q 16.14.

209. *See, e.g.*, Saybolt Int'l B.V. v. Schreiber, 327 F.3d 173 (2d Cir. 2003).

210. H.R. REP. NO. 95-640, at 8.

211. The Unlawful Corporate Payments Act of 1977, adopted by the House and considered by the Conference Committee, originally contained a provision which imposed liability on officers, directors, employees or agents who knowingly and willingly "acquiesced" in an act or practice in violation of the Act. H.R. 3815, 95th Cong., § 30A(c)(1) (1977), *reprinted in* 1977 House Hearings, at 6. During congressional hearings, the Department of Justice and other witnesses objected to using the word "acquiesce," stating that it was too vague a concept upon which to predicate criminal liability. *Id.* at 22–25 (Letter from Patricia M. Wald, Assistant Attorney Gen., Office of Legislative Affairs, U.S. Dep't of Justice); *id.* at 58 (statement of Robert B. von Mehren, Chairperson, Ad Hoc Comm. on Foreign Payments, Ass'n of Bar of City of New York). The reference to "acquiesce" was not included in the final bill passed by the House.

212. *See* Cont'l Baking Co. v. United States, 281 F.2d 137, 149 (6th Cir. 1960); RESTATEMENT (SECOND) OF AGENCY § 43(2) (ALI 1958) ("Acquiescence by the principal in a series of acts by the agent indicates authorization to perform similar acts in the future.").

213. *See, e.g.*, United States v. Richardson, 596 F.2d 157, 162 (6th Cir. 1979) ("mere . . . acquiescence in the object or the purpose of the conspiracy, without an intention and agreement to cooperate in the crime is not sufficient to make one a conspirator.") (quoting United States v. Williams, 503 F.2d 50 (6th Cir. 1974). *Accord* United States v. Rodriguez, 585 F.2d 1234, 1245 (5th Cir. 1978).

214. *See* United States v. Gillen, 599 F.2d 541 (3d Cir.), *cert. denied*, 444 U.S. 866 (1979) (corporate officer convicted of price fixing where he knew of illegal conduct and took no action to prevent subordinates from carrying it out).

215. Pattis v. United States, 17 F.2d 562 (9th Cir.), *cert. denied*, 274 U.S. 750 (1927); *see also* United States v. Wilson, 59 F.2d 97 (W.D. Wash. 1932) (corporation, whose agent made sales of yeast to purchaser known to make illegal liquor, held liable for agent's actions).

216. Deacon v. United States, 124 F.2d 352 (1st Cir. 1941).

217. *Id.* at 357; *see also* Hyde v. United States, 225 U.S. 347, 369 (1911) (to sustain claim of withdrawal, defendant must show an affirmative action to disavow or defeat the purpose of the conspiracy). *Accord* United States v. Chester, 407 F.2d 53, 55 (3d Cir.), *cert. denied*, 394 U.S. 1020 (1969).

218. *See* Q 16.3, *supra* (discussing what an issuer is).

219. Exchange Act § 13(b)(2)(A), 15 U.S.C. § 78m(b)(2)(A).

220. Exchange Act § 13(b)(2)(B), 15 U.S.C. § 78m(b)(2)(B).

221. S. REP. NO. 95-114, at 7 (1977).

222. *See, e.g.*, SEC v. Diebold, Inc., No. 1:13-cv-1609 (D.D.C. Oct. 22, 2013) (ATM provider paid bribes to private banks in Russia); SEC Charges Diebold with FCPA Violations in China, Indonesia, and Russia, Litigation Release No. 22,849 (Oct. 22, 2013), www.sec.gov/litigation/litreleases/2013/lr22849.htm.

223. Exchange Act § 13(b)(2)(A), 15 U.S.C. § 78m(b)(2)(A).

224. Under the Exchange Act, "records" means "accounts, correspondence, memorandums, tapes, discs, papers, books, and other documents or transcribed information of any type, whether expressed in ordinary or machine language." Exchange Act § 3(a)(37), 15 U.S.C. § 78c(a)(37).

225. Exchange Act § 13(b)(7), 15 U.S.C. § 78m(b)(7).

226. S. REP. NO. 95-114, at 7.

227. S. REP. NO. 94-1031, at 23 (1976).

228. Resource Guide at 39 (noting that both SEC and DOJ books and records enforcement actions historically have involved either misreporting large bribes or a systematic pattern of misreporting smaller bribes).

229. *See* Regulation S-K, Selected Financial Data, 17 C.F.R. § 229.301.

230. Exchange Act § 13(b)(2)(B), 15 U.S.C. § 78m(b)(2)(B).

231. Resource Guide at 40.

232. Exchange Act § 13(b)(7), 15 U.S.C. § 78m(b)(7).

233. *In re* BHP Billiton, Ltd. & Billiton Plc, Exchange Act Release No. 74,998 (ALJ May 20, 2015) (order instituting proceedings, making findings, and imposing cease-and-desist order), www.sec.gov/litigation/admin/2015/34-74998.pdf.

234. Exchange Act § 13(b)(6), 15 U.S.C. § 78m(b)(6).

235. *See, e.g.*, SEC v. Peterson, No. 12-cv-2033 (E.D.N.Y. Apr. 25, 2012); Press Release, SEC Charges Former Morgan Stanley Executive with FCPA Violations and Investment Adviser Fraud (Apr. 25, 2012), www.sec.gov/News/PressRelease/Detail/PressRelease/1365171488702.

236. Exchange Act Rule 13b2-1, 17 C.F.R. § 240.13b2-1 ("No person shall, directly or indirectly, falsify or cause to be falsified, any book, record or account subject to [the books and records provision] of the Securities Exchange Act.").

237. *See, e.g.*, SEC v. Jackson, No. 4:12-cv-563 (S.D. Tex. Feb. 24, 2012); SEC Settles Pending Civil Action Against Noble Executives Mark A. Jackson and James J. Ruehlen, Litigation Release No. 23,038 (July 7, 2014), www.sec.gov/litigation/litreleases/2014/lr23038.htm.

238. Exchange Act Rule 13b2-2, 17 C.F.R. § 240.13b2-1.

239. Exchange Act Rule 13a-14, 17 C.F.R. § 240.13a-14 (often called the "SOX certification" rule, for the Sarbanes-Oxley Act of 2002).

240. Exchange Act § 13(b)(5), 15 U.S.C. § 78m(b)(5) ("No person shall knowingly circumvent or knowingly fail to implement a system of internal accounting controls or knowingly falsify any book, record, or account [subject to the books and records provision]."); Exchange Act § 13(b)(4), 15 U.S.C. § 78m(b)(4) (limiting criminal liability to violations committed "knowingly"); Exchange Act § 32(a), 15 U.S.C. § 78ff(a) (limiting criminal liability to violations committed "willfully").

241. H.R. REP. No. 100-576, at 916 (1988).
242. *See, e.g.*, United States v. Jensen, 532 F. Supp. 2d 1187, 1193–94 (N.D. Cal. 2008).

17

Export Controls

*Antonia I. Tzinova, Ronald A. Oleynik &
Jonathan M. Epstein* *

IMPORTANT REGULATORY CHANGES!

Reforms currently in progress, and likely to continue into 2017, are significantly altering the U.S. export control landscape. While the goal of such reform is to reduce the licensing burden for less sensitive items, the rolling changes create challenges for affected U.S. companies as they try and adapt their compliance procedures to keep up with the changes.

The U.S. export controls laws and regulations create a complex framework of obligations for U.S. exporters. Because the U.S. government imposes these controls for reasons of national security, economic interests, and foreign policy objectives, it guards the application of its export controls with heightened diligence. Exporters should remember that exporting is not a right but a privilege that can be taken away from them for a number of reasons.

---

*   The authors wish to acknowledge Christopher A. Myers for his contributions to this chapter.

A good understanding of the export obligations and of the practical procedures to address such obligations reduces the risk of committing a violation and reduces the cost of exporting. An effective compliance program based on a clear statement by management that the company is committed to adhering to export controls laws and policies, coupled with step-by-step procedures, clear role responsibilities, and disciplinary consequences, helps streamline the process of exporting and engages employees at all levels in the complex task of avoiding export controls violations.

Acronyms, initialisms, and abbreviations used in this chapter:

AECA	Arms Export Control Act
AES	Automatic Export System
BIS	Bureau of Industry and Security (U.S. Dep't of Commerce)
CCL	Commerce Control List
CJ	Commodity Jurisdiction
CNC	computer numerically controlled
DDTC	Directorate of Defense Trade Controls (U.S. Dep't of State)
EAA	Export Administration Act
EAR	Export Administration Regulations
ECCN	Export Control Classification Number
ERN	encryption registration number
FCPA	Foreign Corrupt Practices Act
FMS	Foreign Military Sales
IEEPA	International Emergency Economic Powers Act
IRCA	Immigration Reform and Control Act of 1986
ITAR	International Traffic in Arms Regulations
OEM	original equipment manufacturer
OFAC	Office of Foreign Assets Control (U.S. Dep't of Treasury)

SDN List	Specially Designated Nationals [and Blocked Persons] List
TAA	Technical Assistance Agreement
TWEA	Trading with the Enemy Act
USML	United States Munitions List

Overview

Q 17.1   Generally speaking, what do U.S. export laws and regulations aim to achieve?

The U.S. export controls regime is shaped by national security and economic interests, and foreign policy; therefore, U.S. export laws and regulations have various objectives, such as:

- preventing the proliferation of weapons of mass destruction;
- advancing U.S. economic interests at home and abroad;
- aiding regional stability;
- implementing anti-terrorism and crime control; and
- protecting human rights.

Q 17.1.1   How do export controls seek to achieve those objectives?

U.S. export laws and regulations generally restrict the export of products and services based on the type of product and the destination of the export. In both the defense and high-technology sectors, the U.S. government tightly regulates the export not only of equipment and components, but also of technology and technical data. In addition, U.S. economic sanctions laws overlay export controls by generally prohibiting transactions, including the export or re-export of most U.S.-origin goods, to certain countries (including Cuba, Iran, Syria, Sudan, and North Korea), and to certain individuals and entities subject to targeted sanctions.

Q 17.1.2   Which U.S. agencies regulate exports from the United States?

Three principal agencies regulate U.S. exports:

COMPLIANCE FACT

The Obama administration has taken steps toward easing the embargo on Cuba with the goal of improving the lives of the Cuban people. As a result, the Departments of Treasury and Commerce have made changes to their respective regulations authorizing certain transactions with Cuba (such as providing further authorizations of certain travel to Cuba). Additionally, on June 6, 2015, Cuba was removed from the Department of State's list of state sponsors of terrorism. However, most of the restrictions on dealing with Cuba remain and will require congressional action before the embargo can be further eased. Given the extremely politicized nature of the process, we cannot provide a specific forecast as to when the embargo might be actually lifted.

- The Department of State Directorate of Defense Trade Controls (DDTC) administers most defense exports.
- The Department of Commerce Bureau of Industry and Security (BIS) administers dual-use technology exports and less sensitive military items.
- The Department of the Treasury Office of Foreign Assets Control (OFAC) administers exports to certain sanctioned countries and designated persons.

In addition, various other agencies, such as the Department of Justice, the Department of Defense, the Department of Energy, the Nuclear Regulatory Commission, and U.S. Customs and Border Protection, are involved in regulating exports.

Export of Defense Articles and Services

Q 17.2   How are defense exports regulated?

DDTC administers the export of certain defense articles and related technologies (*e.g.*, technical data and defense services) under

TABLE 17-1
United States Munitions List

Category

I	Firearms, Close Assault Weapons and Combat Shotguns
II	Guns and Armament
III	Ammunition/Ordnance
IV	Launch Vehicles, Guided Missiles, Ballistic Missiles, Rockets, Torpedoes, Bombs, and Mines
V	Explosives and Energetic Materials, Propellants, Incendiary Agents, and Their Constituents
VI	Surface Vessels of War and Special Naval Equipment
VII	Ground Vehicles
VIII	Aircraft and Related Articles
IX	Military Training Equipment and Training
X	Protective Personnel Equipment and Shelters
XI	Military Electronics
XII	Fire Control, Range Finder, Optical and Guidance and Control Equipment
XIII	Materials and Miscellaneous Articles
XIV	Toxicological Agents, including Chemical Agents, Biological Agents, and Associated Equipment
XV	Spacecraft and Related Articles
XVI	Nuclear Weapons and Related Articles
XVII	Classified Articles, Technical Data, and Defense Services Not Otherwise Enumerated
XVIII	Directed Energy Weapons
XIX	Gas Turbine Engines and Associated Equipment
XX	Submersible Vessels and Related Articles
XXI	Articles, Technical Data, and Defense Services Not Otherwise Enumerated

the Arms Export Control Act (AECA)[1] and the International Traffic in Arms Regulations (ITAR).[2]

Currently, with limited exceptions, virtually all ITAR-controlled defense articles and technology exported from the United States require a DDTC license. In certain cases, the U.S. company may obtain broad authorization, generally in the form of a Technical Assistance Agreement (TAA), to cover technology transfers, or licenses covering multiple shipments of specified equipment to a specific foreign licensee.

International Traffic in Arms Regulations

Q 17.3 What is the scope of the ITAR?

DDTC administers the export and re-export of defense articles, defense services, and related technical data from the United States to any foreign destination or to any foreign person, whether located in the United States or abroad. Section 121.1 of the ITAR contains the United States Munitions List (USML) and includes the commodities and related technical data and defense services controlled for export purposes. Historically, the ITAR controlled any equipment originally designed for military purposes, and any part or component specifically designed or modified for military purposes. Hence, nuts, bolts, batteries, connectors, and a multitude of minor items were historically also controlled under the ITAR, if specifically designed for military purposes. The keystone of export control reform is to transfer jurisdiction of less sensitive military items currently controlled on the USML to the Commerce Control List (CCL) administered by BIS (*see* Q 17.5.2).

DDTC and BIS have been issuing new rules on a rolling basis, transferring on a category-by-category basis items from the USML to the CCL. As of November 10, 2014, the transfers are complete for fifteen of twenty-one USML categories. In addition, the new rules implement a number of framework changes to the ITAR to facilitate the transition.[3]

Q 17.3.1 What is a defense article?

A "defense article"[4] is any item or technical data designated on the USML.[5] This term includes technical data recorded or stored in any physical form, models, mock-ups, or other items that reveal technical data directly relating to such items. As a result of export control reforms, the USML has largely become a positive inclusive list of sensitive military items (such as fighter aircraft) and specialized military components (such as bomb racks). Less sensitive items, even if specially designed for use with a military aircraft, have migrated to the CCL, which is more flexible in terms of licensing requirements or the availability of licensing exceptions (*see* Q 17.3.5).

Q 17.3.2   What is technical data?

"Technical data" means any information required for the design, development, assembly, production, operation, repair, testing, maintenance, or modification of a defense article. Technical data may include blueprints, operations and maintenance manuals, and the like.[6]

Q 17.3.3   What are defense services?

"Defense services" means providing assistance, including training, to a foreign person, in the United States or abroad, in the design, manufacture, repair, or operation of a defense article, as well as providing military training or advice to foreign military forces. Informal collaboration, conversations, or interchanges concerning technical data are also included in defense services.[7] (Note that DDTC has proposed a revision to the current definition of "defense service" that will remove certain activities currently controlled.[8])

Q 17.3.4   What is "look through" treatment under the ITAR?

With rare exceptions, if an item contains any components that are controlled under the ITAR, the entire item is controlled under the ITAR. For example, a commercial radio that would normally not be controlled under the ITAR becomes a defense article if it contains an ITAR-controlled microchip.

Q 17.3.5   What does the USML cover?

The USML designates particular categories and types of equipment as defense articles.[9] The USML divides defense articles into twenty-one categories, listed above.

Q 17.3.6 How can an exporter determine that an item is ITAR-controlled?

While DDTC has jurisdiction over deciding whether an item is ITAR-controlled, it generally encourages exporters to self-classify. If doubt exists as to whether an article or service is covered by the USML, upon written request in the form of a Commodity Jurisdiction (CJ) request, DDTC will provide advice as to whether a particular article is a defense article subject to the ITAR, or an item subject to Commerce Department controls.[10]

COMPLIANCE FACT

Are "Specially Designed" Components Controlled? While the USML is now largely a "positive" list, for certain subcategories, specially designed parts, and components will still be controlled on the ITAR. A new tiered definition of "specially designed" in the ITAR essentially follows a "catch and release" analysis.[11] An item is initially "caught" if it either has performance capabilities or is used in a defense article controlled on the USML. However, there are then five criteria that may "release" the item from the USML. For example, fasteners and general purpose commodities may be released if they meet the criteria in the definition. Note that such items may then still be controlled and require a license under the Export Administration Regulations (EAR).

Exports and Re-Exports

Q 17.4 What constitutes an export under the ITAR?

The ITAR defines the term "export" broadly. The term applies not only to exports of tangible items from the United States, but also to transfers of intangibles, such as technology or information. The ITAR defines as an export the passing of information or technology to foreign nationals even in the United States—a concept generally referred to as "deemed export"[12] (thus, an export is deemed to have

575

taken place even though no physical border has been crossed). The following are examples of exports:

1. Exports of articles from the U.S. territory:
   - Sending or taking a defense article out of the United States;
   - Transferring title or ownership of a military aircraft to a foreign person, in or outside the United States.
2. Extraterritorial transfers:
   - The re-export or retransfer of defense articles from one foreign person to another, not previously authorized;
   - Transferring the registration, control, or ownership to a foreign person of any aircraft, vessel, or satellite covered by the USML, whether the transfer occurs in the United States or abroad.
3. Exports of intangibles:
   - Disclosing technical data to a foreign person, whether in the United States or abroad, through oral, visual, or other means (commonly referred to as "deemed export"), which could include an electronic transfer by email or fax, discussions or telephone conversations, and information posted on an internal or external website.
   - Performing a defense service for a foreign person, whether in the United States or abroad.

Note that DDTC has proposed new definitions in which sending, taking, or storing unclassified technical data or software secured using certain "end-to-end" encryption would not be considered an export, re-export, or retransfer.[13]

Q 17.4.1   What are re-exports and retransfers?

Under the ITAR, DDTC claims continuing jurisdiction over U.S. defense articles and technical data even after their initial export. This includes the "re-export" of a defense article or technical data from one country to another, or the "retransfer" within a country from the licensee to another entity not previously authorized.[14] Before re-export or retransfer, the U.S. or foreign person who controls the item must obtain authorization from DDTC.

Registration and Licensing

Q 17.4.2   How can a company obtain DDTC authorization to export?

As a general rule, any U.S. person or entity that manufactures, brokers, or exports defense articles or services must be registered with DDTC.[15] A company must generally be registered to apply for a license or take advantage of a license exemption.[16] Once the registration is complete, an exporter may apply for an export authorization by submitting a relatively simple license application for the export of defense articles; or a complex license application, usually in the form of a TAA, for complex transactions that will require the U.S. entity to provide defense services. DDTC uses an electronic licensing system, D-Trade; and most license applications must be submitted electronically (except those relating to classified information).

Most types of applications also contain additional certifications/transmittal letters, supporting documentation, and in some cases, non-transfer and use certificate from the licensee, and in certain cases the foreign government of the licensee.

Q 17.4.3   Are there exemptions to ITAR licensing?

Although there are a number of exemptions in the ITAR, these are often narrow and subject to specific documentation, reporting or other requirements. Some of the most useful license exemptions are the Foreign Military Sales (FMS) exemption (exports under the U.S. government FMS program and other security assistance programs are exempt from DDTC licensing provided the export follows specific procedures to qualify for use of the exemption);[17] the U.S. government use exemption (for exports of defense articles and services by or for the U.S. government); and the Canadian exemption (allowing export of certain defense articles, technical data, and defense services subject to a number of restrictions and requirements). In addition, there are exemptions with the United Kingdom and Australia under certain Defense Trade Cooperation Treaties.[18]

Other license exemptions include certain limited temporary imports/exports; limited value spare parts and components for use on U.S. defense articles already exported; basic maintenance or training. There are also several special exemptions applicable to

Canada, the European Union, the NATO countries, Australia, Japan, and Sweden, and dual nationals of these countries.

Brokering

Q 17.4.4   What are the requirements for brokering defense exports?

The ITAR requires certain persons who "broker" the export or re-export of items subject to the ITAR to be registered with DDTC, and to provide advance notification and/or obtain a license in connection with certain types of transactions. New ITAR brokering rules came into effect in October 2013, clarifying who is required to register and the types of activities that require notification and approval.[19]

Commercial "Dual-Use" Goods and Technology

Q 17.5   How are commercial goods and technology exports regulated?

The BIS regulates the export of commercial products and technology under the Export Administration Act (EAA)[20] and the EAR.[21] These rules cover a wide range of commercial products controlled because of potential dual-use (*i.e.*, commercial and military application) or other strategic value, or when exported to an embargoed country.

Unlike defense items subject to the ITAR, many commercial goods and technologies can be exported to many countries without a license. However, determining licensing requirements is an involved process requiring detailed classification of the product and cross-referencing to the country control chart. In addition, although there are a number of license exceptions, determining their applicability requires careful consideration of the regulations.

Following the export control reform, the EAR now also controls less sensitive military items and most commercial space systems. However, generally such items will require a license for export to most countries (*see* Q 17.5.7).

COMPLIANCE FACT

Most civil aircraft spare parts may be shipped to most (but not all) countries without a license. However, the export of certain "hot section" aircraft engine technologies may require licenses regardless of the destination country.

Export Administration Regulations

Q 17.5.1   What is the scope of the EAR?

The BIS primarily regulates the export of commercial products and technology under the EAR.[22] While there are some parallels to the ITAR, there are also some major differences in how the regulations and the relevant agencies function.

The EAR is similar to the ITAR in that both focus on "technology transfer" and have been increasingly focused on enforcement. They differ in that the EAR covers a wide range of products and technology; the product classification process is highly technical; and most importantly, *the need for a license depends not only on the type of product but on its final destination.*

Q 17.5.2   What categories of items and technology require a license to export under the EAR?

Generally, all commercial items of U.S. origin or physically located in the United States are subject to the EAR. However, only items listed on the CCL may require a license prior to exportation. Items not listed on the CCL are designated as EAR99 items and generally can be exported without a license, except to a sanctioned country, to a prohibited end user, or for certain prohibited end uses.[23]

The EAR requires a license for the exportation of a wide range of items with potential "dual" commercial and military use, or otherwise of strategic value to the United States. The CCL provides a list of very specific items that are controlled. The CCL, divided into ten categories, is similar to the "dual-use" list adopted by other countries under the Wassenaar Arrangement,[24] although the CCL lists additional items, including less sensitive military items. Foreign-manufactured goods not physically located in the United States are generally exempt from the EAR export and re-export requirements if they contain less than a de minimis level of U.S. content by value. The ultimate destination of the export or re-export must be factored into the analysis of whether the de minimis level has been surpassed.

Q 17.5.3   What are the CCL categories?

The Commerce Control List is divided into the following ten categories, as shown in Table 17-2.

TABLE 17-2
CCL Categories

CATEGORY

0	Nuclear & Miscellaneous
1	Materials, Chemicals, Microorganisms & Toxins
2	Materials Processing
3	Electronics
4	Computers
5	Part 1: Telecommunications
	Part 2: Information Security
6	Sensors & Lasers
7	Navigation & Avionics
8	Marine
9	Aerospace & Propulsion

Within each of these categories, controlled items can be grouped into one of five groups:

Commodities. Finished or unfinished goods ranging from high-end microprocessors and airplanes to ball bearings.

Manufacturing Equipment. This includes equipment specifically for manufacturing or testing controlled commodities, as well as certain generic machines, such as computer numerically controlled (CNC) manufacturing and test equipment.

Materials. This includes certain alloys and chemical compounds.

Software. This includes software specifically associated with particular commodities or manufacturing equipment, as well as any software containing encryption.

Technology. Technology, as defined in the EAR, includes both technical data and services. Unlike the ITAR, there is generally no distinction between the two. However, the EAR may apply different standards to technology for "use" of a product than to technology for the "design" or "manufacture" of the product.

Export and Re-Export

Q 17.5.4   What constitutes an export or re-export?

Export is defined as the actual shipment or transmission of items subject to the EAR out of the United States. The EAR is similar to the ITAR in that it covers intangible exports of technology, as well as physical exports of items. The EAR also covers deemed exports defined as the release of technology to a foreign national in the United States. Deemed exports may occur through such means as a demonstration, oral briefing, or plant visit, as well as the electronic transmission of data that is not publicly available.

Similarly to the ITAR, the EAR attempts to impose restrictions on the re-export of U.S. goods—*i.e.*, the shipment or transfer to a third country of goods or technology originally exported from the United States. Some re-export issues may arise out of foreign distributor sales to embargoed countries; the resale of licensed goods to another country; or the resale of goods from a country not requiring a license to one that would require a license.

Licensing

Q 17.5.5   How does an exporter determine if it needs a license to export dual-use goods and technology?

Determining whether a license is required for a particular export is a multi-step process:

1. The product is classified with the proper Export Control Classification Number (ECCN).
2. A determination is made regarding any specific policy controls that may apply to the product, and whether those policy controls restrict export to the specific foreign country.
3. The country chart is checked to determine whether a license is needed.
4. The availability of license exceptions is checked.

Generally, the exporter self-classifies the product. Once it is determined that an item is controlled on the CCL, the exporter must determine its ECCN. The BIS has two assistance procedures when the proper classification or licensing requirements are uncertain. A party can either request that the BIS issue a "classification ruling" for a particular item, in which case the BIS will determine or verify the ECCN of an item. As a less commonly used alternative, a party can request an "advisory opinion" as to whether a license is required or would be granted for a particular transaction.[25] For classification purposes, BIS generally looks at the classification of the complete product being exported rather than at the classification of each subcomponent of the item (*i.e.*, "black box" treatment), as opposed to the look-through treatment under the ITAR.

COMPLIANCE TIP

Commercial software and hardware that utilize encryption are subject to special rules under the EAR. Most commercial software and hardware that utilize encryption can be freely exported to most countries and most end-users if the producer holds an encryption registration number (ERN) and has self-classified the product. However, products that have crypto-analytic capability or use non-standard encryption, and source code and technology, may require formal classification or, in some cases, a license for export.[26]

The EAR contains a number of licensing exceptions. Determining whether a particular exception applies requires a review of the specific exception requirement as detailed in 15 C.F.R. part 740, as well as a review of the notes on applicable license exceptions following the ECCN entry.[27]

Q 17.5.6   How can a license be obtained?

Once it is determined that a license is required, an exporter can apply for export authorization from BIS using the SNAP-R electronic licensing system. Unlike the ITAR, there is no requirement for formal registration prior to applying for export authorization. The EAR has no equivalent to the TAA used in the ITAR. However, the BIS will license relatively broad technology transfers to foreign manufacturers under a single license (*e.g.*, for offshore production of goods).

Q 17.5.7   How are less sensitive military items being incorporated into the EAR, and what does this mean?

In October 2013, the first less sensitive military items migrated from the USML to the CCL. The items and most "specially designed" parts and components for military items not enumerated on the USML will be classified under new "600 series" ECCNs.[28] For example, military cargo and trainer aircraft and many "specially designed" parts and components for these aircraft and USML aircraft will now be classified under one of the subcategories of ECCN 9A610. These will generally require a license to any country other than Canada, unless a license exception applies, while the prohibition on sales to countries subject to arms embargoes (including China) will still apply. Similarly, 500 series ECCNs cover space systems that have been removed from the USML in a similar fashion.

Economic Sanctions Programs

Prohibited Transactions

Q 17.6   What activities are prohibited by U.S. economic sanctions programs?

U.S. economic sanctions broadly prohibit most transactions between a U.S. person and persons or entities in an embargoed country, such as Cuba, Iran, Syria, and Sudan. In addition, restrictions on exports to North Korea impose a de facto embargo on that country as well. This prohibition includes importation and exportation of goods and services, whether direct or indirect, as well as "facilitation" by a U.S. person of transactions between foreign parties and an embargoed country. More limited economic sanctions may block transactions or require a specific license for exports to a number of countries, including the Balkan States, Belarus, Burma, Central African Republic, Côte d'Ivoire, Democratic Republic of the Congo, Iraq, Lebanon, Libya, Russia (the Magnitsky sanctions and Ukraine sanctions), Somalia, Yemen, and Zimbabwe.[29] Economic sanctions programs are country-specific and very detailed.

OFAC maintains the Specially Designated Nationals (SDN) List of known terrorists, narcotics traffickers, and other individuals and entities designated by the U.S. government against whom a number of federal laws impose severe restrictions and sanctions.[30] In addition, U.S. sanctions against Iran and against certain SDNs associated with Iran do apply extraterritorially to non-U.S. persons (*see* Q 17.6.5).[31]

Q 17.6.1   Are there exceptions to the prohibition on exportation to sanctioned countries?

The sanctions regulations for each country may have specific exceptions (called general licenses) that allow certain limited types of transactions, such as those relating to informational material. In addition, the U.S. government will, upon proper application, typically authorize humanitarian- or safety-related transactions, such as the sale of agricultural commodities, medicine, and medical devices to sanctioned countries. In some cases, a general license may authorize a type of transaction without the need to apply for a specific license (*e.g.*, exports of food to Iran and Sudan).

584

Q 17.6.2   What are terrorist and other barred entity lists?

Various U.S. government agencies maintain a number of lists of persons or entities barred or otherwise restricted from entering into certain types of transactions with U.S. persons. Particularly since 9/11, U.S. companies have become more assertive in attempting to place contractual terms on foreign companies related to these lists:

TABLE 17-3
Lists of Barred Entities

Specially Designated Nationals and Blocked Persons List (SDN List)[32]	Maintained by OFAC, this is a list of barred terrorists, narcotics traffickers, and persons and entities associated with embargoed regimes. Generally, all transactions with such persons are barred.
List of Debarred Parties	This is a list of entities debarred from engaging in arms exports under the AECA and is maintained by DDTC.
Denied Persons List	These are individuals and entities (both U.S. and foreign) who have had their export privileges revoked or suspended by BIS.
Entity List	These are foreign entities identified as being involved in proliferation of missile technology, weapons of mass destruction, and related technologies. BIS has expanded the grounds on which it may add persons to the Entity List.[33]
Unverified List	These are foreign entities for which BIS has been unable to verify the nature of their operations. While transactions with these entities are not barred, special due diligence is required.

Excluded Parties List	These are entities that have been barred from contracting with U.S. government agencies. In general, companies cannot contract with such parties in fulfilling a U.S. government contract, either as prime or subcontractor.
Nonproliferation Sanctions	Maintained by the Department of State.

Administration and Jurisdiction

Q 17.6.3   Who administers economic sanctions programs?

The OFAC administers the U.S. economic sanctions programs under the International Emergency Economic Powers Act (IEEPA);[34] the Trading with the Enemy Act (TWEA);[35] and the OFAC Sanctions Regulations.[36]

While most embargo regulations are administered by the OFAC, BIS has jurisdiction over certain exports prohibitions (as is the case with exports to Cuba, North Korea, and Syria).[37] Economic sanctions programs are country-specific and very detailed in the specific prohibitions. In addition, the State Department has taken an increasing role in enforcing certain economic sanctions against Iran that have extraterritorial effect.

Q 17.6.4   Who is a "U.S. person"?

The term "U.S. person" includes any U.S. company, any U.S. citizen or permanent resident alien, and any person or entity physically present in the United States.

Q 17.6.5   What are the jurisdictional limits of OFAC embargo programs?

While generally non-U.S. companies operating outside the United States are not subject to U.S. jurisdiction, there are a number of ways in which U.S. economic sanctions do have extraterritorial effect:

- U.S. sanctions on Cuba and Iran apply to foreign entities owned or controlled by U.S. persons (*e.g.*, foreign subsidiaries of U.S. companies).
- The United States asserts in rem jurisdiction over U.S.-origin goods even after they are exported from the United States. In addition, foreign-made goods containing 10% or more U.S.-origin components by value are considered U.S.-origin for sanctions purposes.
- Because U.S.-dollar wire transactions clear through U.S. banks, a non-U.S. transaction may trigger U.S. sanctions if transfers are made in U.S. dollars. For example, U.S. banks would be obligated to block or reject and report to OFAC most transactions involving embargoed countries or SDNs, regardless of whether a U.S. person was involved in the underlying transaction.
- Non-U.S. persons that engage in certain kinds of transactions with Iran or Iranian SDNs may be subject to extraterritorial sanctions. For example, a foreign bank that engages in a significant financial transaction with an Iranian SDN may be subject to sanctions, regardless of U.S. nexus.
- Foreign private issuers listed on U.S. stock exchanges are subject to certain reporting requirements in dealings with certain sanctioned countries or entities.

Penalties for Export Violations

Q 17.7 What are the penalties for violation of the controls on defense exports?

A person who willfully violates the AECA and the ITAR can be assessed criminal penalties of up to $1 million per violation, or ten years of imprisonment, or both.[38] In addition, the secretary of state may assess civil penalties, which may not exceed $500,000 per violation.[39] The civil penalties may be imposed either in addition to, or in lieu of, any other liability or penalty. The articles exported or imported in violation and any vessel, vehicle, or aircraft involved in such attempt is subject to seizure and forfeiture.[40] Finally, the assistant secretary for political-military affairs may order debarment of the violator, *i.e.*, prohibit the violator from participating in export of defense items.[41]

Q 17.7.1   What are the penalties for violation of the controls on dual-use item exports?

Similar to violations of the ITAR, violations of the EAR are subject to both criminal and administrative penalties. Fines for export violations can reach up to $1 million per violation in criminal cases, $250,000 per violation in most administrative cases. In addition, criminal violators may be sentenced to prison time up to twenty years and administrative penalties may include the denial of export privileges.[42] A denial order is probably the most serious sanction because such order would bar a U.S. company from exporting for a period of up to ten years or bar a foreign entity from buying U.S.-origin export-controlled products for such period.

 CASE STUDY: *BAE Systems plc*[43]

On March 1, 2010, BAE Systems plc, the United Kingdom's biggest defense contractor, pleaded guilty for violating the AECA and the ITAR. In one of the rare cases of assessing criminal penalties, BAE agreed to pay $400 million in criminal penalties.

Q 17.7.2   What are the penalties for exporting to a sanctioned country?

Although potential penalties for violations of U.S. embargo laws vary depending on the country and product involved, an exporter may be subject to a maximum civil penalty of $250,000 per violation under OFAC regulations, with the exception of exports to Cuba.[44] Violations of the Cuban embargo are subject to a maximum civil penalty of $65,000 per violation.[45]

The U.S. government can also seek criminal prosecution where violations are willful and knowing. Such violations may reach $1 million per violation and imprisonment of up to twenty years. In addition, where there is egregious conduct by the offender, BIS (who assists OFAC in enforcing embargoes) may suspend the export privileges of a company.

 CASE STUDY: *Weatherford International Ltd.*[46]

In November 2013, Weatherford International paid approximately $252 million to settle various alleged civil and criminal violations. This case highlights the trend of multiple agencies becoming involved in enforcing export and sanctions laws—in this case BIS, OFAC, and a U.S. Attorney's office in Texas for export and sanctions violations, as well as the U.S. Department of Justice and the U.S. Securities and Exchange Commission for violations of anti-bribery laws.

Q 17.7.3   Who is subject to penalties for export violations?

Generally, any entity that brokers, exports, or attempts to export a controlled item without prior authorization, or in violation of the terms of a license, is subject to penalties. Violators may incur both criminal and civil penalties.

Q 17.7.4   How are penalties determined?

Although there is a maximum amount for a civil or criminal penalty, the actual penalty imposed is often a multiple of that maximum. In general, each shipment might be considered a separate violation, and the BIS and DDTC will often find multiple violations of related restrictions in connection with each shipment (export without a license, false representation, actions with knowledge of a violation, etc.). A series of violations occurring over a period of time may result in hundreds of thousands or even millions of dollars of penalties.

Q 17.7.5   What factors do the DDTC, BIS, and OFAC take into account in assessing penalties?

In assessing penalties, DDTC, BIS, and OFAC will consider a number of factors, both aggravating and mitigating. Mitigating factors include:

1. whether the disclosure was made voluntarily;
2. whether this was a first offense;
3. whether the company had compliance procedures;
4. steps taken to improve compliance after discovery of violations; and
5. whether the incident was due to inadvertence, mistake in fact, or good-faith misapplication of the laws.

Aggravating factors include:

1. willful or intentional violations;
2. failure to take remedial action after discovery;
3. lack of a compliance program; and
4. deliberate efforts to hide or conceal a violation.

TIP: Voluntary disclosure of violations can reduce penalties substantially. In most instances, the BIS reaches negotiated settlements in its administrative cases as a result of voluntary self-disclosures of violations by companies and individuals. Voluntary disclosures constitute a major mitigating factor in determining penalties, reducing the amount of penalty by up to 50%, provided certain conditions are met, such as implementing a comprehensive compliance program.[47]

Similarly, DDTC enforcement actions that result in the assessment of civil penalties are generally resolved by a consent agreement between DDTC and the investigated company. On average, DDTC settles approximately two to four enforcement cases per year.[48] Since 2003, there have been only a very limited number of settlement agreements. In contrast, in 2008,

---

defense companies submitted over 900 voluntary disclosures and 100 directed disclosures to DDTC.[49] This trend at DDTC has continued. With BIS assuming jurisdiction over certain less sensitive military items, companies may need to make disclosures to both agencies. While there is some concern among industry that BIS has historically taken a tougher view of voluntary disclosures, statistically only 3%–6% of voluntary disclosures result in civil penalties.[50]

 CASE STUDY: *ITT Corp.*[51]

While many major U.S. companies have been assessed civil penalties in the millions of dollars, imposing criminal liability on corporate activity is fairly rare.[52] A famous example is the 2007 investigation into the export practices of ITT Corporation, the leading manufacturer of military night vision equipment for the U.S. Armed Forces, resulting in the company's Night Vision Division being debarred from export of defense items for three years. (ITT's ineligible status and statutory debarment were terminated by the Department of State in February 2010.[53]) Pursuant to a plea agreement, ITT also was fined a total of $100 million for violations of defense export laws, one of the largest penalties ever paid in a criminal or civil case.[54] (Note, however, the trend for showcase criminal penalties in the hundreds of millions of dollars in the March 2010 fine charged to BAE Systems plc, discussed in the case study above.)

The ITT guilty plea to defense export violations is a lesson to all exporters. ITT's management cooperation and its willingness to strengthen its compliance program served to save the company from closing down its Night Vision Division. One of the conditions to the plea agreement was the execution of a remedial action plan, under which ITT undertook to:

(1)   strengthen its compliance management structure;
(2)   institute a comprehensive export compliance education/training program for employees and all export compliance managers and security managers;
(3)   strengthen its record-keeping procedures;
(4)   introduce mandatory reporting of violations;
(5)   conduct a complete compliance investigation; and
(6)   provide annual compliance certification stating that the company is in full compliance with U.S. export laws.

In effect, ITT agreed to strengthen its export compliance program. Had it developed and implemented effective export compliance measures to begin with, ITT could have saved an enormous amount of money, time, and energy. The lesson to be learned from this case is that the time to act is *before* the violation occurs.

Effective Export Compliance Programs

Industry Best Practices

Q 17.8   What are the industry best practices related to export compliance?

The export community has identified a number of practices that enhance an export compliance program and streamline the business processes adopted by a company. While each element adds to the effectiveness of a compliance program, the precise implementation will vary based on the nature and scope of exports of each individual exporter.

As discussed in chapter 2, the Federal Sentencing Guidelines advise on the minimum content of an adequate compliance program. The export regulators and the industry agree that an effective export compliance program will comprise all or most of the following elements, discussed in detail below:[55]

- management commitment;
- clear designation of the scope of responsibility of export compliance personnel;
- export compliance manuals;
- training;
- record keeping;
- internal monitoring and auditing;
- detecting and reporting of suspected violations;
- clear disciplinary procedures.

Q 17.8.1   What is the role of management?

The governing body of the company (usually the board of directors) must understand and exercise reasonable oversight of the compliance program. The management commitment must be communicated in a written policy statement and signed by senior management. Senior management must become actively involved in export compliance functions and assume responsibility for export compliance, as well as provide sufficient resources—staffing, IT support, and training funding—to develop and implement the program.[56] Demonstration of management's commitment to export controls compliance is considered a significant mitigating factor in enforcement actions.

Q 17.8.2   What are the roles of those groups recognized as "compliance personnel"?

A good compliance program specifically describes the roles and responsibilities of management; export compliance personnel; employees involved in various aspects of the export transaction (such as technical design of the item, accepting and processing of the purchase order, packaging, and shipment); and employees who do not have direct responsibilities for exports, but who may indirectly contribute to a violation (for example, by allowing foreign nationals access to controlled technology or documentation). Employees must be alerted to the principal risks and their duty to avoid them.

Q 17.8.3   How important is an export compliance program manual?

The export compliance manual is the centerpiece of a good compliance program. The company must establish standards and procedures that are not overly complicated to follow. The manual should include the senior management policy statement and be distributed to all employees. It is a good practice to request a written certification from each employee stating that he or she received a copy of the manual and fully understands his or her responsibilities under the program.

The compliance manual should be easy to follow and provide cross-references that aid the user in applying the procedures under different scenarios. The manual should lay out a description of the export controls regulations, have a separate chapter on all the key elements, and provide ample flow charts and step-by-step procedures to simplify the vetting of the transaction. (The diagram on the following pages illustrates some of the key questions that should be included in such flow charts or checklists to guide the employee through an export transaction analysis.)

Q 17.8.4   What role should training play?

Training should be provided initially at the time of hiring, and periodically thereafter, once or twice a year. The purpose of the refresher training is to communicate new developments in export controls, and new policies and procedures adopted by the company, as well as provide a streamlined method of answering employees' questions on existing policies. Training should be tailored to meet the specific responsibilities of each of the actors in the export transaction, starting from management, export compliance officers, engineers, administrative personnel, etc.

Q 17.8.5   What are a company's record-keeping obligations?

The compliance manual should provide clear guidelines on what documents should be kept and for what period of time. Generally, the various export controls regulations establish an obligation to keep records and have them available for inspection upon request by the governing agency for a period of five years. In addition, an effective compliance program will develop a protocol in establishing a comprehensive filing system that allows easy locating of pertinent documents. If the exporter of record is not the same party that handles shipping, the company may include a procedure in its compliance manual requesting a full record of all products exported for the previous year from the U.S. Bureau of Census, which administers the Automatic Export System (AES) and the mandatory AES filings.[57]

Q 17.8.6   How should companies approach compliance in light of rapid changes in export laws?

Because changes to export controls are occurring on a rolling basis, keeping programs current is and will be an ongoing process. Here are some key tips to survive this process:

❐ Briefing management up front will help ensure that companies have some understanding of the scope and impact of changes and can devote resources to avoid negative impacts with customers and suppliers, who will themselves be implementing these changes.

❐ Updating compliance programs will require a plan of action that will include identifying a transition team, updating manuals, coordinating training, and numerous other steps, including:

• identifying which automated systems will require changes (as software changes may have long lead times);

• determining which product areas are likely to change classifications and reclassifying these items using agreed-upon procedures;

• agreeing on a transition plan for existing licenses and programs that may migrate from the ITAR to the EAR.

❐ Coordinating changes with key suppliers and customers will help ensure that changes in jurisdiction do not come as a surprise or cause logistics problems for business partners.

TABLE 17-4

How to Create a User-Friendly Compliance Manual

Is the Purchaser Barred?

☐ Identify names of all parties involved in the transaction (done by sales rep handling the purchase order).

☐ Ask customer:

  ☐ Who is the immediate recipient of the product?
  ☐ Will the product be transferred in country?
  ☐ ...re-exported in its current form?
  ☐ ...incorporated into an article before re-exportation?

☐ Submit names of parties to the transaction to the export compliance officer to be screened against various denied parties lists. Keep a record of the screening.

☐ Allow the export only if no positive hits are returned or special authorization to export is obtained.

Is a License Needed to Export This Product to This Purchaser?

Usually, the export compliance officer makes this determination based on the screening results, the purchaser's nationality, and its geographical location. Create separate flow charts for the export requirements under the ITAR, EAR, and OFAC regulations. Usually, the determination is based on self-classification; however, if doubt exists, the export compliance officer should have a clearly identified channel for requesting assistance, either from in-house counsel, outside counsel, or by submitting a Commodity Jurisdiction request. Companies with high-volume product sales may develop detailed matrixes of product USML and ECCN classifications.

If a license is required, the manual should provide clear guidance on who is authorized to apply for a license and how the process flows. This step is becoming especially important with the new electronic filing systems introduced by DDTC, BIS, OFAC, and the Census Bureau.

Are Nuclear, Missile, and Chemical/Biological Weapons Screens Necessary?

Not all businesses need to perform such screens depending on the nature of their product. This decision should be made in advance, and once determined, the screen should be integrated into the vetting of the transaction.

Is There Anything Suspicious About the Transaction?

Companies should ensure that an export transaction has been properly screened before they proceed with execution. All regulators impose penalties on companies who deliberately blind themselves with respect to any potential violation. In that respect, BIS has developed a "Know Your Customer Guidance" and a list of red flags to aid exporters in making a determination on whether to proceed with the export.[58] BIS red flags are generally helpful in screening any transaction, regardless of who the relevant regulator is.

What Are the BIS Red Flags?

☐ The customer or its address is similar to one of the parties found on any of the denied parties lists.

☐ The customer or purchasing agent is reluctant to offer information about the end-use of the item.

☐ The product's capabilities do not fit the buyer's line of business, such as an order for sophisticated computers for a small bakery.

☐ The item ordered is incompatible with the technical level of the country to which it is being shipped, such as semiconductor manufacturing equipment being shipped to a country that has no electronics industry.

☐ The customer is willing to pay cash for a very expensive item when the terms of sale would normally call for financing.

☐ The customer has little or no business background.

☐ The customer is unfamiliar with the product's performance characteristics but still wants the product.

☐ Routine installation, training, or maintenance services are declined by the customer.

☐ Delivery dates are vague, or deliveries are planned for out of the way destinations.

☐ A freight forwarding firm is listed as the product's final destination.

☐ The shipping route is abnormal for the product and destination.

☐ Packaging is inconsistent with the stated method of shipment or destination.

☐ When questioned, the buyer is evasive and especially unclear about whether the purchased product is for domestic use, for export, or for re-export.

Q 17.8.7   What is the importance of internal audits?

The compliance program must identify the intervals of regular auditing, the body to conduct the internal auditing, and the authority and responsibilities of the audit officers. In addition, the program should have a built-in mechanism that ensures random document review and tracing of processes. Management should periodically evaluate the effectiveness of the compliance program by taking into consideration the results of the audits.

Q 17.8.8   How should suspected violations be reported?

The compliance program should clearly identify the internal mechanism to report a suspected violation by providing the name and contact information of the person in charge—usually, the export compliance officer.

Q 17.8.9   Why does a company need clear disciplinary procedures?

The compliance program should emphasize the importance of compliance to avoid jeopardizing the company's business and incurring severe sanctions against the company and the responsible individuals. Employees should have a clear understanding of the sanctions for potential violations, as well as the consequences of failing to report a violation once it comes to their attention.

TIP: An important element of the compliance program is ensuring that an employee who simply reports on suspected violations does not get penalized. A successful compliance program provides safeguards against retaliation by management or the employee who may come under an internal investigation due to such reporting.

Designing an Export Compliance Program

Q 17.9   What are the first steps a company should take when drafting a compliance program?

Drafting an effective export compliance program may be a challenge if there are no procedures in place, if the company exports a variety of products, or if it follows procedures that have been in place for a long time. A company should conduct a baseline audit identifying current procedures in various divisions and relevant personnel. Hiring an independent auditor is recommended. An exporter should also try to involve its in-house counsel, the export compliance officers, and employees who are directly handling export transactions in identifying the risks that a company may encounter. Outside counsel may bring a fresh perspective to the table, as well as the experience from similar businesses.

COMPLIANCE TIP

Once the program is drafted, devote resources for the implementation and demonstrate commitment to following through. Start with distributing the compliance manual and initial training of personnel. Institute regular audits and evaluate the effectiveness of the program.

Q 17.9.1   Isn't there a one-size-fits-all program companies can adopt?

No; a company's needs vary depending on the nature and size of the business, the items exported, and the ultimate destination of the exports. A tailored program streamlines the export processing, while at the same time reduces the cost of compliance, prevents delays, and allocates responsibility to the lowest level of personnel possible. Such distribution of responsibilities reduces the risk of violations and is recommended by the regulators. An export compliance program that is tailored to the specifics of the company's business is one of the major mitigating factors if DDTC, BIS, or OFAC determines that there is a violation.

Q 17.9.2   What are the pitfalls to avoid in designing an export compliance program?

The following are some common mistakes made in drafting a compliance program:

❑ References to the ITAR, EAR, or OFAC regulations are too generic.

The compliance manual should explain what the requirements under the specific set of regulations are and provide enough illustrations of possible violations to alert employees to situations to be avoided.

❑ Procedures are overly complex.

Procedures that are not easy to follow will likely be ignored or misinterpreted.

❑ Required information is not readily available.

Each person in the export chain should receive clear guidance where they can find required information, who is responsible for providing it, and what are the channels to request it.

❑ Review of the export transaction is done by front office staff.

This responsibility belongs to the persons who are directly involved instead of being removed to the front office staff, who are usually not familiar with the specifics of a particular transaction.

Q 17.9.3   What key questions should be posed when designing an export compliance program?

A good starting point for designing an effective export compliance program is to identify risks that a specific company faces with respect to export controls, which may dictate certain aspects of the program. Some of the factors to consider are:[59]

TABLE 17-5
Identifying Risk Factors When Designing
an Export Compliance Program

RISK FACTORS	QUESTIONS
Exporter type	*Is the company a manufacturer, a trading company, a purchasing agent, an original equipment manufacturer (OEM), a systems integrator, or a freight forwarder?* Knowledge about the initial design of the article will be readily available to the OEM, but a distributor or freight forwarder may need to identify a specific procedure on how to obtain this information.
Nature of the exported item	*Is the exported item production material, capital equipment, part or component, an end-use item, software (with or without encryption), or a service?* *Is the item specifically designed or configured for a military end-user, or is it a commercial off-the-shelf (COTS) item that does not need any additional modification?* *Is the item built to customer specifications?*
Source of the exported item	*Is the item the company's own manufacture, purchased from the OEM, or purchased from a distributor?* For example, DDTC would accept a Commodity Jurisdiction request from an exporter who is not the OEM only if the OEM is not willing to participate in the process or cannot be reached.
Item sensitivity	*Is the item authorized for export or re-export to all destinations?* *Is there an applicable license exception?* *Is the item subject to the missile technology or nuclear restrictions?*

Does the item have a potential end-use in a weapon?

For example, a company that exports agricultural products may or may not need to screen for nuclear restrictions depending on the product specifics.

Distribution points

Is this a single or multiple point of export?

Are shipments consolidated elsewhere?

Is there a "deemed" export involved?

Exporter size

Is the company a small, medium, or large-size company?

A small company with only a few employees on staff will not require as detailed a description of each actor's responsibility as a medium or large-size company.

End-user

Are you selling to a commercial or military end-user?

Is the item exported to a foreign government?

Location of customer

Is the customer in a country for which there is no export restriction, or in an embargoed country?

Do you have knowledge that the product will be re-exported to a location for which you need prior export authorization?

Exporter/ customer relationship

Do you export to an independent party, your foreign subsidiary or branch, an end-user or a distributor, a new or a well-established customer?

A well-established customer that was previously screened against various denied parties lists will likely not require a new screening with every shipment; however, a company should be extra cautious when shipping to a new customer, especially if no information about the customer is readily available.

Foreign nationals

Does the company employ foreign nationals?

Do they work on projects sensitive to export controls?

Are the foreign nationals also U.S. residents (i.e., green card holders)?

Do foreign nationals visit the company and how often?

A university or an R&D division of a company may need to institute additional procedures to protect its proprietary information from being disclosed to a foreign national. Engineers involved in developing a product to customer specifications must receive special training on what constitutes release of technology or deemed export.

Overlap of control regimes   *Do you have a good procedure in place to identify whether a product is ITAR- or EAR-controlled?*

In addition, OFAC regulations generally apply to any transaction involving, or related to, an embargoed country. Also, watch out for signs that a transaction may be in violation of industrial security regulations, anti-boycott laws, the Foreign Corrupt Practices Act, or anti-money laundering regulations.

Does your customer inquire whether the item contains any Israeli content?

Are you asked to make a payment to a government official to speed up shipment?

Export Controls and Universities

Deemed Exports

Q 17.10   Why should universities be concerned about export controls?

Under current U.S. laws, an "export" is any transfer of an item, *tangible or intangible*, to a foreign country or to a foreign person wherever located. This definition includes the transfer of controlled *information or services* to foreign nationals even when the transfer takes place within the territory of the United States (*see* Q 17.4). As institutions that share and transfer knowledge, universities have come into the sights of U.S. export enforcement personnel. As a result, universities are struggling to square the restrictions of export controls with the openness of the academic environment. The so-called concept of "deemed exports," whereby an export of controlled technical data can take place in the United States if released to a foreign national, has become the modus operandi in determining if research undertaken at a U.S. university will cross the line and deliver knowledge that the U.S. government considers crucial for U.S. national security and, therefore, warranting control. University researchers and administrators need to be aware that these laws may apply to research, whether sponsored or not. However, it also is important to understand the extent to which the regulations do not affect normal university activities.[60]

Many universities and research institutions had high hopes that export control reforms would synchronize definitions between the EAR and ITAR regarding what constitutes fundamental research, how to treat dual nationals, as well as clarifying ambiguities regarding use of publicly available information. The Defense Trade Advisory Group in 2013 issued a white paper analyzing and making recommendations to harmonize the definitions of "fundamental research" and related concepts under the EAR and ITAR.[61]

Foreign Students

Q 17.11   What do export controls concerns related to the defense and high-technology sectors have to do with institutions of higher education?

U.S. national security and economic interests are heavily dependent on technological innovation and advantage. Many of the nation's leading-edge technologies, including defense-related technologies, are being discovered by U.S. and foreign national students and scholars in U.S. university research and university-affiliated laboratories. As the Department of Defense invests less and less of its funding on in-house research and development, university-based discoveries are becoming increasingly vital to national security and other U.S. interests. U.S. policymakers recognize that foreign students and researchers have made substantial contributions to U.S. research efforts, but the potential transfer of knowledge of controlled defense or dual-use technologies to their home countries could have significant consequences for U.S. national interests. As a result, a fine balance has been set up between export controls in general and university endeavors like teaching and research in administering export controls as they relate to universities. The U.S. export controls agencies place the onus on universities to understand and comply with the regulations.[62]

COMPLIANCE FACT

Some 671,616 international students attended U.S. institutions in 2008–09, an increase of almost 8% from a year earlier. In 2008–09, there were 269,874 international undergraduate students and 283,329 international graduate students. Of these approximately 62% came from Asia, with India and China (which predominantly send graduate students) rising to become the top two suppliers of international students to U.S. colleges. Peggy Blumenthal, executive vice president of the Institute of International Education, notes that international students contribute an estimated $17.6 billion to the U.S. economy.[63]

Q 17.11.1   Who is a "foreign student" for purposes of export controls?

A foreign student is any person who is not a U.S. person—that is, any person who is not a U.S. citizen, a person lawfully admitted for permanent residence in the United States (or a "green card" holder), or a protected individual under the Immigration and Naturalization Act (8 U.S.C. § 1324b(a)(3), certain classes of asylees).[64]

Q 17.11.2   Can an institution's treatment of foreign students differ from that of U.S. students?

Generally, an employer cannot refuse to hire someone because of national origin or citizenship status (as long as they are lawfully in the United States). Title VII of the Civil Rights Act prohibits discrimination based on race, creed, color, and national origin.[65] The Immigration Reform and Control Act of 1986 (IRCA) fills the gap to add "alienage" (for example, an individual's current citizenship status).[66] However, under a narrow exception to IRCA, discrimination is allowed:

> based on citizenship status which is otherwise required in order to comply with law, regulation, or executive order, or required by Federal, State, or local government contract, or which the attorney general determines to be essential for an employer to do business with an agency or department of the Federal, State, or local Government.[67]

If U.S. citizenship or permanent resident status is required for a job, then it is a legitimate question to ask for citizenship status.

Q 17.12 What institution activities may fall under the export controls?

Generally, the following should be considered with respect to export controls:

- teaching;
- university research; and
- teaching abroad and foreign campuses.

Regulation of Teaching

Q 17.13 Is all information taught at universities subject to export controls?

It is important to note that many of the activities that a U.S. institution engages in are not subject to export controls or, even if controlled, do not require licensing. Both the ITAR and the EAR have special provisions relating to publicly available information that is not subject to export controls, including limited exemptions regarding the release of information in the context of university research and educational activities. Additionally, the embargo regulations have exceptions for certain information and informational materials.

Q 17.13.1   What information qualifies as "publicly available" and thus not subject to export controls?

The ITAR and the EAR do not control information that is published and generally accessible or available to the public. Even though the two regimes have similar scope, the ITAR and the EAR vary in the specific information that qualifies as publicly available.

ITAR provision: The ITAR describes such information as information in the *public domain*.[68] The information in the public domain may be obtained through:

- sales at newsstands and bookstores;
- subscription or purchase without restriction to any individual;
- second-class mailing privileges granted by the U.S. government;
- libraries open to the public;
- patents available at any patent office;
- conferences, meetings, seminars, trade shows, or exhibitions in the United States that are generally accessible to the public;
- public release in any form after approval of the cognizant U.S. government agency; and
- fundamental research in the United States (*see* Q 17.14).

EAR provision: The EAR does not control publicly available technology if it is already published or will be published.[69] Information is published when it becomes generally accessible to the interested public in any form, including:

- publication in periodicals, books, print, etc., available for general distribution free or at cost;
- readily available at libraries open to the public or university libraries;
- patents and open patents applications available at any patent office; and
- release at an open conference, meeting, seminar, trade show, or other gathering open to the public.[70]

Differences between the two regimes appear in the concept of intent to publish; whether the publication is distributed for a fee; and whether the conference or trade show takes place in the United States or not.

Q 17.13.2   How is educational information subject to export controls?

Both the ITAR and the EAR address the issue of general educational information that is typically taught in schools and universities. Such information, even if it relates to items included on the USML or the CCL, does not fall under the application of export controls.

ITAR provision: The ITAR specifically provides that the definition of "technical data" does not include information concerning general scientific, mathematical, or engineering principles commonly taught in schools, colleges, and universities.[71]

EAR provision: The EAR provides that publicly available "educational information" is not subject to the EAR if it is released by instruction in catalogue courses and associated teaching laboratories of academic institutions.[72]

Therefore, a university graduate course on design and manufacture of very-high-speed integrated circuitry will not be subject to export controls, even though the technology is on the CCL. The key factor is the fact that the information is provided by instruction in a catalogue course. Foreign students from any country may attend this course because the information is not controlled.

Under the fundamental research exception, the information will not be controlled even if the course contains recent and unpublished results from laboratory research, so long as the university did not accept separate obligations with respect to publication or dissemination, for example, a publication restriction under federal funding.[73] (See detailed discussion of the fundamental research exception at Q 17.14.)

Regulation of Research

Q 17.14   Are the results of fundamental research subject to export controls?

No. Both the ITAR and the EAR provide that information published and generally accessible to the public through fundamental research at an accredited U.S. university is not subject to export controls. However, there are certain restrictions. In order to take advantage of this exemption:

- Such information must be produced as part of basic and applied research in science and engineering *and* must be broadly shared within the scientific community (that is, no restrictions on publication/dissemination of the research *results*);[74]
- It is essential to distinguish the information or product that *results* from the fundamental research from the *conduct* that occurs within the context of the fundamental research;
- While the *results* of the fundamental research are not subject to export controls, an export license may be required if during the *conduct* of the research export-controlled technology is to be released to a foreign national; and
- Such export-controlled technology may come from the research sponsor, from a research partner institution, or from a previous research project conducted at the university.[75]

As noted above, in 2013 the Defense Trade Advisory Group issued a white paper analyzing and making recommendations to harmonize the definitions of "fundamental research" and related concepts under the EAR and ITAR.[76]

Q 17.14.1 How does an institution apply the fundamental research exception in practice?

It is helpful to think of a research project in terms of three phases:

(1) pre-existing information;
(2) conduct of research; and
(3) research results.

The researcher must then perform a two-step analysis:

1. Will there be any restrictions on publication or dissemination of the research results? If yes, the research does not qualify as fundamental. If no, then the research qualifies as fundamental and the end results may be released to foreign nationals.

2. Did the researcher use any pre-existing controlled data in conducting the fundamental research? If yes, no foreign nationals may participate in the conduct of the research even if they may receive the end results. If no, foreign nationals may participate in the research itself.

Q 17.14.2   What are the limitations on publication or dissemination of the research results?

Research performed at universities will not qualify as fundamental if the university (or the primary investigator) has accepted publication or other dissemination restrictions. The fundamental research exception does not apply to research whose results are restricted for proprietary reasons or specific U.S. government dissemination and national security controls.[77] University-based research is not considered fundamental research if the university or its researchers accept restrictions (other than review to ensure no release of sponsor-provided proprietary or patent information) on publication of scientific and technical information resulting from the project.[78]

Pre-publication review by a sponsor of university research solely to ensure that the publication would not inadvertently divulge proprietary information that the sponsor has initially furnished or compromise patent rights does not constitute restriction on publication for proprietary reasons. Examples of "specific national security controls" that will trigger export controls include requirements for pre-publication review by the government with right to withhold permission for publication; restriction on pre-publication dissemination of information to non-U.S. citizens or other categories of persons; or restrictions on participation of non-U.S. citizens or other categories of persons in the research.[79]

Q 17.14.3   What are some pitfalls to avoid in negotiating research grants or funding?

Perform extensive screening of an external funding contract's terms to ensure that the sponsor will provide explicit notice that a specific technology/data is export-controlled and will not place any restrictions on publication or dissemination of the research results. Actively inquire whether foreign nationals may participate.

With respect to government contracts, there are several restrictions that you should look for: provisions that declare all information export-controlled; provisions that restrict access to U.S. citizens or even representatives of foreign persons; provisions "incorporated by reference"; and flow-down clauses. Often this is caused by lack of knowledge by the government procurement official. Remember that not all clauses are mandatory flow-down clauses, and you may seek a modification or removal. If you are a subcontractor, review the scope of the flow-down clauses to ascertain the scope of possible export controls restrictions.

Teaching Abroad and Foreign Campuses

Q 17.15 Can a U.S. university professor teach abroad?

A U.S. professor can teach abroad provided that the material is limited to educational information—that is, information that is generally taught in a catalogue course at a U.S. university. Similarly, a U.S. professor may disclose the *results* of fundamental research performed at a U.S. university. With respect to embargoed countries, the information and informational materials exception would cover the information generally released in a catalogue course; however, providing a service in an embargoed country is prohibited under U.S. embargo regulations, and services such as awarding a degree would be prohibited.

Q 17.16 Are there limitations on setting up a foreign campus?

Generally, educational information is not subject to U.S. export controls, and therefore, a class can be taught at a foreign campus provided that such a course is generally taught at a U.S. university. However, there are limitations with respect to fundamental research (for example, the ITAR only recognizes fundamental research if performed at an accredited institution of higher education in the United States). Another limitation on foreign campuses is that a U.S. university may not set up a campus in a country under a U.S. economic sanctions embargo, such as Cuba, Iran, Syria, or Sudan.

Export Controls Compliance

Q 17.17 How can an institution set up successful screening and compliance procedures?

- Minimize limitations on publication and keep an open learning environment.
- Screen against barred entities lists and determine export controls on a project or course material basis.
- Develop a technology control plan for each controlled project and brief the principal investigator, as well as all students involved in the project, on their obligations under U.S. export controls laws and the specific restrictions associated with the project.
- Designate an export compliance officer with sufficient resources to implement export controls procedures and direct access to the legal department and senior management.

 CASE STUDY: *The* Roth *Case*

On July 1, 2009, John Reece Roth, a seventy-one-year-old retired University of Tennessee emeritus professor of electrical engineering, was sentenced to four years in prison for illegal exports of military technical information after a trial that had been followed closely by academic institutions. Roth was convicted of conspiring with Atmospheric Glow Technologies, Inc., a private company, to unlawfully export defense articles to one of his Chinese students in violation of the Arms Export Control Act, 22 U.S.C. § 2778.

The Chinese student was enrolled at the University of Tennessee and was hired by Professor Roth as a research assistant for a project on plasma actuators that were being developed for use in U.S. Air Force drones. What is most intriguing about the *Roth* case is that even though the university compliance officer was instructing the professor that the involvement of the Chinese student was in violation of export controls, the professor chose to continually and stubbornly disregard the advice. While it is sometimes difficult to convince faculty that they must comply with export controls laws—making an effective compliance program even more needed—the fact that the University of Tennessee had an export compliance program and compliance personnel who were actively trying to protect the controlled information determined the results of the case. Roth was convicted and sentenced to jail, while the university was neither charged nor penalized.

Notes to Chapter 17

1. 22 U.S.C. § 2778 *et seq.*
2. 22 C.F.R. pts. 120–30.
3. *See, e.g.,* Amendment to the International Traffic in Arms Regulations: Initial Implementation of Export Control Reform, 78 Fed. Reg. 22,740 (Apr. 16, 2013) (Final Rule, Department of State); Revisions to the Export Administration Regulations: Initial Implementation of Export Control Reform, 78 Fed. Reg. 22,660 (Apr. 16, 2013) (Final Rule, Bureau of Industry and Security); Amendment to the International Traffic in Arms Regulations: Continued Implementation of Export Control Reform, 78 Fed. Reg. 40,922 (July 8, 2013) (Final Rule, Department of State); Revisions to the Export Administration Regulations: Military Vehicles; Vessels of War; Submersible Vessels; Oceanographic Equipment; Related Items; and Auxiliary and Miscellaneous Items That the President Determines No Longer Warrant Control Under the United States Munitions List, 78 Fed. Reg. 40,892 (July 8, 2013) (Final Rule, Bureau of Industry and Security).
4. 22 C.F.R. § 120.6.
5. *Id.* § 121.1.
6. *Id.* § 120.10.
7. *Id.* § 120.9.
8. *See* International Traffic in Arms: Revisions to Definitions of Defense Services, Technical Data, and Public Domain; Definition of Product of Fundamental Research; Electronic Transmission and Storage of Technical Data; and Related Definitions, 80 Fed. Reg. 31,525 (June 3, 2015) (Proposed Rule, Department of State).
9. *See* 22 C.F.R. § 121.1.
10. *See* 22 C.F.R. § 120.4. Although submitted to DDTC, the CJ receives interagency review with input from the BIS and the Department of Defense.
11. *See id.* § 120.41 (definition of "specially designed").
12. *Id.* § 120.17.
13. *See* Proposed Rule, International Traffic in Arms: Revisions to Definitions of Defense Services, Technical Data, and Public Domain; Definition of Product of Fundamental Research; Electronic Transmission and Storage of Technical Data; and Related Definitions, 80 Fed. Reg. 31,525 (June 3, 2015).
14. 22 C.F.R. § 120.19.
15. *Id.* § 122.1.
16. *Id.* §§ 120.1(c), (d), 122.1(c).
17. *Id.* § 126.6.
18. *See id.* § 126.16 (exemption pursuant to the Defense Trade Cooperation Treaty between the United States and Australia); *id.* § 126.17 (exemption pursuant to the Defense Trade Cooperation Treaty between the United States and the United Kingdom).

19. Amendment to the International Traffic in Arms Regulations: Registration and Licensing of Brokers, Brokering Activities, and Related Provisions, 78 Fed. Reg. 52,690 (Aug. 26, 2013) (Interim Final Rule, Department of State) (revising 22 C.F.R. pt. 129).

20. Export Administration Act of 1979, as amended (50 U.S.C. app. §§ 2401–20). From August 21, 1994, through November 12, 2000, the act was in lapse. During that period, the president, through Executive Order 12924, which had been extended by successive Presidential Notices, continued the Export Administration Regulations (EAR) in effect under the International Emergency Economic Powers Act (50 U.S.C. §§ 1701–06 (IEEPA)). On November 13, 2000, the act was reauthorized by Pub. L. No. 106-508, 114 Stat. 2360, and it remained in effect through August 20, 2001. Since August 21, 2001, the act has been in lapse and the president, through Executive Order 13222 of August 17, 2001, which has been extended by successive Presidential Notices, has continued the EAR in effect under IEEPA.

21. 15 C.F.R. pts. 730–74.

22. *Id.* The EAR are promulgated under the Export Administration Act of 1979 (*see supra* note 20).

23. *See* 15 C.F.R. pt. 736 ("General Prohibitions").

24. Information on the Wassenaar Arrangement is available at www.bis.doc.gov/wassenaar/default.htm.

25. *See* 15 C.F.R. § 748.3.

26. The BIS provides guidance and links to relevant regulations on its website. *See Encryption*, BUREAU OF INDUS. & SEC., www.bis.doc.gov/index.php/policy-guidance/encryption (last visited Apr. 24, 2016).

27. 15 C.F.R. pt. 740.

28. Revisions to the Export Administration Regulations: Initial Implementation of Export Control Reform, 78 Fed. Reg. 22,660 (Apr. 16, 2013) (Final Rule, Bureau of Industry and Security).

29. A full list of sanctions programs and summaries of sanctions restrictions are available on the U.S. Treasury website. *See Resource Center: Sanctions Programs and Country Information*, U.S. DEP'T OF TREASURY (June 23, 2016), www.treasury.gov/resource-center/sanctions/Programs/Pages/Programs.aspx.

30. The SDN List is available at www.treasury.gov/resource-center/sanctions/SDN-List/Pages/default.aspx.

31. As of January 16, 2016, many of these extraterritorial Iran sanctions have been lifted under the Joint Comprehensive Plan of Action agreed to by the "P5+1" countries (China, France, Russia, the United Kingdom, the United States, and Germany) and Iran. However, if Iran fails to fulfill certain commitments, these sanctions will "snap back" into place.

32. For additional discussion of SDNs and certain prohibited transactions with them, see chapter 29.

33. Within two or three months after the change that took place in 2008, the Entity List more than doubled.

34. 50 U.S.C. § 1701 *et seq.*

35. *Id.* app. § 1 *et seq.*

36. 31 C.F.R. pts. 500–98.
37. 15 C.F.R. pt. 746.
38. 22 U.S.C. § 2778(c); 22 C.F.R. § 127.3.
39. 22 U.S.C. § 2778(e); 22 C.F.R. § 127.10.
40. 22 C.F.R. § 127.6.
41. 22 U.S.C. § 2778(g); 22 C.F.R. § 127.7.
42. These violations are based on the Export Administration Act of 1979 (*see supra* note 20), and inflation adjustments made in 15 C.F.R. § 6.4. The USA PATRIOT Improvement and Reauthorization Act of 2005, signed into law on March 9, 2006, Pub. L. No. 109-177, 120 Stat. 192, increased the limit of civil penalties available under IEEPA to $50,000. On October 16, 2007, President Bush signed the International Emergency Economic Powers Enhancement Act, Pub. L. No. 110-96, 121 Stat. 1011, which amends IEEPA by increasing civil penalties up to $250,000 per violation, and criminal penalties up to $1 million per violation.
43. *See* Press Release No. 10-209, U.S. Dep't of Justice, BAE Systems PLC Pleads Guilty and Ordered to Pay $400 Million Criminal Fine (Mar. 1, 2010), www.justice.gov/opa/pr/bae-systems-plc-pleads-guilty-and-ordered-pay-400-million-criminal-fine.
44. Violations of most of the Economic Sanction Regulations are set under the IEEPA. *See supra* note 42.
45. The OFAC embargo of Cuba is subject to the Trading with the Enemy Act (TWEA).
46. *See* Press Release No. 13-1260, U.S. Dep't of Justice, Three Subsidiaries of Weatherford International Limited Agree to Plead Guilty to FCPA and Export Control Violations (Nov. 26, 2013), www.justice.gov/opa/pr/2013/November/13-crm-1260.html.
47. For a review of BIS investigations and penalties, see BUREAU OF INDUS. & SEC., EXP. ENF'T, U.S. DEP'T OF COMMERCE, DON'T LET THIS HAPPEN TO YOU! ACTUAL INVESTIGATIONS OF EXPORT CONTROL AND ANTI-BOYCOTT VIOLATIONS (July 2015), www.bis.doc.gov/index.php/forms-documents/doc_view/1005-don-t-let-this-happen-to-you-071814.
48. See DDTC's website at www.pmddtc.state.gov/compliance/consent_agreements.html. For a thorough discussion of penalties imposed under the ITAR in the last few years, see John C. Pisa-Relli, Monograph on U.S. Defense Trade Enforcement (rev. July 20, 2012).
49. Remarks by David Trimble, Dir. of Compliance, Directorate of Defense Trade Controls, delivered at the SIA Fall 2008 Defense Trade Licensing Conference, Washington, D.C., Nov. 12–14, 2008.
50. Remarks of David W. Mills, Bureau of Indus. & Sec., Assistant Sec'y, Export Enf't, Washington, D.C., July 24, 2013.
51. For a detailed account of the ITT Corporation investigation, see Press Release, U.S. Dep't of Justice, ITT Corporation to Pay $100 Million Penalty and Plead Guilty to Illegally Exporting Secret Military Data Overseas (Mar. 27, 2007), www.justice.gov/archive/opa/pr/2007/March/07_nsd_192.html.

52. For a thorough discussion of penalties imposed under the ITAR in the last few years, see John C. Pisa-Relli, Monograph on U.S. Defense Trade Enforcement (rev. July 20, 2012).

53. *See* Public Notice No. 6900, U.S. Department of State, Termination of Ineligible Status and Statutory Debarment Pursuant to Section 38(g)(4) of the Arms Export Control Act and Section 127.7 of the International Traffic in Arms Regulations for ITT Corporation, 75 Fed. Reg. 7650 (Feb. 22, 2010).

54. *See* Bureau of Political-Military Affairs; Statutory Debarment of ITT Corporation Pursuant to the Arms Export Control Act and the International Traffic in Arms Regulations, 72 Fed. Reg. 18,310 (Apr. 11, 2007).

55. NUNN-WOLFOWITZ TASK REPORT: INDUSTRY "BEST PRACTICES" REGARDING EXPORT COMPLIANCE PROGRAM (July 25, 2000), developed for Hughes Electronics Corporation ("Nunn-Wolfowitz Report"). The Nunn-Wolfowitz Report follows closely the recommendations in the Sentencing Guidelines, as well as some of the recommendations provided in the Export Management Systems Guidelines ("BIS EMS Guidelines") developed by the Department of Commerce Bureau of Industry and Security, and in the Guidelines for DDTC Registered Exporters/Manufacturers Compliance Program developed by the Department of State Directorate of Defense Trade Controls.

56. *See* NUNN-WOLFOWITZ TASK REPORT, *supra* note 55, at 8–10.

57. Note that, since 2009, filings relating to an export transaction must be done using the Automated Export System (AES).

58. "Know Your Customer Guidance" is available on the BIS website. *See Know Your Customer*, BUREAU OF INDUS. & SEC. [BIS], www.bis.doc.gov/index.php/compliance-a-training/export-management-a-compliance/23-compliance-a-training/47-know-your-customer-guidance (last visited June 27, 2016).

59. *See also* BIS EMS Guidelines, *supra* note 55.

60. *See* COUNCIL ON GOVERNMENTAL RELATIONS, EXPORT CONTROLS AND UNIVERSITIES: INFORMATION AND CASE STUDIES (Feb. 2004), www.cogr.edu/viewDoc.cfm?DocID=151612.

61. Defense Trade Advisory Group presentations and white papers, as well as other various DTAG documents, are available online. *See The Defense Trade Advisory Group (DTAG)*, U.S. DEP'T OF STATE (June 1, 2016), www.pmddtc.state.gov/dtag/.

62. *See* U.S. GOV'T ACCOUNTABILITY OFFICE, REPORT NO. GAO-07-70, REPORT TO THE COMM. ON THE JUDICIARY, EXPORT CONTROLS: AGENCIES SHOULD ASSESS VULNERABILITIES AND IMPROVE GUIDANCE FOR PROTECTING EXPORT-CONTROLLED INFORMATION AT UNIVERSITIES (Dec. 2006), www.gao.gov/new.items/d0770.pdf.

63. *See* Karin Fischer, *Number of Foreign Students in U.S. Hit a New High Last Year*, CHRON. HIGHER EDUC., Nov. 16, 2009, http://chronicle.com/article/Number-of-Foreign-Students-in/49142/.

64. 22 C.F.R. § 120.15; 15 C.F.R. § 734.2(b). A special question arises with foreign persons who are dual nationals. While BIS looks at the person's most recent citizenship or permanent residence, DDTC also looks at the person's country of origin (*i.e.*, country of birth). Therefore, under the ITAR, an export that

generally may not require a license to a citizen of an EU country will still require licensing if the EU citizen was born in an embargoed country, such as Iran.

65. 42 U.S.C. § 2000e-2.

66. Pub. L. No. 99-603 (1986).

67. 8 U.S.C. § 1324(2)(C).

68. 22 C.F.R. §§ 120.10(a)(5), 120.11.

69. 15 C.F.R. §§ 734.3(b)(3), 734.7.

70. For guidance on BIS interpretation of "published" information, see EAR Supplement No. 1 to Part 734, Questions A(1)–B(6).

71. 22 C.F.R. § 120.10(a)(5).

72. 15 C.F.R. §§ 734.3(b)(3), 734.9.

73. EAR Supplement No. 1 to Part 734, Questions C(1)–(6).

74. 22 C.F.R. § 120.11(a)(8); 15 C.F.R. §§ 734.3(b)(3), 734.8(a).

75. *See* BIS Revisions and Clarification of Deemed Export Related Regulatory Requirements, 71 Fed. Reg. 30,840, 30,844 (May 31, 2006). This interpretation of fundamental research by BIS, while not binding, is instructive as to how DDTC might interpret its regulations.

76. *See* Def. Trade Advisory Grp., DTAG Fundamental Research Working Group White Paper, May 9, 2013, www.pmddtc.state.gov/dtag/documents/plenary_May2013_FundamentalResearch.pdf.

77. 22 C.F.R. §§ 120.11(a)(8), 120.10(a)(5); 15 C.F.R. § 734.8(a).

78. *See* 15 C.F.R. § 734.8(b)(5). However, once the sponsor has reviewed and approved the release, the results may be published as fundamental research.

79. *Id.* § 734.11(b). While the ITAR does not contain such descriptive provisions, the EAR is instructive as to interpreting the limitations on fundamental research.

18

Corporate Political Activity

Christopher DeLacy *

Engaging in lobbying and political activity, while protected by the First Amendment and often essential for business reasons, can create liability for corporations if not carefully managed. At every level of government, laws, regulations, and rules prohibit, restrict, and require disclosure of lobbying and political activities. In many cases, the regulatory regimes are overlapping and are not necessarily intuitive. Accordingly, because of the potential for bad publicity, civil penalties, and even prison time, every corporation that comes in contact with government officials must have a compliance program in place.

The past few years have been particularly active in the areas of lobbying, campaign finance, and government ethics. In June 2015, a political operative was sentenced to two years in prison for illegal federal campaign finance activities involving a Super PAC.[1] The U.S. Attorney's Office for the District of Columbia recently entered into a settlement with a lobbyist that includes a $30,000 fine for missing Lobbying Disclosure Act

* The author wishes to acknowledge Steven D. Gordon and Andrew H. Emerson for their contributions to this chapter.

(LDA) reports. The lobbyist had been facing the prospect of over $5 million in potential fines related to LDA compliance.[2] Similarly, in December 2013, the U.S. Attorney's Office secured a default judgment of $200,000, after seeking up to $33 million in fines against a consulting firm for violations of the Lobbying Disclosure Act of 1995, as amended.[3] In April 2011, the Department of Justice (DOJ) announced that the CEO of a newspaper publishing company pled guilty to a federal felony for submitting to the House of Representatives a Private Sponsor Travel Certification Form that contained false statements.[4] In March 2011, DOJ indicted a former Senate staffer for violating lobbying restrictions.[5] During 2010, the Supreme Court decided one of the most important campaign finance cases in history,[6] and the Office of Congressional Ethics requested documents from numerous companies that had engaged in lobbying and campaign finance activities related to the U.S. House of Representatives.[7]

Impermissible Corporate Political Activities

Q 18.1   May a corporation contribute to a candidate directly out of its treasury?

For more than 100 years it has been illegal for corporations to contribute funds out of the corporate treasury directly to a candidate for federal office.[8] In addition, labor unions[9] and federal contractors[10] may not make direct contributions at the federal level. National banks, corporations organized by a specific law of Congress, and foreign nationals may not make contributions at the federal, state, or local level.[11]

Corporate "soft money"[12] contributions to the national political parties[13] have been illegal since enactment of the Bipartisan Campaign Reform Act of 2002 (BCRA).[14] It is also illegal for corporations to facilitate the making of a contribution to a federal candidate[15] or to reimburse employees for contributions to a federal candidate.[16]

Corporate contributions at the state and local level vary by jurisdiction. Currently, twenty-one states prohibit corporate contributions, while twenty-nine states and the District of Columbia allow some form of corporate contributions.[17]

Permissible Corporate Political Activities

Q 18.2   How may corporations participate in the federal political process?

Corporate employees who are otherwise eligible to contribute in connection with a federal election[18] may contribute directly to federal candidates. Corporations themselves may form political action committees or "PACs,"[19] pay for certain communications about federal candidates,[20] contribute to a "Super PAC" or other third-party political group, invite federal candidates to visit corporate facilities,[21] and fly federal candidates on corporate aircraft under certain circumstances.[22]

Although not expressly political, corporations may also engage in federal, state, and local lobbying activities, including "grass-roots" advocacy, subject to the relevant laws and rules discussed below.

The guidance provided below applies only to *federal* candidates. Each state and some localities have laws and regulations related to campaign finance and lobbying activities that are likely to be different from the federal rules.

Q 18.3   May a corporation expend any resources in support of a candidate for federal election?

Generally, any corporate resources expended in support of a candidate for federal election must be reimbursed by a permissible source—such as an individual, PAC, or campaign.[23] There are, however, several exceptions to this rule, including corporate contributions to Super PACs (*see* Q 18.12), which may make independent expenditures in support of candidates (*see* Q 18.17 *et seq.*).

Political Action Committees (PACs)

Basic Requirements and Restrictions

Q 18.4   What is a PAC?

While there is no definition of "PAC" in federal law, the term is generally used to describe a type of political committee[24] organized to support and encourage the election to federal, state, or local offices of individuals who share a common political view. A political committee can be a PAC, a candidate's campaign, or a political party committee.[25]

The Federal Election Campaign Act of 1971 (FECA), as amended,[26] prohibits corporations from using their general treasury funds for contributions to candidates in connection with federal elections.[27] However, FECA does allow corporations to form political committees called "separate segregated funds" (SSFs).[28] The sponsoring corporation is known as the "connected organization." SSFs are a type of PAC and are usually referred to simply as PACs. The other type of PAC is a non-connected committee, which is not sponsored by a corporation, labor union, membership organization, or trade association.

Q 18.4.1   Are there restrictions on who can participate in a PAC/SSF?

A foreign national, unless an immigrant lawfully admitted for permanent residence in the United States,[29] may not participate in the operation of a PAC, serve as an officer of a PAC, participate in the selection of persons who operate a PAC, or make decisions related to PAC contributions or expenditures.[30] Under certain circumstances, U.S. subsidiaries of a foreign corporation may operate an SSF.[31]

Q 18.4.2   Are there limits and restrictions on how a corporation can support an SSF?

While no corporate dollars may be used for actual contributions to federal candidates, corporations may use treasury funds to establish, maintain, and solicit funds for an SSF.[32] Corporations may pay for office space, administrative support, phone lines, utilities, supplies, and fundraising expenses for an SSF. Generally, there is no limit to the amount a corporation may spend on this support,[33] which is not reported to the Federal Election Commission (FEC). An SSF may also pay its own expenses, but if it does so, such expenditures must be disclosed.

When sending an employee to attend a fundraiser for a federal candidate or political committee, a corporation may pay for that employee's travel and lodging expenses, so long as the employee is delivering a check from the corporation's PAC. These travel expenses are considered an "administrative expense"[34] and are exempt from the definition of contribution under federal law.[35] By contrast, without a PAC, reimbursement for travel or lodging in connection with a fundraiser could be considered an illegal in-kind corporate contribution.

Q 18.4.3   What kinds of restrictions are there on solicitation of contributions to SSFs?

A PAC may accept a contribution from any lawful source,[36] but SSFs are restricted as to who may be solicited for contributions. A corporation and its SSF may always solicit certain individuals known as the "restricted class."[37] Twice a year, a corporation or SSF may solicit employees *not* included in their restricted class, but special procedures must be followed.[38]

All contributions to an SSF must be voluntary. When soliciting contributions, corporations or their SSFs may not use, or threaten to use, physical force, job discrimination, or financial reprisals.[39] Solicitees must be informed of the political purpose of the SSF and their right to refuse to contribute without reprisal.[40] If suggested contribution amounts are provided, the solicitation must also indicate the suggested amount is only a suggestion; that more or less than the suggested amount may be given (no minimum contribution can be specified); and the amount given or the refusal to give will not benefit or disadvantage the person being solicited.[41] SSFs must make "best efforts" to obtain and report the name, address, occupation, and employer for each contributor who gives more than $200 in a calendar year.[42] Solicitations must include a disclaimer indicating that contributions to SSFs are not tax deductible.[43]

Q 18.4.4 Who makes up the "restricted class"?

The restricted class of a corporation includes:

- executive and administrative personnel;
- stockholders; and
- the families of both groups.

Executive and administrative personnel include employees who are paid a salary and who have policy-making, managerial, professional, or supervisory responsibilities[44] as defined by the Fair Labor Standards Act (FLSA).[45]

Stockholders must have a vested beneficial interest in the stock, the power to direct how the stock is voted (if it is voting stock), and the right to receive dividends.[46] Under certain circumstances, members of a corporation's board of directors may be solicited.[47] A corporation may use payroll deductions to raise money for its PAC,[48] but it must have a signed authorization from the employee.[49] Once a signed authorization has been obtained, a corporation should retain that authorization for its records, but may use other records, such as pay transmittal documents, to demonstrate such authorization if necessary.[50]

In addition to soliciting contributions for a PAC, a corporation's restricted class is important for corporate communications purposes (*see* Q 18.6 *et seq.*).

Formation and Operation

Q 18.5   How does a corporation form a PAC?

The FEC required steps are:

- obtaining an Employer Identification Number (EIN) from the Internal Revenue Service (IRS);
- naming a PAC treasurer;[51]
- opening a PAC bank account;[52]
- filing a Statement of Organization with the FEC;[53] and
- filing periodic reports with the FEC.[54]

Though not required by the FEC, other PAC officers typically include a chairman, secretary, and assistant treasurer. During the absence or incapacity of the treasurer, or when circumstances prevent the treasurer from acting, the assistant treasurer[55] performs the duties and exercises the powers of the treasurer.

All federal PACs are required to obtain a unique EIN from the IRS and may not share an EIN with any other entity. A federal PAC must establish and maintain a separate bank account using the PAC's name and EIN. The official name of an SSF must include the full name of the connected organization, including any indications of business entity type (Inc., Corp., LLC). Common business abbreviations and the acronym PAC are acceptable in the official name of an SSF. A non-connected PAC may choose any name, except it may not include the name of any candidate.

Q 18.5.1   What are the disclosure requirements for a PAC?

Federal PACs disclose their receipts and disbursements to the FEC either monthly or quarterly.[56] Receipts from individuals must be itemized if they exceed $200 during the calendar year.[57] Disbursements to candidates and other PACs must always be itemized.[58] In a non-election year, quarterly filers may file semi-annually. During an election year, quarterly filers may have to file a pre-primary and pre-general report and must submit a post-general election report. Monthly filers submit only pre-general and post-general election reports. Accordingly, because state primary dates vary, it is best to file monthly during an election year and quarterly during a non-election year. Both monthly and quarterly filers file a year-end statement. A PAC may change its filing schedule once per year by notifying the FEC in writing.[59]

Once the PAC achieves multi-candidate status,[60] a notification of multi-candidate status must be filed within ten days.[61] A PAC achieves multi-candidate status once it has received contributions from at least fifty-one persons, has been registered for at least six months, and has made contributions to at least five federal candidates, or by being affiliated with a multi-candidate PAC.

Q 18.5.2   What are contribution limits for PACs?

A federal PAC may only accept up to $5,000 from an individual per calendar year.[62] Multi-candidate[63] PACs are permitted to contribute up to $5,000 per candidate, per election.[64] Primaries and general elections are considered separate elections,[65] so multi-candidate PACs can give up to $10,000 per election cycle to a candidate (even if there is no primary). Multi-candidate PACs may contribute up to $5,000 per year to state parties and $15,000 per year to national parties.[66] Multi-candidate PAC contribution limits are not currently indexed for inflation. Non-multi-candidate PACs are subject to the same contribution limits as individuals that are indexed to inflation[67] (*see* Q 18.14).

Q 18.5.3   How can a corporation ensure PAC compliance?

While nothing can guarantee 100% compliance, there are steps a corporation can take to reduce the chances of misappropriation or a mistake that could lead to an audit or fine. Appointing a knowledgeable and proactive PAC treasurer is the most important step. The treasurer is the only officer required by the FEC[68] and is responsible for ensuring compliance with the law as well as preparing and filing reports.[69] The treasurer will be named (either in an official or personal capacity or both) along with the PAC in any FEC enforcement action.[70]

Other steps a corporation should take include:

- adopting bylaws for the PAC;
- creating a PAC budget; and
- establishing a PAC compliance program.

Q 18.5.4   What should a PAC compliance program look like?

A PAC compliance program would include:

- obtaining accounting and FEC filing software;
- auditing the PAC once every two-year election cycle;
- training individuals affiliated with the PAC; and
- providing legal oversight.

The structure and complexity of the compliance program can vary depending on the size and intensity of the PAC's activities. It is recommended that a structure closely akin to the guidance of the U.S. Sentencing Commission on effective compliance and ethics programs be used. (For more on the basic structure of a compliance and ethics program, see chapters 1–5.)

Corporate Communications

Definitions

Q 18.6   What is express advocacy?

"Express advocacy" is a communication that urges the election or defeat of a clearly identified candidate.[71] The term derives from *Buckley v. Valeo*,[72] where the Supreme Court allowed federal regulation of ads that "in express terms advocate the election or defeat of a clearly identified candidate for federal office."[73]

Q 18.7   What is issue advocacy?

In contrast to express advocacy, "issue advocacy" is the discussion of policy issues that stops short of express advocacy. Issue advocacy is technically grass-roots lobbying, although it can blur the line between policy and politics.

Q 18.8   What is an electioneering communication?

"Electioneering communications" are defined as broadcast, cable, or satellite ads that refer to a federal candidate, are disseminated via television or radio within thirty days prior to a primary or sixty days prior to a general election, and reach 50,000 or more persons[74] in the federal candidate's congressional district (for a House of Representatives election) or state (for a Senate election).[75]

In the case of a presidential or vice-presidential candidate, such communications will include any communication that can be received by 50,000 or more persons in a state where a primary election is to occur within thirty days, or by 50,000 or more persons anywhere in the United States within thirty days of the national nominating convention.[76]

Q 18.9   What is an independent expenditure?

An "independent expenditure" is a payment for a communication "expressly advocating the election or defeat of a clearly identified candidate that is not made in cooperation, consultation, or concert with, or at the request or suggestion of, a candidate, a candidate's authorized committee, or their agents, or a political party committee or its agents."[77] An independent expenditure is not a contribution unless it is coordinated with a candidate, campaign, or political party.

Q 18.10   What is coordination?

Coordination includes discussions about expenditures with candidates, political parties, campaign staff, and agents of the foregoing.[78]

Requirements and Restrictions

Q 18.11   What may a corporation communicate about a federal candidate to its employees?

Corporations may communicate on any subject with their restricted class[79] (*see* Q 18.4.4, *supra*). This communication may include express advocacy (*see* Q 18.11.2, *infra*)[80] or solicitations for contributions on behalf of federal candidates,[81] with the following caveats:

- if the corporation spends more than $2,000 per election on these types of communications, it may trigger reporting requirements with the FEC;[82]
- the solicitation should indicate the contributions are voluntary and that the individual has the right to refuse without reprisal;

- the corporation may not provide an envelope or stamps or otherwise "facilitate" the making of the contribution (including collecting or "bundling" checks);[83] and
- the corporation may not copy campaign materials for purposes of the solicitation.[84]

Q 18.11.1 What may a corporation communicate about a federal candidate outside its restricted class?

A corporation may communicate to employees outside its restricted class and to the general public about federal candidates. However, the communication must not be coordinated with a candidate,[85] and it must not contain a solicitation for contributions.[86] A corporation may now pay for communications that contain express advocacy outside its restricted class (*see Citizens United v. Federal Election Commission* case study, *infra*). A corporation's PAC may pay also for express advocacy outside its restricted class.[87] Corporations may also engage in issue advocacy.

Corporate communications to the public may include bipartisan or nonpartisan voting guides, voting histories, and other voter information.[88] Corporations may also endorse candidates by issuing a press release to news outlets.[89]

 CASE STUDY: *Citizens United v. Fed. Election Comm'n* [90]

The Supreme Court handed down a historic decision in *Citizens United v. Federal Election Commission* on Thursday, January 21, 2010. Corporations and labor unions may now use treasury funds to pay for communications that urge voters to support or oppose federal candidates (express advocacy). Corporations and labor unions may still not contribute directly to federal candidates, parties, or PACs. In this historic case, the Court:

- **struck down** the ban on corporate and labor union expenditures contained in FECA;[91]
- **struck down** the ban on corporate and labor union electioneering communications contained in BCRA;[92]

- **overruled** *Austin v. Michigan Chamber of Commerce,*[93] which originally upheld a ban on corporate express advocacy;
- **overruled** the portion of *McConnell v. FEC*[94] that had upheld the electioneering communications provisions contained in BCRA; and
- **upheld** the electioneering communications disclosure and disclaimer provisions contained in BCRA.[95]

On June 25, 2012, the Supreme Court reaffirmed *Citizens United* and overturned a Montana Supreme Court decision that did not adhere to the precedent set by *Citizens United.*[96]

Q 18.11.2   How is express advocacy regulated?

Prior to *Citizens United*, corporations could not pay for express advocacy outside of their restricted classes. See the case study above and QQ 18.11 and 18.11.1 for more details on corporate communications that include express advocacy.

On January 20, 2011, almost one year to the day after the U.S. Supreme Court's landmark decision in *Citizens United*, the FEC deadlocked 3-3 along party lines on a vote to move forward with proposed regulations to implement this decision.[97] The FEC deadlocked again on December 15, 2011.[98] Finally, in October 2014, the FEC adopted a limited regulation implementing the *Citizens United* decision.[99] These regulations acknowledged that corporations and unions may make unlimited contributions to independent expenditure-only PACs (so-called Super PACs, discussed in further detail below), but did not otherwise regulate these entities. The FEC has stated that it will undertake a separate rulemaking on Super PACs, but has not yet done so.

Q 18.11.3   Is issue advocacy regulated?

Generally no, unless it is an electioneering communication, in which case a mandatory disclaimer is required by the Federal Communications Commission (FCC), and the station running the advertisement must collect and maintain certain information in its public files.[100]

Q 18.11.4   How are electioneering communications regulated?

BCRA first defined electioneering communications, banned corporate and labor union payments for electioneering communications, and imposed certain disclaimer and disclosure requirements. After initially being upheld by the Supreme Court in *McConnell*[101] in a facial challenge, the electioneering communications restrictions contained in BCRA were struck down by the Supreme Court in as-applied challenges in *FEC v. Wisconsin Right to Life*[102] (in relation to issue advocacy) and *Citizens United* (in relation to express advocacy). The electioneering communications disclosure and disclaimer requirements were upheld in *Citizens United*.

Q 18.11.5   Is coordination permitted?

Corporations may not coordinate communications with candidates, campaigns, or political parties (*see* Q 18.11.1), as this is considered an in-kind contribution and is subject to the limits, prohibitions, and reporting requirements of FECA. Even after *Citizens United*, corporations are still prohibited from making contributions, including in-kind contributions, directly to candidates or political parties.

Q 18.11.6   What disclosure requirements apply to corporate communications?

Corporations that pay for independent expenditures (*see* Q 18.9) must disclose any aggregate payments that exceed $250 in a calendar year.[103] If total payments for independent expenditures exceed $10,000, disclosure must occur within forty-eight hours.[104] If total payments for independent expenditures exceed $1,000 within twenty days of an election, disclosure must occur within twenty-four hours.[105] Corporations that pay for electioneering communications (*see* QQ 18.8 and 18.11.4) aggregating in excess of $10,000 during a calendar year must disclose certain information within twenty-four hours.[106] Additional FCC[107] and Internal Revenue Service (IRS)[108] disclosure requirements may apply. Independent expenditures and electioneering communications must include the following disclaimer:

Not Authorized by any candidate or candidate committee.
Paid for by [name, permanent address, telephone number,
or Internet address].[109]

Additional disclaimers are required for radio and television ads.

Post–*Citizens United* there has been a flurry of activity related to
the disclosure of political activity:

- On March 25, 2011, the Securities and Exchange Commission
  (SEC) issued a no-action letter rejecting a request from The
  Home Depot, Inc. to exclude from its proxy statement a
  shareholder proposal mandating disclosure of certain political activity, including political expenditures, and requiring a
  non-binding shareholder vote on future political activity.
  NorthStar Asset Management, Inc. had requested that the
  shareholder proposal be included in that year's proxy statement. Home Depot, Inc. had intended to exclude the
  proposal and sought advice from the SEC as to whether this
  was permissible.[110]

- On August 13, 2011, the Committee on Disclosure of Corporate Political Spending, a group of ten academics, filed a petition for rulemaking with the SEC requesting draft regulations
  that would require public companies to disclose to shareholders information regarding the use of corporate
  resources for political activities.[111] The SEC has received
  over a quarter million comments in favor of such a
  rulemaking,[112] and in December 2012 the SEC asked that the
  White House Office of Information and Regulatory Affairs
  include a related rulemaking on the SEC's annual regulatory
  agenda for 2014.[113] However, the SEC did not include this
  proposal on its list of regulatory priorities for 2014,
  suggesting that it is unlikely to take further action in the
  near future.[114]

- On April 21, 2011, Congressman Chris Van Hollen (D-MD)
  submitted a petition for rulemaking with the FEC requesting
  additional disclosure of information related to independent
  expenditures.[115] The FEC deadlocked on the petition on
  December 15, 2011.[116]

- On January 21, 2016, the U.S. Court of Appeals for the D.C.
  Circuit reversed a 2014 district court decision that invali-

dated regulations governing the disclosure of certain donations used to fund electioneering communications.[117] The
regulation in question (11 C.F.R. § 104.20(c)(9)) requires
disclosure of only those donations made for the purpose of
furthering electioneering communications. In reversing the
U.S. District Court for the District of Columbia's 2014 decision, the appellate court upheld the FEC's regulation as a
reasonable interpretation of the disclosure provisions of
FECA.

- On April 27, 2012, the FCC adopted an order requiring broadcast television stations to place their public inspection files
on an FCC-hosted website.[118] The order does not require any
additional disclosure, but previously these public inspection
files had only been available in hard copy at the stations.
Section 315 of the Communications Act of 1934 requires
broadcasters to maintain a public file for any requests for
paid programming—including third-party ads—that refers to
a legally qualified candidate, a federal election, or a national
legislative issue of public importance. A list of the chief executive officers or members of the board of directors of the
entity purchasing the ad must be placed in the public file.

- In December 2013, the IRS proposed new regulations for
501(c)(4) organizations that engage in political activities.
However, the proposals are highly controversial, and more
than 150,000 comments were submitted to the IRS. In 2015,
Congress prohibited the IRS from using federally appropriated funds to implement this proposed regulation or any
similar regulation, revenue ruling, or other guidance not
limited to a particular taxpayer. The IRS is still permitted to
continue to make this determination on a case-by-case
basis.[119]

- At any point, Congress, the FEC, IRS, or SEC may require
additional disclosure of political activity.

In 2011, President Obama reportedly considered an Executive
Order (EO)[120] that would have required the disclosure of certain political spending by entities bidding on government contracts and affiliated individuals and entities. However, after legislative push-back
from the House of Representatives, he reportedly chose to refrain
from doing so for the foreseeable future.[121]

Super PACs

Q 18.12   What is a Super PAC?

Federal "Independent Expenditure-Only Political Committees," also known as "Super PACs," are entities organized to accept almost unlimited contributions and make unlimited independent expenditures (*see* Q 18.9).

Q 18.12.1   Who can make contributions to a Super PAC?

Super PACs may accept unlimited contributions from:

- individuals,
- partnerships,
- Indian tribes,
- corporations, and
- labor unions.

Q 18.12.2   Who is prohibited from making contributions to a Super PAC?

Super PACs may not accept contributions from:

- foreign nationals,[122]
- federal contractors,[123]
- national banks,[124] and
- federally chartered corporations.[125]

Q 18.12.3   What kinds of limitations and restrictions are placed on a Super PAC's activities?

Super PACs may not coordinate[126] with candidates, campaigns, political parties, or agents thereof, and may not make direct contributions to candidates.

Q 18.13   How are Super PACs regulated?

The FEC has not yet adopted comprehensive Super PAC implementing regulations (*see* Q 18.11.2), but it did issue Advisory Opinion 2010-11 (Commonsense Ten) providing guidance regarding Super PACs.[127] Super PACs must register with the FEC and report all contributions over $200 and all expenditures. Furthermore, there is a series of decisions that provide the legal framework for Super PACs (*see* Birth of the Super PAC case studies, *infra*).

Q 18.13.1 Are Super PACs required to disclose their donors?

Yes. Super PACs must report all contributions over $200 to the FEC. So if an individual or organization contributes to a Super PAC, this information will be publicly available. However, while the name of the organization that contributes to a Super PAC will be disclosed to the FEC, the underlying donors to that organization may not be disclosed. For example, corporations or individuals may contribute to 501(c)(4) (social welfare organizations) or 501(c)(6) (business leagues) entities, which may then contribute to Super PACs or pay for political ads directly. Unlike Super PACs, 501(c)(4) or 501(c)(6) entities do not publicly disclose contributor information unless the contribution is earmarked for specific independent expenditures or electioneering communications.[128] In some cases, Super PACs will be affiliated with 501(c)(4) entities.

 CASE STUDIES: Birth of the Super PAC

Citizens United v. Federal Election Commission[129]
- Struck down ban on corporate and labor union independent expenditures.
- Upheld FEC disclosure requirements.
- *Did not* strike down ban on direct corporate and labor union contributions.

SpeechNow.org v. Federal Election Commission[130]
- Struck down individual contribution limits to independent expenditure only political committees.
- Required FEC registration and disclosure.

Commonsense Ten[131]
- Allows independent expenditure only committees to accept unlimited contributions from individuals, political committees, corporations, and labor unions.

Carey v. Federal Election Commission[132]
- Allows both independent expenditures and direct contributions from the same entity (using separate bank accounts).

Q 18.13.2   What steps can a corporation take to vet contributions to third parties?

Corporations should exercise due diligence prior to making a contribution to a Super PAC or other entity that engages in political activity.

1. **Determine the precise identity of the recipient.** It is important to remember that different entities may be affiliated or have similar names. Public databases (such as the FEC, IRS, or state corporation commission) are useful for this purpose.
2. **Confirm the proposed contribution is lawful.** As discussed in QQ 18.1 and 18.12.2, foreign national, federal contractor, national bank, and federally chartered corporation contributions are prohibited in most cases.
3. **Include a cover letter.** It is a best practice to include a cover letter with the contribution clearly indicating the contributor, the recipient, the amount, the understanding that the contribution is legal and will be used in a legal manner, and confirming there are no disclosure requirements that are the responsibility of the contributor. In some cases, particularly for large contributions, it is appropriate to ask for a letter back confirming legality of contribution.
4. **Review public disclosure databases.** Corporations should do this prior to making the contribution to ensure the entity is legitimate and after making the contribution to ensure it was properly disclosed.
5. **Respect the lines between outside groups and campaigns.** Improper coordination can result in civil and criminal penalties.

TIP: While contributions to Super PACs or 501(c)(4) organizations require vetting, even contributions to 501(c)(3) charitable organizations can have political compliance implications. If given in connection with or at the request of a government official, charitable contributions can under certain circumstances be considered bribes,[133] be restricted or prohibited,[134] or require disclosure[135] (*see* QQ 18.19.3 and 18.26.4).

Permissible Employee Political Activities

Q 18.14   How much can individual employees contribute to federal candidates?

For 2015–2016, individuals may contribute up to \$2,700[136] per election to federal candidates and \$5,000[137] per calendar year to PACs. Primaries and general elections are considered separate elections,[138] so an individual can give up to \$5,000 per election cycle to a candidate (even if there is no primary). Individuals may also contribute up to \$334,000 per year to the Democratic National Committee or Republican National Committee or \$233,800 per year to the other National Party Committees (Democratic Senatorial Campaign Committee, Republican Senatorial Campaign Committee, Democratic Congressional Campaign Committee and Republican Congressional Campaign Committee).[139] All the contribution limits above are indexed to inflation every two years, except for contributions to PACs.[140] The FEC will publish new contribution limits for 2017–2018 in early 2017.

 CASE STUDY: *McCutcheon v. FEC*

On April 2, 2014, the Supreme Court in *McCutcheon v. FEC*[141] overturned the federal biennial aggregate limits.[142] Several states, including Arizona, Connecticut, Louisiana, Maine, Maryland, Massachusetts, New York, Rhode Island, Washington, Wisconsin, and Wyoming, and the District of Columbia, had limits similar to the federal biennial aggregate limits.

Q 18.14.1   What other limitations and conditions exist for contributions from individuals?

Under no circumstances may a corporation reimburse employees for campaign contributions, including increasing bonuses to cover the cost of campaign contributions.[143]

Contributions from foreign nationals, unless immigrants lawfully admitted for permanent residence in the United States,[144] are prohibited.[145] This prohibition is absolute and applies to federal, state, and local candidates.

Contributions should never be directly connected to official acts. Giving or offering anything of value to any federal official in connection with an official act could be considered bribery or an illegal gratuity under federal law.[146] Contributions may be made to support candidates because of their general position on issues, but not in return for their support of specific legislation or other official acts.

Q 18.15   What is "bundling"?

The term "bundling" is commonly used to describe the practice of an individual collecting several contributions and delivering them to the candidate or campaign. This common definition is not exactly the same as the new legal definition discussed below.

Q 18.15.1   May corporate employees "bundle" contributions to federal candidates?

No. Although bundling was once a common way for corporations to facilitate the making of a contribution to a federal candidate, it is illegal.[147] Under certain circumstances, individuals acting as volunteers or representatives of PACs may engage in this type of activity,[148] but under no circumstances should corporate employees engage in this activity when acting as an agent or representative of the corporation.[149]

In addition, all contributions bundled by a registered lobbyist must be disclosed.[150] A contribution is "bundled" if it is forwarded by or credited to a registered lobbyist by a campaign committee, leadership PAC, or political party committee. All bundled contributions totaling more than $17,600[151] during a semi-annual period must be reported. Contributions from the registered lobbyist or their family members do not count toward the $17,600 total. Bundled contributions will be reported to the FEC or the Secretary of the Senate by the recipient political committee, not by the bundler. The FEC adopted a new rule to implement this reporting requirement. The $17,600 threshold is indexed annually to inflation.

Q 18.16   May corporate employees engage in political activity related to a federal election while at work?

There is a safe harbor for occasional, isolated, or incidental volunteer activity for corporate employees of one hour per week or four hours per month.[152] The employee must reimburse the corporation to the extent that the activity increases operating costs or overhead.[153] The employee must truly be a volunteer—a superior cannot ask an employee to do volunteer work as part of their regular duties.[154]

Other Permissible Corporate Activities

Q 18.17   May corporate resources or facilities be used in conjunction with a federal election?

Yes, but the corporation must be reimbursed by a permissible source.[155] Fair market value must be paid, *in advance*, for any use of corporate staff, customer lists, or catering services.[156] Fair market value must be paid for any use of office equipment or meeting rooms,[157] but it may be after the fact. These rules do not apply to fundraising activities related to a corporation's PAC.

Q 18.17.1   May a corporation invite a federal candidate to its facility?

Yes, but the rules vary depending on the audience:

If the appearance is before the corporation's *restricted class*, both the candidate and the corporation may engage in express advocacy[158] (advocating the election or defeat of a clearly identified federal candidate) and may solicit campaign contributions.[159] The candidate may collect contributions or otherwise facilitate the making of contributions,[160] while the corporation may not.[161] Corporate expenditures for express advocacy to its restricted class must be reported if costs exceed $2,000 per election.[162]

Corporations need not provide other candidates with a similar opportunity if the audience is limited to the restricted class.[163]

If the appearance is before *all the corporation's employees*, the candidate may engage in express advocacy, but the corporation may not. Post–*Citizens United* (see the case study above at Q 18.11.1), this restriction may eventually be revised or removed by the FEC.[164] The candidate may solicit but not collect contributions and the corporation may not solicit or collect contributions.[165]

Corporations must provide a similar opportunity to other candidates, if requested.[166]

If the appearance is before *the public*, the candidate must appear as a federal office holder or lecturer, not as a federal candidate.[167] Neither the candidate nor the corporation may engage in express advocacy or solicit contributions. (Post–*Citizens United*, this restriction may eventually be revised or removed by the FEC.) The candidate may not make reference to the campaign.

Corporations need not provide other speakers with a similar opportunity if the speaker is not appearing as a candidate.[168]

It is important to note that the IRS has separate rules related to 501(c)(3) charitable organizations and candidate appearances.

Q 18.17.2   May a corporation allow a federal candidate to fly on its private aircraft?

It depends on the status of the federal candidate:

Candidates for U.S. Senate or President	The corporation must be reimbursed the pro rata share of the fair market value of the flight (as determined by dividing the fair market value of the normal and usual charter fare or rental charge for a comparable plane of comparable size by the number of candidates on the flight) within a commercially reasonable time frame.[169]
Candidates for U.S. House of Representatives	A House candidate may not use campaign or leadership PAC funds to pay for a flight on a private aircraft.[170]

Non-Candidate   The reimbursement rate required for a "non-
Campaign   candidate" campaign traveler, including persons
Travelers   traveling on behalf of a political party committee, a
                    PAC, or a leadership PAC (other than a House
                    Leadership PAC) is the first-class, coach, or charter
                    rate, depending on whether the origin and
                    destination cities are served by regularly scheduled
                    commercial airline service.[171] This reimbursement
                    rate does not apply to campaign travelers traveling on
                    behalf of a House Leadership PAC or a House,
                    Senate, or presidential campaign.

House and Senate rules that apply to private aircraft travel by members of the House and Senate are discussed below (*see* Q 18.19, *infra*).

Lobbying Activities

Lobbying Disclosure Act of 1995

Q 18.18   What is the Lobbying Disclosure Act of 1995?

The Lobbying Disclosure Act of 1995, as amended (LDA),[172] is a lobbying disclosure and enforcement statute. It requires certain employers to register and disclose their federal lobbying activities in periodic reports.

The guidance that follows applies only to federal lobbying. Each state and some localities have laws and regulations related to lobbying that are likely to be different from the federal rules.

Q 18.18.1   Who must register under the LDA?

The LDA applies to organizations that employ individuals who make more than one "lobbying contact" *and* engage in "lobbying activities" for 20% or more of their time during any quarterly period. There is also a de minimis expense exception, which is discussed below.

> **TIP:** While the 20% analysis applies to a three-month period, the lobbying contact portion of the definition is not time-limited. The practical effect of this is that an individual may make one lobbying contact on behalf of an employer or client without meeting the definition of a lobbyist (not one lobbying contact per quarter).

Q 18.18.2   What are the penalties for violating the LDA?

The Honest Leadership and Open Government Act of 2007 increased penalties for violations of the LDA from $50,000 to $200,000 and now provides for imprisonment of persons who "knowingly and corruptly" fail to comply with the LDA.[173]

Key LDA Definitions

Q 18.18.3   What is a "lobbying contact"?

A lobbying contact includes any oral, written, or electronic communication to a "covered official" regarding the formulation, modification, or adoption of federal legislation, rules, regulations, executive orders, programs, policies, and positions.[174]

Q 18.18.4   What is not a "lobbying contact"?

There are twenty-six exceptions to the definition of lobbying contact, including statements made by public officials in their official capacities, statements made by news organizations, public speeches, articles and publications, contacts on behalf of a foreign country or political party and reported under the Foreign Agents Registration Act of 1938,[175] testimony, information provided in writing in response to a request for information, information required by subpoena, and comments filed in a regulatory or legal proceeding.[176]

Q 18.18.5   What are "lobbying activities"?

Lobbying activities are lobbying contacts and efforts in support of such contacts, including preparation and planning activities, research, and other background work that is intended, *at the time it is performed*, for use in lobbying contacts.[177]

Q 18.18.6   Who is a "lobbyist"?

A lobbyist is any individual who is employed or retained for financial or other compensation for services that include more than one lobbying contact and whose lobbying activities constitute 20% or more of his/her time engaged in services to that client or employer during a quarterly period.[178]

Q 18.18.7   Who is a "covered official"?

As a general rule, almost every legislative branch employee is a covered official, while relatively few executive branch employees are covered officials. A "covered legislative branch official" includes any member, officer, or employee of the House or Senate. A "covered executive branch official" includes the president, the vice president, officers and employees of the Executive Office of the President, any official serving in level I, II, III, IV, or V of the executive schedule, any member of the uniformed services of pay grade 0–7 (one-star general or admiral) and above, and any Schedule C appointee.[179]

TIP: The Internal Revenue Code (IRC) definition of covered executive branch official is narrower than the LDA definition: president, vice president; executive Schedule I (cabinet-level) and immediate deputies; two most senior officers of agencies within the executive office of the president; and officers and employees of the White House Office of the Executive Office of the President.[180] Under certain circumstances, LDA registrants have the option to use the IRC definitions for executive branch covered officials[181] (*see* Q 18.19.2).

Registration and Reporting Under the LDA

Q 18.19   What is the process for registering under the LDA?

A corporation that employs an in-house lobbyist has forty-five days to register under the LDA on behalf of its lobbyist.[182] The forty-five-day period begins when the lobbyist makes a lobbying contact or is hired to make a lobbying contact. If a corporation is already registered under the LDA, it merely needs to add the new lobbyist on its next quarterly LDA report. For corporations that employ an outside lobbyist, responsibility for registration of the outside lobbyist under the LDA rests with the outside lobbyist or lobbying firm. The registration of an outside lobbyist does not obviate the need for the client to register and vice versa.

All LDA registrations must be submitted to both the Clerk of the House of Representatives and the Secretary of the Senate.

For corporations that employ in-house lobbyists, there is a de minimis expense exception from the registration requirements for employees who would otherwise meet the definition of a lobbyist, if the corporation's total expenses in connection with lobbying activities are $12,500[183] or less during the quarterly period. Amounts are adjusted every four years for inflation.[184] Please note this total is for the entire corporation's lobbying expenses, not only the corporate in-house lobbyist's lobbying expenses. A corporation's lobbying expenses include salary, benefits, and overhead for all lobbyists, lobbying hard costs such as travel and meals, the activities of support staff in support of lobbyists, fees paid to outside lobbyists, the portion of trade association dues used for lobbying, and officers' time and expenses related to lobbying.

Q 18.19.1   What are the contents of the LDA registration?

LDA registrations (Form LD-1) must disclose:[185]

- name and contact info;
- effective date;
- any affiliated organizations;
- lobbyist information (including any former covered federal government positions going back twenty years);

- lobbying issues (general and specific); and
- any foreign ownership or interest.

Q 18.19.2 What are the contents of the LDA quarterly reports?

LDA quarterly reports (Form LD-2) must disclose:[186]

- name and contact info;
- House and Senate IDs;
- reporting period;
- lobbying income or expenses (using either the LDA or IRC accounting methods and rounded to the nearest $10,000);
- lobbying issues (general and specific);
- all entities that were lobbied (House, Senate, and/or executive-branch agency);
- which lobbyists lobbied on which issues;
- any foreign interest in lobbying issues; and
- any updates (contact info, lobbyists, issues, affiliated organizations, and foreign entities).

TIP: LDA registrants have the option to use the IRC method for calculating lobbying expenses.[187] LDA registrations may choose either method, but must consistently use the same method throughout the entire calendar year.[188]

Q 18.19.3 What are the contents of the LDA semi-annual report and certification?

The Honest Leadership and Open Government Act of 2007 amended the LDA to require a semi-annual report and certification from registered lobbyists and entities that employ lobbyists.[189] This is in addition to the quarterly reports.

LDA semi-annual reports (Form LD-203) must disclose:[190]

- name and contact info;
- House and Senate IDs;
- reporting period;
- PAC information; and
- certain federal campaign or certain other political contributions.

The report discloses contributions of $200 and over made to federal candidates, leadership PACs, parties, and presidential libraries and inaugurals. The report also discloses all contributions, regardless of amount, made to entities established, maintained, or named for covered officials, events to honor covered officials, and meetings held by covered officials. Contributions made by registered lobbyists, entities that employ lobbyists, or PACs controlled by either must be reported.

LDA semi-annual certifications (also on Form LD-203) must certify:[191]

- compliance with House and Senate gift and travel rules.

The certification states that the registered lobbyist or entity that employs a lobbyist has read and is familiar with the House and Senate gift and travel rules (*see* QQ 18.26–18.28, *infra*) and has not provided, requested, or directed a gift, including travel, to a member, officer, or employee of either house of Congress with knowledge that receipt of said gift would violate the House and Senate gift and travel rules.

This certification is significant, particularly in light of the fact that it is a violation of the LDA for a registered lobbyist or an entity that employs a lobbyist (and is registered under the LDA) to provide a gift in violation of House or Senate rules. Please note that this prohibition extends to all employees, not just lobbyists.

The Clerk of the House and Secretary of the Senate both provide written guidance about the LDA on their respective websites[192] and informal verbal advice over the phone.

TIP: Submitting inaccurate lobbying information could be considered a violation of the LDA and result in fines of up to $200,000 or even the possibility of prison time.[193] Submitting inaccurate information to the legislative branch is also a violation of the federal false statements statute.[194] In addition, the Government Accountability Office (GAO) is now required to perform audits of LDA filings and report the results to Congress.[195] Accordingly, every corporation must implement a program to ensure compliance with the LDA and House and Senate gift and travel rules.

Q 18.19.4   What is the filing schedule under the LDA?

Initial registrations (Form LD-1)	required forty-five days after the lobbyist makes a lobbying contact or is hired to make a lobbying contact[196] (*see* Q 18.19, *supra*).
Quarterly reports (Form LD-2)	due twenty days after the end of the quarterly period.[197]
Semi-annual reports (Form LD-203)	due thirty days after the end of the semi-annual period.[198]
Termination of registration (Form LD-2)	required if no additional lobbying activities are anticipated.[199]

Q 18.19.5   What if my corporation only lobbied the executive branch?

LDA registrations and filings are required regardless of which federal entity is lobbied—the House, Senate, or executive branch.

The LDA does not require any additional filings with the executive branch.

Q 18.19.6   Does an in-house lobbyist for a foreign corporation also need to register under the Foreign Agents Registration Act?

Not necessarily. The LDA and the Foreign Agents Registration Act of 1938 (FARA)[200] are mutually exclusive when it comes to lobbying. An agent of a foreign corporation[201] is exempt from FARA if the agent is engaged in lobbying activities and registered under the LDA.[202] The definition of an "agent of a foreign principal" under FARA is broader than the definition of a "lobbyist" under the LDA, and the FARA exemption only applies to foreign agent lobbying activities. Therefore, registration under only the LDA will not always satisfy the registration requirements of FARA. Agents working on behalf of a foreign government or political party must register under FARA and not under the LDA.

Q 18.20   Has anyone ever been prosecuted for an LDA violation?

Yes. During 2015, the U.S. Attorney's Office for the District of Columbia announced settlements with lobbying firms that include fines of $30,000 and $125,000 for missing LDA reports. In one instance, the lobbyist had been facing the prospect of over $5 million in potential fines related to LDA compliance.[203] Similarly, in December 2013, the U.S. Attorney's Office secured a default judgment of $200,000 against an LDA registrant that ignored multiple communications from Congress and the U.S. Attorney's Office.[204] Since 2007, the U.S. Attorney's Office has entered into settlements three times—once in 2011 for $45,000, and twice in 2012, for $50,000 and $30,000. Previously, from 1995 to 2007, the U.S. Attorney's Office for the District of Columbia had settled three other LDA enforcement cases for undisclosed amounts.

To date, the Senate has referred 14,010 or more potential LDA violations to the U.S. Attorney for the District of Columbia,[205] resulting in the aforementioned prosecutions, as well as others against individuals under related statutes for post-employment lobbying violations[206] and making false statements to Congress.[207] In addition, according to a GAO LDA report issued in April 2013, the U.S.

Attorney's Office is pursuing criminal penalties for LDA violations for the first time.[208] Finally, the 2014 Second Quarter report from the Office of Congressional Ethics (OCE) indicates that an "entity" has been referred to the U.S. Attorney's Office for failure to register under the LDA. This would appear to be the first time an LDA investigation involved an unregistered lobbyist.

Q 18.21   Will my LDA reports be audited by GAO?

It is very likely GAO will eventually audit at least one LDA report for each registered entity. The GAO has audited over 2,000 LDA filings since 2007.

> **TIP:** During an LDA audit, the GAO currently reviews the following information: lobbying income/expenses, issues lobbied, federal entities lobbied, individual lobbyists, covered positions of lobbyists, foreign entity involvement, individuals no longer expected to lobby, lobbying coalition or association members, open source materials, and FEC records. The LDA contains no specific record-keeping requirement, but it is a best practice to develop and maintain a set of records related to LDA filings that can be turned over to the GAO in case of an audit. These records should include: copies of the past six years' worth of LDA filings, a document detailing the methodology for estimating lobbying income/expenses, a document outlining the issues and entities lobbied, a document detailing individual lobbyist activities, a document outlining the LDA compliance program, and any relevant records such as invoices, expense reimbursements, employee certifications, and time entries. These records should be reviewed and updated in connection with each filing.

Q 18.22   What should an LDA compliance program include?

The following procedures are currently considered industry best practices for an LDA compliance program:

- ensuring all filings are complete, accurate, and submitted on time;
- amending any defective filings in a timely manner;
- responding to any inquiries from the Secretary of the Senate, Clerk of the House, DOJ, or GAO in a timely manner;
- developing and maintaining a set of records to be turned over in case of a GAO audit or DOJ investigation;
- notifying employees regarding the LDA and House and Senate gift and travel rules;
- providing employees with current copies of House and Senate gift and travel rules;
- providing key employees with annual compliance training and updates;
- updating and reviewing internal policies to ensure consistency with the LDA and House and Senate gift and travel rules;
- creating reimbursement certifications regarding House and Senate gift and travel rules;
- collecting accurate LDA data;
- requiring employee House and Senate gift and travel certifications; and
- consulting with counsel on a regular basis.

The structure and complexity of the compliance program can vary depending on the size and level of lobbying activities of the organization. It is recommended that a structure closely akin to the guidance of the U.S. Sentencing Commission on effective compliance and ethics programs be used. (For more on the basic structure of a compliance and ethics program, see chapters 1–5.)

Executive Branch Lobbying Restrictions

Q 18.23   Does the executive branch have any lobbying restrictions?

Executive Order 13490. On January 21, 2009, President Obama issued Executive Order 13490, which banned most gifts from lobbyists and imposed lobbying restrictions. The executive order applies to every full-time, non-career presidential or vice-presidential appointee, non-career Senior Executive Service appointee, or

Schedule C appointee in the executive branch. The key provisions of the executive order are:

1. A ban on gifts to political appointees from lobbyists registered under the LDA;
2. A ban on any political appointee (not just former lobbyists) working on particular matters as a government employee involving specific parties that is directly and substantially related to a former employer or former client in the private sector;
3. A ban on former lobbyists:
   (a) participating in any particular matter lobbied on during the previous two years;
   (b) participating in a specific issue area lobbied on during the previous two years;
   (c) seeking or accepting employment with any executive branch agency lobbied during the previous two years.
4. Extension of the post-employment ban on communicating with employees of the political appointee's former agency contained in 18 U.S.C. § 207(c) from one year to two years;
5. A ban on former employees lobbying any executive branch official or non-career Senior Executive Service appointee for the remainder of the Obama administration.

The EO does provide for waivers of these provisions if the director of the Office of Management and Budget (OMB) deems the waiver to be in the public interest.

Advisory Committee Ban. On October 5, 2011, OMB issued final guidance prohibiting registered lobbyists from being appointed or reappointed to serve on federal boards and commissions.[209] However, a group of lobbyists and former advisory committee members has challenged the ban on First Amendment grounds in the U.S. District Court for the District of Columbia. Although initially dismissed by the district court for failure to state a claim, the U.S. Court of Appeals for the District of Columbia Circuit reversed on the appeal,[210] and on August 18, 2014, OMB issued revised guidance allowing federally registered lobbyists to serve on advisory committees, boards, or commissions so long as they are not acting in an "individual capacity."[211]

House and Senate Gift and Travel Rules

Q 18.24   Who is subject to the House and Senate gift and travel rules?

In addition to the requirements of the LDA, every corporation that has contact with the members or employees of the House of Representatives or the Senate must be aware of relevant House and Senate rules. Registered lobbyists and the entities that employ them can be punished for inducing a member or employee of the House or Senate to accept a gift or travel that violates House or Senate rules.[212] The Honest Leadership and Open Government Act of 2007 provides for fines of up to $200,000 and prison time for knowing and corrupt violations.[213]

Q 18.24.1   Do other government entities have their own rules?

The guidance provided below applies only to House and Senate rules. The executive branch has different rules and each state and some localities have laws, regulations, and rules related to ethics that are likely to be different from the congressional rules.

Q 18.24.2   Are House and Senate rules the same?

No. The House and Senate have similar, but not identical, rules. Corporations must be familiar with both sets of rules. Even when the rules are identical, the House and Senate ethics committees may interpret their rules differently.

Q 18.24.3   How can a corporation obtain information about House and Senate rules?

The House Committee on Ethics (http://ethics.house.gov/) and the Senate Select Committee on Ethics (http://ethics.senate.gov/) both provide guidance about the ethics rules and status updates on rules changes. Both committees will also provide formal and informal ethics advice.

Corporations should seek advice from both committees and from counsel prior to providing any gift or travel to any member, officer, or employee of the House or Senate.

Q 18.25   What House and Senate rules should a corporation be aware of?

At a minimum, every corporation must be familiar with the rules surrounding gifts and travel.

Gift Rule

Q 18.26   What is the gift rule?

The basic rule is that members of Congress and their staffs may not accept any gifts, unless it is allowed by the rules.[214]

Q 18.26.1   What is a "gift"?

A "gift" is "any gratuity, favor, discount, entertainment, hospitality, loan, forbearance, or other item having monetary value."[215] Food and drink, local transportation, travel, and attendance at events are included in this definition.

TIP: Members or employees may not accept a gift offered in appreciation for official action because it could be considered bribery or an illegal gratuity under federal law.[216]

Q 18.26.2   What gifts are acceptable?

Single gifts valued at $49.99 or less, or multiple gifts valued at $99.99 or less from the same source in one calendar year, are generally allowed unless from a prohibited source (see discussion of gifts from registered lobbyists below).[217]

Q 18.26.3   What are some relevant exceptions to the gift rule?

- Campaign contributions;[218]
- Anything provided on the basis of personal friendship;[219]
- Food or drink provided at a fundraiser or campaign event;[220]
- Home-state products;[221]
- Free attendance at a "widely attended event";[222]
- Free attendance at a charity fundraising event;[223]

- A commemorative item;[224]
- Food or drink of a nominal value;[225] and
- An item of little intrinsic value such as a baseball cap or T-shirt.[226]

Note that this list is not exhaustive.

Q 18.26.4   May a lobbyist provide a gift?

The new House and Senate rules[227] prohibit members and employees from accepting a "gift" from a registered lobbyist or a private entity that employs a registered lobbyist unless the gift qualifies under a relevant exception to the gift rule.[228] Several gift rule exceptions apply to lobbyists, including personal friendship, widely attended events, commemorative items, and the reception exception. However, certain gift rule exceptions are not available to lobbyists, including officially connected travel, gifts of personal hospitality, and contributions to legal defense funds. In addition, a lobbyist may not make a charitable contribution to an entity that is maintained or controlled by a member, officer, or employee of Congress.[229]

Q 18.26.5   What is the "personal friendship" exception?

A gift that qualifies for the "personal friendship" exception[230] is not considered a gift under House or Senate rules. However, to qualify for this exception:

- the gift must be given on the basis of the personal friendship;[231] and
- the gift giver must not seek a business reimbursement or tax deduction.[232]

Other factors to consider are whether there is a history of gift-giving and if the gift giver provided similar gifts to other members or employees.[233]

A gift given on the basis of personal friendship may not exceed $250 without first seeking permission from the House Committee on Standards of Official Conduct or the Senate Select Committee on Ethics.[234]

Q 18.26.6   What is the "widely attended event" exception to the gift rule?

This allows members and employees to accept free attendance at an event, including a meal.[235] In order to qualify for the widely attended event[236] exception:

- at least twenty-five individuals from outside Congress must reasonably be expected to attend the event;[237] and
- attendance must be open to members throughout a given industry or profession or to a range of persons interested in an issue.[238]

Once it has been determined that the event is widely attended:

- the member or employee must be a speaker or participant in the event;[239] or
- the event must be appropriate to the official duties or representative function of the member or employee;[240] and
- the invitation must come from the sponsor of this event.[241]

"Free attendance" includes:

- food or drink;
- attendance of one guest (need not be a family member); and
- local transportation.

"Free attendance" does not include:

- entertainment collateral to the event; and
- food or drink provided outside the event.

Q 18.26.7   What is the "charitable event" exception?[242]

Free attendance at a charity event (lunches, dinners, golf or tennis tournaments, races, and cook-offs) is not a gift. In order to qualify as a charitable event:

- the primary purpose of the event must be to raise funds for an organization that is qualified under section 170(c) of the IRC to receive tax-deductible contributions;
- the invitation must come from the event sponsor/organizer (not from the purchaser of a table).

"Free attendance" includes:

- food or drink;
- attendance for a spouse or dependent;
- local transportation; and
- travel expenses, unless the event is "substantially recreational" (and then only local transportation expenses may be accepted).

"Free attendance" does not include:

- entertainment collateral to the event; and
- food or drink taken outside the event.

Q 18.26.8   What is the "commemorative item" exception to the gift rule?

Members and employees may accept a plaque, trophy, or other item that is commemorative in nature and is intended solely for presentation.[243] However, to qualify for this exception, the item must truly be commemorative. Merely placing a plaque on an otherwise useful item such as a golf club or car will not qualify the item for this exception.

Q 18.26.9   What is the "food or drink of a nominal value" exception to the gift rule?

Food or drink of a nominal value not offered as part of a meal may be accepted by members and employees.[244] This is what is commonly known as the "reception exception." Light hors d'œuvres and drinks are standard practice for these types of events. A buffet or sit-down meal will not qualify for this exception.

Travel Rules

Q 18.27   What are the rules for travel?

Expenses paid by a private source for necessary transportation, lodging, and necessary expenses for "officially connected" travel are deemed to be a reimbursement to the House of Representatives or the Senate and not a gift.[245]

Q 18.27.1   What is "officially connected" travel?

It is travel to a meeting, speaking engagement, fact-finding trip, or similar event in connection with a member or employee's duties as an officeholder. This type of travel should not be confused with travel that is paid for by the federal government or by a state or local government,[246] or campaign travel that is paid for by a political committee.[247] The discussion that follows applies only to officially connected travel.

Officially connected travel in the contiguous forty-eight states may not exceed three days under Senate rules and four days under House rules.[248] Travel outside of the contiguous forty-eight states may not exceed seven days.[249]

Officially connected travel may not be "substantially recreational." For example, members and staff may not be reimbursed for golf, tennis, fishing, or skiing.[250]

House and Senate employees must seek advance approval for officially connected travel from the member or officer for whom they work.[251] House members and staff must disclose all travel expenses within fifteen days, while the Senate allows thirty days.[252]

Q 18.27.2   What are "necessary expenses"?

These include "reasonable expenditures for transportation, lodging, conference fees and materials, and food and refreshments."[253] There is no dollar limit on expenses, but they must be "reasonable."

Q 18.27.3   Who may pay for officially connected travel?

Registered lobbyists, private entities that retain or employ registered lobbyists, lobbying firms,[254] and agents of a foreign principal may not pay for officially connected travel.[255]

A corporation that does not retain or employ a registered lobbyist may still pay for officially connected travel.[256] Corporations that retain or employ registered lobbyists may still pay for "One-Day Event Trips."[257]

Q 18.27.4   What are the rules for "One-Day Event Trips"?

- No registered lobbyist may participate in the event;[258]
- A registered lobbyist's involvement in planning, organizing, requesting, or arranging the trip must be de minimis;[259]
- The sponsor must provide written certification as to the funding for and lobbyist involvement with the trip;[260]
- Prior approval must be provided by the Ethics Committees;[261]
- The event must be limited to a single calendar day (exclusive of travel time and an overnight stay);
- A second night's stay will be considered when practically required; and
- The trip may be paid for by entities that retain or employ lobbyists (but not by lobbyists).

 CASE STUDY: Congressional Travel Expenses

On April 14, 2011, the DOJ announced that the CEO of a newspaper publishing company pled guilty to a felony for submitting a Private Sponsor Travel Certification Form to the House of Representatives that contained false statements.[262] The certification claimed that the company alone paid for members' travel expenses to an annual business conference in the Caribbean—and failed to mention that the source of the funds included the foreign host country and a private corporation. The company executive was eventually sentenced to two years' probation, 500 hours of community service, and fined $2,500.

Private Aircraft

Q 18.28   What are the House and Senate rules for travel on private aircraft?

House. Members of the House may not use personal funds, official funds, or campaign funds to pay for a flight on private aircraft.[263]

Under certain circumstances, members may fly on their own aircraft or an aircraft owned by a family member.

Senate. Senators must reimburse the pro rata share of the fair market value of the normal and usual charter fare or rental charge for a comparable aircraft of comparable size, as determined by dividing such costs by the number of members, officers, or employees of Congress on the flight.[264] The Senate Rules Committee has provided additional guidance for flights on private aircraft.[265]

Campaign finance regulations that apply to private aircraft travel by federal candidates are discussed above (*see* Q 18.17.2, *supra*).

State and Local Governments

Q 18.29   What do corporations need to know about state and local laws and regulations?

Each state and some localities have laws and regulations related to campaign finance, lobbying, and ethics that may be different from the federal rules. For example, the majority of states allow corporate campaign contributions, while the federal government does not. Also, some states and localities have implemented "pay-to-play" laws restricting or prohibiting contributions or gifts from government contractors.

Federal law preempts state campaign finance laws in two cases:

- Contributions from foreign nationals, unless an immigrant lawfully admitted for permanent residence in the United States,[266] are prohibited.[267]
- Contributions from corporations organized by a specific law of Congress and national banks are prohibited.[268]

These prohibitions are absolute and apply to federal, state, and local candidates.

State and local laws and regulations are constantly changing. Some are less restrictive than federal laws, while others are more restrictive. The National Conference of State Legislatures (NCSL) maintains an overview of state laws on its website (www.ncsl.org). For more detailed information, consult with the relevant state or local regulating body and/or with counsel.

Pay-to-Play Laws

Q 18.30   What are pay-to-play laws?

Pay-to-play laws ban, restrict, or require disclosure of campaign contributions or gifts by government contractors. While all jurisdictions prohibit bribery, pay-to-play laws go beyond these restrictions to regulate otherwise legal political activity. Congress enacted a federal pay-to-play law in 1940 and made revisions to this law in 1971. California passed the original state pay-to-play law in 1982. Most current pay-to-play laws trace their origin to Municipal Securities Rulemaking Board (MSRB) Rule G-37, approved by the SEC in 1994.[269]

Q 18.30.1   Does the federal government have pay-to-play laws?

At the federal level, the Federal Election Campaign Act of 1971, as amended, prohibits federal contractors from making direct or indirect contributions to political parties, federal candidates, or "any person for any political purpose or use."[270] In addition, the SEC,[271] MSRB,[272] and Commodity Futures Trading Commission (CFTC)[273] have pay-to-play rules. The MSRB was considering an additional pay-to-play rule[274] but withdrew proposed Rule G-42 in September 2011.

Q 18.30.2   Which states have pay-to-play laws?

States with some form of pay-to-play law include:

California	Louisiana	Ohio
Connecticut	Maryland	Pennsylvania
Florida	Michigan	Rhode Island
Hawaii	Missouri	South Carolina
Illinois	Nebraska	Vermont
Indiana	New Jersey	Virginia
Kentucky	New Mexico	West Virginia

Q 18.30.3   Which localities have pay-to-play laws?

Localities with some form of pay-to-play law include:

Albuquerque, NM	Denver, CO	Oakland, CA
Boston, MA	Grand Rapids, MI	Pasadena, CA
Buffalo, NY	Houston, TX	Philadelphia, PA
Chicago, IL	Indianapolis, IN	Salt Lake County, UT
Columbia, SC	Jefferson Parrish, LA	San Antonio, TX
Cook County, IL	Los Angeles City/ County, CA	San Francisco, CA
Culver City, CA	New Orleans, LA	Suffolk County, NY
Dallas, TX	New York City, NY	many localities in New Jersey

Note that, in addition to local ordinances, state law may also apply at the local level.

Q 18.30.4   Do any other entities have pay-to-play laws?

Certain state investment funds and quasi-governmental entities have enacted pay-to-play restrictions, including:

- California Public Employees Retirement System;
- California State Teachers Retirement System;
- California State Lottery;
- Delaware River Port Authority;
- Los Angeles County Metropolitan Transit Authority;
- New Jersey State Investment Council;
- New Mexico State Investment Council, Private Equity Investment Advisory Committee, and State Investment Office;
- New York Comptroller and Common Retirement Fund; and
- Texas Teacher Retirement System.

Q 18.31   How does pay-to-play disclosure work?

Many states require pay-to-play certification and/or disclosure as part of the procurement process. However, certain states, including Maryland,[275] New Jersey,[276] and Pennsylvania,[277] require pay-to-play reporting, and Illinois[278] requires registration outside the procurement process.

Q 18.32   What should a pay-to-play compliance program include?

Pay-to-play laws present some unique compliance challenges. Often it is unclear whether responsibility for pay-to-play compliance should be assigned to government affairs, government contracting, or the general counsel's office. In addition, pay-to-play laws are a moving target, as new laws are being enacted, repealed, and/or altered on a regular basis. However, it is clear that government contractors must implement a pay-to-play compliance program— either as a stand-alone program or as part of a larger corporate compliance program. The actions of just one employee can cause significant legal and financial problems for an entire corporation.

While pay-to-play compliance programs must be tailored to each specific situation, there are several steps that government contractors can take to ensure a baseline level of compliance. Ideally, a pay-to-play compliance program will be integrated into a larger compliance program. Some of the basic procedures to incorporate into a pay-to-play compliance program include the following:

Designate a single pay-to-play point of contact. A single designated employee should be the internal repository of pay-to-play information, coordinate all pay-to-play filings and certifications, and vet proposed contributions in consultation with counsel. This employee does not necessarily need to be located in the general counsel's office, but the general counsel's office and/or outside counsel should be involved.

Provide notice. Individual officers, board members, or employees who may be covered by pay-to-play laws should be provided with annual notice. These individuals must be notified that pay-to-play laws may apply to their personal contributions and to contributions made by their spouse and children and that they must coordinate any contributions with the designated pay-to-play contact.

Provide annual training. Government contractors should provide annual pay-to-play training to relevant employees. This training can be provided internally; however, the pay-to-play point of contact should also attend external training.

Update internal policies. Compliance with pay-to-play laws should be made a condition of employment.

Update expense procedures. Expense forms should be updated to require a certification that the payment does not represent a contribution in violation of pay-to-play laws.

Consider requiring pre-clearance of contributions. This will be unpopular, but may be necessary in some cases.

Require an annual certification. Certain employees should be required to sign an annual statement certifying compliance with pay-to-play laws.

The structure and complexity of the compliance program can vary depending on the size and level of lobbying activities of the organization. It is recommended that a structure closely akin to the guidance of the U.S. Sentencing Commission on effective compliance and ethics programs be used. (For more on the basic structure of a compliance and ethics program, see chapters 1–5.)

Notes to Chapter 18

1.   *See* Matt Zapotosky & Matea Gold, *Republican Operative Sentenced to 2 Years in Landmark Election Case*, WASH. POST, June 12, 2015.
2.   *See* Settlement Agreement, United States v. Alan Mauk Assocs. Ltd., No. 1:14-cv-00409 (D.D.C. Jan. 30, 2015).
3.   *See* Judgment, United States v. Biassi Bus. Servs., Inc., No. 1:13-cv-00853 (D.D.C. Dec. 2, 2013); *see also* Complaint, United States v. Biassi Bus. Servs., Inc., Civil Action No. 13-0853 (D.D.C. June 7, 2013); Christopher DeLacy & John S. Irving IV, *U.S. Attorney Seeks $33 Million Lobbying Disclosure Act Penalty*, HOLLAND & KNIGHT ALERT, June 13, 2013, at 1, www.hklaw.com/publications/US-Attorney-Seeks-33-Million-Lobbying-Disclosure-Act-Penalty-06-13-2013/.
4.   Press Release No. 11-477, U.S. Dep't of Justice, Newspaper Publisher Pleads Guilty to Making False Statement to Congress (Apr. 14, 2011), www.justice.gov/opa/pr/2011/April/11-crm-477.html.
5.   Press Release No. 11-371, U.S. Dep't of Justice, Former Administrative Assistant to U.S. Senator Charged with Making Prohibited Communications to Senate Office (Mar. 24, 2011), www.justice.gov/opa/pr/2011/March/11-crm-371.html.
6.   Citizens United v. Fed. Election Comm'n, 558 U.S. 310 (2010).
7.   Office of Congressional Ethics, Statement of the Office of Congressional Ethics Regarding Evidence Collected in OCE's PMA Investigation (May 27, 2010), http://oce.house.gov/disclosures/OCE_PMA_statement_05-27-2010.pdf.
8.   Tillman Act of 1907, Pub. L. No. 59-36, 34 Stat. 864; 52 U.S.C. § 30118(a); 11 C.F.R. § 114.2(b)(1).
9.   52 U.S.C. § 30118.
10.   *Id.* § 30119.
11.   *Id.* §§ 30118, 30121.
12.   "Soft money" is money not raised in accordance with the Federal Election Campaign Act of 1971; Pub. L. No. 92-225, 86 Stat. 9 (1972).
13.   52 U.S.C. § 431(16); 11 C.F.R. § 100.13; 52 U.S.C. § 30125.
14.   Pub. L. No. 107-155, 116 Stat. 95 (2002).
15.   11 C.F.R. § 114.2(f) (2007).
16.   52 U.S.C. §§ 30118(a), 30122; 11 C.F.R. § 114.2(e).
17.   Nat'l Conference of State Legislatures, State Limits on Contributions to Candidates 2015–2016 Election Cycle (updated Oct. 2015), www.ncsl.org/Portals/1/documents/legismgt/elect/ContributionLimitstoCandidates2015-2016.pdf.
18.   11 C.F.R. § 110.20.
19.   52 U.S.C. § 30118; 11 C.F.R. § 114.5.
20.   11 C.F.R. §§ 114.3, 114.4.
21.   *Id.* § 114.3(c)(2).
22.   Campaign Travel, 74 Fed. Reg. 63,951 (Dec. 7, 2009).

23. 11 C.F.R. §§ 110.1, 110.2, 110.20, 114.2; 52 U.S.C. §§ 30116, 30118, 30121.
24. A "political committee" is any group of people who receive $1,000 or more in contributions and make $1,000 or more in expenditures in connection with a federal election in a year; a Separate Segregated Fund (SSF); or a local political party or a candidate's campaign. 52 U.S.C. § 30101(4); 11 C.F.R. § 100.5.
25. 11 C.F.R. § 100.5(e).
26. Pub. L. No. 92-225.
27. 52 U.S.C. § 30118; 11 C.F.R. § 114.2(b)(1).
28. 52 U.S.C. § 30118(b)(2)(C); 11 C.F.R. § 114.5.
29. An immigrant lawfully admitted for permanent residence in the United States is an immigrant with a "green card." A "green card" is a U.S. government–issued identification card indicating lawful admittance for permanent residence in the United States as defined by 8 U.S.C. § 1101(a)(20).
30. 52 U.S.C. § 30121; 11 C.F.R. § 110.20.
31. Yamaha Motor Corp., FEC Advisory Opinion AO 2013-19 (Oct. 30, 2013); Allison Engine Co. PAC, FEC Advisory Opinion AO 1995-15 (June 30, 1995); CIT Grp. Holdings, Inc., FEC Advisory Opinion AO 1990-08 (June 18, 1990); GEM PAC, FEC Advisory Opinion AO 1989-29 (Dec. 19, 1989); Kuiluma Dev. Co., FEC Advisory Opinion AO 1989-20 (Oct. 27, 1989).
32. 52 U.S.C. § 30118(b)(2)(C); 11 C.F.R. §§ 114.5(a)(2)(iii), 114.5(b).
33. An SSF must reimburse the corporation for any portion of fundraising prizes or entertainment that exceeds one-third of the amount raised in contributions. 11 C.F.R. § 114.5(b)(2).
34. 52 U.S.C. § 30118(b)(2)(C); 11 C.F.R. §§ 114.1(b), 114.5(b).
35. Boeing Co., FEC Advisory Opinion AO 1991-36 (Jan. 10, 1992).
36. A lawful source for a PAC is an individual who is a U.S. citizen or is a permanent resident alien (*i.e.*, has a green card) or another PAC. 52 U.S.C. §§ 30116, 30121; 11 C.F.R. § 110.20.
37. 52 U.S.C. § 30118(b)(4)(A)(i); 11 C.F.R. § 114.2(j).
38. 11 C.F.R. § 114.6; 52 U.S.C. § 30118(4)(B).
39. 52 U.S.C. § 30118(b)(3)(A); 11 C.F.R. § 114.5(a).
40. 52 U.S.C. § 30118(b)(3)(B), (C); 11 C.F.R. § 114.5(a)(3), (4).
41. 11 C.F.R. § 114.5(a)(2).
42. *Id.*
43. 26 U.S.C. § 613.
44. 11 C.F.R. § 114.1(c).
45. 29 C.F.R. § 541.
46. 11 C.F.R. § 114.1(h); *see also* Ashland, Inc. PAC, FEC Advisory Opinion AO 1998-12 (July 16, 1998); USX PAC, FEC Advisory Opinion AO 1996-10 (May 10, 1996); Science Applications Int'l Corp., FEC Advisory Opinion AO 1994-36 (Mar. 24, 1995); Consumers Power Co., FEC Advisory Opinion AO 1994-27 (Oct. 4, 1994).
47. Members of the board of directors who are not shareholders must receive regular compensation. *See* Weirton Steel Corp., FEC Advisory Opinion AO 1985-35 (Nov. 22, 1985).
48. 11 C.F.R. § 114.1(f).

49. Statement of Policy; Recordkeeping Requirements for Payroll Deduction Authorizations, 71 Fed. Reg. 38,513 (July 7, 2006).
50. *Id.*
51. 52 U.S.C. § 30102(a); *see also* 11 C.F.R. §§ 102.2(iv), 102.7.
52. 52 U.S.C. § 30102(h); 11 C.F.R. § 102.5.
53. FEC Form 1; 52 U.S.C. § 30103; 11 C.F.R. § 102.1(c).
54. FEC Form 3X; 52 U.S.C. § 30104(a)(4); 11 C.F.R. § 104.5.
55. 52 U.S.C. § 30102(a); 11 C.F.R. § 102.7(a).
56. 52 U.S.C. § 30104(a)(4); 11 C.F.R. § 104.5.
57. 52 U.S.C. § 30104(b)(3)(A); 11 C.F.R. § 104.8.
58. 52 U.S.C. § 30104(b)(3)(B); 11 C.F.R. §§ 104.9, 104.3(b)(3).
59. 11 C.F.R. § 104.5.
60. *Id.* § 100.5(e)(3).
61. FEC Form 1M; 11 C.F.R. § 102.2(a)(3).
62. 52 U.S.C. § 30116(a)(1)(C); 11 C.F.R. § 110.1(d).
63. 52 U.S.C. § 30116(a)(4); 11 C.F.R. § 110.2. Non-multi-candidate PACs are limited to the contribution limit for a person—currently $2,700 per candidate per election, $10,000 per year to state parties, and $33,400 per year to national parties. 52 U.S.C. § 30116(a)(1)(A); 11 C.F.R. § 110.1; Price Index Adjustments for Contribution Expenditure Limits and Lobbyist Bundling Disclosure Threshold, 80 Fed. Reg. 5750 (Feb. 3, 2015). Non-multi-candidate PAC contribution limits are indexed for inflation. *See* 52 U.S.C. § 30116(c)(1)(C); 11 C.F.R. § 110.17(b)(1).
64. 11 C.F.R. § 110.2.
65. *Id.* § 100.2.
66. *Id.* § 110.2(c), (d).
67. *Id.* § 110.1.
68. 52 U.S.C. § 30102(a); 11 C.F.R. § 102.7.
69. 52 U.S.C. § 30102(c); 11 C.F.R. § 102.9.
70. Statement of Policy Regarding Treasurers Subject to Enforcement Proceedings, 70 Fed. Reg. 3 (Jan. 3, 2007).
71. 52 U.S.C. § 30102(17); 11 C.F.R. § 100.22.
72. Buckley v. Valeo, 424 U.S. 1 (1976).
73. *Id.* at 44.
74. To assist in this determination, the FCC has created the Electioneering Communications Database, which is available on the FCC website at http://gull-foss2.fcc.gov/ecd.
75. 52 U.S.C. § 30118(b)(2), (c); 11 C.F.R. §§ 100.29(a), 114.2(b)(iii).
76. 11 C.F.R. § 100.29(b)(3)(ii).
77. 11 C.F.R. § 109.
78. *Id.* § 109.20 *et seq.*
79. 52 U.S.C. § 30118(b)(2)(A); 11 C.F.R. § 114.3.
80. 52 U.S.C. § 30118(b)(2)(A); 11 C.F.R. § 114.2(b)(2)(ii).
81. 52 U.S.C. § 30118(b)(2)(A); 11 C.F.R. § 114.2(4)(ii).
82. 11 C.F.R. § 100.134(a).
83. *Id.* § 114.2(f).
84. *Id.* § 114.3(c)(1)(ii).

85. *Id.* §§ 109.20, 109.21.
86. *Id.* § 114.2(f)(2)(C).
87. 52 U.S.C. § 30118(b)(2); 11 C.F.R. §§ 114.2(b)(iii), 104.4, 114.5(i).
88. 11 C.F.R. § 114.4.
89. *Id.* § 114.4(c)(6).
90. Citizens United v. Fed. Election Comm'n, 558 U.S. 310 (2010).
91. 52 U.S.C. § 30118.
92. *Id.* § 30118(b)(2).
93. Austin v. Mich. Chamber of Commerce, 494 U.S. 652 (1990).
94. McConnell v. Fed. Election Comm'n, 540 U.S. 93 (2003).
95. 52 U.S.C. § 30104.
96. Am. Tradition P'ship, Inc. v. Bullock, 132 S. Ct. 2490, 2491 (2012).
97. News Release, Fed. Election Comm'n, FEC Votes on Two Drafts of an NPRM on Independent Expenditures and Electioneering Communications, Approves Final Audit Report (Jan. 20, 2011), http://fec.gov/press/20110120Open-Meeting.shtml.
98. FEC certification of 3-3 vote on Agenda Document 11-41 (Dec. 16, 2011).
99. Independent Expenditures and Electioneering Communications by Corporations and Labor Organizations, 79 Fed. Reg. 62,797 (Oct. 21, 2014).
100. FCC regulations require that all paid communications include the following disclaimer notice: "Paid for by ____." Section 315 of the Communications Act of 1934 requires broadcasters to maintain a public file for any requests for paid programming, including third-party ads, that refer to a legally qualified candidate, a federal election, or a national legislative issue of public importance. The file should include information such as whether the ad actually ran, the rate charged, and any free time provided to candidates. A list of the chief executive officers or members of the board of directors of the entity purchasing the ad must also be placed in the public file.
101. McConnell v. Fed. Election Comm'n, 540 U.S. 93 (2003).
102. Fed. Election Comm'n v. Wis. Right to Life, Inc., 551 U.S. 449 (2007).
103. 11 C.F.R. § 109.10(b).
104. *Id.* § 109.10(c).
105. *Id.* § 109.10(d).
106. *Id.* § 104.20.
107. Section 315 of the Communications Act of 1934 requires broadcasters to maintain a public file for any requests for paid programming, including third-party ads, that refer to a legally qualified candidate, a federal election, or a national legislative issue of public importance.
108. All nonprofit corporations annually disclose certain lobbying and political information on IRS Form 990.
109. 11 C.F.R. § 110.11.
110. Home Depot, Inc., SEC No-Action Letter (Mar. 25, 2011), www.sec.gov/divisions/corpfin/cf-noaction/14a-8/2011/northstarasset032511-14a8.pdf.
111. *See* Committee on Disclosure of Corporate Political Spending Petition for Rulemaking (Aug. 3, 2011), www.sec.gov/rules/petitions/2011/petn4-637.pdf.

112. *See Comments on Rulemaking Petition: Petition to require public companies to disclose to shareholders the use of corporate resources for political activities [File No. 4-637]*, U.S. SEC. & EXCH. COMM'N (June 13, 2014), www.sec.gov/comments/4-637/4-637.shtml.

113. *See* Office of Info. & Regulatory Affairs, RIN 3235-AL36, Disclosure Regarding the Use of Corporate Resources for Political Activities, www.reginfo.gov/public/do/eAgendaViewRule?pubId=201210&RIN=3235-AL36.

114. *See* Lucian Bebchuck & Robert Jackson, *The SEC Delays Its Consideration of Rules Requiring Disclosure of Corporate Political Spending*, HARV. L. SCH. FORUM ON CORP. GOVERNANCE & FIN. REG. (Dec. 2, 2013, 9:46 AM), https://blogs.law.harvard.edu/corpgov/tag/rulemaking-petition-on-corporate-political-spending/.

115. REG 2011-01, Independent Expenditure Reporting (2011).

116. Federal Election Commission Statement, Statement of Chair Cynthia L. Bauerly and Commissioner Steven T. Walther regarding Notices of Proposed Rulemakings to Address *Citizens United* (Dec. 15, 2011), www.fec.gov/members/statements/Statement_of_Bauerly_and_Walther_on_CU_Petition_NPRMs.pdf.

117. Van Hollen, Jr. v. Fed. Election Comm'n, 811 F.3d 486 (D.C. Cir. 2016), *rev'g* 74 F. Supp. 3d 407 (D.D.C. 2014).

118. Announcement No. 12-44, Fed. Commc'ns Comm'n, FCC Modernizes Broadcast Television Public Inspection Files to Give the Public Online Access to Information Previously Available Only at TV Stations (Apr. 27, 2012), www.fcc.gov/document/fcc-adopts-rules-transitioning-television-public-files-online.

119. Guidance for Tax-Exempt Social Welfare Organizations on Candidate-Related Political Activities, 78 Fed. Reg. 71,535 (proposed Nov. 23, 2013); Consolidated Appropriations Act, 2016, Pub. L. No. 114-113, 129 Stat. 2242, 2433 (2015).

120. Perry Bacon Jr. & T.W. Farnam, *Obama Weighs Disclosure Order for Contractors*, WASH. POST (Apr. 20, 2011), www.washingtonpost.com/politics/obama-weighs-disclosure-order-for-contractors/2011/04/20/AFBw7qEE_story.html.

121. Mike Lillis, *White House Abandons Push for Federal Contractors to Disclose Political Giving*, THE HILL (Mar. 8, 2012), http://thehill.com/homenews/administration/220453-white-house-abandons-push-for-disclosure-of-political-giving-by-contractors.

122. 52 U.S.C. § 30121.

123. *Id.* § 30119.

124. *Id.* § 30118.

125. *Id.*

126. 11 C.F.R. §§ 109.20, 109.21 (2012).

127. *See also* Citizens United v. Fed. Election Comm'n, 558 U.S. 310 (2010); SpeechNow.org v. Fed. Election Comm'n, 599 F.3d 686 (D.C. Cir. 2010); Carey v. Fed. Election Comm'n, 791 F. Supp. 2d 121 (D.D.C. 2011).

128. 11 C.F.R. §§ 109.10(e)(1)(vi), 104.20(c)(9). Section 501(c)(4) or 501(c)(6) entities must submit annual Form 990 information returns to the IRS disclosing donor information; however, the IRS will redact the name and address of the donor before making the Form 990 public.

129. Citizens United v. Fed. Election Comm'n, 558 U.S. 310 (2010).

130. SpeechNow.org v. Fed. Election Comm'n, 599 F.3d 686 (D.C. Cir. 2010).

131. FEC AO 2010-11, Commonsense Ten (July 22, 2010), http://saos.nictusa.com/saos/searchao?AONUMBER=2010-11.

132. Carey v. Fed. Election Comm'n, 791 F. Supp. 2d 121 (D.D.C. 2011).

133. SEC Litigation Release No. 18,740 (June 9, 2004), www.sec.gov/litigation/litreleases/lr18740.htm.

134. *See* House Rule XXV(5)(e)(1), Senate Rule 35, 2 U.S.C. § 1613; 5 C.F.R. §§ 2635.702, 2635.808(c).

135. 2 U.S.C. § 1604(d).

136. 52 U.S.C. § 30116(a)(1)(A); 11 C.F.R. § 110.l(b); News Release, Fed. Election Comm'n, FEC Chart: 2015–2016 Campaign Cycle Contribution Limits (Mar. 20, 2015) [hereinafter FEC News Release], www.fec.gov/press/press2015/news_releases/20150320release.shtml.

137. 52 U.S.C. § 30116(a)(1)(C); 11 C.F.R. § 110.1(d).

138. 11 C.F.R. § 100.2.

139. 52 U.S.C. § 30116(a)(1)(B); 11 C.F.R. § 110.1(c); FEC News Release, *supra* note 136; Consolidated and Further Continuing Appropriations Act, 2015, Pub. L. No. 113-235, 128 Stat. 2130, 2772 (2014).

140. 52 U.S.C. § 30116(c)(1)(C); 11 C.F.R. § 110.17(b).

141. McCutcheon v. Fed. Election Comm'n, 134 S. Ct. 1434 (2014).

142. 52 U.S.C. § 30116(a)(3); 11 C.F.R. § 110.5; FEC News Release, *supra* note 136.

143. 52 U.S.C. § 30118(a); 11 C.F.R. § 114.5(b)(1).

144. 8 U.S.C. § 1101(a)(20).

145. 52 U.S.C. § 30121; 11 C.F.R. § 110.20.

146. 18 U.S.C. § 201.

147. 11 C.F.R. § 114.2(f).

148. *Id.* § 110.6.

149. *Id.* § 110.6(b)(2)(ii); Fed. Home Loan Mortg. Corp. (Freddie MAC), FEC Matter Under Review MUR 5390 (2006); Westar Energy, Inc., FEC Matter Under Review MUR 5573 (2005).

150. Pub. L. No. 110-81, § 204, 121 Stat. 735; Reporting Contributions Bundled by Lobbyists, Registrants, and the PACs of Lobbyists and Registrants, 74 Fed. Reg. 7285 (Feb. 17, 2009).

151. 52 U.S.C. § 30104(i); 11 C.F.R. § 104.22; FEC News Release, *supra* note 136.

152. 11 C.F.R. § 114.9(a)(2).

153. *Id.*

154. *Id.* §§ 100.134(a), 114.2(f)(2)(1)(A).

155. 52 U.S.C. § 30116; 11 C.F.R. §§ 110.1, 110.2, 110.20, 114.2.

156. 11 C.F.R. § 114.2(f)(2)(i)(A), (C), (E).

157. *Id.* § 114.2(f)(2)(i)(B), (D).

158. *Id.* § 114.3(c)(2)(i).

159. *Id.* § 114.3(c)(2)(ii), (iii).

160. *Id.* § 114.3(c)(2)(ii).

161. *Id.* § 114.2(f).

162. *Id.* § 100.134(a).

163. *Id.* § 114.3(c)(2)(i).

164. *Id.* § 114.4(b)(1)(v).

165. *Id.* § 114.4(b)(1)(iv).

166. *Id.* § 114.4(b)(1).

167. FEC AO 2004-14.

168. FED. ELECTION COMM'N, CORPORATIONS AND LABOR ORGANIZATIONS 84 (Jan. 2007), www.fec.gov/pdf/colagui.pdf.

169. 74 Fed. Reg. 63,951 (Dec. 2009).

170. *Id.*

171. *Id.*

172. 2 U.S.C. § 1601 *et seq.*

173. Pub. L. No. 110-81, § 211, 121 Stat. 735; 52 U.S.C. § 1606.

174. 2 U.S.C. § 1602(8)(A).

175. 22 U.S.C. § 611 *et seq.*

176. 2 U.S.C. § 1602(8)(B).

177. *Id.* § 1602(7).

178. *Id.* § 1602(10).

179. Confidential Policy Personnel as defined by 5 U.S.C. § 7511(b)(2)(B).

180. 26 U.S.C. §§ 162(e)(6), 6033(b).

181. 2 U.S.C. § 1601(a), (b).

182. *Id.* § 1603(a).

183. *Id.* § 1603(a)(3)(A)(ii). Threshold amounts for lobbying firms are $3,000 or less during the quarterly period.

184. *Id.* § 1603(a)(3)(B).

185. *Id.* § 1603(b).

186. *Id.* § 1604(b).

187. *Id.* § 1610(a), (b).

188. *Id.* § 1610(c)(2).

189. Pub. L. No. 110-81, § 203, 121 Stat. 735; 52 U.S.C. § 1604(d).

190. 2 U.S.C. § 1604(d).

191. *Id.* § 1604(d)(1)(G).

192. Guidance from the Office of the Clerk of the U.S. House of Representatives can be found at http://lobbyingdisclosure.house.gov/index.html; the Senate's website offers lobbying disclosure information at www.senate.gov/pagelayout/legislative/g_three_sections_with_teasers/lobbyingdisc.htm.

193. 52 U.S.C. § 1606.

194. 18 U.S.C. § 1001(c).

195. 52 U.S.C. § 1614.

196. *Id.* § 1603.

197. *Id.* § 1604(a).

198. *Id.*

199. *Id.* § 1603(d).

200. 22 U.S.C. § 611 *et seq.*

201. *Id.* § 611(b)(3).

202. *Id.* § 613(h).

203. *See* News Release, U.S. Dep't of Justice, Lobbying Firm Agrees to Pay $125,000 Civil Penalty for Violating Lobbying Disclosure Act (Aug. 28, 2015), www.justice.gov/usao-dc/pr/lobbying-firm-agrees-pay-125000-civil-penalty-violating-lobbying-disclosure-act; *see also* Settlement Agreement, United States v. Alan Mauk Assocs. Ltd., No. 1:14-cv-00409 (D.D.C. Jan. 30, 2015).

204. *See* Judgment, United States v. Biassi Bus. Servs., Inc., No. 1:13-cv-00853 (D.D.C. Dec. 2, 2013).

205. *Cumulative Total*, U.S. SENATE, www.senate.gov/legislative/Public_Disclosure/cumulative_total.htm (last visited June 17, 2014).

206. *See, e.g.*, United States v. Hampton, No. 1:11-cr-00085 (D.D.C. filed Mar. 24, 2011).

207. *See, e.g.*, Press Release No. 11-477, U.S. Dep't of Justice, Newspaper Publisher Pleads Guilty to Making False Statement to Congress (Apr. 14, 2011), www.justice.gov/opa/pr/2011/April/11-crm-477.html; *see also* the case study at Q 18.27.4.

208. *See* General Accounting Office, Observations on Lobbyists' Compliance with Disclosure Requirements (Apr. 2013), http://www.gao.gov/assets/660/653471.pdf.

209. Final Guidance on Appointment of Lobbyists to Federal Boards and Commissions, 76 Fed. Reg. 61,756, 61,757 (Oct. 5, 2011).

210. *See* Autor v. Pritzker, 740 F.3d 176 (D.C. Cir. 2014).

211. Revised Guidance on Appointment of Lobbyists to Federal Advisory Committees, Boards, and Commissions, 79 Fed. Reg. 47,482 (Aug. 13, 2014).

212. 2 U.S.C. § 1613.

213. Pub. L. No. 110-81, § 211, 121 Stat. 735; 2 U.S.C. § 1606.

214. House Rule XXV(5)(a)(1)(A)(i); Senate Rule XXXV(1)(a)(1).

215. House Rule XXV(5)(a)(2)(A); Senate Rule XXXV(1)(b)(1).

216. 18 U.S.C. § 201.

217. House Rule XXV(5)(a)(1)(B)(i); Senate Rule XXXV(1)(a)(2).

218. House Rule XXV(5)(a)(3)(B); Senate Rule XXXV(1)(c)(2).

219. House Rule XXV(5)(a)(3)(D); Senate Rule XXXV(1)(c)(4).

220. House Rule XXV(5)(a)(3)(G)(iii); Senate Rule XXXV(1)(c)(7)(C).

221. House Rule XXV(5)(a)(3)(V); Senate Rule XXXV(1)(c)(12).

222. House Rule XXV(5)(a)(3)(Q); Senate Rule XXXV(1)(c)(18).

223. House Rule XXV(5)(a)(4)(C); Senate Rule XXXV(1)(d)(3).

224. House Rule XXV(5)(a)(3)(S); Senate Rule XXXV(1)(c)(20).

225. House Rule XXV(5)(a)(3)(U); Senate Rule XXXV(1)(c)(22).

226. House Rule XXV(5)(a)(3)(W); Senate Rule XXXV(1)(c)(23).

227. Rules of the House of Representatives, 112th Cong. (2011), Standing Rules of the Senate.

228. House Rule XXV(5)(a)(1)(A)(ii); Senate Rule XXXV(1)(a)(2)(B).

229. House Rule XXV(5)(e)(1); Senate Rule 35, 2 U.S.C. § 1613.

230. House Rule XXV(5)(a)(3)(D); Senate Rule XXXV(1)(c)(4)(A).

231. House Rule XXV(5)(a)(3)(D)(i); Senate Rule XXXV(1)(c)(4)(A).

232. House Rule XXV(5)(a)(3)(D)(ii)(II); Senate Rule XXXV(1)(c)(4)(B)(ii).

233. House Rule XXV(5)(a)(3)(D)(ii)(I), (III); Senate Rule XXXV(1)(c)(4)(B)(i), (iii).

234. House Rule XXV(5)(a)(5); Senate Rule XXV(1)(e).

235. House Rule XXV(5)(a)(4)(D); Senate Rule XXXV(1)(d)(4).

236. House Rule XXV(5)(a)(3)(Q); Senate Rule XXXV(1)(c)(18).

237. House Ethics Manual, 110th Cong., at 41 (2008); Senate Ethics Manual, 108th Cong., at 38 (2003).

238. *Id.*

239. House Rule XXV(5)(a)(4)(A)(i); Senate Rule XXXV(1)(d)(1)(A).

240. House Rule XXV(5)(a)(4)(A)(ii); Senate Rule XXXV(1)(d)(1)(B).

241. House Rule XXV(5)(a)(4)(A); Senate Rule XXXV(1)(d)(1).

242. House Rule XXV(5)(a)(4)(C); Senate Rule XXXV(1)(d)(3).

243. House Rule XXV(5)(a)(3)(S); Senate Rule XXXV(1)(c)(20).

244. House Rule XXV(5)(a)(3)(U); Senate Rule XXXV(1)(c)(22).

245. House Rule XXV(5)(b)(1)(A); Senate Rule XXXV(2)(a)(1).

246. House Rule XXV(5)(a)(3)(O); Senate Rule XXXV(1)(c)(16).

247. House Rule XXV(5)(a)(3)(G)(iii); Senate Rule XXXV(1)(c)(7)(C).

248. House Rule XXV(5)(b)(4)(A); Senate Rule XXXV(2)(f)(1).

249. House Rule XXV(5)(b)(4)(A); Senate Rule XXXV(2)(f)(1).

250. House Rule XXV(5)(b)(1)(B); Senate Rule XXXV(2)(a)(3).

251. House Rule XXV(5)(b)(1)(A)(i); Senate Rule XXXV(2)(b).

252. House Rule XXV(5)(b)(1)(A)(ii); Senate Rule XXXV(2)(c).

253. House Rule XXV(5)(b)(4); Senate Rule XXXV(2)(f).

254. The term "lobbying firm" means a person or entity that has one or more employees who are lobbyists on behalf of a client other than that person or entity. The term also includes a self-employed individual who is a lobbyist. 2 U.S.C. § 1602(9).

255. House Rule XXV(5)(b)(1)(A); Senate Rule XXXV(2)(a)(1).

256. House Rule XXV(5)(b)(1)(A); Senate Rule XXXV(2)(a)(1).

257. House Rule XXV(5)(b)(1)(C)(ii); Senate Rule XXXV(2)(a)(2)(A).

258. House Rule XXV(5)(b)(5)(c)(1)(A); Senate Rule XXXV(2)(d)(1)(B).

259. House Rule XXV(5)(b)(5)(c)(2); Senate Rule XXXV(2)(d)(1)(A).

260. House Rule XXV(5)(b)(5)(d); Senate Rule XXXV(2)(e)(1).

261. House Rule XXV(5)(b)(5)(d)(2); Senate Rule XXXV(2)(e)(2).

262. *See, e.g.*, Press Release No. 11-477, U.S. Dep't of Justice, Newspaper Publisher Pleads Guilty to Making False Statement to Congress (Apr. 14, 2011), www.justice.gov/opa/pr/2011/April/11-crm-477.html.

263. House Rule XXIII(15)(a).

264. Senate Rule XXXV(1)(c)(1)(C), Honest Leadership and Open Government Act of 2007, Pub. L. No. 110-81, § 544, 121 Stat. 735.

265. 154 CONG. REC. S76 (Jan. 22, 2008).

266. 8 U.S.C. § 1101(a)(20).

267. 52 U.S.C. § 30121; 11 C.F.R. § 110.20.

268. 52 U.S.C. §§ 30118, 30119.

269. *MSRB Rule G-37, Political Contributions and Prohibitions on Municipal Securities Business*, MUN. SEC. RULEMAKING BOARD, www.msrb.org/Rules-and-Interpreta-

tions/MSRB-Rules/General/Rule-G-37.aspx; *see also* Exchange Act Release No. 33,868, File No. SR-MSRB-94-2 (Apr. 7, 1994); *Political Contributions and Prohibitions on Municipal Securities Business: Proposed Rule G-37*, 14 MSRB REP. 1 (Jan. 1994).

270. 52 U.S.C. § 30119.

271. Political Contributions by Certain Investment Advisers, 75 Fed. Reg. 41,018 (July 14, 2010).

272. *See* note 269, *supra*.

273. CFTC Rule 23.451, Political Contributions by Certain Swap Dealers and Major Swap Participants.

274. MSRB Notice 2011-04, Request for Comment on Pay to Play Rule for Municipal Advisors (Jan. 14, 2011), www.msrb.org/Rules-and-Interpretations/Regulatory-Notices/2011/2011-04.aspx?n=1.

275. Registration is due upon execution of the contract, and reports are due five days after the end of the semi-annual period. Both registrations and reports use the Contribution Disclosure Form.

276. Business Entity Annual Statement (Form BE) is due annually on March 30.

277. Non-Bid Contract Reporting Form (DSEB-504 or DSEB-504B) is due annually on February 15.

278. Registration is due prior to the effective date of the contract, and amendments for entities with pending bids are due within five business days following changes or no later than a day before the contract is awarded, whichever date is earlier. Registered businesses without pending bids have a continuing duty to report changes on a quarterly basis. Illinois does not require reports. Both registrations and amended registrations use the Business Entity Registration form.

19

Environmental Law

Bonni F. Kaufman & Stacy Watson May *

This chapter discusses the key federal environmental statutes and regulations governing business operations in the United States.[1] These regulations are applicable to industrial, manufacturing, and business operations, universities, farms, feeding lots and agricultural operations, municipal and state governments, as well as construction companies, developers, and property owners. Essentially any business that generates, stores, or uses hazardous substances—such as petroleum, cleaning solvents, grease, and lubricating oils—as well as any business that engages in construction, renovation, and development, is subject to detailed environmental laws.

The purpose of this chapter is to identify and briefly describe the applicable federal laws and the compliance obligations that companies subject to environmental laws must be aware of. In addition, each state has its own authority to enact and enforce the environmental laws as long as the state's law is not in conflict with federal law. However, state environmental laws

*   The authors wish to acknowledge Christopher A. Myers for his contributions to this chapter.

generally follow federal law and must mirror the basic federal requirements that are discussed in this chapter. For questions regarding compliance with state laws, each state's environmental regulations and statutes must be reviewed.

Acronyms, initialisms, and abbreviations used in this chapter:

BOD	biochemical oxygen demand
CAA	Clean Air Act
CERCLA	Comprehensive Environmental Response, Compensation, and Liability Act
CFATS	Chemical Facility Anti-Terrorism Standards
CWA	Clean Water Act (Federal Water Pollution Control Act)
DHS	Department of Homeland Security
EPA	U.S. Environmental Protection Agency
EPCRA	Emergency Planning and Community Right-to-Know Act
FASB	Financial Accounting Standards Board
GHG	greenhouse gas
HAP	hazardous air pollutant
LEPC	local emergency planning committee
LLP	Landowner Liability Protections
MACT	maximum achievable control technology
MD&A	Management Discussion and Analysis
MSDS	material safety data sheet
NAAQS	national ambient air quality standards

NCP	National Oil and Hazardous Substances Pollution Contingency Plan
NESHAP	National Emission Standards for Hazardous Air Pollutants
NHTSA	National Highway Traffic Safety Administration
NPDES	National Pollutant Discharge Elimination System
NPL	National Priorities List
NRC	National Response Center
NSPS	New Source Performance Standards
NSR	New Source Review
OSHA	Occupational Safety and Health Administration
PCBs	polychlorinated biphenyls
PMN	pre-manufacture notice
POTW	publicly owned treatment work
RCRA	Resource Conservation and Recovery Act
SARA	Superfund Amendments and Reauthorization Act of 1986
SEC	U.S. Securities and Exchange Commission
SERC	state emergency response commission
SIP	State Implementation Plan
SPCC	Spill Prevention Control and Countermeasures
SREA	Superfund Recycling Equity Act
TRI	Toxic Release Inventory
TSCA	Toxic Substances Control Act
TSS	total suspended solids
UST	underground storage tank

Federal Statutes and Regulations

Q 19.1   How are environmental issues regulated in the United States?

The U.S. Environmental Protection Agency (EPA) is the federal administrative agency responsible for enforcement of federal environmental laws in the United States. EPA is divided into ten regions, with its headquarters in Washington, D.C. Each region is responsible for administering and enforcing the environmental laws in the states located in its region.

Federal laws are implemented in two stages. First, the statute is passed setting forth the federal requirements, which can be found in the final form in the United States Code. Second, for more technical environmental statutes, EPA is authorized, and often expressly required, to implement regulations (also known as rules) further defining the technical aspects of the law, which are contained in the Code of Federal Regulations. Both the statute and the regulations must be complied with. Where there is a conflict, the statute controls.

Q 19.2   What are the major federal environmental laws with general application to business operations that we need to be aware of and comply with?

The following table lists the major federal laws that apply generally to businesses.

TABLE 19-1
Federal Environmental Laws

Resource Conservation and Recovery Act	regulates use and disposal of hazardous substances;
CERCLA (or Superfund)	requires reporting of spills and other accidental or intentional "releases" of hazardous substances;
Clean Air Act	governs emissions of air pollutants from industrial and manufacturing sources as well as automobiles and other modes of transportation;

Clean Water Act	regulates discharge of pollutants into navigable waters of the United States, including discharges of storm water and filling of wetland areas; and
Toxic Substances Control Act	regulates manufacture and importation of chemicals in the United States as well as disposal and use of asbestos, PCBs, and lead-based paint.

Other environmental laws that regulate specific areas of the environment include the Endangered Species Act, the Federal Insecticide and Fungicide Regulation Act, and the Oil Pollution Act. But because these laws do not have general application to business operations, they are outside the scope of this chapter. Furthermore, be advised that all environmental laws and regulations are subject to frequent revision; the most current versions must be reviewed.

Resource Conservation and Recovery Act

Q 19.3   What is the Resource Conservation and Recovery Act?

The Resource Conservation and Recovery Act (RCRA)[2] regulates the solid and hazardous waste management practices of generators and transporters of solid and hazardous waste, and owners and operators of solid and hazardous waste treatment, storage, and disposal facilities. RCRA establishes a "cradle-to-grave" system governing hazardous waste from the point of generation to disposal. RCRA is a federal statute, but almost all states administer the RCRA hazardous waste program themselves.

The implementing regulations regarding hazardous waste[3] require the entity or person generating the hazardous waste (the "generator") to determine whether its waste is hazardous.[4] If a waste is hazardous, the generator must comply with regulations[5] and properly manage and dispose of it.

Q 19.3.1   What is "hazardous waste"?

Solid waste—garbage, construction debris, sludge, or other discarded material—will be considered a hazardous waste if it is:

(1)   solid waste that is "listed" as a hazardous waste in the regulations;[6]

(2)   solid waste that exhibits one or more hazardous waste characteristics—such as ignitability, corrosivity, reactivity, or toxicity;

(3)   solid waste that becomes a hazardous waste after being mixed with any listed hazardous waste;

(4)   solid waste generated from the treatment, storage, or disposal of a listed hazardous waste.

Q 19.3.2   How does a generator properly manage and dispose of hazardous waste?

If a waste is determined to be hazardous, the generator must and properly manage and dispose of it by taking the following steps:

(1)   Obtain an identification number from EPA (or the state that is implementing RCRA under delegated authority).[7]

(2)   Prepare a manifest for the waste to be disposed of by a licensed hazardous waste transporter.[8]

(3)   Ensure proper packaging, labeling, and placarding of the waste.[9]

(4)   Meet standards for waste accumulation units.[10]

(5)   Maintain proper records of its waste generation.[11]

(6)   Prepare a biennial report by March 1 of each even-numbered year of hazardous waste generated that was shipped off-site for storage, treatment, or disposal (within the United States) for the prior year.[12]

Q 19.3.3   What are the reporting requirements for hazardous waste generators?

Each type of hazardous waste generator has different reporting requirements. Hazardous waste generators are divided into three categories, according to how much they generate in a calendar month:

- **Large quantity generators:** generate more than 1,000 kg of hazardous waste per month or more than 1 kg of acutely hazardous waste per month.
- **Small quantity generators:** generate more than 100 kg, but less than 1,000 kg of hazardous waste per month, or less than 1 kg of acutely hazardous waste per month.
- **Conditionally exempt small quantity generators:** generate less than or equal to 100 kg of hazardous waste per month or less than or equal to 1 kg of acutely hazardous waste per month.[13]

Storage and Accumulation of Hazardous Waste

Q 19.3.4   What are the allowances for hazardous waste storage?

The length of time a generator is allowed to store hazardous waste on-site depends on the generator's classification. For example, a large quantity generator may accumulate any quantity of hazardous waste on-site for ninety days without a permit or interim status authorization. Small quantity generators may accumulate no more than 6,000 kg. Generators count the amount of waste generated by adding up the total weight of all quantities of hazardous waste generated at a particular facility. If waste is accumulated for more than ninety days (for up to 100 kg) or more than 180 days (for up to 1,000 kg), the facility will be deemed to "treat, store, or dispose of hazardous waste" and will be required to obtain a hazardous waste facility permit.[14] Extremely onerous requirements, including financial insurance, detailed record keeping, and numerous inspections, are imposed on hazardous waste treatment, storage, and disposal facilities.

Q 19.3.5   How are underground storage tanks (USTs) for hazardous waste regulated?

The regulations for underground tanks containing petroleum and hazardous substances[15] provide for tank design and release detection requirements, as well as financial responsibility and corrective action standards for USTs. Most states have their own underground storage tank regulations and many states also regulate above-ground tanks.

As of December 22, 1998, all existing UST systems had to be upgraded or closed as set forth in the regulations.[16] Newly installed USTs and related piping must be designed to prevent releases due to structural failure, corrosion, or spills and overfills.[17]

The owner or operator of a facility with underground tanks must notify the implementing agency (typically the state environmental agency) of the following:

1. The installation of a new UST, using EPA Form 7530-1 (Appendix I, 40 C.F.R. pt. 280),[18] which contains a certification of compliance attesting to the proper installation.
2. All releases or suspected releases,[19] spills and overfills,[20] and confirmed releases, exceeding the quantity limits,[21] within twenty-four hours.
3. Corrective actions planned or taken to address a release or spill.
4. Permanent closure or change-in-service.[22]

USTs must have spill and overfill prevention equipment such as a catch basin at the connection of the transfer hose to the fill pipe, as well as equipment such as an automatic shut-off at 95% full or a 90% high-level alarm.[23] USTs and related piping must also have methods of release detection.[24] These methods can include inventory control, manual or automatic tank gauging, tank tightness testing, vapor monitoring, ground water monitoring, and interstitial monitoring. Records of USTs' installation, maintenance, and closure must be available for inspection upon request.

Release of Hazardous Waste

Q 19.3.6   What am I required to do if I release hazardous waste?

Releases or suspected releases must be reported to the implementing agency within twenty-four hours, as well as reported to local and state emergency response commissions as specified at Q 19.6. Suspected releases must be immediately investigated to confirm the suspected release. All spills and releases must be cleaned up immediately.

If a confirmed release exceeds the reportable quantity of a hazardous substance under CERCLA,[25] the facility owner or operator must initiate an RCRA Corrective Action.[26] This includes:

1. Initial abatement measures and site check.

2. Initial site characterization.

3. Free product removal.

4. Investigations for soil and ground water cleanup.

5. Corrective action plan submittal if required.

6. Public participation regarding the corrective action plan, if required.

UST owners or operators must demonstrate financial responsibility to take necessary corrective action and to compensate third parties for bodily injury and property damage. Financial responsibility may be demonstrated by different mechanisms such as satisfying the financial test of self-insurance, by providing a guarantee, surety bond, or insurance coverage.[27]

Q 19.3.7   Is used oil subject to RCRA regulation?

Generators of used oil are subject to storage standards and state and local requirements. Entities that offer storage, transportation, burning, processing, or re-refining of used oil are subject to additional regulatory requirements under both federal and state programs.[28] Generators of used oil must also comply with EPA's Spill Prevention, Control, and Countermeasures.[29] If used oil is stored in underground storage tanks, generators are subject to UST standards.[30]

Q 19.3.8   Is lead-based paint subject to RCRA regulation?

RCRA defines lead-based paint debris as hazardous waste unless it is generated during abatement, renovation, and remodeling of homes or other residences such as apartment buildings. Regulations promulgated pursuant to the Toxic Substances Control Act (TSCA) govern the treatment and disposal of lead-based paint and are discussed below at Q 19.11.

Compliance and Enforcement

Q 19.3.9 What are the penalties for RCRA violations?

Violators of RCRA may be subject to an administrative order, a civil judicial action, and/or a criminal enforcement action.[31] Specifically, EPA or an authorized state can issue orders requiring compliance with RCRA requirements and can assess civil penalties up to $37,500 per day for each day of the violation. Persons convicted of RCRA crimes are subject to fines up to $50,000 per day of violation or imprisonment of up to five years.

It is important to note that any employee, including a plant manager, who fails to comply with any aspect of the RCRA regulations may be held *personally* liable for civil and criminal penalties. To comply with RCRA, all facilities should take care to dispose of all hazardous substances properly and responsibly. Proper disposal means sending materials to the properly permitted facilities, segregating the waste to ensure it is transferred to the appropriate disposal or recycling vendor, properly storing and packaging the waste, and preparing hazardous waste manifests.

CERCLA/Superfund

Q 19.4 What does CERCLA provide?

The Comprehensive Environmental Response, Compensation, and Liability Act (CERCLA), a 1980 law commonly known as "Superfund," authorizes EPA to respond to releases (or threatened releases) of hazardous substances that may endanger public health or welfare, or the environment.[32] CERCLA also enables EPA to force parties responsible for environmental contamination to clean it up or to reimburse the Superfund for response costs incurred by EPA. The Superfund Amendments and Reauthorization Act of 1986 (SARA) revised various sections of CERCLA, extended the taxing authority for the Superfund, and created a free-standing law, the Emergency Planning and Community Response Act (discussed below). In 2002, Congress passed the Small Business Liability Relief and Brownfields Revitalization Act, which expanded EPA's brownfields development program, expanded and created certain defenses for innocent purchasers of contaminated property, and gave liability relief to certain small businesses and municipalities that generated and disposed of de minimis amounts of hazardous wastes.[33]

Release Reporting

Q 19.4.1   What are CERCLA's hazardous substance release reporting requirements?

CERCLA regulations[34] require the *person in charge of a facility* to immediately report to the National Response Center (NRC) any environmental release of a hazardous substance that exceeds a reportable quantity.[35] A release report may trigger a response by EPA or by one or more federal or state emergency response authorities. Failure to provide notice of a release as required by CERCLA, or providing false or misleading information in such notification, may subject the violator to criminal penalties, including fines and imprisonment up to five years.

> **TIP:** Each state has separate state reporting obligations when there is a release of hazardous substances. Furthermore, there are separate obligations pursuant to the Emergency Planning and Community Right-to-Know Act (EPCRA) that require release reporting to local municipal agencies (*see* Q 19.6.1, *infra*).

Property Cleanup Liability

Q 19.4.2   How does CERCLA govern cleanup of property containing hazardous substances?

EPA implements cleanup according to procedures outlined in the National Oil and Hazardous Substances Pollution Contingency Plan (NCP).[36] The NCP includes provisions for permanent cleanups—known as "remedial actions"—and other more short-term cleanups—referred to as "removals." EPA generally conducts remedial actions only at sites on the National Priorities List (NPL). Both EPA and states can act at other sites; however, EPA generally requires responsible parties to conduct removal and remedial actions and encourages community involvement throughout the Superfund response process.

Q 19.4.3 Who is subject to CERCLA liability for release of a hazardous substance?

(1) Current owners or operators of a vessel or facility,
(2) Past owners or operators of a facility at the time a release occurred,
(3) Transporters of hazardous substances to a facility, and
(4) Persons who arrange for the treatment or disposal of hazardous substances at a facility.[37]

Q 19.4.4 Is anyone exempted from liability?

Yes. A "person who arranged for recycling of recyclable material"[38] is expressly exempted from CERCLA liability by the Superfund Recycling Equity Act (SREA), as well as persons who qualify for liability defenses discussed at Q 19.5.3.

Recycling and SREA

Q 19.5 What is the Superfund Recycling Equity Act?

The SREA was enacted November 29, 1999. The purpose of the Act, among other things, is to promote the reuse and recycling of scrap material and to reduce waste while protecting human health and the environment.

Q 19.5.1 What is "recyclable material"?

"Recyclable material" is:

> scrap paper, scrap plastic, scrap glass, scrap textiles, scrap rubber (other than whole tires), scrap metal, or spent lead-acid, spent nickel-cadmium, and other spent batteries, as well as minor amounts of material incident to or adhering to the scrap material as a result of its normal and customary use prior to becoming scrap [except certain shipping containers and materials containing certain levels of PCBs].[39]

Q 19.5.2 What does the SREA consider "recycling"?

A "recycling" arrangement must meet the following criteria under the SREA:

(1) The recyclable material met a commercial specification grade.

(2) A market existed for the recyclable material.

(3) A substantial portion of the recyclable material was made available for use as feedstock for the manufacture of a new saleable product.

(4) The recyclable material could have been a replacement or substitute for a virgin raw material, or the product to be made from the recyclable material could have been a replacement or substitute for a product made, in whole or in part, from a virgin raw material.

(5) The generator exercised reasonable care to determine that the recycling facility was in compliance with substantive provisions of any environmental law or compliance order.

(6) If recycling scrap metal, the metal cannot be melted prior to providing it to the recycler.[40]

In addition, for transactions involving scrap metal, it will only be deemed "arranging for recycling" if the person can also demonstrate that he or she was in compliance with any applicable regulations associated with the recycling of scrap metal (after November 29, 1999) and did not melt the scrap metal prior to the transaction.[41]

Enforcement

CERCLA liability is imposed regardless of fault and regardless of whether the disposal or release of a hazardous substance was authorized by law at the time. In addition to liability for cleanup of releases, facilities may be subject to liability for:

- Punitive damages (up to three times the cost of cleanup) for willful misconduct.[42]
- Natural resource damages.[43]
- Citizen injuries to person or property.[44]
- Criminal penalties, including fines, and imprisonment up to five years, for failure to provide notification of a release of a reportable quantity to the NRC.

Defenses

Q 19.5.3   What are some defenses to CERCLA liability?

The Small Business Liability Relief and Brownfields Revitalization Act provides two defenses to CERCLA liability, in addition to the existing "innocent landowner defense," collectively referred to as the Landowner Liability Protections (LLP). The statute added the contiguous property exemption and the "bona fide prospective purchaser" defense.

Pursuant to these provisions of CERCLA, a property owner will not be responsible for contamination that migrates onto his property from an adjacent site or that pre-existed his purchase. In both cases, the property owner must demonstrate that:

1. he is not responsible for causing the environmental impacts or affiliated with the entity who is;
2. he took reasonable steps to address the threat of release;
3. he is in compliance with any land use restrictions;
4. he did not know of the release prior to purchase and that he properly investigated the property, except that a bona fide prospective purchaser may know of the contamination prior to purchase as long as the other conditions are met.

To avail itself of these liability protections, the purchaser of property must perform "all appropriate inquiry" of the condition of the property prior to purchase. EPA considers all appropriate inquiry to consist of an Environmental Site Assessment conducted in accordance with ASTM Standard E1527-13. This is an assessment conducted by a qualified environmental consulting firm that includes a physical visit to the property, an inspection of surface conditions, a historical investigation of the prior and current uses of the property and adjacent properties, interviews of persons knowledgeable about the property, file searches of public agencies, and a chain of title search. This assessment is referred to as a "Phase I Report" and is valid for six months from the time of the site inspection.

Hazardous Chemical Emergencies and EPCRA

Q 19.6   What is the EPCRA?

The Emergency Planning and Community Right-to-Know Act, also known as SARA Title III, was created by SARA. EPCRA is designed to improve community access to information about chemical hazards and to facilitate the development of chemical emergency response plans by state and local governments. EPCRA required the establishment of state emergency response commissions (SERCs) responsible for coordinating certain emergency response activities and for appointing local emergency planning committees (LEPCs).

Compliance and Enforcement

Q 19.6.1   How does the EPCRA regulate hazardous chemicals?

Manufacturing facilities that store or manage specified chemicals must comply with EPCRA and the EPCRA regulations[45] by providing the following:

- *Extremely Hazardous Substance Notification.* A facility that stores or uses any "extremely hazardous substance" in excess of the substance's "threshold planning quantity" must notify the SERC and LEPC of the presence of the substance. The facility must also appoint an emergency response coordinator.[46]
- *Release Notification.* The facility must notify the SERC and the LEPC in the event of a release exceeding the reportable quantity of a CERCLA hazardous substance or any quantity of an EPCRA extremely hazardous substance.[47]
- *Hazardous Chemical Inventory and MSDS.* A facility must submit to the SERC, LEPC, and local fire department material safety data sheets (MSDSs) or lists of MSDSs and hazardous chemical inventory forms (also known as Tier I and II forms) if the facility has a "hazardous chemical," as defined by the Occupational Safety and Health Act (OSHA), present in an amount exceeding a specified threshold.[48]
- *Annual Toxic Chemical Release Report ("Form R").* A facility with ten or more employees that uses specified chemicals in amounts greater than the threshold quantities must submit

an annual toxic chemical release report.[49] This report, commonly known as the Form R, covers releases and transfers of toxic chemicals to various facilities and environmental media and allows EPA to compile the national Toxic Release Inventory (TRI) database.[50] Pursuant to the Pollution Prevention Act of 1990, also known as "P2," section 8 of Form R requires reporting of waste minimization efforts for each reportable chemical, how much the chemical was reduced, the reduction amount, and how much chemical waste was sent off-site for recycling.

COMPLIANCE FACT

All information submitted pursuant to EPCRA regulations is publicly accessible, unless protected by a trade secret claim.

Q 19.6.2   What are the penalties for noncompliance with EPCRA?

Violations of EPCRA's reporting requirements may be subject to civil and administrative penalties up to $32,500 per day for each violation.

Clean Air Act (CAA)

Q 19.7   What is the intent of the Clear Air Act?

The Clean Air Act and its amendments, including the Clean Air Act Amendments of 1990 (collectively CAA), are designed to "protect and enhance the nation's air resources so as to promote the public health and welfare and the productive capacity of the population." The CAA consists of six titles, which direct EPA to establish national standards for ambient air quality. It requires EPA and the states to implement, maintain, and enforce these standards through a variety of mechanisms. State and local governments oversee, manage, and enforce many of the CAA requirements.[51]

Q 19.7.1   What kinds of air pollutants does the CAA aim to clean up?

The most common are:

- particulate matter,
- ground-level ozone,
- carbon monoxide,
- nitrogen oxides,
- sulfur oxides, and
- lead.

EPA regulates these six "criteria pollutants" using science-based guidelines to set permissible levels. The CAA also identifies 188 hazardous air pollutants (HAPs).[52] The source of pollutants can be stationary (such as gas stations, chemical plants, and power plants) or mobile[53] (such as cars, trucks, buses, and planes).

Q 19.7.2   How does the CAA regulate criteria pollutants?

Pursuant to the CAA, EPA has established national ambient air quality standards (NAAQS) to limit criteria pollutant levels. Geographic areas that meet NAAQS for a given pollutant are classified as "attainment areas"; those that do not meet NAAQS are classified as "non-attainment areas." Non-attainment areas must develop a strategy to bring the areas into attainment of the NAAQS. One useful tool in developing such a strategy is the State Implementation Plan (SIP). Under section 110 of the CAA, each state must develop a SIP to identify sources of air pollution and to determine what reductions are required to meet federal air quality standards. The SIPs contain permitting requirements, source-specific emission standards, and numerous other air-related requirements.

Q 19.7.3   What are some of the ways the CAA regulates HAPs?

EPA establishes and enforces National Emission Standards for Hazardous Air Pollutants (NESHAP), which are national uniform standards designed to control particular HAPs. The CAA requires EPA to develop a list of sources that emit HAPs and to develop regulations for these categories of sources.

EPA has listed numerous categories and developed a schedule for the establishment of emission standards. The emission standards are based on "maximum achievable control technology" (MACT), defined as the control technology achieving the maximum degree of reduction in the emission of the HAPs.

The CAA also authorizes EPA to establish New Source Performance Standards (NSPS), which are nationally uniform emission standards for new stationary sources falling within particular industrial categories. NSPS are based on the pollution control technology available to that category of industrial source but allow the affected industries the flexibility to devise a cost-effective means of reducing emissions.

The CAA also establishes a sulfur dioxide emissions program designed to reduce the formation of acid rain. Reduction of sulfur dioxide releases will be obtained by granting to certain sources limited emissions allowances.[54]

In an effort to protect stratospheric ozone, the CAA also provides for the phasing-out of the manufacture of ozone-depleting chemicals and the restricting of their use and distribution.[55]

Q 19.7.4   How does the CAA regulate greenhouse gas emissions?

In December 2009, EPA issued an endangerment finding under the CAA that greenhouse gases (that is, gases from combustion processes) present an endangerment to the environment, allowing federal regulation of greenhouse gas (GHG) emissions under the CAA.[56]

In addition, on January 1, 2010, the EPA began to require mandatory reporting for large emitters of greenhouse gases. The EPA's rule requires over 10,000 facilities to collect and report data with respect to their GHG emissions, which covers 85% of gas emissions in the United States.[57]

In 2010, EPA and the National Highway Traffic Safety Administration (NHTSA) issued new GHG emission and fuel economy standards for light-duty vehicles manufactured in 2012–16. In 2011, the agencies proposed standards for model years 2017–25. In 2010, EPA issued the so-called tailoring rule establishing GHG emissions thresholds to define when CAA permits are required for new and existing industrial facilities that emit GHGs. EPA currently is working on GHG standards for new fossil fuel power plants and petroleum refineries. These regulations may require mandatory reductions in emissions, which in turn, may increase the cost of fuel, utilities, and petrochemical products for downstream customers.

California and other states have already begun to regulate GHG emissions, and many cities (such as the District of Columbia) are imposing "green building" requirements on new construction.[58] These require building owners to use sustainable materials, alternate forms of energy, and energy-efficient lighting and HVAC systems in commercial and, in some cases, residential buildings.

Compliance/Permits

Q 19.7.5   What kinds of CAA reporting/compliance requirements should businesses be aware of?

New Source Review (NSR). New major sources of air emissions must apply for a permit prior to construction of a source. New sources in attainment areas must obtain a "prevention of significant deterioration permit." A new major source in a non-attainment area must obtain an NSR permit and is subject to stricter control technology requirements, the lowest achievable emissions rate for that industry.

Title V Operating Permit. The CAA requires the following sources (*i.e.*, facilities and equipment) to have a Title V operating permit:[59]

- any major source;[60]
- any source, including area sources, subject to an NSPS under section 111 of the CAA;
- any source, including area sources, subject to a standard for air toxics, except if the source is only subject to the standard because of the risk management program applicability under section 112(r) of the CAA;
- electric utilities that are regulated under the acid rain provision (Title IV of the CAA);
- any sources subject to non-attainment area source review or prevention of significant deterioration programs;
- any other stationary source in an industry category EPA designation pursuant to the regulation.

One purpose of the operating permit is to include in a single document all air emissions requirements that apply to a given facility. States have developed the permit programs in accordance with guidance and regulations from EPA. Once each state's program is approved by EPA, permits are issued and monitored by that state. No state operating permit can be less stringent than the federal requirements. EPA has veto authority over all state-issued operating permits.

Each Title V operating permit will have facility-specific requirements that must be consulted and followed at each facility.

Risk Management Programs. Section 112(r) of the CAA requires facilities to reduce releases of hazardous chemicals into the air, reduce the severity of any accidents that may occur, and improve communication between facilities and the community. The CAA requires all stationary sources that handle extremely hazardous substances or listed substances above certain quantities[61] to take steps to prevent releases or minimize the consequences of such releases. Facilities must generally do the following:

- identify hazards that may result from accidental releases;
- design and maintain a safe facility;
- take steps necessary to prevent releases and to minimize the consequences of such accidental releases.

Facilities that use a listed or extremely hazardous substance in a process[62] must prepare a Risk Management Program and maintain documentation of the program at the facility.[63]

Record-Keeping Requirements. The record-keeping requirements of the air regulations range from two to five years in most cases. Each permit and applicable regulations should be consulted to determine the appropriate document retention period.

Violations and Penalties

Q 19.7.6   What constitutes a violation of the CAA?

- A knowing violation of a state implementation plan.
- A knowing violation of an air toxics, acid rain, non-attainment, or stratospheric ozone provision.
- A knowing violation of a standard associated with a permit.

- A knowing omission of material information on a record required under the CAA.
- A knowing failure to report or notify as required.
- A knowing alteration or concealment of data or files.
- A failure to maintain files or records.
- A knowing failure to install required monitoring devices.

Q 19.7.7   What are the penalties for CAA violations?

Violation of the CAA may be subject to a civil judicial or administrative order, and/or civil or criminal penalties that may include fines of up to $37,500 per day of violation or imprisonment of up to five years.[64] "Knowing Violations" are subject to criminal liability.

Clean Water Act (CWA)

Q 19.8   What is the aim of the Clean Water Act?

The Federal Water Pollution Control Act,[65] commonly known as the Clean Water Act (CWA), is intended to restore and maintain the chemical, physical, and biological integrity of the nation's waters. It directs the EPA to minimize the effects of chemical pollution on fish, shellfish, wildlife, recreation, biological diversity, productivity, and stability.

Q 19.8.1   What kinds of pollutants are regulated by the CWA?

The CWA regulates "priority" pollutants, including various toxic pollutants; "conventional" pollutants, such as biochemical oxygen demand (BOD), total suspended solids (TSS), fecal coliform, oil and grease, and pH; and "non-conventional" pollutants, including any pollutant not identified as either conventional or priority.

Q 19.8.2   How does the CWA protect the nation's waters?

The CWA authorizes the EPA to establish maximum "effluent limitations" for discharges of pollutants from "point sources." It creates various enforcement and permitting mechanisms to achieve effluent limitations, including the National Pollutant Discharge Elimination System (NPDES), which makes it unlawful to discharge a pollutant to "waters of the United States" without first obtaining a permit and complying with its terms.

Q 19.8.3   What are point source discharges?

The CWA regulates both direct and indirect discharges. The NPDES program[66] controls direct discharges into navigable waters. Direct discharges, or "point source" discharges, are from sources such as pipes and sewers.

Q 19.8.4   What are nonpoint sources?

Certain sources of pollution such as storm water runoff from industrial sources or municipal storm drains, agricultural storm water discharges, and irrigation return flows are considered "nonpoint sources." While some of these nonpoint sources are exempted from permit requirements, others—such as certain kinds of storm water discharges—are not. (See the discussion of Storm Water Discharges at Q 19.8.7, below.)

NPDES Permits

Q 19.8.5   What is an NPDES permit required for?

NPDES permits, issued by either EPA or an authorized state, contain industry-specific, technology-based, and/or water quality-based limits, and establish pollutant monitoring and reporting requirements. A facility that intends to discharge into the nation's waters must obtain a permit prior to initiating its discharge.

Q 19.8.6   What are the requirements for a discharging facility to be issued an NPDES permit?

A permit applicant must provide quantitative analytical data identifying the types of pollutants present in the facility's effluent. The permit will then set forth the conditions and effluent limitations under which a facility may make a discharge.

An NPDES permit may also include discharge limits based on federal or state water quality criteria or standards that are designed to protect designated uses of surface waters, such as supporting aquatic life or recreation. These standards, unlike the technological standards, generally do not take into account technological feasibility or costs. Water quality criteria and standards vary from state to state and site to site, depending on the use classification of the receiving body of water. Most states follow EPA guidelines that propose aquatic life and human health criteria for many of the 126 priority pollutants.

For an NPDES permit, facilities must provide the results of biological toxicity tests and any information on its "effluent characteristics." Specific facilities in specific industries must test for certain parameters. For example, the electronics/computer industry must test for all 126 priority pollutants listed in 40 C.F.R. § 122, Appendix D. Facilities must provide quantifiable data only for discharges of priority pollutants which the applicant knows or has reason to believe will be greater than trace amounts.

All manufacturing facilities must satisfy the technology-based effluent limitation guidelines.

Storm Water Discharges

Q 19.8.7   Which kinds of storm water discharges require an NPDES permit?

Facilities that meet certain criteria, such as storing products, inventory, equipment, or hazardous materials outside, must apply for an NPDES permit for its storm water discharges. Storm water discharge associated with industrial activity directly related to manufacturing, processing, or raw materials storage areas at an industrial plant must have a storm water permit.[67]

Agricultural storm water discharges and irrigation return flows do *not* require a permit. Also exempted from permit requirements are storm water discharges from areas located on lands separate from the plant's industrial activities, such as office buildings and accompanying parking lots, as long as the drainage from the excluded areas is not mixed with storm water from the industrial areas. Storm water discharges from construction activities—including clearing, grading, and excavation—that disturb one acre or more *are* subject to the storm water permit program.

EPA has delegated storm water permitting programs in most states, but has retained enforcement authority so that both EPA and the applicable state may bring enforcement action for non-permitted storm water discharges.

Publicly Owned Treatment Works

Q 19.8.8 What kind of permits are required for municipal sewage treatment plants?

The CWA also regulates discharges to publicly owned treatment works (POTWs). Industrial users of POTWs must comply with the national pretreatment program[68] that controls the discharge of pollutants to POTWs. Facilities regulated under section 307(b) must meet certain pretreatment standards. The goal of the pretreatment program is to protect municipal wastewater treatment plants from damage that may occur when hazardous, toxic, or other wastes are discharged into a sewer system and to protect the quality of sludge generated by these plants.

Discharges to a POTW are regulated primarily by the POTW itself, rather than by the state or EPA. EPA has developed technology-based standards for industrial users of POTWs. Different standards apply to existing and new sources within each category. "Categorical" pretreatment standards applicable to an entire industry on a nationwide basis are also developed by EPA. "Local limits" are also developed by the POTW in order to assist the POTW in achieving the effluent limitations in its NPDES permit.

Regardless of whether a state is authorized to implement either the NPDES or the pretreatment program,[69] a state may develop and enforce requirements more stringent than federal standards.

Wetlands Regulation and Development/Dredge and Fill Permits

Q 19.8.9 What other permits are required by the CWA?

Section 404 of the CWA is administered by the U.S. Army Corps of Engineers and regulates the discharge of dredged and fill material into the waters of the United States, which include wetlands in many circumstances. Therefore, any person planning to engage in activities that involve the filling of wetlands (such as construction of buildings in wetland areas) must apply for a permit from the appropriate regional office of the Army Corps of Engineers and present a mitigation plan for any damage to the wetlands. "The scope of waters regulated under the CWA is very broad and can include tributaries that may flow only part of the year as well as wetlands adjacent to those tributaries."[70]

Spill Prevention Control and Countermeasures

Q 19.8.10 What regulations should facilities dealing with oil be aware of?

Facilities that have above-ground oil storage capacity of greater than 1,320 gallons or underground oil storage capacity greater than 42,000 gallons may be subject to Spill Prevention Control and Countermeasures (SPCC) regulations.[71] The CWA requires facilities that store more than 1,320 gallons of petroleum products to prepare a written SPCC plan that requires measures to be implemented to prevent releases of petroleum to navigable waters. The SPCC plan sets forth a facility's response to a discharge of oil. The plan ensures that owners and operators of facilities develop and implement containment and other countermeasures that prevent oil spills that could reach navigable waters. SPCC plans provide for facility practices to reduce the number and volume of spills, such as tank lead detection, spill-overfill protection, external pipe protection, and secondary containment.

Q 19.8.11 What does the SPCC consider "oil"?

The CWA definition of "oil" includes non-petroleum oils as well as petroleum and petroleum-refined products. "Oil" means oil of any kind or in any form, including, but not limited to:

- fats, oils, or greases of animal, fish, or marine mammal origin;
- vegetable oils, including oils from seeds, nuts, fruits, or kernels; and
- other oils and greases, including petroleum, fuel oil, sludge, synthetic oils, mineral oils, oil refuse, or oil mixed with wastes other than dredged spoil.[72]

Q 19.8.12 What must an SPCC plan include?

The plan must include the following components:[73]

- Physical layout of the facility, including facility diagram, marking the location and contents of each container (even if exempted), transfer stations, and piping.
- The type of oil in each container and its storage capacity.
- The discharge prevention measures, including procedures for routine handling of products such as loading, unloading, and facility transfers.
- The discharge or drainage controls such as secondary containment around containers and other structures, equipment, and procedures for the control of a discharge.
- Any countermeasures for discharge discovery, response, and cleanup, including those performed by a contractor.
- Methods of proper disposal of recovered materials.
- Contact list and phone numbers for the facility response coordinator, NRC, cleanup contractors, and all appropriate federal, state, and local agencies who must be contacted in case of a discharge.
- Details about conducting inspections, required tests, and related record keeping.
- Security procedures for the operation, such as fencing, lighting, security of valves, locks on oil pumps, and secure loading/unloading connections of pipelines and piping.
- Proper certification by a licensed professional engineer, unless the facility qualifies as a small business.[74]
- Signature of approval by management.

The SPCC plan must be kept at the facility (except in some cases, it may be kept at the nearest field office).[75]

Q 19.8.13 What other requirements do the SPCC regulations impose?

Each covered facility must train oil-handling personnel in the operation and maintenance of equipment to prevent discharges, procedure protocols, applicable pollution control laws and regulations, general facility operations, and the contents of the SPCC plan.[76] Such training includes an annual discharge prevention briefing for oil-handling personnel to ensure adequate understanding of the SPCC plan for the facility. Each facility must designate a person who is accountable for discharge prevention and who reports to facility management. SPCC plans must be amended whenever there is a

change in the facility's design, construction, operation, or maintenance which materially affects the facility's potential for a discharge
of oil to or upon waters of the United States or adjoining shorelines.[77]

COMPLIANCE FACT

Discharge of Oil regulations, also known as the "Sheen Rule,"
require that certain releases of oil that reach the waters of the
United States must be reported under the Clean Water Act if they
cause a film or sheen upon or discoloration of the surface of the
water or adjacent shoreline.

Enforcement

Q 19.8.14   What are the penalties for CWA violations?

Most states have enforcement authority under the CWA and may
enforce similar or more stringent penalties. Federal penalties may be
in the form of an administrative order, an action for civil penalties, an
injunction, or an action for criminal penalties. Federal penalties may
include:

- *Administrative penalty.* Any owner, operator, or person in
  charge of any vessel may be liable for a discharge of
  hazardous substance or the failure to comply with any regulation under the CWA[78] by administrative penalty up to
  $11,000 per day up to $157,500.
- *Civil penalty.* Any owner, operator, or person in charge of any
  vessel may be liable for a discharge of hazardous substance
  or the failure to comply with any regulation under the CWA
  by civil penalty up to $32,500 per day of violation; may be
  subject to a civil penalty three times the costs incurred by
  the Oil Spill Liability Trust Fund for failure to comply with a
  removal order of the EPA; and may be subject to a minimum
  penalty of $130,000 for grossly negligent or willful miscon-
  duct resulting in a release.

- *Criminal penalty.* Any person in charge of a facility from which oil or a hazardous substance is discharged who fails to immediately notify the appropriate federal or state agency shall be fined (in accordance with title 18) or imprisoned for not more than five years, or both.

Toxic Substances Control Act

Q 19.9   What is the intent of the Toxic Substances Control Act?

The Toxic Substances Control Act grants EPA authority to create a regulatory framework to collect data on chemicals in order to evaluate, assess, mitigate, and control risks that may be posed by their manufacture, processing, and use.[79] TSCA provides a variety of control methods to prevent chemicals from posing unreasonable risk. TSCA standards may apply at any point during a chemical's life cycle.

Q 19.9.1   What substances does the TSCA address?

Under TSCA section 5, EPA has established an inventory of "existing chemicals" whose manufacture or importation is permitted. (Certain substances including food, drugs, cosmetics, and pesticides are generally excluded.) Substances not on the inventory of existing chemicals are referred to as "new chemicals," which are subject to review and regulation by the EPA.

Among the specific chemicals regulated by the TSCA are polychlorinated biphenyls (PCBs), asbestos, chlorofluorocarbons, radon, and lead-based paint.

Q 19.9.2   Are all substances not on the inventory of existing chemicals banned?

Not necessarily. If a chemical is not already on the inventory and has not been excluded by TSCA, a pre-manufacture notice (PMN) must be submitted to EPA for review prior to manufacture or import. The PMN must identify the chemical and provide available information on health and environmental effects. Depending on the risk to human health and the environment, the EPA can ban the manufacture or distribution in commerce, limit the use, require labeling, or place other restrictions on chemicals that pose unreasonable risks. If available data are not sufficient to evaluate the chemical's effects, EPA can impose restrictions pending the development of information on its health and environmental effects. EPA can also restrict significant new uses of chemicals based upon factors such as the projected volume and use of the chemical.

Reporting Requirements

Q 19.9.3   What reporting requirements does TSCA impose?

Under TSCA section 8, EPA requires the producers and importers (and others) of chemicals to report information on the chemicals' production, use, exposure, and risks. Companies producing and importing chemicals can be required to report unpublished health and safety studies on listed chemicals and to collect and record any allegations of adverse reactions or any information indicating that a substance may pose a substantial risk to humans or the environment.

Unless companies manufacture, produce, or import chemicals that are restricted by EPA, they will have no reporting obligations under TSCA.[80]

In spring 2012, the EPA proposed significant new use rules under TSCA to require companies to report all new uses of five groups of chemicals. In addition, EPA proposed a new rule to require electronic reporting of certain information to be reported under TSCA and proposed chemicals for risk assessments under TSCA.[81]

On June 22, 2016, President Obama signed into law the Frank R. Lautenberg Chemical Safety for the 21st Century Act,[82] which substantially amends TSCA. The bill requires EPA to review all existing chemicals in commerce, make an affirmative finding of likely safety for any new chemical, carefully evaluate requests to protect confidential business information from disclosure, and conduct risk-based safety reviews. In addition, EPA must reduce the use of vertebrate animal testing. The new bill also requires EPA to review pre-manufacture notices within ninety days and determine whether the new chemical will meet the safety standard or request additional information.

Regulation of Asbestos

Q 19.10   How is asbestos regulated?

The EPA has passed regulations prohibiting the manufacture, importation, processing, and distribution in commerce of asbestos-containing products[83] due to the health risks from exposure to asbestos. Also, the EPA and OSHA have promulgated regulations for the use and disposal of asbestos, particularly asbestos that is removed from buildings as a result of asbestos abatement projects and/or renovations. OSHA regulates employees' exposure to asbestos and requires specific work practices and engineering controls for removing and handling asbestos. Many states have also established asbestos requirements, particularly for abatement and renovation activities and disposal. Most of the regulations require notice to the appropriate state agency before commencement of asbestos abatement projects and specific work practices to protect building occupants and asbestos removal workers. Building owners with knowledge of asbestos in their buildings are required to comply with other provisions of the OSHA standards, such as maintenance personnel training, signs, and warning labels.

Regulation of Lead-Based Paint

Q 19.11   How is lead-based paint regulated?

EPA has promulgated regulations governing the use, abatement, and disposal of lead-based paint to prevent lead-based paint hazards in buildings, residences, and soils. Although the manufacture of lead-based paint was prohibited in 1978, lead-based paint remains in housing units and buildings constructed before that time. Renovation of such buildings is problematic because scraping of paint results in the release of lead-based paint chips and dust. Emission of lead from cars, smelters, and other industrial sources has also resulted in the contamination of soils in urban areas.

EPA's regulations require lead-based paint that has been released from walls, window frames, and door frames, among other areas, to be abated so that it does not affect human health.[84] The Department of Housing and Urban Development has also promulgated lead-based paint disclosure regulations that require sellers and landlords of pre-1978 housing to disclose any knowledge or information regarding lead-based paint present in the housing to purchasers and all residential tenants.[85]

Regulation of Polychlorinated Biphenyls (PCBs)

Q 19.12 How are PCBs regulated?

With a few exceptions, EPA has banned the manufacture, processing, and distribution of PCBs at concentrations of 50 ppm (parts per million) or greater because they present an unreasonable risk of injury to health within the United States.[86]

Q 19.12.1 What uses of PCB-containing materials/equipment are permitted?

The EPA ban of PCBs does not prevent the use of PCB-containing equipment in which the PCBs are "totally enclosed," such as non-leaking transformers, capacitors, electromagnets, voltage regulators, switches, circuit breakers, reclosers, and cable.

The following uses of PCBs, which are not "totally enclosed," are among those authorized by EPA, subject to certain conditions as noted in the regulation:

- Use in and servicing of transformers.
- Use in mining equipment at concentrations <50 ppm.
- Use in heat transfer systems at concentrations <50 ppm.
- Use in hydraulic systems at concentrations <50 ppm.
- Use in and servicing of circuit breakers, reclosers, and cable at any concentration subject to certain conditions.[87]

The regulation should be consulted prior to the use of any PCB-containing material.

Q 19.12.2 What are some of the requirements for permitted uses of PCBs?

PCB Marking. Materials containing PCBs must be marked as set forth in the regulations.[88] This requirement applies to

- PCB containers,
- PCB transformers,
- PCB large high- or low-voltage capacitors,

- equipment containing a PCB transformer or a PCB large high- or low-voltage capacitor,
- electric motors using PCB coolants,
- hydraulic systems using PCB hydraulic fluid,
- heat transfer systems, and
- PCB article containers.

Importantly, each storage area used to store PCBs and PCB items for disposal, as well as vehicles carrying more than 45 kg of liquid PCBs at concentrations at 50 ppm or higher, must be properly marked.

PCB Storage. Proper storage of PCBs and PCB items with concentrations of 50 ppm or greater is set forth in the regulations.[89] PCBs may only be stored for one year prior to disposal.

PCB Disposal.[90] PCB transformers may be disposed of in an incinerator that complies with 40 C.F.R. § 761.70 or in a chemical waste landfill if all of the free-flowing liquid is properly removed. PCB capacitors that contain PCBs must be disposed of in an incinerator that complies with 40 C.F.R. § 761.70. Other articles that contain PCBs at 500 ppm or greater must be disposed of in an incinerator that complies with 40 C.F.R. § 761.70 or in a chemical waste landfill that complies with 40 C.F.R. § 761.75, provided that all free-flowing liquid PCBs have been properly removed before disposal.

PCBs or PCB items with concentrations greater than 50 ppm may not be exported for disposal without an exemption from EPA.[91]

PCB Waste Manifests. A waste manifest, EPA Form 8700-22, or comparable state form must be properly completed for all PCB waste that is offered for transport for off-site storage or disposal.[92] If the generator is not required to have a storage identification number, the generator should use the generic identification number of "40 C.F.R. Part 761" on the manifest.

PCB Record-Keeping. The record-keeping requirements are more stringent for generators of larger quantities of PCB waste.[93] If a facility stores at least 45 kg of PCB waste, one or more PCB transformers, or fifty or more PCB large high- or low-voltage capacitors, the generator shall develop and maintain all annual records and the written annual document log of the disposition of PCBs and PCB items. The log must be prepared for each facility by July 1 for the previous calendar year and shall be retained at the facility for at least three years after the facility ceases using or storing PCBs and PCB items in the quantities set forth in 40 C.F.R. § 761.180. That section should be consulted for the specific content required in the annual log.

TSCA Enforcement

Q 19.13   What are the penalties for violations of the TSCA?

Failure to comply with a TSCA regulation such as properly maintaining records or submitting reports may be subject the violator to civil or criminal penalties[94] up to $37,500 per day for each violation, or imprisonment for up to one year, or both.

Other Pertinent Regulations

Homeland Security Chemical Storage Rules

Q 19.14   What other federal regulations should businesses be aware of when considering environmental issues and compliance?

The Department of Homeland Security (DHS) recently developed Chemical Facility Anti-Terrorism Standards (CFATS), a comprehensive new regulatory program governing security at chemical facilities.[95] CFATS' scope is large because the definition of "chemical facility" is broad and encompasses many facilities that would not traditionally be thought of as chemical facilities, such as warehouses. CFATS covers any establishment that possesses or plans to possess a quantity of a chemical substance determined by DHS to be potentially dangerous ("chemical of interest").

Q 19.14.1   What are covered facilities required to do under CFATS?

- Prepare and submit security vulnerability assessments and site security plans to DHS for approval;
- Update security vulnerability assessments and site security plans;
- Comply with record-keeping requirements;

- Protect chemical terrorism vulnerability information;
- Conduct background checks.

Q 19.14.2   How does DHS enforce these standards?

DHS may enforce the program through audits and inspections and orders. Administrative penalties of up to $25,000 per day can be assessed for noncompliance. On November 20, 2007, DHS published the final Appendix A of the regulations in the *Federal Register*. With the publication of a final Appendix A, all provisions of 6 C.F.R. pt. 27 are operative and in effect.

SEC Environmental Liability Disclosure Requirements

Q 19.15   What other compliance obligations related to environmental issues should businesses be aware of?

The SEC requires five disclosures related to environmental liabilities. Compliance with the SEC rules governing these disclosures typically requires input from both accounting and environmental professionals.

- Contingent Remediation Liabilities—Rule FASB 5 (and SOP-96-1 and Staff Action Bulletin 92 "SAB-92")
- Environmental Legal Proceedings—Regulation S-K 103 (17 C.F.R. § 229.103)
- Description of Business—Regulation S-K 101 (17 C.F.R. § 229.101(c)(xii))
- Management Discussion and Analysis (MD&A)—Rule S-K 303(a) (17 C.F.R. § 229.303)
- Accounting for Conditional Asset Retirement Obligations— FIN 47

Contingent Remediation Liabilities

Q 19.15.1   What are Contingent Remediation Liabilities?

Examples of probable remediation liabilities requiring disclosure could be (1) cost of cleaning up a spill as a result of an accident or other company operation; or (2) the company's anticipated share of remedial costs at a CERCLA Superfund site in which records show that the company sent hazardous substances to the site.

The SEC requires contingent environmental remediation liabilities to be disclosed and, if possible, estimated and accrued each quarter. Accrual is required if liability is probable and estimable. A company must accrue the best estimate, if one exists. If no estimate is better than any other and there is a range of estimates, the company must accrue the low end of the range. If only part of the remedial activity can be estimated (*e.g.*, investigation), it should be accrued.[96]

Environmental Legal Proceedings

Q 19.15.2   What kinds of environmental legal proceedings must be disclosed?

The SEC requires disclosure each quarter of any pending administrative or judicial proceeding (or one contemplated by the government) arising under environmental laws that meet any of the following criteria:

(1)   is "material" to the company's business or financial condition or

(2)   involves a claim for damages, or involves potential monetary sanctions, capital expenditures, deferred charges, or charges to income, and the amount involved exclusive of interest and costs exceeds 10% of the current assets of the company and its subsidiaries on a consolidated basis or

(3)   has a governmental authority as a party and "such proceeding involves potential monetary sanctions" for which the company reasonably believes the sanctions (not including remedial costs or other costs) will be $100,000 or more.

Examples of administrative or judicial proceedings include (1) formal or informal negotiations with a government agency regarding potential sanctions for an alleged violation; and (2) an administrative proceeding initiated by the company to challenge a permit requirement under an environmental law.

Description of Business Disclosures

Q 19.15.3   What are "Description of Business" disclosures?

The SEC requires annual disclosure of the material effects that compliance with environmental laws may have upon the capital expenditures, earnings, and competitive position of the registrant. The registrant must disclose material estimated capital expenditures for environmental control facilities for the remainder of its current fiscal year, succeeding fiscal year, and further periods the registrant may deem material.

Examples of such expenditures are (1) upgrades to underground storage tanks; and (2) upgrades to a wastewater treatment facility.

Management Discussion and Analysis

Q 19.15.4   What are MD&A disclosures?

The SEC requires a company to disclose and discuss in the MD&A of its annual report "known trends . . . events or uncertainties that are reasonably likely" to have a material impact on liquidity, capital resources, or operating results (even if disclosed elsewhere in the filing)—for example, the potential impact of proposed legislation or regulations. (A company is not required to disclose optional forward-looking information by anticipating a future trend or event.)

Conditional Asset Retirement Obligations

Q 19.15.5   What are "Conditional Asset Retirement Obligations" disclosures?

Financial Interpretation No. 47 (FIN 47) was issued March 2005 and became effective December 15, 2005. FIN 47 is an interpretation and clarification of FASB Statement No. 143, which requires companies to disclose on their financial statements environmental liability that will be realized at a future date. FIN 47 requires an asset retirement activity where the timing and/or method of settlement of an environmental liability are conditional on a future event that may or may not be within the control of the company, such as environmental remediation costs associated with closing or selling a facility. FIN 47 explains that a company is required to recognize an environmental liability for the fair value of a conditional asset retirement obligation at the time it is identified so long as the environmental liability's fair value can be estimated.

An asset retirement obligation can be reasonably estimated if:

(1)   it is evident that the fair value of the retirement obligation is included in the acquisition price,

(2)   an active market exists for the transfer of the obligation, or

(3)   information exists to determine the expected present value, which incorporates uncertainty about the timing and method of settlement into the fair value.

Retirement obligation includes sale, abandonment, recycling, or disposal of a conditional asset. The characteristics of a liability are:

(1)   An entity has a present duty to another entity that entails settlement by probable future transfer or use of assets at a specified or determinable date, on occurrence of a specified event, or on demand;

(2)   A duty obligates an entity, leaving little or no discretion to avoid the future sacrifice; and

(3)   The event obligating an entity has already occurred. Only present obligations are relevant.

Climate Change Disclosures

Q 19.16   What does the SEC require companies to report with respect to the impact of climate change?

On February 2, 2010, the SEC published an interpretive release entitled "Commission Guidance Regarding Disclosure Related to Climate Change."[97] The interpretive guidance does not create new disclosure requirements, but clarifies existing Regulation S-K reporting obligations, particularly existing requirements with respect to the impact of climate change on business operations and profitability. The relevant rules cover a company's climate change disclosure obligations in the risk factors, business description, legal proceedings, and MD&A sections in SEC filings.

Notes to Chapter 19

1. This chapter addresses only legally required programs. Voluntary programs, such as recycling or energy-reduction initiatives, are not included in the chapter.
2. 42 U.S.C. § 6901 *et seq.*
3. Subtitle C of RCRA, contained in 40 C.F.R. pts. 260–99.
4. 40 C.F.R. pt. 261.
5. *Id.* pt. 262.
6. *Id.* § 261.3(a)(2).
7. *Id.* § 262.12.
8. *Id.* § 262.2–.23.
9. *Id.* § 262.30–.33.
10. *Id.* § 262.34.
11. *Id.* § 262.40. Records of hazardous waste handling must generally be retained for three years from the date the waste was received or shipped off-site.
12. *Id.* § 262.41–.44.
13. Not all states recognize conditionally exempt small quantity generators.
14. As set forth in 40 C.F.R. pt. 270.
15. Subtitle I of RCRA, 40 C.F.R. pt. 280.
16. 40 C.F.R. § 280.21.
17. The type of permissible UST construction is specified in 40 C.F.R. § 280.20.
18. 40 C.F.R. § 280.22.
19. *Id.* § 280.50.
20. *Id.* § 280.53.
21. *Id.* § 280.61.
22. *Id.* § 280.71.
23. *Id.* § 280.20(c).
24. *Id.* § 280.40–.44.
25. *Id.* pt. 302.
26. *See id.* § 280.60–.67.
27. *Id.* § 280.94.
28. *Id.* § 279.20–.24.
29. *See* Q 19.8.10 *et seq., infra.*
30. 40 C.F.R. pt. 280. *See* Q 19.3.5, *supra.*
31. 42 U.S.C. § 6928.
32. *Id.* § 9601 *et seq.*
33. EPA's Superfund, TRI, EPCRA, RMP, and Oil Information Center answers questions and provides references to EPA guidance pertaining to the Superfund program. Call them at (800) 424-9346.
34. 40 C.F.R. pt. 302.

35. Reportable quantities are defined and listed in 40 C.F.R. § 302.4-5a. The NRC number is (800) 424-8802; fax (202) 267-2165.

36. 40 C.F.R. pt. 300.

37. 42 U.S.C. § 9607(a).

38. *Id.* § 9627.

39. *Id.* § 9627(b).

40. *See id.* § 9627(c).

41. *Id.* § 9627(d).

42. *Id.* § 9607.

43. *Id.* § 9607(f).

44. *Id.* § 9659.

45. 40 C.F.R. pts. 350–72.

46. EPCRA § 302. (The list of extremely hazardous substances is in 40 C.F.R. pt. 355, Appendices A and B.)

47. *Id.* § 304.

48. *Id.* §§ 311, 312.

49. *Id.* § 313.

50. *Id.*

51. CAA regulations appear at 40 C.F.R. pts. 50–99. EPA's Control Technology Center, at (919) 541-0800, provides general assistance and information on CAA standards.

52. CAA § 112(b), as amended.

53. Reformulated gasoline, automobile pollution control devices, and vapor recovery nozzles on gas pumps are a few of the mechanisms EPA uses to regulate mobile air emission sources.

54. Since 1995, these allowances have been set below previous levels of sulfur dioxide releases.

55. Production of Class I substances, including fifteen kinds of chlorofluorocarbons (CFCs), was to be phased out entirely by the year 2000, while certain hydrochlorofluorocarbons (HCFCs) are to be phased out by 2030.

56. *See Climate Change: Endangerment and Cause or Contribute Findings for Greenhouse Gases Under Section 202(a) of the Clean Air Act*, U.S. ENVTL. PROT. AGENCY, www.epa.gov/climatechange/endangerment/index.html.

57. 40 C.F.R. pt. 98.

58. The Green Building Act of 2006, D.C. Law 16-234 (Mar. 8, 2007).

59. This requirement was created by title V of the 1990 Amendments.

60. As defined at 40 C.F.R. § 70.2.

61. *Id.* § 68.130.

62. *Id.* § 68.115.

63. *Id.* pt. 68.

64. 42 U.S.C. § 7413.

65. 33 U.S.C. § 1251 *et seq.*

66. CWA § 402.

67. 40 C.F.R. § 122.26(b)(14).

68. CWA § 307(b).

69. The general pretreatment requirements that must be followed are found at 40 C.F.R. pt. 413, subpt. B.

70. *See* 40 C.F.R. pt. 230. The EPA published a final rule establishing the definition of "waters of the United States" in the Federal Register on June 29, 2015. Final Rule, Clean Water Rule: Definition of "Waters of the United States", 80 Fed. Reg. 37,054 (June 29, 2015). The Supreme Court ruled on May 31, 2016, in U.S. Army Corps of Eng'rs v. Hawkes Co., 136 S. Ct. 1807 (2016), that approved jurisdictional determinations issued by the U.S. Army Corps of Engineers under the Clean Water Act constitute a final agency action that can be challenged in federal court.

71. SPCC regulations are found at 40 C.F.R. pt. 112. Questions about SPCC regulations can be answered by EPA's Superfund, TRI, EPCRA, RMP, and Oil Information Center at (800) 424-9346.

72. 40 C.F.R. § 112.2.

73. *Id.* § 112.7(a).

74. *Id.* § 112.3.

75. *Id.*

76. *Id.* § 112.7.

77. *Id.* § 112.3(b).

78. 33 U.S.C. § 1321.

79. 15 U.S.C. § 2601 *et seq.*

80. If you are unsure about the status of a chemical, consult the Toxic Substances Control Act Hotline, (202) 554-1404, which answers questions and distributes guidance pertaining to TSCA standards, Monday through Friday, from 8:30 A.M. to 5:00 P.M. (Eastern).

81. *Existing Chemicals*, U.S. ENVTL. PROT. AGENCY, www.epa.gov/oppt/existingchemicals (last visited July 13, 2015).

82. Frank R. Lautenberg Chemical Safety for the 21st Century Act, H.R. 2576, 114th Cong. (2016) (amending the Toxic Substances Control Act).

83 Identified in 40 C.F.R. pt. 763.

84. *Id.* pt. 745.

85. For further information regarding lead-based paint, consult www.epa.gov/lead/pubs/n.lic.htm.

86. 40 C.F.R. § 761.20.

87. *Id.* § 761.30.

88. *Id.* § 761.40.

89. *Id.* § 761.65.

90. Proper disposal of PCB-containing materials is set forth in Subpart D of 40 C.F.R. pt. 761.

91. 40 C.F.R. § 761.97.

92. *Id.* § 761.207.

93. *Id.* § 761.80.

94. 15 U.S.C. § 2615.

95. 6 C.F.R. pt. 27.

96. Rule FASB 5 (SOP-96-1 & SAB-92).

97. Securities Act Release No. 9106 (Feb. 2, 2010), www.sec.gov/rules/interp/2010/33-9106.pdf.

715

20

Consumer Product Safety Act

Charles E. Joern, Jr.

Compliance with consumer product safety laws is not optional. Consumer product safety regulations are both complex and wide-ranging. Failure to comply exposes businesses to significant civil penalties of over $15 million for a related series of violations and, for certain violations, criminal penalties of up to five years' imprisonment. In addition to civil and criminal penalties, failure to comply with the Consumer Product Safety Act (CPSA) can result in nationwide recalls of non-compliant consumer products, which can be extremely expensive and potentially devastating to businesses.

Businesses must know and understand their products as well as the ongoing changes to the CPSA and its implementation. Companies should have a basic, enterprise-wide compliance structure that is flexible enough to accommodate change on an ongoing basis. Compliance with the CPSA requires continuous and diligent efforts by all regulated businesses as well as the assistance of knowledgeable counsel.

To that end, this chapter looks first at the regulatory framework and jurisdiction of consumer product regulation in the United States, before examining the requirements that manufacturers,

717

importers, private labelers, distributors, and retailers of consumer products must comply with, including compliance related to testing and certification of products, reporting non-compliant, defective, and hazardous products, and recalls.

Regulatory Framework

Jurisdiction

Q 20.1   How are consumer products regulated in the United States?

The Consumer Product Safety Commission (CPSC or "Commission") enforces consumer protection laws involving over 15,000 different types of consumer products. The Commission is an independent federal regulatory agency created by Congress in 1972 and charged with protecting the public "against unreasonable risks of injury associated with consumer products."[1]

Q 20.2   What is a "consumer product" for regulatory purposes?

A consumer product is generally any article or component part that is produced or distributed for sale to a consumer for use in or around a household, residence, school, in recreation, or otherwise. Examples of consumer products include, among others:

toys	clothes	jewelry
household appliances	furniture	books
computers	sporting goods	cookware
household chemicals	power tools	children's products

The following items are regulated under other statutes and are not "consumer products":

tobacco products	motor vehicles or motor vehicle equipment[2]
pesticides	firearms and ammunition
aircraft	boats
drugs	medical devices
cosmetics	food

In addition, consumer products do not include any article not customarily produced, distributed, used, or consumed by consumers.[3]

Business Application

Q 20.3   What businesses are covered by consumer product safety laws?

Manufacturers, importers, private labelers, distributors, and retailers of consumer products are all regulated by consumer product safety laws. The Commission has jurisdiction over all such businesses regardless of their size or number of employees. Internet sellers and resellers of used products, such as thrift shops, are also covered.

Statutes

Q 20.4   What consumer product safety laws does the Commission enforce?

The primary governing statute is the Consumer Product Safety Act of 1972 (CPSA) as significantly revised by the Consumer Product Safety Improvement Act of 2008 (CPSIA)[4] and as amended by H.R. 2715, a 2011 "Act to provide the Consumer Product Safety Commission with greater authority and discretion in enforcing the consumer product safety laws, and for other purposes"[5] (*see* Q 20.18). In addition to the CPSA, the Commission enforces provisions of the following acts:

- Federal Hazardous Substances Act (FHSA)[6]
- Flammable Fabrics Act (FFA)[7]
- Poison Prevention Packaging Act (PPPA)[8]
- Refrigerator Safety Act (RSA)[9]
- Virginia Graeme Baker Pool and Spa Safety Act[10]
- Children's Gasoline Burn Prevention Act[11]

Consumer Product Safety Act Compliance

Consequences of Non-Compliance

Q 20.5   How important is consumer product safety law compliance?

Compliance with consumer product safety laws is not optional. Consumer product safety regulations are both complex and wide-ranging. Failure to comply exposes businesses to significant civil penalties of over \$15 million for a related series of violations.[12] Further, individual directors, officers, and agents of a corporation are subject to criminal penalties of up to five years' imprisonment for knowing and willful violations of the CPSA.[13]

The CPSA also mandates the destruction of non-compliant imports. Imported products that do not comply with the CPSA and are refused admission into the customs territory of the United States shall be destroyed (unless the Secretary of the Treasury in response to a special application permits the export of the product in lieu of destruction).[14]

In addition to civil and criminal penalties, failure to comply with the CPSA can result in nationwide recalls of non-compliant consumer products. Such recalls can be extremely expensive and potentially devastating to businesses.

Prohibited Acts

Q 20.6   What constitutes a violation under the CPSA?

Businesses have varying obligations under the CPSA, but generally it is unlawful under the CPSA to

> sell, offer for sale, manufacture for sale, distribute in commerce, or import into the United States any consumer product . . . [that violates any] applicable consumer product safety rule under [the Consumer Product Safety Act], or any similar rule, regulation, standard, or ban under any other Act enforced by the Commission.[15]

721

Other "prohibited acts" include the sale, offer for sale, manufacture for sale, distribution in commerce, or import into the United States of any consumer product that has been recalled in consultation with the Commission, contains a "substantial product hazard" (*see* Q 20.15.2), or is a banned hazardous substance under the FHSA. The failure to report non-compliant products to the Commission, the failure to issue a required product certificate, and other acts and omissions enumerated in section 19 of the CPSA are all prohibited acts.[16]

CPSA Requirements

Q 20.7   What requirements must a business meet to comply with the CPSA?

The CPSA is a complex law. Its interpretation and enforcement are evolving and ongoing. From 2008 through September 2014, the CPSC completed 172 CPSIA-related rulemaking activities. By late 2014, the Commission had issued a total of forty-nine new final rules since the passage of the CPSIA in 2008. Application of the CPSA and related rules and regulations as they currently pertain to specific products requires careful individual analysis. Generally, however, a business must:

- comply;
- test and certify;
- report.

Q 20.7.1   What does it mean for a business to "comply"?

A company must ensure that the consumer product it manufactures, imports, distributes, or sells is in conformity with all applicable consumer product safety rules under the CPSA and any similar rules, regulations, standards, or bans under any other act enforced by the Commission.[17]

Q 20.7.2   What are a business's specific testing and certification obligations?

In most circumstances, domestic manufacturers and importers are obligated to certify, based on an appropriate testing program, that their product meets each applicable consumer product safety rule under the CPSA or similar rule, ban, standard, or regulation under any other act enforced by the Commission.[18]

Q 20.7.3   What are a business's reporting obligations?

If a manufacturer, distributor, or retailer of a consumer product obtains information that reasonably supports the conclusion that a product:

(1)   fails to comply with an applicable consumer product safety rule (or voluntary standard the Commission relied on to develop a rule);

(2)   fails to comply with any other rule, regulation, standard, or ban under the CPSA or other act enforced by the Commission;

(3)   contains a defect that could create a substantial product hazard; or

(4)   creates an unreasonable risk of serious injury or death,

then the manufacturer, distributor, or retailer must "immediately" inform the Commission of such a problem pursuant to section 15(b) of the CPSA.[19]

Regulatory Compliance

Q 20.8   Does the Commission certify that products comply with applicable product safety laws?

No. The Commission will not pre-approve products as compliant with the applicable standards or rules. The Commission does not have the authority to test or certify products for safety prior to their being sold to consumers. Compliance with applicable product safety laws is a business's own responsibility.

Q 20.9   How does a business know what consumer product safety laws apply to its product?

A business should determine (1) if its product falls within the jurisdiction of the Commission and (2) if so, what specific rules, regulations, standards, or bans apply.

Q 20.9.1   How do we determine if our product is a "consumer product" under the jurisdiction of the Commission?

Many products are statutorily excluded from regulation by the Commission. The CPSA specifically defines both the term "consumer product" and the products that are excluded from the definition of a consumer product.[20] If a product is not within the Commission's jurisdiction, the business does not have compliance obligations under the CPSA or other Commission-enforced statutes.

In addition, the Commission's jurisdiction does not include false advertising, fraud, or poor product quality not related to safety. The Federal Trade Commission has the responsibility for handling false advertising, fraud, and product quality complaints.

Q 20.9.2   Once we determine that our product is a consumer product, how do we decide what specific regulations apply?

Proper and complete identification of what rules, regulations, standards, or bans apply to individual products is a difficult task that requires a complete understanding of both a company's products and the CPSA itself. In general, some consumer products are subject to specific regulations, while other consumer products are considered "unregulated." "Regulated" products must comply with specific rules, regulations, standards, or bans applicable to the CPSA or other acts enforced by the Commission (the FHSA, FFA, PPPA, etc.). Examples of regulated products include cigarette lighters, cribs, power lawn mowers, mattresses, toys, and wearing apparel.

Q 20.9.3   What are "unregulated" products, and how are they treated?

"Unregulated" products are consumer products under the jurisdiction of the CPSC, but not subject to specific regulations. Although nominally "unregulated," these consumer products are still subject to the CPSA's general product safety obligations, including the section 15(b) obligation to report defective or dangerous products to the Commission (*see* Q 20.15). Unregulated products also are subject to recall. In fact, many more unregulated products are recalled than are regulated products.

Q 20.9.4   What sources of information can we use to determine what regulations apply to our product?

There are a number of regulations that apply to the CPSA and other acts enforced by the Commission. The Commission's website contains links to regulations for the CPSA and each of the other acts enforced by the Commission.[21] Determining exactly what regulations apply to a particular product requires a detailed analysis of the specific product and the applicable product safety law.

The Commission is aware of the difficulties businesses face in trying to determine how to comply with a complex set of regulations. In addition to the general link to all applicable regulations, the Commission provides a "look-up" table linking specific types of regulated products for which the Commission has issued requirements.[22] The table also provides links to multiple materials relevant to regulatory provisions for the listed products.

In early 2016, the CPSC introduced an online tool designed to help small businesses navigate the maze of regulatory requirements applicable to their products. The "Regulatory Robot" takes the user through a series of questions aimed at identifying the specific nature of the product and the particular regulations applicable to the product.[23]

Ultimately, businesses should consider retaining knowledgeable counsel to assist in determining the regulations applicable to their products under the current law.

Mandatory and Voluntary Standards

Q 20.10   What standards must our product meet?

Many consumer products are subject to mandatory standards, voluntary standards, or both. Businesses must necessarily clearly understand what mandatory and voluntary standards apply to their products. In some instances, the CPSIA mandated that certain voluntary standards be converted to mandatory standards (for example, standards for durable infant and toddler products, all-terrain vehicles (ATVs), and children's toys).[24]

Q 20.10.1   What are mandatory standards?

Mandatory consumer product standards are rules created by statutes or regulations that define the performance and labeling requirements products must meet. Companies must comply with applicable mandatory standards before their product can be manufactured, imported, distributed, or sold in the United States. The CPSC may create a mandatory standard if the Commission determines that a voluntary standard would not eliminate or sufficiently reduce a known risk of injury. Products that do not meet mandatory standards are in violation of the CPSA. They are subject to civil or criminal penalties and may also be stopped at ports and seized. Approximately 200 different kinds of products are subject to mandatory standards.

Q 20.10.2   What are voluntary standards?

Besides mandatory government standards, the CPSA also relies on non-governmental "voluntary" standards. These include industry standards issued by private entities such as ANSI, ASTM, and Underwriters Laboratories. Although voluntary standards do not have the force of law, failure to meet a voluntary standard could lead to a Commission determination that a particular product contains a "substantial product hazard" (*see* Q 20.15.2). Failure to report such a product to the Commission is a "prohibited act" under the CPSA.[25] The CPSC Office of Compliance stated this very position in a letter to manufacturers, importers, and retailers of "hoverboards." Hoverboards that do not meet applicable voluntary standards are considered defective and may be a "substantial product hazard." Such products may be detained and/or seized at import or recalled if present in the United States.[26]

The converse, however, is not true. Compliance with a voluntary standard does not exempt a firm from an obligation to report a product otherwise reasonably suspected to be defective and dangerous.

Voluntary standards also sometimes form the basis for Commission-adopted regulations and may provide useful compliance guidance. In addition, voluntary standards may assist a business in developing a reasonable testing program required for a General Certificate of Conformity (*see* Q 20.12.2).

Children's Products

Q 20.11   Is the Commission's regulation of children's products different from its regulation of general-use products?

Yes, very much so. The CPSIA was Congress's response to a wave of product recalls in 2007, the most highly publicized of which involved the recalls of imported Chinese-manufactured toys containing lead paint. As a result, many new provisions regulating children's products were added to the CPSA.

When trying to determine what regulations apply to a product, it is extremely important to determine whether the product is a children's product or a general-use product. The CPSA defines a children's product as "a consumer product designed or intended primarily for children 12 years of age or younger." The CPSA then lists four factors to consider in this regard.[27] The Commission recognized that the determination of whether a particular product should be classified as a "children's product" is often difficult. The Commission has issued a Final Interpretive Rule designed to provide additional guidance on factors that are considered when evaluating what constitutes a "children's product" under the CPSA.[28] Despite the detailed guidelines, the determination of what is a "children's product" often depends on case-by-case facts unique to each product. A detailed evaluation of the particular product may therefore be necessary to comply with applicable regulations for children's products.

Many substantive and procedural requirements apply to children's products that do not apply to general-use products. Substantive requirements for children's products include:

- rigorous lead-content limits;
- complex and intricate mandatory standards; and
- a ban on the use of certain chemical plasticizers known as phthalates.

In addition, children's products must meet stringent procedural requirements—most notable of which is the independent third-party laboratory testing of children's products.

Testing and Certification

Q 20.12   What testing and certification requirements apply to our product?

Once a company identifies the product safety rules applicable to its product, that company (if it is a domestic manufacturer or an importer) must certify that the product complies with all such safety rules. The certification must be based on an appropriate testing program and must specify each rule, ban, standard, or regulation applicable to the product.[29] Certificates of compliance must also identify: the importer or domestic manufacturer certifying compliance; contact information for the individual maintaining records of test results; the date and place where the product was made as well as where the product was tested; and any third-party testing laboratory on whose testing the certificate depends.[30]

There are two different types of certifications required by the Commission depending on whether the product is a "children's product" or a "general-use" product:

1. A General Certificate of Conformity (GCC) is required for all products (other than children's products) that are subject to specific consumer product safety rules. This type of certification must be based on a test of each product or a "reasonable testing program."[31]
2. A Children's Product Certificate (CPC) is required for all children's products that are subject to applicable product safety rules. This certification must be based on tests done by third-party laboratories that are recognized and approved by the Commission to perform such certification testing required for children's products.[32]

Product-testing certifications must "accompany" each product shipment and be "furnished" to each distributor and retailer of the product. Electronic certificates satisfy these requirements if the certificate is uniquely identified and can be accessed via an Internet URL reference reasonably available to authorities and distributors and retailers.[33]

Q 20.12.1   Are all businesses required to issue certifications?

No. Except as otherwise provided in a specific standard, current Commission regulations require that only importers and domestic manufacturers provide certification. Retailers and distributors are not required to issue certificates of compliance.[34]

Testing General-Use Products

Q 20.12.2   What is a "reasonable testing program" as required for a General Certificate of Conformity?

In order to issue a valid GCC, manufacturers/importers of general-use (non-children's) products must certify, "based on a test of each product or upon a reasonable testing program that such product complies with all rules, bans, or regulations applicable to the product . . . ."[35] However, the Commission has not issued any rule generally defining what a "reasonable testing program" is. The final rule on Testing and Labeling Pertaining to Product Certification "reserved" the subpart defining a reasonable testing program.[36] Nevertheless, the CPSA still requires manufacturers/importers to certify based on a test of each product or a reasonable testing program.[37] Some mandatory standards contain specific requirements for a testing program within that particular standard.[38] Otherwise, manufacturers/importers currently must determine for themselves what a reasonable testing program is.

The previously proposed (but not adopted) testing rule provides some "best practices" guidance in this area.[39] The proposed rule included, among other more specific requirements, that a reasonable testing program provide a manufacturer or importer with a "high degree of assurance" that the product complies with applicable consumer product safety rules and standards. Although the particular requirements of a reasonable testing program are currently undefined, what is clear is that manufacturers/importers without any testing program will be out of compliance.

729

Testing Children's Products

Q 20.13   What testing programs are required for children's products?

Manufacturers/importers of children's products must certify that their products meet safety rules by having an independent third-party CPSC-approved laboratory test a sufficient number of product samples using CPSC-approved testing requirements for each applicable product safety rule.[40]

There are three kinds of testing programs potentially required for most children's products:

(1)   initial certification testing;
(2)   material change testing; and
(3)   periodic testing.[41]

In addition, manufacturers may choose to make use of optional component part testing rules in order to reduce their regulatory burden.[42]

Q 20.13.1   What initial certification testing is required for children's products?

Manufacturers/importers of children's products—with few exceptions—must initially test their products in order to certify that they meet all applicable safety rules. This initial certification testing must be done by an independent third-party CPSC-approved laboratory. Based on the initial certification testing results, the manufacturer/importer must then issue a CPC (*see* Q 20.12) in order to import, distribute, or sell the product.

Manufacturers/importers must submit for certification testing a sufficient number of samples that are materially identical to the products and that are sufficient to provide a "high degree of assurance" that the certification tests demonstrate the ability of the product to meet the applicable product safety rules.

Q 20.13.2   What "material change testing" is required for certification of children's products?

A children's product that undergoes a "material change" in its design or manufacture (including a change in the sourcing of component parts) must also be retested and recertified, if the manufacturer/importer knows, or should know, the change could affect the product's ability to comply with the applicable product safety rule.[43]

Q 20.13.3   What "periodic testing" is required for certification of children's products?

In addition to initial certification testing and material change testing, children's products must also pass periodic testing to ensure continued compliance. Periodic testing is required for children's products that are made in a continuing production. Periodic testing is not required for children's products produced only in limited production runs. Periodic testing must be done by an independent third-party laboratory. The periodic testing must be completed at least once a year, but potentially more often depending on various factors listed in the rule.[44]

There are two exceptions that permit the testing interval to expand beyond one year. First, if a manufacturer/importer implements a written "production testing plan," the testing interval may be a minimum of once every two years. Second, if the manufacturer/importer conducts its continued testing using an ISO/IEC 17025:2005(E) accredited laboratory (that is, a laboratory accredited to meet general testing laboratory requirements), then the testing interval may be extended to a minimum of once every three years.[45]

Q 20.13.4   What are the "undue influence" requirements that a manufacturer/importer of children's products must meet?

Manufacturers/importers are required to establish procedures to safeguard against the exercise of "undue influence" by a manufacturer on a third-party testing lab. These requirements include a written policy, employee training, and signed attestations of training.[46]

Q 20.13.5   What are the record-keeping obligations required for a manufacturer/importer of a children's product?

The record-keeping requirements are extensive. They include the following:

- a copy of the CPC for each product;
- the records of each third-party certification test (the manufacturer must keep separate certification test records for each manufacturing site);
- records of the applicable periodic tests;
- descriptions of all material changes in the product and the related certification tests;
- records of undue influence procedures and training.

The manufacturer must maintain these records for five years and make them available (electronically or hardcopy) to the CPSC upon request. The records may be maintained outside the United States and in languages other than English, if they can be provided immediately to the CPSC and translated within forty-eight hours (or as otherwise negotiated).[47]

Component Testing

Q 20.14   May a company rely on others' testing of component parts in order to fulfill compliance requirements?

Yes. The Commission adopted a final rule in 2011 that allows for certification of compliance based on others' testing or certification of component parts, the testing of another party's finished product, or composite testing. The rule sets out strict testing requirements for test result integrity, sampling protocols, traceability, and documentation. The use of component part testing for compliance purposes is voluntary.[48] A manufacturer/importer that relies on a supplier's test results or certification must use "due care" to ensure the test results or certificate relied on are valid.

Reporting Requirements

Q 20.15   What reporting requirements should a business be aware of?

Section 15(b) of the CPSA requires manufacturers, importers, distributors, and retailers to report to the Commission information that reasonably supports the conclusion that a product:

(1)   does not comply with a safety rule issued under the CPSA (or voluntary standard that the Commission has relied on for a rulemaking);

(2)   does not comply with any other rule, regulation, standard, or ban under the CPSA or any other act enforced by the Commission;

(3)   contains a defect that could create a "substantial product hazard"; or

(4)   presents an unreasonable risk of serious injury or death.[49]

Q 20.15.1   What type of information can trigger a report?

Any information that a company receives, including product returns, customer complaints, quality control data, lawsuits, or other information that indicates a defect, safety rule violation, or unreasonable risk of injury or death, can lead to a reporting obligation. Businesses must even consider information from incidents or sources outside the United States if it is relevant to products distributed or sold in the United States.

Although it is beyond the scope of this chapter, international companies should be aware of their global reporting obligation in countries outside the United States. Canada, Australia, and the European Union (among others) all have requirements to report safety problems with consumer products. Businesses should retain knowledgeable local counsel in those countries to provide compliance advice for companies operating in those jurisdictions.

Substantial Product Hazard

Q 20.15.2   What is a "substantial product hazard"?

Deciding whether a product contains a "substantial product hazard" is a significant determination that may require both forensic engineering and legal analysis. The CPSA defines a "substantial product hazard" as:

(1) a failure to comply with an applicable consumer product safety rule under [the CPSA] or a similar rule, regulation, standard, or ban under any other Act enforced by the Commission that creates a substantial risk of injury to the public, or

(2) a product defect that (because of the pattern of defect, the number of defective products distributed in commerce, the severity of the risk, or otherwise) creates a substantial risk of injury to the public.[50]

The CPSC may also specify by rule that a particular product or class of products contains characteristics that constitute a substantial product hazard. The CPSC has used this authority to issue rules determining that certain classes of products—hand-held hair dryers without circuit interrupters;[51] children's upper outerwear, in certain sizes, with drawstrings;[52] and seasonal and decorative lighting products ("Christmas" lights) lacking certain requirements[53]—each contained substantial product hazards. These products are subject to CPSA reporting and recall provisions and shall be refused entry into the United States.[54]

Q 20.15.3   What should we do if we are uncertain if there is an actual product safety problem with a product?

It is the nearly universal Commission recommendation that companies err on the side of over-reporting. Failure to report can result in significant civil and, in extreme cases, criminal penalties. Businesses should also note that the filing of a report is not an admission of a defective and dangerous product.

Applicable regulations state:

> Subject firms should not delay reporting in order to determine to a certainty the existence of a reportable noncompliance, defect or unreasonable risk. The obligation to report arises upon receipt of information from which one could reasonably conclude the existence of a reportable non-compliance, defect which could create a substantial product hazard, or unreasonable risk of serious injury or death. . . . A subject firm in its report to the Commission need not admit, or may specifically

deny, that the information it submits reasonably supports the conclusion that its consumer product is noncomplying, contains a defect which could create a substantial product hazard within the meaning of section 15(b) of the CPSA, or creates an unreasonable risk of serious injury or death.[55]

Q 20.15.4   How soon must a company report a problem?

The CPSA requires manufacturers and importers distributors and retailers to "immediately inform the Commission" of reportable problems.[56] While there is some reasonable interpretation to the term "immediately," it is imperative that a company move as rapidly as possible in this regard. The applicable regulations state that the Commission will, under ordinary circumstances, allow a maximum of five business days for information obtained by an official of a firm to reach the chief executive officer, official, or employee responsible for filing a 15(b) report to the Commission.[57] In addition, applicable regulations state that an investigation and evaluation should not take more than ten business days unless a company can demonstrate that a longer period is reasonable.[58]

Q 20.15.5   What should a firm do to ensure compliance with CPSA reporting obligations?

Businesses should institute a system that captures any information that reasonably suggests a product safety problem may exist. This system should channel such information to appropriate persons in the company for evaluation and reporting if appropriate. It should be an integral part of a company's formal compliance plan (*see* Q 20.18.3).

Q 20.15.6   If a lawsuit is filed against my company, do I have to file a report with the Commission?

Section 37 of the CPSA requires that manufacturers report to the Commission any product that is the subject of at least three civil actions "filed in Federal or State court for death or grievous bodily injury [within a twenty-four-month period that] results in either a final settlement involving the manufacturer or a court judgment in favor of the plaintiff."[59] Depending on the circumstances, a single lawsuit combined with other information may give rise to a reporting obligation under section 15(b).

Q 20.15.7   If I report a suspected problem, will my business have to recall the product?

Not necessarily. About 60% of the section 15(b) reports result in a recall (including "fast-track" recalls).

The requirement to report a suspected problem is independent of the responsibility to recall a product. In fact, companies are subject to fines "for report failures [even] when a product turns out not to be defective."[60] In short: when in doubt, report.

Recalls

Mandatory and Voluntary Recalls

Q 20.16   When does a company have to recall a product?

Recalls may be mandatory or voluntary. Mandatory recalls can be initiated under the Commission's authority. They are rare. The vast majority of recalls are voluntary. Voluntary recalls are initiated by companies in conjunction with the Commission. In the last several years, nearly 100% of the recalls announced to consumers were voluntary.

More recently, however, the Commission has aggressively pursued mandatory recalls via administrative complaints and other litigation. In these cases, the CPSC has sought to force a recall where companies have refused to voluntarily recall a product (*see* Q 20.18.2).[61]

Q 20.16.1   Under what circumstances does the Commission decide that a recall is not necessary at all?

Once a company files a report with the Commission under section 15(b), the Commission staff investigates the report to preliminarily determine if a product contains a defect that presents a substantial product hazard. If the staff determines such a hazard exists, then the CPSC will require a business to create a "Corrective Action Plan" (which may include a recall). In many cases, however, no Corrective Action Plan/recall is required because the Commission concludes that the reported product does not create a substantial product hazard.

Fast-Track Recalls

Q 20.16.2   What is a fast-track recall?

A fast-track recall is a Commission-created program in which the company filing a section 15(b) report agrees to voluntarily recall the product within twenty working days of the filing of the report. If the company's proposed Corrective Action Plan is acceptable to the Commission staff, the staff will not investigate the product or make a "preliminary determination" that the reported product is defective and creates a substantial product hazard.

Publicly Available Consumer Product Safety Information Database

Q 20.17   Is there a database of consumer product safety complaints?

Yes. The Consumer Product Safety Improvement Act of 2008 required the creation of a new Publicly Available Consumer Product Safety Information Database. In March 2011, the database began operating. The database is a collection of reports of harm relating to consumer products. The reports (or complaints) identify specific manufacturers, importers, or private labelers ("manufacturers") and their products. The database is accessible through the Commission website at www.saferproducts.gov.

The database contains reports of harm that involve not only actual injury, but also reports concerning the risk of injury or death relating to the use of consumer products. The database also includes information the Commission obtains from recall notices and additional information the Commission determines is in the public interest.

Q 20.17.1   Does the database affect businesses?

Yes. The database is a source of self-verified complaints that contain claims about the safety of a company's product. Because the database is Internet-based, reports about a company's products are available to consumers and others worldwide. The reports may therefore have significant impact on the public's perception of a company and its products. In addition, reports submitted to the database could (under certain circumstances) give rise to a company self-reporting its own product to the Commission under section 15(b) requirements.

Q 20.17.2 Is a company notified of reports concerning its products?

Yes. If a company registers with the Commission through the specified electronic business portal, the named company will receive prompt electronic notice of reports before they are published in the database.

Q 20.17.3 Can a company submit anything to the database?

Yes. Within strict designated time frames, companies may submit comments that will be published concurrently on the database with the publication of the complaint. Companies may also submit objections concerning material inaccuracies or confidential company information contained in reports, prior to the time the reports are published. In certain situations, the Commission will correct materially inaccurate or redact confidential information in a report prior to the report's publication in the database.[62]

In a key decision, a federal district court granted a company's request and prevented publication of a database report that the court found was materially misleading.[63]

The district court further allowed the company's request to litigate secretly under the pseudonym "Company Doe" in order to prevent public disclosure in court proceedings of the very allegations the company sought to keep the CPSC from publishing in the public database. The court pleadings were also sealed, and the judge heavily redacted his ruling and eliminated references to the identity of the company and the product.

Although the CPSC did not appeal the district court's rulings barring the database publication, several consumer advocacy groups sought to intervene and appeal the secrecy rulings. The U.S. Court of Appeals for the Fourth Circuit allowed the groups' intervention, overturned the lower court's secrecy rulings, and ordered the court records unsealed. As a result, companies now may be able to sue the CPSC to prevent publication of an inaccurate report, which could harm a product's reputation—but in doing so the allegedly false report itself will have to be revealed in public litigation.[64]

Developments and Outlook

Q 20.18   What aspects of the CPSA have been amended?

In 2011, Congress passed H.R. 2715,[65] which modifies several provisions of the CPSA. The act was signed into law shortly thereafter and gave the Commission new authority and discretion in enforcing consumer product safety rules. Changes included the following:

(1)   Limitations on lead in children's products:
  - Products, product classes, materials, and components may be excepted from lead-content limits if they qualify for a "functional purpose exception."
  - ATVs, as well as bicycles and related products, received exceptions from lead-content limits.
  - Used children's products also received lead-content exclusions with certain designated exceptions.

(2)   Third-party testing requirements:
  - The Commission must seek public comment on ways to reduce the cost of third-party testing. The Commission may then enact rules that reduce the testing burdens.
  - Small batch manufacturers (less than $1 million per year in gross sales revenues of consumer products) may qualify for alternative testing requirements or even exemptions from third-party testing requirements.
  - Ordinary books, ordinary printed materials, and metal components of bicycles are excluded from third-party testing requirements.

(3)   Other changes:
  - The Commission may exclude products or classes of products from tracking label requirements if the Commission determines it is not practicable to label such children's products.
  - The rules for the new public database were modified. If the Commission receives a claim that a report or

comment is materially inaccurate, the Commission will delay publication in the database for an additional five days. Other changes encourage—but do not require—the submission of product model or serial numbers for the product named in the database complaint.

The act made immediate and tangible changes for certain businesses and products. Beyond that, the act also gave the Commission new discretionary powers to grant exceptions concerning other businesses and products. Since 2011, the Commission has made limited progress in finding meaningful ways to reduce the compliance costs and burdens of third-party testing. Recently however, the CPSC was able to reach consensus on a new enforcement policy that will provide an estimated $250 million a year in relief from unnecessary paperwork burdens. The new policy eliminates the need for manufacturers, importers, and private labelers of adult wearing apparel to create a document certifying that certain wearing apparel is exempt from testing under the Flammable Fabrics Act.[66] In other words, such businesses do not have to spend money certifying what they do not have to do in the first place. Hopefully the CPSC will find other ways to implement the 2011 congressional mandate to reduce regulatory costs.

In the meantime, it is unlikely there will be any other legislative changes to the CPSA in the near future. Regulated businesses must therefore monitor the evolving implementation and enforcement of the CPSA in order to effectively comply with the law.

Q 20.18.1   Are any significant rule changes pending?

Yes. Currently there are three potentially significant rule changes pending:

- amendments to the existing rule on certificates of compliance;
- changes to the "section 6(b)" rule on CPSC disclosure of product information; and
- a new "interpretative" rule on voluntary recall notices and compliance programs.

First, the CPSC has proposed changes that could dramatically alter regulations involving almost all consumer products imported into the United States. This long-pending rulemaking would amend the existing regulation on certificates of compliance.[67] The proposed rule would replace the current 16 C.F.R. part 1110 rule and update it to clarify requirements in light of new testing and certification regulations. The new rule would affect requirements for GCC and CPC certificates that must accompany consumer products before they can be imported into or distributed in the United States. The amended rule would, among other things:

- require importers to file only electronic certificates of compliance;
- define importer to mean "importer of record" as defined under the Tariff Act of 1930 (19 U.S.C. § 1484(a)(2)(B)), thus potentially including common carriers that "import" products that consumers buy over the Internet;
- clarify requirements for the form and content of certificates;
- require an importer to provide an "attestation of compliance" that the certificate is based on valid information.

Currently, the CPSC is testing a new e-filing system for all imported consumer products. Results of the "Alpha Pilot" program (expected in late 2016) will likely determine the final certification rulemaking. Regulated businesses—especially importers—should monitor developments in this area.

Second, the Commission has proposed changes to the "section 6(b)" rules on disclosure of information where the identity of the manufacturer can be "readily ascertained." Current section 6(b) rules require the CPSC to take reasonable steps to ensure that such information is accurate and the disclosure is fair. These provisions uniquely protect manufacturers from the damaging effects resulting from public disclosure of inaccurate information by the CPSC. The existing rule, 16 C.F.R. § 1101, requires the Commission to give notice and an opportunity for the manufacturer to comment on the accuracy of the information to be disclosed. The amended rule changes would include:

- narrowing the scope of the information covered by section 6(b) protections;
- deleting section 6(b) notice requirements for "publicly available information";
- removing the addition notice requirement when the Commission re-releases "substantially similar" information;

- requiring manufacturers for the first time to "provide a ratio-nale" why their own comments in connection with a 6(b) notice should not be disclosed.[68]

The proposed section 6(b) rule changes could significantly reduce the protections from unfair CPSC disclosures that manufac-turers now enjoy.

Third, the Commission is considering an "interpretive rule" that would significantly change the way in which voluntary recalls are conducted by businesses. Since 1975, corrective action plans for a company's recall have not been legally binding.[69] The new interpre-tive rule would fundamentally alter past practice and make corrective action plans legally binding. Other changes could limit a business's ability to deny that a reportable issue or a product hazard exists. Additionally, the new rule would allow the CPSC to require formal compliance plans as part of a company's binding corrective action plan—all of which may act as a disincentive for businesses to volun-tarily recall products.[70]

The 6(b) rule changes and the voluntary recall rule changes are in the Final Rules stage of the CPSC's rulemaking agenda. Both are controversial, and as of this writing, it is unclear if both—or either—will be implemented in 2016.

Q 20.18.2 What is the outlook for CPSC enforcement policy?

The CPSC has recently enhanced its enforcement efforts and resources in a variety of ways. These include the following:

- *Significantly higher penalties.* Civil penalties have risen dramatically over the last several years—up on average ten-fold from 2009 to 2015. Now they have reached the maximum amounts increased under the CPSIA in 2008. Current CPSC Chairman Elliot Kaye is publicly committed to imposing the highest possible civil penalties allowed. In announcing a record $15.45 million settlement against a company for late reporting and material misrepresentations,[71] Chairman Kaye warned that the CPSC is "sending a message" that noncom-pliant companies will face similar penalties. In short, expect the CPSC to seek "marquee" penalty amounts whenever feasible.

- *Increased CPSC litigation.* The CPSC is increasingly using litigation as an enforcement tool. Contrary to past practice, the Commission is now filing suits seeking mandatory recalls in cases where the Commission could not reach agreement with companies on the continued distribution of products. The CPSC has filed administrative complaints against companies to force recalls and stop the sale of the questioned products. In one case, the CPSC took the unusual step of adding the CEO of a defunct company as a defendant and asking that he be held personally responsible for the costs of recalling the product.[72]

- *Other enforcement mechanisms.* The Commission also uses informal pressure on retailers to "voluntarily" stop selling products the CPSC believes are hazardous. This effectively takes suspect products off the market without the manufacturers' or importers' agreement or cooperation. The CPSC recently pressured a major online retailer to voluntarily recall hoverboards it sold and to provide customers with a full refund. This effectively eliminated a suspect product from the marketplace while the CPSC was still investigating the root cause of hoverboard fires.[73]

- *Greater port surveillance.* The CPSC is also increasing enforcement activities in conjunction with U.S. Customs and Border Protection agents at major U.S. ports to target and seize high-risk imports that violate safety standards.

Q 20.18.3   Does the Commission's emphasis on enforcement involve formal compliance programs?

Yes. In all recent settlement agreements, the Commission has included provisions requiring the settling business to implement and maintain formal compliance programs.[74] Although there is no official rule or regulation requiring a formal compliance program for all consumer product businesses, the settlement agreements are a reflection of a developing Commission policy. The mandated compliance programs must include at a minimum:

- written standards and policies;
- a mechanism for confidential employee reporting of compliance-related concerns;

- internal training programs on CPSA section 15(b) reporting requirements;
- management oversight of compliance and appropriate personnel responsibility for implementing compliance; and
- a policy to retain all compliance-related records for at least five years and availability of such records to CPSC staff upon request.

The fact that a company has a relevant compliance plan in place at the time of a violation is one of the factors the CPSC considers in determining the amount of any civil penalty. While voluntary at this time, formal compliance plans are a best practice for all businesses under the jurisdiction of the CPSC.[75]

The CPSC will continue to focus on regulatory enforcement and compliance for the foreseeable future. Businesses should therefore take a proactive approach to achieve compliance with the expanded scope and numerous requirements of the CPSA.

Notes to Chapter 20

1.   15 U.S.C. § 2051(a)(3).
2.   For purposes of the Consumer Product Safety Act, the terms "motor vehicles or motor vehicle equipment" are limited to those products "as defined by sections 102(3) and (4) of the National Traffic and Motor Vehicle Safety Act of 1966, sections 30102(a)(6) and (7) of Title 49." 15 U.S.C. § 2052(a)(5)(C).
3.   *Id.* § 2052(a)(5)(A).
4.   *Id.* § 2051 *et seq.*
5.   Pub. L. No. 112-28, 125 Stat. 273 (Aug. 12, 2011).
6.   15 U.S.C. § 1261 *et seq.*
7.   *Id.* § 1191 *et seq.*
8.   *Id.* § 1471 *et seq.* The CPSC does not regulate children's drugs. However, the CPSC regulates child-resistant packaging for both adult and children's drugs as required by the PPPA.
9.   *Id.* § 1211 *et seq.*
10.   *Id.* § 8001 *et seq.*
11.   Children's Gasoline Burn Prevention Act, Pub. L. No. 110-278, 122 Stat. 2602 (2008).
12.   15 U.S.C. § 2069.
13.   *Id.* § 2070.
14.   *Id.* § 2066(e).
15.   *Id.* § 2068(a).
16.   *Id.*
17.   *Id.* § 2068.
18.   *Id.* § 2063.
19.   *Id.* § 2064(b).
20.   *Id.* § 2052(a)(5).
21.   *Electronic Code of Regulations*, U.S. GOV'T PRINTING OFFICE, www.ecfr.gov/cgi-bin/text-idx?c=ecfr&tpl=/ecfrbrowse/Title16/16cfrv2_02.tpl (last visited Aug. 18, 2016).
22.   *Regulations, Mandatory Standards and Bans*, U.S. CONSUMER PROD. SAFETY COMM'N [CPSC], www.cpsc.gov/en/regulations-laws–standards/regulations-mandatory-standards-bans/ (last visited June 1, 2016).
23.   *Safer Products Start Here!*, CPSC, https://business.cpsc.gov/en/Business–Manufacturing/Regulatory-Robot/Safer-Products-Start-Here/ (last visited Aug. 18, 2016).
24.   15 U.S.C. §§ 2056a, 2056b, 2089.
25.   *Id.* § 2068(a)(4).
26.   Letter from Robert J. Howell, Dir., Office of Compliance & Field Operations, U.S. Consumer Prod. Safety Comm'n, to Manufacturers, Importers, and Retailers of Self-Balancing Scooters (Feb. 18, 2016), www.cpsc.gov/Global/Busi-

ness-and-Manufacturing/Business-Education/SelfbalancingScooter-Letter.pdf?epslanguage=en.

27. 15 U.S.C. § 2052(a)(2).

28. Interpretation of "Children's Product," 75 Fed. Reg. 63,067 (Oct. 14, 2010).

29. 15 U.S.C. § 2063.

30. 16 C.F.R. § 1110.11.

31. 15 U.S.C. § 2063(a)(1)(A).

32. *Id.* § 2063(a)(2).

33. 16 C.F.R. § 1110.13.

34. *Id.* § 1110.7.

35. 15 U.S.C. § 2063(a)(1)(A).

36. 16 C.F.R. § 1107 subpt. B.

37. 15 U.S.C. § 2063(a)(1)(A).

38. 16 C.F.R. §§ 1610, 1203, 1204, 1205, 1209, 1210, 1211, 1212.

39. Testing and Labeling Pertaining to Product Certification, 75 Fed. Reg. 28,362 (May 20, 2010).

40. 15 U.S.C. § 2063(a)(2).

41. 16 C.F.R. pt. 1107, subpt. C.

42. *Id.* pt. 1109.

43. *Id.* § 1107.23.

44. *Id.* § 1107.21.

45. *Id.* § 1107.21(c)(1)–(d)(1).

46. *Id.* § 1107.24.

47. *Id.* § 1107.26.

48. *Id.* § 1109.1 *et seq.*

49. 15 U.S.C. § 2064(b).

50. *Id.* § 2064(a).

51. 16 C.F.R. § 1120.3.

52. *Id.*

53. *Id.*

54. *Id.* § 1120.1.

55. *Id.* § 1115.12.

56. 15 U.S.C. § 2064(b).

57. 16 C.F.R. § 1115.14(b).

58. *Id.* § 1115.14(d).

59. 15 U.S.C. § 2084.

60. United States v. Mirama Enters., Inc., 387 F.3d 983, 988 (9th Cir. 2004).

61. *See, e.g., In re* Maxfield & Oberton Holdings, LLC, Docket Nos. 12-1, 12-2, 13-2 (consolidated) (2012); Complaint, *In re* Baby Matters, LLC, Docket No. 13-1 (C.P.S.C. Dec. 4, 2012); Order Granting Plaintiff's Motion for Summary Judgment, United States v. Sen Magnets, LLC & Shihan Qu, No. 15-cv-00955 (D. Colo. Mar. 22, 2016), www.cpsc.gov/Global/Business-and-Manufacturing/Federal%20Court%20Orders%20and%20Decisions/ZenMagnetsordergrantingplaintiffsmotionsummaryjudgment.pdf.

62. 16 C.F.R. pt. 1102.

63. Doe v. Tenenbaum, 900 F. Supp. 2d 572 (D. Md. 2012).

64. Doe v. Pub. Citizen, 749 F.3d 246 (4th Cir. 2014).

65. Pub. L. No. 112-28, 125 Stat. 273 (Aug. 12, 2011).

66. Press Release No. 16-114, Consumer Prod. Safety Comm'n, CPSC Approves Adult Apparel Enforcement Discretion to Reduce Paperwork Requirement on Businesses (Mar. 4, 2016), www.cpsc.gov/en/Newsroom/News-Releases/2016/CPSC-Approves-Adult-Apparel-Enforcement-Discretion-to-Reduce-Paperwork-Requirement-on-Businesses/.

67. Certificates of Compliance, 78 Fed. Reg. 28,080 (May 13, 2013).

68. Information Disclosure Under Section 6(b) of the Consumer Product Safety Act, 79 Fed. Reg. 10,712 (Feb. 26, 2014).

69. 16 C.F.R. § 115.20(a).

70. Voluntary Remedial Actions and Guidelines for Voluntary Recall Notices, 78 Fed. Reg. 69,793 (Nov. 21, 2013).

71. Press Release No. 16-127, Consumer Prod. Safety Comm'n, Gree Agrees to Pay Record $15.45 Million Civil Penalty, Improve Internal Compliance for Failure to Report Defective Dehumidifiers (Mar. 25, 2016), www.cpsc.gov/en/Newsroom/News-Releases/2016/Gree-Agrees-to-Pay-Record-1545-Million-Civil-Penalty-Improve-Internal-Compliance-for-Failure-to-Report-Defective-Dehumidifiers/.

72. *In re* Maxfield & Oberton Holdings, LLC, Docket Nos. 12-1, 12-2, 13-2 (consolidated) (C.P.S.C. 2012); Motion for Leave to File Second Amended Complaints, *In re* Maxfield & Oberton Holdings, LLC (C.P.S.C. Feb. 11, 2013).

73. Press Statement, Consumer Prod. Safety Comm'n, Statement from U.S. CPSC Chairman Elliot F. Kaye on the Safety of Hoverboards and the Status of the Investigation (Jan. 20, 2016), www.cpsc.gov/en/Newsroom/Press-Statements/Statement-from-US-CPSC-Chairman-Elliot-F-Kaye-on-the-Safety-of-Hoverboards-and-the-Status-of-the-Investigation/?utm_source=rss&utm_medium=rss&utm_campaign=Press+Statements.

74. *See, e.g.*, Settlement Agreement, *In re* Ross Stores, Inc., Docket No. 13-C0006 (C.P.S.C. June 21, 2013), www.cpsc.gov//Global/Business-and-Manufacturing/Civil%20Penalties/2013/RossCivilPenalty.pdf; Settlement Agreement, *In re* Williams-Sonoma, Inc., Docket No. 13-C0005 (C.P.S.C. Apr. 25, 2013).

75. 16 C.F.R. § 1119.4(b)(1).